ZWINGLI'S THOUGHT

NEW PERSPECTIVES

STUDIES IN THE HISTORY OF CHRISTIAN THOUGHT

EDITED BY

HEIKO A. OBERMAN, Tübingen

IN COOPERATION WITH

HENRY CHADWICK, Cambridge
JAROSLAV PELIKAN, New Haven, Conn.
BRIAN TIERNEY, Ithaca, N.Y.
E. DAVID WILLIS, Princeton, N.J.

VOLUME XXV

GOTTFRIED W. LOCHER

ZWINGLI'S THOUGHT

NEW PERSPECTIVES

LEIDEN
E. J. BRILL
1981

ZWINGLI'S THOUGHT

NEW PERSPECTIVES

BY

GOTTFRIED W. LOCHER

WITH A FOREWORD BY DUNCAN SHAW

LEIDEN
E. J. BRILL
1981

ISBN   90 04 06420 6

PRINTED IN THE NETHERLANDS

CONTENTS

Author's Preface VII
Foreword, by Dr. Duncan Shaw IX
Abbreviations XVII

1. In Spirit and in Truth. — How worship in Zurich changed at
   the Reformation 1
2. Huldrych Zwingli's Message 31
3. How the Image of Zwingli has changed in Recent Research 42
4. "Christ our Captain". — An example of Zwingli's preaching
   and its cultural setting 72
5. The Content and the Design of Zwingli's Teaching about
   Mary 87
6. Huldrych Zwingli's Concept of History 95
7. Huldrych Zwingli's Doctrine of Predestination 121
8. The Characteristic Features of Zwingli's Theology in comparison with Luther and Calvin 142
9. Zwingli and Erasmus 233
10. Steadfastness. — Zwingli's Final Sermon at the Bern Disputa-
    tion as a Contribution to his Ethics 256
11. Zwingli's Political Activity: It's Motives and Objectives 267
12. "Praedicatio Verbi Dei est Verbum Dei". — Henry Bullinger
    between Luther and Zwingli. An essay on his theology 277
13. The Second Helvetic Confession 288
14. Discord among Guests. — Lessons to be learned from the Re-
    formers debate about the Lord's Supper for a contemporary
    understanding and celebration 303
15. Zwingli's Influence in England and Scotland 340

Selected Bibliography 384
Index of Subjects 386
Index of Writings by Zwingli 390
Index of Names 391

AUTHOR'S PREFACE

This book is concerned with Zwingli's world of thought. Zwingli is an unknown figure. There is no lack of general portrayals, impressions and judgements; but there is a lack of any precise knowledge of his preaching, his motives and his aims. This book consists of a series of individual studies, written over a period of years, which constitute an attempt to achieve a deeper understanding of the reformer. Most of these were given in German and were published in *Huldrych Zwingli in neuer Sicht*, Zurich, 1969. Some, however, reached English-speaking listeners or readers either at the same time or even earlier. "In Spirit and in Truth" were originally lecturers held at Scottish universities; and the principal paper "The Characteristic Features ..." was given at American universities. Finbally I decided to include some papers so far unpublished or difficult to obtain.

Though the occasions were different, there is a basic continuity of theme, so that some repetition could not be avoided. But this may serve to clarify the subject, and care has been taken to vary the references and quotations. The essays and addresses have retained their original form, but they have been revised and brought up to the present, especially with regard to the English and American literature. Only the report on the research work "How the Image of Zwingli has changed ..." did not have any new titles added, because U. Gäbler's comprehensive Bibliography appeared in 1975. However, the discussion and the task has not changed fundamentally since 1969. Since the interpretation of the Zurich reformer which is offered here often differs from some widely-held views, it has been felt necessary to provide a fair amount of documentation.

For hundreds of years, Zwingli has been the subject of over-hasty praise and criticism alike. We have, therefore, exercised restraint in regard to the present relevance of his message. The message itself will speak to the careful reader all the more directly. Zwingli is relevant: one example is his resolute rejection, in the realm of faith, of all attempts to achieve by our own methods what grace has reserved to itself. "God reveals himself by his spirit". Or again, there is the vigorous social and ethical orientation of his faith: "Beware, you tyrants, the gospel makes pious people". In neither case will Zwingli find universal acceptance today. He knows that. "But if someone cries 'Ouch!', then the divine word has certainly hit him: for nobody cries 'Ouch!' unless he has been hit".

I wish to thank, in the first place, the Rev. Milton Aylor and the Rev. Stuart Casson for their translations, which they undertook so enthusiastically and conscientiously, the 16th century Upper German texts posing especially difficult problems. Also the Rev. Duncan Shaw, Ph. D., D. D., whose great labour and pains form a link with the British theologians and historians. And, last but not least, Professor Dr. Heiko A. Oberman, who for many years has taken a great interest in these studies and who has included them in this Series.

Wabern/Berne   G. W. LOCHER

Quotations: Z I 369. II 346. III 379.

FOREWORD

Zwingli Research—the Chasm in British Reformation Studies

More than a decade ago, A. G. Dickens wrote that "the influence of Zwingli upon the earliest English Reformers still needs disentanglement".[1] A similar claim could be made regarding the reformers in Scotland but the problem has never been generally recognised by academic ecclesiastical historians and theologians there.

However, attempts to assess the influence of any foreign reformer in Scotland and, to a lesser extent, in England are more difficult than undertaking a similar task in relation to most of the northern half of Europe. The primary cause is that those who supported major reforms within the old church were effectively excluded from political power in Scotland until the events of 1558 and were not legally in control until 1560, while in England the vacillating policies of Henry VIII did not permit anyone to express their views frankly and, as a result, it was only on the accession of Edward VI in 1547 that the partially submerged movements came to the surface: only to be suppressed a few years later in the reign of Mary Tudor. Consequently, by 1558, the ideas and writings of a host of European theologians and pamphleteers were circulating among all sorts of people, with no particular view holding exclusive sway.

While "we must beware of compartmentalising the torrent of doctrines which by 1530 were flowing into England",[2] we must equally be on our guard against accepting at its face value everything which was labelled 'Lutheran' in official documents and records. As early as 1525, Lutheranism is mentioned in Scotland[3] yet such opinions were known in Scotland, as in England, in the previous decade.[4] Nevertheless, it should not be forgotten that Lutheranism was such a blanket expression[5] that it did not only cover the various continental reformers' views but was applied, on occasions, to beliefs of those who were followers of John Wyclif.[6]

---

1. *The English Reformation*, London, 1964, p. 63.

2. *Ibid.*

3. *The Acts of the Parliaments of Scotland*, ed. T. Thomson and C. Innes, Edinburgh, 1814, ii, p. 295.

4. P. Smith, "English Opinion of Luther" in *Harvard Theological Review*, 1917, x, pp. 133f.

5. N. S. Tjernagel, *Henry VIII and the Lutherans. A Study in Anglo-Lutheran Relations from 1521-1547*, St. Louis, 1965, p. 80.

6. *Original Letters relative to the English Reformation*, ed. H. Robinson, Parker Society, Cambridge, 1847, p. 221.

As most Scottish and English historians have written the history of their countries with the British isles at the centre and the local occurrences dictating the sequence and importance of events elsewhere and because the European reformation has been approached in the light of subsequent developments within Great Britain, the various influences on the period 1520-1550 have often not been brought out with sufficient definition and clarity.[7]

Distortions too have frequently been created by an overemphasis on one tradition or one confessional point of view, often accompanied by a failure, for various reasons, to consider recent research.[8] The most obvious is the perpetuation of an inaccurate tradition where a leap is still often taken from Luther to Calvin without looking for the influence of Zürich from the 1530s onwards.[9]

---

7. E.g. it has been said, 'Scottish Church affairs have perhaps generally been discussed too much in isolation and too little in their proper context of Europe' (G. D. Henderson, *Religious Life in Seventeenth-Century Scotland,* Cambridge, 1937, p. xii) and, "in England, Reformation studies still move slowly, and even in the field of English Reformation study we are cramped by unawareness of what had happened on the Continent". (G. Rupp, *Patterns of Reformation*, London, 1969, p. xiv).

8. This leads to strange pronouncements e.g. "John à Lasco, Martin Bucer, and John Oecolampadius, each disappointed by negotiations between Luther and the Swiss group and likewise confronted with the resurgence of Imperial power, found in the English Church a natural host for their views. With Peter Martyr, Bucer's old colleague, the Edwardian Government collected the most distinguished continental adherents of a reformed position which was expressly intended to mediate between the extreme Protestant camps. The only important exception to this pattern is the interest in Zwingli, but it seems uncommon". (J. K. McConica, *English Humanists and Reformation Politics under Henry VIII and Edward VI,* Oxford, 1965, p. 250) and "Save for the admittedly important doctrine of the Lord's Supper, the Forty-two Articles of the reign of Edward VI and the Thirty-nine Articles of the Elizabethan settlement were and remain Lutheran". (N.S. Tjernagel, *op. cit.*, pp. 252-53). In particular, debates concerning the Westminster Confession often reflect a total neglect of the influence of Zwingli and Bullinger, e.g. H. Ralston, *John Calvin versus the Westminster Confession*, Richmond, Virginia, 1972 (much of this book is taken from his Ph. D. thesis, "The understanding of sin and responsibility in the teaching of John Calvin", Faculty of Divinity, University of Edinburgh), while the references in J. H. Leith (*Assembly at Westminster. Reformed Theology in the Making*, Richmond, Virginia, 1973, pp. 80, 93, 120-21) are insubstantial. The best account of the development of covenant theology is given by K. Hagen ("From Testament to Covenant in the Early Sixteenth Century" in *The Sixteenth Century Journal*, St. Louis, 1972, iii, pp. 1-24): this is an advance on Emanuel Graf von Korff, *Die Anfänge der Föderaltheologie und ihre erste Ausgestaltung in Zurich und Holland*, Bonn, 1908 and O. Ritschl, "Die Entwicklung des Bundesgedankens in der reformierten Theologie des 16. und 17. Jahrhunderts" in *Dogmengeschichte des Protestantismus*, Göttingen, 1926, iii, pp. 412-58, both ignored by Ralston and Leith.

9. All neatly illustrated in the sentence, "Calvinism did not supplant Lutheranism in Scotland: it simply succeeded where Lutheranism failed". (J. S. McEwen, *The Faith of John Knox*, London, 1961, p. 22). English scholars have been less remiss e.g. Pollard notes as early as 1905 that "a loose habit has grown up of speaking about Calvinistic influence in

Additional confusion has arisen because myths, in both countries, have blinkered the outlook of many who have written on the reformation. The Scots have been enticed into interpreting their heritage as being a direct descendant from Geneva by the development of a nationalistic, ecclesiastical ideology which evolved during Scottish resistance to the attempted English domination of the Church of Scotland from the union of the crowns.[10] The Church of England, greatly influenced by an almost pathological fear of Puritanism[11] and an isolationistic imperialism from the time of Elizabeth Tudor[12] (although English imperialism has its beginnings in the reign of Henry VIII),[13] have generally written the history of their small church to emphasise its exclusive inclusiveness, its 'media via',

England during the reign of Edward VI. The Low Church influence of that time was Zwinglian, not Calvinistic; and Bullinger not Calvin was then the oracle of the most advanced Reformers". (A. F. Pollard, *Thomas Cranmer and the English Reformation*, London, 1905, p. 270 n).

10. "The theology of Scotland begins with the Reformation, the first of our great theological writers is John Knox himself... His clear strong mind firmly grasped the Calvinistic system... and he was sufficiently acquainted with its scriptural grounds... to be the expounder and defender of it". (J. Walker, *The Theology and Theologians of Scotland chiefly of the Seventeenth and Eighteenth Centuries*, second ed., Edinburgh, 1888, p. 1) cf. e.g., J. H. S. Burlegh, who taught church history in the University of Edinburgh for over thirty years, makes no mention of the influence of Zwingli or Bullinger in *A Church History of Scotland*, London, 1960.

11. Possibly put most concisely by J. N. Figgis, "Puritanism, like nearly all ascetic ideals, had in it a strong Manichean bias. We know it chiefly by its enmities. It was active for destruction. It destroyed the monarchy, the aristocracy, and finally the representative system; it abolished the drama, it proscribed the Liturgy, it persecuted the bishops, it knocked down statues, overturned altars, and shattered windows. It first abolished tyranny, and then destroyed liberty and finally completed its career of devastation by giving the *coup de grâce* to itself. Few movements have been to all appearances more uniform in their destructive tendencies than was English political Puritanism", in *The Church Quarterly Review*, London, 1903, lvii, p. 125.

12. For the background to this, cf. F. A. Yates, "Queen Elizabeth as Astraea" in *The Journal of the Warburg and Courtauld Institute*, London, 1947, x, pp. 27-82 and *Astraea. The Imperial Theme in the Sixteenth Century*, London, 1974. John Foxe assisted the growth of imperialistic concepts among ordinary people in Elizabethan England. The idealisation of Constantine and the commendation of his example to Elizabeth (*The Acts and Monuments of John Foxe*, ed. G. Townsend, London, 1842, i, pp. 292-304 and his preface to the edition of 1563) and underlined by Foxe's narrative of Constantine's birth in Britain and his mother, Helena, being a daughter of an English king. (*Ibid*, i, p. 312).

13. G. R. Elton, "The Evolution of a Reformation Statute" in *The English Historical Review*, London, 1949, lxiv, pp. 174-97 particularly pp. 178-9. For a critical appraisal of Elton's article cf. G. L. Harriss, "Medieval Government and Statecraft" in *Past and Present*, Oxford, 1963, xxv, pp. 9-12. A useful survey of a lengthy period is given by R. Koebner, " 'The Imperial Crown of this Realm' Henry VIII, Constantine the Great, and Polydore Vergil" in *Bulletin of the Institute of Historical Research*, London, 1953, xxvi, pp. 29-52. Luther played a part in this development, cf. F. W. Henninger, "Luther and the Empire: A Study of the Imperial Ideal in Reformation Politics 1522-1540", University of Nebraska MS Thesis, 1972.

and its 'Anglicanism'.[14] These British idiosyncrasies must be added to the
universal problem of putting modern sectarian interpretations upon sixteenth century concepts, which are on many occasions very different from
the actual reformers' doctrines, as well as the fact that "the historian may
well deplore the fact that sixteenth century misunderstandings still abide,
and that not a few Roman Catholics and Protestants alike have difficulty
in grasping what their opponents are talking about",[15] particularly as to
what Zwingli actually wrote.

There have been occasional specific studies of the influence of the continental reformation on Great Britain[16] but, although one or two studies
on particular topics have appeared,[17] the difficulties already mentioned
have prevented serious consideration of the effect of Zwingli on Scotland
and England.[18] This is all the more significant when the place of Luther
and Calvin, within the English and Scottish reformation, has been
recounted at some length.[19] The research undertaken on these reformers'

---

14. There are many examples of this: e.g. "The works of these Reformation Anglican
fathers are considered in relation to their times and to the ideas of other writers — those
belonging to their own past, present and succeeding generations among Anglicans" (H. F.
Woodhouse, *The Doctrine of the Church in Anglican Theology. 1547-1603*, London, 1954, p. v),
or "The Elizabethan churchmen, the exiles of Mary's reign, carried on the tradition of
Cranmer rather than that of Calvin. Varied in ability, in learning, in character, they were
Anglicans. Theirs should be the credit for preserving Anglicanism during the exile and
reestablishing it upon firm ground in the difficult early years of the new reign". (W. M.
Southgate, "The Marian Exiles and the influence of John Calvin" in *History*, London, 1942,
xxvii, p. 152). More careful scholars are now aware of the problem of using the word
"Anglican" in connection with the English reformation, e.g. D. M. Loades, *The Oxford
Martyrs*, London, 1970, p. 5n.

15. C. C. Richardson, *Zwingli and Cranmer on the Eucharist,* Evanston, 1949, p. 3.

16. E.g. F. J. Smithen, *Continental Protestantism and the English Reformation*, London, 1927.

17. E.g. H. Kressner, *Schweizer Ursprünge des anglikanischen Staatskirchentums*, Gütersloh,
1953; R. Pfister, "Zürich und das anglikanische Staatskirchentum" in *Zwa.*, Zürich, 1958,
x, pp. 249-56.

18. E.g. Zwingli's name does not appear in *Bibliography of British History: Tudor Period,
1485-1603*, ed. C. Reid, Oxford, 1959, second ed.

19. H. E. Jacobs, *A Study in comparative Symbolics; the Lutheran Movements during the Reigns of
Henry VIII and Edward VI, and its Literary Monuments*, Philadelphia, 1908; A. C. Piepkorn,
"Anglo-Lutheran Relations during the first two years of the Reign of Edward VI" in *Concor-
dia Theological Monthly*, St. Louis, 1935, vi, pp. 670-86; E. G. Rupp, *Studies in the Making of the
English Protestant Tradition (Mainly in the Reign of Henry VIII)*, Cambridge, 1947; N. S. Tjernagel, *op cit.;* R. Bonini, "Lutheran Influences in the early English Reformation" in *Archiv
für Reformationsgeschichte*, 1973, lxiv, pp. 206-24; C. D. Crameans, *The Reception of Calvinist
Thought in England*, Urbana, 1949; W. M. Southgate, "The Marian Exiles and the Influence
of John Calvin" in *History*, 1942, new series. xxvii, pp. 148-52 deals with precisely the opposite of what the title appears to suggest; W. S. Reid, "Lutheranism in the Scottish Reformation" in *Westminster Theological Journal,* 1943-5, pp. 91-111; J. H. Baxter, "Luthers
Einfluss in Schottland im 16. Jahrhundert" in *Luther Jahrbuch*, 1958, pp. 99-109; A. Mezger,

affect on Scotland is much less detailed than it could be and is sometimes onesided.

A further area still requiring illumination is the accurate tracing of personal contacts which played such a part in the reformation movement
especially when it was under proscription. Some attempt has been made to
consider the later reformation period[20] but much has still to be done for the
earlier decades.[21] The wide-ranging network is often overlooked. It will be
recalled, for example, that the first protestant martyr who brought
Lutheran ideas to Scotland was incinerated in Paris in 1527[22] and was
almost certainly distantly related through marriage to Pope Leo X.[23] It
will not be forgotten that Myles Coverdale was not proceeded against as a
heretic by Bloody Mary because his Scottish wife, whose sister was married to a Danish royal chaplain, the Scot, John Macchabaeus,[24] secured
the intervention of Christian III, king of Denmark.[25] Connections
between Zwinglians in Scotland and England and the continent have
never been systematically taken in hand and this is reflected in the
historiography of the reformation in Great Britain. As has been said,
"Historians, after all, have every reason to entertain doubts and suspi-
cions about their own methods. Their source material is largely taken from
the special little world of chronicles, documents and official records. There
is no reason to doubt that, while historians scale the peaks of church and

---

John Knox et ses rapports avec Calvin, Montauban, 1905; J. Kirk, "The Influence of Calvin on
the Scottish Reformation" in *Records of the Scottish Church History Society,* 1974, xviii,
pp. 157-79.

20. C. H. Garrett, *The Marian Exiles. A Study in the Origins of Elizabethan Puritanism,* Cambridge, 1938; however, cf. M. A. Simpson, *Defender of the Faith, Etcetera,* Edinburgh, 1977,
Appendix.

21. Scholars have to rely still on work done in Switzerland in the last century as far as
connections between foreigners and local Zwinglians are concerned (J. C. Mörikofer, *Die
Geschichte der evangelischen Flüchtlinge in der Schweiz,* Hirzel, 1896 and T. Vetter, "Englische
Flüchtlinge in Zürich während der ersten Hälfte des 16. Jahrhunderts" in *Neujahrsblatt,*
herausgegeben von der Stadtbibliothek, Zürich, 1893).

22. *Journal d'un Bourgeois de Paris sous le Règne de François Premier,* Paris, 1854, pp. 326-27.

23. Monsieur de la Tour was a gentleman among the men-at-arms of John, duke of
Albany, during one or more of the duke's visits to Scotland between 1521 and 1523.
Albany's mother was Anne de la Tour, third daughter of Bertrand, count of Avergne and
Bouillon, and he married his cousin, Anne de la Tour, countess of Auvergne and Lauragais,
the eldest daughter of John de la Tour, count of Auvergne. His sister, Madeleine de la Tour,
married Lorenzo de Medici, duke of Urbino, nephew of Pope Leo X. The only child of this
marriage was Catherine de Medici, countess of Auvergne and Lauragais, wife of Henry II of
France.

24. Foxe, *op. cit.,* vi., pp. 705-6: cf. H. F. Rördam, *Kjøbenhavns Universitets Historie,*
Copenhagen, 1869, iv, p. 359. No. 261.

25. For the correspondence between Christian III and Mary Tudor, cf. Foxe, *op. cit.,* vi,
pp. 706-8.

government and contemplate constitutional developments and economic trends, they fail to reach down to the everyday life of ordinary folk''.[26]

A substantial amount of partially concealed works of continental reformers, whether appearing as a whole under another name[27] or as long excerpts incorporated in composite works,[28] has been identified but many quotations, *verbatim* or summarised, still await investigation.[29] The actual books too which were read[30] or possessed by British reformers[31] and the marginalia on the books in their own libraries,[32] as well as the listing of such collections,[33] would cast much light on Zwinglian influences.

Thus the interaction of theological thought, writings and personalities, presents a continuing obscurity that will only be cleared by detached, patient and scholarly research by historians, equipped to master the large amount of detail available in several European languages, who

---

26. H. Heimpel, "Characteristics of the late Middle Ages in Germany" in *Pre-Reformation Germany*, ed. G. Strauss, London, 1972, p. 46.

27. E.g. H. Bullinger's *Der Christlich Eestand*, Zürich, 1540, translated by Myles Coverdale, first appeared anonymously as *The christen state of matromonye* in 1541, but in the following year and the next, it was published as *The golden boke of christen matrimony* and Thomas Becon informs us that it was "for the more ready sale, set forth in my name by the hungry printer with my preface, to make it more plausible to the readers". (*Early Works of Thomas Becon, being Treatises published by him in the reign of Henry VIII*, ed. J. Ayre, Parker Society, Cambridge, 1843., p. 29, and cf. A. Weber, *Heinrich Bullingers "Christlicher Ehestand", seine zeitgenössischen Quellen und die Anfänge des Familienbuches in England*, Leipzig, 1929; A. Hume, "William Roye's Briefe dialogue (1527). An English version of a Strassburg catechism" in *Harvard Theological Review*, 1967, lx, pp. 307-21 is a recent example of such research.

28. "Whole sentences occur in different Homilies, so identical with sentences found in treatises on like subjects by Bucer, Peter Martyr, Musculus, Bullinger and others, that it is scarcely possible to regard that identity as accidental". (*Certain Sermons, appointed by the Queen's Majesty to be ... read by all Parsons, Vicars, and Curates ... in their Churches ... Newly imprinted in Parts according as mentioned in the Book of Common Prayers*, London, 1574, ed. G. E. Corrie, Cambridge, 1850, p. xii).

29. Although it should be remembered that readers often used the author's material to reach different conclusions, e.g. Cranmer's use of the *Dialogus* of Oecolampadius. (P. Brooks, *Thomas Cranmer's Doctrine of the Eucharist. An Essay in Historical Development*, London, 1965, pp. 34-35).

30. E.g. it would be interesting to ascertain if there really is any close relationship between the *Catechismus Tigurinus*, Zurich, 1534 and Ponet's *Catechismus brevis*, Zurich, 1553 (C. F. C. H. Garret, "John Ponet and the Confession of the Banished Ministers" in *The Church Quarterly Review*, London, 1944, cxxxvii, pp. 62-64).

31. Lists exist from an early date, cf. e.g., the library of Richard Bayfield (Foxe, *op. cit.*, iv, pp. 684f.).

32. As has been done in the case of George Buchanan (P. H. Aitken, "George Buchanan's Marginalia" in *George Buchanan: Glasgow Quatercentenary Studies. 1906*, Glasgow, 1907, pp. 382-92 or Gabriel Harvey (G. C. M. Smith, *Gabriel Harvey Marginalia*, Stratford-on-Avon, 1913).

33. What is required is Scottish and English studies, similar to R. Doucet, *Les Bibliothèques parisiennes au XVIe siècle*, Paris, 1956, without, like Doucet, stopping at 1560.

are intimate with the writings of Zwingli and who are then able to probe beneath the accepted generalities, which so often hide the truth, to ascertain the facts as far as these are verifiable.

Many scholars, although aware of this situation, shy away from any real attempt at careful analysis. This attitude is illustrated by Derek Wilson, who, when writing of Anne Ayscough, said, "It is undoubtedly wrong to assess the opinions of a heretic like Anne in terms of what elements stemmed from Zwinglianism, what from Lollardy, what from Frith, Tyndale and Luther, etc., her ideas sprang from a much more complicated general background in which it is impossible to distinguish clearly individual elements".[34]

Such an attitude has continued in many instances because previous attempts by scholars seem to have found it impossible to come to an agreed conclusion[35] or because there has been little accurate or detailed knowledge of the theological views of many of the reformers other than Luther and Calvin. It may also be the case that Zwinglianism, since the sixteenth century, and Puritanism,[36] in the twentieth, are words which, both in England and in Scotland, the theologically "respectable" have tended to avoid applying to themselves or to their friends and have, as a result, not been greatly interested in the history, doctrine and practice connected with them.[37] It ought not to be overlooked that ecclesiastical historians generally tend to be interested in the victors and victorious ideologies in history and to leave the defeated in their dust.

Since the end of the second world war, there has been a very considerable growth in Zwinglian studies, particularly in Switzerland,[38] although these have not yet had much influence on the English-speaking world.[39] The appearance of Professor Gottfried Locher's work in English is therefore an inspired undertaking.

---

34. D. Wilson, *A Tudor Tapestry. Men, Women and Society in Reformation England*, London, 1972, p. 270.

35. Cf. e.g., the summary of the conflicting opinions on the sacramental theology of John Frith (W. A. Clebsch, *England's Earliest Protestants 1520-1535*, New Haven, 1964, p. 117).

36. The word is used here in the sense in which critics, often uninformed, use it in this century. The problem of accurate definition for the historian is well known (cf. B. Hall, "Puritanism: the Problem of Definition" in *Studies in Church History*, ed. C. J. Cuming, London, 1965, ii, pp. 283-96).

37. There are, of course, notable exceptions to this generalisation, e.g. for the later period, P. Collinson, *The Elizabethan Puritan Movement*, London, 1967.

38. U. Gäbler, *Huldrych Zwingli im 20. Jahrhundert. Forschungsbericht und annotierte Bibliographie 1897-1972*, Zürich, 1975.

39. Except G. R. Potter, "The initial impact of the Swiss reformers in England" in *Discordia concors. Festgabe für Edgar Bonjour*, Basle, 1968, ii, pp. 391-400.

It is a good omen for the furtherance of Zwinglian studies that the fruits of a scholar, who has been one of the leaders in the resurgence in Zwinglian research during the last quarter of a century,[40] are now made available to a wider circle.

The last chapter, which was written as an introductory sketch with this English translation in view,[41] should encourage younger scholars to follow the signposts and take the road to discover some of the fields mentioned that are yet to be explored in English and Scottish reformation history. The book, as a whole, will help many to identify Zwinglian theological thought which appears disguised in varying forms and to answer some of the questions which inevitably arise in the mind of the careful scholar.

It is to be hoped that Professor Locher's scholarly insights will send the researcher back to read Zwingli's own writings and to ground his subsequent work on the basis of Zwingli himself.[42] There is a real need to do this as there are frequent instances of writers tending to follow one another in citation and interpretation without, one suspects, always referring to the sources and original texts.[43] The continuing need was put succinctly long ago by John Foxe, "Diligence is required and great searching out of books and authors, not only of our time, but of all ages. And especially where matters of religion are touched pertaining to the church, it is not sufficient, to see what 'Fabian' or what 'Hall' saith; but the records must be sought, the registers must be turned over, letters also and ancient instruments ought to be perused, and authors with the same compared; finally, the writers amongst themselves one to be conferred with another; and so with judgment matters are to be weighed; with diligence to be laboured and with simplicity, pure from all addition and partiality, to be uttered".[44]

Old College,   DUNCAN SHAW
The University of Edinburgh.

40. His first considerable contribution to the subject was *Die Theologie Huldrych Zwinglis im Lichte seiner Christologie*, Zürich, 1952.

41. G. W. Locher, "Zwinglis Einfluss in England und Schottland—Daten und Probleme" in *Zwa.* Zürich, 1975, xiv, p. 165n.

42. This is to be hoped for, although a considerable amount of Zwingli's works have been available in English for fifty years (*The Latin Works and Correspondence of Huldreich Zwingli*, edd. S. M. Jackson, W. J. Hinke and C. N. Heller, London, 1912-29, 3 vol.), which does not seem to have been widely read by those writing on the Scottish or English reformation. Little impact could be expected from the small selection appearing in *Zwingli and Bullinger*, ed. G. W. Bromiley, London, 1953.

43. E.g., when expounding Zürich influences on the concept of covenant, L. J. Trinterud ("The Origins of Puritanism" in *Church History*, 1951, xx, pp. 37-57) is followed by Clebsch (*op. cit.*, passim) who is subsequently followed by G. H. Williams (*Reformation Views of Church History*, London, 1970, p. 26).

44. Foxe, *op. cit.*, iii, pp. 376-77.

ABBREVIATIONS

Z   *Huldreich Zwinglis Sämtliche Werke,* ed. Emil Egli, Georg Finsler, Walther Köhler, Oskar Farner, Fritz Blanke, Leonhard von Muralt, Edwin Künzli, Rudolf Pfister. *Corpus Reformatorum,* Vol. LXXXVIIIff., Berlin, later Leipzig, latterly Zürich, 1905ff.

S   *Huldreich Zwinglis Werke. Erste vollständige Ausgabe,* ed. Melchior Schuler and Johannes Schultess, Zürich, 1828ff.

H   *Zwingli Hauptschriften,* ed. Fritz Blanke, Oskar Farner, Oskar Frei, Rudolf Pfister, Zürich, 1940ff.

     References to the above editions of Zwingli's works usually cite simply the volume and page numbers, thus, e.g. Z III 820.

WA   Martin Luther, *Werke. Kritische Gesamtausgabe,* Weimar, 1883ff.

Zwa.   *Zwingliana. Beiträge zur Geschichte Zwinglis, der Reformation und des Protestantismus in der Schweiz,* Zurich, 1897ff.

Th. H. Z. I   G. W. Locher, *Die Theologie Huldrych Zwinglis im Lichte seiner Christologie:* I: *Die Gotteslehre,* Zurich, 1952.

HZnS   G. W. Locher: *Huldrych Zwingli in neuer Sicht.* Zehn Beiträge zur Theologie der Zürcher Reformation. Zürich, 1969.

Zw. Ref.   G. W. Locher: *Die Zwinglische Reformation im Rahmen der europäischen*
im Rahmen   *Kirchengeschichte.* Göttingen, 1979.

1

IN SPIRIT AND IN TRUTH

*How worship in Zurich changed at the Reformation**

I. WORSHIP AND LIFE[1]

It was preaching that gave birth to the Reformation, maintained it, and carried it through to a successful conclusion. This is even more true of Zurich than of the other centres.[2]

In Wittenberg, what happened was that a monk became deeply troubled in conscience concerning the salvation of his own soul and of those whose confessions he had to bear. He was at the same time a German professor, who made revolutionary exegetical discoveries; afterwards, everything had to be examined and reorganised from above.

In Geneva, the city had become Protestant long before Calvin appeared on the scene, through the influence of Zwinglian, Lutheran and Erasmian writings and the discussions of the exiles. It was a pronouncedly lay movement, and it was the man in the street who finally carried the disputation in the church into effect against the will of the episcopal hierarchy. Calvinism has never lost this character. Wherever it has appeared, right down to the present day, it comes with leaflets and pamphlets and militant men and women. There must be a thorough catechism, and a comprehensive and detailed system of theology to clarify and bind together the wave of new thoughts and enterprises.

In Zurich, however, a peculiarly late-medieval and renaissance city, notorious for its immorality, was changed by what happened on one particular day. It was on 1st January, 1519, that the preacher in a certain pulpit in the town set aside the old church lectionary of Scripture readings and instead he allowed the Holy Scripture to speak out in all its living

---

* A lecture, first delivered in September 1952 to the Coetus Reformierter Prediger Deutschlands in Siegen, Westphalia. The theme of the conference was "Preaching in divine worship". The lecture was published in the series *Nach Gottes Wort reformiert*, Neukirchen/Kr. Moers, No. 11.

1. Paul Meyer, *Zwinglis Soziallehren,* Linz/D, 1921: Alfred Farner, *Die Lehre von Kirche und Staat bei Zwingli,* Tübingen, 1930; G. W. Locher, *Die evangelische Stellung der Reformatoren zum öffentlichen Leben,* Kirchliche Zeitfragen No. 26, Zürich, 1950; G. W. Locher, "Staat und Politik in der Lehre der Reformatoren" in *Reformatio,* 1952, No. 4/5.

2. Cf. Walther Köhler, *Huldrych Zwingli,* 2nd ed. Leipzig, 1954, pp. 81-92, "Die Anfänge der Reformation".

coherence, by means of consecutive expository preaching.[3] Zwingli started at the beginning, with the genealogy in Matthew 1, and in his first sermon (like the later exposition of H. F. Kohlbrügge) he emphasised the sinfulness of the female ancestors of the Lord who are named in that passage.[4]

However, we are not concerned here with the history of the reformation in Zurich with reference to the role played by preaching. Anyone seeking an historical survey of that kind will find an excellent one in the third volume of Oskar Farner's wide-ranging biography of Zwingli: *Huldrych Zwingli, Seine Verkündigung und ihre ersten Früchte* (Zürich, 1954).[5] What we are attempting here is to view a current problem of our church from the standpoint of the history of dogma, to consider what help a particular piece of reformation theology can give towards solving a contemporary question. Thus we see our theme as an enquiry into the spiritual, congregational, ecclesiastical and theological *motives* at one of the sources of the reformed church.

We are all familiar with the customary verdict on Zwingli's reformation: that it had its origin in humanistic endeavours for reform rather than in the reformation message; that its aims were of a decidedly political nature, or, at least, that it had slipped to a political level, so that it had no genuinely religious roots—a fact which soon revealed itself in the misuse of religion for political ends. And Zwingli's understanding of the Gospel is alleged to be a mundane, rational-moralistic view, lacking any sense of the mystery of the faith, as is evident from his symbolic doctrine of the Lord's Supper.[6]

These reproaches cannot be dismissed out of hand; there is something in them, as far as the bare facts are concerned. Yet the evaluation of those facts is not correct, either historically or theologically. For this evaluation proceeds from the tacit assumption that the inner development, the way

---

3. *Heinrich Bullingers Reformationsgeschichte*, ed. J. Hottinger and H. Vögeli, Frauenfeld, 1838, Vol. I, p. 12.

4. S VI I 203ff., 395ff.

5. Oskar Farner, *Huldrych Zwingli*. Vol. I: *Seine Jugend, Schulzeit und Studentenjahre*, Zürich, 1943; Vol. II: *Seine Entwicklung zum Reformator*, Zürich, 1946; Vol. III: *Seine Verkündigung und ihre ersten Früchte*, Zürich, 1954; Vol. IV: *Reformatorische Erneuerung von Kirche und Volk in Zürich und in der Eidgenossenschaft 1525-1531*, (edited and completed by Rudolf Pfister), Zürich, 1960; Walther Köhler, *Huldrych Zwingli*, 2nd ed. Leipzig, 1954. G. W. L.: *Zw. Ref. im Rahmen.*, 84-87.

6. Of the numerous works which present the subject in this way, we may mention the following: Paul Wernle, *Der evangelische Glaube nach den Hauptschriften der Reformatoren*. Vol. II; *Zwingli*, Tübingen, 1919; Otto Ritschl, *Dogmengeschichte des Protestantismus*, Vol. III, Göttingen, 1926; Reinhold Seeberg, *Lehrbuch der Dogmengeschichte*. Vol. IV, 1, 4th ed. Leipzig, 1933.

and the doctrine of Martin Luther provide the standard by which every attempt at reformation should be measured. Luther is made the norm for every reformer. Whatever conforms to the phenomenon of Luther is valid, and whatever does not conform is alien. As if it were impossible for the Holy Spirit to lead each one of us, just as we are, in our own way! The essence of the Lutheran reformation, which constitutes the paradoxical secret of its powerful effect, is that it starts at the very centre, with the revelation of Christ in his humanity, and the justification which is there guaranteed for us. It then dwells at length on the personal experience of this justification through faith, whereby justification achieves its end. Then slowly, almost reluctantly, it spreads outwards to the periphery—the re-ordering of the church. The Reformer always regarded the question of the transformation of earthly conditions (where this could not be circumvented) as a nuisance, a diversion from the main business. So it is no wonder that Zwingli did not always agree with Luther! The question is whether one should even compare the two men. For Zwingli actually begins at the circumference. He starts with the political and social questions. From here, he works inwards to the centre—the divinity of God in the Lordship of Jesus Christ—in order to be able to take up politics again, working from this centre outwards. Why should this approach not be possible?

To illustrate this briefly, three points may be mentioned. First, both reformers were awakened to their task through fear of the judgment. With Luther, this meant fear of being punished in hell for his sins; whereas with Zwingli, it was fear that the curse of God must fall upon Christendom, divided and betraying its Lord in bloody wars, and that it must fall in particular upon his beloved Swiss Confederacy, now so arrogant and brutalised.[7]

Second, it is obvious why Zwingli's Christology, with its emphasis on the divinity of Jesus, stands in such contrast to Luther's emphasis on the humanity of Jesus. When the wide field of ethics is so illuminated by the light of the "ascended into heaven", it is inevitable that this same light should also shine brightly in the doctrine of the Lord's Supper.

Thirdly, what does worship mean here? For Luther,[8] worship in the strict sense can only mean that justification is imparted to us in word and sacrament, that we appropriate it by faith and (this must not be neglected) that we bear witness to it by the offering of love. But for Zwingli our

---

7. Cf. "Huldrych Zwingli's Concept of History" (below, ch. 6).
8. Vilmos Vajta, *Die Theologie des Gottesdienstes bei Luther,* Göttingen, 1952.

ecclesiastical service of God must bear the same relation to our everyday service of God as the source bears to the stream, or the root to the tree or its fruit. Thus, of all the reformers, Zwingli is the most conscious reformer—not only of the faith or of the church, or even of the personal Christian life, but rather of the whole life of Christendom. Renewal of life can flow only from the power of the Word of God and from the renewal of church and faith. But never for one moment did it occur to Zwingli that there could possibly be a renewal of the church without a corresponding social and political change. The goal is to produce not some system of liturgical services, but a people that serves God, and does so in that broad field of public relationships which is not an alien element, but rather constitutes the field of real divine service. Thus, in "A Faithful and Solemn Exhortation to the Swiss Confederates" (1524), Zwingli appeals: "Take care that God's Word is faithfully preached among you … and when you see how this alone brings glory to God and the salvation of souls, then further it, regardless of what this one or that one may say. For the Word of God makes you pious, God-fearing people. So you will preserve your Fatherland, even though it displeases the devil. For where there is the fear of God, there is the help of God, Where it is not present, there is hell with all misery and wrong. So listen to the Word of God; for that alone will put you to rights again".[9] The dangerous way in which "liturgism" (that is, concentrating on sacred seasons, buildings, men and vestments) can destroy a true understanding of the service of God is expressed in his exposition of the Fifth Article of 1523: "Where the Spirit of God is, there one knows well … that the highest service of God in the faith is to do good to one's neighbour. Wherever one trusts in God, there is God. Where God is, there is also careful diligence in all that is good … Here I could, indeed, speak of men, whose names I prefer not to mention, who are progressing excellently—eternal praise and thanks to God!—in love to God, in peace with their neighbour, in the knowledge of the Gospel, in simplicity of life, in godly wisdom, in giving alms and help to the poor, in humbling their pride, in forgiving their enemies, in concern for the teaching of Christ, in concern for the prisoners of Christ and in concern for the whole of Christ's people. And though kindling lights, burning incense, making offerings (for the rich priests, I say), babbling prayers, vigils, wailing chants, the sound of masses, dazzling temples, the hoods of the theologians, the colourful robes of the monks and the well-cut coats of the parsons … are not to their liking, they do take pleasure in everything that is pleasing to God.

---

9. Z III 112f.; H VII 121f.

They reduce the rents of their tenants, they pay the labourer more than he dares to demand, they invite the poor and wretched into their homes, they do not indulge in gaming, cursing, buffoonery and all the vanity of the age, and they strive to prepare themselves for eternal life''.[10]

Thus the criterion by which our life is measured is not whether it is "churchly or worldly", "religious or non-religious", "sacred or profane"; it is a question of divine commandment or human ordinance. "Works of man's invention" are by their very nature hypocrisy, "sham works". The good fruits, by which one can recognise the flock of Christ and its true shepherd, are "the things that are found and taught in God's Word", the "works which God has commanded". On this point the reformer can quote John 4: "to worship God in spirit and in truth is the song that pleases him most''.[11]

When Zwingli was called to the office of people's priest at the Great Minster in Zurich, it came about only after a considerable campaign and through the pressure exerted by the craftsmen and their guilds, who recognised him as an opponent of the trade in mercenaries. Foreign military service held such an attraction for young men that trade stood on the verge of collapse because of a shortage of apprentices and journeymen.[12] However, Zwingli had already decided on the course he would take. Despite the very full list of age-old duties which was thrust upon him, he made sure beforehand that duties such as hearing confessions or visiting the sick would not make too great a claim on his time at the expense of his preaching.[13] Then he gave formal notice before the provost and chapter that he hoped to discharge his duties in the following way. He intended "with God's help to preach the holy Gospel according to Matthew in its entirety, section by section (that is, consecutively and in context), and not to follow the piecemeal method of the Evangelia dominica. He would explain it by means of Scripture (interpreting Scripture by Scripture) and not by human opinions, and all to the glory of God

---

10. Z II 47ff.; H III 56ff.; cf. Z IV 121: "From a picture one learns only the facts of what happened, but one learns the story and the efficacy of his suffering only through the Word, and one learns to trust in him only through God who illuminates and draws us ... We are not saved merely by knowing how he was crucified, but by knowing that he was crucified for us, and that he, the crucified one, is our Lord and God. This cannot be learnt from any picture or image, but only through the Word and by the light of God's grace". Cf. Z IV 125-126. "The weaker in faith that a man is, the sooner he succumbs to idols" (127).

11. Z III 51; H I 223.

12. Emil Egli, *Zürich am Vorabend der Reformation*, Zürcher Taschenbuch, 1896; Leonhard von Muralt, *Stadtgemeinde und Reformation in der Schweiz*, Zürich, 1930.

13. Z VII 103; O. Farner, *op. cit.*, Vol III, p. 33.

and of His only Son, our Lord Jesus Christ, as well as to the true salvation
of souls and the edification of pious and honest people".[14] Thus Zwingli
had a set purpose: in order that the people might come to serve God, the
Bible must begin to speak again; therefore the church service must become
a preaching service. That is how worship in Zurich was changed at the
Reformation. To understand this, we must take a brief look at the catholic
service of the late Middle Ages.

II. DIVINE SERVICE IN THE MIDDLE AGES[15]

When medieval man came out of the narrow streets of his city and
entered his cathedral by its great door, he stood on the fateful frontier between this world and the other. That other world would soon surround
him with the colourful grandeur of its mysteries and catch him up into its
solemn silence. But first he must pass through, beneath the feet of the
Christ—Christ in his majesty, or even Christ as judge of the world. From
above, from the side, from the front and from the back the eyes of
prophets, apostles and saints are staring at him—and it must be realised
that for him the stone figures are not mere images, but real symbols. Or
else (and this is even more awe-inspiring) he may notice that all these
figures are unable to look in any direction except towards the One. For
this is their worship, here and above: adoring God, to behold Him; and
beholding, to adore. In fear and trembling, he becomes aware that the
eyes of the One, the Lord, are now turned towards him—or do they scan
the far distance, sweeping over this man who dares to approach His
presence?

He is dismayed to discover that this facade, the face presented by the
church at its frontier with the world, is not just the entrance into the
church's realm, but rather proclaims the church's manifesto concerning
the world. It is much more than an attack; it is the church's clear and
categorical statement of its own order; or rather it is the revelation of
its structure which is founded in creation, basically immovable and which
can never seriously be challenged. Here the man learns about his own
sociological position in the feudal system of everyday life. He learns how
this (together with those exotic ends of the earth which are portrayed
around the portico) is itself sustained, pervaded and overruled by the

---

14. *Heinrich Bullingers Reformationsgeschichte*, Vol. I, p. 12; O. Farner, *op. cit.*, Vol. III,
p. 33.
15. In this section I have made use of various statements and suggestions in C. W. Mön-
nich, *Pelgrimage, Ontmoetingen met de cultuur*, Bussum, 1954; and Julius Schweizer, *Reformierte
Abendmahlsgestaltung in der Schau Zwinglis*, Basle, 1954.

hierarchy of visible and invisible spheres—spheres within which even the devil must take his predestined place, and not even a cherub may step out of line, because of the sublime immutability of God Himself. In other words: whereas the Romanesque church still retained a definite horizontal and therefore a biblical and dramatic element, the late medieval church revealed and proclaimed to the created world its own intrinsically static order, and it represented it as such. It revealed to the created order its theme and its nature, namely, harmony. Worship means: entering into the wonder of creation, this natural-supernatural harmony to which, by virtue of the *analogia entis*, all things belong.

2. Now the medieval Christian makes his way up the nave to the sacred threshold of the choir. The building faces towards the east, so that he can move from the west to where the light rises up from the Lord. In the rose-window above him there may flame the wheel of life with all the signs of the year, of the months, of passing time, which leads up to the heights—but also down into the depths; he has to leave this change-ableness behind him, forgetting both time and world as he gazes on eterni-ty, which redeems him. Already he is stepping, as if through another world, under the multi-coloured light that streams down upon him through the stained-glass windows, amid the sound of voices and music, past the baptistry where once, at the beginning of his life, he was received into this same ark of salvation through which he is now making his way. However, the Christian knows that yonder he is awaited by the priest, the minister of the King of Kings, who, arrayed in his fine, courtly vestments, receives him in accordance with strict ceremonial. Worship means: to leave the world behind, to forget it, to step out of time and stand before the unchangeable throne—to enter the court of God, with all its order.

3. What follows is familiar to us. This minister quickly begins his work as the ordained plenipotentiary, the one with power to bind and to loose. Rudolf Otto has spoken of the "mysterium tremendum ac fascinosum".[16] With fearful adoration the Christian experiences the presence of the Holy One in the transubstantiation. The King appears; he is at hand; indeed, in the communion, the man actually receives him bodily into himself, to strengthen him for this life and to prepare him for eternity. Even more than that, eternity is already present in the sacrament. But here it is manifest that worship is really only what the Priest does when he repeats the unbloody sacrifice. By virtue of his ordination he brings salvation to

---

16. Rudolf Otto, *The Idea of the Holy*, trans. J. W. Harvey, Rev. ed., Oxford, 1936, chap. 21.

the world. He does this symbolically—which does not mean that it is unreal, but that is has its own, sacramental form of reality.[17] Our salvation is achieved through the performance of the liturgy. Whatever discordant element may have caused disorder in the harmony is hereby smoothed out and removed (for scholasticism, sin is primarily "disorder").[18]

The universalism of this view is incapable of bridging the gulf between worship and life—a gulf which it has itself opened up. Certainly the social classes, lands, professions, events—all alike are confronted by the Judge of the world, everything is embraced by the Church, everything is related to the Sacrament. But this only serves to show that the service of God in the outside world does not have its direct origin there, but depends upon the action of the priest in the sacrament. And the corollary is that, since life must nevertheless be taken up into service, the only way left is to establish laws—*human* laws. For salvation cannot dwell outside; it is confined within the church, shackled to the sacrament.

III. PREACHING

1. *Its content*

The theme of the Reformation is grace. The theme of the Reformation is not the harmony between the reality of God and the world of men, even

---

17. "Sacramentum est symbolum rei sacrae et invisibilis gratiae forma visibilis". (A sacrament is the symbol of a sacred reality and the visible form of an invisible grace, Denzinger: *Enchiridon*, No. 876, 1639).

18. Thomas Aquinas states: Ex aversione voluntatis a Deo consecuta est inordinatio in omnibus aliis animae viribus. Sic ergo privatio originalis iustitiae, per quam voluntas subdebatur Deo, est formale in peccato originali; omnis autem alia inordinatio virium animae se habet in peccato originali sicut quiddam materiale. Inordinatio autem aliarum virium animae praecipue in hoc attenditur quod inordinate convertuntur ad bonum commutabile; quae quidem inordinatio communi nomine potest dici concupiscentia. Et ita peccatum originale materialiter quidem est concupiscentia, formaliter vero est defectus originalis iustitiae. (The turning of the will away from God led to disorder in all the other powers of the soul. The loss of that original righteousness, whereby the will was subject to God, thus constitutes the formal element of original sin; all other disorder in the powers of the soul constitutes the material aspect of original sin. The disorder in the other powers of the soul is chiefly to be seen in that they are directed, in a disordered way, towards a transient good. This disorder can be characterised by the customary term "concupiscence". Thus materially, original sin is concupiscence, and formally, it is the lack of original righteousness. *Summa Th.* II, I 82,3).

Original righteousness was the ordained subordination of the lower powers to reason, and the subordination of reason to God (*Summa Th.* I 95,1); since man retains his reason and his freedom, this order is disturbed, but not destroyed. The same is true of concupiscence; it goes beyond the limits of reason, and therefore goes against nature; it is an injuring of nature (vulneratio naturae. *Summa Th.* II, I 85,3). Therefore the disorder must itself bear witness to the validity of the order.

if the supernatural powers by which this harmony is maintained and restored were called grace. The theme of the Reformation is that the reality of God and the world of men stand in direct opposition, and yet are united by the miracle of redemption, the miracle of grace. Grace is God's merciful disposition towards us. Yet it is not a merely general truth, but rather an event. Grace is revealed in Jesus Christ. "The sum of the Gospel is that our Lord Jesus Christ, the true Son of God, has made known to us the will of his heavenly Father, and by his innocence has redeemed us from death and reconciled us to God"[19]—so states Huldrych Zwingli's second Article drawn up for the Zurich Disputation.

This was the main theme of his preaching, and everything else had to be fitted into it or subordinated to it. It was a strongly forensic doctrine of reconciliation, clearly formulated on Anselmian lines. One often has the impression that Zwingli regarded the whole Reformation struggle as a fight for the purity and the consequences of the doctrine of satisfaction.

We do not possess a single manuscript of Zwingli's sermons. He always spoke extempory, and did so daily throughout the years. The writings that have come down to us are mostly in Latin (used as a form of shorthand) and only partially fashioned. A series of special sermons, which he developed and published by request, grew into doctrinal writings. Besides this, fragments of his sermons are to be found in his commentaries.[20] Thus we discover some of the characteristic features of his preaching not only from the numerous testimonies of those who heard him but also from the very nature of his writings. The most important is this: not only did Zwingli add the Saviour's invitation of Matthew 11 ("Come unto me, all ye that labour and are heavy laden, and I will give you rest") to the title-page of all his books, but also all his works, be they concerned with admonition, teaching, comfort or controversy, sooner or later set their particular theme within the greater context of the Gospel, the message of Christ. This is then either more or less fully developed, or else summarised briefly. The heart of the matter is always the reconciliation which Christ achieved for us on the Cross, by rendering satisfaction. No doubt the Reformer spoke in the same way in the pulpit. No sermon without the message of reconciliation. We may take the relevant passage from his

---

19. Z II 27; H III 3.

20. O. Farner, *op. cit.,* Vol. III, pp. 56ff. "Der Nachlass". Further to the problems connected with the transmission of Zwingli's sermons see Farner's introductions to *Aus Zwinglis Predigten zu Jesaja und Jeremia. Unbekannte Nachschriften,* selected and revised by Oskar Farner, Zürich, 1957; and *Aus Zwinglis Predigten zu Matthäus, Markus and Johannes,* selected and translated by Oskar Farner, Zürich, 1957.

treatise "Concerning Divine and Human Righteousness" (1523): "Here
we must show clearly what the Gospel is. We have heard explicitly that
nobody comes to God unless he is pious, pure, righteous and innocent, as
God demands. For in Leviticus 20 he says: be pious, pure or righteous; for
I am pure. As if he were saying: I am righteous, pure and pious.
Therefore, if you would be my people, you must be the same ... All men
must yield to this righteousness; for who is so holy, that his heart is without
temptation and concupiscence? So nobody can dwell with God, for
whoever would dwell with him must be without spot. God has seen this
misery and weakness of ours, he has had mercy on us, and has found the
means whereby his righteousness may be reconciled for us so that we may
dwell with him. It is for this reason that he let his son become man ... and
in that he, who was innocent, suffered death for us guilty sinners, he paid
the price of God's beautiful righteousness, which no man could otherwise
have satisfied. Thus, by his free grace and gift he has made it possible for
us to come to God. Whoever hears this and believes it without doubting
will be blessed. That is the gospel".[21]

This, therefore, is the great change: the break-through from the
liturgical and sacramental action of the church to the word of the completed atonement. The consequences of this for our understanding of
everything that may in any sense be termed service of God are im-
measurable. All our service draws its life from the service that God has
rendered to us. At the beginning of all our service stands the divine service
of Jesus Christ, and that was a service of life, not a liturgy. That he
preached, and taught us to pray, and gathered his disciples around him
certainly belongs to his redeeming work. But it is the atonement he made
for us, which sets us free for that service which permeates our whole being,
as we trust in his guidance (Zwingli's celebrated doctrine of Providence is
rooted in Christology) and obey his will. By his death he purchased the
right to our life. In his sermons, Zwingli described this by his characterisation of Christ as "our Captain".[22] The sixth Article states: "For Jesus
Christ is the guide and captain, promised and given by God to all
mankind". And the seventh Article states: "He is the everlasting salvation
and head of all believers, who are his body, which is, however, dead, and
can do nothing without him".[23]

This preaching, in which the Bible begins to speak again, is therefore
the Word of God. Just as Paul uses the term "Gospel" to describe both the

---

21. Z II 477f.; H. VII 42.
22. Cf. "Christ our Captain" (below, ch. 4).
23. Z I 458f.; H III 4.

content of his message and his own missionary work, so, for Zwingli, the Word of God in Scripture itself, and in the interpretation and proclamation of Scripture, are not to be separated from one another. The Gospel and the Word of God directly characterise the Reformation which sprang from them. These terms denote so much more than part of an order of service—they burst through all the structures and they themselves create the divine service which they seek. It is a splendid example of exposition which is at once both existential and eschatological. For his saying that "the divine righteousness is revealed by the Word of God to our times more than for many centuries"[24] is an eschatalogical phenomenon. Therefore "Do not, for God's sake, suppress his Word!"[25] that is, set evangelical preaching free! "For truly, truly, it will take its course as surely as does the Rhine. It may well be checked for a while, but never stopped".[26] Therefore, to want to offer resistance would be to incur a terrible judgment,[27] although the Word of God has this in common with the Cross of Christ—that it is despised, persecuted and oppressed.[28] But even this is not outside the design of providence, for "God's Word must meet with

---

24. Z II 474; H VII 37. "Huic nostro saeculo vides Christum benignius favere, dum sese clarius aperit quam aliquot retro seculis". (One sees how Christ shows special favour to our age, revealing himself more clearly than to some former ages. Z I 293).

25. Z III 488.

26. *Ibid.*

27. "Our heavenly Father ... has taught us by his Word, especially at this time when the Scriptures are spread to all corners ... As we now see how the magistrates fight against God's Word with all their powers, it is certain that God is angry with us, just as he was with the Jews who would not hear Christ. He says of them in Matthew 13 that seeing they would not see, and hearing they would not hear, for their heart was hardened. But what follows upon that? A wretched destruction and misery worse than had ever been heard. When God's Word is resisted in this same way—as we, alas, well see, for they withstand it with greater wantonness and churlishness than the Jews ever did, then one must accept that the misery and punishment will also follow in similar manner ..." (Z IV 148).

Zwingli also attaches importance to the fact that the threat of judgment contained in God's Word should not be confused with the general anxieties of the age. Because of the unusual conjunction of planets and signs relating to water, astrologers had predicted that there would be immense rainfalls and floods in the year 1524. The resultant panic is strikingly portrayed by Bergengruen in his novel *Am Himmel wie auf Erden,* Zürich, 1947. Zwingli commented in 1523: "As John said in Matthew 3, the axe is laid to the tree ... Even if one wards off (the threat of God's Word) for a time, one cannot escape it in the long run. And this Word does not refer to the flood, as some think, for one should not fear that, but rather say: Lord, thy will be done! For I do not fear what the astrologers predict, nor do I believe it will happen; for they have missed the point up to now. If they talk of cold, one will stifle in the heat; when they talk of warmth, one has to sit by the fire. I hope that one day they will learn and realise that God is Lord". (Z II 453f.; H IV 265).

28. "The Gospel of Christ—that is, the gracious word that God has offered to men and accomplished through his son—has derived its nature from the blood of Christ, in that it thrives on persecution". (Z I 395; H I 128).

resistance so that its power may be seen".[29] So the people of Zürich are confident and expect that within a few years Germany, France, Italy and Spain will yield to the Gospel.[30] For "The Word of God will easily blow all the dust away"[31] and "Nature will change its course, sooner than that the Word of God be not fulfilled and abide secure".[32] In church they learn and confess with thankfulness that "the Word of God is sure and cannot fail; it is clear, and does not leave men to go astray in the dark; it teaches itself, it reveals itself and it illuminates the soul of man with all salvation and grace; it teaches the soul to find comfort in God, it humbles the soul so that it loses itself, or even renounces itself, and cleaves to God. It lives in him. It strives after him and, despairing of all earthly comfort, rests on him alone".[33]

2. *Word and Spirit*[34]

Yet, for all this thankful confidence in preaching and its power, the highest accolade, the one which Martin Luther granted to preaching, was denied to it in Zürich. As the word of man, it is not God himself. Word and Spirit remain clearly distinguished. We know how for Luther everything hangs on the fact that the troubled conscience can find comfort in the concrete human words spoken by a Church official or by one of the brethren: "Verbum, inquam, et solum verbum est vehiculum gratiae dei". ("The Word, I say, and the World alone, is the vehicle of God's grace".)[35] To which Zwingli coolly retorts: "Dux autem vel vehiculum spiritui non est necessarium; ipse enim est virtus et latio qua cuncta feruntur". ("Neither guidance nor vehicle is necessary for the Spirit; He himself is the power and vehicle by which everything is carried along".)[36] In the Roman Church the presence of the Lord depends upon the reading of the Mass. In the Reformation (here we will not go into detail about Calvin; on this point he is nearer to Luther, while making due allowance for Zwingli's reservation)[37] the real presence is ensured by the fact that the Word of God is spoken. Does that simply mean that "someone preaches"? Zwingli denies that. The verbum externum (the external

29. Z II 472; H VII 36.
30. Z IX 130.
31. Z X 153.
32. Z I 355; H I 81.
33. Z I 382; H I 117.
34. Cf. "Praedicatio verbi Dei est verbum Dei" (below, ch. 12).
35. WA II 509.
36. S IV 10.
37. *Institutes* IV. i. 5-6, iii. 1-3.

word) can by itself guarantee neither faith nor the presence of Christ. "No man can come to Christ (that is, believe) except the Father draw him". Zwingli quotes this countless times. If the priest celebrating the Mass could not secure the presence of the Lord in his congregation simply by performing his liturgy, neither can the voice of the preacher secure it instead. To the end of his days Martin Luther marvelled that the Spirit should bind himself to the Word. In much the same way, Zwingli guarded most passionately the truth that the Word is bound to the Spirit. Thus our service of God is continually cast back, beyond all our liturgical ordinances, upon free grace. This is the meaning of the distinction which Zwingli made. He said of the Lutherans; "Hac ratione libertas divini spiritus alligata esset, qui dividit singulis, ut vult, id est: quibus, quando, ubi vult". (In this way the freedom of the Spirit of God would be bound, whereas he imparts to each one as he will; that is, to whom, and when, and where he will.)[38] "Manifestum ergo fit, quod eo verbo, quod celestis pater in cordibus nostris praedicat, quo simul illuminat, ut intelligamus, et trahit, ut sequamur, fideles reddimur... Ab ipso iudicatur exterius verbum. Quod et ipsum deus in medium adferi ordinavit, tametsi fides non sit ex verbo externo". (It becomes clear, therefore, that we are made believers through the word which the heavenly Father himself preaches in our hearts, the word by which he both enlightens us, so that we understand, and draws us, so that we follow... The external word is subject to the judgment of this word. God has certainly ordained that this (external) word should be proclaimed, yet faith does not come by the external word.)[39]

3. *The Alternative*

What caused the men of Zürich to maintain this distinction so stubbornly? The reason was this: if the preaching of God's service to us, which calls us to the service of God—if preaching is the alternative to a service conceived of as liturgy—then this preaching must not itself become a piece of liturgy, or an action to which salvation is bound, for that would be its death. Rather must preaching remain bound to salvation. It testifies to the presence of the salvation which has been wrought by the free grace of the Spirit; but the mere act of preaching does not ensure the presence of that salvation. Zwingli believed that at this point the very essence of the Reformation, as he understood it, was at stake. The controversy about the Lord's Supper only brought the implications of it to light.

38. Z III 761.
39. Z III 263.

As has already been stated, the Reformation in Zurich was sparked off
by social and ecclesiastical grievances. To begin with, Zwingli was
something of a humanistic, idealistic and pacifist Reformer, but then, in
the fearful terror of judgment, he discovered that only the Gospel could
still save his people and Christendom. Now we must name the cause
which, in Zwingli's view, lay at the root of these manifestations of human
selfishness—it is the deification of the creature. This can appear as worldly
greed for gold or power, or it may assume the form of a piety in which one
puts one's trust in earthly things, places, actions or men, seeking God
among these instead of seeking him by himself, that is, in his Word. This
Word tells us, however, that he wants to dwell in us by his Spirit and
thereby to prove himself to be our highest and our only good, the *summum
bonum.* Over against this, economic and religious materialism both stem
from the same root. The man who will not be led by the Spirit of God is
thereby banished every time to the realm of the earthly, the ungodly and
the anti-godly—whether he succumbs to his self—chosen virtues, his
impulses, his greed, his ceremonies or the rules and regulations of a false
church. Luther's Reformation was directed against the Judaistic heresy.
For him, the alternative to faith is works. Zwingli's Reformation was
directed against the false doctrine of pagans. For him, the alternative to
faith is every kind of idolatry, ceremony or *traditio humana* (man-made
tradition). "False religion, false piety is that which trusts in something
other than God. Whoever puts his trust in creatures, no matter how important they may be, is not truly pious. The unbelievers are those who accept the word of man as if it were the Word of God. Therefore, to put men
or councils on a level with the Word of God is madness and the worst kind
of ungodlines. For if these opinions and statutes agree with the Word of
God, it is the Word of God, and not the human statute that should be accepted; and if they do not agree, then one should reject them and flee from
them, just as the children of Israel refused to enter into marriage with the
women of the Moabites and other heathen".[40] Conversely, "True religion
or piety consists in cleaving to the one true God. Pious people listen only to
their Lord, who has torn them away from the flesh and united them with
himself, so that they wish to hear only his voice, and in fervent love they
exclaim with the soul in the Song of Songs "Your voice sounds in my
ears!"[41] ... "Only those who depend wholly on the Word of God are true
believers"...[42] "So those who have the Spirit of Christ do not have their

40. Z III 674; H IX 73.
41. Z III 669; H IX 65.
42. Z III 670; H IX 66.

own spirit. Those who have the Spirit of Christ accept nothing except the Word of the one God, for Christ, who is himself God, cannot accept or tolerate any word other than his own".[43]

So the alternative is this: either the Word of God, spoken into our heart by the Spirit of God himself[44]—or the word of man, whether this word of man comes in the form of divine service, official activity, ceremony, sacrament or—preaching. Similarly, this is the alternative that faces every sermon: service of God or service of the creature.

4. The Contemporary Relevance of Preaching[45]

The Gospel is the most relevant thing there is; in fact, it is the one truly relevant thing in this world. Preaching does not have to be relevant—it is relevant. We must not look for relevance outside, and then slip it into the sermon by artful methods; the mere fact that God allows his Word to be proclaimed imparts a unique urgency to our worship. The eschatalogical character of the Reformation bears the stamp of both the Epiphany and the Parousia. Christ himself is present here;[46] everywhere "the rejected Christ rises again".[47] The reformation sermon makes the resurrection a present reality, it is *christianismus herbescens;* it is, indeed, *Christus renascens* (a new flowering of Christianity, a rebirth of Christ).[48] Preaching is once more God's remedy for his apostate people[49]—to resist him is the sin against the Holy Spirit, the final condemnation. "Since we must personally confess that the whole world is so corrupt, vicious and abominable that it must be radically put right, and since we know that the heavenly Father never fails (us), but always warns and chastises; and since we see at the same time that God has sent his Word in order to heal the deep—rooted trouble and to deliver us from it, so that we do not perish, who will not lift his head to the voice of the Lord? Who can help knowing that the day of the Lord is here? Not, as yet, the Last Day, when the Lord will judge the whole world, but the day when present things are renewed. The prophet

---

43. Z III 673; H IX 70.

44. Z II 110; H III 141 etc. Also the "inspiration of the Spirit" (Einhauchen des Geistes), Z II 76; H III 93 etc.

45. O. Farner, *op. cit.*, Vol. III, pp. 116ff.; cf. also "Huldrych Zwingli's Concept of History" (below, ch. 6).

46. Z I 113, 152, 197, 301; II 19; S IV 33.

47. "Through the Word of God", Z II 445; H IV 253.

48. *Th. H. Z.* I, pp. 20ff.; Paul Wernle, *Die Renaissance des Christentums im 16. Jahrhundert,* Tübingen, 1904; Arthur Rich, *Die Anfänge der Theologie Huldrych Zwinglis,* Zürich, 1949; for "verbum renascens", cf. Z III 675.

49. Z III 631; "pharmacon", 629.

says: 'When the lion roars, who can but fear? The Lord God has spoken, who can but prophecy?' I say; the Most High has let his voice sound forth. Who, then, will not say: I will hear what the Lord God will speak with me? He will speak His Gospel with us which, to our cost, was so long hidden from us, even though we had it among us according to the letter. He has brought this Gospel back to us, in order to cleanse us from the stain of our sins, just as He once gave Deuteronomy to the Jews''.[50]

This relevance is the criterion of whether preaching is the Word of God. As long as preaching does not speak relevantly, it is not a true rendering of the Biblical message "Since it is easy to see that the word which we preach today is in direct conflict with the vices in which we are stuck up to our ears, it must be the Word of God''.[51]

For centuries, Zwingli's preachings has caused foreign mercenary service to be a pressing question of conscience, and particularly the "pension system", and abuse whereby foreign princes, including the King of France and the Pope, granted annuities to individual councillors in the magistracy in return for their support for favourable wage-contracts and for giving permission to recruit. It is said to be the case even today that there are people who have a financial interest in militarism. In 1521, when the all-powerful Cardinal Schinner was staying in Zürich in connection with the renewal of the alliance with the Pope (Schinner was a humanist, who sought to win Zwingli's friendship) the Reformer preached a memorable sermon, as the papal nuncio was sitting in full vestments below the pulpit: "He also spoke against treaties with princes and noblemen which, if they had been made, were closely watched by every good man to see that what had been promised should be done. Therefore one should not conclude any military treaties, and if God helped a people to get out of treaties, they should take care and not enter into them again, for they cost a lot of blood. And I wish, said Zwingli, that someone would punch a hole through the Pope's treaty and stick it on his messenger's back so that he could carry it back home. He also said: they sound the alarm for a wolf that eats animals, but nobody wants to restrain the wolf that destroys people. They do right to wear red hats and cloaks: for if you shake them, ducats and crowns will fall out; and if you wring them, the blood of your son, your brother, your cousin, your good friend will run out''.[52]

---

50. Z III 633; H IX 8.

51. Z III 634; H IX 10.

52. *Heinrich Bullingers Reformationsgeschichte*, ed. J. Hottinger and H. Vögeli, Frauenfeld, 1838, Vol. I, p. 51; Z I 73. Zwingli preached a similar sermon in 1525, after the defeat of the Swiss by Frundsberg's German soldiers at Pavia; cf. *Bullingers Reformationsgeschichte*, Vol. I,

In the malaise which followed the collapse at Kappel, people wanted to forbid ministers to "interfere" in public affairs and to oblige them to restrict themselves to religious matters, as we would say today. It is well known how the young Bullinger bravely and tenaciously refused to succeed Zwingli under these conditions. The Council gave way. The freedom of the pulpit was expressly guaranteed. However, there developed out of these disputes the custom of the so-called "petition" (Fürtrag). When the "ministers of the Churches of Zürich" had a request or a complaint concerning political affairs, it was not necessary to bring the matter into the pulpit immediately. For centuries one would sometimes see all the ministers, wearing their robes, led by the Antistes (Senior Pastor) with a Bible under his arm, walking from the Great Minster along the Limmatquai to the Council House to appear there before the assembled gentlemen. Today the reports still fill several cupboards in the city library and to a great extent are still not researched. To give one example (a military one, to retain a balance): during the Thirty Years' War, when Tilly had occupied the whole of South Germany, and alliances were beginning to arise between Vienna and the Catholic interior of Switzerland, the Reformed peoples were possessed by a severe despair and lack of resolution. Then Antistes Breitinger and his colleagues appeared before the Council of Two Hundred and exhorted them, kindly to put the city defences in order and to do their duty as a christian authority "which bears the sword". Why should not synodical delegations to governments become a permanent institution once more?

5. The Liturgy[53]

Unfortunately, we must forgo a description of the new orders of divine service created by Zwingli and Leo Jud. Julius Schweizer has analysed them for us. A few general observations may be made. The judgment of Schmidt-Clausing, a pupil of Fendt, is that "Luther cleansed, Zwingli created".[54] As yet the Zürich, liturgy is not "reformed and prosaic", but

---

pp. 258-261; Gagliardi in Zwa. III, pp. 339ff.; O. Farner, op. cit., Vol. III, pp. 58ff. For the relationship between the Zürich reformation and the pension system, cf. G. W. Locher, Der Eigentumsbegriff als Problem evangelischer Theologie, 2nd ed. Zürich, 1962. Part I, chapter 3: "Zwingli. Die politische Verantwortung der Christenheit und das Eigentumsproblem".

53. For the practice of the Lord's Supper, cf. Z IV 1ff.; for the order of the Christian Church in Zürich, ibid., 671ff. Fritz Schmidt-Clausing, Zwingli als Liturgiker. Eine liturgiegeschichtliche Untersuchung, Göttingen, 1952. See also the review by G. W. Locher in Musik und Gottesdienst, Zürich, 1955, No. 2; Julius Schweizer, Reformierte Abedmahlsgestaltung in der Schau Zwinglis, Basle, 1954.

54. Op. cit., p. 63.

rich and lively. The ecumenical material is carefully used, but it is
resolutely rearranged. It is no longer acknowledged that the Mass actually
represents the norm of Christian worship. We have the preaching service
and the congregational service. The liturgical elements are not intended to
provide a "frame" for the sermon, and still less an enrichment of it; and of
course nobody would here fall for the absurd idea that the supposed objectivity of the liturgical action has the task of containing and balancing the
subjectivity of the preaching. For what is more objective and yet at the
same time more subjective than the word of reconciliation? The prayers,
lessons, responses (Zwingli had wanted these to be made by men and
women alternately), the Apostles' Creed, the commandments—all this is
simply the congregation's way to the Word, and then the way back from
the Word, and out into life with the Word. And there is one remarkable
feature: Zwingli put the prayer of general confession *after* the sermon, and
immediately before the final blessing, without weakening it with the
customary absolution. So after having received forgiveness the congregation disperses with the confession of sin—which is a shattering vision![55]

6. *Accomplishing the Reformation*

The Reformation was always founded on preaching, and it grew as the
fruit of preaching. In principle the Reformation was established because
evangelical preaching was given free course after the mandates of the
Council in 1521 and 1523. But then all iconoclastic movements were suppressed, and not because of any concern, anxiety or heavy-handedness on
the part of the authorities, but as a matter of principle,[56] and this led to the

---

55. From the position of the confession, Julius Schweizer concludes (*op. cit.,* pp. 38f.,
49f.) that Zwingli sought for a weekly celebration of the Lord's Supper. But it would be difficult to reconcile this intention with Zwingli's doctrine of the Lord's Supper. The position of
the confession arises, rather, from his conception of the prophetic character of preaching. In
his earlier writings Zwingli usually describes the minister as a shepherd, a pastor or a
watchman, episcopus or bishop, whereas in his later writings he almost always speaks of the
minister as a prophet. For Zwingli's concept of liturgical prayer, see Z II 352-354, H 148ff.,
where he emphasises that without "a true exposition of God's Word", it must inevitably
lead to hypocrisy, but from a "good understanding of God's Word" there arises genuine
personal and common prayer. "Farewell, my temple muttering! It is no great harm to me. I
know that you are no loss to me! But greetings to you, pious, inward prayer, awakened by
God's Word in the heart of the believer, even the little groan which arises briefly, and
recognises itself, and will soon listen further. And greetings to you, common prayer, which
all Christians practise for one another, whether publicly in the temple or in their own
chamber, freely and without reward! I know that you are the prayer to which God will give
what he has promised".

56. "One should keep to God's Word alone, and use only that. It will have its effect. For
Christ will slay his enemy, the Antichrist, with the breath of his mouth, II Thess. 2". (Z II
452; H IV 263). "I would also, that all priests would endeavour to present Christ alone; and

tragic division between Zwingli and the Baptists. Fritz Blanke has demonstrated in convincing fashion that the Baptists were originally simply the conventicle of a revival movement that arose out of evangelical preaching,[57] people of a radical mind, to whom the abolition of idolatry appeared too slow a process. But Zwingli, who was sure that the fruit of preaching would ripen sooner or later, issued a warning—not really against impatience, but against legalism. We should not seek to do what the Holy Spirit will do himself; for that would mean replacing popish, human regulations by reformed ones, and would be exactly the same kind of idolatry. It would be dangerous and merciless (and therefore not true to the Gospel) to smash the old faith before the congregations had been established in the true faith. First let there be evangelical faith in Christ alone, and then ceremonies can be abolished.[58] "You can easily persuade an old man to leave his armchair", says Zwingli, "if you first give him a stick to lean on; but otherwise he will never listen to you, because he will think you want to kill him".[59] And so gradually, village by village, parish by parish, it was put to the vote; and then, by the decision of the over-whelming majority, the mass and images were done away with in an orderly fashion.[60]

One little-known detail typifies the conscientious manner in which it was done. After the mass had been discontinued, the question naturally arose as to what should be done with the endowments given for regular masses for the dead, which were sometimes hundreds of years old, and involved considerable sums of money. In Zwinglian territory, such funds were not simply confiscated by the magistrate or the territorial prince.

---

if the Word were preached steadfastly, then in time all the sects, the rabble, the orders and the other abuses would be put away". (Z II 739f.); cf. *Commentarius de vera et falsa religione*, the chapter "De scandalo", Z III 888f.

57. Fritz Blanke, *Brüder in Christo: Die Geschichte der ältesten Taufergemeinde (Zollikon 1525)*, Zürich, 1955.

58. "Everything that has been introduced and added which was not ordained by Christ, is a real abuse. But since one cannot do away with them at a stroke, it is necessary that God's Word should be preached against them, steadfastly and bravely ..." (Z II 788); "Debet doctrina praecedere, imaginum autem abolitio cum tranquillitate sequi; docebit autem omnia in omnibus charitas". (Doctrine must come first, and then the abolition of images will follow peacefully; but in all things love will teach us everything. Z III 906).

59. Z III 891.

60. Cf. the exposition of the Forty-eighth Article, Z II 357ff.; H IV 155ff. It reads: "Therefore the watchmen everywhere should take away the vexation; that is, they should earnestly preach and teach concerning what is forbidden by God, and what by man, so that they do not butcher poor consciences for ever in the prison of human commandments. And thus it will follow that the whole world will listen to God's Word alone, and so piety, peace and joy in the Holy Spirit will increase ..." (Z II 358f.; H IV 157).

Zwingli taught that these funds had to do with the communion of saints. The papal misunderstanding of this wanted to devote them to souls in purgatory. But the evangelical faith understands that the true saints, who have the first claim of the fellowship upon us, are the poor in our congregation. So this money is for the care of the poor. So the new exposition of an article of faith had legal consequences.[61] This was the "Reformation change in divine service" in the broadest sense.

IV. THE LORD'S SUPPER

It is impossible to present in a few sentences all the problems connected with the controversy over the Lord's Supper.[62] And perhaps it would not be superfluous to remark in passing that our attempt to understand Zwingli from the point of view of his own presuppositions and, if possible, to hear a word for our own times, does not mean that we have to defend him at every point. Calvin may well be right in the opinion he expressed in his letter to the Zwinglian Zébédée in Orbe, that Zwingli had not grasped all the richness of what is given to the congregation in the Lord's Supper.[63] Though even in this letter, in which Calvin appears (as so often) as the pupil of Bucer and the propagator of his doctrine, it is clear that Calvin was not aware of how much he had actually received from Zurich by way of Strasbourg. Luther and Zwingli are both concerned about the true and real presence of Christ in the Supper—for Luther it is the *presence* of Christ, for Zwingli, the presence of *Christ*. The problems of the contro-

---

61. The exposition of the Sixty-fourth Article is quite clear at this point—Z II 449ff.; H IV 259ff.; cf. Z III 51; H I 223: "For the sake of God's glory one should clothe the living images of God, the poor Christians, and not idols of wood or stone". "...Henceforth the goods which have been used for the decoration of idols are to be used for the poor, who are the true image of God". (Z III 130). Cf. Z III 178f.; e.g. 179: the veneration of the saints and their images (including St. Ann, "the most worthy Virgin Mary", St. Peter and St. Othmar) "is to the detriment of God's glory, which is venerated when he is honoured in the person of the poor". The church tithes, which even according to papal law were originally intended for the poor, must be restored to them (Z III 392ff.; 454, H VII 147ff., 211).

62. Walther Köhler, *Zwingli und Luther. Ihr Streit über das Abendmahl*, Vol. I, Leipzig, 1924; Vol. II, Gütersloh, 1953; Gottlob Schrenk, "Zwinglis Hauptmotive in der Abendmahlslehre und das Neue Testament" in *Zwa.* V/4 (1930/2); Fritz Blanke, "Zwinglis Sakramentsanschauung", *Theol. Blätter*, 1931/10; Wilhelm Niesel, "Zwinglis 'spätere' Sakramentsanschauung", *Theol. Blätter*, 1932/1; Fritz Schmidt-Clausing, *Zwingli als Liturgiker*, Göttingen, 1952; Julius Schweizer, *Reformierte Abendmahlsgestaltung in der Schau Zwinglis*, Basle, 1954. G. W. L.: *Zw. Ref. im Rahmen.*, 1979, ch. XV.

63. Calvin to André Zébédée, Strasbourg, May 19th, 1539 (*Johannes Calvins Lebenswerk in seinen Briefen...* translated by Rudolf Schwarz. Vol. I, Tübingen, 1909, p. 72); Fritz Blanke, "Calvins Urteile über Zwingli" in *Aus der Welt der Reformation*, Zürich, 1960, pp. 18-47.

versy are rooted in Luther's scholastic conceptions and in Zwingli's spiritualism.[64]

Once it has been understood, we shall never regard this spiritualism as rationalism. Zwingli's protest against Luther's sacramental realism did not arise from rationalism,[65] but from his Christology, out of concern for the complete and exclusive validity of the atonement which was made on the Cross.[66] If reconciliation took place *there*, then the comfort of the troubled soul cannot be made to depend on the celebration of the sacrament[67]—an alternative which Luther never understood, nor could ever recognise on the basis of *his* presuppositions. But for Zwingli, as he was never tired of saying, if the ceremony was more than a testimony to the forgiveness which God has sealed in my heart, through His Holy Spirit, for the sake of Christ—if it constitutes the very act of forgiveness, then it is nothing but "a yearning for the fleshpots of Egypt", the first decline into medieval ceremonialism, in which faith clings to what is visible instead of to Christ, who is both in one, the manifestation and the pledge of grace (*gratia praestita Dei, pignus gratiae*).[68] At this point—Zwingli cannot see it any other way—the whole of the Reformation is at stake.[69]

---

64. Erich Seeberg, "Der Gegensatz zwischen Zwingli, Schwenckfeld und Luther" in *Reinhold Seeberg-Festschrift*, Leipzig, 1929; Helmut Gollwitzer, "Zur Auslegung von Joh. 6 bei Luther und Zwingli" in *Evangelische Theologie*, 1951; *Th. H.Z.* I, pp. 116f.

65. "Absurditatem non metimur ab ipsa re; nihil enim putamus absurdum esse, quod divinis eloquiis traditum est ... si modo recte intelligas ea, quae fidei credenda proponuntur. Quod si quid fidei absurdum, id tandem vere absurdum est". (We do not deduce the absurdity from the matter itself; for we do not consider anything absurd which comes to us from the Word of God ... if only those things which are presented for acceptance by faith are rightly understood. But if anything appears absurd to faith, then it is truly absurd. Z V 618).

66. Zwingli feared that the Lutheran understanding of the Real Presence infringed the concept of Christ's death as the sole source of salvation. "Only by his death does he provide food for the soul, not when eaten bodily". (Z V 279; cf. Z IV 812). On John 6:63 he writes: "Caro Christi caesa plurimum potest, commessa poenitus nihil". (The body of Christ slain has supreme power, but when eaten it has none at all. Z V 356).

67. "Christo dei filio fidere, salutare est contra peccatorum vulnera remedium, non corpus edere! Fidei promissa est salus, non manducationi..." (To trust in Christ the Son of God is the wholesome cure for all the wounds of sin, and not to eat his body! Salvation is promised to faith, not to eating with the mouth. Z V 576). On John 6:63 he writes: "Christus spiritui, hoc est: sibi deo vitam tribuit; carnis ergo esse non potest. Caro igitur manducata ad nihilum prodest". (Christ attributes life to the Spirit, and that means to himself, as God; so it cannot belong to the flesh. Therefore eating the flesh avails nothing. Z V 612).

68. Z III 787 and elsewhere.

69. In his doctrine of the Lord's Supper, Zwingli sought to protect the concept of sola fide against any new manifestations of trust in the creature or in ritual; cf. Z III 781f., 785ff. "Credere ergo Christum, qui carnem nostram induit et in ea mortem pro nobis passus est, filium esse dei viventis, hoc demum est salutare, non credere quod in pane caro Christi corporaliter edatur". (Therefore, to believe that Christ, who assumed our flesh and suffered death in the flesh for us, is the Son of the living God—that is salvation, and not to believe that the flesh of Christ is eaten bodily in the bread. S VI, I 719, commenting on John 6).

Would not certain experiences in our own generation indicate that his watchfulness was correct?

"And so I believe that the sacrament is a sign of the holy thing, that is, of the accomplished grace (*sacramentum esse sacrae rei, hoc est factae gratiae, signum*). I believe, that it is the visible shape or form, that is, the visible, illustrative image (exemplum) of the invisible grace which—let this be well understood—has been effected and given by the gift of God. To be sure, this image bears a certain similarity (*analogia*) to the thing itself, which has been wrought through the Spirit. I believe that the sacrament is a public sign ... and therefore the sacraments should be cherished piously as holy ceremonies—for the word is added to the elements and makes the sacrament (*accedit enim verbum ad elementum et fit sacramentum*—the famous quotation from Augustine). So they should be highly esteemed and handled reverently ... I believe that in the holy Supper of the Eucharist, that is, the Thanksgiving, the real body of Christ is present to the eye of faith (verum Christi corpus adesse fidei contemplatione); and this means that those who thank the Lord for the benefit bestowed on us in his Son recognise that he took real flesh, in which he really suffered, and really washed away our sins by His blood, and that here the entire work of salvation which Christ accomplished is, as it were, present to the eye of faith (et omnem rem per Christum gestam illis fidei contemplatione velut praesentem fieri). But that the body of Christ, that is, His natural body, is essentially and really (per essentiam et realiter) present in the Lord's Supper or can be eaten in our mouth and with our teeth, as is maintained by the papists and by certain people who look back to the flesh-pots of Egypt—this we do not merely deny, but we assert with the utmost earnestness that it is an error that is contrary to the Word of God (qui *verbo* dei adversatur)".[70] Here Zwingli is thinking not only of Scripture, but also of the message of grace seen as proclamation. The Lutherans, who actually ascribed the real presence of the body of Christ (praesentia essentialis) to the power of the Word, must especially have felt the force of this analysis. But the very thing which the Lutherans expected from the Supper, Zwingli expected from Christ and from his Spirit.[71] "Everything indicates ... that after the ascension of

---

70. S IV 11; H XI 273ff. Z VI/II 806.

71. Cf. Z VI 336f.: "In this place (John 6:63) we hear clearly that it can only be the spirit that gives life; and his flesh ... is of no use, however much one would eat of it; for we are speaking here of the fruitfulness of his death, which he suffered in the flesh, and which gives life to the soul ... one would require a Scripture to show that the physical eating of the body of Christ comforts the soul; for in Scripture all consolation is attributed solely to the divine Spirit".

Christ, God wanted to comfort us by his Spirit alone, and not by the bodily eating of his flesh ..."[72]

Today we know that Zwingli did recognise a transubstantiation. Julius Schweizer, a historian of liturgy, has discovered that at the very point where the transubstantiation is effected in the Mass, in Zwingli's orders of service the congregation is addressed as having been changed into the Body of Christ.[73]

V. CONFESSION[74]

Confession and absolution are ancient components of Christian worship in all denominations. How could it be otherwise, when the Gospel brings the message of reconciliation and forgiveness? Though it must not be forgotten that it was at this very point that, at all too early a date, ecclesiastical discipline, authority or lust for power crept into the communication of the divine message of grace and judgment, became entangled in it, and actually usurped its place. But after Luther[75] had set the practice of confession wholly free from Roman sacerdotalism and from the idea of merit, he was able thankfully to continue public and private confession as helpful and comforting forms in which the word of forgiveness is spoken to us; in which that is really said to us, which no man can say to himself; in which reconciliation assumes a form. These are important processes in divine worship.

Zwingli rejects confession—not when it is understood as fraternal discussion and counsel, or as the pastoral method of proclaiming the Gospel, but as an official, liturgical act of absolution.[76] Is it because forgiveness played a minor role in his thought and work as a Reformer? It is the very opposite. What Lutheranism wished to emphasise by its solemn use of confession—namely, the necessity of a personal acceptance of grace—that is what the people of Zürich sought to clarify, represent and embody by withdrawing confession from our worship, ritual, liturgy and

---

72. S II, I 219.

73. Julius Schweizer, *op. cit.,* pp. 103f.

74. Z II 393-404; Z III 820-823; S II, I 22f.

75. Martin Luther, *Resolutiones disputationum de indulgentiarum virtute*, WA I 605; *Evangelium von den zehn Aussätzigen*, WA VIII 336; "Luther continued to maintain the idea of private absolution to which he came in the early years of the reformation" (F. Blanke in Z V 716); Köstlin, *Luthers Theologie*, Vol. II, pp. 245-256; Erich Roth, *Die Privatbeichte und die Schlüsselgewalt in der Theologie der Reformatoren*, Gütersloh, 1952.

76. Article 52: "Hence the confession which is made to the priest or to one's neighbour shall not be held to be a remittance of sin, but as a seeking for advice". (Z II 390; H III 9; H IV 194).

official actions.[77] This, above all, is the special province of the Holy Spirit. It belongs, and this is saying the same thing, to the personal relationship between God and myself. I am reconciled to God through Christ. Therein is the life of all divine service and preaching. It is to this that it bears witness, this is its source, and this is its goal. But it cannot and will not bring this about. The reconciliation is the very heart of life's service of God. In the midst of life it makes this life into a Christian life and takes it into the service of God. The living interrelationship of penitence, redemption and thanksgiving is never a matter of ecclesiastical arrangement and never is it the function of an office. The common divine service of the congregation must reflect the fact that it is the general Law of the Christian life.

Therefore Zwingli argues against Luther as follows: "You have rightly taught that Christ Jesus ... is our salvation ... But as you, besides this (that 'besides' is typical of Zwingli) have always emphasised that the absolution must be spoken to him who would be certain that his sins have been forgiven, and that this same absolution is the keys, then you have not really recognised either the keys or the Gospel. For assurance of faith comes from the Gospel, for we know that the Son of God has paid for our sins with His death. If faith is there, then absolution or acquittal is there also; so there is no need to make man certain, for he can become certain by faith alone, and nobody gives faith save God. And even if a man should say a thousand times: 'Your sins are forgiven you', nobody would be sure of it, except the one who has been assured in his heart by God ... nobody accepts Christ Jesus, unless the Father has drawn him. Thus it follows: as soon as he is drawn, he believes. If he believes, then he is already certain ... so why do we need to make certain or to give him absolution? ... Does not Paul say, in Romans 8: the Spirit Himself bears witness with our spirit...? And in Galations 4:6 ... From the Spirit comes the assurance of our spirit that we are the sons of God, and not from the words of an absolver..."[78]

Behind this verdict there stand six conclusions, each of which marks a major turning point.

1. The Reformation is concerned with the divinity of God. But the divinity of God is revealed pre-eminently and most wonderfully in his gracious act. God has reserved to himself the power to forgive. To ascribe

---

77. Calvinism demonstrates its ecumenical character here also, by maintaining the "both-and", which is better.

78. S II, II 22.

to man the power to forgive would be idolatry. "The fiftieth Article states: God alone remits our sins through Christ Jesus, His Son, our only Lord. The fifty-first Article states: Whoever grants this power to the creature is denying God his glory, and giving it to him who is not God. This is true idolatry".[79]

2. "Nothing is sin, except what is against the Word of *God*. Therefore it must follow that he alone forgives sin; for nobody can forgive on behalf of another".[80]

3. This fact should only be illuminated by our ecclesiastical institutions, and not obscured by them. In order to receive grace, the Gospel points us to Christ, not to office-bearers, or even to the Apostles.[81] The power of the keys, which is committed to all believers,[82] simply consists in proclamation of the Gospel.[83] "To bind and to loose is nothing other than to preach".[84] The institution of confession stands in the way of true absolution.

4. "Faith makes man pious, not auricular confession. The just will live by faith" (*Justus ex fide vivet*).[85] Anyone who wished to consider these matters from the psychological aspect and sought to point out that, for a Luther, temptation belongs with faith, whereas a Zwingli really can enjoy a sure peace in God, could be making a suggestion worthy of note. Yet it needs to be remembered that Zwingli's intention at this point lies in a direction which such a psychology would not expect. For his concern is that one should fight one's way through to a genuine repentance, and then the Spirit of God Himself will lead the heart to peace. Absolution has no business to interfere here, with its premature relief".[86] "But the man who

---

79. Z I 463f.; H III 9.

80. Z II 363f.; H IV 163.

81. Even the apostles are only instruments, i.e. preachers; cf. S IV 96, 117.

82. It is not given to Peter alone; cf. Z II 365-391. According to Matt. 16, Ps. 118:22, Matt. 21:42, I Peter 2:6 and I Cor. 3:11 Christ alone is the rock and "the foundation of the churches, that is, of the faithful" (369); but Peter "gave the answer on behalf of all" (368); "and I say to thee that thou, son of Jonas, shalt henceforth be called Peter, that is, a rock, because of this firm and solid confession" (339); "whence it follows also that the keys have been promised not only to Peter but also to all the disciples, and in them to us, that is, to all believers, if we say with them that Jesus is the Christ, the Son of God" (368). "Those who believe, as the disciples believed with Peter, that Christ is the Son of the living God, are founded upon the rock, and are therefore called rocks" (370; cf. 380).

83. Z II 374f., 380, 385; H IV 174f., 180, 186; cf. Qu. 83 and Qu. 84 of the Heidelberg Catechism; with Qu. 85 compare the exposition of the Fifty-third Article, Z II 405ff.; H IV 204.

84. Z II 386; H IV 187.

85. Z II 402; H IV 200.

86. Z II 400ff.; H IV 200ff.

is just in his faith will confess directly to God every day, or indeed, as often as he sins".[87]

5. In the face of these weighty considerations, all protestations about the usefulness of confession fall to the ground. It has no basis in Scripture. "Nothing is good, save what comes from God. One honours God in vain, when one honours him according to the laws and doctrines of men. It is no use prattling".[88]

6. To see only the negative aspect of Zwingli's protest is a wicked misunderstanding! The "No" he speaks to human tradition is intended only to open the way to his "Yes" to a sincere repentance. We can hear the pastor and the theologian speaking simultaneously—and it would be dishonest if we were so to concentrate on the different consequences which he draws that we overlooked the profound agreement there is with the whole Reformation: "If you want to understand real, true confession, and do it, then lay hold of this. You are a Christian? Yes. Do you believe, without doubt, in the Lord Christ? Yes. What do you believe about him? Answer: That God has made him the one who brings grace for our sin for all eternity. You have judged rightly. So if you have sinned, acknowledge your sin; for confession is nothing other than to surrender and to accuse oneself. And to say with David (Psalms 90; 49; 69) 'Lord, my poor soul is very troubled, and thou, Lord, how long thou hast been away from me. Lord, turn again and redeem my soul. Forgive me my sins through Jesus Christ, in whom thou hast promised to give us all things'. And do not give up crying until God tells you in your heart that you are safe, that he has indeed forgiven through Christ Jesus. Do not give up until you can joyfully say and surely believe: I know that God cannot deny me, for he gave his Son for me, and gave him up so that he should pay for my sins. So it cannot be otherwise: he will forgive me my sins through him; for God is true, he cannot lie. But if God should turn still further away from you, so that you never find peace, then seek comfort from one who can inform you concerning the Word of God, in a better way than you have known so far. See the keys, and he will acquaint you with the Gospel; he will teach you what hope you should have towards God through God's own word. If you believe him, you will be saved; if you do not believe him, you will still be bound in your sins.

And listen to another, shorter confession. Think often in the day about your sinful life; and when you really have to despair over it, then say with

---

87. Z II 402; H IV 201.
88. Z II 403f.; H IV 202.

the publican: O Lord, be merciful to me, a sinner. In my judgment this short cry is a better confession than all the cloister-babbling (German: Baginenblappen) that goes on in some places".[89]

VI. PROPHECY

We have seen that for Zwingli the Reformation began with this—or rather, consisted in this—that the Word of God began to speak once more through the exposition and application of Holy Scripture. His act of reformation was really nothing but a simple change from prescribed passages to a *lectio continua*, thereby shifting the emphasis from the liturgy to the sermon. At the end of 1522 the *Archeteles*, the account which he submitted to the Bishop of Constance, states: "To put you in the picture concerning my preaching activity in Zürich: four years ago I preached right through the Gospel according to Matthew (we know that he started with Matthew, in order to put our Lord's own words before all else.)[90] After the Gospel, I continued immediately with the Acts of the Apostles, for now the Church in Zürich ought to see how, and under what authorities, the further proclamation of the Gospel began. There followed at once Paul's First Epistle to Timothy, which seemed to me to be of excellent benefit to the good flock, because it contains, as it were, the rules of the Christian life. In the meantime, certain persons who had a smattering of knowledge had strayed into such ungodly madness that they had almost brought the name of Paul into disrepute, as they gave themselves airs with their seemingly pious and harmless remarks: 'Who is Paul, anyway? Is he not just a man? Certainly he is an Apostle, but only an additional member, not one of the Twelve; for he never spoke with Christ, and he never composed an article of faith; for my part, I believe a Thomas or a Scotus just as much as a Paul'. So I expounded the two letters of Peter, the prince of the Apostles, so that they might see clearly whether both the Apostles, filled with the same Spirit, did not say the same thing. When I had finished with that, I took up the letter to the Hebrews, in order that they should see more clearly the gracious work of Christ and his glory; here they should learn that *Christ* is the High Priest; and they have already learnt this, to a certain extent".[91] When it had come so far, the break-through of the evangelical mandates and the victorious disputations followed virtually as a matter of course.

It is self-evident that such a renewal and preservation of the church, this turning to Scripture (not as a merely theoretical appeal, but in practice)

---

89. Z II 404f.; H IV 203f.
90. *Th. H. Z.* I, pp. 24ff.
91. Z I 284f.

requires that the interpreters themselves must strive to understand the Bible and to apply it. Therefore the establishment of the "prophecy"—which, to my knowledge, lasted into the eighteenth century—was not a welcome by-product, nor just an arrangement for training ministers, but an integral part of the Reformation change in worship in Zürich—and, perhaps, that which has had the most widespread and profound effect upon Protestantism as a whole. We have already seen how this institution came into being. Here they did not first produce a scientific exegesis, and then ask how much of it, and in what way it could be made intelligible to the sheep; it was the other way round: experience of the relevance of the Bible led to the scientific investigation of it. And at this point the Zürichers were, and remained, convinced Humanists, that is to say, philologists. The method followed by Zwingli, Jud and Bibliander was exactly that of Kittel's *Theologisches Wörterbuch*: this word is to be understood in such and such a way in Pindar; in the context of the New Testament, it changes its meaning in such and such a way.

At seven o'clock in the morning in summer (eight o'clock in winter), on every day except Sundays and Fridays, all the ministers, canons and students gathered in the choir of the Great Minster and took their places in the pews.[92] First, Master Huldrych went to the lectern and said the following prayer:

"Almighty, eternal and merciful God, whose Word is a lamp unto our feet and a light unto our path, open and illuminate our minds, that we may purely and perfectly understand Thy Word and that our lives may be conformed according to what we have rightly understood, that in nothing we may be displeasing unto Thy Majesty, through Jesus Christ our Lord. Amen".[93]

Then Zwingli beckons someone else, who reads the text for the day from the Vulgate. A third man treats the same passage from the Hebrew Bible, and a fourth reads it in Greek from the Septuagint, and throws light on the literal meaning. A fifth presents a Latin meditation in preparation for the sermon; and a sixth, either Zwingli himself or one of his colleagues, then

---

92. Oskar Farner, *Der Reformator Ulrich Zwingli*. Zwinglibücherei No. 60, Zürich, 1949, p. 66. Cf. Z IV 701ff., "Formm, die prophezy ze begon". G. W. L.: *Zw. Ref. im Rahmen.*, 161ff., 625ff.

93. Omnipotens sempiterne et misericors deus, cuius verbum est lucerna pedibus nostris et lumen semitarum nostrarum (Ps. 119:105), aperi et illumina mentes nostras, ut oracula tua pure et sancte intelligamus et in illud, quod recte intellexerimus, transformemur, quo maiestati tuae nulla ex parte displiceamus, per Jesum Christum, dominum nostrum. Amen. Z IV 365, 702. Cf. Fritz Schmidt-Clausing: "Das Prophezeigebet" in *Zwa.* XII/1 (1964/1), pp. 10-34.

delivers the sermon in the German tongue, which is also intended for the ordinary citizens, who have entered in the meanwhile.

The "prophecy" was a model for numerous similar institutions in the Palatinate, in East Friesland, in the Lower Rhineland, in the Netherlands and in other Reformed Churches. John à Lasco who had come to know it in Zürich, introduced it into his refugee church in London, and it spread out from there to play a considerable part in English Puritanism in both the Church of England and the Nonconformist Churches.

From this "Prophecy" there resulted the Zürich translation of the Bible, which made considerable and grateful use of Luther's translation, but which was completed much earlier.[94] Then followed an astonishingly fruitful series of commentaries, some of them contemporary with those of Calvin, and some serving as models for him. These had a great international influence, even in Lutheranism, where, for example, Rudolph Gualther, Zwingli's son-in-law, was held in high esteem. What was the secret of this far-reaching, penetrating power? The Lutheran theologians were soon caught in the toils of the "Loci method". Methodologically all of them, and not only the Philippists, were Melanchthonians. The others merely filled Melanchthon's form with their own gnesio-lutheran content. Whereas the men of Zürich—Bibliander, Ceporin, Rudolph Gualther, Josiah Simmler, Hospinian, Tossanus, Vermigli, Ludwig Lavater (and we have not even mentioned Bullinger)—had learnt and were constantly encouraged to pay attention to the leading themes of the Bible. Zürich's most important contribution to the Reformation is its Biblicism. And, within this context, it is the rediscovery of the Biblical concept of the covenant. This passed from Zwingli via Bullinger to Piscator at Herborn and to Olevian and Franciscus Junius at Heidelberg, thence to the Netherlands where it came to full flower in the shape of Federal Theology. Even those who have no liking for the later forms of this theology may nevertheless admit that when the doctrine of the covenant replaced the dogma of predestination at the centre of Reformed theology—a position which it had held since the time of Beza (not Calvin!)—then this marked one of the few truly great spiritual advances made by Protestantism after the Reformation. For this Biblical sense of involvement in the history of the Covenant and of the Kingdom was bound up with that remarkable sense of responsibility for public affairs which came to life once more and

---

94. Its most important feature is that it is revised approximately every fifty years, and brought up to date as regards changes in linguistic usage and exegesis.

had a lively influence on both Anglican and Puritan England,[95] spreading outwards from there to the whole Reformed world.

This was the Reformation change in divine service in Zürich. "The Lord protects His Church", says Huldrych Zwingli.[96] "Let us see whether God is stronger than the court-dancers".[97]

---

95. Cf. Helmut Kressner, *Schweizer Ursprünge des anglikanischen Staatskirchentums,* Gütersloh, 1953; Ruth Wessel-Roth, *Thomas Erastus. Ein Beitrag zur Geschichte der reformierten Kirche und zur Lehre von der Staatssouveränität,* Lahr/Baden, 1954; W. M. S. West, *John Hooper and the Origins of Puritanism,* Zürich Dissertation, 1956.

96. Quoted from Oskar Farner, *Gott ist Meister. Zwingli-Worte für unsere Zeit.* Zwingli-bücherei No. 8, Zürich, 1940.

97. Z II 322; H IV 110.

2

HULDRYCH ZWINGLI'S MESSAGE*

I. CHRIST'S SOLDIER

Huldrych Zwingli died on 11 October 1531 while fighting bravely and giving comfort to others. His body was burnt, and the ashes were scattered on the water. For some time afterwards, a veiled rumour persisted in Zurich. It was whispered, that after some days the Reformer's heart, still undamaged, had been found by his friends and had been buried in a secret place some time later. Despite every precaution, even the Roman counter-Reformation propagandists got wind of the affair, and they were quick to assert that Zwingli's relics were being venerated in Zurich. Of course that was nonsense; and it is not our concern to pursue the details of this matter now.[1] The important thing is simply this: that this rumour, passed on from person to person, reflected the conviction that Zwingli's heart "could not be killed", that his condemnation was an injustice, that his spirit lives on, even among us, and that his personality has only just begun to have effect. Is this assertion correct? The fact that today he is being commemorated here, in the oldest church in our city, and also further afield throughout the Protestant and Anglican world, is not sufficient proof. There are many dates in the calendar which serve only to remind us that what is past is past. Even the respect and gratitude which we may feel towards the man himself do not constitute an unmistakeable sign that we are actually learning from his spirit. For personal reputation was not important to him. Ten years before he died, he wrote (full of foreboding), as follows "You say: "If you were killed or burnt, that would bring dishonour upon us, even though we should know perfectly well that an injustice had been done you". This is my answer: "Christ, whose soldier (sworn warrior) I am, says in Luke 6: 'Blessed are you when men hate you and when they exclude or revile you, and reject your name as evil on account of the Son of Man! Rejoice in that day, and leap for joy; for be assured that your reward is great in heaven'. Listen to me. The more that men despise my name for God's sake, the more it will be honoured by God. It should be

---

* An address delivered in the Wasserkirche in Zürich on the anniversary of Zwingli's death, October 11th, 1957. *Zwa.* X/10 (1958/2), pp. 591-602.

1. See further G. W. Locher, "Die Legende vom Herzen Zwinglis", *Zwa.* IX/10, (1953/2), pp. 563-576.

the same with you ... Whoever will come to God must consider only what God wants, not men ... They can kill your body, but not your soul ... Christ has shed his blood for our salvation. Whoever will not shed his own blood for his Lord and Captain is a useless warrior, a lazy soldier.''[2]

So, if anything of Zwingli's spirit is still alive, it will mean that his message is understood, and his call to follow Christ is heeded. This is a task which every generation must undertake and solve for itself, according to its own particular circumstances. It is in this sense that we are considering Huldrych Zwingli's message today, and therefore we want to let him speak for himself. Thus we are not concerned about giving an account of his work, or describing his whole world of thought; rather shall we attempt to take note of certain characteristic aspects of his thought which may still be relevant for our faith and practice today, by way of admonition, direction, help or obligation.

II. THE REFORMATION

A brief consideration of the history of our church is essential. Zwingli was a Reformer. What was the Reformation? It was exactly what its name suggests: it was a movement for renewal, the renewal of the one ancient church according to the Word of God. In the course of the centuries the house had partly decayed, it had partly been corrupted and it had partly been spoilt by a top-heavy superstructure. Now it was thoroughly renovated according to the original definitive design. The Reformers found this plan in Holy Scripture. At the Reformation nobody split the church. Nobody founded new churches. Nobody introduced innovations. The fact that it did finally result in permanent divisions and the erection of boundaries within Christendom was due not to the intention of the Reformation preachers and their congregations, but to the negative stance of the Roman Catholic hierarchy. From the Bull against Luther down to the Anathemas of the Council of Trent, one part of the church refused to be renewed according to the Word of God. But the Protestant Christians could only march forward; they could no longer turn back. They were bound in conscience. What separated them from the Papacy was not merely a matter of opinions, about which men could differ in all good faith. It was a matter of a vital experience which could not be changed and could not be disregarded. It was that the Bible had begun to speak once more. More precisely, it was that man had once more recognised the voice of the Shepherd speaking through texts of Holy Scripture as they were ex-

---

2. Z I 394; H I 128.

pounded and applied. The saving presence of the Lord (which the Roman Church claimed to realise in the sacrament through transubstantiation) was now being experienced (and is experienced) by the Protestants through preaching. It was a meeting with the living Lord who calls, warns and comforts us. Faith believes the Word and lives by the Word. This basic belief was common to all the Reformers.

III. LUTHER'S QUESTION

The Reformers were led to this common standpoint by different routes, however. The picture of Brother Martin in his monastery cell, struggling with God and the Devil, has been deeply stamped on Protestantism. Luther was afraid—which was the reason why he was so fearless afterwards. For it is only the man who can be afraid at the right time who can be brave. Luther was afraid of suffering eternal punishment in hell for his sins. There is no evangelical Christian who does not understand these assaults of God's wrath; no genuine faith, which does not have to struggle through the assault in its own way; no answer, without that most personal of all questions: "How can I find a merciful God?" It is only in this assault that we come to know the victory of the Gospel, granted to us by God's act of grace in Jesus Christ, in merciful and free reconciliation through the cross. This was Luther's discovery. And, as has been said, there can be no faith without this experience of turning from the darkness of sin to the light.

IV. ZWINGLI'S QUESTION

Huldrych Zwingli also became a reformer out of fear. But his question was a different one. He was Swiss, and was, therefore, a passionate politician. As a scholarly humanist he was also, for a while, an idealistic and even pacifist reformer. But the profound impact of the rediscovery of the Bible, coupled with his love for his country, did not allow him any peace. He began to view his confederacy and, indeed, the whole of Christendom, in the light of the teaching of the prophets and apostles. And it was at this point that he was afraid—for his own people, and for the whole church. For Master Huldrych judged, and he knew from experience, that in an age when we were developing as a military power, our people were inwardly poor. The booty from military campaigns and raids had made the people rich and the victories had made them proud. The constant opportunity for young men to achieve wealth and honour quickly and adventurously made them reluctant to undertake honest, patient work, and made them rough, even cruel, in character. Even today, in North Italy, mothers will threaten their children with the bogeyman by shouting "The Swiss are coming!" Whole valleys were reduced to poverty because the women, children and old people could not cope with the work while the men were wasting their energy in some war or other, and, as Zwingli put it "were killing people for money". When they came home, they were often wild, ragged, degraded, crippled and diseased. So the freedom of the confederacy, which had been so proudly won and maintained, was lost, even though we were the leading military power in Europe. But the Swiss were always available for hire, and by paying large, regular bribes to the magistrates in the various states of the confederation, foreign princes such as the Dukes of Milan, the Kings of France and the Popes (!) could always secure permission to recruit men. The conviction that God's wrath must be incurred by this state of affairs began to weigh even more heavily on the soul and conscience of the field-preacher from Marignano. "If only the poor people would be content with food and clothing!" he once wrote on Psalm 144.[3] "If only our sons could grow up and not be killed. Murder, murder! What has happened to the Confederacy, that her sons and daughters should be sold like this! Despair, despair! Wretchedness, wretchedness! Sin, sin! .... O Lord, grant us peace ... O Lord, save us from war, so that there is not the screaming in the streets, the lamenting and grief!"

This was Zwingli's discovery: that the injury was so deep that men could not heal it. Only the grace of God could turn away God's wrath from the Swiss people and, indeed, from the whole of Christendom, which was consuming itself in wars and was thereby denying its Lord, the Prince of Peace. Only the Word of God could tear up the evil root of greed and self interest which produced these poisonous fruits (today we would call it materialism). Only Christ, the Lord, could save us by his *Spirit*, who teaches us not to cling to earthly goods.

Everyone is familiar with the charge usually levelled against the Zurich reformer: that he was himself responsible for the catastrophe of Kappel, and that what happened was deserved, because he had mixed religion with politics, and thus profaned the Gospel.

Apart from the question as to whether the defeat at Kappel was wholly a misfortune (which I do not believe), this judgment reveals a failure to understand Zwingli's particular motives. Anyone who talks in this way has not really understood him. Luther's question was purely religious, whereas Zwingli's starting point was the political and social distress. Only

---

3. Z XIII 816.

the Gospel can save us; he recognised that—so that he could take up
politics once more, from the standpoint of faith. His whole inner development made it impossible for him to separate religion and politics, church
and state, inward and outward. When God's judgment stands before the
door, who is going to make such distinctions then? God does not ask about
our distinctions, but whether His commandments are obeyed. And if we
reject evangelical preaching, which is the last chance that God himself still
offers us, then "what happened to the people of Israel would also happen
to us. They refused to heed any warning, until they were taken into captivity. Then they sat furtively beside the waters and bewailed their misery.
May God save us from that ...!"[4] And when he thinks of how the
mercenaries used to wreak havoc as they pleaded their so-called right-of-
war, he is deeply disturbed: "If it should ever come about that we are
measured by the same measure with which we have measured, then we
should not be able to lament our misery enough ..."[5]

V. THE GOSPEL

That was Zwingli's question. And what was his answer? We have called
it the Gospel, because that is how he liked to designate the summary of
essential faith—or "God's Word", as he termed it even more frequently.
But how is this to be understood? Could it be that here the Bible is used in
the service of political ends, and is seen from the distorted viewpoint of our
own desires? No. There must be a complete and genuine about-turn if, as
Zwingli once said, one has to make the choice between the "Word of
God" and the "Word of Greed".[6] When the preaching of the divine word
"puts down selfishness",[7] it is not as simple as correcting an error by
means of better instruction. It comes about through a crisis, in which we
face a wholly personal question. At this point all social, political and other
questions are relegated to the background. We ought to answer him—and
then realise that we have no answer. That is the position in which the
"Gospel" puts us. There is not a single work of Zwingli's, in which the
argument does not at some time work round to this central point, where it
is clearly stated that we find God's divine act, God's question to us, and

---

4. Z I 185.
5. Z I 185; H VII 26.
6. Z V 425; cf. G. W. Locher, *Der Eigentumsbegriff als Problem evangelischer Theologie*, 2nd ed.
Zürich, 1962. Part I, chapter 3: "Zwingli. Die politische Verantwortung der Christenheit
und das Eigentumsproblem", pp. 29-35, 49-53.
7. Z III 112; H VII 121.

God's answer in Jesus Christ. Let this fact be emphasised for once, since it has been veiled all too often in portraits of our reformer. If we were to ask him today, he would declare bluntly: *This* is my message:

"This is the Gospel: after Adam (that is, the human race) had turned away from the light and from the way of the Divine Spirit and had turned to himself, trusting in his own counsel to become great and to be equal to God; and thus, through this sin, had subjected himself and us to the realm or dominion of the law of sin and of bitter death, from which we could then no longer escape; for we were flesh, sinners, subject to death whatever we tried to do, and nobody save God alone could remedy our defect.

Then the merciful God had such deep pity on our suffering and distress, that he wished to save us, not merely by a word of command, but rather by his own natural Son; and to reconcile us wretched men to himself, and through him to make good every defect, as follows:

God is just and He is merciful.

Who can bear God's justice, if he should judge us strictly?... Yet satisfaction must be rendered to his justice, for this is no superficial tolerance, but rather an eternally binding, true and certain judgment.

Since no creature could possibly render this satisfaction, he willed that his own Son should assume our frail nature, (which was not tainted with sin, as it is with us, however) and that he should not merely suffer an ordinary death, but rather that he, though innocent, should suffer the most shameful death for us, in order to redeem us from the cause of death, that is, from sin. He rendered satisfaction to the justice of God, in order that this justice need no longer condemn us for all eternity. Since the innocent Christ was born without sin, of the pure Virgin Mary, and since he is not only true man but also true God and everlasting good, this undeserved suffering, which he endured for us, would provide an eternal merit and recompense for our sin.

For if the one who has suffered for us is the eternal God (as he undoubtedly is) then his suffering must be an eternal merit and bear fruit, satisfying God's justice for all eternity in respect of the sin of all who rely with assurance and trust on what he has done.

God has shown such great mercy to us, willing to redeem us and to kindle our love for him, that, even if his great majesty should not lead us to love him, but rather to fear him, yet the great humility of his son and his goodness to us will compel us to love him and to trust him, if we do not wish to be scoundrels.

For what will God withhold from us, since he has given his son for us?

And whose sins cannot be forgiven, since Christ has made satisfaction to God, provided we truly believe and trust in that?

Behold, this is the sum of the Gospel...

O God of mercy, justice and comfort! How graciously you have pardoned us, wretched thieves and villains, who sought to deceive you and to invade your kingdom! To what sure hope you have raised us! To what great honour you have brought us through your Son! And we do not comprehend it! We are not grateful! We do not believe it!''[8]

We would emphasis three points in this statement. Firstly: there has to be reconciliation. *That* is the central question; until it is answered, there can be no correct answer to any other question about life. There is absolutely no human life at all, which can reach its goal without God. Secondly: reconciliation *has been* accomplished. God has solved the problem. He has done it in his own way, not just with a word, but with a deed, the deed which Christ performed, and by which he proved himself to be the Son of the eternal Father. Thus God's forgiveness is a truly saving act, because it is founded on the *real* cancellation of man's unrighteousness. It has been accomplished, and accomplished sufficiently for all men for all eternity. From Zwingli onwards, this emphasis on the objectivity of the fact of salvation has always given to the Reformed faith its own peculiar strength. Finally: our reconciliation is not just a matter of the soul as distinct from the earthly side of life. If Christ has purchased us by his sacrifice, and has thereby become our Lord, then he wishes now to rule over every area of our life. This is the reason for Zwingli's stress on the *divinity* of the Saviour, and his ascension to the right hand of the Father Almighty. God's salvation and our faith do not stand alongside or behind our practical concerns, but rather encompass them, and should permeate them. But does this include the state?

VI. THE STATE

Among the reformers, it was not Calvin, and certainly not Luther, but Zwingli, who strove for a theocracy; not, that is to say, the establishment of domination by the church or even by the ministers, but rather that even public affairs should be directed by the Spirit of God.[9] As long as he lived, and for a long time afterwards, theocratic elements were active both in the

---

8. Z II 38; H III 42ff.

9. Cf. G. W. Locher, s.v. "Theokratie", *Evangelisches Kirchenlexikon*. Vol. III, Göttingen, 1959, columns 1351-1353.

city and the territory of Zurich. They were planted in other lands also by his disciples and friends—even in Bern, which was antagonistic. To this day the history of England has been influenced by Zwingli. These consequences do not prevent us from realising that here we stand at a boundary which we cannot and do not desire to cross in the way that Zwingli did. Too much has changed in the last four hundred years. In an age when denominations co-exist side by side, an age of tolerance (and of unbelief), Zwingli's directions concerning the state are no longer tenable. Calvin was more far-sighted; he began to separate the responsibilities of church and state. However, having said this, we may still dwell for a moment on this picture of one people in state and church, church and state; not only because it is so splendid, but because it contains and retains certain valid truths. It should be noted that, according to Zwingli, state and church do not coalesce. Their tasks are different, especially in that the church, with its word, not only remains free from the government, but always has also the "watchman's duty" of prophetic criticism. Is this wrong? Have we not experienced the inhuman possibilities which lie dormant in an increasingly powerful political system, if Christians leave it to its own devices? And how the church, which is bound to its Lord, can become, overnight, the last bastion of freedom? Thus, we might say that the relationship of church to state resembles that of the soul to the body. But Zwingli corrects us at this point. He says that both are dependent on the leading of the Spirit of God, as the body depends on the soul.[10] In this sense, then "a Christian is simply a good and loyal citizen, and a Christian state is simply a Christian church".[11] Zwingli maintains that public service is one of the chief activities of the Christian community. Is he right or wrong? Is he not right, especially today? "In their own way the rulers are nothing other than the shepherds of Jesus Christ's sheep".[12] Can that be denied? And is it any less true if those magistrates either do not know it or do not want to know it? A further consequence is found in Article 42: "If they (the civil government, Article 36) are unfaithful, and depart from the way of Christ, they may be removed with God's blessing".[13]

This proclamation of the right to resist has roused powerful echoes in the history of the Reformed Church, and it should not be forgotten in this era of impersonal bureaucracy. Zwingli was of the opinion that the citizen who wrongly tolerated official injustice actually shared the guilt; the Jews

---

10. Z XIV 419.
11. Z XIV 424.
12. Z XIV 527; S IV 58f.
13. Z II 342; H IV 137.

were punished with the Babylonian captivity, he said, because they tolerated the godless King Manasseh.

VII. THE ECONOMY

There is yet another area, which we like to treat as a distinct entity, namely, the economy. Zwingli's message cries: No; the rule of Christ extends to this as well. He asks: What gives us the right to act in so arbitrary a manner at the very point where need, poverty and injustice break out again and again, like wounds that are not properly healed? Who is the Lord? Who is the proprietor? It certainly is not you, if you have any sense at all of the law of God and the Gospel of God; because you belong, with all that you are and all that you have, to him who has purchased you. And that includes your money. "You should not keep your worldly goods to yourself, for you are only the steward",[14] only a trustee. The real owner will demand a reckoning. There is only one certificate which bestows on us some right to our property, and that is hard, faithful work. That is something to think about in this century of speculations on the Stock Exchange and of unearned income of every kind! Property must be the servant of labour, and not the other way round! Work is meaningful in itself, and not merely because of its material reward. For work has to do with man's destiny, with his humanity: "Man is made for toil and work, as a bird is made for flying;"[15] says Zwingli. Indeed, he goes further: even the Creator himself is unceasingly active; therefore at this point we have something in common with God, despite the distance between us.

Agricultural work, in particular, can make us more aware of these things. In those days the farmer was often despised; Zwingli esteemed him highly. "Work is such a good, divine thing; it preserves us from wantonness and vice; it gives good fruit so that man can nourish his body with a good conscience and without worry; and he need not fear that as he eats he is staining himself with innocent blood ... and the best thing of all is this, that fruit and growth follow the worker's hand, just as all things became alive under the hand of God at the beginning of creation. So outwardly at least, the worker is more like God than anything else in the world".[16]

Even at that time it was suggested that Switzerland was a poor land, incapable of supporting its inhabitants. But Zwingli would not hear of this. "It is more fruitful and beautiful and has more virile people than any

---

14. Z II 451; H IV 261f.
15. S VI,I 209, 269.
16. Z III 106; H VII 113f.

other country on earth, and it is fruitful enough to nourish its people, if only we would be satisfied with it".[17]

"Even if it does not have cinnamon, ginger, malmsey, cloves, bitter oranges, silk and such feminine delicacies, it does have butter, medicinal herbs, milk, horses, sheep, cattle, linen, wine and corn in sufficient abundance to enable you to raise fine, strong people. And what you do not have in your own country you can easily obtain by trading with other people who lack what you have".[18]

As we would put it nowadays: with honest work, an export industry can be built up which would balance the necessary imports. But what is remarkable is the significance Zwingli attached to the needs of agriculture.

Because of its relation to the will of God, this whole area of the economy, in which we tend to forget about the Creator (because we are too busy!) must be snatched out of the hand of materialism and brought under the control of the Spirit of God. Woe to those who, by their manipulations behind the scenes, rob the honest worker and his family of their earnings and their savings! Zwingli once said that the politicians who are responsible for inflation deserve to be boiled in oil![19] Often, in an evening in Basle or Zurich, when I see the huge neon advertisements of some of the monopolistic chemical factories, I think of Zwingli's rage at monopolies of every kind, and especially in respect of medicines "because they strive for high prices with their finances".[20] "Now, nearly all commercial goods have come into the hands of some monopoly. If a poor mother in childbed wants to buy some medicine, she may have a hard time of it; for she has to pay the monopolies twice as much as the powder is worth. By such means, they accumulate so much capital that they are acquiring all the money in the world. ..."[21] Thus Zwingli already recognised the economic dangers in concentration of capital—the phenomenon upon which, as is well known, the whole system of Marxism is built ...

VIII. THE LIFE OF FAITH

In conclusion: what did Huldrych Zwingli set against the dangers and wrongs of his time and ours? "Christ is the only treasure of our poor souls!"[22]

---

17. Z I 180; H VII 22.
18. Z III 106; H VII 113.
19. Z III 432ff.; H VII 191-193.
20. Z II 297; H IV 82.
21. Z III 430; H VII 189.
22. Z II 217; H III 285ff.

Basically, he believes that everything is very simple. There is always just one thing that is really at stake. It is always a question of deciding between serving God or serving idols. Because: "Whatever a man trusts in, that is his god".[23]

He staked his life on this message. So whether his heart, which stopped beating on that 11th day of October, is still alive, depends on whether we have given ourselves to the service of God or the service of idols.

"So let us take refuge in the one God, who is our Father. For that reason we can come to him. For what would he deny us, since he has given his only Son to die for us, and has made him an eternal pledge, to pay for our sins? So Jesus himself stands and calls to us (in Matthew 11) "Come to me, all you who labour and are heavy laden; I will give you rest!" See, he calls us to himself... Why, then, should we want to go to anyone but him? Would not that be to despise his free grace and mercy? Such contradiction comes only from unbelief and ignorance. Therefore, all men should earnestly call upon God, that he may increase his light more and more, so that the hearts of men may be enlightened and drawn to the hope of the one God. For it is certain, that he who turns to the creature is an idolator. This brings no small harm to wretched men. May God work out everything for the best; for to him alone will I call in my distress; for I know that he hears me".[24]

That is Huldrych Zwingli's message.

---

23. Z II 219.
24. Z II 221-222; H III 290f.

3

HOW THE IMAGE OF ZWINGLI HAS CHANGED IN RECENT RESEARCH[*][1]

I. THE PROBLEM

The image of Zwingli that prevails today has been formed by three widely-used books: 1) *Die Kirchenratsauswahl*, 1918; 2) Paul Wernle, *Zwingli*, 1919; and 3) Walther Köhler, *Huldrych Zwingli*, 1943/1954. Walther Köhler (1870-1946) was a native of Wuppertal-Elberfeld, a stronghold of the Reformed faith. From 1909 to 1929 he was Professor of Church History at Zürich. He belonged to the liberal school of theology, and was a leading authority not only on the Reformation as a whole but also on the other movements of the sixteenth century, and especially Humanism and the Anabaptist movement. Through his numerous books, articles and reviews, as well as his introductions to the great critical edition of Zwingli's works, he became the doyen of Zwingli research.[2] Even those, like the present writer, who did not know him personally, and who differ from him on essential points, still honour him. The image of Zwingli which Köhler saw, portrayed and disseminated may be characterised by a

---

* This essay first appeared in *Vox theologica*[1], Assen (Netherlands), 32/6 (1962). An amplified version was published in *Zwa.* XI/9 (1963/1), another in *HZNS* 1969. An English version, "The Change in the Understanding of Zwingli in Recent Research", appeared in *Church History*, Oreland, Pa., U.S.A., 34/1 (1965).

1. The editors had requested a survey of Zwingli research during the previous five to ten years. But one must go back further in order to understand the themes and the methodology of this research. It is not a question of merely looking back, but rather of attempting to explain and elucidate, by means of such a survey, the questions and the tasks that face Zwingli research today. The author would point out that his purpose here is to set forth some of the main lines of research, and he would apologise to all concerned for the fact that it has been necessary to make a sometimes arbitrary selection, with the result that some important pieces of work done in recent decades have had to remain unmentioned.

2. *Ulrich Zwingli. Eine Auswahl auf seinen Schriften auf das vierhundertjährige Jubiläum der Zürcher Reformation im Auftrag des Kirchenrats des Kantons Zürich*, tr. and ed. by Georg Finsler, Walther Köhler and Arnold Rüegg, Zürich, 1918; Paul Wernle, *Der evangelische Glaube nach den Hauptschriften der Reformatoren* Vol. II: *Zwingli*, Tübingen, 1919; Walther Köhler, *Huldrych Zwingli*, Leipzig, 1943; 2nd revised ed., Leipzig, 1954.

The progress of Zwingli research is traced in the regular articles and reports in *Zwingliana, Beiträge zur Geschichte Zwinglis, der Reformation und des Protestantismus in der Schweiz* (*Zwa.*), Zürich, 1897ff. It appears twice yearly, published by the Zwingli-Verein, and has been edited since 1934 by Leonhard von Muralt.

For a memoir of Walther Köhler (by Leonhard von Muralt) and a portrait see Z VI, I 1961 (see note 10).

well-authenticated anecdote.[3] One day he praised, in the presence of his students, the well-known monument which stands behind the Wasserkirche in Zurich, which, in a most impressive way, represents the Reformer armed with Bible and sword. But then he added that one must think of the book as having the pages of the Greek New Testament interleaved with pages of Plato's *Dialogues*. His meaning was that Zwingli was and remained essentially a Humanist: "He got the Reformation from Luther"; the antithesis between the humanistic-classical elements and the Biblical-Christian elements runs through his whole being; and, indeed, through his very character.[4] In the brief book mentioned above, which was published in 1943 (2nd. ed. 1954), and which contains the essence of his lifelong researches, Köhler presented the same thesis, though in a more moderate form, and toned down both sides of this "antithesis". Zwingli's independence of Luther is taken into account to a much greater extent, his anthropology is shown to be genuinely Pauline, and the change in his Humanism, in contrast to that of Erasmus, is worked out. But basically the picture of the two different lines in Zwingli's thought, the Biblical-Reformation element and the humanistic element, remains unchanged. They converge only because of the Reformer's "strong will towards unity", but actually they remain separate.[5] It must be emphasised that for Walther Köhler, the establishing of this dichotomy does not in any way constitute a reproach. Rather does this connexion with classical tradition give to Christianity (and to the Reformation in particular) the possibility and the power to influence culture and to ennoble it in the sense of general spiritual progress. It is greatly to Zwingli's credit that he—in contrast to Luther—was conscious of this need. One cannot quite avoid the impression that this great historian, though devoted to a total objectivity, was inspired by a secret longing to find a special father of liberal theology among the Reformers.[6]

But a closer examination shows that this idea of a dichotomy in Zwingli, and the attempt to substantiate it, particularly in German writings on the

---

3. The present writer was told this story by his teacher in Zwingli studies, Oskar Farner, who had heard the dictum personally.

4. Walther Köhler had already arrived at this viewpoint in the studies that provided the foundation for all his subsequent Zwingli research, viz. the section on "Zwingli als Theologe" in *Ulrich Zwingli. Zum Gedächtnis der Zürcher Reformation,* Zürich, 1919; *Ulrich Zwingli und die Reformation in der Schweiz,* Religionsgeschichtliche Volksbücher IV 31/32, Tübingen, 1919; *Die Geisteswelt Ulrich Zwinglis, Christentum und Antike,* Gotha, 1920.

5. Cf. also Walther Köhler's article "Zwingli" in *Die Religion in Geschichte und Gegenwart,* 2nd ed., Tübingen, 1931, Vol. V.

6. Cf. Walther Köhler, *Die Geisteswelt Ulrich Zwinglis,* Gotha, 1920, Foreword and Introduction, pp. 1-4.

history of dogma, are based on an assumption which has been accepted uncritically for four hundred years, namely, that Martin Luther is *the* Reformer. And Luther's inner development, his course, and finally his conception of doctrine provide the yardstick by which all attempts at reformation are to be measured. Luther is made the norm of the Reformer. So whatever fits in with his image is accepted as valid, while anything which does not, is alien. Here we can leave aside the question of whether such an attitude actually does honour to Luther, or even understands him. Certainly it leads one into difficulties with Calvin, and even more with Melanchthon. But when this method is applied to Zwingli (as it is in all the textbooks)[7] it works out as follows: Chapter I: Luther became a Reformer in such and such a way, and then as a Reformer said these things. Chapter II: Zwingli, a Humanist, also became a Reformer, but without sharing Luther's cloister experience or his spiritual troubles. He agrees with Luther at most points, but there are the following differences etc. So these points of difference (such as the doctrine of the Lord's Supper or the doctrine of the state) are wrenched out of their context in Zwingli's thought and are overemphasised. While at the same time, as regards the points of agreement (the doctrine of grace, repentance and the *servum arbitrium*) his own characteristic arguments and aims are overlooked—and this is equally dangerous. In short, Zwingli must be studied in the light of his own motives, and understood on the basis of his own presuppositions. It is possible that there may then emerge a spiritual figure of unexpected integrity which would correspond to the supreme calm and serenity of his style. To my mind, this is the main task of Zwingli research today.

II. EDITIONS

1.   If our generation is to understand the Reformers it is essential to have a critical *edition* of their works, complete with introductions and notes, which meets the requirements of philological and historical science. Zwingli has been fortunate in this respect. The edition of his collected works which was prepared by the theologians Melchior Schuler and Johannes Schultess in connexion with the celebration of the Reformation in Zurich in 1819 has become a model for such undertakings.[8] The texts

---

7. Alfred Adam proceeds along the same lines in the second volume of his excellent *Lehrbuch der Dogmengeschichte*, Gütersloh, 1968, even though he is generally fair to Zwingli.

8. *Huldreich Zwinglis Werke. Erste vollständige Ausgabe*, ed. Melchior Schuler and Johannes Schultess. 8 volumes in 10, Zürich, 1828-1842. *Supplementorum fasciculus*, by Georg Schultess and Kaspar Marthaler, Zürich, 1861. (Since 1958 the hitherto customary abbreviation SchSch or SS has been replaced by the letter S, followed by the Roman numeral of the volume number. See *Zwa.* X, p. 582).

and also, on the whole, the datings are reliable. A number of important writings will be available only in this edition for some years to come.[9] But at the same time, as the new edition progresses, this older one will naturally become less expensive on the second-hand market, so those who are interested should seize this opportunity.

Modern requirements are certainly met by the *Sämtliche Werke*, initiated by Emil Egli.[10] The appearance of this edition was delayed by the two World Wars and by the Iron Curtain and so research was appreciably held up. Nevertheless, despite occasional errors or deficiencies in the notes, no real catastrophes have occurred, such as happened with the Weimar Edition of Luther's works, of which whole volumes can be used only with caution, or with the edition of Calvin's works in the *Corpus Reformatorum*, which was discontinued prematurely. A few years ago the Zwingli Society of Zürich, under its energetic president Leonhard von Muralt, gave a fresh impetus to the publication and consequently the following are now available: Zwingli's writings and documents etc. up to January 1530 (Vols. I-VI, II), his complete correspondence (Vols. VII-XI), four parts of Vol. XII (Marginal Notes) and the complete Vol. XIII and Vol. XIV (Exegetica). Still lacking are the writings of the last years (1530-1531) and the remainder of the Exegetica (on the New Testament). Egli's Prospectus and the appearance of hitherto unknown transcripts[11] will doubtless lead to the publication of some special volumes of sermons—until recently we possessed only a few examples of Zwingli's sermons in a revised and expanded form. A wealth of labour and instructive scholarship is to be found in the notes. The theologian is referred in particular to the short and the longer excurses on the history of dogma by Fritz Blanke. The historian should note the surprising discussion by Leonhard von Muralt and his pupils of Zwinglian politics in the last years.

---

9. This applies especially to the much discussed Marburg sermon *De providentia* and the confessional books *Fidei Ratio* and *Fidei Expositio* in the small volume S IV.

10. *Huldreich Zwinglis Sämtliche Werke. Unter Mitwirkung des Zwinglivereins in Zürich,* ed. Emil Egli, Georg Finsler, Walther Köhler, Oskar Farner, Fritz Blanke, Leonhard von Muralt, Edwin Künzli, Rudolf Pfister. *Corpus Reformatorum,* Vols. LXXXVIIIff., Berlin, later Leipzig, and latterly Zürich, 1905ff. (In the past there has been a great deal of confusion with regard to the designation of the literature. CR with the Roman numeral was apt to be misunderstood or difficult to read. Since 1958 ZW, SW, W, KA, K (= "Collected Works", "Critical Edition" etc.) have all been replaced by Z followed by the Roman numeral of the volume number. See *Zwa.* X, pp. 582).

11. Here as elsewhere we see the consequences of the fact that the Swiss experienced neither a Thirty nor an Eighty Years' War. Compared with the Netherlands and Germany, Swiss archives are rich in documents from the period before the seventeenth century.

2.   Among the editions of selected works, the following should be mentioned: the "Kirchenratsausgabe",[12] to which reference has already been made, still enjoys a wide circulation. But a plain warning about it is necessary for two reasons. First, it gives a one-sided picture, because the writings it contains were abridged in such a way that while the classical quotations and examples which Zwingli adduced to support his arguments are reproduced in full, the even more extensive "testimonia" from Holy Scripture were omitted. Second, the book is full of mistranslations which distort the meaning. The editors, acknowledged as highly conscientious in other respects, were prevented by pressure of time from giving sufficiently close supervision to their collaborators.

Happily, this book has recently been superseded by a good revision.[13] Edwin Künzli has gone back to the old "Kirchenratsausgabe", but has altered it extensively, retranslated whole sections and (what is especially praiseworthy) added a sixth section: "The Bible in the hands of the Reformer", with examples of his translation and exposition. Now at last we have a survey of the real Zwingli in one convenient volume!

The handy *Zwingli-Hauptschriften*,[14] so bravely begun in 1940, have obviously come to a halt because they offer too little to the scholar and expect too much from the layman. Even the present-day Swiss does not find it easy to become accustomed to Zwingli's Upper German. The second half of Blanke's excellent translation of the "Commentarius de vera et falsa religione" finally appeared in 1963. This "Commentarius" of 1523 was the first Protestant work of dogmatics, and it influenced Calvin's *Institutio* at several not unimportant points. What is urgently needed is a selection of Zwingli's writings in the original Latin or German accompanied by a translation in modern German.

We have cause to be grateful for the "token of friendship of a Union Lutheran", Gerhard G. Muras, an experienced editor of texts from the theological history of Protestantism, who has undertaken a modern German translation of the *Anleitung* of 1523 for the Furche-Bücherei.[15]

---

12. *Ulrich Zwingli. Eine Auswahl aus seinen Schriften auf das vierhundertjährige Jubiläum der Zürcher Reformation im Auftrag des Kirchenrats des Kantons Zürich*, tr. and ed. by Georg Finsler, Walther Köhler and Arnold Rüegg, Zürich, 1918.

13. *Huldrych Zwingli. Auswahl seiner Schriften*, ed. Edwin Künzli, Zürich, 1962.

14. *Zwingli Hauptschriften*, ed. Fritz Blanke, Oskar Farner, Oskar Frei, Rudolf Pfister, Zürich, 1940ff. To date eight volumes have appeared: 1-2: *Der Prediger*; 3-4: *Der Verteidiger des Glaubens*; 7: *Der Staatsmann*; 9-11: *Der Theologe*. (Cited as H).

15. *Huldrych Zwingli. Christliche Anleitung*, tr. into modern German and ed. by Gerhard G. Muras, Hamburg, 1962. (Furche-Bücherei, No. 207). The translation is modern and clear, yet does not lose the tone or the finer points of the original. The purpose of the publication is

Unfortunately, Oskar Farner's fine translation of the Reformer's *Letters* remained uncompleted.[16]

Zwingli's political views, which display a theocratic (and, therefore, a republican and critical) attitude towards the state, have once more helped to strengthen our national consciousness and our will to resist during the years when we were threatened by the Third Reich.[17]

Ernst Gerhard Rüsch has produced a new edition of the much-loved *Lehrbüchlein*.[18] It is modern in language and lay-out, in a free yet accurate translation, and provided with a most informative introduction, to which we shall return later.

By contrast, though one may turn expectantly to Oskar Farner's two-volume selection of Zwingli's *Sermons on Isaiah and Jeremiah,* and *Matthew, Mark and John,*[19] one lays them down again with a feeling of disappointment. The fact of the matter is that Emil Egli already knew that in the Central Library in Zürich there were copies of Zwingli's sermons which hearers had taken down in writing. He had already identified the copyist of the sermons on the prophets. According to the notes of Leo Jud, the text was the work of "H. B.", namely Heinrich Buchmann, who was the older brother (by some nearly twenty years) of the famous linguist Theodorus Bibliander. The identity of the person who copied the sermons on the Gospels was still uncertain. Egli had already planned to include these sermons in the Sämtliche Werke (Z).[20] This was all forgotten.[21] Then Leo Weisz discovered anew the manuscript and the writer. Oskar Farner read the pages, made a selection of striking passages, translated them into modern German, and published them. The introductions, which provide clear and exact information about the problems of transmission, make a

---

indicated in the Preface: "On the one hand, it is intended to help the German people come to a better understanding of Huldrych Zwingli as well as Martin Luther... On the other hand, this new edition seeks to make clear the spiritual affinity between the two reformers and to foster the common life of their churches".

16. *Huldrych Zwinglis Briefe,* tr. by Oskar Farner. Vol. I: *1512-1523,* Zürich, 1918; Vol. II: *1524-1526,* Zürich, 1920.

17. *Huldrych Zwingli: Von göttlicher und menschlicher Gerechtigkeit. Sozial-politische Schriften für die Gegenwart,* selected and introduced by Leonhard von Muralt and Oskar Farner, Zürich, 1957.

18. *Huldrych Zwingli: An den jungen Mann. Zwinglis Erziehungsvorschriften aus dem Jahre 1523,* ed. E. G. Rüesch, Zürich, 1957. (Zwingli-Bücherei 82).

19. *Aus Zwinglis Predigten zu Jesaja und Jeremia.* Anonymous transcripts, selected and revised by Oskar Farner, Zürich, 1957; *Aus Zwinglis Predigten zu Matthäus, Markus und Johannes,* selected and tr. by Oskar Farner, Zürich, 1957.

20. Emil Egli, "Die Neuherausgabe der Zwinglischen Werke", *Zwa.* II/9 (1909/1), pp. 269-278. For the "sermones populares", cf. pp. 275-276.

21. Cf. Oskar Farner, *Huldrych Zwingli.* Vol. III, 1954, pp. 56ff. ("Der Nachlass").

real contribution to our knowledge. But as regards the text, one is forced to ask, in connexion with the most significant words: "Is it Zwingli or Farner who is saying that?" The selected items perform an excellent service in making Zwingli's preaching more widely known, but their scientific value is slight.

3. Only a small selection of Zwingli's works is available in French.[22] The large English edition makes slow progress.[23] But the English and Americans now possess a small but representative selection of the works of Zwingli and Bullinger, translated into readable language and of a kind not available in German.[24] In one volume appear "Of the clarity and certainty of the word of God", "Of the education of youth", "Of baptism", "On the Lord's Supper", and "An exposition of the Faith", together with "The sermon of the Holy Catholic Church", the first sermon of the fifth "Decade" of Bullinger's Hausbuch; there are excellent introductions, and a useful bibliography. The General Introduction to Zwingli constitutes a work of true research, and offers an independent contribution which arrives at conclusions very similar to those reached on the Continent. Unfortunately Bullinger's independence is not recognised, and his significance is underestimated. The editor, the Rev. G. W. Bromiley, belongs to the Church of England; which provides an indication of the streams into which the Zürich sources have flowed, in distinction to those of Geneva.

One should not overlook the brilliant Dutch rendering of the *Sixty-seven Articles* and of the Christian Introduction by G. Oorthuys, which provide the high-light of a series of greatly esteemed articles published in "Troffel en Zwaard".[25]

III. BIOGRAPHICAL

Oskar Farner was for decades the pastor who occupied Zwingli's pulpit in the Great Minster in Zürich and President of the cantonal consistory.

---

22. Inter alia: André Bouvier, "Ulrich Zwingli d'après ses œuvres" in *Revue de théologie et de philosophie*, 1931, pp. 205-232; P. Mesnard, "La pédagogie évangélique de Zwingli" in *Revue Thomiste*, 1953, pp. 367-386 (a translation of *Quo pacto ingenui adolescentes formandi sint*); *Huldrych Zwingli. Brève instruction chrétienne (1523)*, tr. by Jaques Courvoisier, 1953.

23. *Selected Works of Huldreich Zwingli*, ed. S. Macauley Jackson, 1901; *The Latin Works and the Correspondence of Huldreich Zwingli. Together with selections from his German Works*, ed. S. Macauley Jackson, 1912ff. (3 volumes to date).

24. *Zwingli and Bullinger*, Selected translations with introductions and notes by G. W. Bromiley. Library of Christian Classics, Vol. XXIV, London, 1953.

25. *Hulreich Zwinglis Zeven en zestig artikelen en Korte christelyke inleiding*, tr. and explained by Gerardus Oorthuys; G. Oorthuys, "Uitleggen en gronden der stellingen..." in *Troffel en Zwaard*, 1909-1911 (reprinted in G. Oorthuys, *Kruispunten op den Weg der Kerk*, Wageningen, 1935).

He was also a Privatdozent (lecturer) and later an honorary Professor at the University. As such, he introduced countless students to Zwingli, and won many of them for research. He was enabled almost to complete his large-scale Biography of Zwingli. The task of completing and publishing the fourth volume was performed conscientiously and capably by Rudolf Pfister,[26] who succeeded Farner at the University. This work supersedes all its predecessors, and may well remain for a long time the standard work on the development and the influence of the Zürich Reformer. Farner's books are characterised by a tireless study of the sources (not a few of which he discovered personally), by a precise knowledge of the state of research and a concise summary of its results, by excellent arrangement of the material and clarity of reasoning, all combined with a brilliant gift for narrative and a forceful style clearly fashioned by Zwingli's own language. The cultural and historical setting of Zwingli's present origins, his scholastic education, his Humanistic development, his decision for the Reformation, and his activities in both the city and the confederacy are all vividly portrayed. One almost feels an eye-witness of the Reformer's relations with opponents and friends, magistrates and people. One can actually see how church history is made, it is all very real and down-to-earth. Yet this very strength of the book has its reverse side. At times, Zwingli's history is confined to a merely local history, so that due attention is not paid either to its wider influence or to its problematics. There was no need for this. For though Farner himself was originally a product of liberal theology, he was led by his work on Zwingli to a truly Pauline faith in Christ and made a firm public stand for the Confessing Church in Germany and its Barmen Declaration. Farner's concentration on Zürich may give the reader cause regularly to consult in addition the mature work by Walther Köhler mentioned above.[27] The difference between the two works can be stated as follows: Farner can tell you the name of the inn where Zwingli sometimes ate supper, and in which tavern his opponents would be gathering at the same time, as well as the reasons (partly very personal ones) why they had a grievance against him. Köhler knows about the trade

---

26. Oskar Farner, *Huldrych Zwingli*. Vol. I: *Seine Jugend, Schulzeit und Studentenjahre 1484-1506*, Zürich, 1943; Vol. II: *Seine Entwicklung zum Reformator 1506-1520*, Zürich, 1946; Vol. III: *Seine Verkündigung und ihre ersten Früchte 1520-1525*, Zürich, 1954; Vol. IV: *Reformatorische Erneuerung von Kirche und Volk in Zürich und in der Eidgenossenschaft 1525-1531* (ed. and completed by Rudolf Pfister), Zürich, 1960. For a memoir (by Fritz Blanke) and a portrait of Oskar Farner (1884-1958) see Z XIV. Oskar Farner, *Erinnerungen*, Zürich, 1954. (Zwingli-Bücherei 68).

27. Walther Köhler, *Huldrych Zwingli*, Leipzig, 1943; 2nd ed., 1954.

relations between Zürich, Venice and Lyons, and who were Zwingli's friends in Paris; he knows what advice they gave him to advance his plans for federation, and which clauses in the enclosed confessional statement would be acceptable to a man like Francis I. Farner is more of a Church historian, whereas Köhler is a historian of dogma also. And whereas in Köhler's work it is the image of the Humanist that predominates, Farner is in danger of letting Zwingli's Humanism disappear behind the picture of the popular politician.[28] It is Köhler who presents Zwingli in the wider context of cultural history.

2.   At this point, we should not overlook two biographies in French, which brilliantly portray the man himself. That by Jaques Courvoisier (about 1952), a masterpiece of brevity and clarity,[29] presents the results of his extensive study of the sources and the literature in the form of a popular, topical narrative. Jean Rilliet depends on Farner for his history, and concentrates on Zwingli's personality and writings, using a sharp Gallic style to depict him against his Alemanic background.[30] As a result the Reformer appears less genial than in Farner, but also more human, fallible, complex, daring and spontaneous, which is by no means inconsistent with his "bon sens". As is stated in the Foreword: "Au XXe siècle, qui rêve d'une foi engagée, le témoin massacré ne saurait demeurer indifférent. Zwingli se présente tout pétri d'humanité et par conséquent d'erreurs. Il a vécu sa conviction dans le relatif des décisions hâtives, caractéristiques d'un temps troublé. Sincère et passioné, curieux mélange de prudence et d'audace, la recherche incessante de Dieu dirige sa vie. Il n'est pas un saint de vitrail. Sa silhouette morale évoque celle d'un prophète combattant comme l'Elie du Carmel".

3.   One further detail: for a long time there hung in the Czernin Gallery in Vienna an old painting of a man's head. Oral tradition maintained a) that it was the work of Albrecht Dürer and b) that it depicted Zwingli. Both ideas were treated with derision. But when the picture was cleaned about 1945 and Dürer's signature was revealed, thereby establishing its origin beyond all doubt, then the question arose as to whether the other part of the tradition might be correct also. In volume II

---

28. Oskar Farner wrote numerous popular studies of Zwingli. In my opinion, the most impressive of these is his *Die grosse Wende in Zürich*, Zürich, 1941. (This work includes pictures of Otto Münch's Zwingli-door in the Great Minster in Zürich). See also his *Der Reformator Ulrich Zwingli*, Zürich, 1949. (Zwingli-Bücherei 60).

29. Jaques Courvoisier, *Zwingli. Labor et Fides Genève* (n.d. 1952?).

30. Jean Rilliet, *Zwingli, le troisième homme de la Réforme*, Paris, 1959. (E. T. *Zwingli, Third Man of the Refomation*, London 1964).

of Farner's Biography, which includes a photograph of the painting, the
Zürich art historian Professor Hans Hoffman, affirms that it is. At an exhibition in Zürich the painting was offered to the city for a million Swiss
francs, but despite the willingness of patrons, no decision was reached
because the historians and art historians could not agree on a recommen-
dation.[31] Today the picture hangs in an American Museum, having been
sold for one million dollars.[32] It depicts a young man with a round head,
sharp features, a strong chin, somewhat sensually curved lips, a broad,
turned-up nose, reddish hair and fiery eyes. The left eye is open slightly
wider, as happens with short-sighted people. The date is AD 1516.[33] This
would be a portrait of the pre-Reformation Zwingli, when he was people's
priest at Glarus, just after he had taken part in a campaign in Upper Italy.
It would be the only portrait of Zwingli painted during his lifetime, and
one of high artistic quality at that. All the known portraits are
posthumous. In the near future I hope to publish proof of the authenticity
of this portrait as well as the possible date and place of origin. In the winter
of 1516, both Dürer and Zwingli were staying in Basle and both
frequented the house of Erasmus of Rotterdam.

4. More important than Zwingli's physiognomy is an understanding
of his spiritual image and his inner development. In Volume II of his
Biography, Oskar Farner (who in his early years, as a student of Wernle,
held views similar to those of Köhler)[34] emphasises the independence of
the Swiss Reformer, and his slowly maturing realisation that his growing
evangelical insight must risk opposing the Papal Church. The break-
through to an irrevocable decision came after his experience of the plague
in 1520; this may be inferred from his famous letter to Myconius and from
the artistic "Plague song" in which he expresses thankfulness for his
deliverance from illness. At about the same time as Farner's work, Arthur
Rich, in a careful and illuminating study, took the discussion of the
problem a stage further, and virtually solved it.[35] Zwingli took up his
position in Zurich on January 1, 1519—but Rich shows that Zwingli's

---

31. The views published in the Zürich press on the occasion of the exhibition are to be
found in Paul Sieber, *Bibliographie zum Zürcher Taschenbuch auf das Jahr 1950*, pp. 187-8. Cf.
Hans Hoffmann, "Ein mutmassliches Bildnis Huldrych Zwinglis" in *Zwa.* VIII, (1948),
pp. 497-501.
32. In the National Gallery of Arts in Washington.
33. A good, coloured postcard-size reproduction is obtainable from the Kunstverlag
Wolfrum, Augustinerstrasse 10, Vienna, Austria.
34. Oskar Farner, "Zwinglis Entwicklung zum Reformator nach seinem Briefwechsel bis
Ende 1522" in *Zwa.* III, 913-1915.
35. Arthur Rich, *Die Anfänge der Theologie Huldrych Zwinglis,* Zürich, 1949.

conception of and programme for the "Christianismus renascens" was
until 1520 determined by Erasmus and by his own humanistic training.
Even the well-known fact that Zwingli read and circulated many of
Luther's writings—which has repeatedly been used as an argument
against his later assertion of his independence—arose from a misunderstanding, in that he saw Luther as a kindred spirit, an ally in the battle for
an Erasmian renaissance of Christianity by means of a *philosophia christiana*. But "from that moment when Zwingli begins to lose faith in this
method of restoring Christianity based on Humanistic education, his interest in the Lutheran writings comes to an end".[36] The Swiss Reformer
was not the student of the Wittenberg Doctor. Certainly, Luther's *example*
did have a great influence upon Zwingli, though, remarkably enough, it
was not that of Worms, but of Leipzig—perhaps just because the Leipzig
Disputation, according to the rules of the late medieval university,
resulted in a defeat for Luther. In his confession Luther, ready to be
sacrificed and showing no concern for the consequences, was in Zwingli's
eyes an "Elijah", a "Hercules".[37]

Beside this basic book by Rich there is also a monograph, whose fifty-six
pages of meticulous work demand patience and close application on the
part of the reader, but which is most rewarding. Joachim Rogge has set
the early writings and letters of Zwingli alongside the corresponding works
of Erasmus and has carefully compared their statements, their train of
thought, their argumentation and even the wording.[38] Luther is cited also.
Rogge is not content with the idea of an "educational form", and rightly
insists on investigating in detail one central theme. So one is able to
observe Zwingli in the process of becoming a Reformer, and to see his
(partly still unconscious) personal and social motives in statu nascendi. In
the way that he changed his position with regard to the question of peace
we can see his development into that unity of Christian and citizen which
was typical of him. "War and Peace" represents not merely the motif of a
passing, idealistic phase in his development, but a permanent "general
theme" in his thought. Unlike the learned author I am of the opinion that
the chaplain from Glarus gives us an eye-witness account of the Pavia
campaign.[39] I base this conclusion not just, as many others have done, on
the vividness of the account, with its numerous personal experiences, but

---

36. Rich, *op. cit.*, p. 93.
37. G. W. Locher, "Elia bei Zwingli" in *Judaica*, Zürich, IX/1 (1953), pp. 62-63.
38. Joachim Rogge, *Zwingli und Erasmus. Die Friedensgedanken des jungen Zwingli*, Stuttgart,
1962. (Arbeiten zur Theologie, ed. by Theodor Schlatter, No. 11).
39. *De gestis inter Gallos et Helvetios relatio* (Autumn 1512) Z I 23-37.

also on the actual language, and the significance of a number of late Latin terms and expressions; but this is not important. Taking all things into account, the results of this North German scholar seem to point in the same direction as our recent Swiss researches; the remarks of the young Zwingli reveal him to be a pupil of Erasmus, not of Luther. "In any case, neither of the Reformers was ever an unconditional Erasmian".[40] Though I should think that, in so far as an ardent confederate could follow a cosmopolitan, Zwingli did so "unconditionally", for a time. But then he was "repelled by the reluctance to face consequences which he found in the great teacher".[41] Though when he turned away from Erasmus it was not only on political or ecclesiastical grounds; Zwingli's "consequence", his decisive stand for reformation, had grown out of the more radical understanding of the Biblical message of God's judgment and God's grace to which he had meanwhile attained, and this understanding went deeper than the Philosophia Christiana of Humanism.

A further remark must be added about the old controversy as to whether the beginnings of Zwingli's Reformation views should be dated in 1520/21 in Zürich (thus Köhler, Farner, Rich, Blanke and others) or as early as the year 1516 in Einsiedeln (as Zwingli himself, Bullinger, and the older school of thought maintained). Basically, this is not an historical but a theological question. It depends upon whether one sees the essence of the Reformation to be Zwingli's conscious doctrinal acceptance of Pauline anthropology (which is not to be found in Zwingli until after his plague experience) or to be the acceptance of the Scriptural principle and the experience of the Christus praesens that is bound up with it (which was Zwingli's own opinion).[42]

IV. THEOLOGICAL

1. Thus we come to the question of Zwingli's *anthropology*, which Luther took up with deep distrust. And ever since then, throughout the centuries, and in almost all the textbooks, there recurs the claim that Zwingli denied original sin, because for him it meant "only" a defect ("presten"). Now there can be no doubt that Humanism exercised a particularly strong influence on Zwingli's anthropology. Throughout his life he advocated a Platonic-Stoic dualism which he combined with his

---

40. Rogge, *op. cit.*, p. 47.

41. *Ib.*

42. Cf. "Huldrych Zwingli's Concept of History" (below, ch. 6) and "In Spirit and in Truth" (above, ch. 1).

Christian spiritualism in his own particular way. But in a dissertation published as long ago as 1905[43] Oorthuys demonstrated that the usual interpretation is a misunderstanding of Zwingli's doctrine of original sin and his denial of "original guilt". Remarkably enough, it was this Dutchman who was the first to notice that Luther, a Middle German, had not really understood the Upper German word "presten", which means a "rent", an irreparable "break". Rudolf Pfister[44] showed that Zwingli came to abandon the traditional doctrine of original sin not because of Pelagian but because of pauline tendencies: personal guilt presupposes divine law, not biological fate. Today the result of the discussion[45] may be stated as follows: according to Zwingli, *morbus* or "presten" characterises sin as "sickness unto death", as the necessity which is laid upon every man a) to sin, and b) to die; and noetically it involves c) our complete blindness to revelation. However, man becomes "guilty" only when he actually commits sin. The intention of this purely theoretical distinction between original sin and original guilt is to deprive the sinner of the possibility of representing his action as the consequence of some fateful destiny, and so passing himself off as innocent, in the last analysis. When understood in this way, Zwingli's formulations do not constitute a weakening but rather a Reformation sharpening of the conception of sin.

2.   The long-established fact that Zwingli, of all the Reformers, was the most extreme exponent of the *doctrine of election* should have served as a warning against that particular misunderstanding. It may be that in his formulation of *Peccatum originale* he was trying to cancel out the impression of determinism to which he had so nearly yielded through his close connexion of providentia and praedestinatio, which he adopted from Thomas Aquinas. So when Calvin drew such a clear-cut distinction between providence and predestination in the *Institutio* of 1559, this could well have been directed against Zwingli, among others.[46] Yet is not the traditional view of Zwingli correct when it detects in his concept of the doctrine of election a moralism, according to which man is able to achieve salvation through his own good powers, even without the aid of the Biblical message? How else could Hercules, Theseus, Socrates and the Catos reach heaven alongside Abraham, Moses and David, as is stated in the famous

---

43. Gerardus Oorthuys, *De anthropologie van Zwingli*, Leiden, 1905.

44. Rudolf Pfister, *Das Problem der Erbsünde bei Zwingli*, Leipzig, 1939.

45. *Th. H. Z.* I, pp. 137-139.

46. Cf. Paul Jacobs, *Prädestination und Verantwortlichkeit bei Calvin*, Neukirchen, 1937, pp. 67ff.

list in the *Fidei expositio*?[47] Is it not understandable that Luther should be angry with Zwingli once more, when this work appeared in 1536—or that Wernle should speak appreciatively of "moral universalism"[48]—and that Köhler speaks of a "humanistic evaluation of man" and of "a break from the exclusiveness of the Christian view of salvation"?[49] Is there not patent synergism here—and, even more, a relativising of revelation?

Rudolf Pfister has devoted a lively and thorough study to this question.[50] He shows, step by step, how Zwingli's statements about the "pious heathen" are to be understood. It is not a question of an anthropological but of a theological statement; it is not a matter of a general possibility which is present in every man, but of the definite election of particular people, outside the Biblical sphere. Secondly, it is not a question of a shift from faith to human subjectivity, but rather a shift of emphasis (which is to be observed in other aspects of Zwingli's development) from faith to election, from the subjective to the objective prerequisite of salvation. There is no genuine faith without election—but the reverse may well be true, as is proved by the case of children born within the covenant, the heathen before they are evangelised, and indeed all of us before our conversion. Thirdly, Christ is not somehow set aside; on the contrary, His glory is increased. For the fact remains: "Whoever would come to God, must come to Him through Christ".[51] "Through election" and "through Christ" mean the same thing: "It is therefore election which saves men, but it is through Christ; that is, through Him, through His goodness and his grace".[52] The sacrifice of Christ is imputed to the elect, even among the heathens. Thus it is in Christ that they are reconciled with the Father and gain salvation.

---

47. S IV 65; cf. S VI, I 583; S VI, II 252; S IV 123.

48. Paul Wernle speaks of the "moral universalism which he (Zwingli) adopted from Erasmus and the Renaissance and which he bore in his heart alongside Paulinism throughout his life" (*Der evangelische Glaube nach den Hauptschriften der Reformatoren*. Vol. II: *Zwingli*, Tübingen, 1919, p. 353).

49. "It was a break from the exclusiveness of the Christian view of salvation, a humanistic evaluation of man, a revival of something from classical antiquity, for this portrayal of the future glorification of great men goes back to Cicero's *Dream of Scipio*". (Walther Köhler, *Huldrych Zwingli*, 2nd ed., Leipzig, 1954, p. 235).

50. Rudolf Pfister, *Die Seligkeit erwählter Heiden bei Zwingli*, Zollikon, 1952; also "Zur Begründung der Seligkeit von Heiden bei Zwingli" in *Evangelisches Missions-Magazin*, Basle, 1951, 95/3, pp. 70-80.

51. John 14:6; cf. e.g. Z V 629, S IV 62.

52. S III 572; cf. R. Pfister, "Zur Begründung der Seligkeit erwählter Heiden bei Zwingli", *op. cit.*, pp. 74ff.

Pfister's argument can be augmented by a further point.[53] When Zwingli speaks of the Atonement, he quotes 1 John 2:2 with unusual frequency: "Christ is the propitiation for our sins, and not for ours only, but for the sins of the whole world". Election and universalism as a principle are mutually exclusive, of course, but Zwingli is trying to say that God's freedom, which is expressed in election, postulates universality and forbids us to set limits according to human standards. The sacrifice of Christ is fundamentally universal. Otherwise redemption would be less than the corruption of sin, and Christ would be inferior to Adam.[54]

This raises the problem of the relationship between *satisfactio* and *praedestinatio*. No reformer has sensed it so keenly or resolved it so boldly as Zwingli. It would have been well if this particular voice had not later gone unheard among the chorus of voices that were raised when the Reformed Church developed its doctrine of election. It would, perhaps, have allowed the light which it possessed to shine more brightly—and that light would not have changed so often into an oppressive darkness. Calvinism draws two lines:[55] God's goodness elects us in Jesus Christ and redeems us; God's justice leaves the rest of mankind in a state of damnation. Zwingli allows only *one* line: God's goodness elects through Christ and this justice imputes to the elect the salvation won by Christ. Since God deals with us according to what Christ has done for us, He is "righteous" both in Himself and in relation to us. "It is of goodness that He elects whom He will; it is of goodness that He adopts and unites the elect to Himself through His Son, who by His sacrifice for us has rendered satisfaction to divine justice".[56] Reprobation is hardly mentioned; it may be understood in the sense of "praeteritio", following the example of the young Augustine.[57]

3.   The expert will already be aware that at the heart of Zwingli's doctrine of predestination is the freedom of the Holy Spirit—one of the chief elements, therefore, of his theology in general, namely, his spiritualism. So we come to the critical part of his doctrine, which from time immemorial has brought down on the name of the Zürich Reformer the most

---

53. For this and for what follows, cf. *Huldrych Zwingli's Doctrine of Predestination* (below, ch. 7).

54. S IV 7.

55. Cf. *Confessio Belgica,* Article XVI.

56. S IV 5ff.

57. See below p. 121ff., for a more detailed discussion of Zwingli's doctrine of election, its place in the history of dogma, and its understanding of the question of supralapsarianism and infralapsarianism, in which it stands much closer to the Bible than does the seventeenth century doctrine.

fame and the most notoriety, the most approval and the most hatred—and which has caused the most misunderstanding among both followers and opponents. For his faith in the exalted Christ and in the Holy Spirit is essential to his doctrine of the *Lord's Supper*. We are aware that friends and foes alike have often simply equated his spiritualism with rationalism, and that they do so still. But it is at this point that we have to be careful.

Köhler's reconstruction of the Marburg Colloquy[58] is a product of the self-denying German scholarship of the old school, and is an achievement that commands the utmost respect. From twenty-seven greater or lesser sources (reports and letters) he reconstructed "a report of the proceedings" of the disputation, which reproduces in a most convincing manner the course and the content of the debate. The modern scholar who does not wish merely to dwell on the exegetical and scholastic-philosophical details, but wants to get to the heart of the matter will be astounded to find how clearly the participants had this aim in sight also. "Oecolampadius: 'Don't hold so much to the humanity and flesh of Christ, but lift up your thoughts to the divinity of Christ!' Luther: 'I know of no God except the One who became man; nor will I have any other' ".[59] Luther's touchiness breaks through repeatedly. "I don't care what you teach in Strassburg. If you don't want me or my doctrine, I can't stand having you as my disciples".[60] The whole complex (and not always unambiguous) relationship between "Humanism", "Reformation" and "the Bible" comes to light. When the discussion turns to Christology, Zwingli quotes Phil. 2:6ff.: "Zwingli: it says "Ος ἐν μορφῇ θεοῦ ὑπάρχων. And: μορφὴν δούλου λαβών. Luther: 'Read it in German or Latin, not Greek'. Zwingli: 'Pardon me for using the Greek Testament. I have been using it for twelve years. I have only read the Latin once' ".[61]

This sometimes "stenographic" reconstruction was a by-product of Walther Köhler's great opus on the controversy about the Lord's Supper "in its political and religious aspects".[62] The importance of those two volumes lies in the wealth of material which has been gathered together

---

58. Walther Köhler, *Das Marburger Religionsgespräch 1529. Versuch einer Rekonstruktion*, Schriften des Vereins für Reformationsgeschichte, Leipzig, 1929, 48/1, No. 148.

59. *Ib.*, p. 27.

60. *Ib.*, p. 38.

61. *Ib.*, p. 30.

62. Walther Köhler, *Zwingli und Luther. Ihr Streit über das Abendmahl nach seinen politischen und religiösen Beziehungen*. Vol. I: *Die religiöse und politische Entwicklung bis zum Marburger Religionsgespräch 1529*, Leipzig, 1924; Vol. II: *Vom Beginn der Marburger Verhandlungen 1529 bis zum Abschluss der Wittenberger Konkordie von 1536*, ed. Ernst Kohlmeyer and Heinrich Bornkamm, Gütersloh, 1953.

from inaccessible archives and correspondence and is presented here in readable language. The reader becomes ever more aware of the great significance of the "satellites" gathered alongside the three chief contestants, and especially the leading role played by Martin Bucer, the Strasbourg Reformer, in the progress of the Reformation. One realises also the significance of the efforts for political unity made by Philipp of Hesse and the Protestant imperial cities, and how they were frustrated by Luther's refusal to oppose the "authority" of the Emperor or to protect the Gospel by any political means at all. One of the main contributions made to research in the first volume is its presentation of the rich store of material of the medieval tradition upon which both parties drew.[63] There is also the thesis (which I have reason to doubt) that Zwingli adhered to the doctrine of the real presence of Christ in the Lord's Supper until 1524 (which is far into his Reformation period, therefore), and that it was only under the influence of the famous letter of the Dutchman Hoen that he came not only to interpret the words of institution tropologically, but also to understand the Lord's Supper symbolically. Finally, there is the fact that "the controversy about the Lord's Supper gave birth to the concept of what is essential in religion,[64] though this was held only by the Zwinglians and not by the Lutherans". "Luther and I have the same faith concerning Christ Jesus our Lord, and in Him" wrote Zwingli to a Roman opponent. The second volume shows how the negotiations to achieve concord were increasingly affected by political factors and soon became completely entangled in them. There is an impressive picture of Luther's stubborn insistence upon the literal word of Scripture and of Bucer's burning, untiring zeal for the unity of the Church, even to the point where his diplomatic adaptability verges on untruthfulness. Both before and after Marburg the debate was carried on with philosophical arguments on both sides—Luther's arguments were scholastic (including that in which he supports the doctrine of the ubiquity of the body of Christ by saying that God is "above mathematics" and that the "dextera dei" is non-spatial); Zwingli likewise used scholastic arguments when on the defensive, but used humanistic and platonic arguments when stating his own case: sense processes can have no effect on the soul.

In his review of the Marburg Colloquy, Köhler remarks in passing[65] that in the difference of opinion about the relationship between spirit and

---

63. E.g. Vol. I, pp. 806-812.
64. *Ib.*, pp. 829ff.
65. Vol. II, p. 137.

nature and about the competence of reason in religious matters, "In Zwingli and Luther humanism and solid Biblicism, Thomas Aquinas and William of Occam (their common teachers in their student days) and even Plato and Aristotle confronted one another". The problem must be formulated more sharply. Seen in terms of the history of dogma, we have a confrontation between the *via antiqua* (Zwingli) and the *via moderna* (Luther) over the exegesis of a text ("this is my body"). There is here an important field for research.[66] [67]

Yet it seems to me that even this does not get to the heart of the Zwinglian protest.[68] This will be revealed only to the person who can free himself from the predisposition to see Zwingli as a rationalist. "We do not judge absurdity according to the matter in itself ... but if anything is absurd to the eye of faith, it is truly absurd."[69] Zwingli's opposition to Luther's sacramental realism arose not from rationalism but from his Christology, with his wish to uphold the complete and exclusive efficacy of the reconciliation accomplished on the Cross. If reconciliation took place *there*, then comfort for the troubled soul must not be made to depend on the celebration of the sacrament—an alternative which Luther could not recognise, because of his own presuppositions. However, the *memoria*, the "memorial feast" is not an intellectual process, and does not merely arouse association with the historical past, but rather (following Augustine) displays the soul's power of actualisation and awareness.[67]

4. Therefore, Zwingli's doctrine of the Lord's Supper is intended to safeguard the "sola fide" of the Reformation against sacramental ceremonialism, which would be a form of idolatry. For this reason, he arranged divine service as a preaching service—though not in the form of ra-

---

66. Important new sources concerning the eucharistic controversy have been brought to light in the careful studies of Joachim Staedtke, "Eine neue Version des sogenannten Utinger-Berichtes vom Marburger Religionsgespräch 1529", *Zwa.* X, pp. 210-216; and Fritz Büsser in his edition of the *Beschreibung des Abendmahlsstreites von Johann Stumpf*, Zürich, 1960.

67. I hope to discuss these matters in more detail in the continuation of *Th. H. Z.*

68. Cf. Gottlob Schrenk, "Zwinglis Hauptmotive in der Abendmahlslehre und das Neue Testament", *Zwa.*, V/4 (1930/2), pp. 176-185; Fritz Blanke, "Zwinglis Sakramentsanschauung", *Theologische Blätter*, 1931, columns 283-290; Wilhelm Niesel, "Zwinglis 'spätere' Sakramentsanschauung", *Theologische Blätter*, 1932/1; F. Blanke, "Antwort auf W. Niesel, Zwinglis 'spätere' Sakramentsanschauung", *Theologische Blätter*, 1932 column 18; F. Blanke, "Zum Verständnis der Abendmahlslehre Zwinglis", *Pastoraltheologie*, 1931, pp. 314-320; "In Spirit and in Truth" (above, ch. 1); G. W. Locher, s.v. "Zwingli. II: Theologie" in *Die Religion in Geschichte und Gegenwart*, 3rd. ed., Tübingen, 1962; Jaques Courvoisier, "Vom Abendmahl bei Zwingli", *Zwa.*, XI/7 (1962/1), pp. 415-426.

69. "Absurditatem non metimur ab ipsa re ... Quod si quid fidei absurdum, id tandem vere absurdum est". (Z V 618).

tional instruction, as some would expect, but in a rich and moving liturgy, in which traditional material was freely used. "Luther cleansed—Zwingli created" that was the surprise revealed in the book by Fritz Schmidt-Clausing, a Lutheran, a student of Leonhard Fendt, and a supporter of the movement for liturgical renewal, who discovered "Zwingli as a Liturgist".[70] One peculiar and unexpected feature of the Zürich liturgy, which demonstrates how patiently and how wisely Zwingli guided the young Reformed congregations (he was not the impatient fanatic so often portrayed!) is that it retained until 1563, in the preaching service, the traditional, so popular, virtually irremovable "Angelic salutation", the German Ave Maria—though it was given a characteristically evangelical introduction: "Let us also consider the incarnation of Christ, which the angel Gabriel announced to the Virgin Mary and which soon afterwards was praised and lauded by the Holy Spirit through Elisabeth in these words: Hail, Mary, thou that art highly favoured.... etc."[71] [72]

The "flood Prayer" used in the Baptism Service, and which has been much discussed, especially in the Netherlands, was modelled on Luther's Baptism Book of 1523.[73] In Wittenberg, "the unfathomable mercy of God" was besought, that the one baptised "might be kept dry and safe in the Holy Ark of Christendom"; in Zürich, it is that he might be "incorporated in Thy Son".

Liturgists were equally delighted with the interpretation of the Zürich Order for the Lord's Supper of 1525 by Julius Schweitzer, Professor of Practical Theology at Basle.[74] He offers an intensive historical, liturgical and psychological interpretation, which opens up to the systematic theologian and the historian of dogma an important new source, namely,

---

70. Fritz Schmidt-Clausing, *Zwingli als Liturgiker. Eine liturgie-geschichtliche Untersuchung,* Göttingen, 1952. See also my review of this work in *Musik und Gottesdienst*, IX/2, Zürich, March-April, 1955.

71. Schmidt-Clausing, *op. cit.,* p. 107.

72. In 1950 there was a controversy in the "Neue Zürcher Zeitung" in connexion with the definition of the doctrine of the bodily assumption of the Virgin Mary. The Roman Catholic side maintained that Zwingli himself had held this doctrine. Here we would mention only the conclusion of the debate: Zwingli says, "All her honour is her Son". (See "The Content and the Design of Zwingli's Teaching about Mary", below, ch. 5). The learned Catholic Karl Federer replied to this in "Zwingli und die Marienverehrung", in *Zeitschrift für schweizerische Kirchengeschichte*, 1951, pp. 13-26; but his views were refuted by the Dominican J. V. M. Pollet, a specialist on the reformation in South Germany and Switzerland, in "Recherches sur Zwingli", in *Revue des Sciences Religieuses*, Strasbourg, Vol. 28, April 1954, pp. 167-169. The Reformers' powerful preaching on this theme is finely displayed in Walter Tappolet, *Marienlob der Reformatoren*, Zürich, 1961.

73. Schmidt-Clausing, *op. cit.,* Index, pp. 152-3.

74. Julius Schweizer, *Reformierte Abendmahlsgestaltung in der Schau Zwinglis*, Basle, 1954.

the actual celebration of the sacrament. For Zwingli's theoretical writings on the Lord's Supper were all polemical. Anyone who has assimilated this description of the emotion and the lively joy with which the congregation participated can no longer maintain that Zwingli paid little heed to the Lord's Supper. Again we may note a typical detail: at the very point where the transubstantiation takes place in the Mass, in Zwingli's order the *congregation* is addressed as having been changed into the Body of Christ.[75] Zwingli concludes the preaching service with a General Confession—without an Absolution. In my view, this is an unprecedented consequence of his prophetism. Schweitzer's conjecture that Zwingli wished the service to be followed by a regular weekly celebration of the Lord's Supper (as the Absolution) may well lead to further discussion. As regards the theology of worship, I think that Zwingli's spiritualism must be underlined once more. The experience of the whole Reformation was that the real presence of the Lord of the Church is to be found fundamentally in the *viva vox evangelii* instead of in the sacrament. But Zwingli adds that the *verbum qua externum* is of no effect unless the Holy Spirit also speaks it inwardly.[76] A discovery made by Oskar Farner shortly before his death is relevant at this point, and should not be overlooked. It was already known that in his total abolition of church singing the (highly musical) Reformer was really striking only at Latin chanting. And now, in an old copy of Zwingli's lectures on the Psalms, Farner found this statement: "If the hymn of praise on Sunday is sung clearly and for all to understand, it is good and praiseworthy".[77] The old assertion "Zwingli was against church singing" holds good no longer. Since then, *"Zwingli's attitude to music in divine worship"* has been effectively illuminated by Markus Jenny in a treatise[78] which discusses all the known statements, suggestions and references (and several newly-disclosed ones also) with a fine judgment based on a comprehensive knowledge of sixteenth century liturgy and music. Zwingli's polemic is concerned exclusively with the medieval Latin choral and priestly chanting and not with the hymns of evangelical congregations or choirs. Zwingli freely allowed vernacular psalm or choral singing. In addition, he even seems to have striven for lively, antiphonal,

---

75. *Ib.*, pp. 103ff.
76. Cf. "In Spirit and in Truth" (above, ch. 1).
77. Z XIII 695, on Psalm 92. It had appeared in S IV 267, but remained unnoticed! Oskar Farner, "Eine neuentdeckte Äusserung Zwinglis über den Gemeindegesang", in *Jahrbuch für Liturgik und Hymnologie*, 1957, p. 130.
78. Markus Jenny, *Zwinglis Stellung zur Musik im Gottesdienst.* Schriften des Arbeitskreises für evangelische Kirchenmusik, No. 3, Zürich, 1966.

unison recitative. The chief thought in his conception of worship was always "conscious attendance and understanding"—"devotion", yet with the lively participation of all concerned.

5.   At the turn of the century Oskar Rückert had already brought to light those forces in the Reformation, and particularly in the Zwinglian Reformation, which made for general, popular education.[79] The tendencies which have endowed Swiss Protestantism with its passion for education are already to be found in Zwingli's doctrine of divine and human righteousness.[80] The educationalist Willi Meister is basically right in saying that "the education and training of the people were rooted in Huldrych Zwingli's Reformation".[81] But the historian Kurt Spillmann is also correct when he warns against drawing too direct a connexion. Zwingli was not concerned with the "German schools", but with prophesying;[82] he was not the forefather of the primary school, but of the college. This is not to deny that Zwingli's thought and efforts led to general educational insights and ideas which found expression especially in the popular *Lehrbüchlein*. When Ernst Gerhard Rüsch sets before us the Humanistic models for this bright little book,[83] then we realise what an achievement of selection and arrangement it is. Walter Gut had already indicated one basic principle: "Here the path no longer goes from ethics to religion, but from religion to ethics".[84] In his fascinating paraphrase, Ernst Gerhard Rüsch emphasises that this change consists in the fact that the relationship of the individual to the community is governed by the self-sacrifice of Christ.[85] Rüsch's introduction to his new edition of the Lehrbüchlein draws attention to the remarkable fact that this official school programme, the prospectus of the Reformed cathedral foundation, should be presented to a fourteen year old stepson as a gift. "By clothing his universal educational wisdom in the garb of a personal gift, he touches on an important secret of educational success: that general rules and instructions are not

---

79. Oskar Rückert, *Zwinglis Ideen zur Erziehung und Bildung,* Gotha, 1900.

80. Leonhard von Muralt, "Von Zwingli zu Pestalozzi", *Zwa.*, IX/6 (1951/2), pp. 329-364. Reprinted in *Der Historiker und die Geschichte*, Zürich, 1960, pp. 118-140.

81. Willi Meister, *Volksbildung und Volkserziehung in der Reformation Huldrych Zwinglis,* Zürich, 1939.

82. Kurt Spillmann, "Zwingli und die Zürcher Schulverhältnisse", *Zwa.* XI/7 (1962/1), pp. 427-488.

83. Ernst Gerhard Rüsch, "Die humanistischen Vorbilder der Erziehungsschrift Zwinglis", *Theologische Zeitschrift,* Basle, 1966, pp. 122-147.

84. Walter Gut, "Zwingli als Erzieher", *Zwa.* VI/6 (1936/2), pp. 289-306.

85. Ernst Gerhard Rüsch, "Die Erziehungsgrundsätze Huldrych Zwinglis", in *Vom Heiligen in der Welt,* Zollikon, 1959, pp. 72-98.

much use, if they do not become the subject of a personal human relationship between teacher and pupil".[86]

6.   It has long been remarked that Zwingli represented a different conception of the *state* from Luther, who believed in loyalty to the civil authority. He was prepared, not only in an emergency, but also in principle, to lay responsibility for the Church upon the Christian magistrate and, at the same time, to charge the Church with the prophetic and critical office of "Watchman" over the government (following Ezekiel 3 and 33). Furthermore, the people have the right to oppose an authority that strays "away from the guidance of Christ". But only now is it gradually becoming clear to our generation that these theses are not just the expression of the Swiss republican tradition but of a basic theological position. The standard work on Zwingli's doctrine of the state is still that of Alfred Farner, a lawyer who died young.[87] It presents the wealth of material in a masterly fashion. His main thesis is that Zwingli—like the whole Reformation—burst apart the medieval social order, the dubiously-termed Corpus christianum. Thus he links Zwingli with the same line that Karl Holl, in his celebrated controversy with Ernst Troeltsch and Walther Köhler, attributed to Luther. Farner's brilliant work caused Paul Meyer's modest but solid dissertation to be forgotten.[88] Simply by collating the sources, Meyer had demonstrated how much Zwingli—and Luther also, for that matter—thought in terms of the Corpus christianum. Anyone who does not just take the Reformers' statements on social ethics in isolation, but considers them in the light of their respective conception of what constitutes the core of their faith,[89] must conclude that the "modern" Troeltsch and his friends had the better grasp of the "medieval" character

---

86. *Huldrych Zwingli: An den jungen Mann. Zwinglis Erziehungsschriften aus dem Jahre 1523,* ed. E. G. Rüsch, Zürich, 1957, p. 6.

87. Alfred Farner, *Die Lehre von Kirche und Staat bei Zwingli,* Tübingen, 1930. The following works deserve mention for their valuable insights into Zwingli's complex political relationships: René Hauswirth, *Landgraf Philipp von Hessen und Zwingli,* Zürich, 1963; René Hauswirth, *Landgraf Philipp von Hessen und Zwingli. Voraussetzungen und Geschichte der politischen Beziehungen zwischen Hessen, Württemberg, Strassburg, Konstanz und reformierten Eidgenossen 1526-1531.* Schriften zur Kirchen- und Rechtsgeschichte, ed. E. Fabian, No. 35, Tübingen, 1968. René Hauswirth, Introduction I to *Quellen zur Geschichte der Reformationsbündnisse.* Schriften zur Kirchen- und Rechtsgeschichte, ed. E. Fabian, No. 34, Tübingen, 1967, pp. 18-22; Kurt Spillmann, *Zwingli und die Zürcherische Politik gegenüber der Abtei St. Gallen,* St. Gallen, 1965; Martin Haas, *Zwingli und der erste Kappelerkrieg,* Zürich, 1965.

88. Paul Meyer, *Zwinglis Soziallehren,* Linz/D., 1921.

89. G. W. Locher, *Die evangelische Stellung der Reformatoren zum öffentlichen Leben,* Kirchliche Zeitfragen, No. 26, Zürich, 1950; "Das Problem der Landeskirche", in *Evangelische Theologie,* 1956/1, pp. 33-48.

of the Reformation. In the territories of its national churches, it set up and continued in a new form the ideal of a unified Christian culture. It was the lawyer Calvin,[90] a refugee and an organiser of refugee congregations, who first began to separate Church and State and to define their respective competencies.

Zwingli's pronouncements on politics should be considered against the background of the dissolution of Imperium and Sacerdotium and of resistance to the seething anarchy (including religious anarchy).[91] The two special studies which have still to be mentioned are not equal in the attention they pay to the concrete situation. The Roman Catholic historian Siegfried Rother takes most account of it in his appreciative and even affectionate dissertation on the foundation of Zwingli's thought.[92] He sees Zwingli as a forerunner of Cromwell, who believes himself called to establish the Kingdom of God by force of arms. This is correct, in so far that for Zwingli faith and political action were not opposites, but were both grounded in the will and providence of God. And it is therefore incorrect to speak of a change in Zwingli's thinking around 1525 out of resignation about preaching. Despite numerous theological deficiencies and incorrect judgments, the book provides a number of useful insights. The most instructive is, perhaps, the attempt (the first ever) to explain Zwingli's intention at Marburg when he preached his remarkably philosophic sermon "De providentia". Rother explains it as a comprehensive exposition of the evangelical faith over against the spirit of the age and its trends, and especially the Renaissance belief in fate. This is worthy of consideration.

Heinrich Schmid, well equipped as a theologian who owes allegiance to no particular school and also as a philologist, delves deeply in his monograph on Zwingli's conception of righteousness.[93] His mastery of the sources, including the often neglected *Exegetica*, is astonishing. In contrast

---

90. G. W. Locher, *Calvin—Anwalt der Oekumene*, Theologische Studien, ed. Karl Barth and Max Geiger, No. 60, Zollikon, 1960.

91. It is not possible to go into the details of the political history of the reformation in Zürich. In place of the older treatments in this subject we would mention the concise but comprehensive contribution by Leonhard von Muralt in *Historia Mundi. Ein Handbuch der Weltgeschichte*, Vol. VII: *Übergang zur Moderne*, 1957, pp. 39-118 "Die Reformation" (Zwingli, pp. 69-74). His essays, "Italienischer Humanismus und Zwingli's Reformation", *Zwa*. X, pp. 398-408, and "Renaissance und Reformation in der Schweiz", *Zwa*. XI, pp. 1-23, afford an insight into the master's workshop.

92. Siegfried Rother, *Die religiösen und geistigen Grundlagen der Politik Huldrych Zwinglis. Ein Beitrag zum Problem des christlichen Staates*, Erlangen, 1956.

93. Heinrich Schmid, *Zwinglis Lehre von der göttlichen und menschlichen Gerechtigkeit*, Zürich, 1959.

to Rother, he maintains that Zwingli did not value the civil law very highly. Yet its imperfect righteousness is still an expression of the preserving and healing will of God. It creates the situation within which the Christian can strive towards the higher righteousness of the Sermon on the Mount. Thus Zwingli goes further than Luther in establishing a social ethic. But over against all this, God's free righteousness is sui generis.

Especially instructive are the reasoned statements made by Helmut Kressner in his chapter on Zwingli.[94] It is true that this book, which was drafted in 1941, still maintains that Zwingli's moralism was grounded in pure Humanism. But it does make it clear that Zwingli's politics arose out of his faith, which demanded practical realisation.

Kressner points out that the "associational" character of the South German towns and of the Swiss communities was similar to the Protestant congregational principle, and thus made it possible for Zwingli "to bridge the gap between the spiritual and temporal spheres".[95] Bernd Moeller's fascinating work[96] examines the relationship between citizenry and the Zwinglian-Bucerian reformation. It gives an account of the powerful advance of Zwinglianism in the South German imperial cities even after the Battle of Kappel in 1531. It was political difficulties, and especially the catastrophe of the Schmalkaldic War (which Zwingli had foreseen) which caused the change to Lutheranism. The collapse of the imperial cities' freedom and the destruction of the associational life went hand in hand with this. Absolutism began its triumphant march, and the German Protestant became a pious "subject".

7.   The very diversity of these features which Zwingli's voice contributed to the Reformation chorus caused renewed enquiry as to the central motive of his awakening,[97] in the hope of discovering thereby that unifying principle of his thought whose existence Wernle and Köhler deny. Humanism shaped his education and his thought, and therefore made a permanent mark upon Zwingli—as it did more or less upon all the Reformers—even Luther, and especially Calvin. But that is not a suffi-

---

94. Helmut Kressner, *Schweizer Ursprünge des anglikanischen Staatskirchentums*, Gütersloh, 1953. Cf. also Erik Wolf, "Die Sozialtheologie Zwinglis" in *Festschrift Guido Kisch,* Stuttgart, 1955.

95. Kressner, *op. cit.,* p. 33.

96. Bernd Moeller, *Reichsstadt und Reformation*, Gütersloh, 1962 (E.T. *Imperial Cities and the Reformation,* Philadelphia, 1972). Cf. also Leonhard von Muralt, *Stadtgemeinde und Reformation in der Schweiz*, Zürich, 1930, a work that is still indispensable.

97. See "Huldrych Zwingli's Concept of History" (below, ch. 6) and "Huldrych Zwingli's Message" (above, ch. 2). Cf. also G. W. Locher, *Der Eigentumsbegriff als Problem evangelischer Theologie*, 2nd ed. Zürich, 1962. Part I, chapter 3: "Zwingli. Die politische Verantwortung der Christenheit und das Eigentumsproblem", pp. 29-35, 49-53.

cient answer, as the example of the revered teacher Erasmus proves. We get further with the patriotism of the confederate concerned about his people's wrongs. And without a doubt, the practice of the late medieval South German Preaching service, the so-called "pronous", and the instruction given by its most eminent theological and liturgical exponent, Johann Ulrich Surgant in Basle, also helped to shape the Zwinglian reformation, as Fritz Schmidt-Clausing has recently shown in an informative treatise.[98] But the decisive factor was Zwingli's turning to the principle of sola scriptura about the years 1514/15.[99] Admittedly, Scripture was still read, for a while, through the eyes of a Humanist; but it led to the experience that in the rediscovered Word of the Bible, in its exposition and its proclamation, the living Christ is Himself present and demands obedience. Zwingli repeatedly dated this experience in the year 1516. The parable of the talents, and the fear of being found as a "lazy servant" "when the Lord comes" played a special part in his sense of urgency in working for reformation.[100] *Here* lies the root of that desire for practical results to which we have already referred. His reading of the prophets led to a further, special experience: the fear of judgment concerning the temporal and eternal salvation of his own people and of the whole of Christendom. Christ, who is present again in the Gospel which is being preached once more, is the last chance, the final proclamation of the right to return home, the "postliminium". This is Zwingli's personal testimony.

This would explain everything: the cultural concern of the Zwinglian reformation, in which Humanism was changed from an end to a means; the spiritualism, which arose from the ethical alternative between the Word of God and self-seeking; the emphasis on the divinity of Christ; and the corresponding efforts to achieve a theocracy. It would follow that any complete study of Zwingli's theology would have to be made in the light of his Christology. The first volume of the writer's work provides the introduction to such an interpretation.[101]

8.   A remarkable new survey of Zwingli's world of thought, from the pen of the Dominican J. V. M. Pollet, has recently been published in the *Dictionnaire de Théologie catholique*.[102] It is both sympathetic and comprehen-

---

98. Fritz Schmidt-Clausing, "Johann Ulrich Surgant, ein Wegweiser des jungen Zwingli", *Zwa.* XI/5 (1961/1), pp. 287-320.

99. "I began to rely entirely on Holy Scripture" (Z I 379).

100. Z I 256, 316.

101. *Th. H. Z.* I.; *Zw. Ref. i. Rahmen.*, ch. XI. (Liter.).

102. J. V. M. Pollet, O. P., s.v. "Zwinglianisme" in *Dictionnaire de Théologie catholique*, Vol. XV, Paris, 1951, columns 3745-3928. This article is summarised and taken further in his article "Zwingli" in *Lexikon für Theologie und Kirche*, 2nd ed., Vol. X, 1965, columns 1433-1441.

sive, treating the Biblical, early Christian and medieval elements in a most exemplary fashion, and including a discussion of the Reformer's own times. The main line of Zwingli's thought is said to be a Christian spiritualism,[103] which, by virtue of Platonic-Stoic-Erasmian influences, developed into rationalism in his doctrine of the sacraments. Zwingli's propheticism is seen as the key to his personality and is treated seriously. But while Zwingli's Christology is correctly presented in its "Nestorian" tendency, its central position is not recognised, nor are his political and social motives. But both in general and in detail it is a reliable work, well documented, and yet lucid. Critically, the influence of Duns Scotus is rated more highly than is usual. It is recognised that Zwingli's reformation set its face against the deification of the creature; but it is maintained that the absolute gulf between creator and creature is not Biblical but heathen in origin, and that Zwinglianism was an attempt "to incorporate within Christian dogma elements which are not Christian, but pagan".

Thus there still remains the task of distinguishing between the Biblical substance of his thought and the Humanistic forms in which it is expressed. The first part of my study of Zwingli's theology has shown that the most numerous and most important concepts in his doctrine of God, which were usually regarded as "Humanistic", actually belong to the Scholastic tradition and should therefore be interpreted in accordance with Thomas Aquinas; that Zwingli's so-called "pantheism" is really the exact opposite, namely an extreme, theistic Monarchianism;[104] that the doctrine of the Trinity, which until now has been virtually denied to Zwingli, plays a fundamental role in his thought;[105] and that his theological and christological statements lead into the covenant theology of the "Deus noster".[106] [107]

Pollet continued his work and produced a happy synthesis of biography and research report in the form of a magnificently illustrated book,[108] in which for the first time a Roman Catholic theologian has provided his

---

103. On Zwingli's spiritualism cf. Erich Seeberg, "Der Gegensatz zwischen Zwingli, Schwenkfeld und Luther" in Reinhold-Seeberg-Festschrift, Leipzig, 1929; Helmut Gollwitzer, "Zur Auslegung von Joh. 6 bei Luther und Zwingli" in Evangelische Theologie, 1951, pp. 143-168.

104. Th. H. Z. I., pp. 95ff.

105. Ib., pp. 99-133.

106. Ib., p. 98; also pp. 33-42.

107. There is a detailed and instructive critique of my book by J. V. M. Pollet in his article "Recherches sur Zwingli", in Revue des Sciences Religieuses, Strasbourg, Vol. 28, April 1954, pp. 156-160.

108. J. V. M. Pollet, O. P., Huldrych Zwingli et la Réforme en Suisse d'après les recherches récentes, Paris, 1963.

church with a comprehensive and sympathetic portrait of Zwingli. And at the same time, in the exhaustive apparatus, the author has traced the course of contemporary research in the whole field of Zwinglianism, even to its most remote ramifications, supplementing it, discussing it or correcting it, always displaying a well-founded point of view, and frequently making surprising contributions. Pollet is highly critical of Zwingli (in distinction from Catholicism and Luther) for weakening Christology and emptying the sacrament of significance. But in contrast to previous Catholic treatment of Zwingli,[109] which was always dependent on Johann Faber, and portrayed Zwingli as an immoral unbelieving rationalist and revolutionary, Pollet does emphasise that he was a "good pastor", that he was throughout his life gripped by the holiness and power of God, that he was a great theologian in his doctrine of predestination and at other points, that he was of a happy disposition, and that he never did away with anything unless he could put something new in its place. Pollet's book is parallel to Joseph Lortz' work in Luther, and even surpasses it in ecclesiological understanding and in detailed knowledge. And it keeps the debate going.

In contrast, Jaques Courvoisier of Geneva has already ventured to summarise Zwingli's theology in a handy compendium.[110] In all those areas in which researchers have been laboriously feeling their way forward for the last twenty years, Courvoisier has taken up a definite position. He has brought together the result of manifold lively studies into a clearly defined shape, mainly by the use of selected literature and a few of Zwingli's writings, namely the *Auslegen,* the *Commentarius*, the *Fidei Ratio* and the *Fidei Expositio.* Along the "Christological axis", "the Word of God", "the Church", "the sacraments" and "Church and State" are impressively presented in the sketch form adopted for this survey. Even those, like the present writer, who believe that with regard to Zwingli's theology we have not yet progressed beyond the phase of preliminary monographs, have to admit that this brave design has turned out well, for the consistent uniformity of the picture it presents it convincing. Though there is another side to it. The praiseworthy attempt to rehabilitate Zwingli and to disseminate his views within the sphere of Calvinism, by presenting him in this comprehensible and concise form, is achieved at the expense of a pro-

---

109. Cf. L. Christiani, s.v. "Zwingli" in *Dictionnaire de Théologie catholique*, Vol. XV, Paris, 1951.

110. Jaques Courvoisier, *Zwingli, théologien réformé.* Cahiers théologiques No. 53, Neuchâtel, 1965.

per historical and dogmatic distinction. Zwingli is drawn near to Calvin and even to Karl Barth.[111] The Scholastic and the Humanistic, which Zwingli combined in himself in such impressive fashion, have completely disappeared in Courvoister. This is one of the exaggerations which have led to a reaction in generally careful Zwingli research of more recent times.

There has been a prompt response in the recent doctoral thesis by Christof Gestrich, who seeks to show the structure of the Reformer's thought in *Zwingli als Theologe*.[112] Three areas of thought are reviewed: "Faith and Knowledge", "God and Man", "Faith and Reality". Of the ensuing paragraphs, we would make special mention of the following: "Faith and Reason", "The Doctrine of God and the Concept of Faith". The problem of the spirit has always been recognised as a particularly important and thorny question with regard to Zwingli; this dissertation allows the reader actually to participate in an intensive attempt to understand the very essence of the Zürich Reformer by concentrating on one central theme. Accordingly, it offers an abundance of individual insights, and especially stimulating suggestions, often drawn from the nineteenth century discussions, which the author continues into the present with a conscious sense of affinity.

For example, the question "Was Zwingli a Rationalist?" is answered in the negative, not on grounds of dogma, but because "Zwingli was not concerned with the autonomy of reason, but with morality".[113] The "hermeneutic circle", which in Luther's case was deliberate and commendable, is with Zwingli a pragmatic "jumping back and forth from faith to Scripture and from Scripture to faith", although the elements of inward faith do predominate.[114] "Zwingli had a different faith from Luther", because "Zwingli thought the heart of the matter was to be found in faith and not in the Word, whereas Luther thought it was in the Word and not the faith".[115] Yet in these extremely instructive pages it becomes clear that the author has not grasped the pneumatological connexion that Zwingli saw between the cross of Christ and faith, between "objectivity" and "subjectivity". It adds up to a confused picture, and

---

111. This is openly stated in Jaques Courvoisier, "Zwingli et Karl Barth", in *Antwort, Karl Barth zum siebzigsten Geburtstag,* Zürich, 1956, pp. 369-387.

112. Christof Gestrich, *Zwingli als Theologe. Glaube und Geist beim Zürcher Reformator,* Zürich, 1967.

113. *Ib.,* p. 57.

114. *Ib.,* p. 78.

115. *Ib.,* p. 145.

the overwhelming impression is that this is due, not to Zwingli, but to the author himself. It is not only that he constantly intersperses his presentation with personal judgments. He also applies uncritically the criteria of "Lutheran" dogmatics, and these, in their turn, are equally uncritically fitted into the framework of modern so-called hermeneutics. As a result, this work provides an unintentional study in how the old reformed theology of election, reconciliation and Spirit burst the bonds of the existentialist standpoint; one has the same experience with Calvin.[116] This is not to say that Zwingli would be outdated. But in this book one reads nothing about the social and ethical impulse of his thinking, for example.

V. ZWINGLI'S ABIDING INFLUENCE

1.   Until recently the origins of the *Anabaptist Movement* lay in darkness. But the subtle researches of *Fritz Blanke* have shown that the first Anabaptist communities constituted a revival movement called into being by the preaching of Zwingli. Starting from Zollikon near Zürich, they made their hard-pressed way through the whole of Europe in search of a church independent of the state.[117] This discovery gave a powerful impetus to Anabaptist research,[118] which would require a report to itself. As a survey of the beginnings of the left wing of the Reformation, its third "denomination", we mention here only the work by George W. Williams, *The Radical Reformation*.[119] It is not free from inaccuracies or one-sidedness in points of detail, but as a whole it presents a splendid and a stirring picture. John C. Wenger who is, apparently, a descendant of the victim of a Bernese persecution has produced a brief introduction to the history and doctrine of the Anabaptist movement.[120] It presents a fine sketch of the faith of these communities, of a kind that is remarkably rare. Today it is generally recognised that the Anabaptists should be included in the Reformation movement.

2.   It is slowly being realised that Zwingli's direct influence was stronger than had long been supposed. Apart from the aforementioned

---

116. G. W. Locher, *Testimonium internum. Calvins Lehre vom Heiligen Geist und das Hermeneutische Problem.* Theologische Studien No. 81, Zürich, 1964. (Including a discussion of Luther and Melanchthon).

117. Fritz Blanke, *Brüder in Christo. Die Geschichte der ältesten Täufergemeinde (Zollikon 1525),* Zürich, 1955.

118. The basic work was *Die Quellen zur Geschichte der Täufer in der Schweiz.* Vol. I: *Zürich,* ed. Leonhard von Muralt and Walter Schmid, Zürich, 1952.

119. George H. Williams, *The Radical Reformation,* Philadelphia, 1962.

120. John C. Wenger, *Even unto Death,* Richmond, Virginia, 1961.

work of Bernd Moeller,[96] reference should be made to an article by
Eekhof;[121] published in 1919, and famous in its time, it is a study of
Zwingli's influence in the Netherlands. Mention may also be made of
the article by van Rhyn in 1950. However, Zwingli's influence there was
soon superseded by that of his great successor Henry Bullinger, who was a
truly ecumenical figure.[122] The bridge with the Church of England was
built by Martin Bucer, by Thomas Erastus, the physician from Aargau,
and by the refugees from Bloody Mary who were received in Zürich.[123]
More important than any particular doctrines of Zwingli, which were soon
overshadowed within the Reformed Church by the integrated theological
system of Calvinism, were the stimuli which he provided. John à Lasco
from Poland, the creator of the Palatinate and Dutch formulae, gratefully
acknowledged throughout his life that his final conversion to the Protestant
faith was due to a brief meeting with Zwingli. Zwingli's "Prophezey" was
imitated in the Netherlands, in the Palatinate and in England. It became
the cradle for a Biblicism which employed philological aids, and which
held its own alongside the "Loci" method of Orthodoxy. And Zwingli's
sense of Christian responsibility for public life, with his specifically social
impact, has continued to inspire religious—social movements in every
land down to the present day. For the special charisma of the Zürich
Reformer was his joyous confidence in the power of God's Word to change
the world:[124] "Truly, the Word of God will take its course as surely as the
Rhine; you can dam it up for a while, but you cannot stop its flow".[125]

---

121. A Eekhof, "Zwingli in Holland", *Zwa.* III/12/13 (1918/2, 1919/1), pp. 370-384;
Maarten van Rhyn, "Die Schweiz und die niederländische Kirchengeschichte", *Theologische
Zeitschrift*, Basle, Vol. VI, 1950, pp. 411-433; *Zw. Ref. i. Rahmen.*, ch. XXIV (Liter.).

122. Walter Hollweg, *Heinrich Bullingers Hausbuch. Eine Untersuchung über die Anfänge der
reformierten Predigtliteratur*, Neukirchen, 1956; Joachim Staedtke, "Bullingers Bedeutung für
die protestantische Welt", *Zwa.* XI/6 (1961/2), pp. 372-388.

123. H. Liermann, "Untersuchungen zum Sakralrecht des protestantischen
Herrschers", *Zeitschrift der Savigny-Stiftung*, Kanon. Abt. 30, 1941; Ruth Wesel-Roth, *Thomas
Erastus. Ein Beitrag zur Geschichte der reformierten Kirche und zur Lehre von der Staatssouveränität*,
Lehr/Baden, 1954; Helmut Kressner, *Schweizer Ursprünge des anglikanischen Staatskirchentums*,
Gütersloh, 1953; W. M. S. West, *John Hooper and the Origins of Puritanism*, Zürich Disserta-
tion, 1955; Rudolf Pfister, "Zürich und das anglikanische Staatskirchentum", *Zwa.* X,
pp. 249-256.

124. Mention may be made here of those spontaneous and less tangible consequences of
the work of the Zürich reformer which include, for example, the tendencies which led to the
Theological Declaration of Barmen in 1934 (cf. G. W. Locher, "Die Stimme des Hirten" in
Oskar Farner, Erinnerungen, Zürich, 1954, pp. 111-115), his distinct contribution to the contemporary discussion about baptism (cf., inter alia, Fritz Schmidt-Clausing, "Zwingli und
die Kindertaufe", *Berliner Kirchenbriefe*, No. 6, October 1962) and, not least, his views on the
subject of Church Councils, which have suddenly achieved a fresh relevance (cf. Fritz
Schmidt-Clausing, "Zwinglis Stellung zum Konzil", *Zwa.* XI/8 (1962/2), pp. 479-498).

125. Z III 488.

4

"CHRIST OUR CAPTAIN"

*An example of Huldrych Zwingli's preaching and its cultural setting**

I. THE PICTURE

On June 26th, 1526, at Wettingen near Baden, a messenger named Johannes Buchli was attacked and overpowered as he was on his way to Zurich with letters from Zwingli's friends in Strasbourg and Basle. The papers were taken from him and opened.[1] They concerned the Baden Disputation,[2] held a short time previously, at which Oecolampadius, the Basle reformer, had concluded a brave and shrewd debate with Dr. Eck, who had been Luther's great opponent at Leipzig. The Zürich Council had refused to give Zwingli permission to participate, since there was reason to distrust the promised safe-conduct. Now, in an attempt to damage Zwingli's reputation, the stolen papers were published in a garbled version, and with malicious comments, by Johann Faber, the Vicar-General of the Bishop of Constance, who had long been one of Zwingli's toughest, most skilful and (because of his political connexions) most dangerous opponents. So the reformer had to take up his pen once more, in order to expose Faber's machinations and to set out the true facts of the matter. Thus there appeared, on 28 July 1526, "Huldrych Zwingli's third essay against Johann Faber". It ends with an urgent appeal to the Protestants to stand firm in the faith, despite all the power and venom of their enemies.[3] And it is here that we find the words that have become famous:[4] "Let all the children of this world boast and make a noise and threaten, for they are unable and unwilling to do anything else; and let every one look to his captain Christ Jesus (Hebrews 12), who will not lead us astray..."[5]

---

* An address given in the Wasserkirche in Zürich on October 11th, 1949, on the anniversary of Zwingli's death, at a commemoration arranged by the Zwingliverein. *Zwa.* IX/3 (1950/1), pp. 121-138.

1. Walther Köhler, Z V 286.
2. Leonhard von Muralt, *Die Badener Disputation 1526,* Leipzig, 1926.
3. Z V 307, 308.
4. Credit must be given to Oskar Farner for bringing some of Zwingli's sayings to our attention in more recent times. See especially his anthology *Gott ist Meister,* Zürich, 1940.
5. Z V 307.

Our Lord is here likened to a captain, and we shall see that Zwingli used this metaphor frequently.[6] He must have used it in the pulpit also, and we know that it made a deep impression on his people.[7] So the meaning of this metaphor is most important for our understanding of Zwingli. In what respects is the Saviour a "captain" and what is involved in the call to "look to" this captain? Zwingli prefaced his writings with the Saviour's call: "Come unto me, all ye that labour and are heavy laden, and I will give you rest". But does not the mood of this invitation, which appeared on the title-page of all Zwingli's works, including the one under discussion, directly contradict this military expression? Did not Zwingli's reformation message declare, from the very beginning, that Jesus would lead into peace this people who had been enmeshed in the troubles and sufferings of war through their mercenary activities? Christ—a captain?

But the "pious, steadfast, careful, worthy and wise representatives of the Confederacy ... gathered at Baden, his gracious and beloved masters",[8] the men who were summoned yet again by this little book,[9] did understand the picture. They were probably all men who were experienced in war,[10] so that such a gathering was virtually, inter alia, like the occasional meeting of a military general-staff, such as no prince possessed; and this contributed in no small degree to the fact that the old Swiss Cantons enjoyed the status of major powers.[11] To a great extent, the "wise men" were probably captains themselves, and the vivid memory of their own overall responsibility in both war and peace would give them an immediate sense of what Zwingli was trying to say when he spoke of Christ as our captain. And the citizens at home, who had sent them to Baden, as

---

6. "Christus et dux et signum est, sub quo militamus". (Christ is the captain and the ensign under which we serve. S V 643).

7. I infer this from the fact that it recurs in the statements made by an ordinary man in the course of the interrogations of the Anabaptists. Many of the ideas to be found in Zwingli's preaching influenced the Anabaptists, albeit in an independent form.

"Lienhart Blüwler says: he is God's servant, and he has no more power or control over himself; he has enlisted under his captain Jesus Christ, and will go to death with him. And whatever he commands and prompts him to do, he will obey and do it". (Emil Egli, *Akten-sammlung zur Geschichte der Zürcher Reformation*, Zürich, 1879, No. 636, p. 284; L. von Muralt and W. Schmid, *Quellen zur Geschichte der Täufer in der Schweiz*. Vol. I: *Zürich*, Zürich, 1952, No. 33). We shall see just how well this member of an Anabaptist assembly in Zollikon had understood the essential meaning of the metaphor.

8. Z V 300.

9. Zwingli published the letter which had previously been addressed to the Diet.

10. Only such men gained civil honours. Cf. Carl von Elgger, *Kriegswesen und Kriegskunst der schweizerischen Eidgenossen im XIV, XV. und XVI. Jahrhundert,* Lucerne, 1873, pp. 28ff., 199.

11. Cf. Johannes Häne, "Die Kriegsbereitschaft der alten Eidgenossen" in *Schweizer Kriegsgeschichte*, Vol. 1, Part 3, 1915.

well as the mercenaries who were actually involved in campaigns, would understand it at once.

However, we live in different times. The company commander of today is quite a different figure from the commander of around the year 1500,[12] with his feather in his hat,[13] with his striped or slashed doublet in either blue and white or red and yellow, and his costly gloves, with cuffs reaching to the elbow (unlike their German counterparts, the Swiss were rather vain about this).[14] This is the figure that Huldrych Zwingli, the onetime chaplain at Monza and Marignano, had in mind, when he spoke of a captain. And we do an injustice to the wonderful vividness of what he was saying, and therefore to its force and impact, if we generalise the image, by explaining it simply in terms of our present-day ideas.

Perhaps some who read this will have already begun to think: "Why do we need a lengthy explanation of this point? 'Everyone should look to his captain'—I understand that at once; it speaks to me directly". But when we examine this more closely, we find that we understand the term "captain" simply as a military leader. So this military leader would represent our leader in life. Our whole generation is still imbued with this idea of the leader (German: Führer) and our intellectual life is governed by it. Not the leader concept of National Socialism, of course, but rather that of idealism. Do we not hear repeatedly from all sides, for example, how Goethe could and should be our leader in so many different ways? So when Christ is described as our captain, we are immediately inclined to understand it in this way, as meaning that Jesus is the one who leads me to a right and true humanity and way of life. His words hold good for me, because they are good and true. And together with this, there is also the

---

12. Though it is perhaps no accident (or else it is a remarkable coincidence) that the title has retained its meaning, or at least it still conveys the same general idea, in one particular respect which is relevant to our theme, in that the captain is the officer who is known by all his soldiers. He is the leader of the individual unit to which the soldier belongs, whether in the field or in the barracks, at the front or at home, and so he is, for the soldier, the day-to-day, visible embodiment of the military hierarchy. Psychologically the captain has a special position and responsibility, derived from the fact that he embodies both the whole and the invididual. He represents the army vis-à-vis the soldier and the soldier vis-à-vis the army (e.g. in granting leave!), and he thus exercises considerable control over the destiny of his subordinates. In this respect, the captain has remained much the same.

13. Cf. the victory song of the German mercenaries after the defeat of the Swiss at Marignano in 1515; Ludwig Erk and Ludwig Böhme, *Deutscher Liederhort*. Vol. II, 2nd ed. Leipzig, 1925, No. 261.

14. The German mercenaries sang: "We'll squander on food and drink, the money the Swiss spend on gloves". (From "Der in Krieg will ziehen..." in Rochus von Liliencron: *Deutsches Leben im Volkslied um 1530,* Stuttgart, n.d., No. 118).

expectation, the demand even, with which we approach all our military superiors; namely, that in their own personal behaviour they should provide a shining and stirring example of what a true soldier should be. So then "Christ our captain" would mean—and this idea also springs to our mind—that Jesus is my example, the one whom I emulate. His deeds of love and self-sacrifice inspire me to unselfishness and devotion. So we may go one step further in defining our understanding of the term: for the democratic Swiss of today, it is the good teacher who embodies this combination of leadership and example. It is his task, by word and deed, to inspire his pupils to every noble act. Times have changed. "Christ our captain"—for Zwingli, it meant a rough warrior; for us, it means an outstanding schoolmaster.

Now it must be understood that, according to Zwingli, it is in no way wrong to see Jesus as a leader, as an example, or as a teacher; it is quite correct. Zwingli says a great deal about the words of Jesus as teaching, and about his life as an example to us.[15] But he would not agree with those people nowadays for whom Jesus is nothing more than a teacher and an example. According to Zwingli, Jesus has binding authority over us as a teacher and an example only because he is something else, something more; namely, he is the Son of God and our redeemer.[16] And to say that he is a captain also tells us something more and something else about him.

II. THE ORIGIN OF THE PICTURE

If we are to examine what this idea really meant for Zwingli himself, then we should ask firstly: where did he get it from, and what meaning did it have for anyone who may have used this picture before him? And secondly: what did it mean to him and his contemporaries?

Did Zwingli actually invent this idea of comparing Christ to an army commander, or did he borrow it from someone else? When we are dealing with a true reformer, we must begin by looking at the primary source of all his thinking, Holy Scripture. In the Old Testament God, the King of the world, is often represented as the Lord of Hosts (Sabaoth), and as the

---

15. For the "doctrina Christi" see Arthur Rich, *Die Anfänge der Theologie Huldrych Zwinglis*, Zürich, 1949 (Index under "Lehre"), and *Th. H. Z.* I, "Die Autorität des Wortes Christi". For the "exemplum Christi" see the section "exemplar vitae" in *Th. H. Z.* I.

16. Zwingli was fond of the term "filius dei". For him, the name Christ denoted the Lord's eternal Sonship; Z VI/I 282; Z. VI/II 167; Z VI/I 462. For statistics concerning the names which Zwingli applied to Christ cf. *Th. H. Z.* I, pp. 18-19. See also the survey of Zwingli's soteriology, pp. 29ff., 134ff.

leader in his own wars, or in the wars of his people. But this is never done
in such a way that God's activity could be compared to that of human army commanders such as Joshua, Saul or David; and, in fact, Zwingli
never refers to this, when he speaks of the captain. Again, in various
places in the New Testament, the life of the Christian is described as a
struggle or war against demonic powers—we may think of Paul's description of the spiritual armour in Eph. 6, for example. But this military
metaphor is never extended to Christ. There is one further text, which we
shall come to later. In the early church, they began to set the service of
Christ (militia Christi) over against the service of Caesar; the idea was
developed further, so that Tertullian, for example, saw the sacrament as
the oath of allegiance which the Christian made to his Lord—a fine interpretation, which we also like to bear in mind in relation to Baptism and the
Lord's Supper.[17] But we do not need to go so far afield. The great and
famous teacher of the reformer was the learned Desiderius Erasmus of
Rotterdam, whom Zwingli never ceased to revere, even though he later
came into sharp conflict with him.[18] In Basle, Erasmus had written a well-

---

17. This had a considerable influence on Zwingli. Cf., for example, Z III 348, where
"sacramentum" is equated with "iuramentum". The Lord's Supper, seen as a sign of
obligation, is a community bound together by oath, "ut frater videat fratrem hoc veluti
iuramento—unde et sacramentum adpellatur—secum in unum corpus, in unum panem, in
unam professionem coaluisse" (thereby a brother may know that, as it were by an oath—for
which reason it is also called a sacrament—his brother has been united with him in one
body, one bread, one confession. Z III 348).

The Lord's Supper is compared to the annual commemoration of the Battle of Murten (Z
III 534) and to the periodic confirmation of the covenant by the Confederates in accordance
with the treaty of Stans (Z III 535).

"A sacrament, as the term is used here, means a sign of obligation; just as, when a man
sews a white cross on his clothes, he shows that he wants to be a confederate; and if, on the
way to Näfels, he also praises and thanks God for the victory which he granted to our
forefathers, then he is declaring publicly that he is a confederate from the very heart". (Z IV
218).

Thus we see how Zwingli's doctrine of the Lord's Supper and his idea of Christ as our
Captain coalesce.

18. The disagreement concerned the doctrine of the freedom of the will and anthropology. In relation to our present subject, the disagreement may be said to concern the
question of Christ as a teacher, and the way in which man is brought to true humanity and
to true humanism—whether it be by man's own powers, or by the Spirit of God. Cf. Z III
649, 665ff. "Quid hic dicent liberi arbitrii adsertores?" (What would the champions of free
will say here? Z III 649). Paul Wernle rightly emphasises that Zwingli responded to
Erasmus' De libero arbitrio (1524) in numerous sections of his Commentarius (1525), without
waiting for Luther's reply De servo arbitrio; (cf. Paul Wernle, Der evangelische Glaube nach den
Hauptschriften der Reformatoren. Vol. II: Zwingli, Tübingen, 1919, pp. 155, 158f., 161, 178).

We may summarise the respective viewpoints as follows: for Erasmus, the grace of Christ
was incorporated in Christ's teaching; the doctrine of Christ, the "philosophia Christi",

known book entitled "The Handbook of the Christian Knight". It contained many early evangelical insights and had a great influence at the time. I am sure that it suggested the theme for Dürer's "Knight, Death and Devil",[19] a famous and mysterious copper etching that has been the subject of much discussion. Erasmus' work deals with the life of the righteous man who has to preserve and save his true humanity, though caught between fear of death and the devilish lusts of the flesh. Here we would expect to find Christ the captain, and a description of his character, and we are not disappointed. In the first part of the work, we already find the idea that the Christian knight (i.e. the Christian seen as a knight) is bound to his commander by oath through his baptism, and this obligation is all the greater because the king has given up his own life for his follower.[20] This refers, of course, to our Lord's sacrificial death. But then we are disappointed, because the figure of Jesus, his death, and, most important of all, his resurrection virtually disappear from view. This no longer has any practical significance for the Christian in his struggle. This is no accident. For despite some evangelical ideas the "Handbook", pious as it is, is not a reformation book; it is a humanistic book. Erasmus' question is: How am I to act in the struggle between the spirit and the flesh, so that I remain or else become a noble person?[21] This falls short of Zwingli's question, which is: How is the Lordship of Christ to make itself felt and to develop in our life? When Zwingli takes up the idea which his teacher had used incidentally, the first and most important change, which we notice immediately, is this difference of theme.

---

was the supreme peak, towards which even the salvation-event was directed. Whereas for Zwingli, the "doctrina Christi" belonged to his grace, to his gracious activity, and it is embraced and surpassed by his grace. "Jesus ... venit docendo sapientam coelestem ... et sese pretium pro peccatis nostris faciendo ... Sed haec omnia nemo accipit, nisi spiritu intus docente illustretur ... Humana doctrina huc pervenire nequit". (Jesus ... came, teaching the heavenly wisdom ... and made himself the payment for our sins ... But nobody receives this, unless the Spirit teaches him and enlightens him inwardly ... No human teaching can achieve this. Z IX 63, 64).

For Zwingli's relationship to Erasmus, cf. Rich, op. cit. Rich also deals with Zwingli's knowledge of the Enchiridion (pp. 120ff.).

19. In 1521, after Dürer had heard the false report that Luther was dead, he wrote in his diary: "O Erasmus of Rotterdam, where art thou?... Hear, thou knight of Christ". (A. Dürer, Tagebuch der Reise in die Niederlande, Leipzig, n.d., p. 46). These well known words of admiration and expectation contain an explicit allusion to the Enchiridion Militis Christiani. For the relationship between Dürer and Erasmus see J. Huizinga, Erasmus, London, 1924.

20. Enchiridion Militis Christiani. Des. Erasmus ausgewählte Werke, ed. H. Holborn, Munich, 1933, p. 24.

21. The Enchiridion is intended as a guide to personal religious and moral edification and conduct. For Erasmus, therefore, the concept of the military leader (dux, duke or prince) corresponds to the idea of Christ as a teacher or pedagogue.

It is equally characteristic of Zwingli that he should change the concept into popular Swiss republican terms. Erasmus speaks of Christ, the military commander, as a king and a general,[22] and speaks of his knight. His book was, in fact, dedicated to an English courtier.[23] Zwingli translates the same Latin by "captain", and preaches in the Great Minster about Captain Christ and his "soldiers" or mercenaries.

But if we were to ask Zwingli himself: "Where did you get this idea from?" he would refer us to the New Testament. We have already seen how he cited Hebrews 12. "Let everyone look to his captain, Christ Jesus (Heb. 12), who will not lead us astray. Just as he suffered inhuman opposition and now sits at the right hand of God, so shall no terror or trouble be able to lead the believer to regret his task. It must be suffered and must be endured in suffering to the end..."[24]

Heb. 12:2, 3 reads: "Looking unto Jesus the author and finisher of our faith; who for the joy that was set before him endured the cross, despising the shame, and is set down at the right hand of the throne of God. For consider him that endured such contradiction of sinners against himself, lest ye be wearied and faint in your minds".

We see that all Zwingli is doing is to quote these words freely from memory.[25] Admittedly, there is no mention of a captain in the Luther Bible or in our modern (German) translations. But a glance at the original text shows how Zwingli came by the idea. The Greek word[26] which is translated by "author", "beginner" or "pioneer" usually means "leader", "general" or "captain".

It is from here, therefore, that Zwingli drew this picture. And the identification of the source is important, because it shows that this picture is not to be understood in terms of humanistic and idealistic ideas about man or educational aims, but rather in terms of the biblical revelation. The passage in Hebrews is not speaking about a teacher, but about the one who was crucified and rose again. Jesus is the captain because he "endured the cross and is set down at the right hand of the throne of God". Zwingli speaks of the fate which the troop shares with its commander in the face of

---

22. Erasmus uses the term "dux" in the sense of feudal lord or prince, using it interchangeably with "rex", "imperator" and "agonethetes" (*Enchiridion*, pp. 25, 44).

23. "Cuidam aulico".

24. Z V 307.

25. The comments in Z V 307 fail to note that Zwingli quotes verse 2b, which is of importance for Christology, in addition to the warning of verse 3.

26. Heb. 12:2 "... ἀφορῶντες εἰς τὸν τῆς πίστεως ἀρχηγόν". The Vulgate has "auctorem" (author, founder), but Zwingli renders it by "respicientes ad fidei ducem" (commander). S VI, II 315.

mortal danger. To Christ, he says, belongs suffering, and it is suffering to the end. For this reason, suffering belongs to us also; and it is suffering to the end if need be, to the bitter end. The reformer does not make his appeal to some aspiration after inner refinement, but to the fact that it is a serious business to have a captain—and in those days, this fact was hammered into every man in the Confederacy from his youth upwards. Because one must remain loyal to the captain, even to death. And it is a good thing to have a good captain. He leads you well, and does not lead you astray.[27]

III. THE BACKGROUND TO THE PICTURE

What was a captain in old Zürich, exactly? It is necessary to take a look at the military system of the Confederacy, and to try to picture what took place prior to one of the numerous campaigns. From time to time[28] there was a general call-up, when all the men in the city or in the country districts who were liable for military service—i.e. all youths and men from sixteen to sixty years of age—were summoned to a certain place (for the citizens of Zürich it would probably be the Lindenhof).[29] This was for the purposes of a careful inspection of weapons and enlistment. This full military call-up only took place at times of the most extreme urgency, when the alarm bells were sounded, as happened in Thurgau at the time of the Swabian War. Generally, it was decided in advance who should immediately rally to the colours at the time of mobilisation, and who should stand in reserve. The names of those who were "drawn out" in this way (often consisting simply of the number of those required from a guild, a village or a parish) are still to be seen on the rolls preserved in the city archives. Together with the officers, who had likewise been determined in advance, these men made up the "troop".[30] (So when Christ's troop is referred to, we should not think of a modern troop of soldiers, but of a company of specially enlisted men). These men were then assigned[31] either to the flag (that is, the advance guard of approximately fifteen hundred men) or to the standard (the main force of at least four thousand

---

27. The old confederates were most aware of how much they owed to good military leadership. Cf. Elgger, *op. cit.*, pp. 205, 206.

28. Cf. Johannes Häne, *Zum Wehr- und Kriegswesen in der Blütezeit der alten Eidgenossenschaft*, Zürich, 1900, p. 21.

29. The suggestion of Häne in "Kriegsbereitschaft", p. 29.

30. Elgger, *op. cit.*, p. 54; Häne, "Kriegsbereitschaft", pp. 26ff.; Häne, *Wehrwesen*, pp. 26ff. Zwingli counsels that "The captain should never let the troop grow lazy" (in his *Plan zu einem Feldzug*, Z III 581).

31. Häne, *Wehrwesen*, pp. 25ff.

men), and then to one of the various weapon companies: the spearmen, who stood in the forefront of the battle, the halberdiers, the crossbowmen, the riflemen etc. Each such group had its own captain, so there was a spear-captain, a rifle-captain, a flag-captain, etc. But the real captain, who was also known as "the chief captain" or "the chief field captain" was at the same time the captain of the main force.[32] At his side stood the standard-bearer as his chief-of-staff, and also the war council consisting of other captains and some members of the Little Council who were experienced in war and who were present as representatives of the government. Under the captain were the lieutenants, who enjoyed a higher status than the lieutenants of today. The sergeant was the man most comparable to the present-day lieutenant. The main force was known by German mercenaries as the "Great Troop", and in Swiss German it was called the "huff",[33] a term which could probably denote the particular weapon-group also.[34] So everyone who had been enlisted in the troop, and then assigned to his "huff",[35] would know what he had to do when the call came. He belonged to his captain. Before they marched off, the solemn oath was taken either in front of the Town Hall or on the Lindenhof. In connexion with this, mention may be made of the fact that the captain swore, inter alia, "not to lead his soldiers astray"[36] (we are reminded of Zwingli's words). Each individual member of the troop promised on oath to renounce every grudge and every thought of revenge against any of his comrades for the duration of the campaign. "They forgive one another for injury and hate".[37] Even though Zwingli never makes any explicit reference to this pledge, we have the feeling that this promise of peace played a decisive part in making it possible for him to compare the military unit and its relationship to its commander with the Christian community and its Lord.[38] But what is worthy of special note in this declaration and subscription of the army regulations is the careful description of and emphasis upon the duty of unconditional obedience to the captain, and the

---

32. Häne, "Kriegsbereitschaft", pp. 26ff.; Elgger, *op. cit.*, p. 187.
33. See the plan of battle in Johannes Häne, *Militärisches aus dem Alten Zürichkrieg. Zur Entwicklungsgeschichte der Infanterie*, Zürich, 1928.
34. Information kindly supplied by Dr. H. Schneider.
35. "The lists of soldiers contained the names of the men who had been enrolled together with the type of weapon they bore". (Elgger, *op. cit.*, p. 54).
36. Emanual von Rodt, *Geschichte des Kriegswesens der Berner*, Vol. I, Berne, 1831, p. 251.
37. Häne, "Kriegsbereitschaft", p. 29.
38. According to Zwingli, it was one of the duties of a true captain to see that there was peace within his troop. (*Plan zu einem Feldzug*, Z III 582).

comprehensive nature of his authority.[39] His powers of punishment, including even the death penalty, were virtually unlimited; though the same was true of his power to pardon.[40] The army regulations provided general legal guidelines, but the captain could "increase or reduce" the penalty,[41] according to the particular circumstances and his findings. We may sense how strong the personal bond between the soldier and his captain must have been. Furthermore, we know from military history that the captains were largely responsible for the condition and for the conduct of their troop. They also felt called upon to represent the interests of their men before the government, with regard to such matters as provisions[42] or the payment of wages.

Of course this applied especially, whether they were serving at home or abroad, to those troops that were composed entirely of mercenaries. In the old Confederacy, there was nearly always, alongside the "troop", another troop of "free mercenaries" under their own captain.[43] For good conduct in battle, these mercenaries would be subsequently rewarded, perhaps by being granted citizenship. In 1491 the sacristan of St. Peter's was present at Dijon as a "free mercenary". He had neglected to have himself enrolled, but thanks to the testimony of his comrades, he was later granted citizenship.[44] These free-lance soldiers were naturally completely dependent on their captain. Whenever there was a campaign, whether with the permission or at the demand of the Council, the captain would make an agreement with the foreign prince concerned, whether it be the Pope, the

---

39. Rodt, *op. cit.*, Vol. I, p. 251; Häne, "Kriegsbereitschaft", pp. 26ff.; Häne, *Alter Zürichkrieg*, pp. 111, 136. "What is striking about the formula is its military character. All the people had to swear allegiance to the *captain*, and the authorities are mentioned only at the end, and in passing". (Elgger, *op. cit.,* p. 184).

40. Elgger, *op. cit.*, pp. 217, 218.

41 Rodt, *op. cit.*, Vol. I, p. 250.

42. Cf. the two letters of complaint addressed to the Council by the captains in the Zürich camp during the First Kappel War (Johannes Häne, *Zürcher Militär und Politik im Zweiten Kappelerkrieg*, Zürich, 1913, pp. 47, 51). The letters do not contain any of the religious and political opposition to Zwingli which Häne reads into them. But they do speak of friction over the supply of bread, and of suspicion that the baker was making an illegal profit at the expense of the soldiers).

43. Häne, *Wehrwesen*, pp. 32-34. Cf. Walter Schaufelberger, *Der Alte Schweizer und sein Krieg. Studien zur Kriegführung vornehmlichen im 15. Jahrhundert*, Zürich, 1952. It is unfortunate that in Schaufelberger the captains appear only peripherally, as men who received the money and paid the wages, and who seem to be men who did not have much to say at the critical moment. His overall picture could be well supplemented by a portrayal of the personal magnetism of famous mercenary commanders such as von Stein or Winkelried, who aroused such enthusiasm among young people. Cf. Liliencron, *op. cit.*, No. 10, strophes 19ff.

44. Häne, *Wehrwesen*, p. 31.

Duke of Milan or the King of France, and he would recruit the number of
soldiers whom he had undertaken to provide.[45] For this purpose he would
receive an agreed sum, and whatever was left over went into his own
pocket. So for him the campaign was not only a military but also a
business undertaking.[46] Examples could well be cited of how the captains
championed the cause of their troops with the foreign princes, but we will
quote an example which lies nearer home. Jörg Göldli[47] was an experienced campaigner and a popular captain, who failed in a surprising manner
when captain of the vanguard in the second Kappel War. This officer had
otherwise shown such a sense of duty towards his men, caring for them to
the best of his ability, that I find it impossible to accept the suspicion
(which is expressed to this day) that he was guilty of treachery in the Battle
of Kappel. In the first Kappel War, he was the captain of six hundred
"free soldiers". From a letter that is still extant we learn of the trouble he
took to have their provisions supplied by the Council, even though they
were not entitled to it. They were suffering great privation. We have a
similar piece of evidence from the Musso War of April 1531, when Göldli
discharged his military duties brilliantly. A letter written in his own hand
shows that he was concerned that his men should not have to wait too long
for their pay; the city should advance the pay; in any case, his men should
not have to suffer. "He took care of their interests with the authorities",
as it would have been put in those days.

It may be added that the captain wore no badge of rank, though he did
like to surround himself with a certain pomp.[48] He was to be recognised by
his particularly expensive armour, he was mounted on horseback, and
(until the simplification of the military system, under Zwingli's influence,
required even the captain to be somewhat more modest) he would have as
many as nine personal adjutants, who were also mounted.[49]

The captain was upheld by the trust of his troop; nobody else could
replace him as their leader.[50] But then he was given up complete freedom

---

45. Elgger, *op. cit.*, p. 203.

46. Elgger, *op. cit.*, p. 72. For the financial power of the captain, even when the troop had
been enrolled by the authorities, cf. *Plan zu einem Feldzug*, Z III 579.

47. Häne, *Zweiter Kappelerkrieg*, pp. 8, 9.

48. Elgger, *op. cit.*, p. 116; Häne, *Wehrwesen*, p. 27. The contemporary "Bildnis eines
Hauptmanns" (Portrait of a captain) by Niklaus Manuel, in Basle, is reproduced in Ernst
Gagliardi, *Geschichte der Schweiz*. Vol. I, 4th ed. Zürich, 1939 and in HZnS p. 56.

49. Häne, *Zweiter Kappelerkrieg*, pp. 34ff.

50. Elgger, *op. cit.*, pp. 198ff., 203ff., 206, 210, 244. For the care taken when filling the
position of captain, cf. Elgger, pp. 206, 211ff. Zwingli declared that "the trust of his men is
the greatest treasure that a captain can have" (*Plan zu einem Feldzug*, Z III 579).

of action. Nobody dare interfere in his handling of the operation; not even the government. "The deployment of the fighting forces was committed to the commanders, and they had to render account to no man, save to their own conscience".[51] As a corollary, the soldier is a good soldier when he remains responsible and obedient to his captain.[52]

IV. THE MEANING OF THE PICTURE

Let us hear Zwingli once more. At the Diet of Augsburg in 1530, the Lutheran alliance, with their confession of faith, had been able to present a respectable opposition. The reformed cities (Strasbourg, Constance, Lindau and Memmingen) with their four-city confession, had gained no support from the Lutherans. They were defenceless, at the mercy of the anger of Emperor Charles V and the power of the Empire. It appeared as if the storm would break first over the brave city of Memmingen.[53] Speaking from Zürich, Zwingli sought to strengthen the resolute evangelical Council of that city: "In the business of the Christian religion and faith, we have long since staked our lives and set our minds on pleasing only our heavenly captain, in whose troop and company we have had ourselves enlisted".[54]

We see that defiance of death was a part of the allegiance due to this captain. Moreover, he who has once begun to venture seriously with Jesus Christ can never again be free from him. He belongs to Christ's troop, and stands in his company. Retreat is no longer possible; we are "enlisted".[54]

Later, the letter continues: "Since (it seems to me) the time has now come when you are required to confess your faith, consider, dear men and brethren, that Christ our Captain threatens that whoever denies him, he will deny before his Father, and on the other hand, whoever confesses him before men, he will confess before his Father (Matt. 10:32). Therefore, confess the truth freely and let the captain Christ Jesus take care of your interests before the highest king, the heavenly Father. He has already led us through minor dangers, so would he forsake us in the decisive battle?

---

51. Elgger, *op. cit.*, p. 211.

52. A different function was exercised by the "captain" resident in Wil, who was appointed for the principality of St. Gallen by the four "protectors" of Zürich, Lucerne, Schwyz and Glarus from 1479 onwards.

53. Walther Köhler, Z XI 187, note 19. GWL: *Zw. Ref. i. Rahmen.*, 473ff.

54. Z XI 186. This letter to Memmingen, together with the two letters to Esslingen (Z V 272ff. and 416ff.) are among the most beautiful and most lucid testimonies to have come from the pen of Zwingli, from both a personal and a reformational standpoint.

Do not worry about yourselves or your opponents, but rather see how strong he is, whose cause it is that you have taken up, and whom you believe and serve. When has he ever forsaken those who trust him?"[55]

If these lines are read carefully, against the contemporary background as we have described it, then we begin to understand why and to what extent Zwingli can apply this military picture of the captain to our Lord Jesus Christ, who still leads those who are weary and heavy laden into peace. There is little talk of teaching or education or of some general ideal of life. It is all about special, concrete things. We notice that Zwingli only speaks of "Captain Christ" when it is a question of dying; or, to be more precise, of being ready to die—of martyrdom. Christ is "captain", because Christianity is something for which one must be prepared to die. Christ is captain, because true faith embodies a pledge of loyalty—even to death, as in the army. Christ is captain, because there are times when the summons is issued, when things are serious ("when you are required to confess"). Christ is captain, because he threatens with his judgment and promises his grace, depending upon how we conduct ourselves in the hour of decision ("confessing him"). He is captain, because he represents our interests before the supreme king, interceding for us with the Father. He has taken our earthly life and our future life into his care; with him, everything is in the best of hands. He cares for us. He is captain because he leads us and is present with us, especially at the decisive moments and in the decisive struggles of our life and of our church. And because he never leaves us. And because he is strong and powerful. And because we trust him. And so, in the light of all this, it is not surprising that there is always linked to this picture of the captain an exhortation to absolute obedience—which means, in Christian terms, self-denial.

One question still remains. It is purely a question of faith. But for this very reason it is the foundation for all these exhortations and consolations. The question is: on what is the captaincy of Christ based? Or, to put it more plainly: what gives him the right to have the same kind of authority over us as a captain has over his soldiers in time of war, even to the point of putting their lives at risk?

Zwingli provided the answer at the very beginning of his career. We first find this metaphor in his splendid "Sermon on the maid Mary" (1522). "Christ shed his blood for the sake of our salvation. Now it is a useless soldier who will not shed his blood for the sake of his Lord and captain, but runs away, when his Lord has already suffered death for him and

---

55. Z XI 187.

before him. The real warriors of Christ are those who are not shy of having their heads broken for their Lord's sake".[56] Therefore: Christ is our captain, because he demands that we should risk our life in his battle. Because he risks our life in his battle. But these lines say more than that. He is our captain because he has power over our life or death on the grounds of *his* self-sacrifice. But at this point, the meaning bursts through the bounds of the metaphor. It must, because the sacrificial death of Christ, through which we become his possession, and he becomes our Lord, is for Zwingli something absolutely unique and incomparable. No metaphor is adequate to unfold the mystery of this miracle.[57]

So Zwingli's talk of Captain Christ, a metaphor boldly taken from everyday life, brings us in a way to that point where faith must become life—or, more precisely, where faith wants to take the form of a committed life. Thus, in true reformation manner, this figure of speech embodies the unity of faith and life. It was only later that this unity was lost, as, on the one side, orthodoxy was thought to represent faith and doctrine, and on the other side, Pietism and the Enlightenment were thought to represent Christian life and Christian morality. We still suffer today from this loss of the unity of faith and life; this is *the* sickness of our church. But here we have it—graphically portrayed in a picture that comes alive for every hearer and reader—still the same living Christ, and everything in the Christian warfare relates to him—believing and living, trusting, obeying and dying, finding comfort and serving. In all these things, the captain takes care of his troops. "Our captain, Christ Jesus, never leaves us comfortless. In times of emptiness, he either comforts us inwardly through his Spirit, who nourishes our faith, or comforts us outwardly by exhorting us to steadfastness..."[58]

Here we must end.[59] In order to formulate the meaning of this metaphor of "Christ our Captain" in such a way as to express both its

---

56. Z I 395.

57. Zwingli commented on Isaiah 53: "Est humiliati Christi mysterium altius quam hominis stilus prosequi possit" (The mystery of the humiliation of Christ is so deep that no human pen can portray it. Z XIV 373). This holds good, even though he developed a carefully constructed doctrine of satisfaction. And in connexion with this one should note his comment on Romans 11 that "these few places provide instruction on how to view and admire the eternal wisdom of God, which He displayed for our salvation; for otherwise nobody could explore or express it". Z II 638; H I 260. Cf. *Th. H. Z.* I., section "Die Soteriologie", pp. 134ff.

58. Z V 276. (Written to Esslingen in 1526). *Zw. Ref. i. Rahmen.*, 471f.

59. A survey of those places where Zwingli speaks of the "soldier" (German "Reiser" = mercenary) of Christ or of God would yield a similar conclusion. The expression signifies self-denial, endurance to the end, and readiness to suffer and to die.

value as good news as well as exhortation, we might summarise as follows:
Zwingli proclaims: We stand with Jesus Christ, the Crucified and Risen
One, sharing a common and inseparable destiny. He has our destiny in his
hands. More than that, he himself is our destiny. And faithfulness to
Christ is the vital question for the city of Zürich, for the "worthy Confederacy" and for all nations. How was it possible for people here and
elsewhere so to lose all sense of the message?

Zwingli carried out his life's work in the service "of the beloved Lord
Christ Jesus, whose soldier I am"[60] as he liked to put it, in full awareness
of this powerful unity between teaching and life. Through the grace of
God there suddenly arose a community that was especially self-sacrificing,
resolute and courageous, a church that was reformed according to God's
Word; and a city that was notorious for its immorality and its neglect
became a lasting source of clean Christian living for many people. The
Battle of Kappel on October 11th, 1531, was a grave setback for this work.
And yet, in the light of the thoughts of the reformer which we have been
considering, must we simply lament that day in 1531? Can we be sorry for
Zwingli because he came to that end which befell him that day? Was not
his end, in fact, a practical recapitulation and a visible representation of
this very picture of the captain?

For years, Zwingli had reckoned with a violent death, on account of the
message that was entrusted to him. Sometimes he had even longed for it a
little, and even, I suspect, had premonitions of his death. It is a great
blessing when our death can be in complete harmony with our faith and
with our work. Huldrych Zwingli could say, not just with his words, but
also through his death: Christ is our Captain. Christ is our destiny.

Today is the anniversary of his death. The church of Jesus Christ
remembers a mighty witness to her Lord. We thank him.

---

60. Z V 133; I 394; H I 128.

5

THE CONTENT AND THE DESIGN
OF ZWINGLI'S TEACHING ABOUT MARY*

1. In the year 1521, Luther wrote a treatise on the Magnificat—one of his finest. Calvin's exposition of the Gospels immerses itself tenderly and warmly in the spiritual life of the "Holy Virgin". Yet, of all the Reformers, it was Zwingli who developed the most explicit teaching about Mary, and who even retained elements of medieval dogma.[1] He did so with "great warmth",[2] and he passionately rejected the reproach that his evangelical preaching diminished the honour of the mother of our Lord. Not only did Zwingli teach the Virgin Birth, i.e. the article of faith, that Mary became the Mother of Jesus solely by the creative power of the Holy Spirit, without the co-operation of any human father—which Zwingli taught[3] in agreement with the New Testament accounts (which were authoritative for him) and the relevant clauses of the so-called Apostles' Creed; not only did he apply the prophesy of Isaiah 7:14 to Mary—in agreement with Matthew 1 and the traditional interpretation of the Church; but also, for Christological reasons, he acknowledged as correct and scriptural the designation "Mother of God" (which originated in the early Church and had been officially recognised since the Council of Ephesus in 431 AD), and he used the term readily;[4] and he also taught, in

---

* This chapter appeared in abbreviated form in the "Neue Zürcher Zeitung" (NZZ), No. 8 and 13, January 3rd, 1951. A fuller version appeared in the "Kirchenblatt für die reformierte Schweiz", 107/3, February 1st, 1951. For the occasion, see above, p. 60, note 72.

1. Cf. the excellent collection of texts *Das Marienleben der Reformatoren (Martin Luther, Johannes Calvin, Huldrych Zwingli, Heinrich Bullinger)*, ed. W. Tappolet assisted by Albert Ebneter, Tübingen, 1962: also Reintraud Schimmelpfennig, *Die Geschichte der Marienverehrung im deutschen Protestantismus*, Paderborn, 1952; Walter Delius, "Luther und die Marienverehrung" in *Theologische Literaturzeitung*, Leipzig, 1954, columns 409-414; Jean Cadier, "La Vierge Marie dans la dogmatique réformée au XVIe et au XVIIe siècle" in *La revue réformée*, 1958/4, St. Germain-en-Laye, pp. 46-58. Further literature is cited in Tappolet.

2. Otto Karrer in NZZ, No. 2546, November 26th, 1950; see also Karl Federer in NZZ, No. 2695, December 10th, 1950.

3. The most important items are: "Eine Predigt von der ewig reinen Magd Maria", Z I 385-428, H I 121-164; in the *Commentarius de vera et falsa religione*, Z III 686-688, H IX 93-97; from the Disputation of Berne, Z VI, I 288-289; from the *Commentary on Isaiah*, Z XIV 181-183; from the *Commentary on Ezekiel*, Z XIV 737.

4. E.g. Z III 687.

agreement with medieval theology, the perfect virginity of the "eternally pure maiden" before, during and after the birth of Jesus. In this connexion there are even hints as to which of the scholastic suggestions he would agree with, regarding how the birth could have taken place.[5] Therefore in agreement with the Roman interpretation which has continued up to our own day, Zwingli does not allow that the "brothers and sisters" of Jesus who are mentioned in the New Testament are children of Mary and Joseph, but understands them to be "relatives", believing that one can appeal to Old Testament usage for this interpretation. There is no trace in Zwingli of the doctrine of the "Immaculate Conception" of Mary by St. Anne,[6] the dogma which was promulgated in 1854, and is celebrated with a Major Feast Day. And this is remarkable in view of the prominent role played by St. Anne in the popular religion of the late Middle Ages.[7] But when explaining the place of honour which Mary holds among all the pious, as a consequence of her important role as the instrument of the incarnation of the eternal Son of God, Zwingli goes so far as to state: "I firmly trust that she is exalted by God above all creatures of blessed men or angels in eternal bliss".[8] This is certainly not an isolated or casual remark, but rather a statement which is in complete harmony with the picture which Zwingli draws of Mary elsewhere. Federer is right to maintain that it is a careful formulation; in the context, Zwingli "believes" that Mary is the Mother of God and a virgin "according to the sure words of the holy Gospel";[9] but he "trusts" that Mary holds the position of honour in

---

5. Until ca. 1525, "Utero clauso" (Z III 688; IV 66); "Virgo perpetua ante partum" (Z XIV 182); "in partu" (*ibid.*), "post partum" (*ibid.*), "ante" and "post partum" alone (Z VI, I 289; Z XIV 737).

6. Federer and Tappolet-Ebneter (p. 251) seek to relate the forceful expressions which Zwingli frequently used to describe Mary's purity ("immaculata", "illibata", "purissima", etc.) to the belief (which Luther shared) that "Mary was, at least at the moment of conception, wholly pure and free from original sin". This attempt fails because Zwingli did not see the problem in this way, for although he recognised the fact of original sin, he did not think in terms of a biological transmission of original guilt. Furthermore, one must take account of statements such as "Et huius (= sancti filii) matrem sic sanctificavit et purificavit deus: nam decebat ut tam sanctus filius tam sanctam haberet matrem" (God has also sanctified and purified the mother (of the holy Son), for it was fitting that so holy a Son should have so holy a mother. S VI, I 546); and "Sanctitas ergo Mariae ex sanctitate nascitur Christi, non contra..." (Thus the holiness of Mary is derived from that of Christ, and not the other way round. S VI, I 639).

7. Cf. the numerous portrayals of St. Ann together with Mary and Jesus, or the spontaneous cry uttered by the young Luther when he was caught in the storm: "Help me, St. Ann; I will become a monk!"

8. Z I 424; H I 159.

9. Z I 424; H I 159.

heaven; it is a theological deduction, "corresponding to the view of the best Medieval theologians" (Federer).

In these circumstances, may not Otto Karrer maintain, "Even Zwingli believed and proclaimed with great warmth the glorification of Mary in heaven"? And when Karl Federer tells us, in his informative essay, that in Zwingli's day the government of Zürich was minded to observe the festival of the Assumption of Mary, can he not claim that the sentence quoted above indicates the Reformer's agreement with the Roman dogma which was defined in 1950? Did Zwingli really believe in the glorification of Mary's body in heaven? And what was the meaning of his teaching about Mary within the context of his Reformation preaching?

2. No, Zwingli "proclaimed", that is, he took as the content of his proclamation, only what he received from scripture. Federer's own discerning grasp of the fine nuances in the wording of our quotation makes this quite clear. That conclusion ("I trust"), for which Zwingli does not claim "the sure words of the holy Gospel", is his private opinion. Because it is not contained in Scripture, it is not binding upon others; but it refutes conclusively the vile slander that Zwingli could have abused Mary from his pulpit; and it is for this reason alone that Zwingli states his opinion here, for in the section quoted he is concerned with rejecting this reproach.[10] The evidence of his other writings confirms the distinction drawn by the Reformer: both in this same sermon, and in all his other writings—everywhere, when Zwingli "proclaims", then Mary does not stand above but alongside the Apostles and Prophets.[11]

But neither in his presentation of the Biblical matter that is necessary to salvation, nor in his own personal reflections upon it, did Zwingli ever contemplate anything other than the spiritual life of Mary with Christ in eternity. Her soul is in heaven. There is no trace of her bodily assumption to be found in Zwingli's writings, not even in the quotation which is discussed above. Certainly Federer thinks that the words can "in practice hardly be understood except as a testimony to the festive secret of 15th August". But then he himself concedes that this assertion must first be proved from Zwingli's practice with regard to the traditional festival of the Assumption of Mary.

---

10. Cf. Z I 423; H I 159.
11. "Therefore the saints of God, Mary, John, Peter and Stephen are equal as witnesses that those who follow after God come to him (Heb. 12)..." *Ibid.*, 427, 163.

On the contrary, it may be shown from other statements of Zwingli that when the Reformer speaks of the blessedness of Mary in heaven, he is thinking of her soul, and, therefore, the quotation in question should also be understood as referring to her soul. More important than any individual references is a basic reminder of one of the chief characteristics of Zwinglian piety and one of his main Reformational concerns, namely: the spiritual nature of faith and of the content of faith. Even if Zwingli is, on the one hand, the Mariologist among the Reformers, yet he is, on the other hand, the one for whom it would be most impossible to accept the bodily assumption. Firstly, because it has no support in Scripture. And secondly, it is intrinsically impossible that the man who constantly and firmly found his reformational basis in the belief that "Christ is the only treasure of our poor souls",[12] should have found any comfort or edification in the bodily assumption of Mary. With this Reformer, whose chief thought, in all his theological endeavours, consisted in the view that "all honour, praise, fear and service may not be rendered to any creature, but only to God"[13] and who therefore says of the veneration of the saints, Mary included, that we "should have no trust in invisible creatures, or imagine that they could comfort us",[14] it is unthinkable that in his theology there should be any foundation for, association with, or even the possibility of a recognition of the idea of the bodily assumption of Mary. Again, when we consider that this is the Reformer who, in contrast to the medieval realism of sacred actions, places and things, wished to cleanse the faith so thoroughly of everything earthly and visible, that in his theology he even attached importance to the distinction that, strictly speaking, only the creator, and not the creation story, could be the object of faith; who, for the same reason, understood the visible event in the Lord's Supper to be only a sign of the act of salvation, and not as the act of salvation itself; who sometimes extended this line of reasoning even to the point that Christ can be our Redeemer only by virtue of his deity; it is unthinkable and intrinsically impossible that this theologian could suddenly, with totally unfounded inconsistency, lay such emphasis on the physical nature of Mary. Likewise, it is basically and intrinsically impossible that this witness to the deity of God in Christ could, in the faith or ordinances of his congregations, give any place to the doctrine of the bodily assumption of Mary.

---

12. Z II 217; H III 285.
13. Z II 192; H III 250.
14. *Ib*.

3. The general character of Zwingli's faith and thought would of itself be sufficient to refute the conjecture that Zwingli believed in the bodily assumption of Mary. But we have, in addition, a piece of direct evidence. The well-known list of those who are among the blessed in heaven, which includes persons from Biblical, Church and world history, together with pious heathen,[15] begins as follows: "We believe that the souls of the faithful, immediately they leave their bodies, rise up to heaven and are united with God in eternal joy". Among these blessed souls who are to be "seen" in the Beyond, without their bodies, is the "Virgin Mother of God", between Isaiah, her prophet, and David, her forefather. That he is thinking only about their souls is further underlined by the fact that there follows immediately a polemic against the doctrine of soul-sleep, which was taught in certain Anabaptist circles.

4. But what about the facts which Federer has brought forward so plausibly—that for a long time the Ave Maria continued to ring out in Zwinglian Zürich, and that in 1526 and 1530 it was agreed to keep the Marian festivals, including the Feast of the Assumption? Anyone who is acquainted with Zwingli's method of reform will not be surprised by this. Zwingli was not a fanatic. It was always his practice, that first there should be the positive planting of evangelical awareness, and then the Catholic traditions and customs should be allowed to fall away. In 1523 he had openly announced this programme, arguing and developing it with regard to the question of the veneration of the saints, including Mary, and he had condemned the opposite approach, which would begin the Reformation by tearing down rather than building up.[16] Zwingli knew how strongly the Christianity of the late Middle Ages clung to the Mother of God, and was the religion of Mary. They could not risk the danger that, as a result of impatience on the part of the Reformers, their preaching of Christ might not be given a hearing.[17] But once the religion of Christ has taken firm root, then everything that is not in keeping with it will fall away of itself. Thus it was a perfectly sensible development in the course of the Reformation, and completely according to plan, that the popular festivals should be kept at first, and then be abolished, virtually without any opposition, under Bullinger. Somewhat unnecessarily, the Council resolution of 1530

---

15. S IV 65.

16. Z II 169-171; H III 218-221.

17. "For, unfortunately, some are so ignorant of the truth, that they repudiate the teaching of Christ as soon as one wishes to do away with their saints". Z II 170; H III 220.

expresses this intention quite openly: The Marian feasts will be kept, for the sake of Christian love and brotherly feeling towards those who still cling to the old way, "until we consider it further".[18]

The decision to abolish the festivals, which Bullinger announced, expressly refers to this proviso.[19] So the resolutions which were passed in relation to the Marian festivals cannot show that Zwingli accepted the bodily assumption of Mary. The same applies to the temporary toleration of the Ave Maria; for those who wished to go on reciting it during the period of transition, Zwingli provided an evangelical exposition and guide to it.[20]

Federer is also of the opinion that it would be a mistake "to conclude *a priori*, from Zwingli's doctrine of the authority of Scripture, that he would reject the assumption of Mary", since there is no Scriptural evidence for Mary's perpetual virginity either, yet Zwingli clearly taught it. Zwingli was aware of the objection that he was violating the Scriptural principle at this point, and relying on tradition. He faced it squarely; he was firmly convinced that he had in Isaiah 7:14[21] and Ezekiel 44:2 a Biblical basis for maintaining that Mary was *semper virgo*, the "eternally pure maid".[22]

Catholic Mariology always points out how the bodily exaltation of the Queen of Heaven is connected with cultic veneration of her. Zwingli was fully aware of the distinction which Roman terminology makes between the veneration of God, and of Mary and of the other saints.[23] He allowed only the worship of God, as that alone is mentioned in Scripture. One can hardly expect to find a man, who shrugged off this whole distinction as a fictitious "fable",[24] and who expressly rejected "Hyperdoulia" as

---

18. Egli, *Aktensammlung*, No. 1656, p. 706.

19. *Heinrich Bullingers Reformationsgeschichte*, Vol. I, pp. 328-330.

20. Z I 408ff.; H I 142ff., 160f.

21. In his exposition of Isaiah 7:14, Zwingli follows the example of the Scholastics in arguing that it would not be a miracle if a virgin were to lose her virginity in becoming a mother. The "sign" promised by the prophet can exist only if the pregnant woman remains a virgin. This is still the Roman Catholic interpretation of the text—cf. Kösters, S. J., in the *Lexikon für Theologie und Kirche*, Vol. VI, 1934, columns 887-894. (The article on "Maria" in the new edition of this lexicon, Vol. VII, 1962, does not mention Isaiah 7 or Ezekiel 44, but this edition is more progressive and not representative). As far as Zwingli is concerned, it should be emphasised that it was on Christological rather than mariological grounds that he attached importance to the perpetual virginity of Mary. In addition, there is a practical reason, in that he believed that if Mary had not remained in a state of virginity, then the original virgin conception and birth would be suspect.

22. Cf. inter alia Z III 687, XIV 181f.

23. *Latreia* denotes the reverence given to God, *doulia* that given to angels and saints, and *hyperdoulia* that given to Mary.

24. Z II 191; H III 248f.

unbiblical, holding a convinced belief in the bodily assumption of Mary. That Zwingli should have shared this belief is out of the question.

5.   How, then, is Zwingli's teaching about Mary to be understood? Zwingli provides the answer himself, clearly and repeatedly. The doctrine of the virgin birth, and indeed the whole of his teaching about Mary are a part of his doctrine of Christ. They are intended to lead us to Christ. Correct Mariology is Christology, and nothing else. It has no independent significance or function, even of a supplementary nature. It may be expressed in the form of a paradox: the honour of Mary consists in the fact that she yields up her honour to her Son. When it is understood in this way, we have the real reason for Zwingli's reformational interest in the Lord's Mother, and for his handling of the question of feast days. "All her honour is her son".[25] What distinguishes Mary is her role at the very beginning of the act of salvation, in its narrower sense, in that our salvation began when she became the Mother of the Saviour.[26] With the miracle of her virginity she stands as a sign[27] which does not point to itself, but to the real miracle, the secret of Christ. She remains the handmaid of the Lord. She herself can never become the subject of church dogmas.

It is certainly not her desire that people should honour her, or believe in her, or trust in her, or call upon her to intercede on their behalf. "Concerning this, let everyone know that the highest honour one can render to Mary, it rightly to recognise and honour the good deed that her Son has done for us poor sinners, and to run to Him for all grace, for God has appointed Him to be the atonement for our sins..."[28] "Indeed, whoever has confidence and trust in Mary's Son, has honoured her most highly".[29] And, conversely, "The eternally pure maid, Mary, cannot bear to be given the honour which belongs to her Son".[30] One honours Mary, by believing in Jesus. Mary is a witness,[31] and as a witness she wants to be taken seriously. Whoever would give her further honour, should take her as a model of faith and obedience.[32]

---

25. Z I 426; H I 161, 162.
26. Z I 425; H I 160.
27. "In order that God's work should have even more faith and honour...", "...from which we clearly learn..." Z I 424, H I 160.
28. Z I 426; H I 161.
29. Z I 426; H I 161.
30. Z II 195; H III 255.
31. Z I 427; Z II 197; H I 163; H III 256.
32. Z I 426; Z II 196f.; H I 162f.; H III 255ff.

To sum up: Zwingli honoured Mary highly, as the instrument of salvation and the mother of the Saviour, and also as a model of Christian living. But he resolutely opposed the religious adoration of her person. To worship her (which the Catholic Church also rejects, in theory)[33] was for Zwingli out of the question. Even to seek her assistance and intercession is contrary to the Reformation belief in Christ as the sole mediator—and is therefore contrary to a proper honouring of Mary herself. If one wished, like Federer, to make Zwingli a party to the view that Mary has a place in the worship and the doctrine of the church such as that expressed in the dogmatic definition of 1950 and its associated ceremonies, then he would let Mary once more speak for herself: "The worthy Mary would say: Let God remain in this rule and power, as through all the ages. You think that I am honoured, when you worship me: that is my dishonour. No one is to be worshipped save God alone. Honour Him, as I have honoured Him".[34]

---

33. To the protestant mind, idolatry begins with the dominant role given to the Mother of God by the clergy and in popular piety (for Zwingli's views on this, see Z II 195-197; H III 255-258); and it continues with the concentration on Mary evidenced by Marian altars, congresses and devotions. We are aware that this feeling is now shared by some within the catholic fold, but we are equally aware that it is sharply rebuffed by the fervent veneration of Mary on the part of Popes (including John XXIII), hierarchs and the faithful—cf. the Second Vatican Council.

34. Z II, 195-196; H III 255-256.

6

HULDRYCH ZWINGLI'S CONCEPT OF HISTORY*

I.

Our theme takes us back far beyond the historical zeal of the nineteenth century. Zwingli was a man of his age,[1] and the sixteenth century neither possessed nor sought a concept of history in the sense of a comprehensive, synthetic and interpretative total view, whereby history assumes the role of the oracle of the truth about mankind. Unless, that is, one were to describe as a concept of history the guidelines derived from the Bible and from church tradition with which that generation contented itself, and which prevented it from forming its own view of the world. These guidelines may be briefly stated as follows: about six thousand years ago, a personal God created the world out of nothing; when sin divided mankind into different peoples, God, of his own free will, chose one of these people, gave them his promise and also faith in his promise; and in the fulness of time he sent his eternal Son to this people in order to reconcile and redeem all mankind; in the not too distant future, at the "Last Day", his Son will visibly come again in order to judge the living and the dead, destroying the old, corrupt creation and raising up the final, new creation; in the meanwhile, the Almighty Father in his providence rules over peoples and individuals by his will and permission.

As none of the parties entertained any doubts about this framework, the Reformation did not seek to break out of it. But it was certainly possible, even within this framework, to have a fresh appreciation of the world and of man, and especially a new view of the details of history, a re-evaluation and re-assessment, a new relationship to the individual events, personalities and patterns of history.

It is recognised that the accomplishment of the Reformation became the central issue in just such a re-evaluation and in the realisation of its conse-

---

* A lecture delivered to the Antiquarian Society in Zürich, February 20th, 1953; published in the *Theologische Zeitschrift*, Basle, July 1953, IX/4, pp. 275-302.

1. This study is related to the need to understand Zwingli in terms of his own presuppositions, and not merely by comparing him with the other reformers and the humanists. The supporting evidence has been drawn primarily from his earlier writings (Z I and Z II) and from his exposition of the Gospel of Matthew (S VI, 1), which likewise belongs to his early period, since these works naturally reveal Zwingli's understanding of the reformation in its most original form, and any suspicion of subsequent interpretation is excluded.

quences—although Martin Luther was never in the least concerned about these things; in this sense he was a reluctant "Reformer".[2] Huldrych Zwingli was quite different. In his relation to history he was typical of the reformation movement. Furthermore, we shall see that his understanding of history is of central significance in his own thought and action.

In order to explain this thesis, we must first of all make a brief review of the elements of historical thought in our culture.

First, we have the laudatory accounts of the mighty deeds and the victories of the Near-Eastern emperors or the Egyptian pharaohs. These lists of facts to be found on temple towers and pyramids do not ask for interpretation or connexion or motivation; they explain and testify to the mythical, strictly unhistorical way of thinking which they serve. They are there to maintain and to guarantee the divinity of the ruler and the eternal validity of the existing order, in much the same way as the array of relations, servants, vassals and prisoners depicted on the accompanying relief, which is equally lacking in perspective. The *Greeks* studied their Egyptian and oriental precursors and consciously broke with them. Even in Homer, the stiff figures have freed themselves from their mythically constricted existence and have become mobile, with a face, a character and a personality; he tells stories of gods and men, though without achieving an historical understanding of existence.[3] But from Herodotus onwards, the Hellene, by virtue of his language, his nationality and his political life, sees himself as a link in an historical chain and, therefore, as one entrusted with a mission. His life has a theme, which hangs together with the theme of his people; he understands himself in historical terms. For our purpose, three things should be mentioned, which the father of historiography and his Greek and Latin successors have impressed upon us. Firstly, that history is not primarily the domain of gods and demons, nor of kings thrust forth from some mythical background, but rather of men, of human peoples and their leaders, their thoughts, their actions and their stories. Whereas the archaic relief leaves man stiffly bowed before the divine throne, Greek sculpture raises him for the first time to an upright freedom and beauty, aware of his own humanity, and even portrays the gods in our image.[4]

---

2. One may recall Luther's hesitation with regard to the reordering of the church, and his aversion to political decisions.

3. Cf. Susi Woodtli-Löffler, "Die Geburt der Intelligenz im griechischen Epos", *Neue Zürcher Zeitung*, February 26th, 1953.

4. The names of Socrates and Euripides characterise the crisis which this violent process of de-divinisation had to undergo.

Secondly, we remember the famous introduction to Herodotus' work.[5] One of the main themes of history, as we know it, is the confrontation between Orient and Occident, the tension between East and West which was to be found even then; to put it in other words: Europe is discovered. The third thing is connected with this, namely, that the man who has found himself, and who therefore feels superior to the barbarians of the East, is the Greek with his intellectual endowment and his intellectual powers. Despite the predominance of war and the clamour of war, our history ever since then, has been in essence cultural history. A later student of Hellenism, a Macedonian (and, therefore, a semi-barbarian), inherits the pride of an upholder of this civilisation, but meets the Eastern enemy on his own ground and does something totally unhellenistic—he founds an empire. But the Roman generals will march along Alexander's roads and surpass their model. The Roman Empire will give Hellenism a political form, a mixture of Greek thought and oriental feeling. What follows is inevitable: that sense of the mythical flows back from the East and culminates in the cult of Caesar as god and lord, the visible representation of the divine order of the empire and the guarantee of its continuance.[6] But the protection of the peace and prosperity of the ecumenical culture against the barbarians of the North and East was still the responsibility of the empire, and it assumed this historic task consciously and proudly.

The second source of our historical consciousness is the *Biblical* tradition, and especially the *Old Testament*. It offers the unparalleled drama of an historical revelation: in a certain place, and at a certain time, God meets with his chosen people, whom he has set free, in order that they may serve him. "I am the Lord thy God, which have brought thee out of Egypt, out of the house of bondage; Thou shalt have no other gods before me".[7] Here also there is a "dedivinisation", but it is different from that already described, and also more radical. For here, history is not at all the domain of men, but the domain of *God's* rule; to correspond with this, we have, not some brilliant sculpture that demands respect and admiration,

---

5. "Ἡροδότου Ἁλικαρνησσέος ἱστορίης ἀπόδεξις ἥδε, ὡς μήτε τὰ γενόμενα ἐξ ἀνθρώπων τῷ χρόνῳ ἐξίτηλα γένηται, μήτε ἔργα μεγάλα τε καὶ θωμαστά, τὰ μὲν Ἕλλησι, τὰ δὲ βαρβάροισι ἀποδεχθέντα, ἀκλεᾶ γένηται τὰ τε ἄλλα καὶ δι' ἣν αἰτίην ἐπολέμησαν ἀλλήλοισι". (Herodotus of Halicarnasssus wrote this history, in order that the memory of remarkable events should not fade among men, and the great and admirable deeds of the Greeks as well as the barbarians should be rightly praised; and in particular to discover also the reasons why they have waged war against one another. *Herodoti Historiae*, Rec. C. Hude, Oxford, 1940).

6. Hendrikus Berkhof, *Kirche und Kaiser. Eine Untersuchung der Entstehung der byzantinischen und der theokratischen Staatsauffassung im vierten Jahrhundert,* Zollikon, 1947.

7. Exodus 20:2-3.

but the uncompromising prohibition of images. The message of the Old Testament is that God has a history with his people, and therefore with all peoples, and that he is leading this history to a goal. From the time of Moses onwards, the task of the people is to learn the lessons of God's guiding in history, and to be true to it in their own historical decisions. There are no independent developments; the necessary actions and changes, the union of the tribes, their centralisation within the monarchy, their division, the prohibition or the concluding of alliances with other peoples all constitute a history that is qualified by its being enacted under the eyes of the Lord of history. Here we find true historiography, strictly concerned with its subject matter even in its details, a far cry from the rambling curiosity of Herodotus. It attains its first literary peak in its description of the drama of guilt and judgment involving the successors of David, the chosen and beloved King who is portrayed, nevertheless, with an unsparing frankness. Alongside this, there is what might be called the demythologising of prehistory. The more Israel conceived of its own history as God's history, so much the more were the legends of the fathers of an earlier age incorporated into its history. Indeed, the contents of the sagas about the origin of the world and of its peoples which were common to the whole of the Near East were fused together and made to serve the one history of salvation, a history which is unfolded stage by stage, and is moving towards its consummation—to be more exact, the history of God's *covenant* with man. But even more typical of the historical existence of the people of God than this picture of the overall history is the figure of the *prophet*, who appears on the scene in certain historical situations—mostly in times of disturbance or danger; he interprets the situation, and proclaims God's Word to it, thus turning it into an hour of decision before God. Thus the prophet is more than a philosophic interpreter of events; he is himself an historical event, the mouth and finger of God. "Shall there be evil in a city, and the Lord hath not done it?" cries Amos. "The lion hath roared, who will not fear? The Lord God hath spoken, who can but prophesy?"[8]

The Old Testament has impressed upon us, in a way that can never be lost, that history has to do with guilt and punishment, and also with grace, preservation and blessing, that it is the domain of the greatest responsibility and testing, and that a higher history is manifested in it, in a purposeful manner.

---

8. Amos 3:6, 8.

Against this background, it is not easy to describe briefly the concept of history to be found in the *New Testament*. For the message of the New Testament is eschatalogical; it causes the end of history to burst out within our history. History is fulfilled in that which is more than history: the Kingdom of God is at hand. Therefore, "μετανοεῖτε, turn and repent!"[9] In the person, word, work and history of Jesus eternity has invaded time; Easter reveals that this is true even of Good Friday. This invasion continues in the community of Jesus and in its Gospel, because the community already bears the spirit of the coming kingdom. It expects a speedy consummation. Yet what is really central to this eschatalogical way of thinking is not the awaited future of the Last Day, but the historically experienced and believed presence of this future: "Behold, now is the accepted time; behold, now is the day of salvation!"[10] That is the early Christian understanding of history, and their message corresponds to it: "Today, if ye will hear his voice, harden not your hearts..."[11]

It must be stated emphatically that Christianity, in the New Testament sense, is in no way (to turn Lessing's own words against him) a "necessary truth of reason", but a "contingent truth of history".[12]

Thirdly, we look beyond, to the end of the ancient world. On the occasion of the fall of Rome in the year 410, *Aurelius Augustinus* began to write his great work, *De civitate Dei*, the "City of God". One hundred years earlier, Christianity had conquered the empire. The long overdue confrontation was inevitable between the Hellenistic, cultural-political understanding of history and the Biblical, immediate-eschatalogical understanding. Now, we may think, there must be a decision: is history to be seen as God's realm or as man's? Which view won? Neither of them; instead, it was once more the unhistorical, oriental-mythical way of thought. The meaning of the decision made by Constantine and his successors is, first of all, that Christ now appears,[13] in the place of Jupiter Sol Invictus, as the protector and guarantor of the empire, and, therefore, of the whole earthly order. But in the eastern empire at least, the emperor, even if he no longer receives offerings, becomes a visible representative of the Kingdom of God, a type of Christ, like the old Testament kings before him.[14] So from this point of view, our sentence should be reversed: the em-

---

9. Mark 1:15.
10. II Cor. 6:2.
11. Hebrews 3:7, 15; 4:7.
12. Lessing, *Über den Beweis des Geistes und der Kraft*. Philos. Bibl. No. 9, Leipzig, p. 94.
13. Berkhof, *op. cit.*, pp. 54ff.
14. *Ib.*, pp. 83ff.

pire has conquered Christianity. But, in the West especially, the heritage of the Bible—prophetic, and therefore theocratic and critical of its cultural milieu—was still lively enough to reach a new peak in this work. It offers, in the form of a portrayal of Roman and world history, that powerful synthesis which the times demanded. When the unjust heathen states are characterised, as "latrocinia magna" (great bands of robbers)[15] and when this same judgment is consistently levelled at Rome, then the whole of history, and in particular that of the empire, is reclaimed for Christ. It takes over from antiquity its cultural tradition and the responsibility of maintaining that tradition over against heathenism, which is seen, from a Christian viewpoint, as the realm of chaotic and demonic powers. It takes over from the Bible the supreme majesty of God and human accountability to his courts. So now it is possible to be a Christian and a citizen. So the empire is granted its most notable role, in that it provides the political framework for the activity of the Church, the indispensable institution of salvation. Thus there arises that strange and mysterious yet effective structure of the Corpus Christianum, that multiplex unity of spiritual and secular whose remains have not yet disappeared. Because of this book, Augustine became the father of the West. By virtue of the spirit of this book, "Europe" will emerge once more from the flood of mass migrations; this book laid the foundation of that which later centuries defended against the Turks, and which has become valuable to us today in various associations made in the face of another danger from the East.

However, this synthesis was made possible only by renouncing the sharp eschatalogical and existential thought of the New Testament, that direct historical encounter with revelation to which the Bible bears witness. The eschatalogy of the Kingdom of God has evaporated into a mild, private hope of a life beyond death. When Christianity is accommodated to the historical reality, to that extent it loses its own historical character, and becomes just one religion among others. It now sets out on its path through history.[16] Once again, a symbolic factor from the history of art may be mentioned: from this point onwards, in numerous sculptures and paintings, Christ is given an imperial orb. Thereafter, both Pope and Emperor wish to be his representative. Since then, the West has always been aware that the fact of Christ is an unavoidable factor in its history.

---

15. *De civitate Dei*, IV, 4.

16. Wilhelm Kamlah makes a similar evaluation of Augustine's work and seeks to show its relevance for our own day in his *Christentum und Geschichtlichkeit. Die Entstehung des Christentums,* Stuttgart, 1951.

II.

1. Yet, amid the confusion, tensions, struggles and confrontations of the 1520's, Huldrych Zwingli wrote in Zurich: "It is, however, God's Word which now arises in the midst of all the evil, and do we not see that this is the work of *God*, who does not wish that his creatures, whom he has bought and paid for with his own blood, should be lost so wretchedly and in such great numbers?"[17] And again, he says "You see, Christ has shown greater favour to our century, for he reveals himself today more clearly than to countless centuries in the past".[18] With Luther[19] one seldom finds such judgments concerning his own time, but they occur repeatedly with Zwingli.[20] What is the reason? Certainly it is not a question of breaking out from the Corpus Christianum, for this is rather given a greater significance in Zwingli.[21] Nor is it a dissolution of the Augustinian synthesis of salvation history and world history. It is that within the traditional framework that *eschatological tension* which had been forgotten, excluded and concealed in the medieval church now bursts forth with inex-

---

17. Z I 293.

18. Z I 203.

19. Though the well-known passage in Luther's letter to the councillors, in which the Word of God is likened to a "moving cloudburst" (WA XV, 32) reminds us that this was a conviction common to the reformers (cf. H. Zahrnt, *Luther deutet Geschichte*, Munich, 1952, pp. 134ff.). But for Zwingli it was of fundamental importance. It is a question of degree.

20. We select the following from the wealth of possible quotations:

"In our times, the divine righteousness is being revealed through the Word of God more than for many hundreds of years previously". (Z II 474).

"Almighty God has punished our sins for so long with false shepherds, who have not nourished us with his Word, and with wolves who have even deprived us of worldly goods, and who have actually made us their own. But now he has rekindled the light of his truth, so that it can be seen and recognised everywhere; so the faithful flock should not resist it, but rather allow itself to be led out of the captivity in which it is held by the wolves ... for the redeemer is here, in order that we should follow him ..." (Z III 60).

"See, what use are your commands or your prohibitions? You issue one order after another, and the more you command, the more the honour of God is increased, and the conscience finds comfort. I could show you a great people which has been subjected to great coercion and suppression, in order that they should not have the Gospel either in writing or in speech. But God has seen to it that they are well acquainted with the Word throughout the land, and that they rightly look to God ... how would you prevent this? Who has awakened the Gospel? Not you, nor the Pope. But since it has come about solely through the dispensation of God, how dare you oppose it, as though you could suppress it?—"Egad! God would be able to maintain it even if we were to exterminate the Christians completely in some places. He sent his own Son into this sinful world. How much more easily will he always be able to find those whom he will send to publish his Word..." "The world clings to the Gospel, even if that might drive you mad. And even in places where you believe that nobody thinks about it, there are sons of the living God". (Z III 438).

21. Cf. G. W. Locher, *Die evangelische Stellung der Reformatoren zum öffentlichen Leben*, Kirchliche Zeitfragen No. 26, Zürich, 1950, pp. 21ff.

plicable power. The word from the "higher history" rings out once more in the midst of history, making it possible to leap across the centuries, bringing early Christianity simultaneously present before the eternal Lord, suspending history, and thus compelling a fresh, genuine, historical decision. Zwingli states repeatedly that the reformation is not something new or unheard of, but is simply "the holy Gospel which is now arising in all Christendom".[22] Therefore the Reformation is not to be confused with any earlier worthy attempts which men undertook to put right the faults in the church or in Christendom. It is rather the work of Christ himself, the negotium Christi. Christ with his truth is no longer the object of our efforts, but rather, according to Zwingli, Christ himself, by his Spirit, is the subject of the movement, he is *the real Reformer*.[23] Thus the reformation message is identical with the preaching of Jesus and his disciples, and actually transports us into the situation faced by the early church.[24] The message is founded upon the eternally valid history of salvation, it is itself a fact of salvation, and hangs closely together with the truth of Easter: today "the rejected Christ rises again everywhere".[25] In his servants Christ preserves his own eternal presence, in accordance with Matt. 28: "He who promised to remain with his people to the end of the world, could not bear their suffering any longer and he called (them) in his own way ..."[26] Zwingli likes to apply to his own age the Johannine saying about the light that came into the world.[27] Another idea which occurs frequently is the proclamation of the right to return home to God,[28] and the parallel with the exodus from Egypt.[29] In my view, reformation theology did not achieve a dogmatic renewal of New Testament eschatalogy,[30] though it did

---

22. Z I 214. To quote one passage among many: "It is now our intention ... to preach the holy Gospel faithfully and in its purity, in order that we may become a good confederacy. For as things stand now, we certainly need almighty God to lead us by his teaching to a better and more pious life, or else it is to be feared that if we should continue in such ways, then finally God would suffer it no longer". (Z I 223).

23. Z I 200; 256. Cf. *Th. H. Z.* I, the section "Christus Reformator", pp. 20ff.

24. Cf., for example, Z I 222. "Haec plantavimus, Mattheus, Lucas, Paulus, Petrus, rigaverunt, deus autem incrementum dedit admirabile". (We have planted, Matthew, Luke, Paul and Peter have watered, but God has given a wonderful increase. Z I 285).

25. Z II 445.

26. Z I 275.

27. E.g., Z I 307.

28. E.g., Z I 152; 197-198.

29. E.g., Z I 88-90; 271; III 9, 403.

30. With all the reformers (though it is least true of Calvin), the events of Easter, Whitsun and the Second Coming are given less prominence than Christmas and Good Friday. The reason for this is that the reformers saw themselves, vis-à-vis the piety of the late Middle Ages, as being entrusted with the task of displaying afresh the wonder and the omnipotence

bring many Biblical truths to light; this is true even of Luther, who, more than Zwingli, lived in the expectation of Last Day. But what is more important is that the eternal was once more present as a spiritual and psychological reality in the self-understanding of the reformers and their followers. When Zwingli can define the goal of the movement as being this: "that the whole of Christendom, universa Christianorum multitudo, should return to its head, which is Christ himself ..."[31], then this is simply the echo, in contemporary terms, of the ancient "The Kingdom of God is at hand".

We notice immediately that this view of evangelical preaching as a present fact, effected by the Spirit, must correspond to an (albeit secondary) *sense of vocation* on the part of the reformer and his friends. Zwingli has often been reproached for claiming divine authority for his preaching. Of course he answered in good evangelical fashion that men have authority before men only in so far as they renounce their own authority and submit to God's authority, letting themselves be guided by the Holy Spirit. But with this proviso, he has to admit: "But with what purpose and will the Almighty God caused this to happen through me, his unworthy servant, I cannot tell; for he alone recognises and knows the mystery of his counsel".[32] This personal experience of his calling, which Zwingli himself

---

of *grace*. —In every one of his writings, Zwingli gives at least a brief statement of his message. The following passage will serve to illustrate his understanding of the content of this newly comprehended "Gospel": "When Christ, the savoiur of all mankind, was born of the holy, undefiled maid Mary, as we read in Luke, chapter 2, the angel spoke to the shepherds: Behold, I proclaim to you great joy, which all the people shall have; for to you is born the saviour, who is Christ the Lord, etc. Thus the gracious act of God, which he has accomplished for us through his Son, is called the Gospel, because in all our need, helplessness and despair, it has been proclaimed to us that the Son of God has come to be the saviour who will heal all our defects. And he is called Jesus, that is, the saviour, because he has made the people well from their sins (Matthew 1). Here we have in brief the whole ground of the Gospel, namely, that after it was impossible for us poor men to come to God by our own merit, God decreed that his Son should take human nature for us, and give himself up to death for us. For he who was wholly perfect and without spot could take away our stains. Whoever believes firmly in this act, and trusts in the precious efficacy of Christ's sufferings, has believed the Gospel and will be saved..." (Z II 638).

31. Z I 198.

32. Cf. Z I 287, and Z I 488: "I hope and I trust, and indeed I know that my preaching and teaching are nothing else than the holy, true, pure Gospel, which God wanted to speak through me by his Holy Spirit inspiring me or speaking in me. But with what purpose..." Such explanations are rarely found in Zwingli, and occur only when they have been provoked, but when they do occur, they are unmistakably clear. Cf. his words concerning the Sixty-seven Articles, still filled with all the zeal of the First Disputation of Zürich (January 29th, 1523): "Before you overturn one of my articles, the earth would burst open, for they are the Word of God". (Z I 557). The same occasion provides another delightful example: "I tell you, Vicar, if you can prove one of my conclusions to be false, according to the Gospel

ascribes to the year 1516,[33] seems to me to have preceded his breakthrough from a humanistic to a pauline understanding of man and salvation, and to have provided the foundation for it. By making this distinction, I suggest that we may resolve, to the satisfaction of both parties, the age-old controversy as to whether Zwingli became a reformer independently of Luther, or not. Zwingli twice speaks of the thoroughly eschatological parable of the talents[34] as the summons which came to him out of eternity, and which he could not escape "so that, when the Lord comes and demands his profit, I shall not appear as a lazy servant, full of fear and shame, bringing him my little bundle that has been buried in the ground and in sloth ..." So it is understandable that he should be convinced to the very end that "The cause is not ours, but Christ's ...",[35] "my teaching is not mine, but God's",[36] that he should call Christ his captain; that is, the one who controls his life,[37] and that, having premonitions of a violent death from the very beginning,[38] he should call himself Christ's "mercenary".[39] Together with all those who hear the Gospel aright, he is a man under constraint—the constraint of historical decision.

This constraint is reflected in a definite spiritual attitude, namely anxiety. In the present day it is seldom realised sufficiently clearly that in the reformation a fear-ridden generation was setting out towards the longed-for consolation. Fear was the spiritual characteristic of the late medieval man, and the reformation was a child of its age. But there was a shift of focus. The medieval Christian was afraid of Christ the Judge, and of suffering in hell and purgatory. Now, with the summons to an evangelical assurance of salvation, there arose the fear that the offer of grace might be rejected through stubbornness or carelessness, thereby incurring the final

---

and the divine scriptures, I'll send you a 'rabbit cheese'!" (This expression "Hasenkäse" was used in sixteenth century Swiss German to treat with irony something particularly costly and sought after; but like many a person since, Zwingli's opponent, Vicar-General Johann Faber of Constance, did not understand the rough Swiss expression, and replied that he did not need a cheese! Z I 565).

33. Z I 256; 379 and 259, etc. For Zwingli's development from humanistic beginnings to reformer, cf. Walther Köhler, *Huldrych Zwingli*, 2nd ed. Leipzig, 1954; Oskar Farner, *Huldrych Zwingli*. Vol. II: *Seine Entwicklung zum Reformator*, Zürich, 1946; and especially Arthur Rich, *Die Anfänge der Theologie Huldrych Zwinglis*, Zürich, 1949 and Fritz Blanke, the Excursus in Z V 613, 713ff.

34. Until now, this has not been noted. See Z I 256; 316.

35. Z I 200.

36. Z I 256.

37. Hebrews 12:2: ἀρχηγός. See "Christ our Captain" (above, pp. 72-86).

38. First in Z I 261; cf. also Z I 324; 397; Z III 40; Z V 357; Z VII 486, etc.

39. Z I 394; Z I 395, etc.

wrath of God.[40] God's wrath, as Zwingli often states, is a power that is effective in history.[41] Does it not actually say in Scripture, concerning the revelation of Christ, that the corner-stone of salvation will dash to pieces whoever takes offence at him?[42] Zwingli frequently quotes this—there is no genuine eschatalogical shock without the seriousness of the judgment. Luther, the monk, has to contend throughout his life with a wholly personal anxiety concerning God's judgment of his own soul; it is characteristic of Zwingli that he remains peaceful and confident in his own life of faith,[43] but that he experiences anxiety concerning God's judgment of Christendom, and especially of the Confederacy.[44] This is one of the strongest motives for his reformation work. "Now that the truth reveals itself on all sides, and meets us everywhere, be careful that you do not neglect it, but rather grasp it singlemindedly. Otherwise, while some delay and others resist and others lose it, the truth might well escape us once more. And the future would be even worse than the past; for to neglect God's warning never brings anything but severe judgment".[45] At the same time, the people's priest is gripped by sympathy for the distracted

---

40. "Truly, the Word of God can never be ignored without great punishment..." (Z 1 222; cf. 221f.). "See what misery follows when man scorns and rejects the Word of God. And notice that if we do not believe the Word of God it is a sure sign that vengeance will soon overtake us". (Z I 361). Zwingli applies to the Bishopric of Constance the lament of Matthew 11:23ff.: "...Num putatis ... impune ablaturos eos, qui herbescentem Christum hodie non tam negligunt, quam impediunt? An non timetis eum, qui dixit Mt. 11: Et tu Capernaum ... Non timetis inquam Germaniae quoque populis aliquando, si praesentem occasionem neglexerint, comminaturum: Et tu Germania, cuius strenuum forteque pectus a belli tumultibus ad veram pietatem traxi ... Ad inferos ... usque detruderis, quod lucem venientem in mundum neglexeris. Quia nulla tam barbara gens est, quae si tot occasionibus ad veram pietatem plantandam invitata fuisset, tanto torpore desedisset..." (Do you believe, you who disregard the revival of Christ in the present day, and who even suppress it, that you can escape unpunished? Do you not fear him who has said in Matthew 11: "And thou, Capernaum..." Do you not fear, I say, that he will threaten the peoples of Germany also, if they neglect the present opportunity? And thou, Germany, whose strong and brave hearts I would raise from the tumult of war to true piety ... you will be thrust down to hell, because you have neglected the light which came into the world. There is no people so barbaric that they have displayed such sluggishness when they have been given such manifold invitations to plant true piety... Z I 307). Cf. Z I 173 (the example of the fate of Sodom and Gomorrah); Z I 186 (the threat of Luke 13:3 applied to the Confederacy), Z II 18-19, etc.

41. Z I 175, 176ff.

42. Z I 314; Z II 19.

43. Cf. *Th. H. Z.* I, pp. 62ff.

44. "The same would happen to us as happened to the people of Israel, who refused to heed any warning until they came into captivity, and they sat secretly by the waters and lamented their misery; may God save us from that". (Z I 185).

45. Z I 317.

and misguided sheep of Christ:[46] so he appeals to the pastoral responsibility of his fellow pastors and of the magistrates.[47]

Zwingli's *prophetic character*, which has hitherto been noted, but never explained, is also grounded in his eschatalogical understanding of his age. The passages in which the reformer expatiates on the nature and the task of the true prophet, and the way in which he differs from the false prophet, are legion, and they increase more and more towards the end of his work. Naturally, people in the sixteenth century were no longer familiar with the history of oriental religion, and there was an enormous psychological difference between the ecstatic and visionary prophet of the Old Testament and a sober, humanistic office-bearer or a cool church politician in a confederate state. Yet latterly, Zwingli made ever-increasing use of the term "prophet" in place of the terms "pastor" or "episcopus" (= watchman) which he had employed previously. And, in fact, the use of this old, sacred title is still appropriate for the minister at the really decisive point; namely, that he is a man who fearlessly and without regard for self, by his word and by his existence, bears witness in his historical situation to the absolute nature of a message which transcends history, thus bringing the present age under the judgment and the promise of eternity. He is impelled by an inner compulsion, by fear of judgment and by a burning love for a lost people: and that is a prophet.[48] He shares the prophetic office of Christ,[49] and yet must do his duty to both high and low, and especially to a tyrannical authority.[50] It is impossible for him not to offend everyone,[51] and yet he is a living symbol of God's goodness.[52] The fact that we should have

---

46. Z I 271.

47. Z I 224; Z I 271; Z III 1ff.; S VI, 1 88. Cf. G. W. Locher, *Die evangelische Stellung der Reformatoren zum öffentlichen Leben*, Zürich, 1950, pp. 21f.

48. In S VI, 1 374, 471 Zwingli described (in connexion with the "woe" of Matthew 23:29) the struggle of the prophet both then and now: "Grave ergo et periculosissimum est officium prophetae" (The task of the prophet is hard and full of dangers). Cf. S VI, 1 305-306; 433-434.

49. "Munus propheticum Christi" (S VI, 1 443).

50. S VI, 1 306-309; S VI, 1 434: "Hinc pugna nostro saeculo, quod evangelium scelera nostra arguit, quod ferre nullo pacto volumus". (Hence the battle of the present day, since the Gospel reveals our sins, and we do not want that by any means).

51. "Omnes ergo offendat necesse est". (S VI, 1 329-330).

52. "Ubicunque ergo deus prophetas veros et fideles mittit, signum est clementiae eius: monet enim in tempore, ut posita impietate populus resipiscat, et non pereat". (Thus, wherever God sends true and faithful prophets, it is a sign of his mercy; for he warns us in good time, in order that the people may return from their impiety and not perish. S VI, 1 306). "...prophetiam rem esse sanctam et singulare donum dei" (the office of a prophet is a holy and special gift of God. S VI, 1 375).

both true and false prophets today is something that is foretold in Scripture as a feature of the last days, and is further proof of the eschatalogical nature of the reformation.[53] [54]

There can be no doubt that this leads to a tremendous tension in Zwingli's thought. For Zwingli was a humanist,[55] and he remained such, at least formally, throughout his life. This is something that should neither be denied nor minimised. And there could hardly be a less prophetic figure than the sixteenth century scholar in his study, who may well ridicule the failings of the age in his superior manner, but who would never let himself be drawn into the field of personal involvement out of dislike of the common herd.[56] The Christianity of Erasmus, for example—and he was a deeply religious man—is unhistorical. In the true philosophy, the philosophia christiana, the humanist is seeking a timeless truth.[57] But he preserves the cultural heritage—perhaps that requires a still room and quiet men. To this day, it is at once the weakness and the strength of Protestantism, and of reformed Protestantism in particular (Calvin was also a humanist!) that this tension between faith and culture, which Augustine and the Middle Ages had resolved, should again be felt, sustained, and rendered productive. Zwingli himself resolved the problem, and this again is something which, in my opinion, should not be denied. Truth and right always come from God, even when the knowledge of them

---

53. Pseudo-prophets (a term which Zwingli came to apply ever more frequently to the Anabaptists) are also an eschatalogical, anti-Christian phenomenon. He liked to apply the contrast between true and false prophets to the reformation struggle. Cf. Z I 288; S VI, 1 384.

54. When the Old Testament prohibition of images was put into effect once more, and the saints (including Mary with her chubby-faced son bearing the imperial orb) disappeared from the walls of churches, it was not due to some fanatical biblicism, but to the conviction that the eternal Son of God was actively present.

55. Apart from particular theological controversies (Zwingli wrote against Erasmus' book on the freedom of the will before Luther did so, for example), there are some passages where he expresses his basic views on the problem of humanistic education. Among these is the autobiographical section of the *Archeteles* (1522), his Apology to the Bishop of Constance, Hugo von Hohenlandenberg, who was also the product of a humanist education. Zwingli explicitly categorises scholastic studies as harmful, and by implication he indicates that humanistic studies are inadequate as compared with the study of Holy Scripture (Z I 259-261). Secondly, there is his well-known preface to an edition of Pindar, in which he deems a knowledge of classical culture and its languages to be useful for exegesis, partly in the sense that it provides a conceptual history of New Testament terminology in comparison with classical usage (Z IV 867-879). Finally (and hitherto unnoticed), there is his exposition of Matthew 23:34 ("prophets, wise men and scribes"), in which the value and the danger of education is evaluated against the measure of the revealed Word (S VI, 1 374-376).

56. For Zwingli's criticism of the self-sufficiency of the educated classes, cf. S VI, 1 376.

57. Cf. A. Rich, *Die Anfänge der Theologie Huldrych Zwinglis*, Zürich, 1949.

is mediated through heathen. This does not mean opening up a second source of revelation. An analysis of the philosophical sections of his works shows that, according to Zwingli, our thinking does not proceed autonomously, but is subject to the judgment of scriptural truth. For the reformer, as for the Middle Ages, philosophy is the handmaid of theology.[58] We even find the express statement that "(humanistic) learning is, as it were, the maid of wisdom, her mistress", and such wisdom consists in a right reverence and love to God.[59]

Zwingli wished to have the *political* instrument of the age, like the spiritual, enlisted in the service of the historical decision. At this point, as is well known, we come up against a feature of his work that proved most momentous and critical, in both its ecclesiastical and historical consequences. We cannot unfold the whole complex of religion and politics in Zwingli's thought.[60] For our present purposes, the following comment must suffice: his prophetic sense of vocation breaks through all his original pacifist tendencies, his theological reservations and his Christian scruples. The exalted and present Christ is the Lord of every part of life, including the political and military spheres, and he wills the renewal of the whole of public life and not just of a small, purified congregation. This is what Zwingli thought, from the very beginning; and his recourse to politics was not, as is sometimes alleged, a necessary expedient from 1525 onwards, after Zwingli had begun to have doubts about the effectiveness of preaching. From the start, Zwingli worked from the political question to the knowledge of faith, and then proceeded to practise politics from this position of faith.[61] His eschatalogical certainty should not be confused with fanaticism, and does not prevent his having a clear grasp of what is actually possible. As early as 1522 he himself gave up the project of a general council, which he had previously supported, because it seemed doubtful to him whether such a council would submit in advance to the principle of scriptural authority which was itself a matter of dispute.[62] At the same time, he was already considering the question of the implementation of the

---

58. Cf. *Th. H. Z.* I, pp. 43-60, where it is shown that this holds true even as regards the intention (not the execution) of his *De providentia*. See pp. 20ff. for the relationship between the Renaissance and "Christus renascens".

59. "Eruditio veluti ancilla est herae sapientiae". (S VI, 1 375).

60. Paul Meyer, *Zwinglis Soziallehren*, Linz/D, 1921; Alfred Farner, *Die Lehre von Kirche und Staat bei Zwingli*, Tübingen, 1930; G. W. Locher, *Die evangelische Stellung der Reformatoren zum öffentlichen Leben*, Zürich, 1950.

61. "Christi spiritus hoc habet, quo civitas maxime indiget". (The Spirit of Christ possesses that which the community has most need of. Z III 868).

62. Z I 127, 134, 149, 235, 306, 320, 497f.

reformation by the princes. He had no fundamental reservations about this, but he did have practical, human reservations. Princes—even Protestant princes—are too concerned for their own advantage, as experience shows.[63] But both at home and abroad, the Swiss republican hopefully entrusted the divine work to the civil magistrates. Zwingli was the first man who recognised clearly that, from the sociological standpoint, the reformation was a bourgeois movement.[64] This was something that Luther, a monk and a prince's man, overlooked—with fatal consequences. Zwingli realised that within the overall course of European history, the era of the bourgeoisie was at hand; the Christian Civic Union (das Christliche Burgrecht) and the secret project to secure for Bern and Zurich the leadership of the Confederacy were both a part of this.[65]

2. It has long been recognised that the eschatalogical view looks to the world to come, and looks at the present in the light of the world to come.

Zwingli's judgment on *his age* occupies a considerable part of his work, and does so to the very end. It is a corrupt age, and God has rightly given it over to even greater corruption. When Romans 1 is held up before Christendom like a mirror,[66] it shows inescapably that we men were always sinners; but the course of history has, inter alia, the effect of exposing sin ever more intensely. Evil must come to full maturity, in order that both judgment and redemption can be effected. Now we have reached this point. This is the age of the Antichrist predicted in the eschatalogical sections of the New Testament.[67] "Today the unbelievers are ten times more

---

63. Z I 320.

64. Cf. Z V 424. (writing to Esslingen): "Take the example of Strasbourg, Ulm, Nuremburg, Augsburg, Constance, Nörlingen and other free and imperial cities; how the Word is increasing among them, and God is rescuing them for ever from persecution". The letter to Blarer in May 1528 (Z XI 451) is discussed by Farner, *op. cit.*, pp. 119f. Cf. also Alfred Schultze. *Stadtgemeinde und Reformation*, Tübingen, 1918; Leonhard von Muralt, *Stadtgemeinde und Reformation in der Schweiz*, Zürich, 1930; Bernd Moeller, *Reichsstadt und Reformation*, Gütersloh, 1962; Bernd Moeller, "Die Kirche in den evangelischen freien Städten Oberdeutschlands im Zeitalter der Reformation", *Zeitschrift für die Geschichte des Oberrheins*, Vol. 112.

65. VI, 1 197-201; S II/III 101f. For the secret memorandum see W. Köhler, *Huldrych Zwingli*, Leipzig, 1943, p. 250; and below ch. 11 pp. 272-274.

66. Z I 486: "...you should know, that in our time ... the serene, pure and clear light, the Word of God, is so masked, adulterated and diluted with human accretions and doctrines, that even the majority of those who profess to be Christians know nothing of the will of God, but go astray through worship, holiness and outward religious ideas of their own invention ... whereas all our blessedness, consolation and salvation lie not in our own merit, nor in such outwardly glittering works, but solely in Christ Jesus, who makes us blessed..." Cf. Z III 633f.; Z I 391ff.

67. This is often stated, together with relevant texts from the Old and New Testaments, and especially in connexion with the general moral depravity, the Papacy, the rules of fasting and priestly celibacy. Cf. Z I 75; 95; 225; 233f.; also Z I 205, 282, 317, Z II 104f.

numerous than the believers''; thank God, a majority is not decisive, ''the majority does not make it true''.[68] The pastor rebukes plainly, even severely, the ever-increasing avarice which springs from unbelief, and the corruption of public life which accompanies it.[69] For where the true God is not known, material things take his place. Or else man is given over to his own lusts. Clergy and laity alike lapse into the late medieval dissolution of all moral obligation. Disunity and fighting—fighting for the sake of money, even, are inevitable. They are a public manifestation of the disobedience of Christendom, its denial of the Prince of Peace and the desecration of the image of God.

It might be objected that similar criticism was voiced by the humanists and indeed, even earlier, within the old church, in the conciliar movement, for example. But it is precisely by such a comparison that the character of the reformation may be clearly seen. For now it does not stop at complaining and criticising. The inner compulsion to obedient action is too powerful for that. The criticism which the reformers level against their age is correspondingly radical. The roots of the present distress are actually laid bare in ''man's wretchedness''.[70] Therefore only his eternal redemption can lead to a solution to the problems of the day. For this reason, Zwingli never tires of exposing the errors of human doctrine, ''humanae traditiones'', as opposed to the exclusive revelation of the Word of God; the error of worshipping the creature, which constitutes so deadly an alternative to the knowledge of the true God in Christ, who alone can be ''the sole treasure of our poor souls''.[71] With reference to

---

68. Z I 375.

69. Z I 39ff.; 70ff.; 155ff.; 210ff.; 385ff. ''In time of danger and distress there is nothing more comforting than the Word of God, and, on the other hand, there is nothing more deceiving than the word of greed, for this looks only to its own advantage and so lets everything else perish'' (V 425, 3). This is a true Zwinglian formulation of the alternatives.

70. Z III 19, 1. Cf. *Th. H. Z.* I, pp. 137ff.

71. Z II 217, 18 (in an autobiographical section). This Zwinglian programme for reform is to be found in principle in all his writings. We select the following examples:

''Summam impietatem puto, cum a deo ad creaturam convertimur, cum humana pro divinis recipimus...'' (It is, I believe, the very essence of ungodliness, when we turn from God to the creature, and acknowledge what is human to be divine. Z I 317).

''Blasphemia est, ubi creaturae damus quod dei est''. (Blasphemy consists in giving to the creature what belongs to God. Z I 299).

''Hi enim 'aliorsum trahunt' qui a Christo ad creaturam avocant''. (The people who ''lead astray'' are those who entice away from Christ to the creature. Z I 316).

''So, from the Old and New Testaments of the Word of God we know only one consolation, one redemption, one Saviour, one mediator, one advocate before God—Jesus Christ. Only in him and through him can we attain grace, help and blessedness, and not from any other creature in heaven or on earth''. (Z I 527. See also Z I 486-488).

previous attempts at reform Zwingli remarks "So far, I have seen nobody who has castigated vices as they deserve"[72]—and it is in connexion with forgiveness that he says this, incidentally. From then on, opposition to all paganising elements remained the particular concern of the reformed Protestants (including Calvin), just as opposition to Judaisers was the special concern of the Lutherans.[73]

So Zwingli does not share the optimism of the humanists concerning the present age. But he is no pessimist. For those whose freedom and whose conscience are under attack, it is a golden age. As Christ rises up again, this—and not the vaunted renaissance of men by the forces of anti-quity—offers a unique opportunity to taste God's goodness.[74] Admittedly, the opponents of the reformation turn it into an iron age also.[75] But truth will gain the victory. In the course of his controversy with Luther, Zwingli appeals on one occasion to a less passionate century, which will agree with him.[76]

3.   In medieval thought, ancient tradition is truth, just as ancient right is the best right. According to this, history is itself revelation. Today we can have no idea of how violent an act it was to break through this historicism with the question of truth. It required a truly eschatalogical power for Zwingli to utter that simple sentence at the first Zurich Disputa-tion: "We want to speak of the truth. Whether a man is to be held guilty according to a divine law which has long been set aside by men. For we believe ... custom should yield to truth".[77] It caused a stir throughout the whole traditional world of thought. We may provide some examples of how things that were historically established were now revalued in the light of eschatology.

Church History. It is full of changes and innovations. So, according to the aforementioned principle of right, in conjunction with the renewed prin-ciple of Scriptural authority, church history cannot have any binding authority, but only a relative one.[78] This is true even of the old

---

72. "Adeoque neminem adhuc vidi, qui pro dignitate flagitia taxaverit". (In the *Archeteles*, 1522. Zwingli clearly felt called to this himself. Z I 317).

73. See note 30. "It is easy to understand that those who lead men away from the creator to the creature are all false shepherds". (Z III 60). "Creator est, quo fidamus ... non creatura esse potest quo fidendum est" (It is the creator, in whom we should trust ... the one in whom we are to trust cannot be a creature. S IV 47).

74. See note 58.

75. Z I 271.

76. Z V 751f.

77. Z I 494. Cf. 290, 366.

78. Everything that has been introduced by human traditions is "recent" and therefore not really valid in law. Z I 290, 368, 319, 320.

Ecumenical Councils, the first four of which are recognised by Zwingli.[79] He dates the beginning of the corruption of the church ca. 500 AD (well after Constantine, therefore!) At that time, human doctrines began to prevail, and so it was the fault of the church itself that the ordinary man was robbed of that assurance of salvation which is given through Christ—and this is a scandal. The line of development leads from human doctrine via the worship of the creature and the ecclesiastical system of penance to the financial exploitation of those who seek pardon.[80] The influence of the Devil makes itself felt more and more.[81] Celibacy and fasting are inspired by him. He is behind the enthronement of the Pope and the Development of his power as the Antichrist. This designation is briefly justified by Zwingli, drawing on relevant New Testament texts;[82] otherwise, they got far less excited about the Pope in Zurich, though they had every reason to be angry because of wages that were still outstanding, than they did in Wittenberg. I have the impression that Zwingli simply took over this application of the title of Antichrist to the Holy Father from the late Middle Ages (from Joachim of Fiore onwards) and that he could largely assume its acceptance. By contrast, the monks feel the full weight of the wrath of the peasant's son, who sees them as nothing but hypocritical idlers.[83] The origin of monasticism was thought of in Zurich as follows: "... One day there came a man who was from a foreign land. He pretended that at home he was a rich man, a nobleman etc., and that he wanted to serve God in the wilderness. It was only so that he could have a good life, and would not have to work. Then people began to provide for him, and from this there arose rich manor houses, dirty, drunkards, rich abbots and imperial princes, and all this under a hypocritical piety ... we believed the priests and monks, that they were saying mass for us, and reaching to heaven with their prayers. So we have let them defile and besmirch our conscience, for the rascal in us likes to be covered with filth".[84] Thus Zwingli maintains that the origin of monasticism was a question of a sleeping rather than a lively conscience—surely he was quite wrong about this. It is surprising that Zwingli, as a humanist and a student of the via antiqua should, like Luther, hold Aristotle responsible for the corruption of

---

79. Z I 302, 304-306, 234.
80. Z I 282.
81. Z I 234, 95.
82. Z II 27; cf. also pp. 50, 67, 71, 104, 108, 111 etc.
83. Z III 831.
84. S VI, I 470.

scholastic thought.[85] But in common with the whole of church history he had a horror of heresy. He was himself very sensitive to the accusation,[86] and he was not free of the old idea which saw the heretic as a morally defective man who devises new teachings out of sheer ambition.[87] And yet he produces a remarkable definition, which is far removed from orthodox formalism and from biblicistic systematising, which matches the richness of revelation, and yet is both profound and clear: "... he is the real heretic, who does not acknowledge Holy Scripture according to the light of Christ, but according to his own light".[88]

In these circumstances, historical research in the realm of the church, following the method of the humanists, should be given completely free rein. Zwingli participates in this. He points out to the scholars of canon law, for example, falsifications concerned with the tradition of priestly celibacy;[89] his researches into local liturgical history show him that in former times the people of Glarus had received communion in both kinds;[90] oral traditions in Switzerland relate how congregations have demanded the marriage of the clergy time and again, and have obtained it.[91] And the expert admits enviously that we have no Christian historiographer, whom we could place alongside those of antiquity.[92]

4. It would be beyond the scope of the present work to include here a survey of Zwingli's new overall view of *biblical history*. It is fundamental for faith and life; it is indispensable, with its threats of judgment and its offer of grace; but its contents are not all equally important to salvation.[93] I do indeed believe, says Zwingli, in the Creator to whom the story of creation bears witness. But the work of the six days of creation as such cannot be the subject of my belief; at the most, it can be something which I hold to be true, and that is not the same thing.[94] If Protestant theology had proceeded

---

85. Z I 126-127, 322.
86. Cf. *Th. H. Z.* I, subject index s.v. "Ketzerei".
87. Z I 322; S VI, I 441.
88. Z I 283.
89. Z I 236f.
90. Z II 133.
91. Z I 247.
92. "I will speak frankly: where do we have an historian since the time of the Apostles, whom we dare set before a wise heathen?" (Z VI, II 241). Zwingli demands of the historian both criticism and self-criticism, a "sympathetic, loving feeling for truth". He must not "mix in what is false and fictional". Thus Zwingli finds fault with the Books of Maccabees, because the author mixed his own opinion with the facts (Z II 419).
93. Cf. *Th. H. Z.* I, pp. 24-29.
94. Z VI, II 193-194.

along these lines in the following centuries, it would have been spared many troubles.[95] Of decisive importance is Zwingli's rediscovery of the biblical concept of the covenant, his presentation of its themes, and the way he applies it to his own age. This marks the beginning of a real, i.e. an historical understanding of the bible and of revelation, and, as this has come down to us through Bullinger, the Dutch, the Federal theologians, Pietism and modern research, it has developed into one of the most fruitful contributions made by Zwinglianism to the intellectual history of Protestantism.[96]

5.   One should learn from the history of the *ancient world*. Indeed, this is the source, according to Zwingli, from which the reformer, the Christian, the pastor, the magistrate, or the student hungry for learning will gain the greatest enrichment, by a determined and critical study of the intellectual heritage of the classical scholars and their philosophy. We shall not enter into the precise nature of this study, though for Zwingli himself this was the most important question. It must suffice to state that Zwingli's own knowledge of classical learning was enthusiastic and thorough, but limited. His knowledge of Greek philosophy was derived wholly from Cicero's De Officiis, or the commentary to it.[97] His knowledge of Roman philosophy was drawn from Cicero, Seneca and Pliny. But ancient history provided him with an inexhaustible source of arguments and examples for Christian truths. Without doing violence to the tradition, the reformer, in the garb of the humanist, puts into practice what he has argued for in theory; truth, wherever it is to be found, including truth expressed by heathen, unconsciously and unrecognised, is pressed into service to confirm the Christian message—just as the Israelite stole the gold of the Egyptians and carried it away, to the glory of God; just as they hung the weapons of their enemies in the Temple to glorify him.[98] Zwingli leaves aside the question of the literary character of the anecdotes he employs. They may be Homeric sagas about the gods, reliable history, mythology, or the pronouncement of some sage or general. Zwingli is firmly convinced

---

95. Emil Brunner, *The Word of God and Modern Man,* trans. D. Cairns, London, 1965, pp. 27f.

96. We would cite just two passages from Zwingli's early period, viz. Z I 200 (1522) and Z II 131f. (1523). These both belong to the period preceding the Anabaptist movement, so it is necessary to correct the assumption made by Schrenk (and generally accepted) that Zwingli adopted the covenant idea from the Anabaptists. Here we have rather an example of early Zwinglian preaching which had a strong influence upon the Anabaptists. Cf. Gottlob Schrenk, *Gottesreich und Bund im ältern Protestantismus,* Gütersloh, 1923, p. 37.

97. Walther Köhler, Z XII 201.

98. *Th. H. Z.* I, pp. 54-61.

of their value for instruction in understanding and conduct, for "God's Spirit was not restricted to Palestine".[99] He regrets that Luther does not take a look round the ancient histories[100]—clearly he means that it would do him good to broaden his intellectual horizons. But having said this, it does not surprise us that it is primarily *warnings* that have to be drawn from ancient history. For example, he underlines his attack on the mercenary activities of the Confederates with the statement that "God punishes evil men with evil"—wars are always a divine punishment. "There is no nation or kingdom which has risen through war, which has not later fallen through war". As examples of this, he cites Israel, Sparta, Athens, the Persians, the Macedonians, the Assyrians, the Medes and the Romans.[101] Jugurtha and Metellus Numicidus provide proof of the fact that "disloyalty strikes her own master and thereby gives him his due".[102] Hannibal's army, like Hector, Paris and Menelaus, serve as a warning to the simple folk of Inner Switzerland of the dangers of softness.[103] We see that it is because of Zwingli's sense of responsibility for his own times that he has an eye for history. He reads history with a view to the present—unlike some humanists who read it in order to escape from the present into a scholarly past. Just as Deucalion confirms the truth of the biblical story of the flood,[104] so do those who have denied humanity, such as Sardanapalus, Nero, Heliogabalus or Domitian, serve unintentionally as proof of eternal predestination.[105] However, the highest attainment of world history is that it gives the laurel wreath to Christ. "See, what man in the world has been greater than Christ? Alexander and Julius Caesar were great, but they still had the world ... only half under their power, whereas men who have believed in Christ have come to him from the East and from the West ... Whose rule and power is as old as the faith of Christ, which will not disappear, even though it should remain only among a few?"[106]

6. As regards the history of *Europe* and of the *Empire*, the choice and the treatment of themes are once more largely determined by the interests

---

99. Z IX 458.
100. Z VI, II 241.
101. Z I 176-177.
102. Z I 182.
103. Z I 183f.
104. Z I 354.
105. Z I 302, 278, 346, 16.
106. Z I 355. A true understanding of the history of mankind is possibly only where there is a Christian understanding of sin (cf. for example, Z I 172). The "humanist" Zwingli never idealised the ancient world (cf. Z I 281). Plato, Cicero (Z III 662, 664) and Seneca (S VI, 1 621) all come in for severe criticism.

of the Reformation. It is true that Zwingli also is motivated by the great
threat to Christendom presented by the Turks. But as with Isaiah and
Jeremiah, God's Word is more pressing than all the external dangers. Furthermore, Zwingli is no friend of the war against the Turks, for the reason
that it would put power into the hands of the Pope, which he would misuse
to suppress the gospel. It is noteworthy that Zwingli considers the
possibility of a missionary enterprise to the Mohammedans as an alternative to war.[107] In fact, it has always been a concern of papal policy, and
especially since the end of the fifteenth century, to create disunity in
Europe and among its princes, to weaken them through war, and thus to
consolidate its own position.[108] Zwingli had a remarkably positive attitude
towards Germany and the Empire—beginning with the fact that he
credited his German mother-tongue with a richness, an expressiveness
and a dignity which neither Greek no Latin could surpass.[109] He praised
the character of the German people for their diligence and courage and
mental endeavour.[110] He deplored the fratricidal Swabian War, and could
not see the need for it; it should have been the duty of the church, and
especially of the Bishop of Constance, to settle it at an early stage.[111] As a
Swiss he shared the age-old feeling of the Germans that they in particular
had been exploited by Rome, and mocked as well.[112]

In 1522, in an anonymous political writing, Zwingli calls himself "a
friend of the Christian state in general, and of Germany in private".[113] So
he likes Germany, but he does not call it the Empire; instead, he speaks of
the Christian state in general, and, as he says in the lines that follow, he
wishes to maintain the liberty of Germany: in other words, he does not like
the Habsburg Emperor.[114] Even in this early writing, the careful reader

---

107. Z I 435, 436f., 439f.
108. Z I 436f.
109. Z VIII 106.
110. "Strenuum forteque pectus". (Z I 307).
111. Z II 282f.
112. Z I 441, 517, 537, Z III 425, note 1; 439.
113. Z I 434.
114. See W. Köhler, *Huldrych Zwingli*, 2nd ed. Leipzig, 1954, for Zwingli's distrust of the
Habsburgs, which permeated his politics from the start (cf. his first writing, the verse-fable
about the ox, Z I 1ff. (1510)). The reformation struggle is augmented by other factors, such
as the old enmity between the Confederates and the royal house of Austria, the feeling on the
part of the Swiss (who had originally been most loyal to the Empire) that the Emperor had
let them down in the Burgundian War, and their successful resistance to Maximilian's efforts at centralisation in the Swabian War. Thus, whereas the possibility of having to oppose
the Emperor presented a severe problem for Luther's conscience, the Swiss had experienced
it so often that Zwingli did not have a second thought about it. The accusation of covenant-

will perceive that twofold political perspective which governed the politics of the reformer to the very end. Firstly, the attempt to suppress the reformation must plunge Europe into grave unrest. Secondly, the victory of Rome over the reformation movement would bring the whole of Europe under the rule of the Pope.[115]

7. "I am Swiss, and I proclaim Christ to the Swiss". "The Swiss should not be counted among the Germans".[116] We would add a further word concerning Zwingli's attitude towards the history of his people. The subject is so instructive, and also of such central importance, that a special treatment would be required in order to do it justice. We select, therefore, just one question; it is the question which led to Zwingli's becoming a reformer, with a profound sense of responsibility, with pain and suffering, and with total commitment;[117] it is the point at which he saw the storm-clouds of divine judgment gathering, namely, the whole question of the mercenary system, and of foreign military service. What was at stake?—freedom, divine favour, everything. The liberation and establishment of the Confederacy had come about "by nothing other than divine power", just like the liberation of the Old Testament people of God from

---

breaking is repeated by the young Zwingli in his account of the Pavian campaign (Z I 37). Fritz Blanke draws attention to a different matter, namely Zwingli's remarkable verdict on Charlemagne (Z III 876), who was generally held in high regard in Zürich. In a list of former princes of exemplary piety enumerated by Zwingli, there appears the comment "Karolus iste magnus, quod ad pietatem adtinet, magister caeremoniarum potius quam pius rex" (Charles the Great, as far as piety is concerned a master of ceremonies rather than a pious king). This sarcastic evaluation of the founder of the Empire may be explained by the fact that Zwingli was not convinced of the genuineness of Charlemagne's Christianity as regards his personal faith and way of life. Therefore his whole work of ecclesiastical organisation seemed to Zwingli to be merely an external thing. As for the "caeremoniae" ("fireworks", as Zwingli liked to call them), he was probably thinking primarily of the old system of disconnected lectionary readings which Charles had established. Because of his doctrine of Scripture, Zwingli set this aside when he began to preach in Zürich in 1519, and replaced it by a system of consecutive readings. Cf. *Lexikon für Theologie und Kirche*, ed. J. Höfer and K. Rahner, 2nd. ed. Freiburg, 1964. Vol. X s.v. "Zeremoniar".

115. Z I 438f.

116. "Helvetius et apud Helvetios Christum profitens". "Helvetii autem inter Germanos non censeantur". (Z I 270). "My whole intention has always been like that of Christ; he also preached first to his own people". (Z IV 159). Cf. Z I 244. "After all, we belong to you, we share your blood and your land, your loyalty and your heart". (Z I 246). Cf. Z I 247, 167, 166.

117. "For my love for the ordinary pious man in the Confederacy of our Fatherland leads me to intervene when someone ventures to blind us and to tear God's truth away from us; even though there are those who take offence at what I say. But God willing, that should not mislead any pious Christian into allowing himself to be turned aside by either the sweet talk or the threats of the papists, so that he does not speak openly what befits the glory of God and the salvation of man". (Z V 178).

the tyrant Pharaoh at the crossing of the Red Sea.[118] Their great historical victories were gifts of God—Morgarten, Sempach and Näfels (the last-named being especially dear to the memory of the one-time pastor to Glarus).[119] God is always "favourable" to *external* political freedom—and especially that of Switzerland! He promotes in particular (I Sam. 8) the *internal*, democratically ordered freedom. And he encourages (I Cor. 7:21) the striving for *personal* freedom also.[120] But then, "as happens so often to all mankind", unfortunately, good fortune made us proud and godless.[121] Foreign military service resulted in money gaining sway, the corruption of rulers, dependence upon foreign princes, epidemics, vice, laziness and impoverishment.[122] And worst of all, the sin of Christians killing Christians for money.[123] Relentlessly and movingly, for he speaks from personal experience, the erstwhile army chaplain portrays the practices of his own people's warriors in Northern Italy where, under the pretext of "the rights" of "war", everything is allowed which God has forbidden.[124] They bring God's wrath upon us.[125] Swiss military service was (and Zwingli means this quite literally) a seduction of the Devil.[126] The divine forbearance still waits to see whether we will mend our ways, but it "will not excuse our pride".[127] Following the example of the cities of Sodom and Gomorrah and the express threat of Jesus: "Ye shall all likewise perish" (Lk. 13:1-3), destruction stands before the door.[128] "Should it come to the point that we are measured by the same measure with which we have measured, then we should not be able to lament our misery enough..."[129]

In view of the great economic importance which foreign mercenary service had at that time, the reformer was duty-bound to say how he thought the life of the valleys could be supported. He answers: through work and a simple life. We see how he would like the history of his people to be re-

---

118. Z I 170, 187.

119. Z I 171. Even in his prereformation period. Zwingli recounts with pride individual military exploits performed by fellow-countrymen in his own day. Cf. Z I 23ff., and especially 34f. for an example of special heroism on the part of a mountain hunter from Glarus.

120. Z I 171. Cf. Z II 19; II 317; S VI, 1 308.

121. Z I 171-172.

122. Z I 168f., 169, 174, 179, 183, 184.

123. Z I 171.

124. Z I 175-176. "The term 'right of war' means nothing else than violence". Z I 179).

125. War is itself a divine punishment. "God punishes the wicked by means of the wicked". (Z I 176).

126. Z I 173.

127. Z I 173; 223.

128. Z I 173, 186.

129. Z I 185.

garded: "The Emperor Julius, after he had conquered the Helvetians, of whom we in our Confederacy form the greater part, commanded that the land should be cultivated again, because it was fruitful. What has happened to it, that it is no longer fruitful, when it was fruitful sixteen hundred and fifty years ago? Indeed, it is more fruitful, more beautiful and has more virile people than any other country on earth, and is fruitful enough to nourish its people, if only we would be satisfied with it...[130] "Although there are enough people, and in addition the soil is good enough to provide abundant nourishment for you ... the reason that you do not have this, is due to your selfishness".[131] "Now you know well what our pious brother Claus von Unterwalden[132] has said, in all seriousness, about the confederacy: that there is no Lord or power could conquer it, except selfishness..."[133] [134]

III.

We conclude by formulating certain overall impressions.

1.   What is essential to the reformation attitude to history is not the picture it draws of history, either as a whole or in detail, but that it stands at a turning point in history, and consciously recognises this.

2.   The eschatalogical vocation which comes to the reformer from the supra-historical realm does not free him from responsilibity for the historical heritage of Christendom and Europe, but, on the contrary, gives an enhanced and binding significance to that responsibility.

3.   For the reformer, history is never itself revelation, and certainly not gospel, and it can mediate and shape truth about man only in the light of revelation.

4.   Conversely, revelation is not merely fitted into history (as the highest level of its development, for example), but it is always bound to history by the fact that is has taken historical form, and, therefore, he who encounters it is compelled to make an historically effective decision.

5.   Finally: since the reformation, this eschatalogical concern has never left our city. It motivated the pastoral spirit of Bullinger as well as the

---

130. Z I 180.

131. Z III 106.

132. Nikolaus von der Flüe (1417-1487).

133. Z III 103.

134. It may be added that one also finds in Zwingli thoughts on religious history (e.g. Z III 203; S VI, 1 539) and cultural history (S VI, 1 588, 621).

theocratic spirit of Antistes Breitinger; Lavater and Pestalozzi, both of whom were gripped by a sense of the absolute, and driven on by compassion, are prophetic figures in Zwingli's sense of the word; and even Leonhard Ragaz was Zwingli's wilful descendant. Whoever lets himself be influenced by historical figures such as these will find a clear pointer to that realm which is at once the fulfilment and the bound of all history.

7

HULDRYCH ZWINGLI'S DOCTRINE OF PREDESTINATION*

I. GRACE, PROVIDENCE AND ELECTION

Huldrych Zwingli plays only a limited role in the work of Karl Barth.[1] This is not the place, nor is it yet the time, to investigate to what extent particular theological motives of Zwingli's continue to make themselves felt, either consciously or unconsciously, in the present day, beyond the atmosphere of the Swiss reformed church,[2] which was shaped by Zwingli's reformation, and from which Barth himself came. We are still only at the beginning of a fresh theological understanding of the reformation in Zürich, Basle and Bern and its particular reformation themes. For four hundred years, people have discussed Zwingli in general terms, writing about him and making their judgments about him too often and far too hastily. We face a problem of historical theology that is by no means easy to solve, and we have to take care that we do not merely replace the humanistic, orthodox or liberal distortion of Zwingli with a dialectical one. This much can be said at once—that Zwingli's theological thinking follows a straight and totally undialectical course, starting out from the unity and the simplicity of God, which were of such importance to him. And when his anthropology concludes with the statement: "Thus it is clear that as we come to God when we climb up from our reason, so when we grasp God, we have already found providence also,"[3] then this sounds too much like the concept of analogia entis for it to be set alongside the Barthian doctrine of revelation. But this selfsame Zwingli also made formal statements such

---

* *Theologische Zeitschrift*, Basle, September 1956, XII/5.

1. The essay "Ansatz und Absicht in Luthers Abendmahlslehre" (1923: *Gesammelte Vorträge*. II, pp. 26ff). does not do justice to Zwingli. But in the *Church Dogmatics* there are sporadic references and quotations which treat him with increasing seriousness. In the chapter on "The Light of Life" (*Church Dogmatics*, Edinburgh, 1961, IV, 3, I, p. 135) Barth acknowledgs that he comes close to one of Zwingli's more controversial theses; and in dealing with the doctrine of baptism (*Church Dogmatics*, Edinburgh, 1969, IV, 4) he feels compelled to enter into serious debate with Zwingli, since he starts from a related concept of the sacrament, yet reaches a contrary conclusion about the baptism of infants.

2. Karl Barth, "Reformierte Theologie in der Schweiz" in *Ex Auditu Verbi. Theologische opstellen aangeboden aan G. C. Berkouwer*, Kampen, 1965, pp. 27-36.

3. "Patet ergo ad hunc modum redascendendo a nostro intellectu ad numen perveniri; quod ubi tenuerimus iam providentia eadem opera pervestigata est". (S IV, 143).

as: "When a man has the faith of Christ, then Christ is his reason, his counsel, his piety, his innocence..."[4] and "God is not where the flesh is, which is nothing other than our knowledge and our reason."[5] As we consider these, we may at least discern a dialectical combination of resolute obedience towards revelation with a complete open-mindedness based on that revelation. On the other hand, Luther's inflexible dialectic of law and gospel was actually levelled out in Zürich (and this was probably a deliberate correction of Wittenberg) by means of an evangelical interpretation of the law, which reminds one in surprising fashion of such works of Barth as the *Church Dogmatics* or *Rechtfertigung und Recht*. "I call gospel everything that God reveals to men and demands of them ... and I prefer to call it gospel rather than law; because it should be named for the sake of the believer rather than the unbeliever; and this also settles and calms the conflict of law and gospel."[6] Also, a fresh understanding of Zwingli may indicate a certain accord which is evident less in the individual themes than in the overall tendency of his dogmatic and ethical works, namely "the triumph of grace."[7] With Zwingli, this arises from the way in which his thought is so clearly governed by the divinity of Jesus Christ, set againt the background of the divinity of God as the summum bonum, the one who bestows mercy and who is the source of all good.

---

4. Z II 82.

5. Z II 95.

"To live spiritually (Romans 8) means: to renounce fleshly reason and power, that is, human nature, and to depend solely upon the Spirit of God". (Z II 81).

"To understand the Gospel (that is, all the goodwill that God has shown to us) does not depend on the wisdom and reason of man, but on the illumination and instruction of the Spirit of God". (Z II 26).

"See how it is with our flesh, that is, with our human or natural reason and wisdom! Nothing good comes from it; for it is evil by nature and by character, as God himself has said in Genesis 8..." (Z II 98f).

"No heart or mind can understand God's word or deed, unless it be enlightened and taught by God... A sure understanding of the Gospel cannot depend upon any man, but only on God who draws and enlightens... Do you hear, that it is the Spirit who leads into all truth? So it must always be that human teaching is not true (in so far as it is human. For in so far as it is of God, though spoken by man, it is not to be attributed to man). For all truth comes from the Spirit of God. Whatever comes from another source is not the truth; for all men are liars, and God alone is true (Romans 3)..." (Z II 22f.).

6. Z II 79 (commenting on the Sixteenth Article, 1523). Cf. also Z II 76, 83, 237. "Therefore it is more appropriate to call it gospel than law. For which man living in human darkness and ignorance would not rejoice, if God revealed his will to him?... The law is gospel to the godly man..." (Z II 232).

7. Cf. G. C. Berkouwer, *The Triumph of Grace in the Theology of Karl Barth*, E. T. London, 1956.

"God is at once just and merciful—although his mercy predominates, for his mercies surpass all his other works."[8]

Here we may refer to one central point, at which it has always proved especially difficult for theologians to maintain this superiority of grace, even when they wanted to teach a theology of pure grace.[9] The difficulty of the *doctrine of predestination* might be said to consist in the fact that the proclamation of salvation by grace alone postulates this doctrine, and yet also surrounds it with a mystery that our thought is incapable of penetrating. For every doctrine of election, of whatever nuance, is nevertheless seen as a double predestination (praedestinatio gemina), and behind the old commonplace objection that the unequal treatment of men is contrary to God's justice, there lurks the problem as to where this lauded grace of God is to be found in relation to the reprobate. Thus, in Barth's identification of the elect and the rejected in the person of Christ, whereby election and reprobation are found together on the Cross,[10] he is not merely going a step beyond the dogmatic tradition, but making an attempt to reorientate the doctrine of election, as compared with the reformers as well as others. Zwingli stands very consciously within the tradition. But within the chorus of those who have sighed over the problem we have mentioned, Zwingli sounded a clearer note, which, had it not been overlooked, would have helped the reformed church to display more clearly the light which she possessed, as she developed the doctrine of predestination in her writings and confessions. Though it is true that the doctrine appeared gloomy only to those who stood outside; for the life of the churches, this doctrine was long a source of comfort, steadfastness and energy.

It could never be denied that Zwingli was a definite predestinarian; and this fact alone should have been sufficient warning against over-hasty accusations that he did away with belief in the biblical revelation. One would also have to interpret his concept of God pantheistically, and his whole doctrine of providence deterministically[11]—and that would be possible on-

---

8. "Qum ergo deus iuxta sit iustus et misericors, tametsi ad misericordeam propendeat (excellunt enim eius miserationes reliqua opera omnia (Ps. 145:9)..." (Z III 677). Further documentation will be provided in the discussion of the concept of faith and of the Christian life in the forthcoming second and third volumes respectively of my *Theologie Huldrych Zwinglis*.

9. This is true even of Calvin, for in passing he sets grace aside in favour of sovereignty when (in defending his doctrine, not proclaiming it) he has to speak of the "decretum horribile". Cf. Paul Jacobs, *Praedestination und Verantwortlichkeit bei Calvin*, 1937.

10. *Church Dogmatics* II, 2.

11. Cf. Paul Wernle, *Der evangelische Glaube nach den Hauptschriften der Reformatoren*. Vol. II: *Zwingli*, Tübingen, 1919.

ly if one disregarded the fact that the terms used by Zwingli did not consist of stoic-humanistic sentiments, but of precise scholastic definitions which expressly excluded such a misunderstanding.[12]

It is true that Zwingli remained faithful to the tradition which had held sway from Augustine onwards, in that he made a close connexion between predestination and providence. Calvin was the first to separate predestination from providence, in the last edition of the *Institutio* (1559), in which he placed predestination at the end of the section dealing with the effects of grace, and before the doctrine of the church. This was a great step, which served to soften the speculative appearance of the doctrine, and to give more prominence to its soteriological and ecclesiological aspects.[13] Yet there is, without any doubt, an indissoluble material connexion between providence and predestination, and this lends point to the arrangement which Zwingli retained. Both speak of a divine appointment which results in a dispensation. The one concerns the eternal salvation of the individual, the other concerns the general government of the world. But while predestination appears formally to be a special case of providence, predestination is materially superior, and the doctrine of providence only acquires a soteriological and Christian character through its relation to predestination.[14] Thus Zwingli is able to state that "providence is, so to speak, the mother of predestination"[15] and also that "God uses for good

---

12. Cf. *Th. H. Z.* I, chapter "Die Gotteslehre", especially pp. 94ff.

13. Cf. Jacobs, *op. cit.*, p. 71, where this viewpoint is clearly worked out. But he does not give sufficient weight to the fact that the separation of predestination from providence is also intended to exclude any falsification of it by the doctrine of foreknowledge, or, to be more precise, to preclude the covert synergism to basing it upon a fides praevisa. I assume that Calvin's polemic in the *Institutes* (III. xxi. 5, xxii. 1, xxii. 4, xxiii. 6) is directed not only against Wimpina and Pighius (who are named in the *Opera Selecta* IV, 374), but also against Zwingli, although the latter's thoroughgoing emphasis upon the fact that it is all of God certainly allows for no synergistic misunderstanding. Those who make prescience the cause of predestination are cavilling. "Ac nos quidem utranque in Deo statuimus: sed praepostere dicimus alteram alteri subiici. Praescientiam quum tribuimus Deo, significamus omnia semper fuisse ac perpetuo manere sub eius oculis ... praesentia ... Atque haec praescientia ad universum mundi ambitum et ad omnes creaturas extenditur. Praedestinationem vocamus aeternum Dei decretum, quo apud se constitutum habuit quid de unoquoque homini fieri vellet..." (We, indeed, ascribe both [prescience and predestination] to God; but we say that it is absurd to make one subordinate to the other. When we attribute prescience to God, we mean that all things were and ever continue under his eye... This prescience extends to the whole circuit of the world, and to all creatures. By predestination we mean the eternal decree of God, by which he determined with himself whatever he wished to happen with regard to every man. *Institutes* III. xxi. 5).

14. For Calvin, cf. Jacobs, *op. cit.*, pp. 67-69.

15. "Est autem providentia praedestinationis veluti parens". (Z III 842).

both good and evil, though with this difference, that with the elect he turns everything to good, even their evil deeds, but not so with those who are rejected".[16]

Here we find already the idea of the force of divine goodness. This becomes even clearer in relation to the other factor which guided Zwingli in his retention of the traditional connexion between the doctrine of predestination and providence,[17] namely, that God is the one God, who alone exercises power and lordship, for otherwise he would not be perfect. If there should be any area or any event, in time or in eternity, which lay outside God's providence, then it would mean that both his power and his goodness were limited—he would not be perfectly good, and the source of all goodness; at best he would be relatively better than we are, but not perfect in the sense that perfection belongs to him alone, and the measure of what is good lies in him, and not in what we may like to regard as good. It is the divinity of God that is at stake. "For we are not speaking here of perfection as theologians generally do".[18]

---

16. "Sic omnibus bene utitur tam recte quam male factis, quamvis interim hoc discrimine, ut electis, etiam quae nequiter faciunt, omnia tamen bene vertat, repudiatis contra". (S IV 137). "Etiamsi electus in tam immania scelera prolabatur, qualia impii et repudiati designant. Nisi quod electis causa sunt resurgendi, repudiatis autem desperandi. Testes sunt David, Paulus, Magdalena, latro, alii..." (Even if one of the elect should fall into such horrible sins as are contrived by the impious and the reprobate; for the elect these are a cause for rising up again, whereas for the reprobate they are a cause for despair. David, Paul, Magdalene, the thief and others bear witness to this... S IV 140).

17. A further point which has a clear bearing upon our subject is Zwingli's rejection of the doctrine of the freedom of the will. "Human wisdom concerning the freedom of the will, which we took over from the heathen, has brought us to the point where we ascribe to our own deed and counsel the work of God, which he works in us; and we do not recognise the almighty providence of God". (Z II 180). Zwingli actually answered Erasmus before Luther did so, in his *Commentarius de vera et falsa religione* (March 1525). "Ex providentiae loco praedestinationis, liberi arbitrii meritique universum negotium pendet". (The whole problem of predestination, of the freedom of the will and of merit depends on the doctrine of providence. Z III 650).

"Providentia ergo dei simul tolluntur, et liberum arbitrium et meritum; nam illa omnia disponente, quae sunt partes nostrae, ut quicquam ex nobis ipsis fieri possimus arbitrari?" (The freedom of the will and merit are both annulled by the providence of God. For if he disposes all things, where is our part, that we could think that anything should come about of ourselves? Z III 843; cf. Z III 844, 649).

18. "Non enim de perfecto hic loquimur ut vulgo theologi". (Z III 647). To quote further from this passage: "Si quicquam esset, quod deum latere posset, illic nimirum sapientia et scientia eius frigeret; si vero quicquam alia providentia quam ipsius disponeretur, iam divina torperet et hac parte manca esset, et perinde nec summa esset nec absolutissima; quacunque enim parte cessaret, ea et imperfecta esset. Quod tam abest a deo, ut nihil aeque cum ipsius ratione ingenioque pugnet, quam imperfectum esse. Nam quicquid imperfectum est, deus non est. Et contra: Hoc solum deus est, quod perfectum est, id est: absolutum, et

Zwingli has thus modified the traditional doctrine of providence in a definitely reformed direction; he has, indeed, traced it afresh with strong, personal lines, though without ever stepping beyond its bounds. But now Zwingli casts a new light on this background, as he seeks to keep it bright.

II. GRACE AND JUSTICE

1.   The classical doctrine of predestination in all its forms is uniformly stated as follows: through his own fault, man fell into ruin (whether the fall of Adam was ordained or permitted by God is controverted) and it is through his own fault that he remains in this state. God displays his *justice* in that he leaves the massa perditionis in the state of condemnation which it deserves, and he reveals his *grace* in that he chooses out of this mass those to whom he will grant salvation. To the objection as to how this mercy can be reconciled with God's justice, the answer is provided by the doctrine of satisfaction.

---

cui nihil desit, cuique omnia absint, quae summum bonum deceant''. (If there were anything that could remain hidden from God, then his wisdom and knowledge would surely be excluded at that point; and if anything should be ordered by some providence other than that of God, then God's providence would be inoperative and deficient in that respect; and it would be, therefore, neither the highest nor the absolute; for wherever it were inoperative, it would be imperfect. But that is foreign to God, for nothing is so contrary to the nature and character of God as imperfection. For whatever is imperfect is not God. And conversely, only that which is perfect is God; that is, whatever is absolute, and lacks nothing and has in itself everything that pertains to the highest good. Z III 647). "Necesse est igitur, ut hoc summum bonum, quod deus est, benignum natura sit ac liberale..., ea liberalitate... qua hoc unum ac solum spectat, ut eorum sit, quae a se facta sunt; gratis enim distrahi vult. Nam ut est fons rerum omnium—nemo enim, priusquam esset, meruit ut ex illo nasceretur—, sic et perenniter liberalis est in eos, quos ad hoc unum genuit, ut liberalitate sua finirentur..." (This highest good, which is God, must necessarily be kind and gracious by nature...that grace...by which he is eager only to belong to his creatures; he wants to give himself freely. For as he is the source of all things—for nobody, before coming into being, deserved to come into being from him—so.he is always gracious to those whom he once created, that they should be perfected by his grace. Z III 650).

"Summum bonum non ita dicitur, quod supra omnia bona sit, quasi vero bona aliqua sint suopte ingenio bona, quae tamen illud bonum superet, quomodo argenti pretium aurum superat, quum ultrumque sit pretiosum. Sed idcirco summum bonum adpellatur, quod solum et natura bonum est, et quicquid bonum esse intelligi potest id ipsum est summum hoc bonum''. (He is not called the highest good in the sense that he is superior to all good things, as though there were any good things which were good in themselves, and which were surpassed only by that highest good, in the same way that gold surpasses the value of silver, although both are valuable. But he is called the highest good because he alone is good by nature, and whatever can be recognised as good is this same highest good. S IV 81).

This scheme is already to be found in Augustine, and all the different variations on the doctrine of election[19] are attempts to find answers to the questions which arise in relation to these twin lines of thought. "God is gracious, God is just. He can redeem some although they do not deserve it, because he is gracious; he cannot condemn anyone unless he deserves it, because he is just", says Augustine.[20] Even the subtle distinction between foreordination and election which is made by Thomas Aquinas, and his introduction of the concept of "permission" rest upon this twofold line of thought, especially in regard to reprobation, where human responsibility and divine justice are made to coincide. "When it is said that the reprobate cannot obtain grace, this must not be understood as implying absolute impossibility; but only conditional impossibility; as was said above, that the predestined must necessarily be saved, yet by a conditional necessity, which does not do away with the liberty of choice. Wherefore, although anyone reprobated by God cannot acquire grace, nevertheless it comes from the use of his free will that he falls into this or that sin. Therefore it is rightly imputed to him as guilt."[21] And Calvin states clear-

---

19. The clearest and most thorough survey is to be found in Gerardus Oorthuys, *De leer der praedestinatie*, 1931.

20. "Bonus est Deus, justus est Deus. Potest aliquos sine bonis meritis liberare, quia bonus est; non potest quemquam sine meritis damnare, quia justus est". (Augustine, *Contra Julianum* III, 18).

"Haec est praedestinatio sanctorum, nihil aliud, quam praescientia scilicet, et praeparatio beneficiorum Dei quibus certissime liberantur, quicumque liberantur. Ceteri autem ubi nisi in massa periditionis justo divino judicio relinquuntur?" (This is the predestination of the saints: it is namely, nothing other than the foreknowledge of God and his preparation of those benefits by which those who are to be redeemed are most certainly redeemed. But where do the others remain, if not in the mass of those who are lost, and that according to God's righteous judgment? *De dono perseverantiae* XIV).

"Quotquot enim ex hac stirpe gratia Dei liberantur, a damnatione utique liberantur, qua jam tenentur obstricti: unde etiam si nullus liberaretur, justum Dei judicium nemo juste reprehenderet". (For all who are delivered from this stock by the grace of God are wholly delivered from the condemnation in which they are held imprisoned; and even if nobody were delivered, none could justly blame the righteous judgment of God. *De correptione et gratia* X, at end).

21. "Cum dicitur quod reprobatus non potest gratiam adipisci, non est hoc intelligendum secundum impossibilitatem absolutam, sed secundum impossibilitatem conditionatam, sicut supra dictum est, quod praedestinatum necesse est salvari necessitate conditionata, quae non tollit libertatem arbitrii. Unde licet aliquis non possit gratiam adipisci, qui reprobatur a Deo, tamen quod in hoc peccatum, vel illud labatur, ex eius libero arbitrio contigit. Unde et merito ei imputatur in culpam". (*Summa Theologica*, I, Q. XXIII. Art. III, 3). For "God does not ordain the reprobate to sin in the same way that he ordains the elect to obtain merit". (*De veritate*, Q. VI. Art. IV).

The manner in which Thomas differentiates allows him to distinguish clearly between the

ly and firmly and no less deliberately: "When you hear the glory of God mentioned, understand that his justice is included. For that which deserves praise must be just. Man therefore falls, divine providence so ordaining, but he falls by his own fault ... the ordination of God, by which they complain that they are doomed to destruction, is consistent with equity,—an equity, indeed, unknown to us, but most certain."[22] "Predestination is nothing else than a dispensation of divine justice, secret indeed, but unblamable; because it is certain that those predestinated to that condition were not unworthy of it, it is equally certain that the destruction consequent upon predestination is also most just."[23]

2.   The justification for this twofold form lies in the fact that unless the tension between God's justice and God's grace is recognised, it is not possible to perceive and understand the wonder of their unity, when justice is revealed as grace at the Cross—which is the theme of the Epistle to the Romans and of pauline theology as a whole. But this manner of treating the doctrine of predestination, so that grace is linked with election and justice with reprobation, does involve the danger that the unity of the two may be lost, and the revelation thereby deprived of its wonder.

Of all the reformers, Zwingli is the one who employed the twin concepts

---

two processes. They do not run parallel; election appears at the first stage, whereas reprobation comes at the third stage.

Election:
1. Election to glory.
2. Predestination to grace (i.e. infused grace) and to merit, which is achieved with the help of this grace.
3. Predestination to glory (as the reward of merit).

A threefold act of divine sovereignty.

Reprobation:
1. Non-election.   Act of sovereignty.
2. Foreknowledge of and permission for the fall and sin.   Act of permission.
3. Reprobation.   Act of justice (voluntate consequente)

Cf. *Quaestio disputata de veritate,* Art. I; C. Friedhoff, *De goddelijke praedestinatie naar de leer van Thomas Aquinas en Calvijn,* 1936, pp. 64ff.; Oorthuys, *op. cit.,* pp. 28ff.

22. "Ubi mentionem gloriae Dei audis, illic iustitiam cogita. Iustum enim esse oportet quod laudem meretur. Cadit igitur homo, Dei providentia sic ordinante: sed suo vitio cadit... Dei ordinationi, qua se exitio destinatos conqueruntur, sua constet aequitas: nobis quidem incognita, sed illa certissima". (*Institutes* III. xxiii. 8, 9).

23. "Si enim praedestinatio nihil aliud est quam divinae iustitiae, occultae quidem, sed inculpatae dispensatio: quia non indignos fuisse certum est qui in eam sortem praedestinarentur, iustissimum quoque esse interitum quem ex praedestinatione subeunt, aeque certum est". (*Institutes* III. xxiii. 8).

Cf. also Calvin's rejection of the idea of permission: "Cur permittere dicemus nisi quia ita vult?" (Why do we say that God permits, unless it is because he wills it? *Ibid.*) However, the nature of predestination is such that the "causa et materia" of reprobation lie in man himself (*Institutes* III. xxiii. 8, 9)—which is somewhat reminiscent of Thomas.

of *misericordia* and *iustitia* most frequently,[24] and he did so consistently through the whole field of doctrine and ethics. It is, therefore, all the more remarkable that he was always concerned with their *unity*, and always held firmly to it. And this is true, not only when he was pursuing a pauline train of thought, which would be directly determined by the event of the Cross, but also when he was employing and developing the traditional doctrine of providence, when he clearly strove to ensure that he said nothing about God, either in his doctrine of providence or of predestination, which did not correspond to the revelation of Christ. Therefore everything is obedient to the message of the Cross, and directly related to it. Thus justice and mercy are both subordinated in principle to the goodness (bonitas) of God; and to Anselm's doctrine of satisfaction, which he valued highly, Zwingli added a second line of thought. According to this, what happened on the Cross meant not only that satisfaction was rendered to justice on the part of grace, but also that satisfaction was rendered to grace on the part of justice.[25]

Zwingli can also grant that God's will has decreed rejection for those who are not to be saved, "in order that they should be an example of justice".[26] But the real design of the chapter (De electione) from which this statement is taken points in quite a different direction.[27] For one thing, there is no decree, such as one finds in Calvin, which would set reprobation alongside election. That there is a state of perdition, and that there are those who are lost, is part of the general, providential and good government of God, which is exercised in justice and in mercy. Zwingli borrows from Augustine the thought that the possibility of injustice must exist, in order that justice may be manifested.[28] But God's true, personal,

---

24. "...nos hoc tantum agere, ut bonitatem resipere non minus quam iustitiam omnia dei opera circa hominem ostendamus". (...we are only concerned to demonstrate that all God's actions in respect to man reveal his goodness no less than his justice. *Sermo de providentia*, Cap. VI De electione. S IV 111). Cf. *Th. H. Z.* I (Index).

25. Cf. *Th. H. Z.* I, pp. 140ff.

26. "Ut sic electio iis tribuatur qui beati futuri sunt, et qui misei futuri sunt non dicantur eligi; quamvis de illis constituat divina voluntas, sed ad repellendum, abiiciendum et repudiandum, quo iustitiae exempla fiant". (Thus, as election is granted to those who are to be saved, one should not speak of election with regard to those who will be lost; the will of God does indeed ordain concerning them, but only to repel, reject and repudiate them, in order that they may be an example of his justice. S IV 115).

27. The heading reads: De electione quam theologi praedestinationem vocant: quod firma sit et immutabilis quodque fons eius sit bonitas et sapientia. (Election, which theologians term predestination; its certainty and immutability; its source in goodness and wisdom. S IV 111).

28. "Iustitiam in deo non cognovisse, summam illius dotem et optimam ingenii illius partem est ignoravisse. At illa quidnam esset, ni esset contraria iniustitia, quum ostendi non

deliberate decree relates to the elect and their salvation. His definition
states: "Election is the free disposition of God's will concerning those who
are to be saved."[29] This special decree of God is expressly limited to those
who are to be saved; in other words, there is a predestination, in the strict
sense, only of the elect.[30] One is reminded of Calvin, in that this disposition (constitutio), which Zwingli terms a "decree" or "sentence", arises
solely from the "majesty and authority" or the sovereignty of God, and
knows no other influence or necessity.[31] The difference from Calvin is that
there is here no corresponding decree of reprobation for the administration of justice. One is reminded of Thomas, in that Zwingli recognises that
the procedure with regard to the elect is different from that concerning
those who are lost; the difference from Thomas is that neither in election[32]
nor in rejection[33] is justice given the decisive word. And Zwingli differs

---

posset: suo bono, quo scilicet in cognitionem iustitiae veniret, lapsus est homo". (Not to
recognise the righteousness of God is to be ignorant of his greatest quality and his highest
characteristic. But how would it be if there were no contrary unrighteousness? It could not
be displayed. So man fell to his own blessing, namely, that he should come to a knowledge of
righteousness. S IV 111).

29. "Est igitur electio libera divinae voluntatis de beandis constitutio". S IV 113.

30. "Est igitur electio libera ... divinae voluntatis ... constitutio cum maiestate et
autoritate, de beandis, non de damnandis". (Therefore election is a free, sovereign and
authoritative disposition of the will of God concerning those who are saved, not those who
are condemned. *Ib.*, 115).

31. "Haec definitio genus habet *constitutionem*, quam pro decreto, sententia aut etiam
destinatione accipimus, quum alias consilium aut deliberationem quoque significet, quae
tamen pro genere ponere non placuit, quum plerumque necessitati subiaceant. Consilium
enim capitur de rebus gerendis, ubi et protinus aliqua prodit necessitas, quae capere consilium iubet quod res postulat, non quod tu maxime velis. Constitutio igitur magis convenit
divinae auctoritati et maiestati, quae longa circumspicientia nihil eget". (This definition has
as its key term the word *disposition*, by which we understand a decree, sentence or even appointment, while the word can also mean a decision or deliberation; but we do not wish to
employ these terms here, as they are mostly connected with some necessity. Thus, one comes
to a decision concerning what is to be done, where there is a prior necessity which causes one
to make that decision which the situation requires and not what one would most desire.
Therefore the term disposition is more appropriate to the authority and majesty of God,
which does not require long deliberations. *Ibid.*, 113).

32. "...et nos cum Paulo in hac sententia sumus, ut praedestinatio libera sit, citra
omnem respectum bene aut male factorum, de nobis dei constitutio". (We agree with Paul
that predestination is the free disposition of God concerning us, independent of any consideration of our works, good or bad. *Ibid.*, 114).

33. It is primarily to safeguard the sovereignty of God that Zwingli opposes the Thomist
doctrine of predestination, which bases election on foreknowledge. He confesses that he had
formerly been under the influence of this view himself, but he had rejected it after making a
deeper study of God's Word. "Credit enim, dei de nobis constitutionem sequi nostram constitutionem". (For it believes that God's disposition concerning us follows our own disposition). It would have God deliberate and decide like a human judge, who knows what is right
only after an investigation. *Ibid.*, 113-114.

from both Thomas and Calvin, in that the question of reprobation and of those who are rejected never really comes into the picture at all; it is mentioned only briefly and in general terms, mostly in subordinate sentences, so that it never constitutes a theme in its own right, either in his preaching, or even in his theology. In these circumstances, what is the place of divine justice?

This brings us face to face with the other special feature of this chapter. The old double line of thought is broken, and justice and mercy alike are subordinated to God's goodness, and together they are made to serve his wisdom—with regard to election. It is no longer simply that the merciful God elects, while the just God rejects; it is the good, merciful and just God who elects in his wisdom and according to his sovereign decree.[34] "It should be clear that it is not only justice that is the source of predestination, as the majority of theologians have thought, but goodness".[35] Zwingli gives three reasons for this; the doctrine of predestination may not be seen as an argument for justification by works;[36] it is quite unworthy of God, for his decision to be dependent on circumstances outside himself;[37] and the unity (simplicitas) of God demands[38] that we should recognise that

34. "Sed quemadmodum legislatoribus ac principibus integrum est constituere ex aequi bonique ratione: sic divinae maiestati integrum est ex natura sua, quae ipsa bonitas est, constituere". (As it belongs to the legislator or prince to dispose according to what is right and good, so it belongs to the sovereignty of God to dispose according to his own nature, as that is goodness. *Ib.*, 113).

35. "...quo manifestum fiat, non solum iustitiam praedestinationis fontem esse, in qua sententia fere theologi fuerunt, sed bonitatem". (S IV, 111).

36. "Sic enim iustitiae operum esset felicitas aeterna". (For in this way, justification by works would mean eternal bliss. S IV, 115).

37. "Ad constitutionem *libertatem* adiecimus, ut numinis hanc constitutionem intelligamus esse liberam, non a nostra dispositione aut constitutione pendere neque nostram constitutionem sequi". We annex *freedom* to disposition, in order that we may understand that the disposition of God is free and does not depend upon our disposition or decision or follow our decision. *Ib.*, 113).

38. "Simplex est numen; nihil ergo potest ab illo fieri, ad quod universae dotes non ex aequo concurrant: nam et illae utcunque pro nostro captu distinguantur, una tamen simplex et indivisa res sunt. Verum tamen alii doti tribuitur quid quod omnium est; et item alii, non secus quam personis quoque sua quaedam tribuantur, quae omnium trium sunt... Sic in destinandis ad salutem hominibus voluntas divina prima vis est; ancillantur autem sapientia, bonitas, iustitia et ceterae dotes". (God is simple; therefore nothing can be done by him, unless all his attributes concur. And although these may be distinguished to enable us to comprehend them, yet they are one, simple and undivided. However, we ascribe to one attribute what belongs to them all, and similarly with some other attribute; just as we ascribe particular attributes to the individual persons (i.e. of the Trinity) although they belong to all three...Thus, in the predestination of men to salvation, it is the will of God that is the prime force, but his wisdom, goodness, righteousness and other attributes assist. *Ibid.*, 114, 115). ("Numen" is a technical term which Zwingli employs in connexion with Trinitarian doctrine to denote the one God in three persons. Cf. *Th. H. Z.* I, pp. 122ff., 128ff.).

when God is active in mercy, his justice is also involved. Behind this last argument, which is typically Zwinglian, there lies Zwingli's real theme: that election is not merely one decision of God's among others; it is actually the triumph of his goodness. God's justice, like his mercy, can only be understood as a manifestation of his goodness—"since it is a form of goodness".[39]

Zwingli discusses the same ideas as Calvin, but they are certainly seen in a different perspective. Reprobation has but scant mention, and is probably to be understood as preterition, as in the earlier thought of Augustine.[40] What is important is that God's justice is no longer set in a dualistic contrast with grace. Since it is related to election, it ceases to compete with mercy.

3.   However, it is not easy to silence the objection that here, as in much of the treatise on providence, Zwingli is simply indulging in speculation, starting from a particular concept of God. This objection can be expressed more concretely in the question as to wherein justice consists in the decree of election, and what role justice plays in it. Zwingli must have been aware of these gaps in his reasoning. In that same year (1530) he had further occasion to clarify these matters; this brings us to the particular formulation to which this essay seeks to direct attention.

In Article 3 of the Fideo Ratio (his Augsburg confession), Zwingli states: "There is one sole mediator between God and man, the God-man Christ Jesus.[41] But God's election stands fast and remains sure. For those whom he chose before the foundation of the world, he chose in such manner, that he chose them for himself through his son. For as he is kind and merciful, he is also holy and just. All his works reveal his mercy and his justice. Therefore election also rightly reveals them both. It belongs to his goodness to have chosen whom he will, and it belongs to his justice to adopt the elect as his children and to bind them to himself through his son,

---

39. "Aperte colligimus, bonitatem harum rerum fontem esse, veluti genus ad iustitiam et benignitatem sive misericordiam, non iustitiam solam quatenus bonitatis species est". (From this we may plainly conclude that goodness is the source of these attributes; it is, as it were, the general concept under which righteousness and kindness and mercy are subsumed; not righteousness alone, for that is only a form of goodness. *Ibid.*, 111). Zwingli is not merely playing with words here, for he is quite prepared to allow righteousness to stand as the general term, provided that it is understood in its Biblical sense ("In iustitia tua libera me"—save me in thy righteousness) for then "eadem erunt bonitas et iustitia" (goodness and righteousness are identical. *Ib.*, 111).

40. Cf. Oorthuys, *De leer der praedestinatie*, 1931, p. 21.

41. For Zwingli, "Christ" denotes the deity and "Jesus" the humanity of our Lord. Cf. *Th. H. Z.* I, pp. 18f.

whom he gave for a sacrifice to render satisfaction to divine justice for us".[42]

With regard to the history of doctrine, it is the second part of the final sentence which contains the surprise. After saying that "it belongs to his goodness to have chosen whom he will", one would expect a corresponding statement to the effect that "it belongs to his justice to pass over (or to reject) whom he will".[43] Therefore we find all the more striking the way in which justice is set in the context of election instead, and the way in which Zwingli defines and substantiates it at the same time. It consists in the application to the elect of the salvation which Christ has won for them. It is "just" that God deals with us according to what Christ has done for us. So it is mercy, which corresponds to justice, which takes the lead. In Article 2, the sending of Christ had been described as the revelation of God's goodness;[44] justice follows goodness, and brings it to completion. But both

---

42. "Hic enim unus ac solus mediator dei et hominum est, Deus et homo Christus Iesus. Constat autem et firma manet dei electio. Quos enim ille elegit ante mundi constitutionem, sic elegit, ut per filium suum sibi cooptaret. Ut enim benignus et misericors, ita sanctus et iustus est. Resipiunt ergo universa opera illius misericordiam et iustitiam. Iure igitur et electio utramque resipit. Bonitatis est elegisse quos velit; iustitiae vero electos sibi adoptare et iungere per filium suum, hostiam ad satis dandum divinae iustitiae pro nobis factum". (S IV 5, 6).

43. Cf. Article XVI of the (Calvinistic) Belgic Confession (*Bekenntnisschriften und Kirchenordnungen der nach Gottes Wort reformierten Kirche*, ed. W. Niesel, 3rd ed. Zürich, n.d., p. 125): "Credimus, posteaquam tota Adami progenies sic in perditionem et exitium, primi hominis culpa, praecipitata fuit, Deum se talem demonstrasse, qualis est; nimirum, misericordem quidem et iustum. Misericordem quidem, eos ab hac perditione liberando et servando, quos aeterno et immutabili suo consilio, pro gratuita sua bonitate in Iesu Christo Domino nostro elegit et selegit, absque ullo operum eorum respectu: Iustum vero, reliquos in lapsu et perditione, in quam sese praecipitaverant, relinquendo. (We believe that after the whole posterity of Adam has thus fallen into corruption and ruin through the guilt of the first man, God revealed himself as he is; that is, as merciful and just. As merciful, in that he redeemed and saved from corruption those whom he had chosen and selected, without any regard to their works, by his eternal and immutable counsel, according to his gracious goodness in Jesus Christ our Lord; as righteous, in that he left the rest in that fallen and ruined state into which they had thrown themselves).

44. "Quum tempus esset prodendae bonitatis, quam non minus ab aeterno quam iustitiam ostendere constituerat: misit deus filium suum ut naturam nostram ex omni parte, quam qua ad peccandum propendet, adsumeret; ut frater et par nobis factus mediator esse posset, qui divinae iustitiae, quam sacrosanctam et inviolatam permanere oportet non minus quam bonitatem, pro nobis perlitaret; quo certus esset mundus et de placata iustitia et de praesente dei benignitate". (When the time had come to reveal his goodness—as he had resolved from all eternity to manifest this no less than his righteousness—God sent his son to take upon him our nature, in every respect except the propensity to sin; in order that, having been made our brother and like unto us, he could be the mediator who could offer an acceptable sacrifice to the righteousness of God, which must remain no less sacred and inviolate than his goodness; so that the world may be sure of the reconciliation of God's righteousness as well as the presence of his goodness. S IV 5).

mercy and justice alike are fulfilled in Christ and grounded in him. This is expressly stated with regard to justice, and as regards mercy, it follows from the context, where election is seen as the peak of God's goodness. But as regards both mercy and justice, this means that election is only to be understood in terms of Christ, and that it depends upon his saving work. Is it equally true to say that his saving work depends upon election?

4.   Article 2 begins with the fact that the divine disposition and the divine decree are independent of any circumstance relating to the creature.[45] This is Zwingli's supralapsarianism. "Therefore at the beginning, in his knowledge and wisdom he created man, who was to fall, and at the same time he determined to clothe his son with human nature in order to repair the fall".[46] That is both supralapsarian and infralapsarian.[47] God's justice is manifested[48] in the fall and the misery of man—in order to lead to the revelation and knowledge of his mercy, which is granted to us in Christ's atoning sacrifice.[49] Thus the foundation is laid.[50] On this basis, it is now established that there can be no more talk of righteousness by works, or of any human mediator,[51] but one may speak of election.[52] Indeed, it is in election and its application that we realise what Christ has accomplished for us by his atoning work. But there can be no election without Christ.

Therefore, our question may be answered as follows: Christ's saving work does indeed rest upon election: the election of Christ. In the revelation of Christ, the eternal counsel of God is realised. On the other hand, our election is expressly related to, and dependent on the redemption won

---

45. "Scio numen istud summum, quod deus meus est, libere constituere de rebus universis, ita ut non pendeat consilium eius ad ullius creaturae occasione". (I know that God, the supreme being, who is my God, disposes freely concerning all things, so that his counsel does not depend upon the circumstances of any other creature. *Ib.*, 4). .

46. "Hinc est, ut, quamvis sciens ac prudens hominem principio formaret qui lapsurus erat: simul tamen constitueret filium suum humana natura amicire, qui lapsum repararet". (*Ib.*, 5).

47. Cf. *Th. H. Z.* I, p. 154.

48. "Manifestabatur dei iustitia". (S IV 5).

49. See note 44. The passage continues: "Cum enim filium suum nobis et pro nobis dederit: quomodo non omnia nobis cum illo et propter illum donabit? Quid est quod nobis de illo non debeamus promittere qui sese huc demisit, ut non tantum nobis par, sed totus quoque noster esset?" (For since he gave his son to us and for us, will he not give us all things with him and for his sake? What is there that we may not surely expect from him who so humbled himself that he did not merely become like us, but became wholly ours? *Ib.*, 5).

50. "Hos Evangelii fontes ac venas esse duco". (These are, I believe, the heart and veins of the gospel. *Ib.*, 5).

51. Article 3 (*Ib.*, 5).

52. Redemption through the Cross or by election are not to be seen as alternatives!

by Christ. This is Zwingli's infralapsarianism. It is always the strength of the infralapsarian viewpoint, that it never makes the revelation of Christ merely a means to some higher end,[53] but rather election is made to serve Christ, just as the elect should serve him.[54]

Thus we have a material (though not temporal!) order: the decree concerning Christ's mission—atonement through Christ—election in Christ and because of Christ. Although the special terms are not used, we recognise the beginnings of the Federal Theology which was to develop later in connexion with Zwingli and Bullinger.[55]

III. THE EFFICACY OF CHRIST'S SACRIFICE AND ELECTION

The way in which the subject of reprobation is set aside will no doubt find expression in a more universalist attitude. But can this be sustained, when Zwingli links election to closely to Christology? Zwingli replies: This link with Christ requires that we should see every man we meet as a candidate for salvation, as one of the elect, until there is proof to the contrary.[56] It is well known that in the discussion which Zwingli provoked, there were two critical questions: the salvation of unbaptised children[57] and of the so-called "pious heathen".[58] We cannot enter into these questions here, but would simply affirm the basic principle: children are free of original guilt through Christ,[59] and not by virtue of their own innocence; and if pious heathen attain to a relative knowledge of the truth, it is not by

---

53. Later, supralapsarian Calvinists would say that Christ died only for the elect. Cf. Alexander Schweizer, *Die protestantischen Zentraldogmen in ihrer Entwicklung innerhalb der reformierten Kirche*, Vol. I, Zürich, 1854; Vol. II, 1856.

54. We would maintain this even in the face of Barth's informative survey and the conclusions which he reaches (*Church Dogmatics,* Edinburgh, 1957, II, 2, pp. 127f. and 68f.).

55. At the Synod of Dort in 1618, it was the representatives of the Church of Bremen and Emden (i.e. those from areas influenced by Zwinglianism (cf. the East Friesian Confession of 1528) and by federal theology) who appealed to Ephesians 1 in an attempt to gain some relaxation of the rigid scholastic attitudes. Cf. Schweizer, *op. cit.*, II, pp. 163, 165, 171ff. and Barth, *Church Dogmatics*, Edinburgh, 1957, II, 2, pp. 127f. and 68f.

56. Zwingli believed that the only conclusive evidence of reprobation would be conscious obduracy, persisting to the very last, on the part of someone who had received the gospel—though even this could only be established by God himself. "...qui fidei rationem exponi audivit et in perfidia perstat ac moritur, hunc possumus fortasse inter miseros abiicere..." (When a man has heard an exposition of the gospel and persists and dies in unbelief, we may perhaps assign him to the reprobate. S IV 123).

57. S IV 7f., 125-127.

58. Rudolf Pfister, *Die Seligkeit erwählter Heiden bei Zwingli*, Zollikon, 1952; also "Zur Begründung der Seligkeit von Heiden bei Zwingli", *Evangelischen Missions-Magazin,* Basle, 1951, 95/3, pp. 70-80.

59. "Ab originali morbo beneficio Christi sunt liberi". (They are free from original guilt through Christ's gracious work. S IV 125).

means of a general revelation or by virtue of their own qualities, but as a result of a special and even personal (relative) illumination by the Holy Spirit;[60] and if they are saved, it is because of Christ's sacrifice.[61] Even Socrates was saved through Christ—and by means of election. Election and universalism (as a principle) are mutually exclusive; but God's freedom, of which election is the expression, postulates universality, and forbids us to impose limits according to our own criteria. For the sacrifice of Christ is fundamentally universal. Otherwise, redemption would be less than the ruin caused by sin, and Christ would be inferior to Adam.[62] "Because of the efficacy of the salvation wrought by Christ, he who assigns them to eternal damnation judges falsely, on account of the aforementioned ground of restoration, and also on account of God's free election".[63]

One has the impression that Zwingli expects the elect to comprise the great majority. The efficacy of the salvation wrought by Christ would, indeed, suffice for all.[64] But election, as predestination, means that even the (subjective) appropriation of the salvation which Christ accomplished does not lie within our powers, but is a miracle.

IV. ELECTION AND FAITH

One final question has long required an answer: In connexion with all this, what about the necessity of faith to salvation? Zwingli replies: "Election is not the consequence of faith, but faith is the consequence of elec-

---

60. *Th. H. Z.* I, pp. 54ff.

61. When speaking of reconciliation, Zwingli quotes I John 2:2 with unusual frequency.

62. "Adamus enim si perdere universum genus peccando potuit, et Christus moriendo non vivificavit et redemit universum genus a clade per istum data: iam non est par salus reddita per Christum; et perinde (quod absit) nec verum: Sicut in Adamo moriuntur omnes, ita in Christo omnes vitae restituuntur". (For if Adam could ruin the whole race by his sin, and Christ by his death has not given life to the whole race, and redeemed it from the ruin which Adam brought upon it, then the salvation won by Christ is inferior; and accordingly (which God forbid!) it is not true that 'As in Adam all die, even so in Christ shall all be made alive' ". S IV 7).

63. "Hoc certe adseveramus, propter virtutem salutis per Christum praestitae praeter rem pronuntiare qui eos aeternae maledictioni addicunt, quum propter dictam reparationis causam, tum propter electionem dei liberam". (*Ib.*, 7).

64. "Nihil enim vetat quo minus inter gentes quoque deus sibi deligat, qui revereantur ipsum, qui observant et post fata illi iungantur". (There is nothing to preclude the possibility that even among the heathen God has chosen some who will honour him and obey him and be united with him after death. S IV 123). Calvin thought differently; cf. his catalogue of the marks of reprobation, (*Institutes* III. xxiv. 12-14), of which the first is the lack of opportunity to hear the gospel. Cf. also the example he gives, that "among a hundred to whom the same discourse is delivered, twenty, perhaps, receive it with the prompt obedience of faith". (*Institutes* III. xxiv. 12).

tion".[65] We could not believe, if we were not elect. The biblical way of saying that we are justified by faith should not mislead us into ascribing to ourselves an achievement[66] which is God's alone. Indeed, its intention is to set aside our own achievement. And although this way of speaking is correct (the "just man" knows that his life rests on faith and springs from faith),[67] yet it ought really to be understood indirectly.[68] [69] It refers back to God's free act of grace, in which our salvation is grounded. To restrict this salvation (and therefore God's freedom) to ourselves would actually be to reverse its meaning. Thus we may say: All believers are elect, but all the elect do not yet believe.[70] Faith is absolutely essential to salvation—for us, who have heard the gospel; unbelief would be a sign of rejection.[71] But God's mercy is not dependent upon our faith; rather is our faith dependent on God's mercy. "If election had not gone before like the blossom, faith could never have followed".[72]

---

65. "Electio ... non sequitur fidem, sed fides electionem sequitur". (S IV 7). "Antecedit electio fidem". (Election preceded faith. S IV 123).

66. "Non quasi fides velut opus sit cui debeatur peccatorum venia". (Not as though faith were, as it were, a work, which would deserve forgiveness of sins". Ib., 122).

67. See the extensive excursus "De fide" in De providentia, Chapter VI, (S IV 118-127). Commenting here on Hebrews 11:1, 10:38 and Habakkuk 2:4 he says: "Apostolus Prophetae verbum: Iustus autem ex fide vivet, huc accomodat, ut iusti vitam in fide illius constitutam esse doceat; quoniam fides scilicet tam efficax, praesens ac vividum sit pharmacum, ut qui illam imbiberit salvus sit ac tutus". (The apostle adapts the word of the prophet "The just shall live by faith" to teach that the life of the just man rests upon his faith. For faith is so efficacious, prompt and lively a medicine that whoever drinks it is safe and secure". Ib., 121).

68. S IV 123, 124.

69. This is because forgiveness of sins constitutes the central point of justification. "Iustificandi verbo pro absolvendi utuntur Hebraei". (The Hebrews use the word "justify" for "forgive". Ib., 121). "Qui fidem habent iusti hoc est absoluti sunt". (Whoever has faith is justified, that is, he is forgiven. Ib., 122). "Quum igitur fides dei donum sit (nemo enim venit ad Christum nisi quem pater traxerit): qui fit ut salus a peccatis et aeterna felicitas tot scripturae locis fidei tribuatur? Si enim et fides donum est, et peccatorum gratia fidei tribuitur: iam dono tribuitur donum". (Since, therefore, faith is the gift of God, (for nobody comes to Christ unless the Father draws him), how is it that in so many places in Scripture salvation from sins and eternal blessedness are attributed to faith? If faith is a gift and if, in addition, the gracious forgiveness of sins is attributed to faith, then one gift is attributed to another. Ib., 121).

70. "Qui enim ab aeterno electi sunt, nimirum et ante fidem sunt electi". (For those who are elect from eternity are surely elect before they believe. Ibid., 7) "Multi sunt electi, qui fidem nondum habent". (Many are elect, who do not yet have faith. Ib., 8).

71. "Quae synecdochice loquuntur de credentibus, quod scilicet soli salvi fiant: hi enim soli hac lege continentur, qui et audierunt et crediderunt. Similiter de incredulorum damnatione: hi enim soli intelliguntur, qui audierunt et non crediderunt". (It is only indirectly true to say of believers that they alone are saved; for this rule applies only to those who have both heard and believed. This is equally true of the condemnation of unbelievers; for this refers only to those who have heard and have not believed. Ib., 123).

72. "Electio ni tanquam flos praecessisset: fides nunquam esset secuta". (Ib., 124).

Far from being devalued by this subordination, the concept of faith is rather heightened in three ways.

First, its decisive character is safeguarded in that one can only speak of faith as being necessary for salvation in the strict sense, when there is preaching of the gospel.[73]

Second, from the start the believer will see not only his salvation, but also his faith as an undeserved privilege. Faith is a gift.[74] It is election which really saves. Faith is the sign, symbol, seal and pledge of election.[75] This has far-reaching consequences for preaching. For one will no longer preach: "You must believe, in order to be saved", but "You may believe that you are eternally saved".[76]

---

73. "Qui non crediderit, inquit Christus ipse, praedicato auditoque Evangelio (praecessit enim: Praedicate Evangelion omni creaturae!), is omnino damnatus est, et huius rei perinde certum signum est incredulitas, atque fides electionis signum est". (Christ himself says "Whoever does not believe the gospel which has been preached and which he has heard (for it says earlier: 'Preach the gospel to every creature') is undoubtedly condemned. And the sure sign of this is unbelief, just as faith is the sign of election". *Ib.*, 123).

74. "At ea vis non est ab ipso homine (sic enim quisque vellet quam grandissimam habere fidem), quum non omnium sit fides; sed a solo deo est: ipsam enim Paulus spiritui sancto refert acceptam. Qui enim terreni sunt, terrena sentiunt; qui autem superne sunt regenerati, coelestia sentiunt. Hominem ergo sibi permittas! unde fidem comparabit aut adsciscet, quum terrena tantum cogitet aut quaerat? Dei ergo solius donum est". (But this power does not come from man himself (for in that case anyone could have the strongest faith at will), for all men do not have faith; it comes solely from God. For Paul ascribes it to the Holy Spirit, from whom he received it. For those who are earthly mind earthly things; but those who have been born again from above mind heavenly things. Just leave man to himself! Whence will he obtain or acquire faith for himself, when he considers and seeks only earthly things? Thus faith is the gift of God alone. *Ib.*, 121). "Dei liberale munus". (God's gracious gift. *Ib.*).

75. "Signum est electionis, qua vere beamur, fides". (Faith is the sign of election, by which we are truly saved. *Ib.*, 124). "Electio est, quae beatos facit, eaque usque adeo libera..." It is election which saves us, and it is wholly free. *Ib.*, 123) "Quocirca, quum fidei lucrum aeternae salutis tribuitur, posteriori ac veluti sigillo tribuitur quod prioris est ac instrumenti... Fidei tribuitur iustificatio ac salus, quum ea solius sint electionis et liberalitatis divinae; fides autem electionem sic sequatur, ut qui illam habeant sciant se veluti per sigillum ac pignus electos esse..." (Therefore, when one ascribes the gaining of eternal salvation to faith, one is ascribing to the consequence, to the seal, that which originally belongs to the title-deed itself... One ascribes justification and salvation to faith, when they really come from the election and grace of God. Yet faith does follow election, in the sense that those who have it know by this seal and pledge that they are elect. *Ib.*, 124). "Fides iis datur, qui ad vitam aeternam electi et ordinati sunt; sic tamen ut electio antecedat, et fides velut symbolum electionem sequatur". (Faith is given to those who are chosen and ordained to eternal life; but in such a way that election has precedence, and faith follows election as a symbol. *Ib.*, 121).

76. "Non quasi fides velut opus sit cui debeatur peccatorum venia; sed quod qui fidem habent in deum sciunt citra omnem ambiguitatem, deum sibi esse per filium suum reconciliatum et peccati chirographum sublatum..." (Not as though faith were, as it were, a work, which would deserve forgiveness of sins; but because those who have faith in God

Finally, the effect of this subordination is to anchor our assurance of salvation in election—or as we must now formulate it, in the light of all that we have said, election anchors our faith in the sacrifice of Christ, and thereby makes it certain. "Therefore it is certain that those who believe know themselves to be elect; for those who believe are elect".[77] And so we already find ourselves in the Christian life.

V. PREDESTINATION AND ETHICS

At this point, predestination once more comes into contact with providence, though without being merged in it. For there is a vast difference between the idea that everything and everyone must serve God's plan, and the idea that the believer renders such service from the heart and sees it as the point of his existence, as the very presence, the real beginning of his eternal election.[78] The believer knows that he does not belong to himself; and that what he does, does not belong to him; therefore it is necessary to deny oneself daily; it is necessary to understand and to give others to understand that faith and love are the same thing.[79] Seen from the standpoint of predestination, the statement that "since good works are the fruit of faith, they are wholly of God and not of ourselves"[80] becomes personal, concrete and beautiful. If providence teaches that "he orders his vessels, that is, us men, as he will ... he can make his creation whole, or destroy it, as he will",[81] then predestination teaches that our life "is nothing other than an active work of God ... so the believer recognises that

---

know without any doubt that God is reconciled to them by his son, and that the bond of sins has been cancelled. *Ib.*, 122).

77. "Constat igitur eos qui credunt scire se esse electos: qui enim credunt electi sunt". (*Ib.*, 123). "Qui vere credant, nemo novit nisi is qui credit. Hic ergo iam certus est se dei electum esse. Habet enim spiritus arrhabonem... Spiritus ille fallere non potest". (Nobody except the believer himself knows whether he truly believes. But he is certain that he is elect. For he has the Spirit as a pledge... this Spirit cannot deceive. *Ib.*, 8).

78. It is to this extent that there is truth in the later reformed doctrine (dating from Beza onwards) of the *syllogismus practicus*. Traces of it are to be found in Zwingli: just as faith is the sign of election, so, under certain conditions, good works can be the sign of faith. "Ut qui fidem habeant sciant se veluti per sigillum ac pignus electos esse: sic qui fidei opera faciunt experimentum dant quum sibi ipsis, dum liberaliter et ex amore dei et proximi, non vana gloria, operantur; tum aliis, quod deum colant, hoc est quod fidem habeant". (Just as believers know by this seal and pledge (faith) that they are elect, so those who perform the works of faith provide experimental proof that they have faith. They show this firstly to themselves, and secondly to others, when they act with generosity and out of love to God and their neighbour, and not out of vainglory. S IV, 124; cf. S VI, I 391).

79. Z III 848-850 (*Commentarius*).

80. *Ibid.*, 849.

81. Z II 180; H III 233 (Exposition of the Twentieth Article).

he is an instrument and a vessel through which God works".[82] And if providence, with its emphasis on divine omnipotence, might appear to make it self-evident that we "are nothing else than the instrument and vessel through which God works",[83] then predestination teaches us that is a grace and a wonder, "because we are evil by nature".[84] Of especial importance is the indication that this service must find its meaning in election itself, and find its happiness in the Lord. There is no promise of the glory of outward success or of the inner satisfaction of the development of spiritual gifts. It may rather befall us that we have to say "Now God lays you aside as a locksmith does with a worn file".[85] That is when belief in election must prove its strength. "You are an instrument and a vessel of God; so he will use you and wear you out; he will not let you lie idle and rust. How blessed are you, that God calls you to be his instrument and uses you".[86] But belief in election will lead to patience, fearlessness, courage and steadfastness.[87] [88] Following our survey, this is extremely significant, for, we may conclude, the one who is elect is moving alone a way in which eternal *justice* does not turn against him, but in mercy and with mercy reveals and gives itself, embraces him, humbles him and comforts him. For justice unites him with Christ, and leads him thereby into the first and the last, the one valid order. "The election of God stands firm and immoveable".[89]

There is no form of the doctrine of election which solves the riddle. It is certainly not its task to explain the inexplicable, but to bring the mystery to our minds, and thus to lead us to adoration and to comfort. Zwingli's formulation of the doctrine is well adapted to awaken that humility and confidence which unite the believer with the angels of God in Dante's Paradise, as they extol the eternal will, because it is good:

---

82. Z II 181; H III 235.

83. Z II 186; H III 242.

84. Z II 186; H III 242.

85. Z VI, I 455; H II 24.

86. "Instrumentum dei es, te vult utendo non otio consumere; o te felicem quem ad operam suam arcessit". S IV 141.

87. "Patientia", "intrepida mens", "fortitudo", "audacia", "aequus animus", "fortissimum pectus" and other terms relating to stoic virtues occur frequently towards the end of Zwingli's *Sermo de providentia* (S IV, 140ff.). They stem from the traditional teaching about providence from Seneca onwards. Zwingli's efforts to incorporate them into a Christian ethic are instructive.

88. And also to "communion with the hosts above". This is a noteworthy factor in Zwingli's ethical teaching. Cf. S IV, 141.

89. S IV 140, 5.

"O how far removed,
Predestination! is thy root from such
As see not the First Cause entire: and ye,
O mortal men! be wary how ye judge:
For we, who see our Maker, know not yet
The number of the chosen; and esteem
Such scantiness of knowledge our delight:
For all our good is, in that primal good,
Concentrate; and God's will and ours are one".[90]

---

90. Dante, *Divine Comedy*, Paradiso, Canto XX, 130-138. (The quotation is from H. F. Cary's translation, revised. Bohn's Standard Library, 1909).

8

THE CHARACTERISTIC FEATURES OF ZWINGLI'S THEOLOGY IN COMPARISON WITH LUTHER AND CALVIN*

I. THE MESSAGE AND THEOLOGY OF THE REFORMATION

1. *The Message*

In the famous introduction to the second part of the Schmalkaldic Articles of 1537, *Martin Luther* writes: "Here is the first and principle article: That Jesus Christ, our God and Lord, died for our sins and rose again for our justification (Romans 4), and He alone is the Lamb of God, who bears the sin of the world... As this must be believed and cannot otherwise be gained or comprehended through work, or law or merit, so it is clear and certain that only such faith can justify us ... (Romans 3) ... One cannot in any way abandon or relax this article, even though heaven and earth should fall and nothing should remain".[1]

In the sixty-seven Articles, which led to the victory of the Reformation in Zürich in January, 1523, Huldrych Zwingli declares: "Article 2: The sum of the Gospel is that our Lord Jesus Christ, the true Son of God, has made known to us the will of His heavenly Father, and through His sinlessness has redeemed us from death and has reconciled God. Article 3: Therefore Christ is the only way to salvation for all who ever were, are and shall be. Article 6: For Christ Jesus is the guide and captain promised and given by God to all mankind".[2]

In the Third Book of the *Institutes*, John Calvin gives the following definition of faith: "it is the firm and sure knowledge of God's favour toward us, which is founded on the truth of the free promise of grace in Christ, and is revealed to our minds and sealed in our hearts by the Holy Spirit".[3]

---

* Lectures delivered at universities and theological seminaries in North America in Autumn 1966. The present version also provides the documentation for the article "Zwingli. II: Theologie" in *Die Religion in Geschichte und Gegenwart*, 3rd ed., Vol. VI, Tübingen, 1962; also *Zwa.* XII/7/8 (1967/1/2), pp. 470ff., 545ff. An abbreviated version, "The Shape of Zwingli's Theology, a comparison with Luther and Calvin", appeared in the *Pittsburgh Perspective*, Vol. VIII/2, June 1967.

1. The Schmalkaldic Articles (1537), in *Die Bekenntnisschriften der evangelisch-lutherischen Kirche*, Göttingen, 1930, Vol. I, p. 415.

2. Z I 458.

3. *Institutes* III. ii. 7.

It is not easy to define in a few words the essence of the Reformation message. We have decided, therefore, to concentrate upon the Reformation understanding of justification by faith, or, to express it more precisely, the relation of faith to Jesus Christ as the sole Redeemer and Saviour. We could proceed immediately, and begin to distinguish the three main Reformers in the light of these quotations, which are characteristic of each of them. In order to compare the Reformers and, indeed, to gain a deeper understanding of them, it is necessary to distinguish them from one another. But as soon as we do this, there is the danger of overestimating the differences and of laying more emphasis upon the points at which they differed than on what they had in common. In reality, the differences between them—with which we are dealing here—can be theologically understood only against the background of their common basis. Common to the whole Reformation movement is the escape from fear and troubles of conscience to Jesus Christ, the one who was crucified and raised again for us, and the comfort which is to be found in Him. Common also is the rediscovery of the Saviour of sinners in contrast to the medieval picture of the inexorable judge of the world. Therefore the Reformers have in common the "sola gratia", in contrast to the never-ending religious and moral demands made by Rome and medieval scholasticism and also to the various stages of the mystical way of salvation which could never be enforced. They share also a more exact definition of the concept of the grace of justification "sola fide"—that is, by excluding any natural or supernatural property or any natural or supernatural co-operation of man, even if such a property or co-operation should be termed "grace". For only the pure gift can give us complete assurance. Therefore they also have in common the personal concept of grace, as opposed to "gratia infusa", which is infused into man by means of the sacraments. They have a common understanding of the church as the assembly of believers, as against an organisation of salvation which is infallible with its hierarchical offices and its doctrinal and legal tradition. And common to all their work is the awakening of the "viva vox" of proclamation based solely on Holy Scripture; though even the "sola scriptura" is but a form of testimony to the presence of the one to whom Scripture bears witness, the "solus Christus". Come to Christ and trust yourself to him in life and death. No comfort is to be found in men. That is the message of the Reformation.

2. *Theological Motives*

It is clear that the interpretation of this message is influenced in two ways. Firstly, by the exposition of Holy Scripture—here, the points of agreement predominate. Secondly, by the respective starting-points of the Reformers and their churches, and by their different experiences. So when we pose the question of the motives of the Reformation movement, the diversity of the answers and their consequences should not surprise us. If anything, we should be amazed at the outstanding abundance of what they have in common. Though we need to be careful at this point. The presentation of Reformation theology, especially in the German language, has all too often taken Luther's teaching as the standard guide, and has then simply noted the points of agreement or difference in Zwingli and Calvin. The result is that in some cases the differences are exaggerated, and at other times, when the formulations sound similar, differences of intent are overlooked. To achieve a better understanding of the Reformers, it is necessary to consider their motives historically and objectively. Then we come to the very heart of their theology. We shall attempt to state their views briefly.

Luther

Luther's words concerning justification by faith (cited above) continue as follows: "On this article is based everything that we teach and live in opposition to the Pope, the Devil and the world. Therefore we must be quite certain about this, and not doubt. Otherwise, everything is lost and the Pope and the Devil and everything will gain the victory and the right over us".[4] Thus Luther's teaching struggles not only against the Pope (that is, the representative of a church principle that denies the "solus Christus", and therefore bears the character of Antichrist) but also against doubt and despair, against the way of the world, with its reason and its sin, and against eternal damnation and the Devil. We are surrounded by these powers day and night and exposed to seductions. Yet they unleash their most dangerous powers in our inner selves. In my conscience, the Devil appeals to God's law and says "You are lost". Luther's message is addressed to the man who despairs of his own good works and is in fear of hell. Or, to put it in modern terms, it is addressed to the man who, despite all his efforts to achieve a meaningful and useful life, does not succeed in realising the presence of God in his existence, or his eternal bond with God. There is a psychological side to this existence. The Protestant must never forget the picture of Brother Martin wrestling with God in his monastery cell. Here Luther was afraid, and that is the reason why he could appear so fearlessly before the state and the church. He experienced

---

4. The Schmalkaldic Articles, in *op. cit.,* (note 1), p. 416.

fear about his election, about the worth of his works, about the purity of his views; and fear of being condemned for his sins. There is no true evangelical faith which does not know the onslaught of God's wrath, and is not in some way affected by this attack. For only the conscience which is attacked[5]—this was Luther's way—holds to the Gospel against the Law, holding to the promise of grace in the cross of Christ, which contains in itself both the condemnation of God's wrath and the assurance of God's love. As we have said, there is no faith without this turning from the darkness of guilt to this light which is kindled for us in the word of preaching—in Word and Sacrament. When understood in this sense, that oft-quoted question "How can I find a merciful God?" surely expresses the most personal and most profound of all human questions, as well as being the central motive of Lutheran piety.[6] The comprehension of the promise of grace takes place in personal faith; and indeed, this faith, which is created by the Word, is itself the goal of God's revelation to us, with its constantly new way from Law to Gospel. It stands in opposition to either despair or works.

Zwingli

Huldrych Zwingli also became a Reformer out of fear[7]—fear in the face of God's wrath. But it is important to realise at once that there was another reason for his fear. It has frequently been asserted that Zwingli did not know those distressing spiritual conflicts which Luther had to suffer throughout his life. This is not true.[8] But whereas Luther's religion

---

5. "I have certainly had experience of the devil, especially when he comes with Scripture; so that he has brought me to the point where I no longer knew if I was dead or alive. He drove me to such despair that I did not know whether there was a God, and I almost despaired of our God..." Martin Luther, *Tischreden,* WA TR I 1059; cf. WA I 557. See also Paul Bühler, *Die Anfechtung bei Martin Luther,* Zürich, 1942; Paul Althaus, *Die Theologie Martin Luthers,* Gütersloh, 1962, pp. 58-65.

6. For Luther's doctrine of justification, cf. H. J. Iwand, *Glaubensgerechtigkeit nach Luthers Lehre,* 3rd ed., Munich, 1959; Ernst Wolf, "Die Christusverkündigung bei Luther", in *Peregrinatio,* Vol. I: *Studien zur reformatorischen Theologie und zum Kirchenproblem,* 1954, pp. 30-80, and "Die Rechtfertigungslehre als Mitte und Grenze reformatorischer Theologie", in *Peregrinatio,* Vol. II: *Studien zur reformatorischen Theologie, zum Kirchenrecht und zur Sozialethik,* Munich, 1965, pp. 11-21.

7. Cf. G. W. Locher, *Die evangelische Stellung der Reformatoren zum öffentlichen Leben,* Zürich, 1950; also "Huldrych Zwingli's Message" (above, ch. 2) and "Huldrych Zwingli's concept of History (above, ch. 6).

8. Cf. the *Supplicatio ad Hugonem episcopum Constantiensem* (1522), Z I 189ff., for Zwingli's confession of the sexual distress which compulsory celibacy caused to himself and his colleagues during his pre-reformation period; and the Reformer openly describes his trouble with the phrase "as we forgive them" in the Lord's Prayer (Z II 225). Cf. Fritz Blanke,

reflected to the very end the desire of the true monk, struggling for the salvation of his soul, the Zürich Reformer was a people's priest, responsible for the souls of his congregation; furthermore, he was a confederate, and therefore a passionate politician and a fiery democrat. The task of proclamation is a prophetic one.[9] One must preach the Word of God in a way appropriate to the times, interpreting the hour. However, the public and private life of the present is determined by two factors. These are the corruption of the times and the Reformation movement.[10] This means on the one hand a general and fearful apostasy of the peoples of Christendom and their Church from the commandment of God, and their plunging into self-destruction through bloody wars, which are a betrayal of Christ. And Zwingli's beloved confederacy in particular, which had grown proud in the wars of liberation, had burdened itself with an indelible guilt through its greedy mercenary campaigns.[11] The punishment which threatens will

"Zwinglis Urteile über sich selbst" in *Aus der Welt der Reformation, Fünf Aufsätze*, Zürich, 1960, pp. 9-17.

9. Cf. e.g. *Der Hirt* (The Shepherd, 1524), Z III 23, 27-33. "From this (i.e. the example of Elijah) the shepherd can well learn that he is obliged to stand manfully by the Word of God, even though the whole world should be against him; and also that he should not let himself be frightened by the great host of the priests of Baal" (Z III 33). "If the shepherd reads the prophets, then he will find nothing but an everlasting struggle with the mighty and with the vices of this world". (*Ib.*, 35).

10. For all his high regard for Luther (which he retained to the last), the Reformation, as far as Zwingli was concerned, did not begin with Luther's appearance on the scene, but with the (gradual) discovery of the principle of Scriptural authority. Cf. Z II 144, 145ff.; Z V 815-817.

11. "My whole teaching, my heart and my soul all serve to maintain the Confederacy, that they might follow the example of our forefathers, in having respect for themselves rather than for foreign princes, and so live and continue together in peace and friendship. But the warlike and insatiable pensioners (i.e. those involved in the mercenary system) talk as if I were guilty of inciting to rebellion, just because I lead people to repentance—but it is Christian repentance—so that one may suffer much for God's sake, and one does not run after foreign princes for the sake of money, to harm, slaughter and ravage people and lands that have never done us any harm. Will my detractors treat it as heresy when I teach so pointedly against waging war for money, or against pensioners? When I say, 'If a wolf enters a country, the alarm is sounded, and all the people suddenly join together to catch it. But when a captain or a recruiter enters a country, people raise their hat to him. The wolf carries off the first sheep he can lay hold of. The recruiter makes his choice from the most handsome and strong, and leads them off to risk both body and soul'. It is Holy Scripture which teaches me to speak and chastise in this way. For with regard to this question, it declares in Isaiah 1, and elsewhere, 'Your hands are full of blood' etc. We can in no way deny that our hands are stained, not only with the blood of enemies, but also with our own blood; for we have let our own folk be led away for the sake of money. Is that not rough and hard speech? (Pious man, don't take it to yourself!)". (Z III 484-485).

For the arrogance of the Swiss, cf. Z I 172-173 ("...nobody can resist us ... it is just as though we were made of iron and other people were pumpkins..."). With regard to mercenary service seen as one of the devil's wiles against the confederates, cf. Z I 173-174. Concerning the wrath of God which threatens because of this, cf. Z I 175-178; S VI, I 563 (on Luke 3:14).

be disastrous. In "The Shepherd" (1524), the Reformer addresses himself to the clergy: The shepherd knows that he "should rebuke and hinder the wanton waging of war by the princes". "Where do the papists, the high bishops and the whole crowd of so-called clergy stand? How have they acted? For fifteen years they have caused chaos by setting the greatest and strongest nations against one another;[12] the honour, the life and the property of so many souls have been destroyed that it is beyond measure; and it is getting worse all the time. Whenever they have started to talk of peace, it was always with a view to their own advantage, and afterwards the war was worse, so that even today one shudders when they begin to talk of peace. What they have in mind is to bring destruction into the world. In brief, let him who wants peace accept God's Word now, as it is brightly revealed at this time. Otherwise he will never enjoy peace, for the axe is laid against the tree".[13] For God has bestowed the Gospel afresh in our day; He allows His Word to be preached. It is the last chance to return to the Father.[14] But if we resist the Gospel, what judgment will come upon us? It must be final. "Do you not think, O pious Christian, that God reveals His Word with special zeal in this sinful age, in which there has arisen among the majority of the rulers such wantonness, such destruction of true piety, of justice, chastity and loyalty, and so much shameless grasping, robbery, profiteering, usury and devaluation of money. Since the very beginning of the Christian faith, the Word of God has never been so clearly revealed everywhere as it is in these times, so let us realise that it is for our salvation and to rid us of the hypocrisy of human doctrines. Therefore, in this age when even the children and simple folk can speak, woe to the shepherd who keeps silent, who hides the light under a bushel, who is negligent in the work of God and who does not help to set free God's people".[15]

The man who turns away from the commandment of God is given over to his own selfishness. Resistance to the Gospel (Reformation preaching) is rooted in man's obstinate clinging to his own ideas and traditions. In both cases, he is making the creature his god, instead of worshipping the

---

12. "An allusion to the policies of Julian II and Leo X, which provoked the bloody wars of Milan" (Z III 34, note 12 by Georg Finsler).

13. Z III 34-35.

14. Cf. Z III 633-634 in the Preface to the *Commentarius* addressed to Francis I of France. In the "Gospel" (= Reformation), Christ proclaims to the world the "postliminium" (the right to return home). (Z I 152; cf. also Z I 197-198).

15. Z III 27-28.

one true God, who is spirit.[16] Here lies the root of the pneumatological emphasis in Zwingli's theology. For the present, we may say that, for Zwingli, "belief in the Gospel" means not only a personal laying hold of the gracious promise of eternal salvation, but also a decision to make a total change in the whole social and political spheres of life. In practical life, the opposite of faith is "self-interest",[17] and in the field of religion it is human teaching and tradition.[18] "There can be no doubt that if a man thinks he can know what is good by his own reason, and does not learn what is right and good simply from God and his Word, then he is setting up an idol within himself, namely, his own reason and judgment. This idol is difficult to overthrow, because it presents a magical effect, shining with a false glitter, selling itself to others as true and right. And just as a monkey is pleased with her young, so is man pleased with his inventions".[19]

It must not be forgotten that with Zwingli, as with Luther, the ground and the possibility of faith are to be found in Christ alone. That oft-quoted book "The Shepherd" explains how faith and love are one in the face of the divine grace that is revealed in Christ. "When a man is sure that Christ does not deceive him with his promises, then he has a real trust and faith in God. Where this exists, it is impossible for godly love not to follow. For who would take God as the merciful, true and highest good, and yet not love him, and especially when he has assured us in so costly a way of his grace through Jesus Christ, his son?"[20]

16. "Manifestissime patet, quod quincunque adhuc in creaturis haerent, uno, vero, soloque deo non nituntur". (It is most evident that whoever still cleaves to creatures is not relying upon the one, true and only God. Z III 841).

17. Z III 112-113; Z V 425.

18. "Adulterinas doctrinas esse arbitror, quae ab hominibus adfectibus suis deditis confictae pro divinis venduntur..." (I regard those doctrines as false, which are devised by men who are given over to their own emotions, and which are then sold as divine. Z I 287).

"Human teaching and commandments are vain; for the word of Christ simply cannot lie". (Z VIII 19).

"Therefore the shepherd must not fashion himself according to doctrines of human invention, but according to the Word of God, which he preaches; for otherwise he plants nothing but hypocrisy". (Z III 20).

"Veterum traditiones quanto magis sunt euangelio conformes, tanto magis suspici merito debent. Quas vero dicitis antiquorum traditiones? nonne eas quas quorundam cupiditas recens invenit?" (The more that the traditions of the ancients are conformed to the Gospel, the more they are deserving of honour. But what do you in fact term traditions of the ancients? Is it not those which have recently been devised by the avarice of certain people? Z I 290).

"Quae a deo profecta non sunt, sed ab hominibus, mala sunt". (Whatever has not originated from God, but from man, is evil. Z I 313).

19. Z III 29.

20. Z III 44.

Calvin

We have seen the significance for the first reformers of the "Word of God"—their experience of the living proclamation of the Word, springing from the rediscovered Bible. For John Calvin, a man of the second generation, the vital power of God's Word was itself the motive for the reformation movement.[21] Fear played no role here; a true reverence for God loves and fears him spontaneously, "even if there were no hell".[22] Confronted by the mighty reality of the Word of God, our situation becomes basically quite simple and clear: it is a matter of glorifying God in the life of the Church of Jesus Christ. One cannot quite escape the impression that Calvin is criticising even Luther, whom he esteemed highly, when he emphasises that the glory of God is even more important than our salvation.[23] With Calvin also, Christ is the revelation of grace, and, therefore, constitutes for us the wonderful possiblility of believing. But we must recognise that trust itself represents a part of that attitude of obedience to which the Holy Spirit leads us. The opposite of faith is unbelief in all its forms, which is always disobedience.

3. *The Task*

Our task is to understand the individual character of the Zurich reformer and his thought within the framework of this reformation awakening which was brought about by preaching Christ. We are, however, only just beginning. During the last hundred and fifty years, Zwingli has always been portrayed (both historically and theologically) in comparison with the Wittenberg reformer, and has been measured against him, whether for blame or for praise. This could never lead to a right understanding. Moreover, in the Reformed Church, his memory has been obscured for four hundred years by the world wide influence of the teacher and organiser from Geneva; though there are certainly good historical and factual grounds for this. Whether contemporary theology has reason to consider Zwingli's role afresh, and should strive to understand it, and whether perhaps his particular contribution to the reformation message would serve to make that message valuable for us today are questions that can be decided only when we know the man himself. But his doctrine of the Lord's Supper must be presented for once, within the framework of his theology, and not the other way round!

---

21. For what follows, cf. G. W. Locher, *Calvin, Anwalt der Ökumene*, Theologische Studien No. 60, Zürich, 1960, pp. 9ff.

22. *Institutes* I. ii. 2.

23. E.g., contra Cardinal Sadoletus, OS I 463f.

II. HULDRYCH ZWINGLI'S DEVELOPMENT

1. *Life and Work*

Let us consider briefly Zwingli's life and work: Born on January 1st, 1484, in Wildhaus, Toggenburg (which stands some 3,500 feet above sea level), he was the son of a free mountain farmer and official. At the age of five he was given into the care of his uncle, Bartholomew Zwingli, the principal priest of the parish of Weesen on Lake Walen. At the age of ten˙ he was sent to the Latin School in Basle, and two years later moved to Bern. In 1498, when he reached the age of fourteen, (by which time he was already living in the Dominican monastery)[24] his uncle sent him to the famous University of Vienna. In 1502 he moved to Basle, where he graduated as Master of Arts in 1506. In September of the same year, in Constance, he was ordained priest by Bishop Hugo of Hohenlandenberg. From 1506 to 1516 he worked as a priest in the small but important town of Glarus. During this period he made a pilgrimage to Aachen, and also acted as a chaplain on two campaigns in Italy. As a supporter of the alliance with the Pope he had to give way to the French party, and so he became a minister in Einsiedeln, a well-known place of pilgrimage. By now an opponent of mercenary service, he was called on New Year's Day, 1519, at the request of the guilds, to the post of people's priest at Zürich Cathedral. He broke with the traditional order of lessons and introduced evangelical preaching, based on consecutive exposition of complete books of the Bible. The mounting enthusiasm caused some of his friends to break the rules of fasting—and Zwingli defended them. The inactivity of the Bishop led the city council to call the First Zürich Disputation in January, 1523, to discuss the principle of Scriptural authority. Zwingli's successful defence of his sixty-seven Articles marked the first's breakthrough for the Swiss Reformation. His *Exposition and Justification of the Articles* constitutes the first Protestant dogmatic theology in the German language, and is Zwingli's most comprehensive work. There follows a second disputation (concerning images and the Mass) and a gradual renewal of the church: the pastors were obliged to base their preaching on Scripture; individual congregations should be governed according to the wishes of the majority; images should be removed; endowments made for masses for the dead should be used for schools and for the care of the poor; there was the

---

24. Zwingli was not merely "almost" a novice, as one often reads, but probably already a novice. In writing later "how I was a monk in the Dominican monastery at Berne", Zwingli corrects the date, but does not deny the fact (Z III 486). Cf. O. Farner, *Huldrych Zwingli*, Vol. I, p. 172.

development of the "prophesy" (a seminar for Biblical exposition together with a sermon for the congregation); and from 1525 onwards, there was an evangelical administration of the Lord's Supper. In the same year there appeared Zwingli's *Commentarius de vera et falsa religione*, his largest Latin work. His writings on the eucharistic controversy with Luther followed soon afterwards. The main political and theological disputes took place during the next few years: with the peasants, the Anabaptists, the loyal Papists of inner Switzerland, and with Luther. Zwingli experienced his greatest triumph at the Disputation of Bern in 1528, which won the powerful city over to the Protestant side, and also brought the Reformation to Geneva. The meeting that carried the greatest consequences for the history of Protestantism itself was that with Martin Luther at Marburg in 1529, when they reached agreement at every point except their understanding of the Lord's Supper. The real point of difference was whether this doctrinal difference must lead to ecclesiastical division; Zwingli denied this. The increasing confessional and political tension with the Cantons, who felt threatened, led to bloody attacks being made by them. Zwingli's aim was to secure a free path for evangelical preaching. But the harsh and clumsy measures taken by Zürich and Bern drove the inner Swiss to a desperate counter attack, which found the Protestants unarmed. The outnumbered Zürich army was destroyed at Kappel on October, 11, 1531; the army chaplain fell, "fighting bravely". The result was that the Reformation movement suffered a severe setback. But thanks to the outspoken determination of Zwingli's colleague, Leo Jud, and the courage and wisdom of his young Successor, Henry Bullinger, Zürich, Bern, Basle and Schaffhausen remained Protestant, together with their territories.

2. *His Inner Development*

In so far as it is possible to survey Zwingli's inner development, the following phases may be traced.[25]

From his home background Zwingli inherited a fervent love for his country, his people, his community and the church. His "trivium" schooling was conventional, though the Latin schools in Basle and Bern, under the influence of Humanism, already fostered ancient history. His studies at Vienna and Basel would provide a thorough introduction to late-medieval scholasticism; there may even have been a semester in Paris,

---

25. For a more detailed account, together with the necessary documentation and comments, I would refer to my book *Die Zwinglische Reformation im Rahmen der europäischen Kirchengeschichte*, Göttingen 1979.

which would serve to explain the influence of Thomism. Although the Faculty of Arts was still opposed to Humanism at this time, the student would still gain his first impression of Humanism in Vienna, and from the viewpoint of Eastern Europe, which concentrated more strongly on the exact sciences.

Zwingli's period in Glarus nurtured his patriotism towards the Confederacy, and also saw his meeting with the revered Erasmus, the representative of West European Humanism, which paid homage to the individualistic and cosmopolitan ideal of learning. At this time Zwingli went through a period of pacifism. At the same time, he and his friends formed a circle of a unique kind; it was a Swiss Humanism, which combined educational zeal with a desire for political and ecclesiastical reform.[26] During his years at Einsiedeln came the study of Greek and Hebrew, of the Fathers, an intensive study of the Greek New Testament, and, latterly, that of Augustine. About the end of 1516, the principle of the supremacy of Scripture burst forth, as the direct result of his encounter with the living Christ. The duty of renewing the Church is conceived as a holy responsibility, to be seen in the light of the Parable of the Talents. In later years Zwingli regarded this as the beginning fo his evangelical path. Apart from an essentially Christocentric doctrine of redemption, the development of a Reformation theology made slow progress. Luther's early writings around the year 1520 were still interpreted in the sense of humanistic reform. On the other hand, he did regard as exemplary Luther's resoluteness at the Disputation of Leipzig. The hymn which Zwingli composed after the plague reveals a deeper personal faith in divine providence and a readiness to offer himself as an instrument of God.[27] The experience must have furthered his understanding of the Pauline doctrine of man and of sin. Since 1522 he produced a lively new formulation of the Reformed doctrine of grace and of freedom.[28] From this point onwards, until his death, Zwingli's theology remained wholly consistent, and it was

---

26. Cf. *ibid.*, for the significance of this phase in Zwingli's development.

27. But not, as yet the reformation doctrine of justification by faith. In this I agree with Fritz Blanke, against many interpreters both old and new, including, most recently, Markus Jenny, "Des Reformators Kampf und Sieg", in "Neue Zürcher Zeitung", November 6th, 1966.

28. To state my view briefly, in comparison with the views of my revered teacher Oskar Farner and my friend Arthur Rich: I, like Zwingli himself, would place the reformational turning-point essentially earlier in his life, and the completion of his development into a reformer considerably later. Cf. O. Farner, *Huldreich Zwingli. Vol. II: Seine Entwicklung zum Reformator 1506-1520,* Zürich, 1946; Arthur Rich, *Die Anfänge der Theologie Huldreich Zwinglis,* Zürich, 1949.

only in points of detail that it was amplified, varied or made more profound—as, for example, through the Christology of the Epistle to the
Hebrews, through the discussions with the Anabaptists, and through the
debate with Luther about the sacraments.

III. THE MAIN ASPECTS OF ZWINGLI'S THEOLOGY

1. *Elements and Motives*

Zwingli's thought can be described as follows: The constant elements,
co-existing in a state of tension are: his scholasticism, in the sense of the *via
antiqua*, predominantly Thomist, but with Scotist overtones;[29] Erasmian
Humanism, which, even after his turning to Reformation views, continued to exercise an influence, as revealed in his Platonistic understanding of the spirit and the soul,[30] and which led also to the historical,
critical and philological methods of exegesis of the Biblical texts, involving
the examination of the change in concepts vis-à-vis secular authors.[31]
Viennese Humanism drew his attention to the historical and geographical

---

29. Cf. *Th. H. Z.* I. The failure to give due attention to the scholastic elements in
Zwingli's thought, and confusion of the scholastic and humanistic terminology are among
the main reasons why researchers have hitherto failed to achieve a homogeneous understanding of Zwingli's theology. But Fritz Blanke, as the editor of *Huldreich Zwinglis Sämtliche
Werke*, has, in his annotations, brought a vast amount of scholastic material to our notice,
and has thereby done much to prepare the ground for a fresh understanding of Zwingli.

30. As is well known, Walther Köhler has consistently emphasised this feature in
Zwingli's thought, so that anyone who wishes to gain some idea of Zwingli's humanism need
only pick up the *Kirchenratsausgabe*. The writings edited by Walther Köhler constitute a (one-
sided) selection in which the humanistic arguments are presented almost exclusively. (*Ulrich
Zwingli. Eine Auswahl aus seinen Schriften, auf das vierhundertjährige jubiläum der Zürcher Reformation
im Auftrag des Kirchenrats des Kantons Zürich*, translated and ed. by Georg Finsler, Walther
Köhler, Arnold Rüegg, Zürich, 1918).

31. Cf. especially Zwingli's *Epistola* to Ceporin's edition of Pindar (Z IV 873-879) and
Walther Köhler's assessment of it in his introduction (Z IV 865). As a striking example of
the many places where Zwingli endeavours, in a way that is philologically correct, to
elucidate New Testament texts with the help of the Hebrew Old Testament, we may note
one that Ludwig Köhler has brought to our notice—that δικαιοσύνη (Matt. 3:15) corresponds
to the Hebrew מִשְׁפָּט (Gen. 40:13), with the meaning of "order" (Z XIII 241. Cf.
Ludwig Köhler, *Kleine Lichter, Fünfzig Bibelstellen erklärt*. Zwingli-Bücherei No. 47, Zürich,
1945, No. 19, pp. 70-73. See also S VI, I 213). Edwin Künzli has provided an instructive insight into the way that Zwingli worked as an expositor of Scripture, in the helpful section on
this which he has added to his new and improved edition of the *Kirchenratsausgabe (Huldrych
Zwingli, Auswahl seiner Schriften*, ed. Edwin Künzli, Zürich, 1962, pp. 311-326, "Die Bibel in
der Hand des Reformators 1525-1531"). Further works which are easy of access are Oskar
Farner's *Aus Zwinglis Predigten zu Jesaja und Jeremia* and *Aus Zwinglis Predigten zu Matthäus.
Markus und Johannes*, both Zürich, 1957.

environment of the New Testament.[32] Swiss Humanism adopts the stoic ideal of virtues and uses both classical and national history as a source of examples.[33] The Fathers, and especially the Cappadocians and Augustine, are all read with discrimination, in the light of the Bible.[34] In the Old Testament, his sympathetic understanding of the Prophets comes as a surprise; in the New Testament, he gives the central place to Matthew because of the Lord's teaching, John because of the Christology, the Epistles to the Romans and to the Galatians because of the doctrine of grace and the Epistle to the Hebrews because of its concept of sacrifice.

The motives of Zwingli's striving for reform lie; in his adoption of the widespread, mildly-rationalisitc reforming ideas of Humanism[35] (though with the observation that they are not sufficient to save social and church life);[36] in his republican patriotism;[37] in his pastor's passion for Christendom and its congregations;[38] and in his experience that in the rediscovered

32. Zwingli knows and uses, for example, the works of Flavius Josephus; e.g. Z XII 388; Z VIII 139, 678.

33. Zwingli's own understanding of humanism is well illustrated in letter No. 514 (probably 1526), addressed to an unknown person (possibly a student), which contains suggestions for a course of study. The political wisdom and the knowledge of human nature displayed by the ancient writers may well serve as a dessert after "the main course of the Word of the Lord" (Coena verbi dominici). They provide examples for the truth of the Gospel (Z VIII 677f.; see also "Huldrych Zwingli's Concept of History", above, ch. 6).

34. The standard work is still Johann Martin Usteri, "Initia Zwinglii, Beiträge zur Geschichte der Studien und der Geistesentwicklung Zwinglis in der Zeit vor Beginn der reformatorischen Thätigkeit", in *Theologische Studien und Kritiken*, 1885/4 and 1886/1.

35. Johann Martin Usteri, *Zwingli und Erasmus*, Zürich, 1885; Joachim Rogge, *Zwingli und Erasmus. Die Friedensgedanken des jungen Zwingli*, Stuttgart, 1962; Joachim Rogge, "Die Initia Zwinglis und Luthers, Eine Einführung in die Probleme", *Luther Jahrbuch*, Hamburg, 1963, pp. 107-133.

36. Cf. the whole thematic arrangement of the *Commentarius de vera et falsa religione*. The aloof, theoretical attitude of humanism and its self-confidence are throughout treated under "falsa religio". See in particular the Preface, written in the rhetorical form of a humanistic oration (addressed to Francis I of France, a Renaissance Prince), which states that the only help out of the corruption of the contemporary world and church is provided by the Gospel, which God has sent afresh in our day in a most wonderful manner (Z III 628-637, especially 633).

37. "For love of the pious, ordinary man in the Confederacy of our Fatherland drives me to take preventive action whenever anyone tries to dazzle us and to snatch the divine truth from us". (1526, to John Eck; Z V 178).

"There is no people on earth for whom Christian freedom is more fitting, than the praiseworthy Confederacy". (Z II 19).

38. "Which is Christ's church? That which listens to his word". (Z III 223).

"Therefore have no doubt or worry. Christ does not forsake his people, his church or his sheep; he will always instruct them, carry them through and make them victorious, even though all the power of hell should be against them. He certainly shows this in our own day, as he reveals his word so clearly and irresistibly". (Z III 223).

"Now the prophets should stand against all ungodliness and save God's people, or else the sheep that die will be required at their hand... But all flesh behaves in this way; as soon as

Word of the Bible, its exposition and its proclamation Christ is present[39] and demands obedience.[40] Bound up with this is the conviction that, as the Word of God rings out in the Reformation movement, the present moment must be recognised as an eschatalogical time of decision for the church, for the nations and for the individual.[41] The Reformer himself states his motives, more than once, in a varied yet harmonious formulation: the glory of God, the welfare of the Christian state, and the comfort of the troubled conscience.[42]

---

one touches its sore spot, it cries out: 'What has my dealing or my buying, my adultery or my drinking to do with the parson?' This is the way the demons often spoke out of those who were possessed: 'Jesus, what have we to do with you?' but what do you think—did he have power over them?'' (Z III 432).

"When the prophet trifles and chats sweetly, then all righteousness and public freedom perish''. (S VI, I 408). "What good is a shepherd who does nothing but keep watch, and does not fight when the wolf appears? To have no shepherd at all, and to have one who does not fight amount to the same thing''. (Z III 80).

"But if someone cries 'Ouch!', then surely the divine word has struck home; for nobody cries 'Ouch!' unless he has been hit''. (Z III 379).

"If the prophet should not speak the truth in the congregation, then one might just as well install a musician with his pipe or lute, then we would all listen gladly, and nobody would get angry''. (S VI, I 402).

"Fight like a proper soldier! Don't leave your place or your post!'' (from an unpublished manuscript, quoted in *Gott ist Meister, Zwingli—Worte, für unsere Zeit*, selected by Oskar Farner, Zwingli-Bücherei No. 8, Zürich, 1940, p. 15).

39. Cf. the Excursus at the end of this section.

40. Similarly in the *Archeteles* (Ch. 60): "Explorabimus omnia ad lapidem euangelicum et ad ignem Pauli. Ac ubi euangelio conformia deprehenderimus, servabimus; ubi difformia, foras mittemus; quiritentur licet ii quibus rei quiddam decedit; non audiemus hos stentores, ac Sirenes obturata aure praeteribimus, 'Deo etenim obedire oportet magis quam hominibus' [Act. 5, 29].'' (We will test everything by the touchstone of the Gospel and the fire of Paul. Where we find anything that is in conformity with the Gospel, we will preserve it; where we find something that does not conform to it, we will put it out. Those who lose something in this way may complain; we will not listen to those stentors, and we will pass by the sirens with our ears stopped. Because one must obey God rather than man. Z I 319).

41. "You see, Christ grants a greater favour to our century, for he reveals himself today more clearly than in countless centuries previously''. (Huic nostro saeculo vides Christum benignius favere, dum sese clarius aperit quam aliquot retro seculis. Z I 203). Similarly, "In our days, the divine righteousness reveals itself through the Word of God more than in many previous centuries...'' (Z II 474). "...Who could ignore the fact that the day of the Lord is here? Not the last day, on which the Lord will judge the whole world at once, but the day on which he puts the present to rights...'' (Z III 633 and 633-634 generally).

42. The *Commentarius de vera et falsa religione*, the first comprehensive statement of reformation theology, concludes with the words: "Nos enim quicquid diximus, in gloriam dei, ad utilitatem reipublicae Christianae conscientiarumque bonum diximus''. (For everything that has been said here, is said to the glory of God, the good of the Christian commonwealth and the blessing of consciences. Z III 911).

The reformer writes his *Divine Exhortation* (May 1522) "out of fear of God and out of love for an honourable Confederacy''. (Z I 167). "Now all our work in preaching the gospel at this time is to this end, that people should find the assurance of our salvation in the death of

Excursus

The most striking proof of how deeply Huldrych Zwingli himself was conscious of this motivation is to be found in the *Archeteles* of August, 1522, in which he gives an account of his activities to the Bishop of Constance, Hugo von Hohenlandenberg, a man of Humanistic sympathies in whom Zwingli placed a certain amount of confidence (cf. Z IV 60). In the Foreword he inserts a note on his own inner development (it might be expressed in modern terms as: from Roman Catholic via Humanist to Reformer). Of all Zwingli's autobiographical statements, this section (Z I 259-261) seems to me to give the deepest insight. Its significance has seldom been fully recognised; it is not mentioned by Walther Köhler, *Huldrych Zwingli* (1943), or by Oskar Farner, *Huldrych Zwingli,* Vol. II: *Seine Entwicklung zum Reformator* (1946), or by Arthur Rich: *Die Anfänge der Theologie Huldrych Zwingli* (1949).

It is to the credit of August Baur, *Zwinglis Theologie,* Vol. I (1885), that he quotes it extensively, and sometimes word for word (pp. 121-124). Unfortunately, Baur's translation is faulty, and overlooks important allusions to special Biblical texts. Even the editors of Z I did not notice, for example, that on p. 261 Zwingli is referring to Eph. 5:13 and Jn. 1:9, so that both the Christological and the autobiographical turning-point alike pass unnoticed. We shall attempt an improved translation (which is difficult!) but would refer the reader to the Latin text.

The account is announced in Z I 259 (the Reformer wishes that his opponents at the Court of Constance would consider "what I myself have *God himself* considered so long, *quae ipsi nobiscum reputavimus tam diu"*, "until the Spirit *(the pneu-* of God has assured them of what he has effected in us"). Then he begins *matological* with "Haec videlicet" and concludes (Z I 261:38) with "Viden quid me *presupposition)* coëgerit?" "Do you now understand what it is that compels me to reject the bloodless *paraenesis* of these people (i.e. at the episcopal court)?"

---

the living Son of God". (Z III 140). "God keep you, and be assured that we in Zürich will so regard and present God's Word that it will serve only for the glory of God and the healing of consciences". (Z III 143). "...All Christian hearts will openly confess that we undertake nothing but to uphold God's glory, to promote his Word and to improve our poor consciences; and that we do this, not by means of our mind, our reason or our strength, but by the clear, everlasting Word of God..." (Z III 155). "God will direct all your zeal to his own glory, to repentance and to the peace of your consciences. Don't worry. So long as you live in a Christian way and do not just chatter about Christianity, God will direct his Word so powerfully, with the increase of everything good, and the decrease of everything evil, that all the world shall see the salvation of the Lord (Ps. 98:3)". "Since I gave myself completely over to God's Word, I have directed all my teaching towards the goal of promoting the right and true glory of God and planting Christian living and peace". (Z III 465). "My whole meaning, earnestness and diligence have been directed towards the purpose of promoting the glory of God and building up many in Christ". (Z IV 708).

"It is a question of the following. We see how the human race worries and frets its whole life long about attaining salvation hereafter, not so much because we are by nature so conscientious, but rather as a consequence of the desire for a life, whose breath God the Creator breathed into us at the beginning of the creation of our race (Gen. 2:7). However, it is by no means obvious how this blessedness is to be found. For if one turns to the *philosophers*, there is so much controversy about salvation among them, that anyone would be vexed. If one turns to the *Christians,* one finds people among whom there is even more confusion and error than among the heathen: some strive to attain salvation by means of human traditions and the elements of this world (Gal. 4:3, 9; Col. 2:8, 20), that is, according to their own human ideas; others rely solely on the grace and promise of God; and both groups work their fingers to the bone in the attempt to gain recognition for their own view. Having come to this crossroads, which way should I turn? To men? If you reply: 'To men', then I reply: 'I will just give it a try. Does it mean those men who were once considered wise, at the time of the early church; or those who, shortly before our own time, displayed more folly than wisdom?' Then our opponent will break into a cold sweat and lapse into silence, just like the Jewish leaders when Christ asked them where John's baptism came from (Matt. 21:25ff.). If you press him yet further, he will admit that one should go to the Ancients (*ad veteres*), since he grants them a greater significance both because of their age and because of their holiness of life. But if you proceed still further: 'Even with the Ancients one can find all kinds of things that differ from the evangelical and apostolic Scriptures, or even contradict them; so which of the two should one accept?' Then, if he is not either a blockhead or a beast, he will answer: 'That which has come by inspiration of the Spirit of God'. For whatever springs from human wisdom can deceive us, even when it appears in brilliant splendour or adornment; but whatever proceeds from divine wisdom will never deceive. This is the mainspring of faith. Whoever does not possess this will vacillate, grow weary, and fall. And so, sir, while I was considering this tirelessly and from every side, and at the same time imploring God to show me some way out of my doubts, He spoke to me: 'You fool, why do you not remember', 'The truth of the Lord endures for ever' (Ps. 119:90; 100:5). You should hold on to this truth! And: 'Heaven and earth shall pass away, but my words shall not pass away' (Matt. 24:35). What is human is done away with, the divine remains unchangeable. And 'In vain do they honour me, teaching the doctrines and commandments of men' (Matth. 15:9); as though our advice were necessary, in order to obey God! So that what we devise, and

The soteriological question

Scholasticism

Fathers (Erasmian Humanism)

Holy Scripture

The Alternative

what appears to us at first glance to be beautiful, good, even holy, must gain his approval without further ado. As if it were not much more important that we should depend wholeheartedly upon him, and not upon that which pleases us, or which we contrive for ourselves, after the manner of lazy servants who deserve a good beating because they do what they will, and not what their Lord will!

So it came about that I finally set aside everything else, and I placed trust in nothing and in no word other than that which has come from the mouth of the Lord. And since wretched mortals, forgetting both themselves and God, dared to offer their own (inventions) as though from God, I began my own quest to see whether some yardstick (*ratio aliqua*) could be found, by which one might determine (punitively) whether the human or the divine has precedence (sc. in the statements of those who offer what is 'divine', but are, in fact, passing off their own inventions as divine); especially when I saw how not a few of them forcefully demanded that simple people should accept their inventions as divine, even when those inventions did not agree, or even contradicted one another. In the course of my search it (the text) came to my mind: Everything will become clear in the light (Eph. 5:13; which says literally, according to the original text: everything becomes clear, in that it will be punitively revealed by the light); that is, in that (light) which says 'I am the light of the world' (Jn. 8:12) and which also 'lightens every man who comes into this world' [Jn 1:9]. And again that word 'Do not believe every spirit, but prove the spirits, whether they are from God!' (I Jn. 4:1). And while I was searching for the (touch-)stone,[42a] I found no other than the stone of stumbling and the rock of offence (I Pet. 2:7f.) against which all stumble who, after the manner of the Pharisees, revoke God's law for the sake of their own tradition (Matt. 15:6).

Thus, after I had compared those assertions in this way (i.e. with Christ!), I began to examine every doctrine against this stone,[42b] and if I

The hermeneu- tic criterion

Jesus Christ (Reformation)

42a. Pliny, with whose works Zwingli was familiar, speaks of the "lapis" (Lydius), the flint or whetstone, as the touchstone, which was used in ancient and medieval chemistry and by goldsmiths to test the precious metal content of ores and alloys.

42b. "Cepi *omnem* doctrinam ad hunc lapidem explorare". (I began to test *every* doctrine by this stone—my italics). The section that follows is not a repetition of the previous one; "cepi" marks the beginning of an account of a further step in his development; from now on, Zwingli does not measure only the self-contradictory, arrogant doctrines which he has just mentioned, but *all* the doctrines that he encounters, against the touchstone of the reality of Christ.

The development here described is that which Zwingli dates at the end of 1516 (the Einsiedeln period) in various brief but concurring accounts. The memory of the "illumination" which he experienced always breaks through. Thus, in his work *Of the Clarity and Certainty of*

found that the stone gave out the same colour, or rather, that the doctrine could tolerate the clarity of the stone, then I accepted it; if not, then I rejected it. As time passed, I could tell from the first scratch whether there was some foreign additive or impurity in it; and no power or threat could ever again bring me to put the same faith in the human, however pompous it might appear, or however great a significance it might claim, as in the divine.

Now if those people gave orders that their own inventions must be ac- *The existential* cepted, even though they conformed in no way to the divine appoint- *Reformation* ments, but were rather contrary to them, then I barked at them the saying *action* of the Apostle, 'One must obey God rather than men!' (Acts 5:29), until those people who had the highest regard for their own thoughts, but little or no regard for what is of Christ, came to cherish the very worst opinion of us—which was for us, of course, the surest indication that this course of action is pleasing to God and will bring me to salvation. For 'Woe to you'; he says, 'when all men speak well of you' (Lk. 6:26) and 'You will be blessed (*eritis*) when men hate you, when they revile your name and despise you for the Son of Man's sake, and your names are written in heaven!' (Lk. 6:22; 10:20).

So if your opponents should accuse us before your Excellency, saying that I pay too little attention to human traditions, or even despise them, then you should know that it comes about because I have investigated closely the difference between them and the divine, and the way in which they contradict the divine. And that I shall not fear what man may do to me (Ps. 56:12; Vulgate 55:11). For if my name is hissed at, I am certain it

the Word of God (September 1522) he writes: "...I know for certain that God teaches me, for I have experienced it. But in order that you do not mistake my words, you must understand how I know that God teaches me. In my younger days I certainly acquired as much human teaching as many of my age, and when, some seven or eight years ago, I began to devote myself entirely to the Holy Scriptures, philosophy and theology of the squabblers always raised difficulties. But eventually I came to the point where, led by the Scriptures and the Word of God, I realised that I must lay all these things aside and learn the teaching of God directly from his own simple Word. Then I began to pray to God for his light, and the Scriptures began to become much clearer to me—although I did not read anything else—than if I had read many commentators and expositors. You see, this is a sure sign of God's leading, for I would never have reached this point by my own feeble mind". (Z I 379).

This conviction of having been guided by the living Christ himself in the reading and exposition of Holy Scripture is described in a pithy manner in the *Archeteles* (Ch. 22), at the end of the well-known account which Zwingli gives of his preaching activity in Zürich: "Ego, inquam, nullis captiosis fomentis, dolis vel hortamentis, sed simplicibus ac apud Helvetios natis verbis ad vulneris sui cognitionem quosvis traxi, id a Christo ipso doctus, qui praedicationem suam hinc orsus est". (I declare that I have led each one to see his wound, not with deceptive comforts, tricks or encouragements, but with good, simple Swiss-German words; and I have learnt this from Christ himself, who began his preaching at this point... Z I 285. Cf. Z I 266).

will be glorious with God. For God's name is never more gloriously hallowed, than when our name has the worst repute among men. And when the body falls, He must grant eternal life to the soul.

It is to this treasure (*thesaurus*), namely, the certainty of the Word of God, that we must direct our heart (Matt. 6:21) ..."

2. *The Reformation Decision*

The reformation decision consists, therefore, in turning away from idolatry to the true God.[43] It is this same worshipping of the creature which manifests itself in the religious life in the supreme importance attached to human authorities, doctrines and traditions,[44] especially in

---

43. "A man's god is that to which he turns for help, his only consolation and his treasure. Therefore the one God is the refuge of the faithful, and those for whom he is not a refuge are not believers; they may well be believers, but not in the true God. If their hopes rest on creatures, then they are idolators... When our comfort reaches out to anything other than God, we are idolators..." (Z IV 89). "It is certain that whoever turns to the creature is an idolator..." (Z II 222; cf. Z I 299; Z II 192; Z IV 76; Z IV 93; S II/I 204).

44. "Controversia est divinis obtemperare an oporteat an humanis. Hic inter saxum et sacrum statis; nam si dixeritis, humana cedere divinis debere, concidit corbona, conciderunt tituli; si humanis divina, incidistis in summam impietatem". (The dispute concerns whether one should obey divine laws rather than human ones. Here one is in a dilemma; for if you say that the human must give place to the divine, it is the end of your treasury and titles; but if the divine must yield to the human, then you have fallen into the worst godlessness. Z I 314).

"Cicaniam adpellant humanas constitutiones, adde scoriam, quisquilias, scobem, quicquid a mente Christi est alienum, quicquid ab hypocrisi, a cupiditate, a φιλαυτίᾳ profectum est". (They (i.e. Protestants) call human ordinances weeds; and in addition dross, refuse, sawdust, everything that is foreign to the mind of Christ, and everything that stems from hypocrisy, greed and egoism. Z I 272).

"Per vos deos deasque omnes oro, quandoquidem hoc contravertitur, humanis traditionibus quantum divinis deferri debeat necne, an non vobis aliquando in mentem venit hoc: 'omnis homo mendax'; et e diverso illud 'Deus verax est' Joan. 3 (33) Rom. 3 (4)..." (By all the gods and goddesses, I ask you: whenever it is debated, whether one ought to comply with human traditions as much as with divine ones, whether this text has ever occurred to you: "All men are liars", and conversely "God is true", Z I 274).

"Qui fieret, ut divina ab humanis autoritatem caperent?" (How could it be, that the divine should derive its authority from the human? Z I 294).

"We learn from Christ that God is the teacher of believing hearts...as he says in John 6 (v. 45): 'Every man that has heard and has learnt of the Father, comes to me'. Nobody comes to the Lord Jesus Christ unless he has learnt to know him from the Father. Listen how the schoolmaster is called: not doctors, not fathers, not pope, not cathedra, not council; he is called the Father of Jesus Christ". (Z I 366).

44, 45, 46. Zwingli wrote to the Toggenburgers, July 18th, 1524: "Was it not great blindness that we allowed ourselves to be persuaded that a man was our earthly god, and that entry into heaven or hell lay in his hands, and that what he thought should be believed by all men, even though it be contrary to the divine word? Was it not great blindness that God Almighty, who created us, has so often made known to us that he is our Father, and finally even gave his Son for us; and he himself stands there and calls us poor sinners, saying 'Come

sacramentalism[45] and justification by works;[46] and it manifests itself in social life in avarice, war and licentiousness.[47] The newly-proclaimed

---

to me, all who are weary and heavy laden and I will give you rest'. And we went and turned to the creature, and thought God to be so rough and cruel that we dare not come to him, and though we called him Father, we did not do so in the spirit of Christ; that is, we did not regard him as Father and we did not expect all grace from him; for we did not recognise the secret of his grace, in that he gave his Son for us; and we did not ascribe salvation to the grace of God, even though his only Son Jesus Christ, true God and man, has redeemed us by virtue of his suffering, which he bore for us. But we have inferred our righteousness, and therefore our salvation, from our own works, which were so besmirched, done for our own advantage, selfish and foolish. So we have been blind judges in our own affair, just like a man who, on the basis of his own judgment, regards himself as a good singer or a wise man. When the divine truth, Jesus Christ, speaks these two words together: 'You are my friends, if you do the things that I command you' and 'They honour me in vain, when they teach the doctrines and commandments of men' (John 15:14; Matt. 15:9), then is it not great blindness when we neglect everything that God has commanded, and accept everything that man has prescribed for us? God commands us to love one another as we love ourselves, and for the purpose of such an agreement he gave us the sacrament of his body and blood, in order that we should all be agreed therein, which would at least have protected us from the chief vices. Then the false gang of clergy came and turned the sacrament of agreement into a sacrifice, which they pretended to offer for us; and we were so blind that we believed them, so that we might keep our desires and our temptations and meanwhile attain salvation in our sleep, so to speak, as the monks and priests read mass. And even though he says it is vain we still want to be saved by trusting in the priests' vestments, singing, murmuring, even gluttony, whoring and greed, but not to touch the laws of God with even a finger". (Z VIII 207-208).

45. "The error, that the mass is a sacrifice, has comforted and planted all the vices; for all the robbers, usurers, traitors, killers and adulterers have thought that provided they had a mass held for their misdeed, everything would be all right. And it cannot be otherwise, than that they have sinned through counting on this..." (Z II 660).

"Fides ergo opus est, quod beat, non corpus corporaliter edere". (Therefore it is faith that saves, and not the physical eating of a body. (Z III 340).

"Therefore baptism must be an emphatic sign, which obliges us to live a new life, and thrusts us into Christ". (Z IV 245, on Romans 6).

45, 46. Zwingli writes in 1527, in his warning to Luther, who did not, in his opinion, make a sufficiently radical break with Rome: "Eo reciderunt quidam, ubi nuper erant, qui cerimoniis atque operibus fidebant". (For this cause certain people have fallen away, who recently placed their trust in ceremonies and works. Z V 614).

46. "Now when I really believe, and indeed know that so great a salvation is kept for me in Christ Jesus, then I am no longer oppressed by the first commandment: You shall love God with all your strength and heart and soul and mind; notwithstanding I know that I do not fulfil it; for Christ compensates for all my failings; and the commandment lifts me up into a holy amazement at the goodness of God, and says within me: See, God, the highest good, is so high and worthy and good that all our desires should yearn for him, and that is for our good. Besides that, the good news is always comforting: What you cannot do—what you really cannot do, Christ will do it all; he is all; he is the fore and aft". (Z II 39). For the "meritum Christi" as against the "opera meritoria" cf. Z II 174.

47. "I have gained all my enemies through fighting against robbery, war and violence" (Z V 62).

"...Paul calls covetousness idolatry (Col. 3:5), because those who are covetous have put their trust in money. Thus, whatever a man trusts in, that is his god". (Z II 219). Cf. also Z I 155-188; Z I 210-248; Z II 458-525; Z III 97-145; Z III 355-469.

"Word of God" or "Gospel" bears a spiritual character,[48] therefore, for it summons the human spirit to God's Word,[49] calling it away from human emotions to God's command.[50] It teaches that God Himself is our highest and only true comfort and possession: the *summum bonum*.[51] It is spiritual, because the living Christ himself is present in it.[52] Thus the offer of grace

48. "God reveals himself through his spirit, and nothing can be learned about him except by his spirit. He reveals himself essentially to every man who comes to him without reservation". (Z I 369).

"The word of God can certainly be understood by men without the instruction of men; not that it is the understanding of man, but rather that of the light and spirit of God, which so shines and breathes in his words, that in his light one sees the light of his meaning; as it states in Psalm 35 (Ps. 36:9): 'With thee, Lord, is the fountain of life, and in thy light do we see light'..." (Z I 365).

"By 'God's Word' you should understand only that which comes from the spirit of God". (Z I 382).

49. "Faith does not come from human reason, art or perception, but only from the spirit of God who illuminates and draws us". (Z IV 67).

"First of all, lay aside all your reasoning, which you would apply to Scripture on your own..." (Z I 376).

"If they had the love of God in them, they would believe no other word but his; for he is the light which lightens every man, who comes into this world (John 1:9); and philosophy is not such a light". (Z I 378, on John 5:41).

"God wants to be the only schoolmaster". (Z I 381).

50. "...Haec vera pax est, quae in deo habetur, non quae in suis adfectibus, qui non minus quam Euripus aestuant". (That is true peace, which one has with God; not that in your own feelings, for they are as stormy as the Euripus canal. Z I 278, on Isaiah 48:18).

"Where there is sin (that is, the breach that comes from Adam), there is also desire and temptation. Where there are fleshly temptations, one cannot fulfil the pure, clean, spiritual law, the will of God. These defects are not present in Christ; therefore only he, living in conformity to the will of God, can come and make satisfaction... This merciful redemption of God through his Son we call Gospel". (Z II 235).

51. "Hic est religionis nostrae fons, ut deum agnoscamus esse qui increatus creator rerum omnium est quique idem unus ac solus omnia habet, gratis donat. Hoc igitur primum fidei fundamentum evertunt quicunque creaturae tribuunt, quod solius creatoris est. Fatemur enim in symbolo, creatorem esse quo fidamus; non ergo creatura esse potest quo fidendum sit". (This is the fount of our religion: to acknowledge God, the uncreated creator of all things, who solely and alone possesses all things, and who gives all things freely. All who ascribe to the creature that which belongs only to the creator, are overturning the first fundamental of the faith. For we confess in the creed, that it is the creator, in whom we should trust. Therefore it cannot be a creature in whom one puts trust. S IV 47).

"Our faith, trust and confidence stand only in him, who is the true and highest good, the life, being and strength of all things, and we put our trust in no good other than him, who is the original good, so that nothing can be good, other than that which comes from him. All comfort from the creature falls to the ground here, for as soon as we trust in creatures, we mistrust God..." (Z VI, I 452).

52. "Scripturam capi volumus non literam occidentem (2 Cor. 3:6) sed spiritum vivificantem". (By 'Scripture' we are not to understand the letter which kills (2 Cor. 3:6) but the spirit who gives life. Z I 306).

"...You imagine that when one speaks of the 'gospel', one means the gospel writings. But it is not so; one means rather God's gracious act and message to the poor human race

and the grace that is offered coincide. "Gospel" or "Word of God" often simply denote the reformation movement.[53] When understood in this way, it naturally lays claim to the whole of life, including public life.[54] Zwingli did not "confuse" church and state, religion and politics, but neither did he consider for a moment that there could be any sphere of life that lay outside the influence of God's Word.[55] He always thinks theocratically, in terms of the medieval *corpus christianum*.[56] But the decision between "God or Creature" is always a personal one.[57] The Humanists had also

---

through his own Son. So Christ is the message, the messenger, the pledge of grace, the one who reconciles and who is reconciled. So to speak of believing the gospel means the same as believing in Christ, trusting Christ, resting on the mercy of Christ" (Z IV 68).

53. E.g. "See to it that God's Word is truly preached among you" (Z III 112). "When you see that it serves only for the honour of God and the salvation of souls, then promote it" (Z III 113). Cf. *Th. H. Z.* I, pp. 15-42; cf. also Z I 197; Z I 200; Z I 441; Z III 16; Z VI, I 35 Z VI, I 141; Z V 79.

54. Cf. the letter No. 720, May 4th 1528 to Ambrosius Blarer (a long treatise in Z IX 451-467; cf. also G. W. Locher, *Die evangelische Stellung der Reformatoren zum öffentlichen Leben*, Zürich, 1950; G. W. Locher, *Der Eigentumsbegriff als Problem evangelischer Theologie*, 2nd ed. Zürich, 1962, pp. 29-35, 49-53: "Zwingli, die politische Verantwortung der Christenheit und das Eigentumsproblem".

55. It is not often that the reformer emphasises the tangible moral renewal that is effected by the Word of God, but when necessary he does so most forcefully; cf. e.g. Z IX 462 and S IV 18; Z V 63. "In danger and sadness there is never anything that is more comforting than the Word of God, and, on the other hand, there is nothing more seductive than the word of greed; for this looks only to its own advantage and to that end lets everything else go by the board. But the Word of God looks to the common good, it makes one comforted and manly in God, it provides good counsel and in short, whatever is built on God's Word is undaunted, stands upon a rock, and no storm can harm it". (Z V 425; cf. Matt. 7:24-27).

56. "Nos huc solum properamus, ut probemus (sc. contra Lutheranos et catabaptistas, Z IX 462; Z IX 466) Christi regnum etiam esse externum; ...Vult ergo Christus etiam in externis modum teneri, eumque imperat; non est igitur eius regnum non etiam externum". (We are concerned only to prove (against the Lutherans and Anabaptists) that the kingdom of Christ is also external; ...it is Christ's will, therefore, that the measure should also apply in external things, and he appoints it; therefore his kingdom is by no means not external Z IX 454). Cf. also G. W. Locher, article "Theokratie", in *Evangelisches Kirchenlexikon*, Vol. III, 1959, columns 1351ff.

57. "Nunquam pax futura est his, qui Christi sunt, cum his qui carnis". (There will never be peace between those who belong to Christ and those who belong to the flesh. Z I 279,4).

"Atque, ut clarius dicam, non est sententia res aliqua, quae solo figmento humano constet, aut ambigua opinione; sed manifestum experimentum est, quo homo experitur intra se, quantam fiduciam habeat in ea, quae non videntur. Est ergo certa experientia, qua homo intra se infallibilem de deo, et ad deum, in quem speratur, sententiam fiduciamque sentit". (To speak more plainly, this decision is not something which rests solely on human imagination or on uncertain opinion; it is rather a manifest fact of experience, whereby a man proves inwardly how much faith he has in that which he does not see. It is therefore a sure experience, whereby a man feels within himself an infallible conviction concerning God and trust in him, the one in whom he sets his hope. Z IV 491, referring to Hebrews 11:1).

emphasised the spiritual nature of God. But Zwingli went beyond the Humanists, by recognising that man cannot of himself either conceive or attain "the comfort of the soul in God alone",[58] and that to overcome corruption requires not merely a principle of spirituality, but an act of redemption on the part of God himself.[59]

3. Gospel

God has himself undertaken this spiritual invasion into our world of sinful dependence upon ourselves and the creature. The decisive event is the atoning death of Christ Jesus on the cross—a fateful event both for the universe and for each individual. Objectively, it constitutes redemption; subjectively, it creates the possibility of our faith.[60] Therefore it is seen strictly in terms of the Anselmian doctrine of satisfaction, for when it is so understood, it comprises the very kernel of God's Word, often termed "the Gospel".

"The Gospel is the pledge and assurance of God's mercy: Christ Jesus. And it is therefore so called. Because of Adam's fall, the poor human race is so proud, selfish and arrogant (for it follows after its father) that there is no man conceived in sin, Psalm 50 (51:7) who does not bear this fault. From this it follows that whatever he conceives, does, or leaves undone, is directed towards his own advantage or honour; even, indeed, when he does serve God, he does not serve him out of love, but for personal gain or from tyrannical fear. So no service of God that man performs can count as right according to God's righteousness; for all our service is so stained that it is worthless before God. Whereas God is such a clean, pure, unstained, innocent, genuine good, free from all pride, selfishness, greed and such like, that nothing can abide with him that is not clean and pure in his way.

---

58. "The word of God should be held in the highest honour by us—by the word of God we understand only that which comes from the Spirit of God—and such a trust should not be accorded to any other word. For this word is certain and it cannot fail. It is clear, and will not allow us to wander in the darkness; it teaches its own truth, it reveals itself, and it shines upon the human soul with all salvation and grace; it leads the soul to find comfort in God; it humbles the soul, so that it loses itself, and even rejects itself, and takes hold of God; the soul lives in him, and strives after him; it despairs of all creaturely consolation, and finds its only comfort and confidence in God; without him the soul has no rest, for it rests only in him, Psalm 77: 'My soul did not want to be comforted, then I thought of God and was filled with joy'. Indeed, there is blessedness even at this time, though not in a present form, but in the assurance of a comfortable hope; may God increase this in us, and never let it fall away". Z I 382.

59. See the Excursus at the end of section 1. See also Zwingli's work *Of the Clarity and Certainty of the Word of God* (e.g. Z I 379).

60. *Th. H. Z.* I, pp. 140-152.

Since man, in all that he undertakes, does, or leaves undone, stains all his works with the vices which we have mentioned, it follows that, whatever he does, he cannot come to God. And the more vehemently a man denies such faithlessness and roguery, the greater hypocrite and rogue he is; for Adam's nature does not fail—we all possess it ... God saw our weakness and took such deep pity on it, that he wished to redeem us with his only-begotten Son, that our hope in God should not waver or weaken. For if he had given us any other pledge of his grace than his only Son, we might have been in doubt about it, but not about his Son. Since he has given him for us, there is no sinner so great, that he need despair of God, when he sees that he has given his Son for us. This is the reason why God wanted to bring us to himself by his son, as is taught in II Thess. 2 (v. 13-17) ... for the one who is to be a sacrifice for our sins must be free from all reproach of sin. So, after he had lived long enough in this world to provide us with an example of how we should live, he was given over to a violent death by the members and children of the devil, the innocent one was killed and offered up for us sinners; and by this sacrifice the righteousness of the heavenly father was satisfied, paid and reconciled for all eternity for the sins of all believers. For as all men are created through him, so are all redeemed through him; for as all men can be created only through him, so they can be restored and saved through none except him.

This is, in brief, the sum of the Gospel, namely: that God has given us a Saviour to pay for our sins, even his only-begotten Son''.[61]

In contrast to the Anselmian tradition, Zwingli makes the new suggestion that not only God's righteousness but also his mercy postulates the need for satisfaction: a forgiveness that consisted merely of a remission of the punishment would be at best an arbitrary act of kindness, and not the complete divine grace which carries assurance with it.[62] And to complete the picture, it must again be emphasised that neither angel nor man nor any other creature could reunite human kind to God for all eternity; only the eternal Son of God could do that.[63]

4. *Faith*

Since Christ gave up life for us, he has thereby bought our life, and possesses the right of life and death over us. Zwingli uses a military expres-

61. Z IV 64-66.
62. Especially in the *Fidei Expositio* of 1531, S IV 47-48; cf. *Th. H. Z.* I, pp. 147f. In the Paris MS of the *Fidei Expositio*, which comes from Zwingli's own hand, I found (in connexion with the statements about God's goodness, S IV 54) the terse marginal comment "Bonitas continet iustitiam et misericordiam". (Goodness includes justice and mercy).
63. Z II 38-40; S IV 47f.

sion: he is our "Captain", and we are his "soldiers", mercenaries sworn in allegiance to him.[64] In the late Middle Ages there existed a relationship of solid trust between a captain and his troop. In wartime the captain had an almost total authority, so that every man was dependent upon his care and placed at his disposal. This is the model for the Christian's faith. The acceptance of reconciliation with God will in faith evidence itself as trust in his control of our everyday life. It has always been remarked how strongly Zwingli emphasises providence, and it has been possible to see in this some connexion with Renaissance philosophy.[65] For the reformer himself, this belief in providence does not compete with faith in Christ, but rather constitutes the consequence and proof of that faith. This is shown by the fact that, whether he cites extra biblical evidence or not, he usually rests his argument on dominical sayings such as Matt. 6:25ff and Matt. 10:28ff or on Romans 8:32.[66] Zwingli likes to appeal to the fact that certain pious heathen, such as Socrates and Seneca, when they had advanced towards monotheism, had, by the illumination of God's Spirit, gained a profound insight into the concept of providence.[67] But with the classical philosophers, as well as the medieval theologians who were under their influence, and also the humanists, the principle of free will precluded a true grasp of divine providence.[68] To comprehend the basis and nature of divine providence it really requires the decision of evangelical faith, which means more than making a theoretical correction; it means surrendering pride in one's supposed free will and bitterly renouncing the merit of personal action. "Faith is nothing else than the certain assurance with which man relies on the merit of Christ ... that man himself contributes nothing, but believes that all things are directed and ordered by God's providence, and this comes only from giving himself to God and trusting in him completely; that he understands in faith that God does everything, even though we cannot perceive it".[69]

---

64. Cf. "Christ our Captain" (above, ch. 4).

65. Cf. Christoph Sigwart, *Ulrich Zwingli, Der Charakter seiner Theologie mit besonderer Rücksicht auf Picus von Mirandola dargestellt*, Stuttgart/Hamburg, 1855. Against this background, Zwingli's expanded Marburg sermon appears to be an ambitious attempt at a reformational confrontation with the spirit of the age. Cf. *Sermonis de providentia dei Anamnema*, S IV 79-144; cf. also Siegfried Rother, *Die religiösen und geistigen Grundlagen der Politik Huldrych Zwinglis*, Erlangen, 1956, pp. 139-148.

66. E.g. Z III 649-653 (in the *Commentarius*).

67. Rudolf Pfister, *Die Seligkeit erwählter Heiden bei Zwingli*, Zollikon, 1952.

68. "Human wisdom concerning the freedom of the will, which we have imbibed from the heathen, has led us to the point where we ascribe to our own deed and counsel the work which God works in us, and we do not recognise the almighty providence of God". Z II 180.

69. Z II 182.

Thus providence cannot be separated from God's omnipotence, but for this very reason, our awareness that we are God's instrument is not something that can be taken for granted. "As it is God's nature to order and direct all things, the believer recognises that he is an instrument and implement through which God works, and he does not ascribe anything to himself, but knows that he himself and all that he does are God's. Yet what your words are really saying is that you are an idle, unfruitful tree, as you do nothing. And if you do something, it is clear that you ascribe it to yourself. Therefore your work—as you call it—is your condemnation, since you ascribe to yourself what belongs to God".[70]

Thus, in Zwingli's concept of faith, humility and the will to act are bound together.[71] Both spring from trust. No other reformer emphasised so strongly that the genuineness of our faith in Christ's atonement will prove itself as trust in God in the course of daily life. "It is not possible, that he who has given his own son for us, will ever refuse us, or that he has not opened up to us the fulfilment of all our needs in him. As Paul says in Romans 8: If God is for us, who can be against us? As he has not spared his own son, but gave him up for us all, will he not give us all things with him? This is Paul's belief: God is on our side and he stands by us; therefore nobody can harm us. But in order that we should be certain how kind and merciful he is towards us, and that we should be assured that he will refuse us nothing, he has not even spared his own son for our sake, and has given him up for us. So how could he refuse us anything? For he has nothing greater nor dearer nor worthier than his own son. So why should he deny us anything? For whatever he should give us must be less than his own son. Therefore, since he has given him for us, we should come to him with all our needs; for he will never again deny us".[72]

---

70. Z II 181. The passage continues: "And although God works through you, God's work has its own end and order, and if you should ascribe it to yourself, then through your arrogance you would be untrue to the work of God, and would be condemned". (Z II 181; the same thought is repeated in Z II 186).

71. "Indeed, there is nothing so small with regard to us or in all creation, that it is not ordained and sent from the omniscient and omnipotent providence of God. So how much more do all our works come about by the ordination of God. Z II 179, with reference to Matthew 10:28-31 ("Fear not; you are of far more value than many sparrows").

72. Z II 193 (from the exposition of the Twentieth Article). The letter to Memmingen in 1530 (Z XI 185-188) and the two letters to Esslingen in 1526 (Z V 272ff. and 416ff.) provide impressive examples of words of encouragement, spoken in a time of grave danger, and which spring from this attitude of faith; for an example of comfort tendered to a person who is seriously ill, see the letters to Michael Cellarius and to Johannes Wanner, both written in 1526 (Z VIII 715f. and Z VIII 768ff. respectively).

5. *God*

Clearly, it is the concept of God that lies behind all this. God is "the highest good", the *summum bonum*.[73] Scholasticism had also described God in these terms, and the adoption of this description has had far-reaching consequences for the relationship of theology to philosophy, and, therefore, for the whole history of culture. But as far as Zwingli is concerned, certain important facts should be borne in mind. Firstly, the neutral character of this expression, which to our mind verges on an abstract idea, or even pantheism, was not seen in this way in the sixteenth century, and Zwingli is completely bound by biblical theism. His God is a personal God who judges, reconciles and acts in history.[74] Secondly, when Zwingli speaks of the "highest good", he is saying, like the Scholastics,

---

73. For what follows, cf. *Th. H. Z.* I, pp. 43-98.

74. Cf. *Th. H. Z.* I, pp. 46ff., 65, 72. The later Zwingli was conscious of a tension between the Biblical concept of God and the use of the Greek concept of οὐσία, which has been linked with Exodus 3:14 from the Early Fathers onwards. Zwingli does, in fact, follow the orthodox tradition in linking his own arguments to "Ego sum qui sum", but then he detects from the words that follow ("I am has sent me to you") that the second "sum" in the first sentence does not denote a static being, but rather an active, communicating, self-authenticating being; he translates אהיה by "Existo", and uses this word as a proper noun: "Mosi percontanti nomenclaturam dei, responsum est coelitus: Ego sum qui sum. Et addidit numen: Sic dices filiis Israel, *existo* misit me ad vos. Quae verba sic intelligi debent, ut in *ego sum qui sum* posterius *sum* κατ' ἔμφασιν intendatur...Habet igitur secundum *sum* hanc emphasin: Qui *vere* sum; aut: Qui sum ipsum *esse* rerum omnium; quomodo patres numine adflati ante nos olim expediverunt. Quamvis hoc ipsum id quoque ostendat, quod se mox velut *Existonem* adpellat, ut qui non modo ipse existat, verum etiam universis quae existunt existentiam suppeditet. Nam si quicquam suis viribus existeret: iam deus nihil plus dixisset, quam siquis se legatum esse affirmaret alicuius qui existeret. *Existonem* igitur sese vocat hac ratione, quod et per se ipsum existit ex aliis ut sint atque existant sese fundamentum ac solum suppedidat, ut iam nihil aut sit aut existat quod non ex illo et in illo et sit et existat. Abhorreremus plane a figmento inusitatae vocis, nisi videremus plus dicere eum qui *Existonem* deum vocat, quam qui existentem; et nisi ad Hebraicae vocis אהיה ingenium propius accederet". (When Moses desired to know the name of God, the answer came from heaven: 'I am who I am'; and God added: 'Thus shall you say to the children of Israel, I am (existo) has sent me to you'. These words are to be understood as follows, namely, that the words 'I am who I am' point emphatically to the 'I am' which follows. Therefore the second 'I am' has this emphasis: 'I who truly am' or 'I who am the being of all things'. This is how the Church Fathers, inspired by the Spirit of God, have interpreted these words in times past. Though the fact that God at once speaks of himself as 'Existo' indicates that he not only exists in himself, but that he imparts existence to everything that exists. For if anything existed by its own powers, then God would have said nothing more than if a person were to affirm that he was the envoy of someone who existed. Therefore, God calls himself 'Existo' in the sense that he exists of himself and that he also gives himself to other things, as their basis and foundation, in order that they may exist; so that nothing is or exists which does not have its being and existence from him and in him. We should certainly avoid coining this unusual expression, if we did not believe that to call God 'Existo' is to say more than that he exists, and if it were not closer to the Hebrew term אהיה S IV 91).

that for man God is greater and more important than all that the world can offer, and that fellowship with him means salvation.[75] But Zwingli goes beyond Scholasticism, in that the *summum bonum* does not merely constitute an enhancement of what we know as good in other ways, but rather indicates a totally new category, quite beyond our own judgment, which teaches us for the first time what "good" really is.[76] God alone is by nature essentially good.[77] Everything that can be called good in the realm of creation has been given this property "through participation, or, rather, by bestowal" (*participatione, aut potius precario*) and must be measured against God's revealed goodness.[78] At the beginning of his work *De Providentia*, the reformation dialectic of Zwingli changes the Scholastic concepts quite drastically, as if to exclude from the very beginning any interpretation along the lines of a "natural theology". God is received as the personal giver of all goodness, the course of all good, the *fons omnis bonitatis.*[79]

The same way of thinking can already be seen in regard to the concept of being, which in Scholastic logic naturally takes precedence over the "good", whereas in Zwingli's thought the two concepts are interwoven in a typical manner. There exists nothing that does not have its being from God as the first good gift of the Creator.[80] Having been created by God, all being is good.[81] But God alone exists of himself; he is the one true being,

---

75. "For who could regard God as the gracious, undeceiving and highest good, and yet not love him? Especially since he has so dearly assured us of his grace through his son Jesus Christ". Z III 44.

76. "Nam quicquid imperfectum est, deus non est. Et contra: Hoc solum deus est, quod perfectum est, id est absolutum et cui nihil desit, cuique omnia adsint, quae summum bonum deceant. Non enim de perfecto hic loquimur, ut vulgo theologi". (Whatever is imperfect is not God. And conversely, only that is God which is perfect, that is, which is complete and lacks nothing, possessing everything that belongs to the highest good. For we do not speak here of being perfect in the sense that theologians generally do so. Z III 647).

77. "'...Sicut enim solum est, et seipso est, ita et solum ... se ipso bonum est, verum, rectum etc...'" (For as he alone has being, and that of himself, so is he alone of himself good, true, right etc... Z III 645).

78. S IV 81.

79. "Omnium bonorum fons et scaturigo". Z III 645. In Z I 313, God is described as the ground and source of all good. ("ratio atque origo").

80. "Esto ergo solus deus, qui seipso est, quique omnibus esse tribuit atque ita tribuit, ut esse nulla ratione, nulloque momento possent, nisi deus esset, qui omnibus tum esse tum vita est, omnia sustinet, omnia regit". (Therefore, it must be God alone who exists of himself, and who imparts being to all things, and does so in such a manner that they could not exist in any way, or for one moment, if God did not exist, who is being and life to all things, who sustains all things and who directs all things. Z III 645).

81. Z III 645 (see note 77). The passage continues, in lines 19-22: "Si nunc omnia, quae fecit, vehementer bona sunt etiam se iudice, et nihilominus nemo bonus est nisi solus deus sequitur, quod omnia, quae sunt, in ipso et per ipsem sunt". (If everything which God made

for he exists by his own power; the concept of aseity is fundamental to Zwingli's concept of God.[82] Again, we note that he does not recognise any all-embracing concept, no *essentia* which comprehends both creator and creative alike; instead, like Thomas Aquinas, he sees the relationship of creator and creative in their dissimilarity, and their dissimilarity in their relationship.[83] This is an important piece of evidence for the influence that the *via antiqua* exercised upon the reformer. But he emphasises with every word that this relationship is established by the creator, and that it remains dependent upon him.[84]

The result is that the aseity of God is united with his biblical Lordship,[85] and must serve as a basis for it, while the conceptions of God as the highest good and as pure being flow into the biblical concept of the Father.[86] Starting from this point, providence (*providentia, prudentia*) is then described as the immediate, comprehensive activity of the living God, for *providentia* is identical with *moderatio, gubernatio, ordinatio* and also *praedestinatio*.[87] To deny providence is to limit the deity of God; thus it

---

was exceedingly good even in his judgment, and yet nobody is good except God alone, it follows that everything that exists exists in him and through him).

82. "Cum Moses a domino peteret Exo 3, ut ei nomen suum manifestaret, quo dexterius agere videretur cum filiis Israel, dixit dominus ad eum: 'Ego sum, qui sum'. Quo verbo se deus totum exhibuit; perinde enim est, ac si dixisset: Ego is sum, qui meipso sum, qui meopte Marte sum, qui esse ipsum sum, qui ipsemet sum". (When Moses asked the Lord, in Exodus 3, to reveal his name to him, in order that he might deal more readily with the children of Israel, God said to him, 'I am who I am'. God revealed himself fully by this word; for it is as if he had said, 'I am he who exists of himself; I exist by my own power; I am being itself; I am my own being'. Z III 643. Cf. Z III 644).

83. See the quotations in notes 78 and 82. In the passage quoted in note 74 there is a definite rejection of the interpretation "quam siquis se legatum esse affirmaret alicuius qui existeret". (than if a person were to affirm that he was the envoy of someone who existed. S IV 91).

84. "Ex quo ... facile inducimur, ut liquido videamus omnia a deo, quaecunque tandem, quae videmus, non a seipsis esse posse, sed ab alio, ex illo essendi fonte et vena, deo videlicet esse et constare". (Thus we are readily led to see clearly that everything is from God; that ultimately everything that is visible cannot have its being of itself, but rather has its being and its existence from another, the source and root of being, namely God. Z III 644).

85. Z III 644, combining Exodus 3:14 ("I am") and 3:16 ("The Lord God of your fathers").

86. See, for example, the exposition of the First Article in the first sermon at Bern, Z VI, I 451-456; cf. *Th. H. Z.* I, pp. 75f.

87. "Ergo verissimum hoc erit, quod etiam temere, ut nobis videtur, contingentium autor deus sit". (Therefore it is most true that God is the author even of those events which seem chance to us. Z III 650).

"Nascitur autem praedestinatio, quae nihil aliud est, quam si tu dicas praeordinatio, ex providentia, imo est ipsa providentia". (Moreover, predestination, which is nothing other than foreordination, proceeds from providence, and is indeed itself providence. Z III 843).

Cf. Z II 539; Z III 649f.; Z IX 30-31.

turns God into an idol, and is therefore a denial of God.[88] The traditional attributes of God (wisdom, all-sufficiency, omnipotence, omniscience, etc.) are then derived from this conception of providence,[89] and here we find a certain determinism, which indicates the influence of Thomism. Zwingli's emphasis on the simplicity (*simplicitas*) of God[90] may be directed against Luther's Occamistic distinction between the "hidden God" and the "revealed God" (*Deus absconditus, Deus revelatus*). God is always undivided. In his revelation he offers himself to us in his entirety.[91] The same is true of the distinction which Zwingli makes between God's justice and God's mercy (*iustitia, misericordia*),[92] which is not to be confused with the Lutheran antithesis.[93] Because for Zwingli, they both find their being and their truth only in their mutual relationship and in their ultimate unity: both emanate from the goodness (*bonitas*) of God, and are subordinate to it.[94] Thus grace retains its supreme position, "...for his mercies surpass all his other works" (*misericordiae eius omnia opera eius superant*) says Zwingli, quoting Psalm 145:9.[95] Thus, in Zwingli's doctrine of God, all the more or less static concepts of Classical Stoicism or medieval Scholasticism are

---

The term "providentia" expresses the idea that God, as the "summum bonum" denotes an overflowing goodness. "Breviter: hoc bonum illud ab aliis, quae videntur bona distat, quod haec se ἀμισθωτί, id est: gratuito, non expendunt, utpote sordida et egena; illud contra nisi gratuito impendi nec velit nec possit; ... infinitum enim est, ac distrahi amat". (In short, this 'good' is distinguished from others, which are regarded as 'good', in that they do not give themselves freely, base and deficient as they are; whereas this good will not and cannot do other than give itself freely ... for it is infinite and loves to bestow itself. Z III 650).

88. Z III 647; Z IX 30-31; S IV 98, 143.

89. Z VI, I 453f.; S IV 82.

90. E.g. Z II 158; S IV 114; cf. *Th. H. Z.* I, p. 64.

91. "Qui enim sese nobis dat, quid reliquum fecit quod non dederit?" (For if someone gives himself to us, what would remain that he would not have given to us? S IV 47, 48).

92. "... Numen enim paterno adfectu erga nos tangi, quoniam non minus mite et mansuetum sit atque iustum et sanctum; et in huius rei testimonium natum suum unicum hominibus dediderit, ut sciant sibi apud se omnia esse speranda. Quae plane est rei Christianae summa". (For God is moved by a feeling of fatherhood towards us; for he is as mild and gentle as he is just and holy. As proof of this he caused his only son to be born and given to men, in order that they may know that they may hope for all things from him. This is assuredly the very essence of the Christian faith. S VI, I 5). Cf. Z XIV 422; *Th. H. Z.* I, pp. 97f.

93. "Debent ergo iustitia et misericordia dei simul iungi et permisceri in corde credentium". (Therefore the righteousness and the mercy of God should unite and mingle together in the heart of believers. S VI, I 531). Such a statement is totally different from Lutheran formulations. Cf. *Th. H. Z.* I, p. 96.

94. "Hac enim ratione bonitas illius ex omni parte manifestata est. Ista enim quum in se misericordiam et iustitiam contineat ..." (For thus his goodness is revealed on all sides. For it encompasses both mercy and righteousness. S IV 5, 47; cf. note 62).

95. E.g. Z III 676-677.

made to serve the Biblical, historical way of thinking; everything is directed towards the fact that God is our God, "Deus noster".[96]

6. The Trinity

Close study reveals that, for Zwingli, the early church doctrine of the Trinity stands within this soteriological context. Therefore he does not simply take over a traditional dogma without further thought, but rather gives us a vital reinterpretation of it.[97] For in Zwingli's view, the doctrine of one God in three Persons serves to maintain and describe the divinity of God in his historical activity. This emphasis on divinity must inevitably elevate the notion of the unity of the Trinity to the level of dogmatic statement, and thus Zwingli is more clearly aligned with the western, Augustinian tradition of the "economic" Trinity than is Luther, who stresses revelation and incarnation and thereby gives greater prominence to the distinction between the three persons of the Godhead. Even though Zwingli treats the doctrine only briefly, he clearly gives his own particular emphasis to the official formulae. Thus the introduction to the *Fidei Ratio* consciously echoes the Nicene-Constantinople formula, and yet varies it in a characteristic manner: "I believe and know there is one only God. He is by nature good, true, mighty, just and wise. He is the creator and sustainer of all things visible and invisible. There are the Father, Son and Holy Spirit, three persons, but they have one simple being. And, in general, in accord with the exposition of the Nicene and Athanasian creeds ..."[98]

---

96. Following an extended discussion of the concept of God, in relation to Mark 12:29 ("The Lord thy God is one Lord"), he states: "Sed praecipue noster factus est per Christum, aut declaravit se nostrum esse hoc pretioso pignore". (But chiefly he has become ours through Christ; or rather, he has declared that he is ours by this precious pledge. S VI, I 530). Cf. *Th. H. Z.* I, p. 98.

97. Cf. *Th. H. Z.* I, pp. 99-133. For this whole question, see Jan Koopmans, *Das altkirchliche Dogma in der Reformation*, Munich, 1955.

98. "Credo et scio unum ac solum esse deum, eumque esse natura bonum, verum, potentem, iustum, sapientem, creatorem et curatorem rerum omnium visibilium atque invisibilium; esse patrem, filium et spiritum sanctum, personas quidem tres, sed essentiam horum unam ac simplicem. Et omnino iuxta expositionem symboli tam Niceni quam Athanasiani ..." Zwingli continues: "... per singula de numine ipso deque nominibus sive personis tribus sentio". (So I think of God's being itself in the singular, and of three names or persons. S IV 3). Like the other reformers, and Augustine also, Zwingli was fairly free in his terminology; the important thing is to keep to the right sense, even if the way in which it is expressed may sound heretical. (Cf. the marginal comment on Cyril of Alexandria made by the young Zwingli, Z XII 230. See also J. M. Usteri, in *Theologische Studien und Kritiken*, 1886, pp. 97f. For "essentia" or "deitas" Zwingli likes to use the term "numen", thus strengthening the biblical and personal aspect of the Godhead. He renders the controverted term "personae" by "nomina" (sc. dei). There is an unmistakable tendency to

7. *Christology*

Within the doctrine of the Trinity, it is the connexion with Christology that is of importance to the reformer.[99] He holds firmly to the "vere deus, vere homo" formula of the early church. What this means, namely, that Jesus is the Christ (i.e. the Son of God), can be described only in terms of the Trinity and of soteriology.[100] It was only the eternal Son (not the Father, nor the Spirit) who "per assumptionem carnis" took human nature and united it with his deity in the "hypostatic or personal union".[101] On this point, Luther and Zwingli are in agreement. But Zwingli emphasises that in this "assumptio" the divine nature is active whereas the human nature (as a creature) is passive, and the divine nature enters into the human, but is not absorbed by it. For Luther, the deity and manhood of Christ coincide, virtually to the point of identity. In the reformation debate, this meant that whereas Luther emphasised the humanity, Zwingli put the divinity in the forefront. Luther stresses the *revelation* of God, Zwingli, the revelation of *God*. Here, to my mind, lies *the* difference between the reformations in Wittenberg and Zurich. It was only a question of different emphases within a common, fundamental Christological doctrine, but it had far-reaching consequences: here lie the roots of all the discussions about the sacraments, the Lord's Supper, baptism and confession, about the Word and the Spirit, about the Church, the State, about "authority" and the right of resistance, and about the relationship of faith and politics in general.[102] But, on the other hand, we would dare to speculate[103] that this difference need not have led to division between the

---

modalism—as there is with Calvin, and also with Karl Barth (who even speaks of "modes of being"). Zwingli ventures further than Calvin into the scholastic ideas of "notions" and "appropriations". He suggests that the use of the concept of "alloiosis" (taken over from Plutarch) renders it possible to make statements concerning the individual persons while maintaining the unity of the Godhead. Cf. *Th. H. Z.* I, pp. 127, 128ff., 130f.

99. Further details and documentation will be provided in *Th. H. Z.*, Vol. II.

100. "Dei cognitio natura sua Christi cognitionem antecedit". (The knowledge of God naturally precedes the knowledge of Christ. Z III 675). In its context, this statement has to be understood in a strictly trinitarian sense. Contrary to a common misinterpretation of these words, which has remained widespread to this day, they do not teach the idea of a natural theology having priority over Christology. Cf. *Th. H. Z.* I, p. 55, note 14.

101. S IV 3-4.

102. This difference in emphasis had far-reaching consequences, extending to music and liturgy on the one hand, and social ethics on the other. See G. W. Locher, *Die evangelische Stellung der Reformatoren zum öffentlichen Leben*, Zürich, 1950.

103. We say this with some reserve, for we are well aware that in historical science the question "What would have happened if ...?" is permissible only for the purposes of elucidating what did actually happen.

churches if only Wittenberg had recognised in time that the Zurichers should not be regarded as enthusiasts or as chiliastic anarchists, but rather as fervent preachers of the self-same reformation testimony to Christ—albeit with their own characteristic theological emphasis; and that they really stood much nearer to one another than appeared to be the case after earlier unfortunate events.[104] Never is an argument more violent and more damaging than when it occurs at the wrong point. Had the debate been about Christology from the very beginning, then their closeness would have been presupposed without question, and the controversy over the Lord's Supper would not have gained such fateful significance.[105]

Because Zwingli's Christology started out from this point, it lent a "Nestorian" colouring to the relationship of the two natures.[106] These remain quite distinct (if polemically stated, "separate"), and are only joined together in the "person" of Christ, and this is identical with his divinity.[107] This identity in the concept of Christ's person means that Zwingli's Christology fits effortlessly into the doctrine of the Trinity, thus lending great force to this doctrine. It is true that Zwingli develops the details of the gospel tradition of Jesus' earthly life more thoroughly than any other reformer.[108] But this is due to the fact that not only Jesus' healing miracles, but also his teaching and the authority of his words are associated with his divinity.[109] In order to render satisfaction, the eternal Son of God had to take human nature.[110] It had to be truly *our* nature, for

---

104. E.g., the role of Karlstadt; Bucer's edition of Luther's *Postille*, which offended Luther (cf. Z V 571, note 2; 975, notes 6 and 16); Luther's illness, etc.

105. When it was recognised on both sides, at Marburg in 1529, that the real controversy lay in the realm of Christology, it was too late, partly because of the questions of prestige which had meanwhile become associated with the debate.

106. The reproach of "haeresis Nestorii" had already been raised by John Eck.

107. "... id autem hoc modo, ut totus ille homo in unitatem hypostaeos sive personae, filii dei, sic sit adsumptus, ut peculiarem personam homo non constituerit, sed adsumptus sit ad filii dei personam ..." (...but in such a way that he is taken, in his total manhood, into the unity of the hypostasis or person of the Son of God, so that as man he does not constitute a distinct person, but is taken into the person of the Son of God... S IV 3; S IV 48).

108. In the section "De religione christiana" in the *Commentarius de vera et falsa religione*, Z III 681-691; H IX 87-102.

109. "Dei se filium testatus est cum docendo tum inaudita miracula faciendo". (He has shown himself to be the Son of God both by his teaching and by his remarkable miracles. Z III 689; Z III 141).

110. "Carnis ergo indutus paludamento summi regis filius prodit, ut hostia factus (nam pro divina mori natura non potest) inconcussam iustitiam placet ac reconciliet his, qui suapte innocentia sub intuitum numinis propter scelerum conscientiam venire non audebant". (The Son of the most high King came clothed in human flesh in order to be the sacrificial lamb (for he cannot die according to his divine nature) and thus to render satisfaction to God's inviolate righteousness, so reconciling him to those who, being conscious of

otherwise he could not really have come to us, he could not be *our* redeemer.[111] But it had to be a *pure* human nature, untainted by original sin, for otherwise he could not be our *redeemer*.[112] It was, without any doubt, to safeguard this teaching that Zwingli so firmly maintained the mariological doctrine of the "semper virgo".[113] But the saving power of the human nature of Jesus Christ does not lie in itself, but in the fact that it is the organ of his deity.[114] With regard to the human nature of Jesus, there is a definite subordinationism. "Christ Jesus is our Saviour"—that simply means that "Only God can save"; for, Christologically speaking: He could suffer only in his human nature, but only through his divine nature could this suffering bring about eternal salvation. The "pro *nobis*" is firmly anchored in his humanity, but the "*pro* nobis" springs from his divinity.[115]

their own sins, could never dare to come into the presence of God trusting in their own righteousness. S IV 47; Z III 124).

111. "Jesus Christ our Redeemer came in a manner so humble, kind and lowly, so that we should see that he is ours, and is our friend. For if he had done nothing other than take our nature, that would be friendship enough; but over and above that, he died a most shameful death. And all this was to the end that we should learn to suffer and to bear poverty for his sake. If you are sick, he has been sick also; if your head aches, a crown of thorns has pierced his head; if you are hated, so was he; if you are betrayed, so was he. See and perceive in particular and in general how Christ the Son of God is like you because of sin, for it is a disease. So if a person sees Christ in this way, then Christ brings healing and comfort to him, and the path of suffering in this world becomes light and insignificant". (With reference to Matthew 17:22, quoted in *Gott ist Meister*, ed. O. Farner, Zürich, 1940, p. 45).

112. "Huic ergo tam desertae causae nostrae tandem volens succurrere creator noster misit, qui suae iusticiae sese pro nobis litando satisfaceret, non angelum, non hominem, sed filium suum, eumque carne indutum, ne aut maiestas a congressu deterreret, aut humilitas a spe deiiceret. Quod enim deus deique filius est is, qui sequester ac mediator missus est, spem fulcit. Quid enim non potest aut habet, qui deus est? Quod autem homo, familiaritatem, amiciciam, imo necessitudinem et communitatem promittit; quid enim negare potest, qui frater est, qui imbecillitatis consors?" (When at last our creator wished to help us in our lost state, then he sent the one who could render satisfaction to his justice, by offering himself as a sacrifice for us; not an angel, nor a man, but his son, clothed in human flesh, so that his majesty should not deter anyone from coming to him, and his lowliness should not deprive anyone of hope. For the fact that the one who was sent to be our representative and mediator is God, the Son of God, strengthens our hope. For what is there that he cannot do or have, since he is God? And since he is man, this assures us of his brotherhood, his friendship, and, indeed, his solidarity and fellowship with us; for what could he deny us, when he is our brother, and shares our weakness? Z III 681).

113. Z III 686. See Z I 391-428 and also "The Content and the Design of Zwingli's Teaching about Mary" (above, ch. 5).

114. "He has redeemed us by his death, by reason of the fact that he who died was God; and redemption belongs to the deity; but the suffering of death must be born by the humanity alone". Z IV 118. Cf. note 110.

115. "Now it does not save us to know how he was crucified, or that he was crucified, but that he was crucified for us, and that he who was crucified is our Lord and our God". Z IV 121.

In the course of the debate among the reformers, caused especially by the Lutheran assertion of the possibility of a "ubiquity", i.e. the omnipresence of the body of Christ, there developed the controversy concerning the *communicatio idiomatum*, the interchanging of the properties of the divine and human natures. After God has become man in Christ can one or must one conclude that God has thereby become finite, even mortal, and so on—and that the man Jesus has simultaneously become infinite etc.? The more consistent Lutherans affirmed this, while the Reformed theologians (as well as the Philippists) denied it. Zwingli admits only the *communio naturarum*; and it is only with regard to the *person* of the God-man that one can assert per alloiosim[116] the properties of both natures alike—as, for example, "Christ is the eternal God" and at the same time "Christ died for us".

The reformed side maintained this position for the sake of the true *humanity* of Jesus. Thus the lines of battle crossed one another. The reformed theologians insisted as a matter of principle that if Christ be truly our brother, then his human nature is finite, and remains finite even in its glorified state.[117] This finite nature is always joined to the infinite divine nature, but the divine nature surpasses the human. This is what was later to be called the "Extra Calvinisticum"; it is already formulated by Zwingli, clearly and emphatically—and in agreement with Augustine and the older Scholastics, incidentally.[118] Whereas Roman polemic in the sixteenth century, like Luther, argued against this, on the lines of a neo-monophysite Christology. This has its common roots in late-medieval mysticism and in nominalism.[119]

We may refer to two brief quotations from Zwingli, which are chosen deliberately because they are not directed against Luther.

---

116. See the final part of note 98; also Z V 354; Z V 564.

117. "Nos autem intelligimus et scimus nos vera et firma dicere, cum L. S. testimoniis, tum divi Augustini sententia fulti, qui Christi corpus in aliquo coeli loco ponit propter veri corporis modum". (But we perceive and know that we are stating a sure truth, supported by the testimony of Holy Scripture and by the teaching of St. Augustine, who teaches that the body of Christ, because of his true corporeality, is in some heavenly place. S IV 38).

118. "...Et humanitatem in uno loco esse, divinitatem ubique, ita non dividit personam..." (It does not divide his person to say that the human nature is in one place and the divine nature is ubiquitous. S IV 12). Cf. Z V 354; *Institutes* II. xiii. 4; Heidelberg Catechism, Questions 47-48; Karl Barth, *Church Dogmatics*, II/I; E. D. Willis, *Calvin's Catholic Christology. The Function of the so-called Extra Calvinisticum in Calvin's Theology*, Leiden, 1966.

119. Heiko A. Oberman, *The Harvest of Medieval Theology, Gabriel Biel and Late Medieval Nominalism*, Cambridge/Mass., 1963, pp. 235-254 and 259-280 (especially pp. 261-264).

1) "His humanity is the sacrificial lamb, which takes away the sin of the world; not because he is man, but because he is God and man; but according to his humanity he could suffer, and according to his divinity he makes alive".[120] Here we see clearly both the dyophysite formulation and the soteriological intention which stands behind it.

2) Zwingli attacks *Johannes Eck* with acerbity, saying that his assertions pervert and darken the Word of God and are "Insults and belittlings of the glory and honour of Christ, who sits at the right hand of the Father, and are confusions of the two different natures of Christ, of which the divine penetrates everything and is ever-present; whereas the human can be in only *one* place, according to God's direction and decision ..."[121] Again we may see how these points of view overlap. Here the reformed standpoint underlines the true *humanity* of Jesus; the "confusion" of the natures infringes upon the concept of *vere homo*, and with it the miracle of the incarnation and the grace therein revealed, as well as the real historicity of our Lord, and the depth of his suffering.

Thus the scope of this Christology is the assurance that God is really to be found and received in the man Jesus. In addition, it seeks to protect Christ's humanity against any decline into monophysitism or docetism. It maintains most determinedly that the Lord who is exalted and proclaimed, the object of faith, is completely identical with the historical Jesus. Finally, it concerns the promise that we shall personally share everlasting life with the glorified Lord who sits "at the right hand of the Father".[122] In order to counteract a widespread misunderstanding which aroused Luther's ire, it should be stated that the phrase in the Apostles' Creed about the "right hand of God" was not understood by Zwingli to mean a "place", any more than it was by Luther.[123] "He sits at he right hand of God the Father Almighty" is figurative speech, by which one understands that Christ Jesus is equally powerful with the Father".[124] In brief, Luther's Christology belongs to Christmas, while Zwingli's belongs

---

120. Z V 489.
121. Z V 226.
122. Z III 691; Z IV 907; S IV 49-50.
123. "In this context, Scripture uses the word 'hand' in the sense of 'power!'" Z V 480.
"Dexteram patris non esse circumscriptam nemo negat, sed humanam Christi naturam circumscriptam esse oportet ... In homine deus est. Homo circumscribitur, deus minime gentium". (Nobody denies that 'the right hand of the Father' is infinite, but the human nature of Christ must be finite ... God is in the man. The man is finite, God is in no way so. Z V 354). For Luther, see below, section 20, note 366.
124. Z V 481.

to Easter or to the Ascension. Its theocratic force is latent in that it speaks of him to whom "all power is given in heaven and on earth".

8. *Pneumatology*

But this emphasis upon the deity of God, which we have so far treated in relation to soteriology, theology, the Trinity and Christology, concerns above all that characteristic feature of Zwinglian thought which is generally described as spiritualism. But since the reformer does not maintain some principle of a free spirit, or even of a free psyche, but rather a doctrine of the Holy Spirit and his relationship to the human spirit which is clearly determined and controlled by his trinitarian doctrine, we prefer to adopt the felicitous suggestion of Fritz Schmidt-Clausing,[125] and speak of the *pneumatological* character of Zwingli's theology.

Even before the Fall, from the moment of his creation onwards, man was dependent upon the Holy Spirit—that is, that God should unceasingly and graciously attend to him, guide him and communicate with him[126]—which could well constitute one of the sharpest reformation rejections of the medieval teaching about *habitus*. But since the Fall, "man is deceitful"[127] and since then all knowledge of the truth, as well as of "the law of nature" is dependent upon the work of the Spirit of God.[128] And the knowledge of God and of oneself, which are inseparably bound together, and which the *homo mendax* resists with all his strength, can only be gained as the Spirit of God creates a new entrance for the Word of God.[129] Like

---

125. Fritz Schmidt-Clausing, "Das Prophezeigebet", *Zwa.* XII/1 (1964/1), pp. 10ff.; Fritz Schmidt-Clausing, *Zwingli* (Sammlung Göschen 1219), Berlin, 1965. The author provides a lively historical survey, and his attempt to portray Zwingli as the "Theologian of the Holy Spirit" is, in itself, laudable. Unfortunately, the work contains numerous historical and theological inaccuracies, the latter being largely the result of the author's exaggerating his own interpretation at the expense of the doctrine of God, and, in particular, of Christology.

126. Z II 34; Z II 38.

127. "Omnis homo mendax" (Psalm 116:11, Romans 3:4, Vulgate). Z II 76; cf. Z II 96 and passim.

128. Z II 326; Z II 634.

129. Z III 640; Z II 630.

"Constat, quod a solo deo discendum, quid ipse sit..." (It is certain, that it is only from God that one can learn what he is. Z III 643).

"Solius divini spiritus est, ut homo sese cognoscat". (It is only by the spirit of God that man can know himself. Z III 692). Cf. Z III 654; Z III 661.

"No heart or mind can understand God's word and action, except it be illumined and taught by God. But if this happens, than man becomes so sure and brave and certain with regard to God's Word, that he relies on its truth more surely than on any seal or letter". Z II 22; S VI, I 321.

every consistent theologian of the Spirit from Paul onwards,[130] Zwingli draws two consequences which are mutually exclusive from the theoretical standpoint: the line of strictly predestinarian salvation-history,[131] and a universal overall view of mankind.[132] But when the Holy Spirit himself has acted, then the unity of these two lines of thought is perceived from within. The Spirit of God is God in his freedom, and the one who is "elect", (that is, taken hold of by the Spirit) is the very one who can never wish to maintain that the Spirit and the freedom of God are bound to the history of salvation in the narrow sense,[133] and that Christ is not effective either for the heathen or among the heathen.[134] Zwingli's enumeration of pious heathen, whom he looks forward to meeting in heaven one day, is famous.[135] Though it is important to note that even here there is no question of human ability or achievement. The heathen's fragmentary knowledge of the truth and the devoted obedience that corresponds to this relative knowledge, such as one finds with Socrates or Seneca, can always be traced back to special communications from the Holy Spirit.[136] If one is inclined to speak of Zwingli's liberalism at this point, one should remember that Zwingli's himself speaks of the freedom of the Holy Spirit.

In particular, faith in Christ is the free gift of the Spirit of God.[137] "No man can come to me, except the Father draw him" (John 6:44) is one of the Biblical texts which Zwingli quotes most frequently.[138] The right

---

130. E.g. Augustine, Calvin, Pascal, Vinet.

131. "So faith always springs from God's election. And faith is nothing other than reliance upon God; for thus has God made his covenant with all the elect, that they should worship only him, honour only him (as their God), and hold only to him, which is what the Lord Jesus Christ threw in the Devil's face, as it says in Matthew 4". Z V 781.

132. "His sinlessness can pay and render satisfaction for the sins of the whole world". Z III 124. (Zwingli frequently quotes 1 John 2:2 in this connexion).

"It is certain that by his suffering Jesus Christ has won access to God, peace with God and salvation for the whole human race". Z II 172.

133. "Non continebatur tum religio intra Palaestinae, terminos, quia spiritus iste coelestis non solam Palaestinam vel creaverat vel fovebat, sed mundum universum". (The fear of God was not limited to the boundaries of Palestine, for the heavenly Spirit did not create and bless only Palestine, but rather the whole world. Z IX 458).

134. "Pietatem ergo etiam apud istos aluit, quos elegit ubiubi essent". (Therefore he has nourished faith in those whom he has chosen, wherever they might be. Z IX 459). Cf. S IV 95.

135. S IV 65; cf. Rudolf Pfister, *Die Seligkeit erwählter Heiden bei Zwingli*, Zürich, 1952.

136. "Thus the heathen did not know the law of nature by virtue of their own reasoning, but by the illuminating Spirit of God, even though he was not known to them... Since they did not have faith, but did understand the law of nature, this must have come from God alone..." Z II 327; S IV 93, 123.

137. "Thus it must always follow that nobody comes to know Christ through human instruction, doctrine or opinion, but only as the Father draws him". Z II 23.

138. Z II 22, passim.

knowledge of Christ according to his divine and human natures also depends upon the gift of the Spirit.[139] And what is decisive is that Christ himself is present in the Spirit by virtue of his divinity. Thus it is that he grants forgiveness, faith, comfort, assurance, peace with God and newness of life. "The spirit of man cannot do this".[140] No man can understand the Word of God, unless he is enlightened by the Spirit. "Without the Spirit, flesh perverts the Word of God into the very opposite".[141]

Conversely, the marks of the Holy Spirit include (1) conformity to Holy Scripture, which is itself inspired by the Spirit; (2) striving after God's honour; (3) the humility of man.[142] Zwingli's sacramental doctrine will guard against the idea that the Spirit of God can be bound to the creature,[143] even if the creature is concealed in religion, faith, church or office. We have to recognise that this is not merely a question of drawing conclusions from the premises of an idealistic ontology, but that it is a soteriological necessity: the gracious presence of God is the pre-requisite of faith, and not the other way round.[144]

9. Religion

These premises, which are derived from revelation, constitute a singular, dialectic, yet very clear conception of religion.[145] Firstly, it ex-

---

"But we learn from Christ that God is the teacher of the hearts of believers ... when he says in John 6: 'Every man that hath heard, and hath learned of the Father, cometh unto me'. Nobody comes to the Lord Jesus Christ, unless he has learned to know him from the Father. And see who the schoolmaster is—not doctors, nor fathers, nor pope, nor cathedra nor council, but the Father of Jesus Christ. And you cannot say, 'May one not learn it from a man also?' No. For immediately before this, he says: 'No man comes to me, except the heavenly Father draws him'. And even if you were to hear the Gospel of Jesus Christ from an apostle, you would not act upon it, unless the heavenly Father should teach you and draw you by his Spirit. The words are clear: it is the teaching of God that gives clear illumination, instruction and assurance, apart from all human wisdom". Z I 366.

139. Z IX 63f.
140. "The human spirit cannot give life..." Z V 968.
141. S V 773.
142. E.g. Z II 62.
143. "I will not bind the freedom of the Spirit of God". Z II 110.
"Friget ergo ista opinio ... quae putat sacramenta talia esse signa, ut, cum exerceantur in homine, simul intus fiat, quod sacramentis significetur. Nam hac ratione libertas divini spiritus alligata esset, qui dividit singulis, ut vult, id est: quibus, quando, ubi vult". (We cannot accept that view ... which holds that the sacraments are signs of such nature that when they are administered then they simultaneously accomplish inwardly that which they signify. For this would bind the freedom of the Spirit of God, who divides to men severally as he will; that is, to whom and when and where he will. Z III 761.
144. Z V 583.
145. Z III 639-640; Z III 665-674.

cludes, as a basis of faith, any "natural theology" which would lie within man's capacity,[146] since all truth, even in non-Christian religions, depends upon the communication of the Holy Spirit.[147] Again, man is, in his very religion, an inveterate idolater, a worshipper of self, and a liar.[148] Since the Fall, in any case, religion exists only in statu corruptionis.[149] Yet man is not simply left in this state by God; religion is rather the steady repetition of God's most gracious call: "Adam, where art thou?"[150] The origin, the possibility and the promise of "religion" rest upon the fact that the heavenly Father, in *his* "piety", has not given up the lost son, but has held on to him in his godless flight, by calling him.[151] "Thus piety springs forth from God to this very day, but (only) for our benefit".[152] Thus proper "piety or religion"[153] on man's part can only consist in grasping the word spoken by the gracious "piety" of God and clinging to it[154] "as if to a ship's plank".[155] Any "religion" which fails to do this is thereby continuing Adam's sin of "following his own ideas" and his despairing and stubborn flight.[156] Therefore, thirdly, evangelical Christianity constitutes at one and the same time the crisis of all religion, the criterion by which it is measured, and the one true religion. "True religion or piety is that which holds solely and exclusively to God".[157] "False religion or piety is where one trusts in something other than God. Therefore, whoever puts his trust in any creature, cannot be truly pious. That man is ungodly who receives

---

146. Z III 639; H IX 18.

147. Z III 643; H IX 24. Romans 1:19, 20 and Romans 2:14, 15 do not present any problem for Zwingli, as he understands the revelation to be dynamic rather than static, and he equates φύσις, the "natura naturans" which proceeds from the creator God, not with our "our nature", but with the "continuous and perpetual working of God" (S VI, I 241). Cf. S VI, II 82. "Nature is nothing other than the continuous working of God". (S IV 297; Z XIII 797, with reference to Psalm 134:7). Cf. Z III 641; also *Th. H. Z.* I, p. 56.

148. Cf. the section on the origin of false religion, Z III 638; H IX 17. "Quisque enim sibi deus est". (For every man is his own God. Z III 667; H IX 62).

149. "Religionem originem sumpsisse ... videmus, ubi deus hominem fugitivum ad se revocavit qui alioqui perpetuus desertor futurus erat". (We perceive that religion began when God recalled to himself the runaway man who would otherwise have remained in apostasy for ever. Z III 667; H IX 62).

150. Z III 667.

151. "Iam erga impium filium, parentis pietatem vide!" (But now behold the Father's love towards his unloving son. Z III 668, 11f., with reference to Genesis 3:9; H IX 63).

152. "Oritur ergo pietas a deo usque in hodiernum diem, sed in nostrum usum". Z III 668; H IX 63.

153. Z III 668; Z III 669.

154. Z III 668; Z III 669; Z III 672; Z III 673.

155. Z III 670.

156. Z III 667; Z III 668; Z III 674.

157. Z III 669.

the word of man as if it were from God''.[158] Religion is therefore the proof that man lives in relationship to God, and so constitutes the kernel of his humanity.[159] Without God, man becomes a wild animal,[160] and his communal life becomes either chaos or tyranny.[161] Zwingli adopts the Thomistic distinction, according to which man knows of himself "that" God is, though not "what" or "who" God is. But then, by means of a circular argument based on the "who", he asserts that it is only by His Word that we can even know "that" our God exists![162]

10. Sola Fides

In substance, the chapter "De religione Christiania"[163] contains the whole "Gospel": reconciliation achieved through the Cross—for it is this that determines (objectively) our relationship to God. The title of the short chapter that follows, *Evangelium*,[164] means the "Kerygma"—it is concerned with the preaching of the Gospel and its appropriation. *Faith* is "peace and assurance through the merit of Christ".[165] It is inaccurate to

---

158. Z III 674. "Is cultus, ea pietas aut religio vana est, quae ex humana inventione aut lege proficiscitur". (The worship, piety or religion which has its origin in human invention or precept is vain. Z III 672, with reference to Matthew 15:8).

159. "Ex omnibus animantibus nullum est praeter hominem quod notitiam habeat dei". (Of all living things, only man has any conception of God. S VI, I 241).

160. "Nisi sit deus (homini deus), nihil est homo quam belua". (Unless God is God to man, man is nothing but a beast. Z III 673).

"Numinis reverentiam ex humanis tolle, et eadem opera ex hominibus beluas, quod Circen fabulae perhibent, feceris". (If you take away from men the fear of God, then you turn them into beasts, as the fable of Cicero describes. Z XIV 417).

161. "Tolle a magistratu religionem, tyrannis est, non magistratus". (Take away religion from the government, and it is not a government, but a tyranny. Z IX 458).

162. Compare Z III 640 with Z III 642!

163. Z III 674-691.

164. Z III 691-701.

165. Z II 182. Zwingli has his opponents say, "Iactamus Christi sanguinem, quod pro nobis fusus sit, sed si quis eo fretus firmiter crediderit sibi perpetuo eius gratia deum ignoturum, hunc mox haereticum pronunciamus". (We boast that Christ's blood was shed for us; but if anyone firmly believes that God will forgive him for ever by his grace, then at once we accuse that man of heresy). Zwingli answers, "Constanter, o viri, perseverate in isto verbo, quod vobis sive de industria sive casu excidit: est enim salutis verbum, Christum scilicet ecclesiam sanguine suo parasse. Quicunque id firmiter crediderit ex ecclesia Christi est ea, quam suo sanguine paravit; nam fides sola salutis causa est". (Please, gentlemen, stand firm by the word which you let slip, whether it was by intention or by accident, for it is the word of salvation, namely, that Christ has founded his church by his blood. Whoever firmly believes this belongs to the church of Christ which he has founded by his blood, for faith is the only ground of salvation. Z I 319).

"As he himself says in John 11, 'I am the resurrection and the life; he that believeth in me, though he were dead, yet shall he live; and whosoever liveth and believeth in me shall never die' ". Z II 49.

say that faith "saves", for faith knows that it is not faith but grace which redeems.[166] Faith is a gift of electing grace, and is the sign of that grace, though it is not always indispensable (as in the case of children, for example).[167] So the corrections which Calvin made with regard to Luther's mode of expression[168] were made by Zwingli also.[169] Instead of "justification" (Rechtfertigung), Zwingli likes to render the Greek more literally as "making righteous" (Gerechtmachung).[170] For him, it coincides with forgiveness.[171] When taken together with his adherence to the "securitas" of faith, it shows that the dimension of the troubled soul does not have for him the theological relevance that it has for Luther. Accordingly, there is no sign of those sharp Lutheran formulations of an "outward" justification. For Zwingli, the justification that comes through faith is primarily inward and spiritual, and this provides the basis for the outward justification.[172] Grace is the great liberation from all despair concerning one's own

---

"Fides enim est quae deo per Christum nititur". (That is (true) faith, which rests upon God through Christ. S IV 57, and passim throughout Zwingli's writings. "Faith" is often equated simply with "coming to Christ" (e.g. S IV 121).

166. "Accipitur enim fides pro dei electione, finitione, vocatione, quae omnia fidem antecedunt, sed in eodem ordine". (Faith is to be understood as God's election, predestination and calling, which all precede faith, in that order. Z VI, I 174). Cf. S IV 119; also Heidelberg Catechism, Qu. 61.

167. "Fides iis datur, qui ad vitam aeternam electi et ordinati sunt; sic tamen ut electio antecedat, et fides velut symbolum electionem sequatur". (Faith is given to those who are chosen and ordained to eternal life, but in such a way, that election comes first, and faith follows election as a kind of sign. S IV 121).
"Fides electionis signum est". (Faith is a sign of election. S IV 123; Z VI, I 172).

168. Calvin, *Contra Sadoletum*, OS I, p. 469; *Institutes* III. xi. 1-2 (see note 172).

169. "Per fidem autem diximus remitti peccata, quo nihil aliud volumus quam dicere, solam fidem certum reddere hominem de remissis sceleribus". (We said that sins are forgiven through faith. By which we wish only to say that faith alone makes a man sure of the forgiveness of his sins. S IV 60).
"The faith which we have in God, in and through Christ Jesus, makes us whole. This is true. But this is not because our faith, which has actually arisen from within ourselves, can achieve this, but because whoever believes has been chosen by God from all eternity, and has been drawn by him, as it says in John 6:44..." Z V 781.

170. E.g. Z II 172, referring to Romans 5:1, and Z II 642.

171. "Iustificandi verbo pro absolvendi utuntur Hebraei". (The Hebrews use the word 'justify' for 'forgive'. S IV 121). "Qui fidem habent, iusti hoc est absoluti sunt..." (Those who have faith are justified; that is to say, they are forgiven. S IV 122).

172. For Luther, see H. J. Iwand, *Glaubensgerechtigkeit nach Luthers Lehre*, 3rd ed., Munich, 1959. As is well known, Luther attaches importance to the fact that it is not security (securitas), but rather assurance (certitudo) that is promised to faith. Luther speaks of "iustitia Christi pro nobis extra nobis" (the righteousness of Christ for us and outside of us)—though he sees it, in fact, as something that is very "inward"! With this we may compare some words of Zwingli: "Christus solus veram iusticiam non tantum sicut alii praeceptores docet, sed etiam largitur ac praestat. Ubi tamen praetereundum nobis non est, quo minus in memoria teneamus, quanam iustitia ditet, aut qualem doceat. Docet autem inter-

achievements,[173] and from all ecclesiastical regulations.[174] Trusting in one's own works belongs to creature-worship.[175] By contrast, Spirit, faith and love are vividly described as the sources of the new *works*.[176] The believer abhors sin.[177] And it is true that "the more faith grows, the more the doing of all good things grows also" for the believer is "moved to such action by God".[178] It is characteristic of the Swiss reformer that, in this connexion, he never paints an individual picture of a saint or of some paragon of virtue, though he does on occasion speak of the visible fruits of

---

nam istam, quae nihil aliud est, quam spiritus, haec est: fides et veritas, atque eam gratis donat. Docet et externam esse, misericordiam facere, fidem servare, ius suum cuique reddere: sed et istam donat; ex priore enim tamquam fonte dimanat". (Christ alone not only teaches true righteousness, as do other teachers, but actually effects and bestows it. But we must not fail to take note of the nature of the righteousness which he teaches and bestows. He teaches that inward righteousness, which is nothing other than spirit, that is, faith and truth, and he bestows it freely. He also teaches that it is external—to show mercy, to hold the faith, to render to every man his due. But he bestows this righteousness also, for it flows from the former righteousness as from a spring. Z V 625). Cf. S IV 121.

The way in which Zwingli speaks here of the righteousness of faith is similar to Calvin's statement: "Summa autem haec fuit, Christum nobis Dei benignitate datum, fide a nobis apprehendi ac possideri, cuius participatione duplicem potissimum gratiam recipiamus: nempe ut eius innocentia Deo reconciliati, pro iudice iam propitium habeamus in caelis Patrem: deinde ut eius Spiritu sanctificati, innocentiam puritatemque vitae meditemur". (The whole may be thus summed up: Christ, given to us by the kindness of God, is apprehended and possessed by faith, by means of which we obtain a twofold and most important benefit; first, being reconciled to God by the righteousness of Christ, we have, instead of a judge, a gracious father in heaven; and secondly, being sanctified by his Spirit, we aspire to integrity and purity of life. *Institutes* III. xi. 1).

(It might also be observed that the above quotation from Zwingli excludes the possibility of a "liberal" interpretation of the reformer).

173. "Faith is such a treasure, that man has never encountered anything more joyful or worthy, and he values nothing so highly. Therefore believers would lose life and limb rather than abandon their faith, in which they find peace for their conscience and comfort in their security as children and heirs of God". Z III 446. Cf. especially the *Kurze christliche Einleitung* (Z II 626-663) and the *Exposition of the Articles* (Z II 1-457, passim).

174. Cf. Z I 74-136; H I 5-57.

175. "So reconciliation is not ours, but Christ's. And it is an insult to Jesus Christ, when one attributes to any creature that which belongs to him alone; therefore he is called the healer". Z II 172.

176. "Quanto maior est fides, tanto plura maioraque facimus opera..." (The greater our faith is, the more and greater works we are able to do. S IV 62).

"Fides enim cum spiritus divini sit adflatus: quomodo potest quiescere aut in otio desidere, quum spiritus ille iugis sit actio et operatio? Ubicunque ergo vera fides est: ibi et opus est, non minus quam ubi ignis isthic et calor est". (Faith means being moved by the Spirit of God—how could it rest or settle down in inactivity, since this Spirit is constantly working and acting? Therefore there is work wherever there is true faith, just as there is heat wherever there is fire. S IV 63). Cf. Z II 39-40; Z II 42; Z II 433; S IV 61.

177. Z III 701; H IX 118f.

178. Z II 183; Z II 187.

faith as displayed in communal life.[179] In this sense, there sometimes appears in Zwingli's work the *syllogismus practicus* which is generally regarded as a typically Calvinistic doctrine.[180] What is more important is that faith itself, being the work of the Spirit, is seen as *experientia* (experience)[181] and as *fiducia* (trust)[182] and must be clearly distinguished from *fides historica* (accepting as true) and *opinio* (personal opinion).[183] Faith is of divine origin, and in the strictest sense, it can only have God as its content.[184] Thus, it is the deity of Christ which makes it possible "to believe in him",[185] and faith "in God" and "in Christ" are identical. And so the Trinitarian circle is completed.

11. *"The Word"*

Therefore, we must receive faith from God (or "Christ") himself. Men cannot bestow it[186]—not even the Apostles.[187] Therefore the true word,

---

179. E.g. S IV 18.

180. Good works are a sign of faith, just as faith is a sign of election. "... Sic qui fidei opera faciunt experimentum dant quum sibi ipsis, dum liberaliter et ex amore dei ac proximi, non vana gloria, operantur; tum aliis, quod deum colant, hoc est quod fidem habeant". (Thus those who perform works of faith provide practical proof that they serve God, that is, that they have faith. They show this firstly to themselves, and then to others, when they act with generosity and out of love to God and their neighbour, and not out of vainglory. S IV 124). Calvin states: "Sancti opera non aliter quam Dei dona intuentur, unde eius bonitatem recognoscant, non aliter quam vocationis signa unde electionem reputent". (Believers regard works only as gifts of God, in which they recognise his goodness, and as signs of their calling, in which they discern their election. *Institutes* III. xiv. 20). Cf. Heidelberg Catechism, Qu. 86; also Leo Jud, "Der kürzere Katechismus", in Leo Jud, *Katechismen*, ed. Oskar Farner, 1955, p. 293; August Lang, *Der Heidelberger Katechismus und vier verwandte Katechismen*, 1907, pp. XCIV and 80; W. Niesel, "Syllogismus practicus?", in *Aus Theologie und Geschichte der reformierten Kirche*, Festgabe für E. F. K. Müller, Erlangen, 1933, pp. 158-179; G. Oorthuys, "De beteekenis van het nieuwe leven voor de zekerheid des geloofs, volgens Calvyns Institutie", in *Onder Eigen Vaandel*, 13/4, Wageningen, October 1938, pp. 246-269.

181. Z IV 491. "Res enim est ac experimentum fides, non sermo aut ars". (For faith is reality and experience, not talk or craft. Z XIII 145).

182. Z IV 495; S IV 55.

183. S IV 55; Z IV 496; Z V 786; Z V 902.

184. "Non modo ex scripturis, sed etiam ex ipsius fidei natura manifestum fit, quod nullius creaturae verbum pro verbo dei recipi potest, quia in creaturae verbo non redditur quieta pacataque conscientia". (It is plain not only from scripture but from the nature of faith itself that no word of a creature can be received as the word of God; for the conscience finds no rest or peace in the word of a creature. Z III 671).

185. "It follows that trust in the Lord Jesus Christ is founded basically upon his divinity alone, upon the fact that he is true God ... But what about his humanity? It is a sure pledge of grace; for it was his human nature that was given up in death, in order to satisfy the divine righteousness and to reconcile it to us..." Z V 782.

186. "It is not man who causes men to believe, but the Spirit". Z II 111.

187. "Even if you were to hear the gospel of Jesus Christ from an apostle, you would not follow it, unless our heavenly Father should instruct you by his Spirit, and draw you", Z I

out of which faith stems, is the inner word, the "verbum internum" which is "spoken into" man or "breathed into" him by the Spirit of God.[188] Because of *Luther*'s fundamental experience of being troubled in conscience, for him everything depends on the fact that the word of promise and the Gospel are no less external to us than the law.[189] There is no relying on the inner man and his wavering condition.[190] He receives assurance only when faith can cling to that which is outside oneself. It is for this reason that God has established within his church the office of preaching and administering the sacraments, for no one can pronounce forgiveness to himself.[191] *Zwingli's* fundamental experience of the danger that threatens men through worship of the creature means that he sees this overemphasis on the "verbum externum" not as upholding the freedom of grace, but as endangering it. The external word is ordained by God; it denotes the highest mandate in Christendom.[192] But it is always dependent upon the fact that the Holy Spirit should accompany the human word and open the mind of the hearer.[193] *Rome* vouchsafes the presence of the Lord through the sacrament. Zwingli's dialectic warns that this cannot be guaranteed, on the Protestant side, merely by the sermon instead. The Lord's presence can only give itself. Luther sees, in grateful wonder, how the Spirit binds himself to the word. Zwingli anxiously watches that the word remains bound to the Spirit, and that the proclamation of the Word

---

366. This is true even of Jesus Christ himself, as far as his human nature is concerned:— "The greater part of those who heard Christ himself remained unbelievers ... Wherefore faith comes ... only from ... the Spirit of God, who draws men". Z IV 66.

188. Z II 76; Z II 110.

189. Paul Althaus comments that "this follows from the fact that Christ is God's presence with us in his humanity, that is, in his historicity. When he became man and assumed bodily form, he came to man in the human-historical manner of the "external word' ''. Althaus quotes Luther's statement that "Christ is not known except by his word", (WA X/III 210) and "to preach the gospel is nothing other than to bring Christ to us, or to bring us to him". (W X/I 1). The following well-known passage in the Schmalkaldic Articles is directed against Zwingli:—"In these places which concern the spoken, external word, it is firmly to be maintained that God does not give his Spirit or his grace to anyone save through or with the preceding external word; whereby we guard against the Enthusiasts or Spiritualists, who boast of having the Spirit before or without the word". *Die Bekenntnisschriften der evangelisch-lutherischen Kirche*, Göttingen, 1930, Vol. 1, pp. 453ff.; Paul Althaus, *Die Theologie Martin Luthers*, Gütersloh, 1962, pp. 42-47.

190. "Our heart thinks there is nothing but an empty 'No', but it is not true. Therefore it must turn away from such feelings, and with a firm faith in God's word grasp and cleave to that deep, hidden 'Yes' which lies beneath and above the 'No'..." WA XVII/II 203.

191. "God will not give either his Spirit or faith to any man apart from the external word and sign which he has appointed for this purpose..." WA XVIII 136.

192. Z II 352.

193. Z II 110.

is aware that it is dependent upon free grace. The sermon bears witness to salvation, but the Spirit reserves to himself the actual bringing of salvation.[194] We may recognise how the Christological presuppositions are thus developed by both sides.

At this point, *Henry Bullinger* made a considerable contribution towards the building of a bridge between Zurich and Wittenberg. The first article of the Second Helvetica Confession deliberately sets aside the question of principles, and emphasises the identity of the one who causes both the external and the internal word to be spoken.[195] *John Calvin* emphasises the sanctity of ecclesiastical office to a far greater extent than Zwingli. It is not without reason that Highchurch-men have always been able to appeal to him. Yet in his view the honour of the ministry rests in the fact that it is the foundation and the instrument of the Spirit. Upon closer examination, he is simply continuing the line followed by Zwingli in this matter: it is only through the Holy Spirit that the word effects faith in us,[196] and only the Holy Spirit can lead us to Christ.[197] He does not, however, differentiate between himself and Luther, but rather takes his experience of testing and his experience with the (external) word and draws it into the realm of the Spirit's activity. "Therefore, as we cannot possibly come to Christ unless

194. "Quod auditur, non est ipsum verbum, quo credimus. Si enim eo verbo, quod auditur et legitur, fideles redderemur, omnes plane essemus fideles ...; sed contra videmus et audire et videre multos, nec tamen fidem habere. Manifestum ergo fit, quod eo verbo, quod caelestis pater in cordibus nostris praedicat, quo simul illuminat, ut intelligamus, et trahit ut sequamur, fideles reddimur ... Et exterius verbum deus in medium adferri ordinavit, tametsi fides non sit ex verbo externo". (What one hears is not the word by which we come to believe. For if we were made into believers by the word which we hear and read, we should all be believers ...; but we see, on the contrary, that many hear and see who do not have faith. Therefore it appears that we become believers by means of that word which our heavenly Father preaches in our hearts, by which he enlightens us, so that we understand, and draws us (John 6:44) so that we follow ... God has ordained that the external word should be proclaimed, although faith is not produced by the external word. Z III 263). Cf. also "In Spirit and in Truth" (above, pp. 12-15).

195. "Qui enim intus illuminat, donato hominibus spiritu sancto idem ille praecipiens dixit ad discipulos suos: Ite in mundum universum et praedicate Evangelium omni creaturae". (For the one who illuminates men inwardly, by giving to them his Holy Spirit, is the one who commanded his disciples, saying, 'Go into all the world and preach the gospel to every creature' ". Confessio Helvetica Posterior, cap. I, in *Bekenntnisschriften und Kirchenordnungen der nach Gottes Wort reformierten Kirche*, ed. W. Niesel, 3rd. ed. Zollikon, n.d., p. 223). Cf. "Praedicatio verbi dei est verbum dei" (below, ch. 12); Joachim Staedtke, ed., *Glauben und Bekennen. Vierhundert Jahre Confessio Helvetica Posterior*, Zürich, 1966 (see pp. 235-250, E. A. Dowey, "Das Wort Gottes als Schrift und Predigt"; pp. 251-257, J. Staedtke, "Die Gotteslehre"; pp. 300-336, G. W. Locher, "Die Lehre vom Heiligen Geist" (especially pp. 324ff.).

196. *Institutes* III. ii. 33.

197. *Institutes* III. ii. 34.

drawn by the Spirit, so when we are drawn we are both in mind and spirit exalted far above our own understanding".[198] And it is because the Spirit is ever giving new strength to our faith that it is not stifled by troubles and doubts, but rather is firmly preserved in peace, and "perseveres to the end".[199] Thus speaks Calvin, in Book III of the *Institutio*. In Book IV he will explain how the Spirit uses the external word and the sacraments to this end. If Bullinger found a point of union with Lutheranism in the identity of the author, Calvin found it in the identity of the content of the *verbum internum* and *externum*.[200]

12. *Sola scriptura*

Zwingli sees no contradiction between his basic pneumatological standpoint and the definite reformation principle of the authority of Scripture. On the contrary, the Spirit demands obedience towards Scripture, in contrast to all human authority.[201] Firstly, because the Apostles and the prophets wrote their word as those who were filled by the Spirit,[202] and secondly, because Scripture is the concrete, historical form of the fact that the Word of God (as the "inner word") is not our own word.[203] So, on the one hand, one finds in Zwingli expressions which verge on the later orthodox doctrine of verbal inspiration;[204] on the other hand, he stresses that Scripture points back behind itself to its meaning, which can be grasped only in the Biblical context.[205] The exposition of an individual problematic

---

198. *Institutes* III. ii. 34.

199. *Institutes* III. ii. 37, 40. Cf. Jürgen Moltmann, *Prädestination und Perseveranz*, Neukirchen, 1961.

200. Cf. Edmond Grin, "Quelques aspects de la pensée de Calvin sur le Saint-Esprit, et leurs enseignements pour nous", and "Expérience religieuse et témoignage du Saint-Esprit", in *Théologie Systématique en Suisse Romande*, 1966, pp. 48-63, 64-82; also, G. W. Locher, *Testimonium internum. Calvins Lehre vom Heiligen Geist und das hermeneutische Problem*. Theologische Studien, No. 81, 1964.

201. "I think it necessary to explain the matter from Scripture so that everyone, relying on divine Scripture, may stand fast against the enemies of Scripture. So read and understand, open the eyes and ears of your heart and listen and see what the Spirit of God says to us". Z I 91.

202. "The divine word does not come from men, but rather those who spoke it were instructed by God". Z III 206.

203. Thus he can term the Bible the "divina lex" (Z I 305 etc.) Similarly, he speaks of "in via ac lege dei bene ac inoffense, sine humanarum traditionum fascino, currere ..." (walking, in the way and the commandment of God, sure and without stumbling, without being bewitched by human traditions ... Z I 306).

204. Z IV 841; Z VI, I 24; Z VI, I 361.

205. "The shepherd must learn the word of God only from the Holy Scriptures of the Bible. But it is vain for him to learn the letter, unless God draws his heart, so that he places trust in the word, and does not wrest it according to his own desires, but gives it free rein, in keeping with its divine inspiration". Z III 22.

text must accord with the context—therefore "faith is the master and the interpreter of the words".[206] This may be compared with Luther's famous insistence upon the "est". This certainly does not mean that the exposition of scripture must be accommodated to our reason: "Let the Word of God have its own nature ... and let all your intelligence lie!"[207] The Bible expounds itself;[208] one experiences this, as one is led from the easier texts to the more difficult ones.[209] In doubtful cases, the right exposition will be the one that honours God and humbles us.[210] Christ himself is the "clarity" of Scripture.[211] There are different levels of authority within Scripture; on the highest level stand the words of Jesus and (similar to Luther) the Gospel of John.[212] The Apocrypha are excluded,[213] as is also the Apocalypse, as it is adjudged, on the basis of content and style, "not a biblical book".[214] Nor is it accidental that when speaking of the Bible as a whole, Zwingli prefers the order "New and Old Testament".[215] The qualification about the possibility of being better instructed through the Scriptures, which found its way into all the reformed confessions, and which is a classical sign of the principle of scriptural authority (pneumatologically understood), goes back to Zwingli (cf. *The Sixty-seven*

With regard to the question as to "how one tests the Scripture or the letter of the Gospel", cf. Zwingli's vivid picture of the old countryman of Uri, who is familiar with the ancient law of the land. "The faithful old man is the believer upon whose heart God has written his law, and in whose mind God has put his commandment (Jeremiah 31:33), so that, by virtue of this inward faith and knowledge which God has given him, he can test the external letter, whether or not it is conformable to the true laws of the land, that is, the true teaching of God". Z IV 71. Cf. also Z I 558, and the quotations in notes 52 and 58.

206. "Fides ergo magistra et interpres est verborum". Z V 663.

"... Scripture is to be understood by faith alone; and to see whether faith is true, it must be tested only against Scripture, which is rightly understood by faith ... so you see that one must have faith and Scripture side by side". Z V 773; Z V 774. Zwingli expressly says "Potior est, ingenue agnosco, spiritus". (The Spirit is more important, as I freely acknowledge. Z V 734).

207. Z I 375f.

208. "Scripture interprets Scripture". Z I 561. He states, immediately prior to this "I understand Scripture only in the way that it interprets itself by the Spirit of God. It does not require any human opinion". Z I 559.

209. Z III 309; Z IV 831.

210. Z II 62; Z III 264; Z III 280; Z III 848; Z III 408.

211. Z I 365; Z III 194; Z V 564. See *Of the Clarity and Certainty of the Word of God*, Z I 328-384. (English translation by G. W. Bromiley in *Zwingli and Bullinger*, London, 1953, pp. 49ff.).

212. Cf. *Th. H. Z.* I, pp. 24-28; Z I 471; Z IV 283.

213. Z II 203f.; Z XI 599; Z VI, I 402.

214. Z II 208; Z VI, I 395.

215. E.g. Z VI, I 462.

Articles and the *Christian Introduction*).[216] As the message of the Spirit, it is, be it noted, the natural meaning of Scripture that is definitive.[217] The typological interpretation of the Old Testament derives its power from the New Testament, and is therefore kept within bounds.[218] Allegory is allowed occasionally, "as a dessert".[219] It is important to follow the great lines of salvation history. The exposition of disconnected individual texts leads to heresy.[220] Like all the reformers, he accepts without reservation that the dogmas of the early church constitute a legitimate summary of the Biblical message.[221] But when these are then applied in their turn, to the exegesis of Scripture, then even with Zwingli it gives rise to systematisations which lay far from the New Testament.[222] Because Scripture is "spiritual", the Holy Spirit is needed for its correct exposition,[223] as well as for the proclamation of its message.[224]

13. *Repentance*

By means of the challenge and the example of Christ which Scripture presents, the Holy Spirit is ever leading us to repentance.[225] Repentance precedes faith,[226] and also follows it.[227] One has the impression that repen-

---

216. Z II 457; Z II 629; Z III 758; Z III 790.

217. "One should not set some other cap on the Word of God, but leave it with its right and natural sense. And whoever grasps this has grasped the Spirit's meaning". Z III 205.

218. Z III 193-195.

219. Z XIII 225; Z XIII 310. Following the example of Paul, allegory must remain within the bounds of the analogy of faith. Z XIII 310, 373.

220. Z IV 899.

221. Zwingli emphasises that dogma does not stand alongside Scripture; the Fathers based their decisions on Scripture, as in the Arian controversy, for example. Z I 560-561.

222. E.g., in the christological sections of the *Fidei Ratio*, S IV 4.

223. Z I 559, 561.

224. Z III 22 (note 205) is addressed to the shepherd as preacher!

225. *De vera et falsa religione commentarius*, Cap. VIII, "De poenitentia", Z III 701-706; H IX 119.

226. "So the man, of whom I am speaking, who despairs of salvation because of the wounds of sin, turns to the mercy of God and makes his appeal to it; and as soon as he glimpses Christ, he knows that he may hope for everything, 'for if God be for us, who can be against us?' (Romans 8:31). So now he who was prostrate can stand up; he who was dead, and who in agony knew and felt himself to be dead, is alive!" Z III 702; H IX 121. Cf. the summary of the "sermon" of the "shepherd" (1524): "By this means (i.e. the word of God) the shepherd will show to those who are entrusted to him their sinful weakness; and when they have understood this, and realise that they cannot be saved by their own strength, then he will direct them to the grace of God ..." Z III 22. Cf. also the example of Zwingli himself in the *Christliche Einleitung* (1523); see the sections "Bessrend üch" (Z II 630) and "Evangelium" (Z II 636).

227. In the *Commentarius* (March, 1525), the chapter "De poenitentia" follows those on "De religione Christiana" and "Euangelium". The Holy Spirit, who is comprehended only

tance and faith arise together, each grounded in the other.[228] With this, one may compare the decisive way in which Luther maintains that repentance is the basis of faith, and remains so,[229] while Calvin emphatically declares that without faith there can be no repentance.[230] More particular-

by faith, precedes both repentance and faith. "Nisi enim fides adsit, qua homo credat omnem vocem a deo prolatam veram esse, tam longe aberit a sui cognitione, quantum inter spiritum carnemque interest. 'Per legem enim cognitio peccati'. Est autem lex spiritualis, nos autem carnales. Nisi ergo spiritus se nobis ingerat, perpetuo carnales erimus". (For if faith is not present, by which a man believes every word spoken by God to be true, then he is as far from knowledge of himself as the spirit is from the flesh. 'For by the law is the knowledge of sin'. (Romans 3:20). For the law is spiritual, but we are carnal. Therefore if the Spirit does not enter into us, we shall remain carnal for ever. Z III 661). This whole section is relevant. It makes it clear that man is incapable of true self-knowledge because of is impenitence. "Per Christum ergo confit, ut vitae pristinae nos poeniteat; nam satis declaravimus in consideratione hominis, quod is se citra dei gratiam tam non cognoscit, quam illum sine illa non agnoscit". (Thus it is Christ who causes us to repent of our former life; for in our consideration of man we have made quite clear that apart from the grace of God he knows himself as little as he knows God. Z III 692).

228. "To summarise what I think, I term 'Gospel' everything that reveals God to men and makes demands of them". Z II 79.

"For this reason the shepherds should abound in the word of God, and should so preach the gospel, which cannot be understood apart from the law, that good and bad alike may know the way that leads to God". Z II 653.

Cf. Z III 18. See below, note 265.

229. *Luther*: "Dominus et magister noster Jesus Christus dicendo: Penitentiam agite etc. omnem vitam fidelium penitentiam esse voluit". (Our Lord and Master Jesus Christ, in saying 'Repent ye, etc.' meant the whole life of the faithful to be an act of repentance. 1st Thesis, 1517. WA I 233).

"Quando deus incipit hominem iustificare, prius eum damnat, et quem vult aedificare, destruit, Quem vult sanare, percutit, quem vivificare, occidit ... Hoc autem facit, quando hominem conterit, et in sui suorumque peccatorum cognitionem humiliat ac tremefacit ... Sic convertuntur peccatores in infernum, et implentur facies eorum ignominia ... In ista autem conturbatione incipit salus. Quia initium sapientiae timor domini ... Hic denique operatur opus alienum deus, ut operetur opus suum. Haec est vera contritio cordis, et humiliatio spiritus gratissimum deo sacrificium". (When God begins to justify a man, he first condemns him; whoever he wishes to build up, he destroys; whoever he wishes to heal, he smites; whoever he wishes to make alive, he kills ... He does this when he crushes a man, and humbles and terrifies him with the knowledge of himself and his sins ... Thus sinners are turned to hell, and their faces are filled with shame ... But salvation begins with this very anguish. For the fear of the Lord is the beginning of wisdom. Here God works his strange work, in order that he may do his proper work. This is that true brokenness of heart and humility of spirit, which is the sacrifice well pleasing to God. WA I 540).

In the first Disputation with the Antonimians (1537), Luther states: "First Thesis: By common and true consent repentance is sorrow for sin combined with the intention to lead a better life. Second Thesis: Strictly speaking, this sorrow is nothing other, and can be nothing other than the effect or sense of the law in the heart of conscience". WA XXXIX/I 345.

In the third series of Theses against the Antinomians (1538) Luther states: "Fifth Thesis: The penitence of those who believe in Christ goes beyond their sinful acts; it is constant, and continues throughout the whole of life, until the very end. Sixth Thesis: For it is incumbent upon them to abhor to the end the sickness or sin of nature". WA XXXIX/I 350.

230. *Calvin*: "Poenitentiam vero non modo fidem continuo subsequi, sed ex ea nasci, ex-

ly, Zwingli sees repentance as consisting in sorrow for sin (not just over the consequences and punishment of sin),[231] in the breakdown of all trust in oneself as regards spiritual things,[232] in the knowledge of self[233] and the

---

tra controversiam esse debet. Quum enim venia et remissio per Evangelii praedicationem ideo offeratur, ut a tyrannide Satanae, peccati iugo, et misera servitute vitiorum liberatus peccator in regnum Dei transeat: certe Evangelii gratiam nemo aplecti potest quin ex erroribus vitae prioris in rectam viam se recipiat, totumque suum studium applicet ad poenitentiae meditationem. Quibus autem videtur fidem potius praecedere poenitentia quam ab ipsa manare vel proferri, tanquam fructus ab arbore, nunquam vis eius fuit cognita ... Nam dum in hunc modum concionantur Christus Dominus et Johannes, Poenitentiam agite, appropinquavit enim regnum caelorum: annon resipiscendi causam ab ipsa gratia et salutis promissione ducunt?... Neque tamen, quum resipiscentiae originem ad fidem referimus, spatium aliquod temporis somniamus quo ipsam parturiat: sed ostendere volumus, non posse hominem poenitentiae serio studere nisi se Dei esse noverit. Dei autem se esse nemo vero persuasus est, nisi qui eius gratiam prius apprehenderit ..." (That repentance not only always follows faith, but is produced by it, ought to be beyond controversy. For since pardon and forgiveness are offered by the preaching of the gospel, in order that the sinner, delivered from the tyranny of Satan, the yoke of sin and the miserable bondage of iniquity, may pass into the kingdom of God, it is certain that no man can embrace the grace of the gospel without betaking himself from the errors of his former life into the right path, and making it his whole study to practise repentance. Those who think that repentance precedes faith rather than flowing from it, or being produced by it, as the fruit by the tree, have never understood its nature ... For when Christ our Lord and John begin their preaching thus: 'Repent, for the kingdom of heaven is at hand', do they not deduce repentance as a consequence of the offer of grace and promise of salvation?... Still, when we attribute the origin of the repentance to faith, we do not dream of some period of time in which faith is to give birth to it; we only wish to show that a man cannot seriously engage in repentance unless he knows that he is of God. But no man is truly persuaded that he is of God until he has first embraced his grace... *Institutes* III. iii. 1-2).

231. *Zwingli*: "... And a man does not live in himself, but Christ lives in him, and so much so that if he even thinks of some wickedness, he grieves about it from that moment on, and reproaches himself for his wantonness". Z I 118. Cf., inter alia, the final chapter of the *Commentarius*, Z III 909-910 (a section dealing with the subject of how man is freed from despair by the grace of God).

"See, how we are nothing at all, and can do nothing because of the flesh. Wherefore, after his preceding words, in which he has accused himself of being led into captivity to sin, St. Paul cries out, 'O wretched man that I am! who shall deliver me from the body of this death?' (Romans 7:24). By which he means that the bondage of the inner man is death". Z I 351. Cf. also note 233.

232. "This consolation (i.e. the gospel) saves us from despairing of God; we must despair of ourselves". Z II 481.

"Where God's grace is not present, there is no salvation, but rather total despair". Z II 631.

"We are only flesh, as God says in Genesis 6 ... therefore it follows that by nature we can do nothing that is either right or good..." Z II 632.

"However much we endeavour to satisfy the demands of his word, and to follow it, we always find that we are helpless..." Z II 482.

233. "Whoever learns to know himself discovers within himself such a Lernaean Hydra of wickedness, that he is not merely racked with pain, but driven to terrible despair and

denial of self[234] and in guarding against a possible relapse.[235] It involves constantly resorting to the mercy of Christ,[236] for (like all the reformers) he applies Romans 7, with its cry of "wretched man that I am", to the one who is born again.[237] Sin "always" dwells in the believer, "although it is

---

death ... Therefore repentance is one aspect of the gospel—not partial repentance, but that repentance in which a man who has come to know himself, blushes and is ashamed of his former life. He is ashamed for a twofold reason; firstly, because he is so displeased with himself, and feels such grief concerning himself; and secondly, because he sees that it does not in any way befit a Christian to fall into those vices from whch he is so glad to be saved". Z III 701.

234. "...The more my name is despised among men for God's sake, the more honourable it will be in God's sight ... Christ shed his blood for our salvation. He is a worthless soldier who cannot shed his blood for his Lord and captain, and who flees to the rear, when his Lord has already suffered death before him and for him. The true warriors of Christ are those who are not afraid to have their heads crushed for their Lord's sake..." Z I 395.

"To deny oneself is a great sacrifice; for man is great in his own eyes". Z II 129. Cf. the whole section, Z II 128-130.

"Vita Christiana innocentia est, ut saepe iam diximus. At innocentiam nullus ager foelicius proferet, quam contemptus sui ipsius..." (The Christian life is one of uprightness, as we have often stated already. And in no field does the fruit of uprightness grow better than in that of self-denial. Z III 845).

"Innocentia" (uprightness) is to be understood in the sense of a guileless self-forgetfulness, as is shown by the context, and also by the later statement: "Constat ergo, quod, qui pii sunt, opera sua non aestimant: nunquam ergo de mercede eorum digladiantur. Contra vero, quod qui aestimant, impii sunt. Pius enim non est, qui se ipsum non abnegavit". (Thus it is plain that anyone who is pious does not have a high opinion of his own deeds; he never fights about the reward they should receive. On the contrary, it is the impious who set a high value on themselves. For whoever does not deny himself is not pious. Z III 850).

235. "If we rely on Christ, then this has come about by the power of God. Where God is present, there is an effort to get away from sin". Z II 641.

"Istud quoque patet, quod poenitentia peccata non abluit, sed spes in Christum; quodque poenitentia custodia est, ne in ea recidas, quae damnavisti". (It is also plain that it is not penitence which cancels sin, but faith in Christ; but penitence keeps guard to ensure that we do not fall back into that which has been cast off. Z III 705). Cf. also Z III 701.

236. "The knowledge of sin ... brings only despair with regard to ourselves, and drives us forcibly to the mercy of God. But we can be sure of that, for God has given his Son for us". Z III 18.

"Since we are never without sin, as it says in I John 1:8 ... and yet it is our duty to live according to God's will, which we can never fulfil, we can only cry out with St. Paul, 'O wretched man that I am! who shall deliver me from the body of this death?' and then we answer ourselves, 'The grace of God through Jesus Christ our Lord' ". Z I 351.

"Yes, indeed, all true believers experience this struggle ... However, it is obvious why God has suffered us to have such a struggle, namely, that in our sinful weakness we should be compelled by necessity to flee to him". Z II 47.

237. Inter alia, Z I 350-352; Z II 46-47; Z III 711-715; Z V 968.

mastered and held captive by Christ".[238] Thus Zwingli clearly expresses
the idea of the Christian's being "just yet a sinner at the same time",[239]
even though it may not be so prominent as it is with Luther.[240] We are

---

238. Z I 351; cf. Z II 47.

239. Z II 47. "...Discamus, quid vero eis eveniat, qui Christo fidunt, quomodo videlicet
per fidem salutis securi sint, per infirmitatem autem carnis nunquam non peccent, quanquam ea, quae peccant, vi fidei non imputentur". (We learn what befalls those who trust in
Christ, namely, that by faith they are assured of salvation, but by reason of the frailty of
their flesh they remain sinners, but by virtue of their faith their sins are not imputed to them.
Z III 706).
"These two things exist side by side: to be holy, and not to be free from sin ... whoever
rests on God with a true faith commits no sin that can condemn him. Yet he is not without
sin as long as he is in this world; but it is washed away by daily repenting, firmly believing
and turning to God in faith". Z IV 83.

240. The formula is already to be found in Luther's Lectures on Romans and in his first
Lectures on Galatians, e.g. WA II 497: "simul ergo iustus simul peccator". Cf. Paul
Althaus, Die Theologie Martin Luthers, Gütersloh, 1962, pp. 211-213; also Rudolf Hermann,
Luthers These Gerecht und Sünder zugleich, 1930, and Gesammelte Studien zur Theologie Luthers und
der Reformation, Göttingen, 1960, (pp. 391-427, especially pp. 401-405); H. J. Iwand,
Glaubensgerechtigkeit nach Luthers Lehre, 3rd ed., Munich, 1959; W. Joest, Gesetz und Freiheit,
1951, pp. 55ff. It should be born in mind that for Luther and Zwingli this formula and its
parallels do not simply constitute an anthropological statement that the converted man, as
he struggles against his sinful nature, is "partly this and partly that"; they constitute rather
a theological statement that man in his totality is at once wholly sinful and wholly righteous
in the sight of God. (To Althaus' illuminating exposition it should be added that the concept
of man as "totaliter peccator" is not merely an empirical observation but a divine verdict).
Upon closer examination, we find the same idea in Calvin. "Docemus itaque in sanctis,
donec mortali corpore exuantur, semper esse peccatum: quia in eorum carne resided illa con-
cupiscendi pravitas quae cum rectitudine pugnat". (Accordingly, we hold that there is
always sin in the saints, until they are freed from their mortal frame, because depraved concupiscence resides in their flesh, and is at variance with rectitude. Institutes III. iii. 10).
Calvin continues: "Praestat hoc quidem Deus, suos regenerando, ut peccati regnum in iis
aboleatur: (virtutem enim Spiritus subministrat, qua superiores in certamine victoresque
fiant), sed regnare tantum, non etiam habitare desinit ... Et illas (sc. reliquias peccati)
quidem fatemur non imputari, acsi non essent: sed hoc simul Dei misericordia fieri conten-
dimus ut ab hoc reatu liberentur sancti, qui merito alias peccatores et rei coram Deo
forent". (In regenerating his people God indeed accomplishes this much for them: he
destroys the dominion of sin, by supplying the agency of the Spirit, which enables them to
come off victorious from the contest. Sin, however, though it ceases to reign, ceases not to
dwell in them ... We admit that these remains (of sin) are not imputed, just as if they did not
exist; but at the same time we contend that it is owing to the mercy of God that the saints are
not charged with the guilt which would otherwise make them guilty sinners before God. Institutes III. iii. 11). Earlier editions of the Institutes contain the statement: "Itaque fidelis
anima, a regeneratione, in duas partes divisa est, quibus perpetuum inter se est
dissiduum..." (Thus the soul of the believer, from regeneration onwards, is divided into two
parts, between which there is a perpetual conflict. OS IV 63f. It was, perhaps, to avoid this
misleading idea of "parts" that this section was to thoroughly revised for the final edition to
1559/1561. In Zwingli's Christliche Einleitung (Z II 641f.) we find argumentation similar to
that of Calvin in the Institutes III. iii. 9ff.

never finished with our sin in this life,[241] but the struggle is not hopeless, since "all good works increase the more, the more one gives oneself to God".[242] The most dangerous temptation for the Christian is a self-appointed way of sanctification, for it is a pious means of avoiding God's command.[243] Real Christian living means simply keeping to the law of God[244] and the example of Christ[245] and in this way striving constantly for "purity".[246]

---

241. Zwingli declares: "Whoever does not alter his life day by day after he has been restored in Christ, is mocking the name of Christ, and makes it contemptible and shameful in the sight of believers". Z III 19.

"Est ergo tota Christiani hominis vita poenitentia. Quando enim est, ut non peccemus?" (Thus the whole life of a Christian man is repentance. For when does the time come when we are not sinners? Z III 695. Note the verbal resemblance to Luther's First Thesis, note 229). Cf. Z III 702.

242. Z II 93. "Though we may be aware that we are still far from perfection, we nevertheless feel that the measure of good in us is growing according to the measure of faith and trust in Christ". Z II 649.

"The believer believes by the Spirit of God. Where God is present, the good always grows and increases". Z II 644.

"Pugna igitur est vita Christiana, tam acris et periculosa, ut nusquam sine damno cessetur. Rursus perpetua quoque victoria est; nam qui hic pugnat, vincit, dummodo a capite Christo non deficit". (Thus the Christian life is a fight so fierce and dangerous that it can never be broken off without injury. But at the same time it is also a constant victory. For whoever fights this battle is victorious, provided he does not forsake Christ, his head. Z III 910; cf. the quotation from Calvin in note 240). The causes and the origins of the Zwinglian reformation (see above, ch. 1 and ch. 2) explain why Zwingli, despite his total rejection of the idea of human merit, should so forcefully exhort Christians to live a new life, as something inseparable from faith and repentance. He deals with this extensively in his early writings. Cf. Z II 45-50; Z II 640-644; Z II 486-493; 497-522.

243. In connexion with monastic vows, cf. Zwingli's warning against ἐθελοθρησκία (Colossians 2:23; AV "will worship", RSV "Rigour of devotion"): "quae nihil aliud est quam propria voluntate adinventa religio, quae nihil est quam hypocrisis ac legis divinae contemptus ... Aperte loquar et vere: Haec vota castitatis, paupertatis et obedientiae fuga sunt et declinatio legis divinae..." (which is nothing but a religion devised by one's own will, hypocrisy and contempt of God's law ... I will speak frankly and truly: these vows of chastity, poverty and obedience are a flight and a declension from the law of God... Z III 829).

"Qum ergo haec sola requirat a nobis deus: fidem et innocentiam, non potuit nocentior pestis excogitari, quam varius dei cultus nostra industria inventus". (Since God requires from us only faith and uprightness, it is not possible to conceive a worse pestilence than devising various forms of worship of God by our own efforts. Z III 910). Cf. also note 244.

244. "Si opus nostrum sit et non fidei iam sit perfidia, quam deus abominatur. Fides autem ut supra monuimus a solo dei spiritu est. Qui ergo fidem habent, in omni opere ad dei voluntatem velut ad archetypum spectant. Ex operibus ergo reiiciuntur non tantum quae contra legem dei fiunt, sed etiam ista quae sine lege dei fiunt. Lex enim est perpetua voluntas dei. Quae igitur sine lege, hoc est sine verbo et voluntate dei fiunt: non sunt ex fide. Quae non sunt ex fide, peccatum sunt; si sunt peccatum, iam aversatur illa deus. Unde adparet, ut etsi opus, quod deus praecepit, puta eleemosynam, quis faciat absque fide, opus illud deo non sit gratum. Quum enim inquirimus quisnam fons sit huius eleemosynae quae non ex fide orta est, invenimus eam ex vana gloria vel cupiditate plus recipiendi, vel aliquo alio affectu malo scaturivisse. Et eiusmodi opus quis non credat displicere deo?" (If the work

14. *The Law*

The law does not become meaningless for the disciple of Christ, for it is the unchanging will of God.[247] External commandments are indeed repealed through Christ; this includes those contained in the Bible, and especially the ceremonial law.[248] But that which concerns the inner man has been endued with eternal validity by Christ himself, the divine lawgiver.[249] This is the commandment of love, to which the "natural law"

---

is of ourselves, and not of faith, then it is unbelief, which God abhors. But faith, as we have already stated, comes only from the Spirit of God. Thus, in all their works, those who have faith look to the will of God as their pattern. Therefore they reject from their works not only those which are done contrary to the law of God, but also those which are done apart from the law of God. For the law is God's constant will. Therefore, whatever is done without the law, that is, without the word and will of God, is not of faith. Whatever is not of faith is sin (Romans 14:23). If it is sin, God rejects it. Whence it follows that if someone performs a work which God prescribes, such as giving of alms, but does so without faith, then that work is not pleasing to God. For if we inquire after the cause of this almsgiving which has not come from faith, we find that it has sprung from vanity, or the desire to gain more in return, or some other evil disposition. And who would not believe that a work of this kind is displeasing to God? S IV 61).

245. "That man alone is a Christian, who has died to himself and to the world, and who walks in God's way, that is, according to the law of Christ". Z III 381.

"To be a Christian is not a matter of chattering about Christ, but of following in the way he went". Z III 407.

Zwingli calls on the brethren in Augsburg to act in truly reformed manner: "Endeavour yourselves daily to be changed into the likeness of Christ". Z III 502.

Zwingli exhorts the "shepherds" in particular: "The shepherd must not be conformed to teachings of human invention, but to the word of God which he preaches; otherwise he will plant nothing but hypocrisy. And since Christ is such a perfect model, he must see to it that he conforms to his pattern". Z III 20.

246. Cf. notes 234, 243. "Vera pietas nihil aliud est quam ex amore timoreque dei servata innocentia". (True piety is nothing other than uprightness, preserved by the love and fear of God. Z III 775).

"Vita Christiana innocentia est, ut saepe iam diximus". (The Christian life is one of uprightness, as we have often stated already. Z III 845).

247. "Lex est perpetua voluntas dei". (The Law is God's constant will. S IV 61).

"Lex est numinis iussus, illius ingenium ac voluntatem exprimens. Atque si lubet concisius loqui, dicito: Lex est perpetua voluntas dei". (The law is God's command, the expression of his character and his will. In short, the law is God's eternal will. S IV 102). Cf. Z II 634.

248. "Lex vetus est abrogata quatenus ceremonialis est et iudicialis". (The old law is abrogated, in so far as it was ceremonial and judicial. Z I 291). Cf. Z II 496; S VI, I 99.

249. "Thus the law has been both renewed and also abolished by Christ. Renewed, in that Christ has stated and commanded what God requires of us more precisely than ever before. Abolished, in that the transgression of the law can no longer condemn us, if we steadfastly believe that Christ has fulfilled it, and has paid the ransom price to gain access to God for us for all eternity". Z II 496. Cf. Z II 237; Z II 492. With reference to the law of love, Zwingli speaks of "Christus ipse legislator" (Christ is himself a lawgiver. Z III 707).

had pointed, albeit in vain.[250] But the "Law of Christ" belongs to our salvation, equally with forgiveness.[251] The one who is filled with love rejoices in it; and so it loses its legal character[252] and is revealed as an aspect

---

250. "The law is nothing other than the revelation of God's will. Just as the will of God is eternal, so the law is also eternal. We are speaking now only of that law which promotes the piety of the inner man. This is, indeed, nothing other than the revelation of God's eternal will. For example, the law 'Thou shalt love thy neighbour as thyself' (Leviticus 19:18, Matthew 22:39) is nothing other than the law of nature, which states: 'Whatsoever ye would that men should do to you, do so to them' (Matthew 7:12, Luke 6:31), and conversely, 'See thou never do to another what thou wouldst hate to have done to thee' (Tobit 4:16). Indeed, this law of nature, which God has sweetened with love, must come only from God. And even if the heathen also accept it, it does not come from human reason, whatever they may say. For human reason looks to itself, and does not think of belonging to others; it thinks that others should belong to it and serve it. Therefore every law that makes the inward man pious can come only from God. But understand this, that laws do not have the power to make a man pious or righteous; they only show him what a man should be if he, living in accordance with the will of God, wishes to be pious and come to God. Romans 7:12 states that the law is holy; and the commandment is also holy. Now it could not be holy, unless it came from someone who is holy. If it came from us, it would not be holy, for we are not holy. Therefore Paul says again a little later (Romans 7:14): 'We know that the law is spiritual'. But since we are carnal, it is clear that the law cannot come from us. This all points to the conclusion that the law, which teaches us true inward piety, must proceed from the will of God alone". Z II 634. Cf. Z II 262; Z II 294; Z XIII 268.

251. "Here I understand to be gospel everything that God has made known to us through his only Son. It is gospel even when he says, "You should not be angry with one another' (Matthew 5:22), or when he says that one commits adultery simply by lusting (Matthew 5:28), or when he says that one should not resist the person who harms one (Matthew 5:39), and similar laws; which many people will no doubt consider inappropriate. But my opinion is that a man who rightly believes is delighted and nourished by every word of God, even though it may be contrary to the desires of the flesh; whereas the unbeliever regards every word of God as false and untrue". Z II 76. Cf. Z I 99.

"Constat igitur legem, ut propius accedamus, numinis ingenium, voluntatem et naturam esse, quod ad essentiam legis attinet. Quo fit, ut ubicunque lex dei pronuncietur, admirandum in modum reficiatur quicquid dei cognitionem habet. Eodem fit, ut quae dei notitiam non habent ex auditu legis nihil voluntatis aut commodi capiant. Quum ergo deus per legem voluntatem suam homini communicat; iam ista traditione sua duorum nos certos facit: unius quod ad deum cognoscendum nati; alterius quod ad illo fruendum destinati sumus". (It is clear that if we consider it more closely, the law is in essence the character, will and nature of God. Whence it comes, that wherever the law of God is declared, everything that has knowledge of God is renewed in a remarkable manner. And at the same time, everything that has no knowledge of God gains no inclination or profit through hearing the law. Since God makes his will known to men by the law, he teaches us two things in giving us the law: first, that we are born into the world in order to know God; and secondly, that we are intended to enjoy fellowship with him. S IV 105).

252. "Sic sumus liberati: Qui amat, libere omnia facit, etiam gravissima". (Thus are we set free; whoever loves does everything gladly, even the hardest things. Z III 710). "The believer keeps the commandments out of love, the godless man hates them. The believer does not keep them by his own strength, but God effects in him the love, the decision and the deed". Z II 237.

Cf. the section "Vom abthuon des gsatztes" (The abolition of the law) in the *Christliche Einleitung* (1523), Z II 646-654. Here we quote a part: "If this law (sc. the law of love, Matthew 22:37ff.) were abolished, then faith would be abolished, for it is nothing other than a

of the Gospel.[253] Free from the law, we stand on the side of the law.[254] Clearly opposing the sharp antithesis made by Luther, Zwingli affirms

constant clinging to God ... The law kills us ... Therefore everyone feels that he is rightly condemned according to God's righteousness. But Christ renders satisfaction to God—for he is our righteousness—so see how we are redeemed from the law; that is, we are set free, so that the law cannot kill us; the law remains fixed for eternity—all the law remains unabrogated for all eternity, as far as the inner man is concerned ... The believer already lives in Christ and Christ lives in him. For having such faith is not due to human reason or powers, but to the hand and power of God. And see, such a believer needs no law, for his whole life is fixed on Christ ... He who lives in grace, lives in God, and God lives in him. For all that God demands of him is sweet and acceptable and pleasing to him in the inner man, even though he cannot fulfil it because of his weakness. For he holds fast to the grace of God. And what pleases God pleases him also, even though the flesh cannot follow in this..." Z II 647-649.

253. "The law is nothing other than the eternal, unchanging will of God, who wills nothing but what is just and good. Now how can the will of God be known to us, unless he declares it to us? We call this declaration law, because it is contrary to our flesh, which will not suffer anything save what pleases it. But truly, it is in itself nothing other than gospel, that is, a good and certain message from God, in which he reveals his will to us. And how could a pious man be anything but happy when God reveals his will to him? Thus the law teaches us what is pleasing to God. If the law is pleasing to us, then the Spirit of God is in us, for otherwise the law could not please us. For in us there is no good thing, as Paul says in Romans 7..." Z II 159.

254. The reformation preacher finds some extremely vivid and down-to-earth illustrations for this paradox of the eternal validity of the law and the believer's freedom from the law. "An example will make him clear. 'Thou shalt not steal' is an eternal commandment. If someone has committed a theft, and you arrange with the judge to save him from the gallows, he is now freed from the law; that is, he is freed from the penalty of the law. But he is not free in the sense that he may henceforth steal contrary to the law. And even if one were to save him from the gallows whenever he stole, yet he would never be free in the sense of not being obliged to keep the law". Z II 647.

"To give another example: if a town should forbid its citizens, on pain of being impaled or broken on a wheel, to receive payment, gifts or presents from any foreigner, the order would be received in different ways. Those who would not wish to transgress the law, out of love of righteousness or for love of their town, would not find it burdensome; for even if there were no such law, they would still not accept gifts. But the law weighs down upon the selfish, and so they oppose it. The pious man is not under the law, but the selfish man is; for the pious man lives happily and freely in his love of righteousness, whereas the selfish man lives only under the pressure of the law, which comes about because he has no love of piety. So the man who enjoys the freedom of the gospel is not under law; the Spirit of God, who has led him into the knowledge of evangelical freedom, is his guide. The Spirit makes him glad to do everything that God wants; and it does not upset him that some things are commanded or forbidden; for the Spirit of God, who has already inspired him, shows him what God wants..." Z II 83.

"If we are completely surrendered to God, we no longer need any law. For it is God himself who leads us; and as God himself needs no law, so the man in whom God lives needs no law either, for God leads him..." Z II 649.

In Zwingli's understanding of freedom from the law we may trace the beginnings of the Calvinist concept of the "third use of the law". E.g. "What is the law of the living Spirit? Answer: the guidance and instruction which God gives us through a right understanding of his word, provided that we trust in him..." Z II 649.

"Eos qui in Christum credunt non damnat, sed ducit potius lex". (The law does not condemn those who believe in Christ, but rather leads them. S VI, II 90).

that "The law is a gospel for the man who honours God".[255] For Martin Luther, the distinction between Law and Gospel is a basic principle of his entire theology and of his preaching.[256] "The whole of Scripture and the

255. Z II 232. "The law means only what is eternally right and good; for the law is good, righteous and holy, as it says in Romans 7. Do you want to know why? It is because it is nothing other than a revelation and declaration of the will of God, and we see from the word of commandment what God wants and demands. Thus it may more appropriately be called gospel rather than law. For what man, living in human darkness and ignorance, would not rejoice if God revealed his will to him? And would that not be good news, if the will of God were made known to man? You must say 'Yes', if you would speak the truth. For if an earthly prince were to reveal his foolish secret to you, you would regard it as a great favour. And that is why I said that the law is gospel to the man who loves God. But if the law, which is holy, good and righteous, is not loved, and does not delight us, or make us fruitful, that is not because it is the nature of the law in itself to frighten or oppress or sadden those who hear it. It is because of the sadness of our flesh. Therefore, I should appreciate it, if some who write about the law in our own day, saying that the law terrifies us, and causes us to despair and to hate God, would correct what they say with more appropriate words. For despair and hatred of God are not caused by the law, but by the sinful weakness of our flesh, which cannot fulfil the law, and therefore acts in the way that helplessness is wont to do: it begins to hate what it cannot attain. Paul has stated this truly in Romans 7: 'We know that the law is spiritual, but I am carnal, sold under sin'... See, whether it is not more appropriate to call it gospel rather than law? I say this now for the sake of proper understanding. I do not want the names 'law and gospel' to be so mixed up that one cannot tell one from the other. As has already been said, what could bring more joy to the human mind, than for God to reveal his will? But we call it law, because our flesh squirms under it, and feels impatient: but the law in itself is spiritual and righteous, and so nobody can attain to it or fulfil it unless he is spiritual". H III 306-307; Z II 232-233.

"To summarise: I call everything gospel which God reveals to men and demands from men. For whenever God reveals his will to men, those who love God rejoice; and thus it is for them a sure and good message; and for their sake I call it gospel, and I prefer to call it gospel rather than law; for it is more fitting to name it after the believer than the unbeliever. This also puts an end to the dispute about law and gospel". Z II 79.

This early criticism of Luther, which dates from 1523 (in the *Exposition*) may be compared with the later one to be found in Zwingli's *De providentia* (1530): "Constat igitur ut, quum lex iussus dei sit, expressa sit illius voluntas; quumque illius est voluntas, ipse quoque illius sit sententiae quam nobis praecipit ... Hinc apparet, nostra tempestate quosdam primi, ut ipsi credunt, nominis non satis circumspecte locutos esse de lege, quum nihil aliud de ea quam quod terreat, quod damnet dirisque addicat, prodiderunt; quum re vera lex ista prorsus non faciat, sed contra numinis voluntatem et ingenium exponat: cui quid comparari potest? Si credit rex aut imperator sententiam suam, consilium et ingenium decurioni aut tribuno: quomodo ille non exilit et gestit prae laetitia?..." (Thus it is certain; if the law is God's command, it is the expression of his will; and since it is his will, he is himself of that same mind which he prescribes for us ... Wherefore it is apparent, that in our day, certain people who consider themselves to be most eminent have not spoken of the law with sufficient care, since they have stated only that it terrifies, and condemns men and consigns them to hell. Whereas in reality the law does not do that at all, but rather sets forth the will and intention of God. What is to be compared to it? If a king or an emperor entrusted his decision, his counsel and his intention to an official or an officer, would not that man spring up and leap for joy?... S IV 102-103).

256. Cf. Theodosius Harnack, *Luthers Theologie mit besonderer Beziehung auf seine Versöhnungs- und Erlösungslehre*, 1862; new edition, ed. W. F. Schmidt, Munich, 1927, Vol. 1, pp.

knowledge of the whole of theology depends, so to speak, upon a right understanding of Law and Gospel".[257] The fact that his reformation faith had its origin in the troubles of his soul continually comes to light at this point, because for Luther, the devil and the law go together: the devil actually appeals to the law of God in order to cast the sinner into despair. "The chief trick of the devil is that he can make law out of the Gospel ... The distinction between the law and the Gospel, that does it, because the devil beats one over the head with a word; if one sticks with the law, one is done for ..."[258] So it is not by chance that one finds in his Table-talk this further ironic comment. "Whatever Scripture is, it is either Law or Gospel; one of the two must triumph, either the law, leading to despair, or the Gospel, leading to salvation. I'm learning this every day, and Zwingli and Duke George can do it".[259] As is well known, for Luther this tension developed into the tension between God's wrath and God's mercy. But whereas Luther found it helpful to distinguish the two, *Zwingli*, having experienced *his own* troubles, and having laid hold of salvation through the cross of Christ in *his own* way, found it helpful to join them: "Therefore the justice and mercy of God ought to be joined and integrated in the heart of believers".[260]

If we glance ahead to John Calvin once more, we find a similar attitude. He allows Luther's point, but does not fall into line behind him by making the opposition of Law to Gospel *the* theme of theology. Calvin characteristically shifts the problem into the realm of salvation history, and explains that in this way "we see the error of those who, in comparing the Law with the Gospel, represent it merely as a comparison between the merit of works, and the gratuitous imputation of righteousness. The con-

---

444-461; Paul Althaus, *Die Theologie Martin Luthers*, Gütersloh, 1962, pp. 218-238; for a lucid summary by Luther himself, see the Preface to the *First Disputation against the Antinomians*.

257. "Pene universa scriptura totiusque Theologiae cognitio pendet in recta cognitione legis et euangelii". (WA VII 502). Cf. *Luther's* words to Erasmus: "Obsecro te, quid ille in re Theologica vel sacris literis efficiat, qui nondum eo pervenit, ut, quid Lex quid Euangelion sit, norit, aut, si norit, contemnat tamen observare? Is omnia misceat oportet, coelum, infernum, vitam, mortem, ac prorsus nihil de Christo scire laborabit". (I pray you, what man have to say with regard to a theological question or Holy Scripture who has not yet reached the point where he knows the difference between law and gospel—or, if he does, pays slight attention to it? Such a man must confuse everything—heaven and hell, life and death—and find himself in the difficulty of knowing nothing at all about Christ. WA XVIII 680; Clemen III, 172).

258. Luther, *Tischreden*, No. 590 (Clemen VIII, 76f.).

259. *Tischreden*, No. 626 (Clemen VIII, 79f.).

260. "Debent ergo iustitia et misericordia dei iungi et permisceri in corde credentium". S VI, I 531; cf. note 62, above.

trast thus made is by no means to be rejected .... (Paul) appropriately represents the righteousness of the Law and the Gospel as opposed to each other. But the Gospel has not succeeded the whole Law in such a sense as to introduce a different method of salvation. It rather confirms the Law, and proves that everything which was promised is fulfilled. What was shadow, it has made substance ..."[261]

Zwingli is also linked with the later reformed tradition in that the famous division of the *Heidelberg Catechism* could already be felt as the pulse-beat of his faith.[262] In March 1524, he could still recommend that the "shepherds" should follow the Lutheran order of "Law and Gospel" in their preaching, "for the sickness must be recognised, before one takes the medicine".[263] But by December of that same year, in a basic dogmatic study intended for "Franz Lambert and the other brothers in Strasbourg", he was moving on to formulations which, while alluding to Luther, actually go beyond him, and anticipate Karl Barth's order of "Gospel and Law".[264] Because of his emphasis on the spiritus prae-veniens, this had to come sooner or later: "We have to preach faith constantly, so that it can form the foundation on which the Law can be built up ... for where there is no faith, you will sing your little song about the Law in vain".[265]

---

261. *Institutes* II. ix. 4. *Calvin's* criticism is directed against Luther as well as the Antinomians.

262. *Zwingli's* writings often foreshadow the famous tripartite exposition of "the only comfort in life and in death" which was provided by the Heidelberg Catechism of 1563, viz.: "The Misery of Man", "The Redemption of Man" and "Thankfulness". One finds verbal similarities, for example, in a single sentence in *The Shepherd* (1524): "If a man has acknowledged his misery, and has thereupon found salvation in Christ Jesus, then it is no longer fitting for him to live in sin". Z III 19. In the same work Zwingli summarises the Word of God, with regard to the preacher's task, as follows: "Man's sinful weakness"—"the grace of God", Jesus Christ—"to live henceforth according to God's will", Z III 22. The verbal resemblance between Question 12 of the Heidelberg Catechism and certain sentences in the *Christliche Einleitung* is so striking that one is bound to conclude that the latter had a direct influence upon the former. Cf. Z II 637.

263. "Nobody improves himself if he does not know how bad he is. Therefore man's weakness must be preached first, and then salvation. And let nobody make the mistake of thinking that in Matthew 10 and Mark 16 Christ bids us only to preach salvation, or the gospel; for a man must recognise his weakness before he will take the medicine". Z III 18.

264. The first formal statement is to be found in Barth's *Evangelium und Gesetz*, Theologische Existenz Heute, No. 32, 1935 (reprinted Munich, 1961).

265. "Perpetuo igitur praedicanda est fides, ut ea fundamentum fiat, supra quam aedificetur lex. Sed quid hic dico, fidem legis esse fundamentum? inusitatus est hic sermo. Nemo offendatur! verum est, quod dicimus. Nam fides nisi adsit frustra legis cantilenam canes, ut iam patuit, quia ii modo pastoris vocem audiunt, qui sunt ex ovibus eius. Legem vis a quoquam recipi? doce fidem ac ora deum, ut ipsum trahat, alioqui littus arabis. Hoc tamen interim observamus, ut propter fidelium varietatem simul legem ac fidem

15. Sin

The Law reveals our "wretchedness"[266] to us; and it does this most forcibly through the word and the example of Christ, which show us the radical, spiritual significance of the commandments.[267] Our whole knowledge of our *sin*[268] presupposes instruction by the Spirit and faith.[269] Zwingli retains the traditional distinction between original sin (*peccatum originale*) and actual sins (*peccata actualia*).[270] The former he termed "sickness" (south Germanic "prästen"), which was his rendering of the word "morbus" employed by Augustine. But Zwingli's term has been

praedicemus ... Fides igitur sic perpetuo firmanda inculcandaque erit, ut lex tamen nusquam omittatur, qua fides delectatur; beatus enim, qui in lege domini meditatur die ac nocte; ubi vero fides alget aut desidet, extimulatur. Nam quod hactenus de lege omnes dicimus, quod terreat, sic verum est, quod eos modo terret, qui deo fidunt; nam impii, dum in profundum peccatorum, ut Salomon inquit, veniunt, contemnunt. Lex dei, si quenquam terret, eum terret, qui hunc deum suum esse confitetur, cuius legem audit, creditque hanc ipsam legem a deo esse. Lex igitur nusquam omittenda, nusquam negligenda est, sed hac ratione, ut studium eius, quod lex iubet, ex fide oriatur". (Therefore faith must be preached constantly, so that it can form the foundation upon which the law can be built up. But what am I saying here? That faith is the foundation of the law? This manner of speaking is unusual. Let nobody be offended. What we say is true. For if there is no faith, you will sing your little song about the law in vain. This follows from the fact that only those who are his sheep hear the voice of the shepherd. Do you want someone to accept the law? Then teach him faith, and pray to God that he will draw him, otherwise you will be labouring in vain. Though I would remark, incidentally, that because of the differences among believers, we have to preach law and faith at the same time ... Thus faith is constantly to be established and to be inculcated in such a way that the law is never omitted, for faith delights in the law. For blessed is the man who meditates in the law day and night! But where faith grows cold or idle, it must be stimulated. For all that we have said thus far concerning the law, namely, that it should cause fear, is true only in so far as it frightens those who believe in God. For the godless despise it, if they have fallen into the depths of sin, as Solomon says (Proverbs 18:3). If the law of God frightens anyone, it frightens the man who confesses that this God whose law he hears is his God, and who believes that this law itself is from God. Therefore the law is never to be omitted, and never to be neglected, being mindful that zeal for what the law requires springs from faith. Z VIII 263, 264. (Zwingli himself draws attention to his change of view).

266. "But since our mind cannot of itself recognise what is right and godly, God has revealed his law to us, so that we may see thereby what is right or wrong. For as Paul says in Romans 7: 'I had not known sin, but by the law' ". Z II 634. Cf. note 262.

267. Cf. e.g. Z I 103; Z II 477; Z II 479-487; Z III 707.

268. Z III 708-720.

269. See notes 227 and 228 above.

270. "One should here note that the word 'sin' is taken to mean something like this: the weakness of our broken nature, which is always inciting us to the temptations of the flesh, and which can therefore fittingly be called 'the irreparable breach' (präst) ... thus sin is this sinful breach, from which the various sins grow like branches. Therefore adultery, whoremongering, gluttony, avarice, arrogance, envy, ill-will, discord and murder are the fruit and the branches of this sinful weakness, which Paul also calls 'the flesh' in Galatians 5:19 and many other places; for these gullies spring from our broken flesh as from a fount". Z II 44; Z II 235.

consistently misunderstood. It does not mean merely "infirmity" or "defect", but rather an "incurable breach".[271] Since Adam, our nature is "broken", and completely so.[272] Everything in us is evil; even our spiritual existence is "flesh".[273] And so it remains, even though in Zwingli's later writings the soul (*mens, anima*), and not the understanding (*ratio, intellectus*), is seen as that part of man to which the Holy Spirit primarily addresses himself.[274] As with Augustine and Luther, original sin is love of self (*amor sui*) and turning in upon oneself.[275] It always means

---

271. Z II 99; Z II 493; Z II 631. Cf. also *Th. H. Z.* I, pp. 137-140.

272. Cf. notes 270 and 271 above. "See how things stand with our flesh, that is, our human or natural reason and wisdom. Nothing good comes from it, for it is evil by its very nature and character, as God himself has said in Genesis 8..." Z II 98.

"Thus it follows that by nature we are as incapable as was Adam of doing anything that is either right or good ... And this is the real original sin: the fall, trespass, impotence, loss of God, sinful breach, sin or whatever you want to call it..." Z II 632.

Cf. Z II 176f. "Nothing good comes from man". Z II 177, 30. Cf. also Z III 658.

273. "God is not present where the flesh is (this is nothing but our own knowledge and reason)". Z II 95; cf. Z II 633.

"Mala igitur mens, malusque est animus hominis ab ineunte aetate, quia caro est". (The mind of man is evil, and his spirit is evil from the moment his life begins, because he is flesh. Z III 659).

"Loquitur Paulus non de ea carne, quam cum camelis habemus communem ... Sed de toto homine, qui, utut ex anima corporeque rebus nature diversis compactus est, caro tamen adpellatur, quod pro ingenio suo nihil quam carnale mortiferumque cogitet." (Paul is not speaking of that flesh which we have in common with camels ... but of the whole man; and although he consists of soul and body, two elements which are different by nature, yet man is called 'flesh', because by disposition his mind is set only on what is carnal and deadly. Z III 660). A similar saying is to be found in Z III 713, with the difference that he refers to oxen instead of camels.

274. Cf. Z V 820, where Zwingli says, in connexion with Romans 8:16: "Fides est illud firmum et essentiale animi, quo fertur in deum..." (Faith is that true steadfastness of the soul by which it is lifted up to God).

Cf. also S IV 119, in reference to Hebrews 11:1: "Fides est essentiale ac firmum illud in animis nostris quod ab deo datum est..." (Faith is that true steadfastness in our souls which is given to us by God). Similarly, "fides lux et securitas animi" (faith is the light and the security of the soul) and "fides lux et pastus animi" (faith is the light and the food of the soul), S IV 121.

In connexion with John 3:6, Zwingli states, "Spiritu spiritus generatur, non re corporea". (The spirit is begotten by the Spirit, and not by any corporeal thing. S IV 13). See further S IV 34f., with quotation from Augustine, and S IV 55, with reference to the Lord's Supper. If the Holy Spirit does not first bestow faith, then the sacrament can mediate at best a "fides historica". Conversely, "corpus" and "sensus" furnish dangerous openings for sin; cf. S IV 57; S IV 99-100 (where the influence to Pico della Mirandola is to be seen). In the eucharistic controversy, Luther must have noted this "spiritual metaphysics" and rejected it. Cf. Helmut Gollwitzer, "Zur Auslegung von Joh. 6 bei Luther und Zwingli" in *Evangelische Theologie*, 1951.

275. "Therefore the will of the flesh, that is, of our broken human nature, struggles constantly against God. If God bids us die, or suffer, or be patient, then we all know well how

turning away from the divine Spirit to oneself and to the creature.[276] Physical death is the consequence and the picture of that eternal death of which we already partake.[277] The biological notion of "hereditary sin" is scarcely to be found,[278] as it recedes behind the judicial and ethical conception of our situation in peccatum originale.[279] It is quite clear from all

---

sweet that seems to us! It all springs from the sinful weakness of man's first fall and his self-centredness". Z II 633.

"Adam turned away from the light and guidance of the Spirit of God, and turned to himself, and trusting in his own counsel he thought to become great and like God. Through this sin he brought himself and us under the dominion or slavery of the law of sin and of bitter death". Z II 38.

Cf. Z III 661-662. "Misera conditio lapsi hominis, qua perpetuo sui amans ac studiosus est". (The wretched state of fallen man, in which he is continually taken up with love and concern for himself. Z III 662).

For original sin as "amor sui" cf. S IV 6.

276. "Peccatum in nobis inhabitans aliud non est, quam vitium corruptae carnis, quae amore sui perpetuo concupiscit adversus spiritum. Spiritus enim rei publicae studet, caro privatae ... Amor sui haec omnia invenit atque concinnat. Ipse ergo morbus aut vitium est, ex quo tot mala velut ex equo Troiano prodeunt". (The sin which dwells in us is nothing other than the defectiveness of our corrupt flesh, which because of its self-love is filled with constant longings that are in opposition to the spirit. For the spirit seeks the common good, whereas the flesh seeks its own ... Self-love contrives and hatches everything. It is the sickness or defectiveness from which all evils come, as though from a Trojan horse. Z V 377).

"Man falls by nature on that which is presented to his senses". Z IV 92.

277. "Peccati enim mors corporeae mortis parens est". (The death which consists of sin is the parent of physical death. Z III 657). Cf. Z II 34f.

278. Zwingli states, "Istud originale peccatum per conditionem et contagionem agnasci omnibus qui ex adfectu maris et feminae gignuntur, agnosco, et nos esse natura filios irae scio, sed gratia, quae per secundum Adamum, Christum, casum restituit, inter filios dei recipi non dubito". (I acknowledge that because of their condition and by infection, original sin is innate in all who are born of the desire of man and woman; and I know that we are by nature children of wrath. But I do not doubt that we are received among the children of God through the grace of God in Christ, the second Adam, which has remedied the fall.). But even this statement is to be found in the context of our being descendants of a rebel who has been imprisoned and enslaved, S IV 7. "Criminis igitur tanquam causae, non nativitatis, est humana calamitas; nativitatis vero non aliter quam eius quod ex fonte et causa sequitur". (It is sin, therefore, and not human descent, which is the cause of man's wretchedness; it is due to human descent only in so far as this follows from the real cause. S IV 6).

279. "Primum parentem nostrum perdere cum posset vel aequitate iubente, melior tamen deus supplicium in conditionem vertit, ut servum faceret quem plectere potuisset. Hanc conditionem nec ipse nec quisquam ex ipso natus quum tollere posset (nequit enim servus nisi servum gignere): omnem posteritatem exitiali gustu in servitutem coniecit ... Peccatum originale ... morbus igitur est proprie et conditio. Morbus, quia sicut ille ex amore sui lapsus est ita et nos labimur; conditio, quia sicut ille servus est factus et morti obnoxius, sic et nos servi et filii irae nascimur et morti obnoxii..." (It would have been right and reasonable for God to have had our first parent destroyed. But in his mercy God changed this death sentence into the condition wherein he whom God might have killed was made into a slave. And neither he nor his offspring could alter this condition, for a slave can only

Zwingli's terminological, exegetical and dogmatic statements about "original sin"[280] that he certainly has no desire to conceal the depth of human sinfulness or to mitigate the gravity of human guilt,[281] in the way that Lutherans have mistakenly represented him, right down to the present day. He is, rather, concerned to prevent us, as far as possible, from taking refuge in the idea of fate, and to bring us to a sense of personal responsibility for our guilt. "Guilt" in the strictest sense is never a general concept, but is always "my guilt". "Just as Adam fell through love of self, so we fall also".[282] As a humanist he was familiar with the attitude of fatalism that was so widespread in the Renaissance era; it is as though he could foresee how easily the Lutheran formulation of the doctrine of original sin would be transformed into a melancholy metaphysics, in which "guilt" would turn into a tragic inevitability. Compared with Luther himself, there may be a difference in the terminology and in the argumentation but there is not (contrary to first appearances) any material contradiction.[283] According to Zwingli, the "sickness" has two aspects: (1) Ontologically: the necessity of sinning; (2) Noetically: blindness to God and to his revelation.[284] "Man is deceitful"—Zwingli emphasises this factor with especial vigour as against the optimistic search for truth of the humanists.[285]

Within the overall tradition of the history of dogma, Zwingli belongs to those theologians who have most consistently taken up the cudgels against

---

beget a slave; so by that deadly bite he plunged the whole of his posterity into slavery ... Original sin ... is really, therefore, a sickness and a state. It is a sickness, because just as he fell through self-love, so do we; it is a state, because just as he became a slave, and subject to death, so we are born as slaves and children of wrath and subject to death..." S IV 6).

280. E.g. Z II 44, 55, 96, 99, 163, 177, 186, 235, 365, 485, 493, 633. Cf. De peccato originali declaratio (1526), Z V 359-396; S IV 6-7.

281. Cf. Z III 658. For Zwingli's criticism of the Vulgate, which dilutes the clear Hebrew truth of Genesis 8:21 by its rendering "prona ad malum" (Douai version: "prone to evil"), and also his polemic against the related scholastic anthropology, Z III 661; similarly Z II 98f.

282. S IV 6. (Note 279 above).

283. Article IV of the Marburg Articles acknowledged the agreement at this point. Cf. Z VI, II 521.

284. Z II 96-99.

285. "Of ourselves, we know no more of God than a beetle knows of man. Indeed, the infinite and eternal deity is more remote from man than man is from a beetle, because it is more fitting to compare creatures with one another than to compare creatures with the creator ... We leave to Lucifer and Prometheus the impudence of presuming to know what God is, other than by the Spirit of God. Therefore, whatever theologians bring forward from philosophy regarding the question of God is deception and false religion..." Z III 643; H IX 23f.

"From this have arisen wanton opinions concerning free will, our own ability and the light of our understanding..." Z II 99.

dualism. He does not confer on the mystery of evil that erratic autonomy to which theology almost always resigns itself. Instead, he makes a resolute attempt to locate it within the mystery of God instead. Sin does not fall outside the realm of providence;[286] with the resultant danger that God might almost appear to be the author of sin.[287] Two things are to be said on this point. First, the formal reason that the Lawgiver can never be made a transgressor by the Law.[288] This means: God is always good, and

---

286. "... quin fit, ut non ... dei providentia sic omnia geri ac disponi confiteamur, ut nihil citra ipsius voluntatem aut imperium fiat? Curiosi sumus: Veremur enim, ne cogamur deum esse malorum quoque autorem confiteri". (Why do we not confess, that everything is so governed and ordered by the providence of God, that nothing happens apart from his will or command? We are over-cautious; for we are afraid lest we be compelled to confess that God is the author of evil also. Z III 842).

"... dum quaedam fiunt, quorum causam et finem ignoramus, nolumus in eis divinam providentiam agnoscere, quae nobis utitur, imo rebus cunctis pro sua libertate. Nec illi turpe est, quod nobis". (When things happen, of which we do not know the cause or the end, we are unwilling to recognise therein God's providence, which freely makes use of us, and, indeed, of all things. What is evil for us is not so for it. Z III 843). Cf. S VI, I 416f.

287. "... sic omnia quae circum hominem fiunt, sive ad corpus, sive pertineant ad animum, a deo sunt, tamquam vera et sola causa, ut nec peccati opus ab alio sit quam a deo; quantumvis illi non sit peccatum..." (Thus everything that happens with regard to man, whether it concerns his body or his soul, comes from God, the real and sole cause; and even the work of sin comes from none other than God; although it is not sin for him. S IV 125).

"Nec illi turpe est, quod nobis. Quae enim nobis turpia sunt, ex eo provenit, quod lex nobis imposita est. Lex autem hac causa est posita, quod adfectus nostri modum excedebant. Hi autem in deo qum non sint, legi non est obnoxius, sed hoc ipsum est, quod a nobis per legem exigit. Unde turpe apud illum non est, quod nobis turpe est ... Ne ergo curiosi simus ac timidi, a providentia dei quaedam liberantes, quasi eam minime decentia. Quae enim nobis turpia sunt, illi non sunt, et quae nos perniciosa esse arbitramur, alia parte proficua sunt". (What is evil for us, is not so for him. That it is evil for us derives from the fact that the law is imposed upon us. But the law was imposed upon us, because our desires knew no bounds. But since there are no such desires in God, he is not subject to the law; he is himself that which he demands of us through the law. Therefore what is evil for us, is not evil for him ... Therefore let us not be over-cautious and anxious, and take certain things away from God's providence, as though they were unsuited to it. For what is evil for us is not so for him, and what we consider disastrous is, from another aspect, profitable. Z III 843).

288. See notes 286 and 287. "Quae nobis leges sunt, deo lex non sunt: quis enim legem ei ferret qui summus est, aut quis eum doceat qui lux est? Illi ergo natura et ingenium sunt, quae nobis lex sunt. Et quum praecipit: Me unum ama! primum discimus eum, non ex lege quam illi ponere nemo potest, sed natura et ingenio amare. Secundo discimus et nos illum iure amare debere. Ita ut ipse supra legem sit, nos sub lege; ut ille sit amor qui nobis praecipitur ... Constat igitur legem ... numinis ingenium, voluntatem et naturam esse, quod ad essentiam legis attinet". (What are laws for us are not law for God. For who could prescribe a law for the supreme being? or who could instruct the one who is light? Therefore, what is law for us is his very nature and disposition. And when he commands, 'Thou shalt love me alone' we learn firstly, that he loves, not by reason of a law (which none could impose upon him), but by his nature and character; secondly, we learn that it is right that we should love him also. Thus, as he is above the law, we are under it; and he is that love which is prescribed for us ... Therefore it is clear that the law ... is in essence, the disposition, will and nature of God. S IV 104-105).

only God is good. There is nothing that is good in itself, which would be superior to God. What is good is good because God wills it.[289] Second, the material reason that in the providence of God everything stands in a new light. Without the murder of Uriah, David would not have repented; without the fall of Adam, the redeemer would not have come.[290]

---

289. With reference to James 1:13-16 he writes, "Whatever comes down from heaven or from God is good, and must be good. Therefore you should not lay the blame for sin upon God". S VI, II 255.

"Quae enim a domino fiunt, prius iure et recte facta esse debemus cognoscere, quam causas cur sic fecerit exigere". (For we should first acknowledge whatever is done by the Lord to be just and right, before we seek the reasons why he has done it. S IV 126).

Zwingli has here incorporated an important Occamistic element in his otherwise Thomistic and rationalistic system. Cf. Heiko A. Oberman, *The Harvest of Medieval Theology*, Cambridge, Mass., 1963, pp. 96-98. As a consequence, there is agreement at this point between Zwingli and *Luther*, who states: "Anyone who does not understand that there is no law for God should remain silent. With God it is simply will, will, will". (WA XVI 148). In *De servo arbitrio*, Luther, writes: "Deus est, cuius voluntatis nulla est caussa nec ratio, quae illi ceu regula et mensura praescribatur, cum nihil sit illi aequale aut superius, sed ipsa est regula omnium. Si enim esset illi aliqua regula vel mensura, aut caussa aut ratio, iam nec Dei voluntas esse posset. Non enim, quia sic debet vel debuit velle, ideo rectum est, quod vult, Sed contra, Quia ipse sic vult, ideo debet rectum esse, quod fit". (God is he for whose will there is no cause or ground which might be prescribed as its rule or standard; for there is nothing that is equal or superior to it; it is itself the rule of all things. If there were any rule or standard, any cause or ground for it, it could not be the will of God. For what he wills is not right because he is or was bound so to will. On the contrary, what happens must be right because he so wills. WA XVIII 712). Cf. Paul Althaus, *Die Theologie Martin Luthers,* Gütersloh, 1962, pp. 244f.; Martin Luther, *Ausgewählte Werke,* ed. H. H. Borcherdt and Georg Merz, Ergänzungsreihe I: *Vom unfreien Willen,* with theological introduction by H. J. Iwand, Munich, 1954, pp. 258f. *Calvin*'s objection (though terminological rather than factual) applies to Luther and Zwingli alike: "Pii homines ... reputent quantae sit improbitatis, causas divinae voluntatis duntaxat percontari: quum omnium quae sunt, ipsa sit causa, et merito esse debeat. Nam si ullam causam habet, aliquid antecedat oportet, cui veluti alligetur: quod nefas est imaginari. Adeo enim summa est iustitiae regula Dei voluntas, ut quicquid vult, eo ipso quod vult, iustum habendum sit ... Neque tamen commentum ingerimus absolutae potentiae: quod sicuti profanum est, ita merito detestabile nobis esse debet. Non fingimus Deum exlegem, qui sibi lex est (French: Nous n'imaginons point aussi un Dieu qui n'ait nulle loy, veu qu'il est loy à soymesme.): quia (ut ait Plato) lege indigent homines qui cupiditatibus laborant: Dei autem voluntas non modo ab omni vitio pura, sed summa perfectionis regula, etiam legum omnium lex est. Verum negamus obnoxium esse reddendae rationi..." (The pious ... should consider how sinful it is to insist on knowing the causes of the divine will, since it is itself, and justly ought to be, the cause of all that exists. For if his will has any cause, there must be something antecedent to it, and to which it is annexed; this it were impious to imagine. The will of God is the supreme rule of righteousness, so that everything which he wills must be held to be righteous by the mere fact of his willing it... We, however, give no countenance to the fiction of absolute power, which, as it is heathenish, so it ought justly to be held in detestation by us. We do not imagine God to be lawless, seeing that he is a law to himself; because, as Plato says, men labouring under the influence of concupiscence need law; but the will of God is not only free from all vice, but is the supreme standard of perfection, the law of all laws. But we deny that he is bound to give an account of his procedure...*Institutes* III. xxiii. 2).

290. S IV 134; S IV 136.

Thus the doctrine of sin also flows into the Gospel, which is redemption from sin. The "unforgivable" sin against the Holy Spirit is simply the refusal of forgiveness itself, the rejection of the Gospel, unbelief.[291]

16. *Election*

Against this background, Zwingli held the doctrine of the enslaved will, the servum arbitrium, in opposition to medieval semi-pelagianism and humanistic optimism.[292] In the "Commentarius" he had answered Erasmus' "De libero arbitrio" before Luther did so.[293] Redemption takes place through grace, on the basis of *election*.[294] Predestination is logically established as a special case of providence, and as its peak, which follows from a right concept of God.[295] But its significance extends further: it is the basis for assurance of salvation.[296] Zwingli's formulation of it con-

---

291. Z II 409; Z III 720-723.

292. E.g. Z II 180; Z II 272; Z III 650.

293. Erasmus' *Diatribe de libero arbitrio* appeared in September 1524, Zwingli's *De vera et falsa religione commentarius* in March 1525 and Luther's *De servo arbitrio* in December 1525. For a discussion of Zwingli's arguments, see Paul Wernle, *Der evangelische Glaube nach den Hauptschriften der Reformatoren*, Vol. II: *Zwingli*, Tübingen, 1919, pp. 155f., 222f.; also Walther Köhler, *Huldrych Zwingli*, Leipzig, 1943, pp. 129, 157; cf. also Z III 650; Z III 842f.

294. See further "Huldrych Zwingli's Doctrine of Predestination" (above p. 000).

295. "Est autem providentia praedestinationis veluti parens". (Providence is, so to speak, the parent of predestination. Z III 842).

"Nascitur autem praedestinatio, quae nihil aliud est, quam si tu dicas praeordinatio, ex providentia, imo est ipsa providentia". (Predestination, which one may also call foreordination, springs from providence, and is, indeed, itself providence. Z III 843).

In the final (1559) edition of the *Institutes* Calvin separated the doctrine of predestination from the doctrine of providence (cf. Paul Jacobs, *Prädestination und Verantwortlichkeit bei Calvin*, Neukirchen, 1937, pp. 67-71). This was an innovation vis-à-vis the whole dogmatic tradition from Augustine onwards. Calvin's aim was to develop the christological and soteriological aspect of election, and its relation to ecclesiology. His separation of the two doctrines also involves an implicit correction of Zwingli, whose doctrine is not free from deterministic, philosophical elements. Calvin does not seem to have recognised the decisive connexion which Zwingli makes between election and christology.

296. "Sic scriptum est in Actis: Et crediderunt quotquot ad vitam aeternam ordinati erant. Qui ergo credunt, ad vitam aeternam sunt ordinati. At qui vere credant, nemo novit nisi is qui credit. Hic ergo iam certus est se dei electum esse. Habet enim spiritus arrhabonem, iuxta Apostoli verbum, quo desponsus et obsignatus scit se esse vere liberum et filium familiae factum, non servum. Spiritus enim ille fallere non potest. Qui si dictat nobis deum esse patrem nostrum, et nos illum certi et intrepidi patrem adpellamus, securi quod sempiternam hereditatem simus adituri, iam certum est spiritum filii dei esse in corda nostra fusum. Certum est igitur eum esse electum qui tam securus et tutus est: qui enim credunt ad vitam aeternam ordinati sunt". (As is written in the Acts of the Apostles, 'as many as were ordained to eternal life believed'. Therefore, those who believe are ordained to eternal life. But nobody knows who truly believes save he who believes. And he is already sure that he is elected by God. For, as the Apostle says, he has the earnest of the Spirit, and by this pledge and seal he knows that he is truly free and has been made a child of the family, and not a slave. For this Spirit cannot deceive. If he tells us that God is our father, and we call him

stitutes one of his most original achievements. In God's eternal decree, the revelation of Christ, and therefore the election of Christ, has precedence. On the basis of this, God's mercy chooses us men and unites us to himself, whereupon God's justice declares us righteous for the sake of Christ, and adopts us as children.[297] Thus he follows a different course from that of *Calvin's* doctrine of predestination, according to which, on the one side there stand the reprobate, under the judgment of God's righteousness, and on the other side are the elect, under God's mercy. Here we have the supreme example of that unified way of thinking which Zwingli derived from the *simplicitas* of God, and which he maintained against Luther also, as we have already seen. God's mercy and his justice come towards us along the same course. God is "just" in that he deals with us in accordance with what Christ has done for us.

The question of those who are rejected is peripheral. Until there is proof to the contrary, we should believe that our fellow men are among the elect. And as a rule such proof is impossible.[298]

---

father with assurance and without fear, assured that we shall have access to an eternal inheritance, then it is certain that the Spirit of the Son of God has been poured into our hearts. Therefore it is certain that whoever has this sureness and security is elect; for those who believe are ordained to eternal life. S IV 8).

"Constat igitur eos qui credunt scire se esse electos: qui enim credunt electi sunt". (Therefore it is certain that believers know that they are elect; for those who believe are elect. S IV 123).

"Hi ergo sic electi sunt, ut non soli deo nota sit ipsorum electio, sed illis ipsis quoque qui electi sunt". (Their election is such, that it is known not only to God, but also to the elect themselves. S IV 122; S IV 140).

297. "Hic enim unus ac solus mediator dei et hominum est, Deus et homo Christus Iesus. Constat autem et firma manet dei electio. Quos enim ille elegit ante mundi constitutionem, sic elegit ut per filium suum sibi cooptaret. Ut enim benignus et misericors, ita sanctus et iustus est. Resipiunt ergo universa opera illius misericordiam et iustitiam. Iure igitur et electio utramque resipit. Bonitatis est elegisse quos velit; iustitiae vero electos sibi adoptare et iungere per filium suum, hostiam ad satis dandum divinae iustitiae pro nobis factum". (There is one sole mediator between God and man, the God-man Christ Jesus. But God's election stands fast and remains sure. For those whom he chose before the foundation of the world, he chose in such manner, that he chose them for himself through his Son. For as he is kind and merciful, he is also holy and just. All his works reveal his mercy and his justice. Therefore election also rightly reveals both. It is of his goodness that he has chosen whom he will, and it is of his justice that he adopts the elect as his children and binds them to himself through his Son, whom he gave for a sacrifice, to render satisfaction to the divine justice on our behalf. S IV 5-6).

298. "... Non est igitur universale, quod qui fidem non habeat, damnetur; sed qui fidei rationem exponi audivit et in perfidia perstat ac moritur, hunc possumus fortasse inter miseros abiicere ... libera est enim electio Dei..." (It is not, therefore, a universal rule, that whoever does not believe is condemned; but whoever has heard the faith expounded and explained and yet persists and dies in unbelief may, perhaps, be reckoned among the reprobate ... for God's election is free. S IV 123, with reference to Mark 16:16). Cf. S IV 127.

17. The Church

Election and covenant find their expression in the existence of the church.[299] The church is born of the Word of God,[300] and it is ruled from the throne at the right hand of God;[301] the Pope is therefore the Antichrist.[302] The government of the church is effected through the Spirit, whom every believer possesses.[303] But after his controversy with the Anabaptists, the Reformer goes on to say that the Spirit maintains the church in unity and order by means of appointed offices,[304] which may also be discharged by magistrates.[305] It is this relationship of trust to the state, rather than any question of doctrine, that caused the tension that has often resulted in conflicts within the reformed church in countries where Zwinglianism continued to exercise influence alongside the spreading force of Calvinism.[306] Because of the absolute authority of the Word of God, both Zwingli and Calvin demand unrestricted freedom of preaching, and are imbued with a keen sense of the prophetic role of the preacher vis-à-vis those who bear office. But Calvin, the lawyer, sees the approach of modern secularism and individualism, and teaches his congregation to stand on their own feet. He aims at a free church, because it is only when the church has freedom to determine its own forms and to exercise its own discipline over doctrine and life that the freedom of proclamation and the building up of lively congregations can be assured.[307] Zwingli still retains

---

299. Z III 741-757; S IV 8f.; 58f.

300. "Which is Christ's church? That which hears his word". Z III 223.

"That is the Christian church, which heeds only God's word, and which allows itself to be led and directed only by that word, as Christ teaches by the parable of the shepherd and the sheep, in John 10..." Z III 168.

"The word of God creates the church; the church cannot create the word of God". Z III 217; Z IV 734.

301. Z I 295.

302. Z II 67; Z IV 123; Z IV 801 etc.

303. Z I 376 for the priesthood of all believers (1 Peter 2:9). Cf. also Z I 496; Z I 499; Z III 259f.

304. Z IV 369-433, especially Z IV 390; Z II 439; Z II 282.

305. For a detailed treatment of this question, see Zwingli's letter no. 720, May 4th 1528, addressed to Ambrosius Blarer in Constance, Z IX 451-467. The "magistrate" may, "if he is a Christian magistrate", order the external affairs of the church, "with the consent of the church". Z IX 455-456.

306. For Geneva and Vaud, see the biographies of Calvin, such as Ernst Stähelin, *Calvins Leben und ausgewählte Schriften,* Vol. II, Elberfeld, 1863, pp. 91-159; for England, cf. Helmut Kressner, *Schweizer Ursprünge des anglikanischen Staatskirchentums,* Gütersloh, 1953; for the Palatinate, cf. Ruth Wesel-Roth, *Thomas Erastus,* Lehr/Baden, 1954; also Walter Hollweg, *Neue Untersuchungen zur Entstehung des Heidelberger Katechismus,* 1961; for the Netherlands, cf. Walter Hollweg, *Heinrich Bullingers Hausbuch,* Neukirchen, 1956.

307. *Luther* himself wished to see churches that were independent, founded on the basis of ecclesiastical office and the priesthood of all believers. But because he "did not have the peo-

the medieval vision which sees a Christian community as the political expression of the Christian church.[308] In the foreground stands the pastor, who has the preaching office, and who is also termed "shepherd", or

ple; and the Bishops rejected the reformation, he recognised the territorial princes as "Emergency bishops" (*Sämtliche Werke* (Erlangen edition) 55, 223; 8, 370). Since the external organisation of the church was never a question of faith as far as Lutheranism was concerned, and because of its own general conservatism, and also because of the political development of absolutism, it was relatively easy for Lutheranism to accept the government of the church by the princes.

Zwingli was the one reformer who was a convinced advocate of a close link between "state" and church. He was influenced firstly by the medieval concept of the Corpus Christianum, which meant, in its new Protestant form, that reformation means not merely the renewal of the "church", but of the whole life of society; and secondly, he was influenced by his own personal experience of such a renewal in the town and council of Zürich, as a consequence of reformation preaching.

The relation of "church" and "state" (though when understood in Zwingli's sense they might better be termed "the Christian community in its ecclesiastical and its political forms") is that of soul and body. For this very reason, the church must remember that her power is of a spiritual nature, and that her task is to serve and not to rule. Ministers are to be firmly integrated into the civil legal system. The development of their position of worldly power is a characteristic of the perversion of the church under the papacy. "Hic videmus etiam sacerdotes, tametsi ex eorum ore lex dei cunctis requirenda sit, subditos esse magistratibus. Quem ordinem (ut omnia) Antichristus Romanus pervertit, non solum se suosque a iure et potestate magistratus eximens, sed principibus et regibus se quoque praeferens". (Here we see (Exodus 4:16) how the priests are subordinate to the magistrates, even though the whole law of God is to be ascertained from them. The Roman Antichrist has perverted this ordinance, like all the others, not only by removing himself and his people from the law and the power of the magistrates, but also by setting himself above princes and kings. Z XIII 313). See also Articles 34-36 (Z I 462) and the exposition in Z II 298-311.

If Zwingli's Zürich is to be described as a theocracy, then it must be qualified by the adjective "prophetic"; it was certainly not an ecclesiocracy. Conversely, the government and care of the church exercised by Christian authorities is itself a service to the church which is necessary because of rough, godless people and hypocrites. "Summa: In ecclesia Christi aeque necessarius est magistratus atque prophetia; utcunque illa sit prior. Nam sicut homo non potest constare nisi ex animo et corpore, quamquamvis corpus sit humilior pars atque abiectior: sic et ecclesia sine magistratu constare non potest, utcunque magistratus res crassiores et a spiritu alienores curet ac disponat". (In short, in the church of Christ the office of the magistrate is as necessary as that of the prophet, though the latter has precedence. For just as a man must consist of both soul and body, though the body is the humbler and lesser part, so the church cannot exist without the magistracy, even though it should only take care and dispose of the more worldly matters, which have less to do with the spirit. S IV 60).

It must be remembered that the total incorporation of the church in the government political (as happened in Bern, where a strong civic consciousness had been quickly developed) was not really in keeping with Zwinglian policy, even though the opposition to it in Geneva and Vaud was regarded as anti-Zwinglian. By contrast, *Calvin's* endeavours to secure a free church arose from his clear insight into new political developments (as the medieval "rulers" were transformed into an impersonal "state") and from his personal experience and work—in France he had the task of counselling a persecuted minority church as it sought to establish itself in the face of the power of the state.

308. See below, section 21.

"watchman" (his translation of "bishop").[309] Three usages of the term "church" are to be distinguished. (1) The whole of Christendom, including unbelievers; (2) The "communion of saints" in the sense of the Apostles' Creed. This church is without blemish, because it is cleansed by the blood of Christ, and it does not err;[310] (3) The individual congregation.[311] The congregation watches over the conduct of its members and the word of the shepherd.[312] It has the right to reform itself.[313] Those guilty of serious sin are to be excluded from the Lord's Supper, and in this connexion attention is to be paid to unchristian behaviour in commercial or financial matters.[314] But the *power of the keys*, in the true sense, consists in preaching[315] (as the Heidelberg Catechism states).[316] To grant forgiveness belongs exclusively to God's right and power; the institution of confession would obscure this fact[317]—as Zwingli maintains in the face of the high value that Luther sets on confession.[318] As regards the form of its ordinances, the church is free, provided only that they conform to the message of Christ.[319] But in the light of Ezekiel 3, the church is charged with the inescapable task of acting as the prophetic watchman over public

---

309. Z I 231; Z I 495; Z III 5 etc.

310. Z III 255f.; Z III 745f. For the slight difference between Zwingli's concept of the invisible church and that found in Melanchthon's *Apology* for the Augsburg Confession cf. G. W. Locher, "Das Problem der Landeskirche", in *Evangelische Theologie* XVI/1 (January 1956), pp. 33-48, especially p. 40; cf. Z I 538; Z III 257f.; Z III 259; S IV 9.

311. Zwingli calls it the "Kilchhöre". Cf. Z III 253, 255, 257f., 261, 267f.

312. Z III 259; Z III 262f., etc. "If the shepherd is false, then do not listen to him; and if the whole congregation realises that he is false, then agree to get rid of him". Z III 64.

313. Z IV 149. In practice, by a majority decision. "It has always been the custom throughout the confederacy" that in church affairs "the whole congregation" should vote. S II, III 86; Z VI, III No. 171.

314. Z III 267f.; Z IV 31. Cf. Roger Ley, *Kirchenzucht bei Zwingli*, 1948.

315. Z II 368ff.; Z II 374; Z II 380-391; Z III 723-741. "Verbum ergo dei, quo nos ipsos cognoscere discimus, quoque deo fidere docemur, claves sunt, quibus ministri verbi liberant; nam qui eo docti omnem fiduciam in deum collocant, iam vere liberi sunt". (Therefore the word of God, by which we learn to know ourselves, and which teaches us to trust in God, is the keys, by means of which ministers of the word set people free; for whoever, having been taught by the word, sets his whole trust in God, is truly free. Z III 738).

316. Heidelberg Catechism, Questions 83 and 84.

317. Cf. "In Spirit and in Truth" (above, p. 000ff., section 5).

318. Z V 819f.

319. Z II 623. "Habeat quaelibet ecclesia suum morem; non enim omnia omnibus conveniunt, sed debent omnia, quod ad fontem attinet, ex eadem pietate proficisci; ac quae contra ex ipsa non proficiscuntur, cum tranquillitate aboleri". (Every congregation may have its own usages, for not everything is suitable for all. Basically, however, everything must spring from the one faith; and whatever does not spring from that faith is to be done away with peacefully. Z III 855). Cf. Z IV 129.

life. If the church should neglect its duty, then church and people alike will come under the wrath of God.[320]

320. The first function of this office of watchman consists in establishing and maintaining peace.

"One sees here (I Timothy 2:1ff.) the work of true bishops, namely, to be one watch, being diligent to ensure that we live peaceably". Z II 313.

Cf. Z II 282-284, for the idea that the church, and the Bishop of Constance in particular, should have prevented the Swabian War.

Cf. Z II 313-318, for the duty of the watchman to oppose mercenary service for the Pope (with Zwingli's personal testimony).

"Since hypocrisy has now reached the point where it is so rich and strong that it no longer needs to hide, but actually dares to protect itself publicly with a powerful hand, what do you think is to be done, pious servant of God? If you remain silent, then the blood of those who are killed will be requested at your hands, as it says in Ezekiel 3..." Z III 23.

"... Non desunt hodie prophetae, non desunt optimi consultores, sed omnem exhortationem, omnem admonitionem spernimus, gentibus etiam stultiores et duriores. Nihil ergo nobis quam extremum supplicium expectandum est". (There is today no lack of prophets or of excellent councillors. But we are more foolish and obdurate than the heathen, spurning every exhortation and every warning. Therefore we cannot expect anything but the most severe punishment. Z XIII 245).

"Nunquam non dedit multum damni neglecta dei admonitio". (To disregard divine admonition has always caused much harm. Z I 318).

"Expectat quidem longanimiter poenitentiam deus; quod si non resipiscimus, veniet tandem et horribili poena multabit contemptores. Requiretur nihilo minus perditorum sanguis de manu eorum, qui vel verbo admonere ac corripere peccantes, vel qui gladio sontes plectere ac e medio tollere debuerant. Hi enim, qui episcopi sunt, qui custodes ac pastores Christianae gregis, qui ministri publicae iusticiae, si non circumspiciunt, si hostem advenientem non abarcent, si lupum irruere vident ac non monent, si non se sceleribus ut aheneum murum opponunt, neglecti officii dignas luent poenas". (In truth God waits patiently for repentance; but if we do not come to our right mind, then finally he comes and punishes most fearfully those who scorn him. Nevertheless, the blood of those who are lost will be required at the hand of those who should have admonished or rebuked the sinners with the word, or who should have punished and destroyed the guilty with the sword. For if those who are overseers, the guardians and pastors of the flock of Christ, the ministers of public justice, are not on watch, if they do not ward off the enemy when he approaches, if they see the wolf breaking in and do not give warning, if they do not set themselves against sin like a brazen wall, then they shall have to pay the just penalty for their neglect of their duty. Z XIII 117).

"As we now see how the magistrates fight against God's word with all their powers, it is certain that God is angry with us, just as he was with the Jews who would not hear Christ. He says of them in Matthew 13 that seeing, they would not see, and hearing, they would not hear, for their heart was hardened. But what follows upon that? A wretched destruction and misery worse than has ever been heard. When the word of God is resisted in this same way,—as we, alas, well see, for they withstand it with more wantonness and churlishness than the Jews ever did—then one must accept that calamity and punishment will follow in like manner. Dear Valentine, I know so well the God who is our God, that I know full well that he will not fail us. But we are worse than the senseless beasts. We hear and we understand, but we do not want to understand; we shut our ears; but divine wisdom will laugh at our downfall, as it says in Proverbs 1, for we mock all his warnings and admonitions". Z IV 148.

"God wants to make this evil world better by his own word, as he has always done in every age. When Sodom and Nineveh, or the whole world in the days of Noah, or the

18. Sacraments

All these factors, among which the exposition of scripture should once more be given pride of place, prepare the way for a distinct concept of the sacraments.[321] It was only with reluctance that Zwingli used this term, because it is foreign to the Bible, and because it is saddled with the Roman concept of grace.[322] One feels that in the later confessions he prefaces his

---

children of Israel were at their worst, he sent the prophets and his word to them, and those who improved their ways survived: those who despised his word were most wretchedly destroyed or imprisoned. Do we not see, in our own times, how the world is so evil in every land and among all classes, that we are filled with horror? But since the word of God is now being revealed amidst all this wickedness, do we not see that it is God's doing? He does not wish his creatures to suffer such wretched and widespread loss, when he has bought them and paid for them with his own blood. If you set this great wickedness and the true word of God against one another, you will find that the wickedness wants to be left alone. So if the one to whom the word of God is entrusted should give way, he will have to give account of those who are lost, because, as Jeremiah says, he has seen the sword coming and has not given warning. But if he resists the pomp of this world, he will be shut out, reviled and scorned and even killed by the world. Which would you prefer? That I remained silent and tolerated the evil which I ought to resist, and so fell into the devil's power for the sake of peace and reputation in this world? I well know what you will say: 'No, but punish us in moderation!' Just listen! Do you think your present vices are so small that my words are too rough? If you thought that, you would be mistaken. They are so great that the roughest words of the prophets and of God's wrath could not reproach you sufficiently". H I 127; Z I 393.—A most impressive example of how the reformer himself put these principles into effect is to be found in his work *Wer Ursach gebe zuo Uffruor* (1524), H VII 123-228; Z III 355-469. In a most expert and concrete way he gives an insight into the machinations of an age of transition from a natural to a monetary economy, of early capitalism, of the rent system, and of the manipulation of inflation and deflation. And the tone is always the same: "You say, 'what has that to do with the gospel?' Much in every way! ... But it is the same with all flesh. As soon as you touch its sore point, it cries out, 'What business of the parson is my dealing or my buying, my adultery or my drinking?' Just as the devil often cried out of those who were possessed, 'Jesus, what have we to do with you?' But what do you think? Did he have power over them?' H VII 190-191; Z III 431; Z III 432.

321. Z III 757-762; S IV 9-11, 30-36, 56-58. Cf. Walther Köhler, *Zwingli und Luther, ihr Streit über das Abendmahl nach seinen politischen und religiösen Beziehungen*. Vol. I: *Die religiöse und politische Entwicklung bis zum Marburger Religionsgespräch 1529*, Leipzig, 1924; Vol. II: *Vom Beginn der Marburger Verhandlungen 1529 bis zum Abschluss der Wittenberger Konkordie von 1536*, ed. Ernst Kohlmeyer and Heinrich Bornkamm, Gütersloh, 1953. In addition to the better known works, special reference may be made to Julius Schweizer, *Reformierte Abendmahlsgestaltung in der Schau Zwinglis*, 1954. Zwingli's sacramental writings were polemical, and this inevitably affected their balance. But by analysing the formulations which provide a positive expression of Zwingli's views, Schweizer achieves a new and surprising insight. G. W. L.: Zw. Ref. 1. Rahnen., ch. XV., (Litw.).

322. Z II 120-122ff.; Z II 126-127; Z III 486-487. "Vocem istam 'sacramentum' magnopere cupiam Germanis nunquam fuisse receptam, nisi germane esset accepta. Cum enim hanc vocem 'sacramentum' audiunt, iam aliquid magnum sanctumque intelligunt, quod vi sua conscientiam a peccato liberet". (I very much wish that the Germans had never taken this word 'sacrament' into their language, or at least had taken it only in the germane sense. For when they hear the word 'sacrament', they think at once of something great and holy, by whose power the conscience is freed from sin. Z III 757).

individual exposition of the two sacraments with a discussion of the general concept only after he has first gained from the New Testament a clear idea of Baptism and the Lord's Supper in particular. But for ecumenical and apologetic reasons he accepts the traditional concept, and takes up a widely-recognised summary of Augustine's sacramental doctrine: "A Sacrament is a sign of a sacred thing".[323] Zwingli explains immediately: "I believe the sacrament to be the sign of a sacred thing, that is, of effected grace".[324] This interpretation maintains three things: (1) The sacrament-sign is a human action and is part of the church's confession. It is a public "sign of duty".[325] (2) This confession relates to the

---

323. "Sacramentum est sacrae rei signum". Z II 121; Z III 757; Z IV 218; Z IV 793; Z VI, II 200; S IV 11.

324. "Credo sacramentum esse sacrae rei, hoc est factae gratiae, signum". S IV 11—with reference to another, equally accepted "Augustinian" formula, "Sacramentum est invisibilis gratiae visibilis figura sive forma" (a sacrament is the visible figure or form of an invisible grace). Cf. Z VI, II 200. Characteristically, Zwingli qualifies "gratia" thus: "quae scilicet dei munere facta et data est" (grace which is, of course, granted and bestowed by the goodness of God).

325. "Sacramentum means, strictly speaking, an oath". Z II 120. Cf. Z III 123-125.

"This sacrament is an inward and an outward agreement among Christian men". Z III 124.

"We find the practice of the ordinary man, in so far as he is rightly instructed in the faith, is that with this seal and sacrament each individual, together with his Christian brethren, bears public witness to his faith in the death and the redemption of Jesus Christ". Z III 127. For an extensive treatment of the sacrament as a community act and as a sign of Christian duty, see Z III 226 228. For the equation of "sacramentum" and "iuramentum", cf. Z III 348.

"Here is a parable. Confederates have a covenant with one another. They are mutually obliged to keep it, and if they keep it, they are confederates. If they do not keep it, they are not confederates, even though they bear the name. But every five years, the covenant and the oath must be renewed, so that the people everywhere are truly aware of their duty and obligation to one another, and once again profess their commitment to one another. Similarly in the sacrament, a man publicly binds himself to all believers". Z III 535; cf. Z IV 292; Z V 471f.

Cf. Z III 759 for the terms "initiatio", "oppignoratio" (giving a pledge) and "publica consignatio" (public attestation). "Sunt ergo sacramenta signa vel ceremoniae—pace tamen omnium dicam, sive neotericorum sive veterum—quibus se homo ecclesiae probat aut candidatum aut militem esse Christi, redduntque ecclesiam totam potius certiorem de tua fide quam te". (The sacraments are, therefore, signs or ceremonies (pace all church teachers, ancient or modern) by which a man testifies to the church that he is either a candidate or a soldier of Christ. So they confirm your faith to the church rather than to you. Z III 761).

Cf. Z III 761f. and 807f. for the idea that the congregation of the faithful is the subject of the sacramental act. "When we hear this word 'sacrament', we Germans imagine that it means something which takes away our sin or makes us holy. But that is most false; for nothing can take away the sin from us Christians, or make us holy, except Jesus Christ alone; and no external thing can do so. But because of this misunderstanding, some cry 'They want to take away from us the holy sacraments, the comfort of our poor souls!' But

event of the cross, where our pardon was accomplished; the sacrament points beyond itself to the "effected grace".[326] (3) Therefore it is impossible for the sacrament itself to dispense grace, or to relieve the afflicted conscience.[327] It presupposes faith.[328] Yet there is still a symbolic analogy be-

nobody wants to take them away, but simply to use them properly, and not pervert them. Those people pervert them, who ascribe to them what they do not possess. As used here, the term 'sacramentum' means a sign of obligation or pledge. Just as, when a man sews a white cross on his clothes, he shows that he wants to be a confederate. And if, on the pilgrimage to Näfels, he praises and thanks God for the victory which he granted to our forefathers, then he is declaring publicly that he is a confederate from the very heart. So whoever receives the mark of baptism wants to listen to what God has to say to him, to learn God's ordinances, and to live according to them. And whoever joins with the congregation in saying thanks to God in the remembrance, the supper, is publicly declaring that he rejoices from the heart at the death of Christ, and is therefore giving thanks to him. So I ask those who complain to allow the sacrament to be a sacrament, instead of saying that sacraments are signs which actually are that which they signify. For if they were what they signify, they would not be signs. For the sign and the thing signified can never be one and the same thing. Sacraments—as even papist teachers say—are simple the signs of holy things. Thus baptism is the sign which pledges us to the Lord Jesus Christ. And the remembrance signifies to us that Jesus Christ suffered death for us. They are signs and pledges of holy things". H XI 16f.; Z IV 217.

326. Z IV 217f. (note 325). "So Christians should be like a body, and confest to one another by means of this sacrament, that they believe that they have been redeemed by the death of Christ and by the shedding of his blood, and that they have been made children of God. And they should do this so often as the individual church or congregation pleases, with praise and thanksgiving to God for redeeming us through his son Jesus Christ. This is what it means to proclaim the Lord's death: to recognise that he has redeemed us, and to give him praise and thanks for this. Just as each year, on the Day of Ten Thousand Knights, confederates give praise and thanks to God for the victory which he granted to us at Murten, so in this sacrament we should give praise and thanks to God for saving us by the death of his only son, and for redeeming us from the enemy. This is to proclaim the Lord's death". Z III 534.

Even as early as the *Auslegung* Zwingli attacks the mass on the grounds that the assertion that the mass is a sacrifice infringes upon the one complete sacrifice of Christ upon the Cross, which is the "testament", the "legacy", the "inheritance", the "covenant", the "agreement". The only understanding of the Supper which corresponds to the "testament" is that of "a sure remembrance of the sacrifice of Christ offered once for all" (Z II 130), "a sincere thanksgiving for his goodness and a remembrance of his suffering in humility". (Z II 137; cf. Z II 128-137).

"Now since ... it is true that Christ should and could be sacrificed only once—for it is fitting, that, having offered himself to God, he should be a propitiation for the sins of the whole world for all eternity—it follows that the mass is not a sacrifice, but rather a remembrance of the sacrifice, which could be offered only once; and it is an assurance to the weak that Christ has redeemed them..." Z II 127.

327. "Sacramentum ergo, qum aliud porro nequeat esse quam initiatio aut publica consignatio, vim nullam habere potest ad conscientiam liberandam". (Therefore, since the sacrament cannot be anything more than an initiation or a public attestation, it cannot possess the power to set the conscience free. Z III 759).

"Credo, imo scio omnia sacramenta, tam abesse ut gratiam conferant, ut ne adferant quidem aut dispensent ... Nam gratia ut a spiritu divino fit aut datur (loquor autem Latine, quum 'gratiae' nomine utor pro venia scilicet, indulgentia et gratuito beneficio): ita donum

tween the sign and the thing signified, and this gives to the Sacrament an impact that surpasses that of the word.[329]

---

istud ad solum spiritum pervenit. Dux autem vel vehiculum spiritui non est necessarium: ipse enim est virtus et latio qua cuncta feruntur, non qui ferri debeat; neque id unquam legimus in scripturis sacris, quod sensibilia, qualia sacramenta sunt, certo secum ferrent spiritum; sed si sensibilia unquam lata sunt cum spiritu: iam spiritus fuit qui tulit, non sensibilia". (I believe, and indeed I know, that all sacraments, so far from conferring grace, can neither impart nor bestow it ... For since grace is effected or given by the Spirit of God (I speak Latin, using the word 'grace' in the sense of forgiveness, remission of sins or undeserved favour), only the Spirit can bestow this gift. The Spirit needs neither guidance nor vehicle, for he is himself the power and the means by which everything is carried. He does not have to be carried. And we do not read anywhere in Holy Scripture that things that are perceptible to the senses, such as the sacraments; must necessarily carry the Spirit with them. If sensible things ever appear together with the Spirit, then it is the Spirit who is bears them, and not they the Spirit. S IV 9-10; S IV 55).

"Gratia sic per Christum facta est, ut perpetua sit ... Non ergo per sacramenta, non per aliud precium itur ad patrem, quam per Christum". (Thus grace is so effected by Christ as to be eternal ... Therefore one does not come to the Father by means of the sacraments, or at any other price, but only through Christ. Z VIII 233).

328. "Therefore I say with Christ: if a man, before he comes to the Supper, has not already put faith in his Word, as we believe, that is, wholly relying upon him as the Saviour, then the body of Christ is of no value to him". Z II 143. "Spiritus sua benignitate adest ante sacramentum, et perinde gratia et facta et praesens est antequam adferatur sacramentum. Ex quibus hoc colligitur ... sacramenta dari in testimonium publicum, eius gratiae, quae cuique prius adest". (The Spirit in his goodness is present before the sacrament. Likewise, grace is effected and present before the sacrament is administered. Wherefore it is to be concluded ... that the sacraments are given as a public testimony to that grace which is already present for everyone. S IV 10).

329. "See therefore, pious Christian, that the body and blood of Christ are nothing other than the word of faith; namely, that his body, which was slain for us, and his blood, which was shed for us, have redeemed us and have reconciled God. If we firmly believe this, then our soul is nourished and refreshed with the body and blood of Christ. But in order that the essential gospel should be more comprehensible to simple folk, Christ has given an edible form, namely the bread, for his body, and the cup or drink for his blood, in order that their faith might be confirmed by a visible act; just as in baptism, being dipped in the water does not wash away sin, unless the person who is baptised believes in the salvation of the gospel, that is, the gracious redemption won by Christ". H III 184; Z II 143.

"... In sacramentis viva et loquens est invitatio. Loquitur enim dominus ipse, loquuntur et elementa, atque idem loquuntur et suadent sensibus, quod menti sermo et spiritus". (The sacraments contain a lively and eloquent invitation. For the Lord himself speaks, and the elements also speak; they speak and bear testimony to our senses of that which is spoken to our minds by preaching and by the Spirit. S IV 35).

"Credo, sacramentum esse invisibilis gratiae, quae scilicet dei munere facta et data est, visibilem figuram sive formam, hoc est visibile exemplum; quod tamen fere analogiam quandam rei per spiritum gestae prae se fert". (I believe that the sacrament is the visible figure or form of an invisible grace, which is effected and bestowed by the goodness of God. That is, it is a visible example, which bears, to be sure, a certain likeness to that reality which is effected by the Spirit. S IV 11; cf. S IV 32).

Cf. also S IV 56-57 for discussion of the "duplex analogia eucharistiae" and of the exercise of the obedience of the senses.

19. Baptism

Baptism[330] points to the promised baptism of the Spirit.[331] It is probable, if not certain, that infant baptism goes back to the apostolic age.[332] What is decisive is that children belong within the divine covenant, and the outward sign of this, according to Col. 2., is baptism, just as for Israel it was formerly circumcision.[333] It is unthinkable that the children of Christians should be less favoured than the children of those within the old covenant.[334]

At the beginning of his time in Zürich Zwingli must have entered into a examining discussion with close friends as to whether infant baptism was Scriptural.[335] When they went on to establish their own conventicles, practising adult baptism, Zwingli turned against them, to the deep distress of both sides.[336] From the Baptist side, the connexion between church and

---

330. Z III 763-773; S IV 10-11, 66-67; *Concerning Baptism, Rebaptism and Infant Baptism* (1525) Z IV 188-337 (an English translation of part of this work is provided by G. W. Bromiley in *Zwingli and Bullinger,* London, 1953, pp. 129ff.); *Refutation of the Tricks of the Catabaptists* (1527) Z VI, I 1-196.

331. Z IV 224, 225; cf. Z IV 671-717 for the oldest Zürich Church Order, an undated work (Joachim Staedtke is inclined to date it in 1532, i.e. after Zwingli's death). It contains a baptismal formula in which the first prayer for the child, which precedes the baptism, asks "that the outward baptism may be effected inwardly by the Holy Spirit through the water rich in grace..." (Z IV 680). Contra Walther Köhler's Introduction, this intercession is actually looking to the future, and is the expression of a desire that is central to Zwingli's thought. But it is to my mind inconceivable that the phrase "water rich in grace" could have come from Zwingli's pen (cf. Z IV 334). There are parallels, however, in the careful teaching of Leo Jud and in the ecumenical and irenic formulations of Henry Bullinger.

332. Z IV 298, 312, 318; Z VI, I 49. Infant baptism is not expressly commanded in the New Testament, but neither is it forbidden. "But when one examines the nature of baptism, one finds that it is appropriate to children" (Z IV 317). Zwingli appeals to Origen (Z V 452) and Augustine (Z IV 318, 321ff.) and also makes a somewhat surprising reference to the allegory in I Corinthians 10: "The figure of the cloud and the sea signified baptism, as Paul himself indicates ... and one sees that Paul also recognised baptism as the common sign of allegiance for all the people of God, for believers and for their children". (Z IV 306).

333. Z III 410f.; Z IV 326, 327; Z VI, I 171. "Being physically born of Abraham, Isaac and Jacob meant that the children, while still in their childhood, followed in the way of their fathers. How much more should the children of the new generation, which is under grace and not under law, be counted with their fathers among the people of God, and live with their fathers under the sign of allegiance, no less than those of former times". (Z IV 326). "Baptism is the sign of the people of God". (Z V 194). Zwingli criticised Luther's teaching concerning the faith of infants and set against it (in the common front against the Anabaptists) his own doctrine of the covenant. Z V 649f. Cf. Z IV 228 (contra Walther Köhler, Z IV 672).

334. Z III 410ff.; Z IV 317, 333, 639; S IV 7.

335. Cf. Oskar Farner, *Huldrych Zwingli.* Vol. IV, Zürich, 1960, pp. 102ff.; Z IV 207; Z VI, I 36ff.; Z IV 160-175.

336. The works cited in note 330 provide examples of Zwingli's argumentation. See also his *Answer to Balthasar Hubmaier's Baptism Book* (1525), Z IV 577-647 and his *Opinion concerning Baptism,* Z V 448-452.

state was called into question for the first time since Constantine, and the ideal of the independent congregation was upheld.[337] On the Reformer's side the theme was not, as has been generally supposed,[338] concern for a national church and a Christian culture. Instead, his argument at this point is again typically Zwinglian: whoever makes being a Christian to depend upon the manner or fact of baptism is falling into sacramentalism and legalism.[339]

Zwingli (like Calvin after him) derives the covenant concept from the French-humanistic tradition (Budaeus), strips it of its predominantly judicial character, and raises it to the position of a leading thought in the understanding of Scripture.[340]

---

337. Fritz Blanke, *Brüder in Christo*, Zürich, 1955; *Quellen zur Geschichte der Täufer in der Schweiz*. Vol. I: *Zürich*, ed. Leonhard von Muralt and Walter Schmid, Zürich, 1952, No. 14, pp. 13-21, "Konrad Grebel und Genossen an Thomas Müntzer; Blanke, *op. cit.*, p. 15, "Die älteste Urkunde protestantischen Freikirchentums". Grebel and his friends demanded that true believers should withdraw not only from the national church, but also from national life (cf. Blanke, *op. cit.*, p. 15). The movement must have been aware that there was a basically anarchic and disruptive force in their spiritualism. Felix Manz admitted that "there is more behind baptism than can be revealed at the present ... for it will finally put down the government". (Farner, *op. cit.*, pp. 113, 530).

338. E.g., by Walther Köhler in his introductions to Zwingli's works on baptism and that on the office of a preacher (Z IV 369ff.; cf. especially Z IV 378f.). See Walther Köhler, *Huldrych Zwingli*, Leipzig, 1943, pp. 139ff. Oskar Farner also presents this as the main feature of Zwingli's attitude (in his work *Huldrych Zwingli*, Vol. IV, Zürich, 1960).

339. Z IV 325, 330; S IV 119. "All this simply leads one to realise that Scripture baptism is understood in different ways, and that salvation does not depend upon any form of outward baptism. Therefore we learn that water baptism is a ceremonial sign, to which salvation is not tied, as has already been proved by the example of the dying thief and others". (Z IV 224). "Thus the inward baptism of the Spirit is nothing other than the work of teaching which God performs in our hearts, and his calling, whereby he comforts our hearts in Christ, and gives us assurance. None save God can give this baptism. And nobody can be saved without it. But it is quite possible to be saved without the other baptism of external teaching and immersion in water. The proof of this is that the murderer on the cross was not taught or baptised outwardly, but he was saved". (Z IV 225). "Non spectant catabaptistae liberam electionem dei, et salutem putant cum pontificiis alligatam esse symbolis". (The catabaptists have no regard to the free election of God, and like the papists they think that salvation is tied to the symbols. Z V 387).

Zwingli's feeling that the reformation message of justification was at stake was quite correct, as is evident from the complaint of Grebel in 1524 that "people are preaching about grace too much". (Z III 405; cf. Farner, *op. cit.*, p. 106).

340. In his exposition of the words of institution in the Lord's Supper, Zwingli's emphasis on the "testamentum" was taken over from Luther, as Zwingli himself states (Z II 137). But here Zwingli sees the "covenant" in its full scope as the fundamental reality which determines the whole faith and life of the people of God, today, just as in Old Testament times. Thus the concept of the covenant is given an ethical, historical and also legal character. See further Josef Bohatec, *Budé und Calvin, Studien zur Gedankenwelt des französischen Frühhumanismus*, 1950 (inter alia, pp. 246ff.).

20. The Lord's Supper

In the 18th Conclusion and his exposition of it (in July 1523),[341] we find that Zwingli was already disputing the sacrificial character of the Mass, on the basis of the ἐφάπαξ of the Epistle to the Hebrews.[342] He attacked transubstantiation explicitly, and the idea of a substantial reception of the body of Christ implicitly. The Lord's death is the food of the soul, and thus the notion of a real presence of the body of Christ in the elements falls to the ground.[343] The Lord's Supper[344] is "a remembrance of the sacrifice (of Christ) and an assurance of the redemption which Christ has given us".[345] [346] It is stressed that this understanding of the sacrament must not

---

341. Z II 111ff., 119ff.

342. Hebrews 7:26f., 9:11f., 9:24f., 10:10; Z II 112-119.

343. In the Exposition of the Eighteenth Article we find these words: "Simple folk should learn hereby that the dispute is not about whether the body and blood of Christ are eaten and drunk (for no Christian doubts that), but whether it is a sacrifice or only a remembrance". (Z II 128). It can only be on the basis of this one sentence that Köhler (e.g. in the introduction to *Zwingli und Luther. Ihr Streit über das Abendmahl nach seinen politischen und religiösen Beziehungen*. Vol. I, Leipzig, 1924, pp. 1ff.) and Fritz Blanke (e.g. in *Die Religion in Geschichte und Gegenwart*, 3rd ed., Vol. VI, 1962, column 1955) state that Zwingli had still not disputed the corporeal real presence of Christ, and regard Zwingli's eucharistic doctrine as beginning to develop at this point. See, however, the explanation of "eating and drinking" the body and blood of Christ, which follows immediately upon the words quoted above: "I do not worry about what theologians have invented regarding the transformation of the wine and bread. It is enough for me, that I firmly know by faith that he is my redemption and the food and comfort of my soul". (Z II 144). This does not only exclude transubstantiation; on closer examination, it excludes consubstantiation also. In general, according to Zwingli, the flesh and blood of Christ are to be understood in the sense of John 6, "when the soul believes they are its salvation, its pledge, its merit and its satisfaction in the sight of God". (Z II 143). Here "flesh and blood" stand for the death of Christ and its redemptive significance. "It also means, that if you do not find your comfort in the body and blood of Christ, that is, in his death, which is your life, then there is no life in you". (Z II 142).

Cf. also the letter of June 1523 to Thomas Wyttenbach (Z VIII 84-89) in which Zwingli, when writing to a friend, speaks more plainly, but urges caution in the development of reformation preaching. Cf. also the *Commentarius* of 1525 (Z III 773f.) in which (contra Köhler, *ibid.*, p. 606) Zwingli retracts nothing, but states that at that time, in 1523, he had not wanted to say everything that he believed, out of concern for the weaker brethren. The whole question of a "development" in Zwingli's eucharistic doctrine requires fresh examination. Cf. also Z V 84, 486.

344. The most important of Zwingli's works relating to this are the exposition of the Eighteenth Article (Z II 111-157); the chapter "De Eucharistia" in the *Commentarius* Z III 773-820); Articles 7 and 8 of the *Fidei Ratio* (S IV 9-15); and part of the *Fidei Christianae Expositio* (S IV 51-52). Of Zwingli's polemical writings, special mention may be made of the "Freundliche Verglimpfung über die Predigt Luthers wider die Schwärmer", 1527 (Z V 763-794).

345. Quoted from the Eighteenth Article (Z I 460; cf. Z II 111).

346. The first part of the corresponding section of my article in *Die Religion in Geschichte und Gegenwart*, 3rd ed., Vol. VI, 1962, column 1967, needs to be corrected in the light of what is said here.

be set in opposition to that of Luther (as Zwingli construes it). Luther calls the Lord's Supper a "Testament" "from its nature and property"; Zwingli calls it a "remembrance" "from its use and procedure".[347] The two terms complement one another, and Zwingli will "gladly give way" over his own[348]—on the assumption, of course, that Luther recognises the agreement between them.[349] Soon, however, there arises opposition to the Lutheran doctrine of the consubstantiation.[350] A Dutchman, Cornelius Hoen,[351] had addressed himself to Luther, Zwingli and Oecolampadius simultaneously, and it was from his letter that Zwingli took over the figurative interpretation of the words of institution (understanding *est* in the sense of *significat*).[352] Although Zwingli himself did not come to the famous rendering "signifies" by means of some liberating exegetical discovery, but by relating the Supper to the Old Testament Passover[353]—which was likewise a public feast of remembrance and thanksgiving for past deliverance and for the eternal covenant. Zwingli does not regard this interpretation as an impoverishment, but as progress. In the 18th Article he was already concerned about this reference to the eternal salvation that has been wrought for us: it is a "remembrance". Now the doctrine is speedily developed in more detail on the basis of the biblical texts ("do this ...!") The Lord's Supper is (1) public thanksgiving (eucharist) for Christ's gracious sacrifice; (2) a memorial celebration of it; and (3) a common meal that involves witness and commitment.[354]

---

347. Z II 137, 150.

348. Z II 137, 138.

349. One has the impression that even in 1523 Zwingli was not completely sure of Luther's agreement. Not only does the whole exposition of the Eighteenth Article look rather like an attempt to achieve concord, but it is also in this very context that we find the great and well-known declaration of independence vis-à-vis the "true servant of God, Martin Luther" (Z II 144-150), whom Zwingli "esteems as highly as any man living", but "I did not learn the doctrine of Christ from Luther, but from the Word of God itself". (Z II 149). In particular, his doctrine of the Lord's Supper did not go back to any Lutheran teaching; Zwingli had already maintained it for years, and had come to know Luther's teaching only "after some time" (Z II 137).

350. At the latest, in the *Epistola ad Matthaeum Alberum* of November, 1524 (Z III 322-354).

351. Z IV 512-518.

352. Z IV 560. (Zwingli speaks of finding a "costly pearl" here). Cf. the Excursus by Fritz Blanke, Z V 739f.

353. In a dream which occurred on the night of April 12th, 1525, Zwingli was pointed by an unknown person to Exodus 12:11: "It is the Lord's passover" (Z IV 483, in the *Subsidium*). Cf. *ibid.* 448f. for Walther Köhler's extremely illuminating summary of Zwingli's reasoning. It should be remembered that the *Subsidium* (a "supplement" to the *Commentarius*) was not directed against the Lutherans, but against the Catholic opposition in Zürich.

354. In the "Christian Answer of Zürich to Bishop Hugo" of August 1524 the meaning of the Lord's Supper is defined for the first time as 1) a communal meal 2) a sign of allegiance

As opposed to Luther (and Calvin), the actor of the celebration is not Christ, but the congregation.[355] It is not the "This is ..." but rather the "Do this ..." which is emphasised. This difference could well be much more significant than the whole controversy about the elements. But the following points should be noted. (1) This "remembrance" is not a merely intellectual process; and it does not awaken association with the past, but rather with the present. *Memoria,* as understood by Augustine (like ἀνάμ-

---

3) a memorial meal 4) a meal of witness before men and God (Z III 227-228).

Similarly, in the *Epistola ad Matthaeum Alberum* of November, 1524, the Lord's Supper is described as 1) commemoratio 2) communicatio 3) iuramentum ("wherefore it is also called a sacrament". Z III 346-349).

The *Commentarius* develops the argument for the various aspects, and then comprehends them under two points: "Est ergo sive 'eucharistia' sive 'synaxis' sive 'coena dominica' nihil aliud quam: commemoratio, qua ii, qui se Christi morte et sanguine firmiter credunt patri reconciliatos esse, hanc vitalem mortem annunciant, hoc est: laudant, gratulantur et praedicant.

Iam ergo sequitur, quod, qui ad hunc usum aut festivitatem conveniunt, mortem domini commemoraturi, hoc est: annunciaturi, sese unius corporis esse membra, sese unum panem esse, ipso facto testentur ... Qui ergo cum Christianis commeat, qum mortem domini an-nunciant, qui simul symbolicum panem aut carnem edit, is nimirum postea secundum Christi praescriptum vivere debet; nam experimentum dedit aliis, quod Christo fidat ... Erat sacramentum, quod nos Christo addictos esse apud ecclesiam testabatur..." (Thus the 'eucharist' or 'solemn assembly' or 'Lord's Supper' is nothing other than a commemoration in which those who firmly believe that they are reconciled to the Father through the body and blood of Christ proclaim this life-giving death, namely by praise and thanksgiving and preaching. It follows, therefore, that those who come together for this festal occasion, in order to commemorate—that is, to proclaim the Lord's death, thereby confess that they are members of one body, that they are one bread ... Therefore whoever joins with Christians when they proclaim the Lord's death, and eats the symbolic bread or flesh, is thereafter assuredly bound to live according to the commandment of Christ; for he has shown to others that he believes in Christ ... It was the sacrament which testifies to the church that we belong to Christ. Z III 807).

The reply to Th. Billican and U. Rhegius (March, 1526) states in a single sentence that "We say that the sacrament ... is an act of thanksgiving for the gracious gift bestowed once for all, a commemoration, giving of praise, and finally, the assembly of the mystical body, which is the church". (Z IV 902). Cf. Z IV 938; Z V 471f., 777; S IV 10f.

355. See above, note 325, see also Z V 711.

"Grace is not visible to us; but we have a visible symbol or sign of grace, the Supper, to extol and praise the grace which has been shown to us". (Z VI, II 200).

"For Christ is offered to us not only in the Supper, but also in his birth and death; and he has given us a sacramental sign of this in the bread and the wine. And he does not give himself truly and essentially or substantially; but rather Christian believers, who hope and trust in him, bring Christ with them to the Supper by faith. Therefore our Supper is not vain or empty, but Christ is present in it through the faith of the believing, God-loving soul. For before the bread or the wine is presented, our faith must be set on Christ as the one who was born and suffered and died for us, and must be assured that this took place to redeem us and to gain eternal life for us. And so we confess that Christ is present in the Supper to the believing, God-loving soul". (S II, III 93).

νησις in Plato) describes the soul's power of realisation and of consciousness in general; it often means the same as *conscientia*. According to this tradition, remembrance does not denote our ability to set ourselves back into the immediate or the remote past, but the way in which the past is brought into our present time, becoming contemporary with us and effective in us. Zwingli thinks in the categories of this Platonist-Augustinian anthropology; though for him this power to "render present" the death of Christ as our salvation does not lie within our soul, but in the Holy Spirit, on the basis of the eternal efficacy of the Lord's sacrifice; the organ by which it is received is faith, or rather the conscious contemplatio of faith.[356] "Thus it is seen from the strong proofs of scripture that the Lord's Supper, if it is not a sacrifice for the soul, is a remembrance and renewal of that which once happened, which is valid for all eternity, and which is dear enough to render satisfaction to God's justice for our sins. This proof stands in Christ's own words ... He says: Do this in remembrance of me; that is: Do this among you, so that you eat and drink my body and blood in remembrance of me; that is: that by commemorating it, you renew the kindness I have shown you".[357] In this act of remembrance, the congregation does not transport itself back 1500 or 2,000 years to the place of the historical event, but rather, the one who was crucified for us comes to us in the present.[358] (2) Secondly, Zwingli emphasises that the whole Christ,

---

356. S IV II, 31, 33, 38, 39, 57.

357. "But since the sacrifice is not offered in our own day, it is not a sacrifice, but a remembrance and renewal of that sacrifice which Christ made once for all, thus saving us for all eternity. Thus it is seen from the powerful proofs of Scripture..." (Z II 136).

"Eat and drink his flesh and his blood in this faith, and acknowledge that these are given you as an assurance that your sins are forgiven just as though Christ had just died on the Cross. Christ is present in such power at all times, for he is the eternal God. Therefore his suffering is eternally efficacious, as Paul says in Hebrews 9: 'How much more shall the blood of Christ, who through the eternal Spirit offered himself without spot to God, purge your conscience' etc. Here Paul does not say for nothing that Christ offered himself to God through the eternal Spirit; though we read in the Latin (i.e. the Vulgate) 'per spiritum sanctum', through the holy Spirit; For Paul explains in this same place that Christ, having offered himself once for all, is a precious and abiding sacrifice for the sins of mankind for all eternity, and he shows, since he is the eternal Spirit and God, that his suffering is efficacious for all eternity". (Z II 127-128).

"Thus we do not say that there is no value in the sacrament, but rather do we recognise that in the sacrament the death of Christ is proclaimed with the bread and wine, not only with words, but in our hearts. This belongs to the sacrament of the Supper". (Z VI, I 371-372).

358. In addition to the passages quoted in notes 356, 357 and 359, we would mention the following sections in which this concept of "remembrance" is to be found: Z II 137, 138, 141, 144, 150; Z V 726 (with reference to I Corinthians 11:26—'meminisse' (remember) = 'adnunciavisse' (proclaim).

"... omnem rem per Christum gestam illis fidei contemplatione velut praesentem fieri"

including his corporeal nature, is present to the faithful in the Lord's Supper.[359]

Finally, the character of the Lord's Supper as a *gift* is clearly stated.[360]

As a consequence of discussion with Luther and with Rome, this feature is worked out ever more clearly, until finally we have a parable that comes

---

(Thus the whole salvation wrought by Christ is, as it were, present to them by the contemplation of faith. S IV 11. The 'velut' signifies not that the presence is inferior, but that it is spiritual as distinct from corporeal and local).

"... Ista cum recoluntur, sacramentis non tantum ante oculos ponuntur, sed in mentem usque penetrant. Verum, quo duce? Spiritu!" (When they remember it, it is not merely brought before their eyes by the sacraments, it enters into their soul. But who accomplishes this? The Spirit! S IV 32). This important question naturally requires more detailed elucidation and documentation, which I hope to provide in the continuation to my *Theologie Huldrych Zwinglis*. Meanwhile, the brief exposition in *Die Religion in Geschichte und Gegenwart*, 3rd ed., Vol. VI, 1962, column 1967 (similarly in *Zwa*. XI, p. 576) should be supplemented by what is stated above—with the further comment that if it were expressed in medieval categories, Zwingli is here following the path of realism rather than nominalism (cf. J. V. M. Pollet, *Huldrych Zwingli et la Réforme en Suisse*, Paris, 1963, p. 87).

359. Z III 341; Z V 587, 588. "Spiritualis est ista corporis praesentia", states Zwingli (This presence of Christ's body is of a spiritual nature). According to Zwingli, the controversy is not about "the real presence of the body of Christ", but about the form of the presence—whether it is "a spiritual presence of the body and blood of Christ in the souls of the faithful" or a "corporeal presence". Cf. Z VI, II 202; S IV 11, 32f.

"Sic in coena Christi corpus tanto praesentius est fidei contemplatione menti, quanto maior est fides et caritas Christi". (Thus the stronger our faith in Christ and our love for him, so much the more is the body of Christ present to our souls in the Supper by the contemplation of faith. S IV 39).

360. In discussing the "subjectiveness" of Zwingli's sacramental doctrine, this "objectiveness" should not be overlooked, for it is basic to it. When Zwingli disputes the idea that administering the bread and wine causes the body of Christ to be present, he is not thereby maintaining that the body of Christ is not present, but rather that it is *already* present. "There has never been a sacrament which caused what it signifies to be present. Thus circumcision did not make people into children of God; but those who were already children of God according to promise received circumcision as a sign and a testimony of the covenant in which they stood. Similarly, the paschal lamb did not bring the passover with it (for that had taken place only once), but those who were eternally grateful for it bore their testimony to this, and they brought their believing, thankful hearts to the lamb, bearing the passover in their hearts. Similarly, baptism does not make people into children of God; but those who are God's children already receive the sign and the testimony of the children of God. And likewise the Supper of Christ, or the bread and the wine, do not cause the body or the death of Christ to be present; but those who acknowledge the death of Christ, who suffered once for all, to be their life, bring this to the Supper in their thankful hearts; and there, together with their fellow members, they receive the sign which Christ instituted, in order that it should be received by those who confess his death, and be a testimony for them". (Z VI, II 202). Cf. Z II 143; S IV 15; and Z III 805. These passages appear to me to have provided the model for Questions 75, 79 and 80 respectively in the Heidelberg Catechism.

From the way in which Zwingli bases the presence of Christ so strictly upon the activity of the Holy Spirit, and relates it exclusively to faith, it follows that he (like Calvin and contra Luther), denies that unbelievers partake of the body and blood of Christ. See e.g., Z VI, II 238f.

very close to *Calvin*. "If a man is about to travel to a far country, and he gives his wife his finest ring, on which his likeness is engraved, saying: "Here you have me, your husband; hold to me even when I am absent, and rejoice in me" ... then he is giving much more than if he had merely said "Here you have my ring" ... He is really saying: "I want you to be sure that I am wholly yours..."[361] But here also it is quite clear that the meaning which the "sacrament of the altar" had for Luther is attributed by Zwingli to Christ himself and to his Spirit.[362] The main arguments against Luther are: (1) the evidence for figurative speech in Scripture (e.g. "I am the vine");[363] (2) John 6:63;[364] and (3) the bodily ascension of Christ.[365] In the debate, both sides used philosophical as well as exegetical arguments. Luther used scholastic arguments,[366] while Zwingli employed

---

361. S IV 38f.

362. Z III 760, 782. Zwingli writes, with reference to John 6:63: "Caro Christi omni modo plurimum imo immensum prodest, sed, ut diximus ceasa, non ambesa. Caesa nos servavit a caede, sed comesa poenitus nihil prodest". (The flesh of Christ is most profitable, indeed exceedingly so. But, as we have said, it is the flesh slain, not eaten. Slain, it has saved us from death; but when eaten, it is of no profit at all. Z III 782).

"Obiter patet, eucharistiae esum non tollere peccata, sed symbolum eorum esse, qui firmiter Christi morte exhaustum et deletum esse peccatum credunt et gratias agunt". (It is clear that eating the sacrament does not take away our sins, but it is the mark of those who firmly believe that sin is removed and destroyed by the death of Christ, and who give thanks for that. Z III 351).

"It is trusting in him that saves; not eating, seeing or feeling him". (Z IV 815).

"Caro Christi caesa plurimum prodest, comessa poenitus nihil". (Slain, the flesh of Christ is most profitable, but when eaten, it is of no profit whatever. Z V 350). "Christo dei filio fidere, salutare est contra peccatorum vulnera remedium, non corpus edere! Fidei promissa est salus, non manducationi, nisi allegoricae, quae nihil est quam fidere". (To trust in Christ, the Son of God—that is the wholesome remedy for the wounds of sin, and not eating his body! Salvation is promised to faith, not to eating—unless that be understood allegorically, which would simply mean faith. Z V 576). "Constat sacramenta non iustificare aut gratiam facere posse: nescimus enim aliam iustificationem quam fidei". (It is certain that the sacrament cannot justify, nor can it produce grace; for we know no justification other than that of faith. S IV 33; Z V 688).

"Here (in John 14:26) you can see, dear Luther, that it is the Holy Spirit who is the Comforter, and not physical eating". (Z V 897; Z V 962).

363. Z III 795-798; Z IV 842-847; Z VI, II 31-46.

364. Z II 141-144; Z III 782-785, 790-792; Z VI, I 336f.; Z VI, II 181-191.

365. Z IV 467, 827-841, 904-909; Z V 695; Z VI, I 372, 478f., 482; S IV 38.

366. Cf. e.g. the debate in Z V 667ff., and Fritz Blanke's note thereon. Luther's statement that "the right hand of God" does not denote a place, but rather omnipotence, appears at first sight to be very modern, but it was really a piece of late scholastic philosophy, as Luther himself was well aware. It is based on logical distinctions relating to the problem of space (esse localiter, esse definitive, esse diffinitive, esse circumscriptive, esse repletive) and it envisages that within creation a certain limitation is imposed upon the laws of mathematics by the omnipotence and infinity of God. According to William of Occam, divine omnipotence can cause a substance (in this case, the body of Christ) to be so condensed as to be without dimensions, like a mathematical point; and it can at the same time confer

those of humanistic platonism: that external, material things can have no saving effect upon the soul.[367] But such thoughts are always subservient to the decisive Christological question: if atonement has been made on the

---

upon it the possibility of ubiquity. This was the idea that was taken up by Luther. Cf. A. W. Hunzinger, Article "Ubiquität" in *Realencyklopädie für protestantische Theologie und Kirche*, 3rd ed., Vol. XX, Leipzig, 1908, pp. 182-196; Reinhold Seeberg, *Lehrbuch der Dogmengeschichte*, Vol. IV/I, Leipzig, 1933, pp. 463-475; Ernst Bizer, Article "Ubiquität" in *Evangelisches Kirchenlexikon*, Vol. III, 1959, columns 1530-1532; H. L. Martensen, Article "Ubiquitätslehre" in *Lexikon für Theologie und Kirche*, 2nd ed., Vol. X, 1965, columns 442f. See also Bernhard Bartmann, *Lehrbuch der Dogmatik*, 5th ed., Freiburg, 1920, § 32: "Die Unermesslichkeit und Allgegenwart Gottes"; Hermann Schultz, *Die Lehre von der Gottheit Christi-Communicatio idiomatum*, 1881, pp. 202-215; Gerhard Esser, Article "Ubiquitätslehre" in *Wetzer und Weltes Kirchenlexikon*, Vol. XII, Freiburg, 1901, especially column 177.

367. "... spiritu spiritus generatur, non re corporea". (The spirit is born of the Spirit, and not of material things. S IV 13, with reference to John 3:6).

"Spiritus spiritum docet. Spiritus dei miserum hominis spiritum dignatur ad se trahere, sibi iungere, alligare ac prorsus in se transformare. Ea res mentem pascit, laetificat, certamque salutis reddit". (The Spirit teaches the spirit. The Spirit of God deigns to draw the wretched spirit of man to himself, to join it to himself, to bind it to himself, and to transform it into himself. This fact satisfies the soul, gladdens it, and gives it assurance of salvation. Z III 782).

"We were formerly led into complete blindness, when we sought comfort for our soul in outward things". (Z IV 284).

"Negamus corporis carnalis ad animam adhibitionem quicquam ad iustificationem facere, cum, quod corpore carneo vesci anima nequit, tum, quod Christus ipse spiritum esse oportere, quod iustificet; carnem autem nihil poenitus prodesse luculentissime disseruit". (We deny that applying a physical body to the soul can contribute anything to our justification. Firstly, because the soul cannot be fed with phsyical flesh; and secondly, because Christ himself has stated most clearly that it must be the Spirit who justifies, whereas the flesh is of no avail. Z V 626).

"Spiritum esse oportet, qui mentem vicificet, quique ad eam penetret, corpore pasci abhorret". (It must be the Spirit who gives life to the soul, and who enters into it; it refuses to be nourished by flesh. Z V 622).

"If we physically eat the body of Christ, then it must produce something in us. So we ask, whether the soul can be nourished with flesh? One has to answer, 'No'. For whatever is to renew and comfort and revive the spirit must be spirit, as it says in John 6:63". (Z VI, I 476).

"Quae in homine interno sunt, ut nemo nisi solus deus novit, ita immutare nemo alius potest, quanto minus res aut verba". (None except God alone knows what is within man. Therefore nobody else can change it. How much less can anything or words do so. Z XIV 174).

"Spiritus ubi vult spirat et operatur in corde credentium, non res externae". (The Spirit breathes and works in the hearts of believers; not outward things. S VI, I 569).

"Si spiritus est, quod in quaestionem venit, iam certa relatione contrariorum sequitur, corpus non esse; si corpus, iam certus est, qui audit, spiritum non esse. Unde corpoream carnem spiritualiter edere nihil est aliud, quam quod corpus sit, spiritum esse adserere. Haec ex philosophorum fontibus contra istos adduximus, qui philosophiam, quam tamen Paulus cavendam esse monet Coloss. 2., verbi dei magistram ac praeceptorem fecerunt, ut liquido videant, quam probe nonnunquam placita decretaque sua expendant. Breviter: Fides non cogit sensum sentire fateri, quod non sentit, sed trahit ad invisibilia et spes omnes in ista confert. Non enim versatur inter sensibilia et corporea, neque aliquid cum his com-

cross, then the comfort of the troubled soul cannot depend upon the celebration of the sacrament.[368] This is an alternative which Luther, because of his presuppositions, could not recognise, and therefore never understood. Yet Zwingli's protest was not rationalistic, but Christological. "We do not derive the absurdity from the thing itself ... what is absurd to *faith* is truly absurd".[369] Christ himself is both the fulfilment of grace and

mune habet". (If it is the spirit that is being spoken of, then it follows, from the law of opposites, that it cannot have to do with the flesh; if it is the flesh that is spoken of, then whoever hears is sure that it does not mean the spirit. Therefore, 'to eat bodily flesh after a spiritual manner' is to maintain that flesh is spirit. I have drawn this from the philosophers' springs, in order to refute those, of whom Paul warns in Colossians 2, who make philosophy the mistress and teacher of the Word of God. I have done this, in order that they might see clearly how well they sometimes think through their doctrines and their principles. In short: faith does not compel our senses to declare that they perceive something they do not perceive, but rather draws us to the things that are invisible, and sets all our hope on them. For faith is not concerned with what is corporeal and perceptible to the senses, nor has it anything in common with such things. Z III 787; H X 81f.). "Nam inter naturale sive corporale, et spirituale non est medium. Etiamsi universa, creatorem et creaturas, in unum cogas; aut spiritus erunt aut corpus". (There is nothing intermediate between what is natural or corporeal and what is spiritual. And even if you bring together everything, both creator and creatures, then they are either spirit or body. S IV 37).

368. "If physically eating the body of Christ could redeem the soul, then it would not have been necessary for him to die". Z VI, I 476.

"Non capiebant mentem verborum Christi, quod non esus, sed caesus nobis esset salutaris. Sic enim mentem humanam reddi certam misericordiae dei, quum videt eum filio suo non pepercisse". (The Jews did not grasp the meaning of Christ's words, namely, that he would not save us by being eaten, but by being slain. For the human soul is assured of God's mercy when it sees that he has not spared his son. Z III 780).

"It is the Spirit of truth who will comfort, not flesh that is physically eaten". (Z VI, II 117, with reference to John 14:16). "Falsa religio est, quae docuit symbolici panis usum peccata delere; nam Christus solus delet peccata, qum moritur". (It is a false religion which teaches that consuming symbolic bread cancels sins. For it is only Christ and his death that atones for sins. Z III 803).

"Fide constat salus, non corporali manducatione, neque ea fide, qua te fingas credere, quicquid finxeris, sed qua fidis filio dei pro te in cruce impenso". (Salvation consists in faith, not in physical eating; neither does it consist in that faith whereby you think to believe what you have imagined, but rather in that faith whereby you trust in the Son of God who hung on the cross for you. Z IV 467).

369. "Absurditatem non metimur ab ipsa re; nihil enim putamus absurdum esse, quod divinis eloquiis traditum est ... si modo recte intelligas ea, quae fidei credenda proponuntur. Quod si quid fidei absurdum, id tandem vere absurdum est". (We do not deduce the absurdity from the matter itself, for we do not consider anything absurd, which comes to us from the Word of God ... if only those things which are presented for acceptance by faith are rightly understood. But if anything appears absurd to faith, then it is truly absurd. Z V 618).

"We are not speaking here of fleshly reason, but of the reason of the inner man, that is, of the believer, as Paul does in the seventh chapter of Romans..." (Z V 502).

"We are not speaking of the worthlessness or ineptness of merely human understanding, but of the clear understanding of faith". (Z V 880).

"In reply to the accusation which is levelled against us by Luther, that we deny the physical body of Christ, and that this is contrary to reason, we give ... this answer: we have

the pledge of grace.[370] When faith is once more bound to a ceremony, then for Zwingli the whole reformation is at stake.[371]

21. The State

The same trust in the power of the Spirit leads to a theocratic ideal; the reformation of the church must also bring about the renewal of the State.[372] [373] The boundaries are fluid. "A Christian town is the same as a

---

always said that it is not so to the believing mind, because it contradicts faith and scripture". (Z V 884).

According to Zwingli, belief in a corporeal real presence is contrary to the essential nature of faith, which is trust, and also to the content of faith. Cf. Z V 882f., 885-904; Z VI, II 206-211.

370. "Christus est gratiae pignus, imo est ipsa gratia". (Christ is the pledge of grace; indeed, he is grace itself. Z III 675).

"The Gospel is the pledge and the assurance of the mercy of God, Jesus Christ". (Z IV 64).

Cf. Th. H. Z. I, Index, s.v. "pignus". For Zwingli, the term "pledge of grace" was reserved for Christ himself, and could not, therefore, be applied to the sacrament; a fact which undoubtedly rendered the union of Zwinglianism and Calvinism more difficult. In the latter, the function of the sacraments as "pledges" and "seals" plays a fundamental part. Cf. Institutes IV. xiv. 12: IV. xvii. 1. The Consensus Tigurinus of 1549 speaks of "sigilla" (seals) but avoids the term "pignora" (pledges) in referring to the sacraments (cf. E. F. K. Müller, ed., Die Bekenntnisschriften der reformierten Kirche, Leipzig, 1903, pp. 159-163). The same is true of Bullinger's Confessio Helvetica Posterior, which states in Article XIX that by means of the sacraments God seals his promises ("promissiones suas obsignat". W. Niesel, ed., Bekenntnisschriften und Kirchenordnungen der nach Gottes Wort reformierten Kirche, 3rd ed., Zürich, n.d., p. 259). The idea that the sacraments are seals and pledges is to be found in the Heidelberg Catechism of 1563, Questions 66, 73 and 79; in the Confessio Gallicana of 1559, Article 34; and in the Confessio Belgica of 1561, Article XXXIII. Cap. 21 of the Confessio Scotica of 1560, despite a decidedly anti-Zwinglian statement, speaks of the sacraments only as "sealing" the assurance of God's promise in the hearts of believers; this was taken over by Bullinger.

371. In his doctrine of the Lord's Supper, Zwingli wishes to guard the doctrine of "sola fide" against any fresh outbreak of the tendency to trust in the creature rather than the creator. Cf. Z III 781ff., 785ff.; Z IV 812; Z V 279, 576, 591, 614, 625, 671, 706, 708, 711, 783. Sensing a yearning for medieval catholicism and its ideas of sacramental grace, he declares that Luther's words "begin to reek of the garlic and onions of Egypt" (Z VI, II 70, 94 etc., with reference to Numbers 11:5).

372. Z I 155-188; Z I 210-248; Z II 458-525; Z III 97-113; Z III 355-469; Z XIV 5-14; Z XIV 417-425; Z IX 451-467; Zwingli Hauptschriften. Vol. VII: Zwingli, der Staatsmann, ed. Rudolf Pfister, Zürich, 1942; Huldrych Zwingli: Von göttlicher und menschlicher Gerechtigkeit. Sozial-politische Schriften für die Gegenwart, selected and introduced by Leonhard von Muralt and Oskar Farner, Zürich, 1934; Paul Meyer, Zwinglis Soziallehren, Linz/d., 1921; Alfred Farner, Die Lehre von Kirche und Staat bei Zwingli, Tübingen, 1930; G. W. Locher, Die evangelische Stellung der Reformatoren zum öffentlichen Leben, Zürich, 1950; Siegfried Rother, Die religiösen und geistigen Grundlagen der Politik Huldrych Zwinglis, Erlangen, 1956; Heinrich Schmid, Zwinglis Lehre von der göttlichen und menschlichen Gerechtigkeit, Zürich, 1959. G. W. L.; Zw. Ref. i. Rahmen., 167ff; 540ff (Liter.).

373. Zwingli confidently hoped for a majority of believers in both the church and the nation. Cf. Z IV 478; Z VI, I 31ff., 35ff; Z IV 207. He hoped also to see a speedy victory for

Christian congregation'',[374] and the magistrates must know that the responsibility for "Christ's sheep" is entrusted to them.[375] They govern according to imperfect "human justice", which at best gives "to each his own", whereas divine justice gives us what does *not* belong to us.[376] But within this framework, God himself restrains chaos by means of law and authority.[377] To work in politics or trade is to serve God[378], while preaching should be always relevant in its demands and should press for improvement in the conditions.[379] In this connexion, Zwingli teaches that those in positions of responsibility have the duty to resist, and this is carefully worked out on the basis of each person's position.[380] Zwingli, the democrat, maintained that the Babylonian captivity was God's punishment upon the Israelites for their failure to depose the godless tyrant Manasseh.[381]

22. *Education*

This same theocratic character even gained control over Zwingli's humanism.[382] "Learning is, as it were, the handmaid of wisdom, which is

---

the reformation in Italy, France, Spain and Germany (Z IX 130). To Luther, this was presumption (cf. Luther, *Tischreden*, No. 2891a and b, and No. 4043; also Oskar Farner, *Das Zwinglibild Luthers*, Tübingen, 1931, pp. 16f.).

374. "Sic principes vestri non turgent fastu, sic prophetae commode, fideliter ac erudite docent, sic plebs tranquilla et doctrinam et imperium capit, ut iam dixisse olim non poeniteat Christianum hominem nihil aliud esse quam fidelem ac bonum civem, urbem Christianam nihil quam ecclesiam Christianam esse". (Your patricians (in Strasbourg) are not swollen with pride, your prophets preach with skill, faithfulness and learning, and the people quietly accepts both teaching and government; therefore I need not repent of having once said that a Christian man is nothing other than a good and faithful citizen, and a Christian city is nothing other than a Christian church. Z XIV 424; Cf. Z VI, I 139, 141).

375. Z IX 455f.; Z XIII 117, 308; cf. S IV 58f.

376. Z II 475; Z VI, I 140f.

377. Z II 305, 328; Z VI, I 131.

378. S VI, I 285f.; Z XIII 169, 195, 239f., 244; Z XIV 424f.

379. The Word of God demands the reformation of the whole of public life (Z III 633, 636); reformation preaching serves to save, maintain and support the Confederacy (Z III 112f.). See what is said above with regard to the office of "watchman"; also note 320; and see Zwingli's attitude to numerous contemporary problems, such as the question of property (cf. G. W. Locher, *Der Eigentumsbegriff als Problem evangelischer Theologie*, 2nd ed., Zürich, 1962, pp. 29-35, 49-53), of mercenary service, of rents, of inflation, of monopolies and his opposition to Luther's role in the Peasants' War (Z VIII 382) *Zw. Ref. i. Rahmen.*, 499ff.

380. Z II 344; Z XIII 308, 414; Z XIV 388; S IV 16, 59.

381. "If the Jews had not allowed the wantonness of their king to go unpunished, God would not have punished them". (Z II 344).

382. Zwingli's much-lauded and much-maligned humanism requires a thorough study, which would need to begin by establishing precisely which ancient and contemporary authors he was familiar with. After a period of research in which the reformer long stood in the shadow of the humanist, it is now once more necessary to speak a word of warning

her mistress"—whereby wisdom consists in the proper reverence and love of God.[383] [384]

IV. SUMMARY AND CONCLUSIONS

1. *The character of the Zurich Reformation*

The characteristics of the Zurich reformation are as follows: a theocentric and theocratic way of thinking combined with a pneumatological Christology; an emphasis upon the objectivity of salvation in election and the atonement, together with the application of salvation in Spirit and in

---

against the opposite error of neglecting Zwingli's humanism. Both formally and methodologically, Zwingli remained a humanist to the end of his life. He was a reformer in a humanist's gown, just as Luther was a reformer in a monk's habit.

383. "Iugenda est eruditio sapientiae, et rursus sapientia eruditioni: nam altera sine altera aut manca est, aut perniciosa. Eruditio veluti ancilla est herae sapientiae, quae scrutatur omnia vasa, omnem supellectilem, sed debet servire sapientiae, reginae. Sunt qui abutantur sua eruditione ad vanam gloriam, mancipia fiunt aurae popularis, ventris, gloriae, pecuniae. Hi non secus faciunt, quam si quis pro hera et legitima uxore ancillam accipiat, et cum ea adulteretur. Pessima res est et odiosissima, si ancilla hera fiat. Hanc eruditionem quidam negligunt, quidam vero perverse deamant. Eruditio pessimis rebus iungi potest, et ipsa fieri pessima, quasique toxicum et venenum. At sapientia nunquam, non enim potest esse nisi optima. Eruditio et doctrina petitur ex historiis, ex philosophia, ex legibus. Haec est enim vera eruditio, quum homo ex divinis et humanis literis (nam et saecularis, ut vocant, eruditio ex deo est) quaerit ac investigat honesta, necessaria, utilia quaeque, quae in se derivet, et deinde utatur, in aliosque transfundat, ut et illos eruditos faciat. Sapientia vero est deum nosse summum bonum, sapientissimum, justissimum, optimum, misericordissimum, cognitumque colere et amare". (Learning must be joined to wisdom, and conversely, wisdom to learning; for the one without the other is either defective or destructive. Learning is, as it were, the handmaid of wisdom, which is her mistress. She examines every vessel and every utensil; but she should serve wisdom, which is the queen. There are those who misuse their learning for their own vainglory; they then become slaves to popular favour, to their belly, to prestige or to money. They are acting no differently than if a man were to take to himself the maid in place of the mistress, his legitimate wife, and lived in adultery with her. It is a very bad and most abominable thing when the maid becomes the mistress. Some neglect learning, while some are completely enslaved by love for her. Learning can be joined to the worst things, and thereby become a bad thing herself, like a poison or a drug. But it can never be so with wisdom; for wisdom cannot be anything but good. Learning and instruction are sought from histories, from philosophy and from laws. For true learning is found when a man applies himself to divine and human sciences (for even so-called secular science is from God), seeking out and exploring whatever is honest, necessary and useful, absorbing it, and then using it, passing it on to others, in order to educate them also. But wisdom means knowing God in his supreme goodness, wisdom, righteousness, kindness and mercy; and knowing him, to worship and to love him. S VI, I 375, with reference to Matthew 23:24).

384. In accord with the nature of this survey there should naturally follow at this point a section dealing with Zwingli's ethical teaching, but this must be reserved for a later study. Such a study might well contrast the precedence which Zwingli gives to social ethics with Luther's concentration on personal ethics, and Calvin's emphasis upon church discipline.

faith; responsibility for community life in church and state, as well as a humanistic-pedagogic tendency. All in all, it was a reformation that broke out on the periphery, which penetrated to the spiritual centre, and from there worked outwards to the periphery again. Nor should we forget its cheerful soberness: "If you find that the fear of God is beginning to make you more happy than sad, then that is certainly the work of God's Word and Spirit".[385]

2. *Comparisons*

Luther sees before him a troubled man, and proclaims to him the solus Christus, Christ pro me. *Zwingli* sees before him the deceitful, selfish man, and the disruption of his social life. He cries to the solus Deus, the Deus noster in Christus noster.[386] *Calvin* sees before him man as a disobedient individual. He calls him to order and to salvation under the glory of Christ in his church: "*Domini sumus*—we are the Lord's!"[387] In their doctrine of the Word, Luther and Calvin stand close together; Zwingli goes his own way. In Christology, Zwingli and Calvin agree, and Luther stands alone. The same is true of the doctrine of the Spirit, and of the relationship between Spirit and Word. Though, compared with the other reformers, it is Zwingli who has the strongest and most vital pneumatology. In his teaching on election, it is he who has found the most helpful formulation, and it is a pity that in the reformed tradition this should have been displaced so soon by the systematic theology of Calvin. In their understanding of the church, Zwingli and Luther are united by the medieval concept of the Corpus Christianum, while Zwingli's theocratic purposes were, in fact, realised more effectively by the far more modern outlook of Calvin, who worked towards a free church.

3. *Tasks that remain*

In our responsibility for handing on our reformation heritage in a productive way, a right understanding of Zwingli's theology can stimulate, challenge and also help us to a surprising extent. We may name the following examples:

1) his open and uninhibited attitude to philosophy, which arose out of his faithfulness to the biblical message, and not in spite of it.

---

385. Z I 384. *Zw. Ref. i. Rahmen.*, ch. XXIII.
386. For the centrality of this idea in Zwingli's thought, cf. *Th. H. Z.* I, pp. 33ff., 98ff.
387. *Institutes* III. vii. 1.

2) A similar natural openness towards the world of religion, even though accompanied by a sharply critical attitude.

3) The ethical dynamic which he combines with a cultic asceticism in connexion with everything that can be termed "divine service".[388]

4) The exemplary way in which he sets social and ethical problems at the very centre of faith—in contrast to that religious individualism from which neither Lutheranism, nor Rome, nor later Protestantism has been free.

5) Finally, I know of no other reformer who has so consistently anticipated the modern ecumenical and missionary programme of the church, which really is the church only when it opens its doors to public life, and becomes the "church for the world".

In all these ways, the voice of the oft-misunderstood reformer from Zurich has important things to say to us. "For God's sake, do something brave!"[389] cries Huldrych Zwingli. "Truth has a happy face".[390]

---

388. Cf. "In Spirit and in Truth" (above, pp. 1-6, section 1. Worship and Life).
389. Z X 165.
390. "Laeta est veri facies" (Z III 820).

9

ZWINGLI AND ERASMUS*

The names Erasmus and Zwingli signify a perennial problem for Reformed Protestantism, and indeed for Christian theology in all traditions. Since their personal relations have been treated extensively in such fundamental studies as those of John Martin Usteri,[1] Walther Köhler,[2] Arthur Rich,[3] and Joachim Rogge,[4] I shall not attempt to cover this ground again but rather will select for comment a few main issues concerning the relations between Erasmus and Zwingli and between humanism and the Reformation.

I. THE ANTITHESIS FROM THE PERSPECTIVE OF HISTORY

The problem of this antithesis is contained in the fact that both Erasmus and Zwingli were humanists. Zwingli was first influenced by the quite distinctive eastern European humanism[5] represented by men like Konrad Celtes and Joachim Vadian. However, when he returned from Vienna, he became an enthusiastic reader of the works of Erasmus, whose grateful and devoted student he felt himself for the rest of his life.[6] Even after the painful break with Erasmus, Zwingli remained a humanist. Apart from Luther, all of the reformers were more or less humanists. This was cer-

---

* This article is a revised version of an anniversary lecture given at the University of Zurich, 22 January 1969. German-language versions appeared in *Zwingliana* 1969, XIII/1 37-61 and in *Scrinium Erasmianum*, Leiden 1969, II 325-50. Translation by Sherman Isbell, Duncan Shaw, and Erika Rummel. Erasmus in English, A Newsletter published by University of Toronto Press, 10/1979-80, pp. 2-10.

1. J. M. Usteri, *Zwingli und Erasmus. Eine reformationsgeschichtliche Studie*, Zurich 1885.

2. W. Köhler, *Zwingli und Luther. Ihr Streit über das Abendmahl nach seinen Politischen und religiösen Beziehungen*, Leipzig 1924, I, Gutersloh 1953, II; "Erasmus von Rotterdam als religiöse Persönlichkeit" in *Voordrachten gehouden ter herdenking van den sterfdag van Erasmus. Bijdragen voor Vaderlandsche Geschiedenis en Oudheidkunde*, 's-Gravenhage 1936, VII 213-25; *Huldrych Zwingli*, Stuttgart 1952.

3. A. Rich, *Die Anfänge der Theologie Huldrych Zwinglis*, Zurich 1949.

4. J. Rogge, *Zwingli und Erasmus. Die Friedensgedanken des jungen Zwingli*, Stuttgart 1962; "Die Initia Zwinglis und Luthers. Eine Einführung in die Probleme" in *Luther Jahrbuch* 1963, 107-33.

5. W. Näf, *Vadian und seine Stadt St. Gallen*, 1944, I 109-205.

6. In 1528, in a letter to Ambrosius Blarer, Zwingli regretted that he had made a personal enemy of Erasmus several years previously by defending Lutheran paradoxes ("paradoxa") against him in (Z IX 451 17 - 452 15).

tainly true of Calvin, who cites Erasmus without hesitation and does not discuss the difficulties of combining humanism with the Reformation: a member of the second generation of reformers, he no longer felt this to be a problem.

The historian recognizes differences between humanism and the Reformation, but not merely contrasts. Viewed historically, the Reformation sprang largely from humanism. It was largely carried by the humanistic ideal of individualism and its quest for personal freedom and was set ablaze by the humanists' caustic criticism of late scholasticism and the abuses of the church.

The Reformation is regarded in another light by theologians, who draw attention to Luther's major controversy with Erasmus in 1525.[7] This dispute concerned the question of freedom or bondage of the will of man. The recognized prince of humanists disappointed the high hopes of the evangelical party by remaining in the old church. These facts make it clear (so the theologians claim) that humanism and the Reformation were fundamentally opposed movements. This view has governed theological literature, both Protestant and Catholic, since Luther.

Although Erasmus is certainly representative of humanism, his name is not synonymous with humanism as a whole; additional points could be raised about his confessional tenets, yet it is correct to give a high priority to his position in matters of Christian anthropology. The question at stake is whether sinful man is able by his natural abilities and powers to make God the goal of his life and reach him.

Neither Luther nor Erasmus denied human responsibility or divine grace. But Luther's argument began with grace and led as a consequence to the *servum arbitrium*. Erasmus argued then, as Kant did in a later age, that the existence of law presupposes man's freedom to decide. Despite the profusion of humanistic principles which flowed into Lutheranism through Melanchthon, Luther's church hardened the breach doctrinally by making the controversy of 1525 its final judgment on humanism.[8] The

---

7. *De libero arbitrio sive collatio per Desiderium Erasmus Roterodamum*, ed. J. van Walter in *Quellenschriften zur Geschichte des Protestantismus*, Leipzig 1910, Heft 8; D. Erasmus, *De libero arbitrio. Discourse on the Freedom of the Will*, ed. W. H. Woodward, Cambridge 1904; M. Luther, *De servo arbitrio* in *Werke*, Historisch-kritische Gesamtausgabe, Weimar 1833f., xviii 600f.; *Luthers Werke in Auswahl* ed. O. Clemen, Berlin 1933, 94-293; *The Bondage of the Will*, ed. J. I. Packer and O. R. Johnston, London 1957; *Dass der freie Wille nichts sei. Antwort...an Erasmus von Rotterdam* in *Martin Luthers Ausgewählte Werke*, Munich 1954, Ergänzungsreihe I, trans. B. Jordahn and intro. H. J. Iwand.

8. Since the Formula of Concord of 1580, solida declaratio, II De libero arbitrio sive de viribus humanis. In *Bekenntnisschriften der evangelischen-lutherischen Kirche*, Göttingen 1963, 889.

Reformed church took the same course when the Synod of Dordrecht excluded the Arminians, in whose theology a certain humanistic synergism was sensed.[9] Is everything essential to an understanding of the relationship of humanism and the Reformation thereby determined? We think not.

II. FROM HUMANISM TO REFORMATION

Post-Petrarchian humanism has justly been described as a *scholarly* movement.[10] In contrast to the surviving, but simplified, ecclesiastical Latin of the Middle Ages, the Ciceronian style was once again fostered. The Aristotelianism of the scholastic school was challenged by a return to Platonic philosophy, now studied in the Greek original. On philological grounds, Hebrew was also added to the program of studies. For Old Testament and old Christendom which was viewed as a religion of classical antiquity were included in the watchword *Ad fontes*, 'to the sources'. Man's renewal was sought in the origins of civilization rather than in tradition. All this is well known, and the importance of the so-called *tres linguae* for the exposition of holy scripture is obvious. The movement was propagated through the rise of the art of printing.

It should be observed that this zealous literary activity was already a result of humanistic activity. The movement sprang from the demand of Renaissance man for personal experience and his desire for individual self-realization at the risk of breaking through the dogmatic and social boundaries derived from the medieval *ordo*. Many humanists were aware that this new and autonomous experience of life had long been nourished by the Christian "rebirth" taking place within mysticism and the *devotio moderna*.[11] Erasmus' vision of a comprehensive *Christianismus renascens* was

---

9. "The Canons of Dordrecht" in *Die Bekenntnisschriften der reformierten Kirche...* ed. E. F. K. Müller, Leipzig 1903, 843-61; the *Sententiae Remonstrantium* in the introduction LVIII-LXIV; J. C. S. Locher, *De Dortsche Leerregels uitgelegd*, Amsterdam 1956.

10. On the problem of humanism: P. Wernle, *Renaissance und Reformation*, Tübingen 1912; J. Huizinga, "The Problem of the Renaissance" in *Men and Ideas. History of the Middle Ages, the Renaissance*, trans. J. S. Holmes and H. van Marle, New York 1959, 243-87; A. von Martin, *Soziologie der Renaissance. Zur Physiognomik und Rythmik bürgerlicher Kultur*, Stuttgart 1932; *Rencontres internationales de Genève. Pour un nouvel humanisme*, Neuchatel 1949; W. Näf, *Die Epochen der neueren Geschichte. Staat und Staatengemeinschaft vom Aufgang des Mittelalters bis zur Gegenwart*, Aarau 1945, I; H. S. Nordholt, *Het beeld der renaissance*, Amsterdam 1948; J. M. Romein, "Ancien et nouvel humanisme" in *Comprendre. Revue de la société européenne de culture*, 1956, XV 93-100; "Versuch einer neuen Interpretation des Humanismus" in *In Memoriam Werner Näf. Schweizer Beiträge zur Allgemeinen Geschichte*, Bern 1961, XVIII/XIX 254-66; P. Ricœur, "Que signifie humanisme?" in *Comprendre*, 1956, XV; H. Baron, "Moot problems of Renaissance Interpretation" in *Journal of the History of Ideas*, 1958, XIX 31-34; W. Kaegi, *Humanismus der Gegenwart*, Zurich 1959.

11. Rich, Anfänge 9-24.

intended as a response to this experience of life. The formation of man
after the authoritative human model of Jesus made humanism an educational movement.

The literary slogan *ad fontes* can also be understood in this connection.
What was actually new was not the recent discoveries in philology, but the
new spirit in which old sources were read. Virgil, Galen, Caesar, and
Cicero had been known for centuries. What was new was the idea of im-
itating Aeneas by embarking on sea voyages to distant lands; of carrying
out experiments to confirm the principles of traditional science and
medicine and to build on them; of approving desire for power and glory as
political and social motives of action. *Ad fontes* was a call to the "essential
matter", to the realities of life as reported in the literary sources, to one's
own experience *e fontibus*, out of the actual fountains of life.[12]

What happens if this search for the essential matter is applied to the
"sources" of "original" Christianity? What happens, if after the literary
preparation of the Greek New Testament by Erasmus, a Zwingli breaks
out of the literary situation of these writings, and hears in them the Word
of God, the gospel, indeed *Christus renascens* himself, and sets out to live
according to these sources? When this happens we have the authentic and
legitimate transition from humanism to the Reformation. For Erasmus
too intended not literature, but spiritual experience and practice.

Before accepting this conclusion we must consider a point which Hans
von Greyerz made almost forty years ago, and which, in spite of convincing evidence in its favour, received scant attention.[13] It is well known that

---

12. What today we would call the realm of depth psychology was also drawn into the field
of personal exploration. Here belong Dante's Inferno and Purgatorio in which the poet
himself experienced the journey to the underworld reported by his predecessors. He acted
not only like Homer or Virgil, but like Odysseus and Aenaes. The visionary experiences of
Dante are datable: on Good Friday, 1300, Dante fell into a deep sleep and had a vision
which lasted ten days (Dante Alighieri, *The Divine Comedy* I, *Inferno* parts 1 and 2 trans. with a
commentary C. H. Singleton, Princeton 1970. Canto 21 lines 112-14 and comment). The
history of religions and depth psychology provide innumerable instances to demonstrate intellectual ecstatic and apocalyptic experiences. Thus the dating given by Dante is not to be
regarded as a poetic fiction, as for example, according to A. Buck, "Dantes
Selbstverständis" in *Dante Alighieri. Vorträge an der Universität Bern zur Feier seines 700. Geburts-
tages*, Bern 1966, 12 (cf. E. Moore, *The Time-References in the Divina Commedia*, London 1887).
What Buck sets forth impressively on the following pages, about the experience of inspiration as "the decisive impulse of the poetic work", contradicts that judgment.

13. H. von Greyerz, "Studien der Kulturgeschichte der Stadt Bern am Ende des Mit-
telalters" in *Archiv des Historischen Vereins des Kantons Bern*, Bern 1940, XXXV/2 431f.; W.
Näf, "Schweizerischer Humanismus. Zu Gareans 'Helvetiae Descriptio' " in *Schweizer
Beiträge zur Allgemeinen Geschichte*, Aarau 1947, V 186-98; W. Näf, *Vadian und seine Stadt St.
Gallen*, St. Gallen 1944-57, I 335-60, II 55-121.

the cosmopolitan educational ideal of humanism contended in many countries with an early nationalism. Greyerz and Näf have shown that alongside this cosmopolitanism there was, for several years in Switzerland, a Swiss humanism with its own characteristics, in which an enthusiastic exchange of ideas took place and a methodical program was pursued. The significant achievements of its protagonists included the dangerous first ascent of Mt Pilatus by Vadian, Myconius, Grebel and others in August 1518;[14] Myconius' edition of the funeral oration for a captain of the papal guard in Rome;[15] and Glarean's description of Switzerland in hexameters with a commentary by Myconius, published in Basel in 1519 by Froben.[16]

Vadian's dedicatory poem explains the significance of this volume: Helvetia, the cradle of liberty, long renowned in Italy, Gaul, and Spain for its military power, has at last found her herald in Glarean and in Myconius her commentator. Thus her spiritual minority is ended. In succession to Mars, Pallas Athene now also bestows upon the land her good will, and Apollo's muses climb the mountains of Switzerland. *Libertas* has her refuge only where she is defended *armis animisque* (intellectual national defence in the sixteenth century!).

Zwingli's early writings and letters also belong to this Swiss humanism. The leading figures of this movement (Vadianus in Vienna, Glareanus in Paris, Xylotectus and Myconius in Lucerne, Zwingli in Einsiedeln and others) used to send one another their numerous students for further education. Their correspondence reveals a common practical goal in education and politics—unusual in the intellectual world of humanism which had adopted Horace's principle: *Odi profanum vulgus et arceo*. But within this circle, the aim was not to construct a scholars' republic, but rather to create a Swiss cultural nation.

The period of euphoria was brief. The reasons for this are both external and internal. Those involved encountered not only changed circumstances, but also a new value-system. The moment, so significant for Swiss cultural history, when the young Swiss humanist circle consolidated itself and began to clarify its program, coincided with Zwingli's call to Zurich, where his preaching in the Grossmunster initiated another move-

---

14. W. Brändly, "Wann war Vadian auf dem Pilatus?" in *Zwingliana*, 1947, VIII/7 425f.

15. E. Egli, *Schweizerische Reformationsgeschichte*, ed. G. Finsler, Zurich 1910, 41.

16. H. Glareanus, *Descriptio de situ Helvetiae et vicinis gentibus per eruditissimum virum Henricum Glareanum Helvetium, poetam laureatum. Idem de quatuor Helvetiorum pagis. Eiusdem pro iustissimo Helvetiorum foedere Panegyricum. Cum commentariis Oswaldi Myconii Lucernani...Joachimus Vadianus medicus, orator et poeta laureatus Helvetiam alloquitur*, Basel 1519; H. Glareanus, *Descriptio de situ Helvetiae...*, ed. and trans. W. Näf, St. Gallen 1948.

ment. Zwingli's reformation activity might at first appear to be closely related to the concerns of the humanist circle, but it soon reduced to secondary importance everything which was precious to the humanists: literary publishing, critical editing, poetry, skilful Latin style, mutual admiration within the circle of pupils and like-minded colleagues, title, gown, and poet's laurel.

III. THE CRISIS IN THE RELATIONSHIP BETWEEN ZWINGLI AND ERASMUS

It is enough to draw attention to the following points in the relationship between Zwingli and Erasmus.[17] The secular priest of Glarus and Einsiedeln had eagerly read the works of the esteemed master of spiritual renewal and had absorbed both his thought and his style, responding appropriately with merry laughter at Erasmus' ridicule of stupidity and hypocrisy in science, church, and secular world. But from the beginning, with perhaps too much of the sincerity of the Swiss peasant, Zwingli failed to appreciate the scepticism which lay behind Erasmian irony and this intellectual divergence always held the threat of a crisis in their relationship.

Walther Köhler has recorded which books by Erasmus were in Zwingli's library; many of them bear signs of intensive reading.[18] Still more impressive are Zwingli's grateful autobiographical testimonies, especially from the years after their friendship had broken down.[19] The most persuasive evidence lies in the numerous elements in Zwingli's theology whose Erasmian origin can be proved. (With some detailed research, even a literary dependence can be established).

Zwingli visited Erasmus in Basel in the winter of 1515-16. Of the correspondence which ensued, only Erasmus' letters are extant, because Erasmus later destroyed those he had received from Zwingli, and transcripts of only a few of them survive. Like all true humanists, Zwingli frequently quoted from the *Adagia*—after all, the collection was intended as a sourcebook. The line from Erasmus' poem *Expostulatio* ("Jesus' Lament to Men"), that "Christ is the only solace of the needy soul", Zwingli took to heart and made the basis of his reformation impulse, consciously understanding it as an alternative to the adoration of the saints in a far

---

17. The relevant biographical material is, as one would expect, admirably collected and related by O. Farner, *Huldrych Zwingli, IV...1525-1531,* ed. R. Pfister, Zurich 1960, 214-27.
18. Z XII 253-75.
19. E.g. Z VIII 334: 2f.; Z V 719-23 (with notes by F. Blanke); Z V 816: examples of how the later Zwingli utilized Erasmus' philological work, Z XI 456; Z VI/7 231.

more radical way than Erasmus had intended.[20] We can identify direct influences from the *Enchiridion*, the *Praise of Folly*, the *Colloquies*, the *Querela pacis*, the Prefaces to the New Testament, *Ratio verae theologiae*, the *Paraphrases* of the New Testament, and other writings.

However, the deepest influence which Erasmus exercized on Zwingli was admittedly not through his own original ideas, but through the publication of the Greek New Testament in 1515-16. Bullinger tells how the pastor of Einsiedeln subsequently committed to memory the Pauline epistles in the original language.[21] Today almost no one wishes to take this literally; in my opinion, the report is all the more trustworthy in that the disciple was carrying out the advice which is to be found twice in the writings of the master.[22]

The response of Erasmus to Zwingli's reforming writings and actions was increasingly to caution, to inhibit, to reject.[23] On the appearance of the *Archeteles*, Zwingli's petition to the Bishop of Constance in 1522, Erasmus reacted instantly in the middle of the night with a note motivated by apprehension and fear, and also by an ill concealed resentment because the disciple had not consulted him beforehand on so important a matter.[24] About the *Commentarius* of 1525, the first comprehensive dogmatics of the Reformation, Erasmus complained (as before, in the case of Luther's writings)[25] that whatever was true in the work he himself had already frequently propounded.[26] Inadvertently the scholar's sensitive mind touches upon a central theological problem: there are sentences which, though they contain a more or less correct statement, nevertheless do not have the authority that characterizes truth. It is often a question of how a thing is said and who says it. Zwingli recognized this when he drew a distinction with an almost Erasmian pun: Luther was an Elijah who smashed the

---

20. II 217; 5-21. The song was later translated into German by Leo Jud, and was published in 1522 by Froschauer in Zurich.

21. *Heinrich Bullingers Reformationsgeschichte*, ed. J. J. Hottinger and H. H. Vögeli, Frauenfeld 1838-40, I 8.

22. *Erasmus von Rotterdam. Ausgewählte Schriften* (Latin and German) ed. W. Welzig, Darmstadt 1967f., I 373 (in the *Enchiridion*); III 68, 458. Erasmus himself traces this advice back to Augustine *De doctrina christiana* II 9 (*Patrologiae Latinae cursus completus*, Paris 1844-64, XXIV 42).

23. Even in friendliest humour the forefinger is waved: *Tu pugna, mi Zwingli, non modo fortiter, verum etiam prudenter; dabit Christus, ut pugnes et feliciter* (Z VII 581 236). No. 256 is a veiled refusal. The letters, Z VIII 315 and 316 of 1523, are exceptional, in which Erasmus attempts to set the *eruditissimus Zwinglius* against Luther, and to prejudice him against Ulrich von Hutten.

24. Z VII 582.

25. Z VIII 118: 2f.

26. Z VIII 333: 26f.

altars of idolatry, while Erasmus was only an Eli, too weak to prevail even upon his own circle to accept what he had recognized as the truth.[27]

Zwingli, with many of his companions, long retained his confidence in Erasmus, and hoped that he might yet publicly join the Protestant camp. When in 1522 their friends became aware that the differences between Luther and Erasmus threatened to break out into the open, Zwingli wanted to bring about a reconciliation.[28] He ensured that Erasmus, who was having difficulties in Basel, was invited to emigrate to Zurich and was offered citizenship by the town council.[29] Three years later, however (that is, prior to Luther's criticism), Zwingli published his *Commentarius* in which he opposed Erasmus' teaching on the *liberum arbitrium*.[30] The breach became generally known in the European scholarly world when Erasmus, with hate-filled letters, caused Ulrich von Hutten to be chased from one city to another until Zwingli secured him asylum on the Ufenau in August 1523.

Erasmus expressed, in no uncertain terms, his pleasure at the deaths of Zwingli and Oecolampadius.[31] As is well known, he moved to Freiburg im Breisgau after the victory of the Reformation in Basel. He remained faithful to the papal church—or at least so his biographers say—but the Franciscan polemic against this first agent of unrest in the church had mounted inordinately since the Imperial Diet at Augsburg.[32] Erasmus declined a cardinal's hat. At an advanced age he returned once again to Basel and died there. Myconius conducted the funeral service according to the rites of the Reformed church. Erasmus' considerable fortune was left as an endowment for students at the Reformed university in Basel.[33] The Council of Trent placed his books on the Index.

Once again let us examine the first letters which Erasmus and Zwingli exchanged in 1515-16 after the latter's visit in Basel.[34]

---

27. Z I 440: 17f. Cf. G. W. Locher "Elia bei Zwingli" in *Judaica* 1953, IX/1 62f.; and F. Blanke in Z V 721 n4.

28. Z VII 496-98 No. 199 (letter to Beatus Rhenanus).

29. Farner *Huldrych Zwingli* 216 and 539; Z VII 580.

30. Z III 649f.; 843f.; moreover, clear anti-Erasmian statements are already found in the *Usslegen* of 1523 (e.g. Z II 180: 26, "Human wisdom's suggestion of a free will, a suggestion we imbibed from the heathen...").

31. *Erasmi Opera*, ed. J. Clericus, Leiden 1703-6; reprinted 1961-2, III, *Epistolae*, col. 1422 B.

32. R. Stähelin in *Realencyklopadie* 1898, third ed. V. G. B. Winkler in *Erasmus ... Schriften*, ed. Welzig, III/39.

33. C. Roth, "Das Legatum Erasmianum" in *Gedenkschrift zum 400. Todestage des Erasmus von Rotterdam*, ed. Historische und Antiquarische Gesellschaft zu Basel, Basel 1936, 282-98.

34. Z VII 35f., 37f.; cf. Z V 741f. n5. *Zw. Ref. i. Rahmen.*, 68-77. (Liter.).

What is the explanation for Zwingli's frank enthusiasm and the reserved coolness of Erasmus' reply? The answer lies in Zwingli's praise for Erasmus as the editor and expositor of holy scripture, whereas Erasmus wanted to be admired as a person.[35] He sensed already in Zwingli a radical theological objectivity, and sought to stifle it by adopting a condescending manner and expressly praising his devoted Glarean as the banner carrier of Swiss humanism. The relationship between Erasmus and Zwingli was doomed from the beginning.

IV. CHRISTIANISMUS RENASCENS

Erasmian elements in Zwingli's theology

The elements in Zwingli's thought whose origin or affinity can be traced to Erasmus are the following.[36] There is first the emphasis on the spirituality of God and the consequent differentiation between creator and creature and, in connection with this, the accentuation of the spirituality of man's nature in a glittering blend of Platonism and Stoicism. Related to this is Zwingli's representation of man in whom reason struggles with the emotions, which stand morally on a lower level. In his representation of God, the traditional attributes are rigorously reduced to the two concepts of justice and mercy, of which the latter carries greater weight (for Erasmus, in fact, it predominates exclusively).

As far as the relationship to tradition is concerned, there is here a certain proximity to Thomas Aquinas, while the Scotists are spurned as modern-day sophists, although a few of their tenets are adopted.[37] The influence of both schools of thought is overshadowed, however, by a return to the church Fathers, among whom admittedly Origen and Jerome are pre-eminent for Erasmus,[38] whereas for Zwingli the highest authority resides in Augustine. In addition, the two men shared a high estimation of antiquity, though it is popular philosophy which receives particular attention from Erasmus, and historical writings from Zwingli.

On this basis sincere feelings and freedom of the mind are set over against observance of ceremonies, divine truth against human precepts.

---

35. Zwingli at the climax of the letter, "...ut sanctae litterae a barbarie sophismatisque ... in perfectiorem aetatem grandescant ..." (Z VII 36.17f.). Erasmus, Lucubrationes (containing, among other things, the Enchiridion), "...nostras tibi probari, viro tam probato, vehementer letor..." (37: 7f.).

36. Cf. above ch. 8.

37. Erasmus shared the freedom of the will with the Scotists whom he hated so much.

38. Apparently Erasmus chose the first name Desiderius from a correspondent of Jerome (J. Huizinga, Erasmus, London 1952, 6).

Within this framework innumerable particulars might be alluded to: influences on the doctrine of the Lord's Supper, the study of the three languages as a theological and prophetic skill,[39] the rejection of congregational singing in the name of inner concentration and heartfelt devotion,[40] the salvation of the pious heathen. Not the least of their common concerns was peace in Christendom, a life-long theme for both of them. And the *philosophia christiana* was, at the beginning as at the end, being drawn from the teaching and example of Christ. It was ultimately of central importance for Zwingli and the entire Reformation movement that Erasmus thought, in his own way, christocentrically and acknowledged the authority of scripture.

Confronted by such substantial agreement, we ask ourselves the question which already bewildered their contemporaries: why did Erasmus not become a reformer? We could give a quick, final answer: because he does not understand the reformer's doctrine of justification or the corresponding doctrine of grace, *sola gratia*. But this is the crucial point in our discussion and we must have a clear understanding of it. Those elements—some evangelical, some humanist-classical—have a different context in the thought of the great reforming theologian than in the teachings of the reformers. They have a different motive, a different goal. A brief summary may clarify this point for us.

V. PHILOSOPHIA CHRISTIANA

Basic Concepts of the Intellectual World of Erasmus[41]

1. *The Criterion: Humanitas*

Erasmus teaches that man is in essence a spiritual being, endowed with *ratio*, which makes him concious of his origin and destiny, and leads him through life along his self-determined course: *Consultor ille divinus, sublimi*

---

39. Cf. e.g. Zwingli, Z IV 393-98, and Erasmus, *Erasmus ... Schriften,* ed. Welzig, III 124, "*Paulus enarrantionem arcanae scripturae non philosophiam, sed prophetiam vocat*". This sentence is the basis for the designation of Zwingli's exegetical-theological institution "Prophesyings". The procedure employed represents the use of the model which Erasmus (ibid. III 140f.) cites from Augustine *De doctrina christiana*.

40. M. Jenny, *Zwinglis Stellung zu Musik und Gottesdienst*, Zurich 1966; O. Söhngen, "Zwinglis Stellung zu Musik im Gottesdienst. Eine Antwort an Markus Jenny" in *Theologie in Geschichte und Kunst. Walter Elliger zum 65. Geburtstag*, Witten, Ruhr 1969, 176-92. Söhngen's reply seems to me in fact to correct and deepen, but not to contradict, Jenny's valuable allusion to Erasmus *Annotationes* on I Cor 14:19 (1516-19).

41. *Erasmi Opera,* ed. J. Clericus, Leiden 1703-6; reprinted Hildesheim 1961-2, 10 vols; *Opus Epistolarum ...,* ed. P. S. Allen, H. M. Allen and H. W. Garrod, Oxford 1906-58, 12

in arce praesidens, memor originis suae, nihil sordidum, nihil humile cogitat ("The divine counsellor, who has his seat in the highest citadel and is ever conscious of his origin, entertains no base or vulgar thoughts").[42] Man's existence is fundamentally intellectual: he conceives plans and is conscious of experiences. This fact has always been reflected in man's search for a philosophy.[43] But a closer look at Erasmus' use of the term "philosophy" indicates that he did not refer to a weltanschauung but to a practical art of living in the Stoic sense.[44] Its content is the human striving for happiness.[45] The philosophy of the ancients succeeded in a high degree in developing the necessary morality. But it found its perfection when Christ appeared in order to teach us the heavenly philosophy, the *philosophia celestis*.[46] The proof of the validity of this philosophy lies in its simplicity and in the founder's being in accord with his teaching.[47] It presents us

vols; *Ausgewählte Werke*, ed. H. Holborn, Munich 1933; I have quoted from the easily accessible edition, *Erasmus von Rotterdam. Ausgewählte Schriften*, ed. W. Welzig, Darmstadt 1967f., vols II, III, V, VI already published. (This stylistically excellent German translation must sometimes be checked for accuracy against the original text.) *Stultitiae laus Des. Erasmi Rot. Declamatio*, ed. J. B. Kan. *Insertae sunt figurae Holbeinianae*, The Hague 1898; *Gespräche des Erasmus*, ausgewählt, übersetzt, eingeleitet H. Trog, Jena 1907; W. Köhler, *Desiderius Erasmus. Ein Lebensbild in Auszügen aus seinen Werken*, Berlin 1917; *Erasmus*, Auswahl und Einleitung F. Heer, Frankfurt am Main and Hamburg 1962; J. Huizinga, *Erasmus*, London 1952; R. H. Bainton, *Erasmus of Christendom*, New York 1969; B. de Ligt, *Erasmus begrepen uit de geest der renaissance*, Arnhem 1936; R. Lichtenhan, "Erasmus von Rotterdams religiöses Anliegen" in *Zwingliana* 1937, VI/8 417-37; J. Lindeboom, "Erasmus' Bedeutung für die Entwicklung des geistigen Lebens in den Niederlanden" in *Archiv für Reformationsgeschichte*, 1952, 1-19; J. Lindeboom, *Erasmus*, Wiesbaden 1956; E. W. Kohls, *Die Theologie des Erasmus*, Sonderband 1/1 and 1/2 of *Theologische Zeitschrift*, Basel 1966 (extensive bibliography); J. W. Aldridge, *The Hermeneutic of Erasmus*, Richmond Va 1966; R. H. Bainton, "The Paraphrases of Erasmus" in *Archiv für Reformationsgeschichte* 1966, 67-76; C. Augustyn, *Erasmus en de Reformatie*, Amsterdam 1962; C. Augustyn, *Erasmus. Vernieuwer van Kerk en theologie*, Baarn 1967. From the 1936 Erasmus anniversary, J. von Walter, "Das Ende der Erasmus-renaissance" in *Theologische Blätter* 1936, XV 7; L. von Muralt, "Erasmus-Literatur" in *Zwingliana* 1937, VI 7 409-414, VI 8 363f.

42. *Ausgewählte Werke*, ed. Holborn 44.

43. Many writings and colloquies of Erasmus proceed on this assumption: cf. e.g. *Ausgewählte Schriften*, ed. Welzig, III 9, 41 (*Praefationes* to the NT); *Ib.* VI 20f. (*Convivium religiosum*); *Ib.* VI 554f. (*Epicureus*), and elsewhere.

44. Cf. *ib.* I/25; III/3 n4 (by Winkler). It should be added that when Erasmus wishes to express himself precisely, he always speaks of *studium caelestis philosophiae, studium verae pietatis*, or in admonitions. His philosophy does not signify an objective truth, but a being perpetually caught up in an existential involvement. *Studium* and *vita* are identical (*Ib.* I 92). Christianity is an ideal; cf. here the *Epistola ad Paulum Volzium*.

45. *Ib.* III 22f. Here and for what follows, cf. especially the *summa ac compendium* in the *Ratio ... verae theologiae. Ib.* III 170f.

46. *Ib.* III 10, 18-22, 24, 28, 170.

47. *Ib.* III 12, 22, 218.

with the weapons appropriate to the path of virtue, the *virtutum iter*.[48] These weapons are meditative prayer, which brings us into harmony with God, and knowledge, *scientia*, which overcomes evil.[49] So the Christian in his own way strives for happiness. Indeed no one lives more happily, *iucundius*: he is the true Epicurean.[50]

This remains true despite the heavy demands which Christ's teaching makes: nothing less than the *mortificatio carnis*,[51] that is, the mastering of the passions, and the *transformatio*,[52] the moulding of man by the Spirit. But this struggle of Spirit and flesh is a way of life not without hope. The Pauline anthropology is thoroughly identified with a Stoically foreshorten-ed Platonism, with its contrast of the noble soul and the dangerous physical-sensual existence.[53] Man is indeed weak so long as he remains ignorant, but he is capable of betterment.[54] Betterment was the goal of Christ's incarnation;[55] he himself passed through a development, was *Christus proficiens*, in order to introduce us to development.[56] He is the innocent lamb who takes away the sins of the world, promising innocence to men.[57] His life was the pattern of perfect humility;[58] in death he demonstrated the credibility of his teaching;[59] he rose in order to manifest immortality to his own;[60] he ascended into heaven, that we should know whither we aspire;[61] and sent his Spirit that his disciples 'might be made what Christ desires them to be'—to initiate the process of development.[62] We see that Erasmus doubts none of the biblical narratives, but he sees the whole story of Christ as essentially moral or ethical in content. Also, he does not impugn the early church's doctrine of the two natures: the deity of Christ guarantees the truth of his teaching, his humanity provides us with an example.[63] Admittedly he never speaks of the personally present

---

48. *Ib.* I 56.
49. *Ib.* I 76, 101.
50. *Ib.* III 170: VI 590: 11, 594.
51. *Ib.* The pricipal theme of the *Enchiridion* ("dagger" and "manual") *militis christiani:ib.* I 50-274; NB 156.
52. *Ib.* III 22 and elsewhere, I 86: *transfiguratio* III 42: ... *ut transformeris in ea quae discis.*
53. *Ib.* I 108f., 126, 140f.
54. *Ib.* III 180: cf. especially here the essay by Lindeboom, footnote above.
55. *Ib.* III 170f., 218.
56. *Ib.* III 218.
57. *Ib.* III 216.
58. *Ib.* III 218.
59. *Ib.* III 218, 257.
60. *Ib.* III 218f.
61. *Ib.* III 220.
62. *Ib.*
63. *Ib.* III 234-37.

or even of the coming Christ. But this is the impressive christocentrism of the theology of Erasmus; it naturally determines the understanding of the authority of Scripture,[64] and indeed finds in Christ a standard within the scriptures.[65] (Erasmus is led to criticize not only the Apocalypse, a point in which Zwingli followed him,[66] but also the Epistle to the Hebrews,[67] which Zwingli as a reformer especially esteemed). Thus Christ is the true wisdom.[68]

2. *Education and development*

Christ initiated the process of development; 'imitation of Christ' is man's corresponding task. Erasmus spent his youth with the Brethren of the Common Life; *imitatio* occurs in his thought, and his writings breathe to the last the style and mood of the piety of Thomas a Kempis or Gerard Groot. But we must be careful to distinguish between *transformatio* and *imitatio*. The latter contemplates the earthly history of Jesus. But that gradual conversion to spiritual humanity [Geistes-Humanität] which Erasmus had in mind refers to an eternal truth, which through the *philosophia* imparted by Christ has the power to make him who knows it like itself. It has to do with a comprehensive and continuous process of education and development after an eternally valid pattern. This essentially unhistorical way of thinking, which the humanist Erasmus shares with high scholasticism, explains the energy with which, though a conscientious philologist and historian, he went beyond the literal meaning to arrive at the allegorical exposition of the scriptures.[69] According to the teaching of Christ himself, which we find only in the Bible, the *Bible* is the primary instrument of this educational and formative process. But because its truth lies not in its historical testimony, but in its timeless ethics, in its "spiritual" meaning,[70] it is only understood and interpreted with difficulty; for this reason Erasmus' attitude towards translations into the vernacular was at least reserve (this question is a matter of controversy).[71] A pure and

---

64. *Ib*. III 295.
65. *Ib*. III 222; I 295.
66. *Ib*. III 222.
67. *Ib*.
68. *Ib*. I 100; III 10.
69. *Ib*. I 84, 88, 190-95; III 60f.
70. *Ib*. I 180f.
71. The short excerpt from the *Paraclesis*, which recommends translation into the vernacular for the laity (*Ib*. III 14: *vehementer ab istis dissentio, qui nolint ab idiotis legi divinas litteras in vulgi linguam transfusas* ...) is put in Erasmus' highly diplomatic way. He only goes so far as to say that the first step is always an outward acquaintance (*cognoscere* does not mean "understand"). When biblical sayings are recited by a woman, a man or a weaver, an un-

devoted heart is requisite,[72] together with a large measure of human and pagan wisdom, in order to judge and scale this peak.[73] One is obliged to enter upon the study, not of the scholastics, but of the church Fathers, and Origen and Jerome in particular.[74] Erasmus persistently appeals to the Fathers and to scripture in the same breath, despite his concession that the Fathers are to be judged by the scriptures and his occasional detailed correction of them. For the Fathers were still acquainted with the "spiritual" or allegorical meaning of the text, and were thus equipped to defend the teaching of Christ.[75] Erasmus, in short, could not acknowledge the Reformed *Scriptura sui ipsius interpres*—scripture as its own interpreter.[76] An acquaintance with the three languages is indispensable; only the humanist trained in *bonae litterae* can comment on the scriptures.[77] But to the humanist perusing the scriptures, *humanitas*, the meaning of existence, discloses itself. For study and life are one; the *philosophia coelestis* takes the "studies" of its devotees as its presupposition and goal.[78] It leads us to inner modesty, *modestia*, and to a gentleness, *mansuetudo. Mansuetudo nos divini spiritus reddit capaces* ("Gentleness makes us receptive of God's Spirit").[79] It is evident that along these lines grace appears chiefly as educational-formative, as a power assisting the attainment of self-control and prudently guarding against arrogance.[80]

3. *Individualism*

That humanism grew out of the Renaissance experience of life is reflected in the profound individualism of these trains of thought intended

---

concious influence is exercised on them. "We are what our everyday chatter is". Erasmus has in no way retracted his demand that we should "leave the literal meaning far behind us" (*Ib.* I 89). On the relationship of the *Paraclesis* to the *Methodus*, cf. Winkler in *ib.* III/20f.

72. *Ib.* I 86: Summa animi puritas; III 40.

73. *Ib.* I 84.

74. *Ib.* I 88; III 70, 74f.

75. *Ib.* III 76.

76. The section in the *Methodus* (*Ib.* III 62-68), which counsels the collection of Bible texts unto definite *loci theologici*, still does not draw the consequence of self interpretation of Scripture. In the context, Erasmus wishes to demonstrate how allegory is to be handled. The conclusion explains how a dark passage is to be made clear through comparison with another (dark passage!), and "a mystical writing clarified by a mystical". The *Ratio* deals with the same question (*ib.* III 66, 454f.). Here examples are introduced, with the result that *verbis alium subesse sensum*, "another meaning must lie under the words". (The interpretation of Winkler [*ib.* III/28], sets Erasmus more in accord with the Reformation than he would wish to be.)

77. *Ib.* III 84, 142, 160; cf. 78.

78. *Ib.* III 42 etc., n45.

79. *Ib.* I 104.

80. *Ib.* I 132 takes II Cor 12:9 as an educational guide.

very much for an élite. The deep piety of Erasmus did not conceal its other side: there are many unmistakable expressions of his contempt for the common people.[81]

4. *Cosmopolitanism*

Like all men who are basically individualists, Erasmus was a citizen of the world.[82] He compared peoples, languages and customs, and as a philosopher he acknowledged no boundaries. It is not true that Erasmus was a secluded person. He describes countries and their inhabitants in a very realistic manner. His accounts of the differing reception of a stranger in English, French and Germans inns might still be enlightening to a hotel manager today.[83] In psychological observation and closely related matters of educational advice, he was far ahead of his time. However, he is not concerned with variables, but with constants, not with individual men, but with Man. For this reason he disdained the national pride of many humanists and scorned the national languages and vernaculars.[84] This scorn extended even to his native Dutch, into which he involuntarily lapsed in prayer on his deathbed to the astonishment of those present. Toward Swiss humanism in its individuality, he displayed a patronizing benevolence.[85] Unremittingly he warned of the thirst for fame, at times in complex Latin sentences in which his own vanity was barely concealed.[86]

5. *The church*

On these presuppositions, Erasmus' approach to the great conflict in the church is not difficult to understand, and ought not to be seen as the hesitation of a scholar who cannot make up his mind. Erasmus followed a well-defined policy. The church is the great educational institution. It has declined, and must be re-organized by responsible people whom Erasmus will instruct to this end. His concern is the improvement of the individual Christian, which is possible. There is no need for that miracle of a fundamentally inexplicable process of reformation out of the Word of God,

---

81. E.g. *ib.* I 240f., 244; III 194; VI 258.

82. To Zwingli, *Ego mundi civis esse cupio, communis omnium, vel peregrinus magis. Utinam contingat asscribi civitati coelesti.* Z VII 580.

83. *The Colloquium: Diversoria*, "Concerning Inns". Cf. Trog, *Gespräche* (see footnote 41 above) 42-50.

84. Semilinguae miseranda balbuties: (*Ib.* III 42, 132. Cf. J. Huizinga, "Erasmus über Vaterland und Nationen" in *Gedenkschrift zum 400. Todestage des Erasmus*, Basel 1936, 34-49.

85. Z VIII 37: 8f., distancing himself, but with a pertinent characterisation of the cultural programme.

86. Z VIII 334: 1f., Zwingli regrets Erasmus' habit of drawing attention to himself.

which was the experience of the Protestants. The congregation as such nowhere enters the picture. The church ought not to give offence, but rather to adapt itself,[87] as did the *Proteus Christus*[88] and his apostle, "the chameleon Paul".[89] Christ is lord over the bishops; they are his representatives.[90] One can dismiss the pope as scathingly as does Erasmus in his conversation between Julius II and Peter at the gates of heaven[91] and yet remain true to the papacy.[92] An act of schism is unnecessary; unity ought to be possible on the basis of simple declarations, as for example the Apostles' Creed.[93] (Here Erasmus is playing church politics; for, unlike the early Reformers, he already knew that the so-called Apostles' Creed was not composed by the apostles.)[94] The short-sightedness of his apparently lofty attitude reveals itself sadly in the *Colloquia familiaria*. These jewels of polished Latin were meant for connoisseurs. They exposed with overpowering sarcasm the superstitions of the common people and the clergy. But when they appeared in the 1520s, the common man's life was at stake in Wittenberg, Zurich and elsewhere. Erasmus, his thought orientated to the timeless, was insensitive to the *kairos* of the hour.

History has five phases,[95] whose careful consideration (*distinctio*) is necessary to establish the timeless truth and its moral applications in each case: (1) "The time before Christ"—no distinction is made between the Old Testament and antiquity. (2) The years of John the Baptist and the first sermons of the disciples, with their higher level of spirituality. (3) The age of Jesus, the apostles and the Fathers: the gospel imparts what irrevocably belongs to being a Christian, and abrogates external laws and ceremonies, but is still frail, and Judaism and paganism retain their hegemony. Ecclesiastical sacraments, ceremonies and rules come into use, including those which are incompatible with the gospel. (4) After the end of the persecutions, "considering the altered situation, new laws are introduced, several of which appear to be in contradiction to the statements

---

87. The church ought also to accommodate the Protestants by modifying its rules (*Ausgewählte Schriften*, ed. Welzig, VI 346).

88. *Ib.* III 230.

89. *Ib.* III 258.

90. *Ib.* I 285; III 194.

91. *Dialogus. Julius exclusus e coelis* (*ib.* V 6-109).

92. *Extra Ecclesiam est, quisquis non agnoscit pontificem Romanum __ Non reclamo* (*ib.* VI 346).

93. *Ib.* III 222. Cf. *Inquisitio de Fide. A colloquy by Desiderius Erasmus. 1524*, ed. with introduction and commentary C. R. Thompson, New Haven 1950 and H. Baron in *ARG* 43 (1952) 254-6.

94. On the other hand, he groups it together with the Nicene Creed (contrary to Zwingli; *ib.* III 222).

95. *Ib.* III 186-93.

of Christ". (5) In the Middle Ages began the *tempus ecclesiae prolabentis ac degenerantis a pristino vigore Christiani spiritus.* But because of *bonae litterae*, conditions were becoming better in the present.

Erasmus knew nothing of a special or eschatological distinction for the century in which he lived. Rather he warned against a sequential and progressive view of history,[96] and postulated instead concentric *circuli* to be found in the church in all ages.[97] In the middle are Christ and His teaching, around Him stand first the priests and "the purest element", and further out the worldly rulers "whose weapons and laws serve Christ after their own fashion". In the outer circle are to be found the *promiscuum vulgus*, to whom a few ceremonies and a not excessive adoration of the saints should be allowed,[98] and who require some coercion and perhaps occasionally a "Platonic lie".[99] It is the learned wise men of the *philosophia coelestis* who recognize in this arrangement the manner by which men are permanently conducted to a religion of the spirit.[100]

6. *Politics*

Erasmus was non-political, even more unequivocally so than Luther. He gave expression to a few sporadic political thoughts[101]—such as that princes and magistrates are representatives of Christ[102]—but this does not make up for the fact that his pamphlet on the education of a prince's son proves only how oblivious the author was to everyday political problems.[103] This individualist also knew nothing of the intensive concern for rights in bourgeois circles and peasant communities, either in his Batavian homeland or in his adopted Switzerland. The cosmopolitan man had a few broad perspectives: the true defence of the Christian West against the Turkish threat would be missionary activity.[104] In fact Erasmus' only

---

96. Ne tanta temporum, personarum ac rerum varietas involvat lectorem ... (*Ib.* III 192).

97. *Ib.* I 20-29; III 192-209. The Platonic doctrine of classes is used.

98. Thus the *Colloquia* passim (*ib.* VI 451). Cf. especially the *Convivium religiosum* (*ib.* VI 20-123).

99. "... by which the wise deceive the common people to the people's benefit" (*ib.* III 208). Here belong the doctrines of papal infallibility and the pope's power to release souls from purgatory.

100. *Omnibus pro sua cuique portione ad Christum est enitendum* (*ib.* I 26). The heavenly philosophy has given no credence to human precepts (*ib.* I 20; III 200).

101. R. Liechtenhan, "Die politische Hoffnung des Erasmus und ihr Zusammenbruch" in *Gedenkschrift zum 400. Todestage,* Basel 1936, 144-65.

102. *Ausgewählte Schriften*, ed. Welzig, I 285.

103. *Institutio Principis Christiani* (*ib.* V 111-357): also the introduction by G. Christian (*ib.* V/18).

104. *Ib.* I 111. Zwingli took over the thought, as for example in Z I 439f.

political principle is world peace. The *Querela pacis*, the widely read appeal for peace, dared for the first time to call into question the *iustum bellum*, "the just war". Erasmus suggested an internation court of arbitration![105]

7. *The unresolved question*

The Reformation, including the movement led by Zwingli, consciously left behind the educational program of Erasmus because there was no time to await the fruits of education. For Erasmus the education of man to *humanitas* absorbed the concept of redemption. Erasmus did not concern himself with the dimension of evil. He emphatically claimed never to have stirred up the dregs of depravity, "as did Juvenal".[106] He denied that Paul referred to himself in Romans 7 ("What a wretched man I am! Who will rescue me from this body of death?") and asserted that he only spoke hyperbolically.[107] The Reformation by contrast was a movement of repentence, proceeding from the despair which believing Christians felt when their educational ability and capacity for development proved impotent against the reality of the forces which opposed spiritual life and God. "The justification of the sinner by grace for the sake of Christ", which for the protestant faith were the great tidings of salvation, remained for Erasmus a process of development within the context of overcoming the passions.[108]

This objection had to be raised against Erasmus from the standpoint of the whole Reformation. Zwingli repeated it on the level of community life: church, nation, and world, the communities of men, were the operating grounds of sinister demons which could not be brought under control by the aid of education alone.

V. THE WORD OF GOD

Zwingli's theology in comparison with Erasmus' theology[109]

The historian of dogma judges that Luther (fruitfully) misunderstood Paul and Augustine. The dogmatician replies that Luther drew the ex-

---

105. *Querela Pacis undique Gentium ejectae profligataeque (ib.* V 359-451). Cf. R. H. Bainton, "The *Querela Pacis* of Erasmus, Classical and Christian Sources" in *Archiv für Reformationgeschichte*, 1951, XIII 32-48.
106. Praefatio to *Stultitiae laus* (cf. Kan, *Stultitiae* VII; Heer, *Erasmus* 86).
107. *Ausgewählte Schriften*, ed. Welzig, III 184f.
108. *Ib.* III 282-92f.
109. On what follows, cf. above ch. 6. For instructive comparison, cf. E. Staehelin, "Erasmus und Oekolampad in Ihrem Ringen um die Kirche Jesu Christi" in *Gedenkschrift zum 400. Todestage des Erasmus*, Basel 1936, 166-82.

istential consequences from this encounter and arrived at an application of his predecessors' thought. Rich has proven line by line how Zwingli misunderstood Luther until around 1520 by reading him with the eyes of a humanist. Here we would add that he also misunderstood Erasmus. For Zwingli, in whom the formal principle of the Reformation was already established, read Erasmus in a sense that would constrain one to reformation activity. Zwingli related in September 1522: "I probably took in as much of human teaching in the days of my youth as any of my contemporaries"—he was thus a stout-hearted *studiosus proficiens* on the Erasmian model. "And when now some six or seven years ago"—that brings us to 1515, the beginnings of his contact with Erasmus, the first correspondence and the publication of the Greek New Testament—"I applied myself to holy scriptures, but philosophy and theology always interrupted me with their contentious voices. Finally, guided by the scriptures and the Word of God, I thought: You must lay all that aside and learn the will of God simply from his own literal Word. Then I prayed to God for his enlightenment, and the scriptures began to be much clearer for me by simply reading them than if I had studied many commentaries and expositions. Observe that this is a certain sign of God's intervention, for with my small understanding I would never have been able to arrive at this".[110] That is the Reformation principle: the Bible is interpreted by the Bible itself. According to Zwingli, the guidance of the Spirit of God is antithetical to a perfecting of reason, to *ratio* and to a scholarly education. This concept is totally anti-Erasmian, and Zwingli knows it. The Erasmian philosophy is among those which are to be silenced—it appears in the same breath with scholasticism. Zwingli wrote at the same time: "No one comes to the Lord Jesus Christ except he has been given by the Father to know him. Do you hear who the schoolmaster is? Not doctors [scil. *ecclesiae*, i.e. among others Jerome and Augustine], not the fathers [Origen, etc.], not popes, not chairs, not councils, but rather the Father of Jesus Christ".[111]

This enlightenment gripped the pastor of Einsiedeln and Zurich and never left him. It was an event and it rendered accessible the historical character of the biblical narrative. When *scripture* explains itself, there is no use for allegory. One learns "the will of God from his *literal* Word". Precisely the literal sense is the Word of the Holy Spirit, and the "clarity and certainty of God's Word" is open to everyone, even to the unlearned.[112] For now its *mysterium* (so Erasmus), its spiritual content, is

---

110. Z I 379, 21f.
111. Z I 366, 24f.
112. Z I 376f.

no longer a timeless verity; rather it is a witness to an historical reality. *Christ* Jesus, also teacher and example, is now primarily redeemer—is in his own person a divine event: "That in brief is the sum of the gospel, namely that God has given us the Saviour and the ransom for our sins, his only Son".[113] The *gospel* is not in the first place doctrine, but proclamation of history, itself history[114] and creating history,[115] demanding historical decision. Zwingli uses the word "gospel" precisely as does Rudolf Bultmann his *kerygma*. "Give heed to the gospel, an assured message, response or assurance. Christ steps forward with open arms, inviting you and saying: Come to me all you who are weary and burdened and I will give you rest. How joyful the message, for it brings with it a light that we should discern and believe the Word to be true!"[116] *Grace* also is no longer an impersonal power, but an event: the reconciliation on the cross and the forgiveness of sins, "which he earned for us that we might come to God out of his free grace and gift".[117] There is no more confidence in reason; the Psalm text, *omnis homo mendax* ("all men are liars"), was one of Zwingli's most frequently cited texts.[118] Any optimism regarding *humanitas* is gone; the reformer, citing Romans 7, sees man's 'ruined nature' far too realistically.[119] But faith trusts all the more confidently in the operation of the *Spirit*, because this Spirit is now understood to be altogether the Spirit of God,[120] at work in nation and state and *society* as well as in the individual. "The gospel will draw pious people":[121] And "Who is Christ's *church*? They who hear his Word".[122]

These are declarations from the years after Zwingli's experience of the voice of the living Christ speaking in the holy scripture which opens itself to our understanding. This unfolding of an authentic Reformation theology required time, and was often the consequence rather than the presupposition of the deeds of the Reformation. Zwingli's development is a splendid example of the unity of the formal and material principles of the Reformation: *solus Christus* and *sola scriptura* are mutually dependent concepts.

---

113. Z IV 66, 25f.
114. Z I 372.
115. Z I 382.
116. Z I 372, 12f.
117. Z II 468, 3f.
118. E.g. Z II 76, 96.
119. Z II 94-101; Z I 350f.
120. Z I 366, cf. above pp. 178-180.
121. Z II 346, 10.
122. Z III 223, 6.

One can maintain with good reason that around 1516 Erasmus had a much fuller understanding of the Gospel than Zwingli. Why then did the teacher not become a reformer, though the student did? Because the student knew himself obliged to labour with the limited talents entrusted to him, to proceed to action, in order "not to be found the slothful servant" at the coming of the Lord.[123] Because he did not despise the common people, but mourned for them, as did his Lord. Because for him forgiveness was not simply a matter of course;[124] rather he was terrified by the approaching judgment of God upon his native Switzerland and the whole of Christendom.[125] Because he knew that only God's Spirit can "beat down selfishness".[126] Because he perceived the eschatologically laden hour of *Christus renascens*: "today the rejected Christ rises again everywhere".[127]

VI. THE PROBLEM

The continuing problem which the names of Erasmus and Zwingli symbolize for Protestantism is the relationship of education and faith.

Erasmus belongs to all of Christendom. He belongs to the Roman Catholic party in so far as he desired to strengthen the unity of the church by his fidelity to bishop and pope. If one ponders the liberty of his spirit and his merits in restoring scriptural texts one must number him among the initiators of Protestantism, which, by the way, the Reformed church has always done.

Erasmus was a great scholar, theologian, and Christian, the Christian witness to *humanitas* for the new age. This *humanitas* he anchored deep in metaphysics. He was able by his *philosophia christiana* to extend the conversation between Christians and non-Christians to broadly common themes.

---

123. Z I 256, 316.

124. The consolation which Erasmus offers to the tempted is an ethical imperative (*Ausgewählte Schriften*, ed. Welzig, I 306). In the *Colloquium Funus* (Two Deaths), a good Roman Catholic dies with almost Lutheran words in his mouth (Trog, *Gespräche*, 133f.). But the appeal to the mercy of God releases one from fear before the divine righteousness, rather than mercy overcoming righteousness. One can say that Erasmus will neither be counted with either the Roman Catholic or the Protestant interest: or should one describe him, as does Heer, as "a third force"? The same question is raised at the end of the *Colloquium Epicuraeus* (*ib.* VI 596).

125. How deeply the motive and the program of action for the renaissance of Christianity (*Christianismus renascens*) changed from Erasmus to Zwingli appears most clearly in the preface (still in humanistic language) of the Commentarius dedicated to Francis I (Z III 628-37: German translation by F. Blanke in *Zwingli Hauptschriften*, ed. F. Blanke, O. Farner and R. Pfister, Zurich 1941, IX 1-14).

126. Z III 112f.

127. Z III 445. 6.

He charged the conscience of the church and of Western culture with tasks which are even now unfulfilled, and continue to weigh heavily upon our minds: world peace, the interdependence of truth and freedom, the humanity of man. The Italian humanists had drawn boundaries, both peaceful and polemic, between Christianity and the classical tradition. It was Erasmus' historical achievement[128] to break down these boundaries and to establish an alliance between the two cultural powers. Christianity was to be the dominating party. Peace would be brought about by integrating Christianity into, and basing it upon, *humanitas*.

Zwingli was a reformer—and a humanist. He opposed with holy wrath the endeavour to adapt the Christian life of faith and obedience to a comprehensive human system. The personal lordship of Jesus Christ would thereby be impugned and the freedom of God's Word denied. Zwingli's historical achievement is twofold. First he set beside the individualism of the Erasmian humanist ideal the concept of community life as a basic and irreducible element in the realization of *humanitas*. Pangs of conscience over social responsibility were a major motif of his Reformation. Moreover, he never abandoned the educational goal and task in his reformation protest. On the contrary, he postulated the integration of education into the Christian faith. *Eruditio ancilla sapientiae.*[129]

Now *faith* means an act: the breaking through of God's grace and its intervention in human life. On the other hand, *education* means a continuous evolution of human life. Therefore faith and education can never be brought together in an intellectual system. Nor will it be of any avail to classify people in a psychological way, distinguishing those belonging to the group of faith and those belonging to that of education. Faith and education must be brought together practically in a responsible way,[130] amid the scientific activity of the twentieth century more so than ever.

There is one very important text in which Erasmian and Zwinglian piety came together in a convincing manner. When in the course of his work in Zurich, Zwingli founded the so-called *Prophezei,*[131] the germ of the present-day University of Zurich, he used to open his lectures with a

---

128. F. Wehrli, "Vom antiken Humanitätsbegriff" in *102. Neujahrsblatt zum Besten des Waisenhauses in Zurich für 1939*, Zurich 1939, 3f.

129. Z VI 375.

130. Here one thinks of John Heinrich Pestalozzi and Friedrich Daniel Schleiermacher: both are spiritual descendants of Erasmus, as well as of Zwingli.

131. For the development of prophesying or the exercise in England, cf. I. Morgan, *The Godly Preachers of the Elizabethan Church*, London 1965, passim; in Scotland, cf. G. D. Henderson, *The Burning Bush: Studies in Scottish Church History*, Edinburgh 1957, 42-60.

prayer in which the inheritance of the early church and of humanism are joined in Erasmian terms with the concerns of the Reformation: "O merciful God, heavenly Father! Because your Word is a candle for our feet and a light that should illuminate our way, we pray that through Christ, who is the true light of the whole world, you will open and enlighten our hearts that we should clearly and purely understand your Word and form our entire lives accordingly, that we do not displease your exalted majesty, through our Lord Jesus Christ".[132]

132. Z IV 365, 702 4f. For the Latin text, cf. n. 52 above.

10

STEADFASTNESS

Zwingli's Final Sermon at the Bern Disputation as
*a Contribution to his Ethics**

1. The Great Disputation, held from 6th to 26th January, 1528, in the church of the Franciscans in Bern,[1] led to the victory of "the Gospel" in this, the most powerful city-state of the Empire. Its repercussions, not only within the old Swiss Confederation, but also on the whole of Western Europe, proved to be most significant. The shrewd Bernese magistrates were well aware of the fact that this array of reformers from the southern parts of the German-speaking area was politically important as well. Charles V, who had strictly forbidden the disputation to take place, was informed that His Imperial Majesty's letter carrying the ban had arrived too late.[2] Furthermore, the bishops who had been invited, but did not appear, lost all ecclesiastical authority within the territory of the proud republic.[3]

The events make it clear that it was not so much the weight of the personalities of Haller, Kolb, Zwingli, Bucer, Oecolampadius and others that tilted the decision, but the change of heart on the part of the citizens. Although Zwingli contributed frequently, and forcefully to the discussions, he was on the whole very restrained. "It would be saying too much, if one called Zwingli the real reformer of Bern.[4] He was not even the foremost participant in the deliberations. That is true, for example, in the case of the first and second theses. Neither can one say that he gradually came to control the meeting. Of course Zwingli played a leading role, but so did others. He followed the debate with utmost attention, even when he did not contribute himself. Nevertheless, one cannot ascribe the Bern Disputation or the reformation in Bern to the impact made by one per-

---

* Translation by Sherman Isbell and Duncan Shaw.

1. K. Guggisberg, *Bernische Kirchengeschichte*, Bern 1958, 101-120. G. W. L.: *Zw. Ref. i. Rahmen.*, ch. XIV.

2. R. Steck and G. Tobler, *Aktensammlung zur Geschichte der Berner Reformation 1521-1532*, Bern 1923, Two Vols., No. 1428 and 1453.

3. *Ib.* No. 1375, 1385, 1449, 1462, 1494 (p. 618), 1513, (p. 630f.), 1560, 1587, 1593 etc.

4. W. Köhler does that in *Zwingli und Bern, Sammlung gemeinverständlicher Vorträge...No. 132*, Tübingen 1928, 20f.

sonality''.[5] Guggisberg's observation remains valid even when one also considers that, for a long time, Zwingli had given advice, encouragement and a sense of direction to Haller, who was not a born leader.[6] Furthermore, the text of the classic first thesis of the Bern Disputation—''The holy Christian Church, whose one head is Christ, is born out of the word of God, remains in the same, and does not hear the voice of a stranger''[7]— is even verbally dependent on Zwingli.[8] Finally, we know from a recently-discovered manuscript written by Zwingli on paper made in Bern, that before his departure Zwingli gave the decisive counsel for Bern's much-admired reformation mandate of 7th February, 1528, and thus the plan for the organisation of the Bernese church.[9] One has the impression that the nine sermons preached from the pulpit of the Cathedral influenced the mood, the convictions and the final decision taken by the city council and the citizens of Bern as much as did the disputation which they accompanied. There spoke in succession: Ambrosius Blaser from Constance, Huldrych Zwingli from Zurich (on the Apostle's Creed), Martin Bucer from Strasbourg, Johannes Oecolampadius from Basle, Konrad Sam from Augsburg, Thomas Gasser from Lindau on Lake Constance, Conrad Schmid from Küssnacht and Kaspar Grossmann from Zurich.[10] ''Finally, on 30th January, Zwingli gave a brief address in the Bernese Cathedral, from which the images had already been removed. He urged the Bernese to persevere in a thorough work of reformation. Neither the resistance of the enemy nor consideration for those who are outraged by

---

5. Translated from Guggisberg, *op. cit.*, 102f.

6. Guggisberg, *op. cit.*, 102.

7. *Die Bekenntnisschriften der reformierten Kirche*, ed. E. F. Müller, Erlangen 1903, 30.

8. The text does not just go back to Johannes Comander's ''Ilanzer Thesen'' of January, 1526, as claimed in most of the literature. K. Lindt, ''Der theologische Gehalt der Berner Disputation'' in *Gedenkschrift zur Vierhundertjahrfeier der Bernischen Kirchen-reformation*, Bern 1928, I, 301-344, 313-315. Cf. also G. W. Locher, ''Die Stimme des Hirten'', in O. Farner, *Erinnerungen*, Zwingli Bücherei 68, Zürich 1954, 111-115. There I traced the text to Zwingli's *Commentarius* (1525) and to his paper against Emser (20th August, 1524). I will add here another quote from Zwingli which is even clearer. In the *Christliche Antwort Zürichs an Bischof Hugo von Konstanz*, Zwingli says: ''The Christian church listens only to the word of God, and allows itself to be led and guided by that word alone. Thus Christ teaches, in John 10, in the parable of the shepherd and the sheep: The sheep will not follow a stranger. Neither will they recognize his voice, but only that of the true shepherd.'' (Z III, 168, 6-10).

9. Steck and Tobler, *op. cit.*, No. 1513; also Guggisberg, *op. cit.*, 115-120. The text of Zwingli's ''Anschlag'' was first published in Z VI/1, No. 117, 504-508; which was not yet available when Guggisberg wrote his church history. (L. von Muralt, ''Einleitung zur Anweisung für das Berner Kirche'', in *Mélanges d'Histoire et de Littérature offerts à Monsieur Charles Gillard*, Lausanne 1944, 325-330).

10. Details in T. de Quervain, ''Geschichte der Bernischen Kirchenreformation'', in *Gedenkschrift...* I, 151 n. 8; Guggisberg, *op. cit.*, 112; Bullinger, *Reformationsgeschichte*, I, 435f.

the work of destruction should be a determent. God, who enlightened the Bernese, may in his time lead the other members of the Confederation to accept the gospel''.[11]

We know Zwingli's last sermon in Bern[12] from a copy which, although obviously fragmentary towards the end, still reflects the vividness of the spoken word. The document closes with the remark: "Written with the greatest brevity".[13] The reformer undoubtedly agreed to its publication.[14]

2.   Zwingli himself introduced the theme. "Since you, my beloved, have acknowledged the victory of the truth and are therefore already engaged in doing away with images, altars and other things, it would seem to me fruitful before my departure to speak to you about *steadfastness and perseverance* in virtue''.[15] It was clear to the preacher that in Bern, still yet hesitant, not all resistance had been overcome. Thus he felt obliged to warn the Bernese against the danger of stepping back into old ways, and to urge them to stand by the gospel and remain thoroughly loyal.[16] His argument appeals to the experience of the statesmen in the audience. Without steadfastness "nothing will be done right, nor will it be completed".[17] Like all virtues, steadfastness without faith and the fear of God is mere hypocrisy. Therefore "we should ensure that it be learned not from ourselves, but from God in whom we wish to abide".[18] Steadfastness, rightly understood, is rooted in our abiding in God.

To this end, instruction and an example is offered by the work and the words of Christ. Gethsemane, the crucifixion and, of course, Matthew 10:22 ("But he who endures...") are mentioned. He who wishes to live according to the will and word of Christ must suffer temptation and persecution. "But all these things will be conquered by constant endurance. Even the heathens said, '*Ferendo vincitur fortuna*', which means: 'Misfortune must be repulsed and overcome solely by enduring and bear-

11. Translated from Guggisberg, *op. cit.*, 112.

12. Z VI/1 493-498; S II/1 226-229; H LL, 67-78.

13. Rudolf Gwalthers translation reads as follows: "Copiosius haec coram ecclesia exposita sunt, quorum potissima capita hic attingere, Christiano lectori satis fore putavimus. *Huldrychi Zwinglii sermo ultimus, quem apud Bernenses de constantia habuit. Latinitate donatus Rod. Gwalth. interprete* (*Opera Zwinglii* 1544, II 537b).

14. "Die predigen so vonn den frömbden Predicanten die allenthalb här zuo Bern uff dem Gesprach oder disputation gewesen beschehen sind ... Getruckt zuo Zürich durch Christophorum Froschauer jm DMXXVIII jar." (Z VI/1 448).

15. Z VI/1 493, 2-5.

16. Farner, *op. cit.,* H II 69.

17. Translated from Z VI/1 493, 7.

18. Translated from Z VI/1 493, 11.

ing it' ".[19] Ezekiel 3:20 leads to the consideration of Luke 14:28 (on building a tower) and Luke 9:62 ("No one who puts his hand to the plough and looks back is fit for the kingdom of God".) "Here we see that he will have us to be ever forging onward".[20] Zwingli points in the Old Testament of Moses' courage when having to make himself unpopular; no hostility could deter him from his resolute intention to do good for his people. For forty years he could not be moved "for the sake of his friends either to omit or do anything which would be against God and the common good".[21] The nomadic leader becomes the model for republican aristrocats. David, even when he was persecuted, he kept his integrity in striving for justice and peace. Then follows the determination of the youthful Scipio major after the catastrophe of Cannae. "As now your estimable wisdom and love has moved you to eliminate the idols, the mass, ornaments and other things, you need no better or further counsel or leverage than steadfastness".[22] For on the one hand Zwingli was faced with the serious criticism that "one should first remove the idols from the heart and only then from before the eyes".[23] This was Zwingli's own conviction as to how the reformation should proceed.[24] This argument had been used against Zwingli by his friend Komtur Schmid at the Second Zurich Disputation in October 1523.[25] But now the reformer is in a position to appeal to the conscience of his hearers: the fact that they are undisturbed while they watch the destruction of their once beloved idols proves that the idols have already been removed from their hearts. Changes cannot wait until no one takes offence at them any more; otherwise Christ would have done wrong in cleansing the temple (Matthew 21:12, John 2:18).

On the other hand, Zwingli had considered the opponents: those who do not hear the word of God and those who do not accept it. Their machinations could be dangerous. One has to trust the word of Christ, who has assured us that he has overcome the world (John 16:33) and makes his people victorious. God allows us to be threatened by dangers so that we

---

19. Translated from Z VI/1 493, 25-494, 3: "Superanda omnis fortuna ferendo est" (Virgil, *Aeneid*, 5, 710).
20. Z VI/1 494, 14f.
21. Translated from Z VI/1 494, 17f., 24f.
22. Z VI/1 495, 15f.
23. Z VI/1 495, 20f.
24. The chapter De scandalo, in: Commentarius de vera et falsa religione, Z III, 888ff. G. W. Locher, "In Spirit and in Truth". above ch. 1, pp. 18ff.
25. Z II, 704, 24f.

may be tested. Only when we need him do we realize how he is able to help.

The real horror, which is bound to seize us in the fact of the broken débris of altars and images, reveals the internal bondage and external display which used to tie us to them.[26]

The disputation was intended to give the Christian congregation and the government the legitimate authority "to act from now on unperturbed and without being ridiculed, honourably and in accordance with God's will",[27] i.e. to proceed to action. But the disputation was not an end in itself; it "does not enrich the understanding of those who are quarrelsome or weak".[28] To sum up: a government which has the courage to take responsibility must not be hindered *ad infinitum* either by the quarrelsomeness of some or by the insecurity and weakness of others. From now on a "well prepared and resolute spirit" will recognise "what colour truth has". You have in your midst God-fearing, pious and learned "prophets", preachers of the Word of God. Courage and loyalty are required more than anything else to stand steadfast in the liberty which Christ gives us (Galatians 5). Even as our forefathers protected our physical freedom, much more must we remain immovable in the freedom "which here liberates our consciences and there makes us eternally joyful".[29] In his time God will enlighten our confederates so that we will be united as never before. "May God grant that to all of us, who has created and saved us all! Amen".[30]

3.   The few pages reveal the whole Zwingli: passionate initiative for the gospel, seriousness and cheerfulness, sternness and popularity, courage and moderation, skilful diplomatic approach to the thinking of his hearers

---

26. "There lie the altars and the idols in the temple. He who fears them now, does so not out of a steady conscience, and easily understands whether or not we once put a high value on them. This rubbish must be cast out, so that the inestimable worth which you, above all men, ascribed to these foolish idols may be ascribed to the living image of God." (Z VI/1, 497, 3-8). This can be interpreted in various ways. Gwalther too seems to have been unclear about the meaning; he translates: "Quisquis ergo hanc rerum faciem horret, non autem pie animi conscientia motus, facile intelligit, num in pretio aliquo aut honore muta ista idola apud nos fuerint, vel minus. Caeterum...", *op. cit.*, 537a. I have the impression that Zwingli at this point argues against the objection that the offensive destruction of the images was superfluous because no one put his faith in them anyway. Zwingli says: the outrage over the destruction of the images is sufficient proof of the religious significance they actually had.

27. Translated from Z VI/1 498, 2f.

28. Translated from Z VI/1 497, 16f.

29. Translated from Z VI/1 498, 23f.

30. Translated from Z VI/1 498, 29f.

and, at the same time, consistently safeguarding his message. In these brief sentences all the characteristic motifs and emphases of Zwingli's *theology* are to be found.[31] Here are his pride in his native land and his zeal for its renewal, even when he is in conflict with "our dear neighbours".[32] There is evidence of his humanistic education, which allows him to sprinkle the central passages of his preaching with Latin proverbs. We see how skilfully he illustrates prophetic admonition with scenes from the Bible, from antiquity and Swiss history. It is remarkable how in all this he does not seem to lose contact with the people. The determination, which permeates the whole, ensures the reformation of the spiritual and ecclesiastical life while, at the same time, civic life too.[33] The concentration on the lordship of Christ whose triumph knows no delimitation between the internal and external, the here and hereafter.[34] The foundation of this salubrious lordship in his vicarious death on the cross.[35] The verification of faith in the Saviour in an unshakable trust in the Father's providence—"that you will see, that he works powerfully with you and protects you; that all things depend on him alone."[36] The alignment of faith to the revealed word,[37] with its origin in the elective work of the Holy Spirit.[38] Against this background, the reformation alternative for the individual heart as for public life: the choice between the true God and false gods of every description.[39] For Zwingli, a false god is anything, in my feeling, thinking, and acting which occupies the place which solely belongs to God.[40]

This brings us to the passages which are particularly characteristic of Zwingli's second sermon in Bern. They are concerned, explicitly and implicitly, with the basic principles of Zwingli's *ethics*. We select three

---

31. Cf. W. Köhler, *Die Geisteswelt Ulrich Zwinglis*, Gotha 1920; G. W. Locher, The Characteristic Features…, above ch. 8.

32. "Undoubtedly the God who enlightened and attracted you (John 6:44) will also in his time win our dear neighbours, the other confederates, so that our friendship will be firmer than ever before. This God is well able to do." (Z VI/1 498, 25f.).

33. Cf. especially Z VI/1 498, 2-9.

34. Cf. Z VI/1 496, 13-16.

35. Cf. Z VI/1 16f. and 498, 13-19, "You know what distress of conscience we suffered when we were led from one false comfort to another, which did nothing more than burden the conscience. They could not free or comfort us. Now you see what freedom and consolation you have in knowing and trusting God alone through Jesus Christ, his only begotten Son."

36. Z VI/1 496, 20, 26; 496, 18-497, 2.

37. *Ib.*, 493, 10-14; 498, 4-9.

38. *Ib.*, 498, 25, 27.

39. *Ib.*, 495, 15-496, 8.

40. "In whoever a man places his confidence, he is his God." (Z II 219, 13).

aspects, leaving aside the frequently discussed special relationship between church and state in the Bernese reformation.

4.   Firstly, the summons to *steadfastness*[41] is not merely a suitable contemporary theme, understandable both to followers and opponents. More significantly, a characteristic feature is consciously raised for the first time which reformed education has been driven to work out in later centuries. For Zwingli himself, the transition from genteel theorising detachment to decisive and consequential action accords with the transition from humanism to reformation.[42] In his popular writings, he continually reiterates this exhortation to this fundamental virtue of the Christian man, especially to pastors.[43] Furthermore, he expands it in a strikingly detailed way in the *Exegetica.*[44] Here, alongside the Lord's saying about "enduring to the end",[45] there is revealed the other source of this fascinating challenge: Seneca, and all other Stoic philosophy, which linked *constantia* to self-control, and has exalted the *civis Romanus* as a pattern for one's attitudes.[46] That progression of Zwingli from humanism to reformation, did not involve the sacrifice of concepts, they were, however, assimilated into the biblically based testimony.[47] It can be clearly substantiated from the life and history of the church that the virtue of steadfastness was handed down, not in the Zwinglian communities, which were soon relatively

41. "Let your love be aware that, without steadfastness, nothing right can be done or completed. Without it, a man will be accounted as a woman and a woman neither pious nor faithful. Neither is there any piety or faithfulness without it. Without it no one's country can be defended, nor protected against shame and ridicule." (Z VI/1 493, 6f.).

42. Cf. pp. 103-104, 151-164.

43. Cf. e.g., "Der Hirt", 1524, (Z III 1-68: H I 165-242). "Vom Predigtamt", 1525 (Z IV 369-433). "...the shepherd must continue manfully by the word of God. Although the whole world should stand against him, he must not allow himself to be frightened by the great horde of Baal's priests." (Z III 33, 12f.). "Fearlessness is the armour." (*Ib.*, 36, 16).

44. Matthew 11:29, for example, "Qui vero Christo serviunt, leve onus gestant. Quantumvis enim foris adfligantur et persequutionibus exagitentur, intus tamen mirabili gaudio perfusi, laeto et constanti animo omnia propter deum perferunt..." (S VI/1 283).

45. Z VI/1 493, 21f.; Z III 66, 28f.

46. Stoic philosophy is reflected, for instance in the following sentences, taken from the *Praefatio* to *Brevis commemoratio mortis Christi*, "Discamus et nos talia, ut fortes intrepidi et constantes simus, si quid patiendum est pro Christo, pro veritate, pro iustitia, ut infracto animo feramus ignominias, contumelias, mortem, ut nihil sit tam arduum, nihil tam grave, quod pro ipso ferre non simus parati. Hoc est conformem fieri Christo, pati quod ipse passus est..." (S VI/2 3).

47. With regard to Matthew, 24:13, "Qui perseveraverit in finem...": Constantia et perseverantia sal est quod conservat, et condit omnes virtutes..." Then he describes how the *constantia* is given to those who contemplate the love of Christ and whose adfectiones carnales are consumed in the fire of love for the summum et aeternum bonum. (S VI/1 380f.).

secure, but in the Calvinist congregations, pressing forward under bloody persecution, in which the tradition of this principle for conduct was assimilated, indeed revitalised and carefully conserved. Here again stoic anthropology and biblical pneumatology coincide. Calvin himself edited a treatise by Seneca before he became the theologian of election. Concerning Calvin, one sentence addressed to Charles V is sufficient here, "The possibility of the renewal of the church must not be measured according to men's inclination or the auspiciousness of the situation; one must break through all despair".[48] The abundance of expressive faces upon whom he has left his mark, as is evident from those in the portrait gallery of the Genevan Reformation Museum, has often been pointed out: the Huguenots' "Stoicism", which grew out of education and faith, has often been discussed: one need only mention Gaspard de Coligny or Agrippa d'Aubigné. William of Orange is reputed to have said, "Il ne faut pas espérer pour entreprendre ni de réussir pour persévérer". His life was an illustration of that. I find, in a biography of Masaryk that, in his youth, there was still a proverbial phrase in Bohemia, "That holds as strongly as Helvetian faith".[49] Undoubtedly the training in defiant determination among those who were severely persecuted, but subsequently appearing within society as rather successful minority churches, not infrequently developed at the expense of that depth and serenity which one can recognise in the Lutheran type of piety. But, Zwingli's exhortation in Bern acquired a seriousness and a depth in the course of the centuries which no one foresaw at the time. What does it mean today? For those in the front rank of politicians who face this question, duty conscientiously fulfilled with fundamental truthfulness has not become easier in an age of the formal, democratic power game.

5. Secondly there remains the question concerning the source of such determination. A reformed theology will never answer it otherwise than with the sober affirmation. "We ought to ensure that we learn steadfastness not from ourselves, but from God in whom we long to abide".[50]

What is meant by "from God", is indicated in what immediately follows, "Thus we find that our Lord Jesus Christ has been an example

---

48. Calvin, "...per mediam desperationem prorumpere convenit." (CR Calv. Opp., VI, 510f.).

49. K. Capek, *Gespräche mit T. G. Masaryk*, Munich 1969, 29. The point here is the tradition and style of piety. Cf. J. Moltmann, *Praedestination und Perseveranz. Geschichte und Bedeutung der reformierten Lehre "de perseverantia sanctorum"*, Neukirchen 1961.

50. Translation from Z VI/1 493, 12f.

and taught in deed and word''. Steadfastness is received by means of a living fellowship with Christ. From there on, it is supremely in a familiar acquaintance with the Holy Scriptures about which the preacher then devotes four pages to the citation of numerous biblical texts.[51] Accordingly, he says expressly towards the end, ''You are provided with God-fearing, pious and learned prophets and preachers. Therefore listen to them earnestly''. ''They set forth God's promises and warnings, so that your minds will always be assured by God's word in all your conduct and behaviour, and prevent you from going astray''.[52] [53] Here we see distinctly how Zwingli envisages the *ethical decision-making process* for the evangelical Christian. The will of God is certainty itself. Nearness to Christ leads to continual alertness to the expounded Bible, i.e. the immediate, responsibility-charged reality therein contained, and this requires the total commitment of pious and learned exegetes: even so, they can only expound.[54] The goal, however, lies throughout in what happens to the seeking heart: it becomes ''assured by God's word the whole way''. It becomes certain of the will of God and thereby of its affairs and of itself. It makes a decision and is thus able to stand by it: the heart becomes steadfast in God. Careful observation also shows that Zwingli, while calling men to the word of God and Scripture from the pulpit, waits for the Holy Spirit who must speak the inner word.[55] Thus the ethical demand is essentially a summons to grace.

At the same time, we maintain that, according to Zwingli, the threat belongs no less to the office of the prophet-preacher than the promise.[56] In other words, the law, with its announcement of judgment, is also the gospel,[57] for with it, God will protect us from the ruination which we are preparing for ourselves and one another when we do not keep his gracious commandments. Yet, as the Bern sermon demonstrates, a realistic

---

51. That was a general habit of Zwingli. Even in consecutive exegesis, he always brings a balanced combination of numerous other biblical passages.

52. Zwingli does not in any way mean, ''No misfortune will befall you''. He has in mind here the conciliar and ruling function of the magistrates. Gwalther translates, ''ut omnium vestrum animi certissimis divini verbi rationibus instructi non unquam errare aut falli possint.''

53. Z VII/1 498, 4-9.

54. Gwalther, ''exponunt''.

55. See pp. 125, 185-188.

56. ''Hence, the prophetic office, the episcopal or pastoral office, the office of the evangelist, is all one office'' (Z VI, 398 1f.; 394, 1-3). Cf. also, F. Büsser, ''Der Prophet—Gedanken zu Zwinglis Theologie'' in *Zwingliana*, 1969/1, XIII and in *450 Jahre Zürcher Reformation*, Zürich 1969, 7-18.

57. See above p. 196-201.

seriousness, which takes into account the Christian's experience of resistance, danger and want, also belongs to the prophetic proclamation. It is remarkable how, today, these two elements have disappeared from preaching! Zwingli means that the word of God, i.e. the evangelical sermon, has enemies who "every day bring new fears and trials".[58] By these are not only meant personal difficulties, but also social and political constellations and machinations. Whether one likes it or not the Reformation is a *politicum* just as the entire medieval ecclesiastical system was a political power. According to his thought, which aspired throughout to a Protestant mono-culture, he affirms the church's mandate for public affairs and its office as a watchman. This bears, of necessity, Old Testament emphases. Zwingli, more fundamentally than the other reformers, is clearly aware that the church of the sixteenth century is less to be compared with the church of the apostles than with that of the prophets.[59] With this appropriate way of approach, which takes account of the different context in time in which to fulfill the biblical commission, he poses the question for us as to how the prophetic witness is to be understood, formulated and authenticated in the secularized society of today. In commitment to justice and freedom, we keep ourselves on the move along the lines Zwingli intended.[60] Here Christians ought not to allow themselves to be surpassed in demonstrating their steadfastness.

6.   "Therefore acknowledge the freedom which Christ has given you, and stand fast, as Paul says in Galatians v. 1, and do not submit again to a yoke of slavery and servitude".[61] Tenacity to the Reformation decision is imperative because *freedom* is at stake. What freedom? In many ways, Zwingli is extraordinary in that he seeks ways which lead from the inner freedom of the Christian into the area of political, of "temporal freedom".[62] Furthermore, he has depicted the personal "assurance of the heart" and free submission to the will of God which was not only taken up by Paul but is reminiscent of Kant. Here however, he goes in the other direction and points to the prerequisite which the free Christian can never surrender and to the event which the centre of their faith apprehends—liberation through Christ. "Now you see what freedom and

---

58. Z VI/1 496, 12f.

59. He said that openly in St. Gallen (E. Egli, *Analecta Reformatoria*, 1899, I, 114).

60. G. W. Locher, "Theokratie und Pluralismus—Zwingli heute" in *Wissenschaft und Praxis* (formerly *Pastoraltheologie*), 1973, LXII, 1, 11-24.

61. Translated from Z VI/1 498, 10f.

62. Z VI/1 498, 22.

consolation you have in knowing and in trusting that you have them from God alone through Jesus Christ his only begotten Son. Never let yourselves be lured from this freedom and redemption of the soul".[63] There are clearly times when far-reaching political decisions are to be made in the light of such central religious problems which touch the innermost core of humanity: the commitment of men to that freedom which is identical to their being children of God. The understanding of that commitment is seen in the hermeneutical context of our inner experience missing or wrecking it completely. "You know what tribulations we have suffered in our consciences when we have been led from one false consolation to the next".[64]

Some say that this formulation of the question belongs to the sixteenth century: today, we are concerned with the problem of social structures. That is true. Huldrych Zwingli, however, the reformer committed to the renewal of society, perceives profound inter-relationships. Can one address one's contemporaries, can one, as this text does, challenge the politician with his conflicts of conscience—thereby sparking off the all-embracing liberating power of the gospel of Christ? Can one do so in an environment in which one must laboriously discuss with politicians and lawyers whether the actions of political opposition can, in good conscience, be well founded?

It seems to us that the situation then was not so different from today, when nobody wants to know or speak about conscience. Men today will once again become aware of conscience and all its inner conflicts, if the message is firmly pointed out. "We have been led from one false consolation to the next, from one decree to another".[65] The politically involved are well acquainted with this. Here, especially, steadfastness and perseverance are essential requirements for the representatives of the Christian faith. "More courage is required in this than in any other undertaking".[66]

---

63. Translated from Z VI/1 498, 16f.
64. Translated from Z VI/1 498, 13f.
65. Z VI/1 498, 14f.
66. Z VI/1 498, 20f.

11

ZWINGLI'S POLITICAL ACTIVITY:
ITS MOTIVES AND OBJECTIVES*

I. SURVEY

1. The Reformation in Southern Germany and Switzerland was a religious movement aimed at the renewal of social life as a whole. The Reformers were well aware of the fact that such social regeneration depended upon the renewal of doctrine and structure of the church and a reorientation of church activity. Such ecclesiastical reform included and presupposed a refocussing of the faith of the individual, a process which must have caused much anguish and insecurity during the transition from the Middle Ages to modern times. This, however, was not at the centre of public debate. Such debates focussed on public affairs, without drawing fundamental distinctions between ecclesiastical, political or economic problems. The controversies about tithe and image worship show this quite clearly. Religion and politics had always been intertwined. Thus contemporary citizens could have no doubt from the start, that the Reformation was a political phenomenon. It was demonstrated time and again by the fact that the only authority capable of implementing church reform was the political authorities such as a reigning prince or a town council.

2. Zwingli's 1519 appointment as a secular priest in Zurich was a political appointment. The guilds approved of his opposition to the mercenary system. In Zurich his political influence grew as much as his understanding of the bible and the power of his preaching. The town council supported him in the "dispute about fasting". It also organized three[1] public discussions of Christian doctrine culminating in the declaration of the unrestricted authority of the Holy Scriptures. Finally, the town council entrusted Zwingli with the drawing up of a confession of faith—the "Christian Introduction", and had it published. By political decision and

---

* This paper was given at Session 48, 14th International Congress on Medieval Studies, Kalamazoo Mich., May 4th, 1979. A more detailed German form containing further references, proofs, and notes, has been published in the *Theologische Zeitschrift* Basel in 1980. Translation by Alfred Braunschweig and Uli Locher.
1. In January and October 1523. The debates of the 13th and 14th of January 1524 were of equal importance. *Zw. Ref. i. Rahmen.*, ch. IX (Liter.).

legal enactment, the council laid down that ministers had to preach according to the Holy Scriptures, that images had to be removed and that mass
had to be abolished. The councils decided that the Lord's Supper was to be
celebrated according to Zwingli's proposals. They also organised the
Christian education of the young people, Christian welfare work, the
institution of the synod and an order of discipline in the matrimonial
court ("Ehegericht").

3.   Soon the preaching of the gospel had even more far-reaching
political consequences. The repudiation of the alliance with France in
1521 and the prohibition of mercenary service in 1522 were mainly the
results of the evangelical preaching of Zwingli. The members of the council were leaders with political experience; they were very well aware that
Zurich risked a dangerous political ecclesiastical isolation. This isolation
was felt particularly at the time of the Disputation of Baden in 1526 and
did not end before 1528, when Berne joined the Reformation movement.

4.   Spreading the ideas of the Reformation was an essential part of
foreign policy, even during those difficult years of isolation. The protestant movement grew strong in the cities of Berne, Basle and St. Gall, and
could thus no longer be crushed by the Federal Diet. The same is true for
Southern Germany and other parts of the Empire: "protestantism"
became intertwined with the opposition of free imperial cities against the
ever increasing absolutist aspirations of the reigning princes.

5.   The spreading of protestant doctrine in the "*Condominiums*" was of
particular political importance. These were territories belonging to several
sovereign cantons and governed by governors whom each of them appointed in turn. The majority of these governors protected the Catholic
status quo. Protestants in the condominiums were oppressed and turned to
protestant Zurich for help. To quote them, "Their hope and hold were
God's word and Zurich".[2] The spreading of the Reformation thus altered
the balance of power within the Swiss Confederation. This became
especially evident after 1528 when Zurich assumed the offensive. The first
peace of Kappel one year later already established a new balance of power.

6.   The fate of the oppressed protestants in the condominiums became
an issue both in Zurich and Berne. Political leaders felt morally and
politically obliged to extend a helping hand—an obligation which was
welcomed as an oppurtunity in Zurich but resented as a burden in Berne.

7.   Zurich's political goal throughout was to guarantee the free
preaching of the gospel both in the condominiums and, eventually, in the

---

2. Bullinger, *Reformationsgeschichte* II, 31.

catholic cantons. This would, in Zwingli's view, itself lead to further changes: forced conversion to protestantism was thus unnecessary.[3] It was never his goal.

8. A similarly vital sense of solidarity developed in the catholic cities and cantons of the Swiss Confederation, especially in the central heartland. Political leaders there felt morally obliged and politically compelled to protect Roman catholic doctrine against heretical propaganda. Having the majority in the Federal Diet and among the governors of the condominiums, they could forbid evangelical preaching within their own borders and suppress it in the condominiums.

9. Thus the Reformation inevitably conflicted with established law and order. Zwingli must have felt this conflict between his loyalty to the Swiss Confederation and the revolutionary effects of his movement. A new order was in the making.

10. The situation in the German Empire and in the whole of Europe was not different from that within the Swiss Confederation. Zwingli as well as Landgrave Philipp of Hesse, who later on became his good friend, were among the very few clear-sighted people who realised early that the real—and really dangerous—enemy of the Reformation was none other than the German Emperor himself. Zwingli knew that the hour was imminent when Pope and Emperor would come to an understanding and join in action against all those whom they called "Lutherans" since the Diet of Worms in 1521.

All Zwingli's political activities, from the years 1528 and 1529, have to be understood as the endeavour to prepare Protestantism for this danger. His lack of patience towards the Confederates in the central and eastern parts of Switzerland was the result of his desire to cover his rear in the coming conflict with Habsburg. The Christian Civic Union—i.e. the alliance of the protestant cities and leaders in Switzerland and southern Germany—and the even more farreaching negotiations, were nothing but an attempt to unite all the forces which were against the House of Habsburg. Defending Protestantism was thus synonymous with resisting Habsburg political power.

11. As a citizen of the Swiss Confederation, Zwingli was deeply impressed with the anti-Habsburg feeling that had already been part of the Swiss tradition for generations. I think that Zwingli, for this reason, underestimated the loyalty towards the Empire of the imperial cities of southern Germany. They could only hope to resist the avarice of the ter-

---

3. Z X 153 20-24.

ritorial princes by siding with the Emperor—whether they liked it or not. Zwingli also underrated the power of the traditional system of alliance, whereby the old cantons were enabled to protect their own interests.

12. To summarize, the objective of Zwingli's political activity was identical with the objective of his preaching and writing: to protect, strengthen and spread faith in the gospel within a society whose true corporate identity was that of a Christian community.

II. THE RELIGIOUS BASIS OF ZWINGLI'S POLITICAL ACTIVITY

1. In the years 1529 and 1531, Zwingli published commentaries on the books of Isaiah and Jeremiah of which he was the co-author along with his friends and collaborators of the theological school of Zurich, the so-called "Prophezei". Isaiah and Jeremiah inspired him to give politically outspoken sermons.

a) In his *preface* of 1529, he dedicated the *Commentary on Isaiah* to the cities of the Christian Civic Union. There he says: "If we want to preserve the freedom we have inherited from our forefathers, let us appeal to religion and equity for good counsel and help... Let us, first of all, care for religion and equity, my dear fellow-citizens: for without them no civil community may be durable, much less a Christian community".[4]

We find the same principle in Roman law as represented by Cicero. "Religion" is Zwingli's word for what Cicero called "legitimus cultus". But Zwingli gives the word a Christian meaning: for him "religion" is not the formal act of public worship, but the fulfilment of personal devotion. Furthermore Zwingli deliberately speaks of *"aequitas"*, of equity, not of *"justitia"* (= justice). He is fully aware of the fact that conflict between the Reformation and certain valid legal systems is inevitable. It is just for this reason that the Christian Civic Union was concluded. *"Libertas"* means for Zwingli the liberty and privilege of communities, such as the old cantons of the Swiss confederation or the free imperial cities. Protestantism and liberty depend on each other—an idea that was up to date in the year of the "protestation" of Speyer. Zwingli's foreign policy, therefore, was determined by domestic political considerations. As he saw it, the cities of the Christian Civic Union are related to one another in much the same way as the citizens of one urban community.

b) We find a particularly clear expression of these ideas in the *preface* to Zwingli's *Commentary on Jeremiah*, published in 1531 and dedicated to the city of Strasbourg which had just joined the Christian Civic Union. Zwingli

---

4. Z XIV 13 1-3, 39-41.

had been in Strasbourg on his way to Marburg and knew it quite well. He praises the city: where patricians are so unassuming, ministers so conscientious and the people so peace-loving, we may say, "A Christian is none other than a loyal, good citizen; a Christian city nothing else than a Christian community".[5]

Indeed, this sentence is, of course not meant to express the obvious. It is an ideal and Strasbourg comes close ot it.

2. Quite a different mood prevails in the "Appeal"[6] of 1530. A year before the preface to the commentary on Jeremiah, Zwingli had made this appeal to the governments of the Five Cantons. It resembles the "Exhortations" of 1522 and 1524, but sounds like a final summons to turn back and be reconciled. It was read out, in a period of highest political tensions, at the Diet at Baden in October 1530, "in the name of the ministers of the gospel of Strasbourg, Zurich, Berne and Basle". Although almost unknown, this document is the clearest exposition of the motives for Zwingli's political activity within the Swiss Confederation.

The appeal contains the following propositions: The Confederation is going to pieces because of discord between the Confederates. The "common weal" which we need is "an attribute of God". The will of God is only to be learned in his word. Therefore "we urge you, in God's name, to have the bright and clear word of God, according to the Holy Scriptures of the New and Old Testament, preached freely among you". Three further reasons support this plea: 1) Our forefathers have never claimed to be the master of the word of God, as it is done nowadays "on account of the wiles of the papists". 2) Discipline and virtue alone, as taught by the word of God, maintain authority. 3) Honour, welfare, and freedom are promised by God to those who adhere God's Word and Law, whereas those who do not obey are threatened with ruin. The discord with the cities is not more than a "friendly squabble" and will disappear, immediately when "you allow God's word to be freely preached, you accept it and amend your life according to it". The only thing that separates us is that which is forbidden by God's word. If this obstacle is removed then "we hope of almighty God, He will give his grace so that you will be united again in all love and friendship as all your faithful forefathers were ..."

Those who are in government must listen to this exhortation of the "prophets" or "the wrath of God will come over you". If this last admonition be ignored, the prophet will be justified nevertheless: he has done his best for reconciliation.

5. Z XIV 424 20-22.
6. S II/III 78-80.

Zwingli's appeal was not well received. The leaders of the Catholic cantons had long been convinced that they ought to remain faithful to pope,
the mass and the saints precisely for Zwingli's reason: namely, to escape
the wrath of God. Zwingli's appeal possibly failed because it was such a
cogent summary of his position. It showed how freedom, unity, the free
preaching of the gospel, the fear of God and God's judgement and blessings are all interconnected. This is protestant preaching; the Catholic
authorities would have nothing to do with it.

3.   Zwingli saw his 1530 appeal fail and thought he knew the culprits,
namely, the "oligarchs", i.e. those demagogues and condottieri who
pocketed fat premiums for every mercenary hired and prevented the
preaching of the gospel in their territories. He realized that they could only
be overthrown by force. He therefore urged a quick military intervention
in order to get rid of those corrupt despots. He vigorously denounced the
embargo on victuals which the protestant cities adopted in its place, since
it would hit innocent women and children.[7]

4.   We now turn to the document which is often considered to be the
most important relating to the subject under discussion. In the course of
deliberations at Bremgarten, during August 1531, Zwingli wrote down the
"*secret advice*" entitled "What Zurich And Berne Ought To Consider In
Their Quarrel With The Five Cantons".[8] This document has been the
subject of much debate. It is generally interpreted as exhibiting Zwingli's
true political objectives concerning the Swiss confederation: to subdue the
five old cantons by force, to "root them out" if necessary and, to govern
them as condominiums of Zurich and Berne. One sentence in the document even implies the possible toleration of "pensions", if they were
received in secret. It is understandable that it has left many readers
bewildered. The champion of freedom and corporate responsibility
appeares to condone a practice as crude as institutionalized bribery.

Closer examination of the original document, however, makes it quite
clear that it does not contain much serious "advice" at all. Its proposals
are incomplete and its suggestions are frequently incomplete and lack
reasonable argumentation. Furthermore, it is not clearly stated to whom it
is addressed. Obviously it must have been restricted to a most trusted
circle of close political friends in Zurich and Berne. We also feel that
the writer was at best drawing up an initial outline, a very rough draft
of heterogenous impressions and considerations, divided into seven

---

7. Bullinger II, 384, 388.
8. S II/III 101-107.

paragraphs of unequal length and several appendices. The document, which Zwingli calles a "hurried attempt", starts several times all over and is further marred by inconsistent terminology. To sum up: what we have here is by no means a piece of well-reasoned "advice". On the contrary, it is a series of loosely connected notes, probably memoranda of confidential discussions retaining diverging ideas and utterances. If these observations are correct, we must not hold Zwingli responsible for every word in this paper.

What remains of the document, after precise observation, is the following argument: 1) "A Confederation is the same as a city, a state or a community".[9] Here Zwingli speaks as a "prophet"—and, as a man from the Toggenburg, native of a condominium; but this would never have been what was felt by a citizen of Zurich, Berne of Uri. For the Thirteen Cantons the Confederation was, on the contrary, a proven instrument to protect their own independence and sovereignty. They cherished its decentralized structure. — 2) Bad housekeeping by one of the brothers will ruin the whole household, unless the family intervenes. All those tolerant of ungodliness and public offences, share in the guilt.[10] — 3) The five old cantons of central Switzerland have lost their honour as the founders of freedom and have decayed through pride and arrogance. They offend against God and the law by their persecution of evangelical faith and their maladministration and despotism in the condominiums.[11] — 4) "Wherever the law is neglected, this is done under the eyes of God. No lawbreaking nation will be left unpunished".[12] "If then, the behaviour of the five cantons is ungodly and harmful to a worthy Confederation, it is our duty to have them punished or we shall be rooted out together with them".[13] — 5) After the failure of the embargo on victuals the options for this punishments are three:[14] a) to renounce the covenants; b) war (going as far as "rooting out" according to God's law in the Old Testament)[15]; c) to "reduce the votes"—the catholic votes that is—by denying them the right to govern the condominiums. — 6) However, the first two proposals would not attain their aims and would be "too harsh for many people"; the only reasonable alternative would be the cession of the (German-

---

9. S II/III 103.
10. *Ib.* 106, 103.
11. *Ib.* 102, 103, 104, 106.
12. *Ib.* 103.
13. *Ib.* 103.
14. *Ib.* 104.
15. *Ib.* 102. Deut. 13:6 etc. Jud. 20:13. I Kings 9:7.

speaking) condominiums to Zurich and Berne alone (proposal c).[16] —
7) By this, so the document continues, the two cities would attain the
supremacy commensurate with their merits and their importance. If they
remain united, they "will be, for our Confederation, like a pair of oxen
together drawing the cart and joined together by one yoke".[17] A quick attack should force the five cantons to give up the condominiums, because
they could not hope for any help from the Habsburgs at the time. Furthermore, "there are many good and godly people among them, whose heart
is more on our side than on the side of their governments". And, for the
time being, the cities are better armed, on account of their artillery. Thus,
victory is certain.[18]

The real aim of all this is to rid Northern Switzerland of Catholic governors. This aim is connected with the somewhat nebulous idea of an inner
recovery of the Confederation by saving it from the wrath of God. A vague
outline of a new political order of the Confederation based on its unity can
also be detected. This idea was not absolutely utopian at that time. The
"Crown of France" and the "House of Habsburg" were political
realities. For the vital and unquestioned federalism in Switzerland,
however, any centralizing designs came three centuries too early. The
document could nowhere meet with approval. There is no trace that it was
ever officially discussed. We may assume that the author(s) never revealed
it to anybody. The document gives a glimpse at some of Zwingli's thinking
after the failure of his "appeal". But, politically, it remained an irrelevant
piece; historically, it is an interesting fragment of doubtful value which
should not be allowed to lead us to premature conclusions.

III. APPRAISAL OF ZWINGLI'S POLITICAL ASPIRATIONS

1.   Zwingli's far-reaching political plans correspond, *theologically,*[19] to
this intense concentration on the cross of Christ on one hand, and on the
divinity of Christ, on the other. The pneumatology requires a pattern of
the Christian community which is the same as that for a community of free
citizens. God's grace, as well as ethical guidelines, are announced in the
preaching of the biblical Word of God. Public proclamation through
preaching, gives "religion" a political significance. "Religious" standards become significant for politics.

---

16. *Ib.* 104.
17. *Ib.* 105.
18. *Ib.* 104, 106.
19. Cf. *The Characteristic Features of Zwingli's Theology...*, above pp. 173 s. 228 s. *Zw. Ref. i.
Rahmen.*, 540ff. (Liter.).

2.   From the point of view of practical *politics* however, we feel obliged to be critical over against both Zwingli himself and those who, up until now, have written about him. a) Zwingli was right in his analysis of the situation. He foresaw the peace treaty between Pope and Emperor as well as its practical consequences. He also saw quite clearly that the war of the Habsburg Emperor against protestantism had the objective of subduing the free imperial cities. We cannot help but sympathize with Zwingli's urge to safeguard the alliances and to have a free hand for the approaching decisions. Nobody could then foresee (not even the Emperor Charles V), that the Turks would for a while save the Reformation. When however the Smalkaldic war eventually broke out in 1546/47, German protestants were not sufficiently prepared for it politically and militarily, while spiritually, they were completely unprepared.—b) Zwingli's vision of a coalition of all the natural opponents of Habsburg from sea to sea,[20] i.e. from Venice to Scandinavia, including France and Western Germany, was not at all utopian. It was almost fully realised in the alliance that, from a human and historical point of view, saved protestantism, when brought about by William of Orange and, later, by Gustavus Adolphus. The question is whether Zwingli's ideas came fifty or a hundred years too early or whether Protestantism woke up late.—c) *Zwingli's politics failed at home,* in Switzerland. By the first Kappel peace of 1529, Zurich and Berne had won a very strong position within the Confederation. Unfortunately, Zwingli then abandoned his former practice of allowing time so that newly converted individuals and communities could strike down roots within protestantism. Zurich became overextended in frequent mobilizations. The loyalty and reliability of Berne were overrated. Berne had joined the Reformation only two years previously and moreover was threatend by Savoy. On the other hand, certain important factors were underestimated; e.g. the inevitable loyalty of the imperial cities in southern Germany to the Empire; and last, but not least, the religious loyalty of the conservative people in the Five cantons to the Church to which Niclaus Manuel had drawn Zwingli's attention[21] for a long time already.—d) To come return to the *theological* problems: we consider that Zwingli underrated the power of the Word of God to penetrate, by its own force, into areas where it was prohibited.

3.   All this cannot be a final word about *Zwingli's political thought and action.* Zwingli's example has been deeply impressed upon the tradition of

---

20. Z VI/II 607f., VI/I 201.
21. J. P. Tardent, *Niclaus Manuel,* 1967, 243.

the Reformed Church that freedom for the preaching of the Word of God, as well as the shaping of society, belongs to the responsibilities of the faithful. But this has also been a negative example: We have to be more cautious and peace-loving in using political instruments. Furthermore we learn that, at times, political failure and even defeat may be a blessing in disguise. The mini-battle of Kappel 1531 was the first victory of the counter-reformation and was immediately understood in this sense all over Europe. It effectively hindered the spreading of the Reformation. But it also taught the young protestant churches what it means to be an evangelical Christian and what risks we have to be prepared to take for our faith. Zwingli's defeat added a dimension to his work no victory could have achieved.

12

"PRAEDICATIO VERBI DEI EST VERBUM DEI"*

Henry Bullinger between Luther and Zwingli

An essay on his theology[1]

I.

The influence exercised by Henry Bullinger over his own age and over posterity has never been properly understood or recognised. It would be difficult to overestimate it. Bullinger's correspondence with scholars, princes and diplomats had a profound and immediate effect on politics in general as well as on church politics. His letters and writings were read from the Balkans and the Russian border to Scotland, and then in America and India also. The stamp of his personality was felt throughout the old reformed church and beyond it in a way fully comparable to that of Calvin. It was only after the Synod of Dordrecht (1618) that in Holland and elsewhere the Zuricher was relegated to a place below that of the Genevan, because the Remonstrants who were condemned at Dordrecht had appealed to Bullinger.[2] Until then, Bullinger's *Hausbuch* (or *Decades*), his sermons on the Apostles' Creed, the Ten Commandments, the Sacraments and the Lord's Prayer, had been the most widespread devotional book in Holland and England.[3] Every ship belonging to the Dutch East India Company was required by the States-General to carry a copy along with the Bible. Thus it is that the pigskin folios are to be found to this day in the cottages of Geldre and Overyssel as well as in the huts of Ambonese or Malayan Christians—and they continued to be read, moreover, at least into the present century.[4]

---

* *Zwa.* X/1 (1954/1), pp. 47-57.

1. With reference to the Confessio Helvetica Posterior, cap. I, 1. Cf. the Latin text in the edition of E. F. K. Müller in *Die Bekenntnisschriften der reformierten Kirche*, Leipzig 1903, p. 171, and of W. Herrenbrück in *Bekenntnisschriften und Kirchenordnungen der nach Gottes Wort reformierten Kirche*, ed. W. Niesel, 3rd ed., Zollikon, n.d., p. 223. An English translation is to be found in: A. C. Cochrane (ed.): *Reformed Confessions of the 16th Century.* Philadelphia 1966, pp. 220-304. *Zw. Ref. i. Rahmen.*, ch. XXII (Liter.).

2. Much to the distress of the orthodox, who contested the propriety of appealing to Bullinger in defence of Arminius, Episcopius and Grotius.

3. Walter Hollweg, *Heinrich Bullingers Hausbuch*, Neukirchen 1956.

4. I know this from personal observation, as well as from information given me by the learned Dutch theologian Dr. Gerardus Oorthuys, who possessed a collection of editions.

Equally profound, but possibly even more extensive[5] was the influence of a small private composition which the reformer had never intended for publication. In the year 1562, in anticipation of death, and as a matter of personal need, Bullinger quietly set down in writing his own confession of faith.[6] His friend Peter Martyr Vermigli (who died on November, 12th, 1562) was able to have a look at it before his death. In 1564, when the plague was raging in Zürich, and Zwingli's successor had also fallen sick, he designated this work as his spiritual testament, with the instruction that after his death it should be handed over to the Council as evidence that he had truly maintained the faith. But in 1566 Elector Frederick the Pious of the Palatinate sought counsel from Geneva and Zurich with regard to the Diet of Augsburg, which presented a threat to him, since it wanted to exclude the Reformed Christians from the confessional peace.[7] Eventually, Bullinger sent him his Confessio, as it contained the evidence that its supporters should be considered to be Christian and orthodox according to the terms of the imperial law. The little book aroused spontaneous enthusiasm on every side, and began a veritable victory march.[8] Even if it were not so officially, the work became in practice the confession which, alongside the

---

5. *Glauben und Bekennen. Vierhundert Jahre Confessio Helvetica Posterior. Beiträge zu ihrer Geschichte und Theologie*, ed. Joachim Staedtke, Zürich 1966. (In the first part, Rudolf Pfister, Gerhard Goeters, Jaques Courvoisier, Grete Mecenseffy and Barnabas Nagy describe the spread of the Confession). The line extends to the present day—cf. Joachim Staedtke, "Die historische Bedeutung der Confessio Helvetica Posterior", in *Vierhundert Jahre Confessio Helvetica Posterior, Akademische Feier Bern*, with contributions by Joachim Staedtke and G. W. Locher, Berner Universitätsschriften No. 16, Berne 1967.

6. E. F. K. Müller, *op. cit.*, p. XXXI. Our study will show that Müller is not wholly correct in his remark that the document was composed "without any regard to the contemporary dogmatic and ecclesiastical struggle." For the origin of the Confession cf. Ernst Koch in *Glauben und Bekennen* and Fritz Blanke in *400 Jahre Zweites Helvetisches Bekenntnis, Geschichte und Oekumenische Bedeutung*, a Commemoration on June 8th, 1966, in the Great Minster of Zürich, Zürich 1966.

7. Walter Hollweg, *Der Augsburger Reichstag von 1566 und seine Bedeutung für die Entstehung der Reformierten Kirche und ihres Bekenntnisses*, Neukirchen 1964.

8. In addition to the literature already cited, cf. Heer and Egli, *Realenzyklopädie für protestantische Theologie und Kirche*, 3rd ed., Leipzig 1908, Vol. III, p. 546; E. F. K. Müller, *ib.*, Vol. VII, pp. 645ff.; and especially R. Zimmermann and W. Hildebrandt, *op. cit.*, pp. 124ff. The extended list of those who subscribed, in the second edition of the Confession (1568), provides a telling picture of its early history:

"Subscripserunt omnes omnium Ecclesiarum Christi in Helvetia ministri, qui sunt Tiguri, Bernae, Scaphusii, Sangalli, Curiae Rhetorum et apud confoederatos in Ecclesiis Evangelium profitentibus cis et ultra Alpes, Mylhusii, et Biennae, quibus adiunxerunt se et ministri Ecclesiae, quae est Genevae et Neocomi etc. Sed et consenserunt in ipsam iam editam ministri Ecclesiae Polonicae, quae sunt in Ducatu Zathoriensi, et Ossuiecimensi, Scoticarum quoque Ecclesiarum ministri, qui Nonis Septemb. Anno Domini 1566 scriptis ad clariss. virum D. Theodorum Bezam literis, inter alia dicunt, Subscripsimus omnes qui

Heidelberg Catechism, united all the reformed churches.[9] It presents an astonishing sight for anyone who has observed the endeavours to achieve common formulae that were made in the sixteenth century—efforts that were earnest but mostly laborious, grim, and often encumbered with unspiritual considerations. For here is a great and very diverse part of the reformation movement suddenly finding the word that it was seeking. It is a warning from church history for all who look for salvation only from conferences. Could it be that this became a common word, for the very reason that it originated as a wholly personal word?

---

in hoc coetu interfuimus, et huius Academiae sigillo publico obsignavimus. Praeterea Debrecini in Hungaria, edita et impressa est Confessio una cum articulis quibusdam, Septemb. 1. Anno Domini 1567. et inscripta Sereniss. Principi et Domino D. Joanni 2. Dei gratia electo Hungariae Regi, etc. In qua inter alia haec leguntur verba, Omnes Ecclesiae ministri, qui in conventu sancto ad 24. Februarii, Anno Domini 1567 Debrecinum convocato, cis et ultra Tibyscum, inter reliquas Confessiones recepimus, et subscripsimus Helveticae Confessioni, Anno Domini 1566. editae, cui et Ecclesiae Geneven. Ministri subscripserunt, etc." (There have subscribed: the ministers of all the churches of Christ in Switzerland, those in Zürich, Berne, Schaffhausen, St. Gallen, Chur in the Grisans, with the confederates in the churches which confess the Gospel on both sides of the Alps, in Mühlhausen in Alsace and Biel, and they have been joined by the ministers of the churches in Geneva and Neuchatel, etc. Since the publication of the Confession, it has gained the acceptance of the ministers of the church in Poland, in the Dukedoms of Zathor and Auschwitz, and also of the ministers of the Scottish Churches, who, in a letter written on September 1st, AD 1566 to the renowned Dr. Theodore Beza, state inter alia that 'All of us who were present at this synod have subscribed, and have sealed it with the official seal of this University.' In addition, the Confession, together with other articles, was printed and published in Debrezen in Hungary on September 1st, AD 1567, and addressed to His Highness, the Prince and Lord John II, by the grace of God King of Hungary, etc. Here one finds, inter alia, these words: 'All the ministers of the churches on both sides of the Theiss, present at the sacred convocation summoned to Debrezen on February 24th, AD 1567, have accepted and subscribed, among other confessions, the Helvetic Confession, which was published in 1566, and has been subscribed by the ministers of the church in Geneva, etc.' Niesel, *op. cit.*, p. 219, quoting from *Confessio Helvetica Posterior*, ed. E. Böhl, Vienna 1866).

Thus the subscribers included the protestant confederates, together with those affiliated to them, and the Reformed churches in Poland, Scotland and Hungary. (With regard to the Confession's reception in Scotland, the literature of the last 150 years (including Zimmermann and Hildebrandt, *op. cit.*, p. 127) has been haunted by a General Assembly in "Glasgow", although the reference to "Adrianopolis" naturally denotes St. Andrews. For fuller details, cf. Duncan Shaw, "The Inauguration of Ministers in Scotland, 1560-1620", in *Records of the Scottish Church History Society*, Glasgow 1966, Vol. XVI, pp. 35-62).

The Huguenot Synod of La Rochelle subscribed in 1618. Basle, on the other hand, did not do so until 1642. Apart from the opposition of Antistes Sulzer, a man of Lutheran tendencies, a further factor may well have been their pride in their own Second Confession of Basle, the *Helvetica Prior* (1536). Glarus and Appenzell subscribed from 1644 onwards.

9. It was expressly recognised as such by the Synod of Dordrecht in 1618. There were numerous editions of translations into German, French, Italian, Romanic, English, Dutch, Hungarian and Polish (cf. the remarkable list in Zimmermann and Hildebrandt, *op. cit.*, p. 135). There was even a Turkish and an Arabic edition for the religious struggle in Hungary. Joachim Staedtke's bibliography in *Glauben und Bekennen* lists 113 editions.

II.

The significance of Bullinger does not only lie in the fact that he led the Zürich reformation through its gravest crisis with resolution, courage and wisdom, but also that through the association with Geneva[10] and his interest in the worldwide endeavours for renewal, he was able to break through the political and ecclesiastical isolation. Through Bullinger, a considerable part of the Zwinglian heritage achieved a wider, ecumenical impact. His own original contribution should not be underestimated, but his real strength (like that of John Calvin) lies in his careful grasp of the theological output of the reformation struggles, sifting, clarifying and deepening it. Both show themselves to be typical and faithful administrators and representatives of the second generation. The difference between them, which should not be overlooked, is not to be found primarily in their personal character, for they actually have some features in common, but in their respective intellectual origin and milieu. Both are humanists, but the one is a product of the devotio moderna, the other of jurisprudence; the one works peacefully within the protected and circumscribed bounds of his state church, whereas the other has to work in the midst of strife to establish his church-state as the revolutionary centre for many lands; and at the same time, the one is living in a place where the abiding memory of the victories and defeats of the early years imposes a certain obligation, whereas the other is in many respects quite free to make a fresh start. This last factor made a decisive difference to the impact of Calvinism, in terms of theology and organisation. To give but one example: both had to deal with the question of Zwingli's controversy with Luther. But in Geneva one is naturally more remote from that bitter struggle and, consequently, more free. It is, therefore, very much to the credit of Henry Bullinger that they did not simply settle down behind the old lines of battle in Zurich either; they were duly grateful for all that had come down to them from Zwingli, but they still strove for an independent and mature solution to the problem.

We may gain some idea of the freedom and the restraint, the character and the method of Bullinger's theological work by looking at one of the most momentous sections of his most influential writing.

In the first chapter of the second Helvetic confession, it states[11] (De

---

10. We would draw attention to the Consensus Tigurinus of 1549, E. F. K. Müller, *op. cit.*, p. 159. Cf. O. E. Strasser, *Zwa.* IX (1949/1), p. 1.

11. Confessio Helvetica Posterior I, 1; E. F. K. Müller, *op. cit.*, p. 171; Niesel, *op. cit.*, p. 223. "Ipse in Evangelio dixit Dominus: Non vos estis loquentes illi, sed spiritus patris mei

Scriptura Sancta, vero Dei Verbo): "The Lord himself has said in the Gospel (Mt. 10:20; Lk. 10:16; Jn. 13:20): 'For it is not you who speak, but it is the spirit of your Father, who speaks in you. Therefore, whoever hears you, hears me, and whoever rejects you, rejects me'.

The preaching of the Word of God is the Word of God.

Thus, when this Word of God is proclaimed in the church today, by a preacher who has been lawfully called, we believe that the Word of God itself is proclaimed and is received by the faithful, and that no other Word of God may be devised or expected from heaven. And now we must have regard to the word itself, as it is preached, and not to the minister who preaches it. Even if he is a wicked man and a sinner, the Word of God remains no less true and good. And it is by no means our opinion that one may regard external preaching as useless, because instruction in the true religion depends upon inner illumination by the Spirit, because it is written: No one will teach his neighbour. For all will know me (Jer. 31:34). And: The one who waters is nothing, nor the one who plants, but God who gives the increase (1 Cor. 3:7). For though no one can come to Christ unless he is drawn by the heavenly Father (Jn. 6:44) and inwardly illuminated by the Holy Spirit, yet we know that God wills that the Word of God should be published abroad. Of course God could have instructed

---

loquitur in vobis. Ergo qui vos audit me audit, qui autem vos spernit, me spernit (Matth. 10:20; Luc. 10:16; Ioan. 13:20).

Praedicatio verbi Dei est verbum Dei. Proinde cum hodie hoc Dei verbum per praedicatores legitime vocatos annunciatur in ecclesia, credimus ipsum Dei verbum annunciari, et a fidelibus recipi, neque aliud Dei verbum vel fingendum vel coelitus esse expectandum: atque in praesenti spectandum esse ipsum verbum, quod annunciatur, non annunciantem ministrum, qui etsi sit malus et peccator, verum tamen et bonum manet nihilominus verbum Dei. Neque arbitramur praedicationem illam externam tanquam inutilem ideo videri, quoniam pendeat institutio verae religionis ab interna spiritus illuminatione: propterea quod scriptum sit: Non erudiet quis proximum suum. Omnes enim cognoscent me. (Ierem. 31:34). Et: Nihil est, qui rigat aut qui plantat, sed qui incrementum dat Deus 1. Cor. 3:7. Quamquam enim nemo veniat ad Christum, nisi trahatur a patre coelesti (Ioan. 6:44), ac intus illuminetur per spiritum sanctum, scimus tamen Deum omnino velle praedicari verbum Dei etiam foris. Equidem potuisset per spiritum suum sanctum, aut per ministerium angeli, absque ministerio S. Petri instituisse Cornelium in Actis Deus, caeterum reiicit hunc nihilominus ad Petrum de quo angelus loquens: Hic, inquit, dicet tibi quid oporteat te facere. *Interior illuminatio non tollit externam praedicationem.* Qui enim intus illuminat, donato hominibus spiritu sancto, idem ille praecipiens dixit ad discipulos suos: Ite in mundum universum, et praedicate Evangelium omni creaturae. (Marc. 16:15) Unde Paulus Lydiae apud Philippos, purpurariae, praedicavit verbum exterius, interius autem aperuit mulieri cor Dominus (Act. 16:14): idemque Paulus collocata gradatione eleganti ad Rom. 10:17. tandem infert: Ergo fides ex auditu est: auditus autem per verbum Dei. Agnoscimus interim Deum illuminare posse homines, etiam sine externo ministerio, quos et quando velit: id quod eius potentiae est. Nos autem loquimur de usitata ratione instituendi homines, et praecepto et exemplo tradita nobis a Deo."

Cornelius, in the Acts of the Apostles, by his Holy Spirit, or through the ministry of an angel, without the ministry of St. Peter; but nevertheless he was directed to Peter, of whom the angel said: He will tell you what you should do.

Inner illumination does not make external preaching superfluous.

For the one who illuminates men inwardly, by giving to them his Holy Spirit, is the one who commanded his disciples, saying: Go into all the world and preach the Gospel to every creature (Mk. 16:15). Therefore, at Philippi Paul preached the external word to Lydia, the seller of purple, but inwardly the Lord opened her heart (Acts 16:14). And likewise, in Rom. 10:13-17, after a fine development of his thought, Paul concludes: Thus faith comes by hearing, and hearing by the Word of God. We freely acknowledge that God is able to illuminate men, even without an external ministry, illuminating whomsoever and whenever he will, for that is within his power. But we are speaking of the usual way in which men are to be instructed, as it has come down to us from God, by precept and by example''.

"The preaching of the Word of God is itself the Word of God"—here we have one of the fundamental reformation insights, expressed aptly and with a brilliant conciseness. It was in the name of the Word of God that they ventured upon the great renewal of church and of life. This is the source, where all the reformation currents are one; and it is here that all the differences have their starting point. In saying this, we are thinking not only of differences in exposition, but also of the fact that the actual significance of the Word of God is sought in different directions, corresponding to the respective reformational tendencies of those concerned. As some simplification is inevitable, we may state their different views as follows: for Erasmus, the significance of the Word consists in the divine instruction it gives concerning a right knowledge of life; for Luther, it lies in the power of its promises to bestow personal assurance; for Zwingli it consists in the way that it brings the eschatological tension into the present, imposing a public obligation; for Calvin, it lies in the fact that it reveals the will of God for our faith and life—the will of a God who acts in judgment and mercy.[12] So the opposite to the Word of God consists for Erasmus in error; for Luther, in the contradiction of conscience, of reason or of experience: for Zwingli, in the deification of created things or of human opinions; for Calvin, in disobedience. Accordingly, for Erasmus

---

12. Cf. G. W. Locher, *Die evangelische Verantwortung der Reformatoren für das öffentliche Leben*, Zürich 1950, and "Huldrych Zwingli's Concept of History" (above, ch. 6).

the keyword is Philosophia christiana; for Luther, Certitudo; for Zwingli, Euangelion, God's Word, or Spirit; for Calvin, Doctrine. However, they are in fundamental agreement in asserting and maintaining, as against the medieval tradition, that salvation is experienced as God speaks, rather than in the sacramental act of the priest, and that this takes place within the community of those who are addressed and called, rather than in the church as an institution. In Roman Catholicism, everything depends on the reading of the Mass; in Protestantism, it depends on the speaking of God's Word.

Does that mean "preaching"? According to Zwingli's view, the answer would be a definite "Yes". He is passionately convinced that the ministry of preaching is essential for the life of Christendom,[13] and it is a part of the Zwinglian heritage that the Confessio does not defer the subject of preaching until it deals with the doctrine of the church and the means of grace,[14] but speaks of it in the introduction, and, for this very purpose, passes to quickly from the word written to the word preached. And yet Bullinger's definition, which he enunciates on behalf of the whole reformation, contains a declaration and a restriction at the same time. According to the section quoted above, the Verbum Dei is contained primarily in the Holy Scripture, and our preaching is the Word of God only because it expounds and applies the Word of the Bible. There is a clear demarcation line here, which is often overlooked when this famous statement is quoted. The emphasis is chiefly on the second and third words; not every conceivable sermon is a divine word, and certainly not that which is merely a display of personal opinion. Only that preaching which hands on the message of the prophets and apostles is the Word of God. But when it does do this, then the simple human word shares in the eternal presence of God's Word; for the words of the prophets and apostles contained in the biblical books are not just witnesses to the past, but instruments of God's activity in the present.[15] Thus, while the biblical message has precedence over our preaching, and constitutes its yardstick and its guideline, one cannot overlook the fact that Bullinger actually gives them both the same

---

13. Cf. Z I 328ff.; II 626ff.; III 5ff., 112f., 355ff., 691ff.; S IV 13-16. "Credo prophetiae sive praedicationis munus sacrosanctum esse, ut quod ante omne officium sit summe necessarium." (I believe the office of a prophet or preacher to be a sacred office, and that it is, indeed, the most necessary of all forms of service). S VI, I pp. 1ff.

14. As e.g. the Augsburg Confession, Article V, or Calvin's *Institutes*.

15. Confessio Helvetica Posterior I, 1: "Deus ipse loquutus est patribus, prophetis et apostolis, et loquitur adhuc nobis per scripturas sanctas." (God himself has spoken to the patriarchs, the prophets and the apostles, and he still speaks to us through the Holy Scriptures).

basis, and ascribes to both the same dignity: "Whoever hears you, hears me!"

This miracle of the real presence of the Spirit of Christ in feeble human words was the great trust of the reformation—comparable only to the fervent manner in which the Roman Catholic believer immersed himself in the mystery of the corporeal presence of the Lord in transubstantiation. The Confessio declares this confidence to the opposing side without any polemic, and at the same time confesses that it is fundamental for the evangelical church.

Next, there must be a word for those standing within the sphere of Protestantism, for despite the basic unity, much detail remained unclarified.

In brief, the Confessio first distinguishes itself from various forms, tendencies and aspirations to be found among the "Enthusiasts", who were so detested by Luther, and among the Anabaptists who first sprang up in such embarrassingly close proximity to the Zurich reformation.[16] From the days of the early church right down to the present, there have always arisen, in the wake of revival movements, communities in which the Word of Scripture and its preaching have been supplanted by an interest in the inner word or in inward illumination, in visionary revelations or other kinds of direct manifestation of the Holy Spirit. Until the Marburg Colloquy in 1529, Luther had always regarded Zwingli in this light, alongside Karlstadt and Müntzer, and even later, despite the radical course of action that Zurich took against the Anabaptists, the old Lutherans always had a keen eye for the spiritualistic aspect in Zurich theology.[17] Zwingli's casual tale of how the connexion between the words of institution and Exodus 12:11 suddenly came to him in a dream in the early hours of the morning provided a target for the calumny that the Zurichers did not base themselves on the Bible, but on subjective private revelations.[18] So, in a word: "No other Word of God may be expected from heaven". But, in fact, the statement in the Gospel of John concerning the Spirit, who alone can give life,[19] was of cardinal importance not

---

16. Fritz Blanke, *Brüder in Christo. Die Geschichte der ältesten Täufergemeinde (Zollikon 1525)*, Zürich 1955; Heinold Fast, *Heinrich Bullinger und die Täufer*, Schriftenreihe des Mennonitischen Geschichtsvereins, No. 7, Weierhof 1959; John Yoder, *Täufertum und Reformation in der Schweiz. I. Die Gespräche zwischen Täufern und Reformatoren.* Schriftenreihe des Mennonitischen Geschichtsvereins, No. 6, Weierhof 1962.

17. Cf. *Th. H. Z.* I, pp. 116f.; also G. W. Locher, "Die Lehre vom Heiligen Geist in der Confessio Helvetica Posterior" in *Glauben und Bekennen*, pp. 300-336.

18. Z IV 483, 559.

19. John 6:63.

only for Zwingli's doctrine of the sacrament, but for the whole of his thought and action. When one thinks of the young Zwingli's trust in how the Spirit "speaks in" and "breathes in" (inspiration), and when one considers statements such as: "The same God who illuminates him (sc. the teacher) will also give you to understand that what he says comes from God"; and "the Word of God should be held in highest honour by us—the Word of God understood only as that which comes from the Spirit ... it teaches itself, reveals itself and shines into the human soul ... so that the soul grasps God in itself ... in this it lives ... and abandons hope of finding comfort through any created thing ... indeed, eternal bliss actually begins here in this world"—is it so inexplicable that his radical pupils should forget, for once, that such statements[20] all referred to the exposition of Scripture? Was it mere chance that they should at least put into practice the possibility for which Zwingli had allowed, namely "that the worst of men may speak on Scripture"?[21] So now, in agreement with what Zwingli said later, after years of confusing and painful experiences, Bullinger finds it necessary to add—not just out of a concern for church order, but simply out of pastoral faithfulness—that preaching enjoys God's mighty promise only when it is carried out "by preachers who have been duly called".

So Bullinger now stands in the midst of the controversy with the true Zurich tradition. No doubt the concession which is to be found at the end of this section, that "God can, if he desires, illuminate without external proclamation", expresses a good Zwinglian sentiment,[22] and similarly, the appeal to Jn. 6:44 and related texts is to be found repeatedly in Zwingli's writings, from the earliest to the latest.[23] But Bullinger contests the idea that one should begin with such texts when one is concerned with the knowledge of divine truth and the building up of the church. He is less amazed at the power of the Spirit than at the miracle of the Word. Do we have here a rapprochement with Luther?

Yes and no. Anyone who can recall the discussion of the reformers cannot fail to remark that the writer of these lines has listened to Wittenberg attentively, carefully and dispassionately. Because Luther's whole faith lives by the Word alone, he could not tolerate the slightest separation of

---

20. Z I 382.

21. *Ib.*

22. Cf. e.g. S IV 8, 16. In contrast to this, Luther's Schmalkaldic Articles of 1537 declare: "In these places, as concerns the spoken, external word, it is firmly to be maintained that God does not grant his spirit or his grace to any man except through or with the preceding external word." (WA, Vol. L, 245; *Die Bekenntnisschriften der evangelisch-lutherischen Kirche*, Göttingen 1930, Vol. I, pp. 453f.).

23. Cf. inter alia, *Th. H. Z.* I, Index.

Spirit and Word, and so he declared: "The Word, I say, and only the
Word is the vehicle of God's grace". Zwingli, whose word believes in the
living Spirit alone, soberly replies: "The Spirit needs neither guidance nor
vehicle, for he is himself the power and the means by which everything is
carried".[24]

The Lutheran solution to the relationship of Spirit and Word had been
simple. All too simple, as it seemed to the reformed theologians. Certainly
it accorded a high honour to the Word, but it failed to safeguard the
freedom of the Spirit. With Zwingli's separation of Spirit and Word, on
the other hand, it was impossible to provide a true theological basis for the
public preaching to which Zwingli himself had given so much prominence.
Now Bullinger takes up the theme, starting from Zwingli's standpoint, but
then, in his treatment of it, he takes a decisive step towards Luther, in that
he is equal to Luther in his trust in the Verbum externum, and, indeed,
almost surpasses him. So the particular concerns of both Luther and
Zwingli are fully recognised, but the solution is new. It does not lie in the
metaphysically determined relationship of the natures of Spirit and Word,
but in the identity of God, who is at one and the same time the one who
gives the Spirit and who sends the Word, using both in order to reveal
himself to us. "It is the same person, idem ille, who illuminates inwardly
and who gives the command: Preach the gospel!"

Bullinger's independence of Luther and Zwingli alike is considerable—although he would not separate himself from either. We can
understand what a liberating effect his work must have had in
innumerable places where they had not yet bound themselves to old
formulae. The wrestling of the minds had not been in vain. Alongside
Calvin's *Institutio*, the Helvetica posterior helped to ensure that the
reformed church would always count Luther among its fathers and
teachers.

A few further details may be mentioned. "Even if the minister of the
divine word is a wicked man, the Word of God remains true and
good"—because God is good and the message of Scripture is true. Once
again, we can best understand this thesis by comparing it with the cor-

---

24. "Verbum, inquam, et solum verbum est vehiculum gratiae dei." (Luther, WA II
509). "Dux autem vel vehiculum spiritui non est necessarium; ipse enim est virtus et latio
qua cuncta feruntur" (Zwingli, S IV 10).

These sentences had far-reaching consequences for their eucharistic doctrine. I hope to
treat this and the Christological background in more detail in *Th. H. Z.* II. It is clear that
Bullinger's "Praedicatio verbi Dei est verbum Dei" is also modelled on the interpretation of
John 1:14 in terms of the doctrine of the two natures of Christ. Even more important is that
faith in the living and present Christ which underlies the sentence.

responding Roman thesis. It is true that there can be no talk of an indelible character as far as the Protestant pastor is concerned, but the sermon, like the Roman sacrament, achieves its effect *ex opere operato, non ex opere operantis, et virtute Spiritus Sancti.*[25] But this work of the Spirit stands in a totally new context. "We believe that the Word of God is preached in the church today, even if the servant is a sinner". Whoever has an eye for such things will again recognise here the great riches of Luther's hard-won doctrine of justification—though here it is not applied to the troubled individual, but to the life of the church, which was the consuming passion of Zwingli and Calvin.

"We are speaking of the usual way in which men should be instructed according to divine precept and example". The Confessio is not concerned with the abstract possibilities of divine omnipotence, but with the practical building up of the congregation. For the reformed churches,[26] this is by no means merely a matter of expediency, but of obedience. A confession also speaks of concrete organisation, and the chapters on the church (XVIIIff.) treat this extensively.

III.

Even in an age which has long since abandoned, and with good reason,[27] any obligation to confessions, the one who reads in a teachable spirit cannot escape from the lasting admonition which issues forth from the sentences we have discussed. It lies in the call to that sober, sure and clear faith which is bound to the Word; in the call to that preaching and hearing which lives by the biblical objectivity of the message, and not by the subjectivity of religious experience; in the call to have courage, even though weak and fallible men, to receive and to hand on the great tidings; and in the call to build up the church by means of its true powers,[28] which do not consist in organisational skills or in nervous activity, but in that compassionate faithfulness with which the revelation makes itself known even today: "And he still speaks to us".[29]

---

25. Denzinger 1608/851, 3488/2089, 793/424.

26. At this point the emphases are different from Lutheranism.

27. Cf. "The Second Helvetic Confession" (below, p. 299-300, sections 15 and 16).

28. A modern confirmation of Bullinger's thesis may be seen in the fact that a fresh consideration of the nature of preaching became one of the most fruitful elements in the development of dialectical theology. Cf. Karl Barth, *Not und Verheissung der christlichen Verkündigung,* 1922; Emil Brunner, *Die Mystik und das Wort,* 1924; Eduard Thurneysen, *Die Verkündigung des Wortes Gottes in unserer Zeit,* 1941.

29. "Et loquitur adhuc nobis" (see note 15). Cf. E. A. Dowey, "Das Wort Gottes als Schrift und Predigt im Zweiten Helvetischen Bekenntnis", in *Glauben und Bekennen,* pp. 235-250, especially p. 240.

13

THE SECOND HELVETIC CONFESSION*

1. In Zurich, Berne and Debrecen the years 1966 and 1967 saw the commemoration of the Confessio Helvetica posterior, which was professed with a fearless courage four hundred years ago and which still remains, next to be Heidelberg Catechism, the most widespread and vigorous catechism of our church. In German and French Switzerland, in the Palatinate and in East Friesland, in Hungary, Austria and Slovakia there were knowledgeable individuals and congregations who turned to this little book eagerly and gratefully. As recently as 1967 it won the support of a major church in the new world, at the Synod of the United Presbyterian Church of the U.S.A., held in Boston. While it is not our task to trace the course of this unique document through the centuries, a look at how it originated will help us to understand it better. To this end, some consideration of the general situation of Protestantism around the year 1566 is necessary.

Zwingli had foreseen the coming of that dangerous moment when Emperor and Pope would unite, and he wanted to prepare Protestantism for it. Despite his warnings, however, the catastrophe of Schmalkald (1545/46) found Protestantism still unprepared. Neither in the political-military field nor in the theological realm was it ready for the beginning of the suppression of the reformation movement by means of all-out force. And in particular, it was unprepared with regard to its religious creed. Melanchthon realised this when he consented to the Interim (1548), which at least made allowance for the evangelical doctrine of justification within a catholicism reformed along erasmian lines. It should be noted that the two Electors who formally introduced the Interim at the "Armoured Diet" of Augsburg were Joachim II of Brandenburg and Ottheinrich of the Palatinate, whose "reformations" had always been most concerned with preserving tradition as far as possible, while avoiding any revolutionary decisions. Hardest hit was the Reformed movement in Upper Ger-

---

* An address given to the Evangelisch-kirchlicher Pfarrverein and the Theologische Arbeitsgemeinschaft of Berne on the Quatercentenary of the Confessio Helvetica Posterior in 1966. Published in the "Kirchenblatt für die reformierte Schweiz", 122/15, 16, Basle, July 21st and August 4th, 1966, and in the "Reformierte Kirchenzeitung", 107/23, 24, Neukirchen-Vluyn, December 1st and 15th, 1966. *Zw. Ref. i. Rahmen.*, 602ff (Liter.).

many, which aimed at a complete renewal of ecclesiastical and social life, and which had expanded greatly since Kappel, despite having lost the military assistance of the Swiss. But now this Reformed movement was compelled to depend, both politically and theologically, upon the loyal Lutheranism of the Electorate of Saxony. The imperial city of Constance, with its prophetic preaching service, its flourishing wealth of songs, its ecclesiastical and moral culture, its lay congregational system and its republican council had developed an extraordinary evangelical power, and was in a position to develop into a northern "Geneva". But it fell in 1548 and sank to the level of a little Habsburgian country town. The confusion after the Interim, with the change of front by the treacherous Moritz of Saxony (who, for the sake of his own petty private interest, fought first on the Emperor's side and then with the Protestants), finally led, after unspeakably great suffering, to the Peace of Augsburg, with its principle of *cuius regio, eius religio*. This gave the ruler the right of reform, but with a "religious reservation" for the lands of the ecclesiastical princes, and it was expressly restricted to Roman Catholic or "Augsburg related" religions. Once again it was the Turks who, by the providence of God, "saved the Reformation". The Emperor was dependent on the support of the Protestant ranks, on the princes' soldiers and the cities' wealth. Therefore, in 1555 Augsburg brought peace to the Empire, but it was a peace bought at the price of bringing the Reformation to a standstill. From this point onwards, the chief agent of any further advances by the Protestant faith was that movement which had its headquarters in Geneva, but which received its character from France, the Calvinism which advanced fearlessly across all boundaries, propagated by means of pamphlets, by books in Latin and by refugees. The secret of its strength was that it was, from the very beginning, a prohibited church. For Calvin, the French refugee, Geneva was simply the base for the front-line ranks of the persecuted confessors of the faith.

2. The textbooks tell us that in 1563 Elector Frederick III of the Palatinate (afterwards named "the Pious"), who had succeeded the less earnest Ottheinrich, went over to Calvinism, together with his lands. On the basis of what has already been said, the following comments may be made:

I. What happened in the Palatinate, the most important of the secular electorate, under Frederick the Pious, was not a matter of defining a position vis-à-vis Lutheranism, but merely that the Reformation was now implemented in a systematic and thorough manner. Up to this time it had, as in many other places, stopped halfway, and it had penetrated only to a moderate extent into the consciousness of the congregation—the retention of the traditional altars, ceremonies and vestments having contributed not a little to this state of affairs. The events in the Palatinate gave Reformed Christians to believe (as they do to this day) that they represent the more thorough and complete reformation and that they belong to a church which places more emphasis on readiness for reform than on the maintenance of unity by preserving tradition. The Scottish Church, which was establishing itself at about the same time, has a similar feeling in relation to the Church of England.

II. Frederick the Pious did, in fact, have a strong sense of the international nature of the Reformation movement and he had, therefore, sought to unite his territorial church with it and at the same time he made his own church useful to the whole movement. Again and again he and his family took up, at considerable sacrifice to themselves, the cause of the suppressed or embattled Huguenots and the Dutch. He lost a son, for example, in the terrible defeat suffered by William of Orange at Mookerheide at the hands of the Spanish.

These two points meant that, on German soil also, the Reformation began to overflow the dams which had been erected in its path, and started to move once more.

III. In spite of all this, Frederick always declined to be called a "Calvinist". He frequently stressed that he had not even read Calvin. He maintained this even though Calvin's *Catechism* was translated and printed (anonymously!) in Heidelberg, and though a work of Beza's, which was likewise published in Heidelberg, provided an important model for the *Heidelberg Catechism*. There were also links with Beza himself, who travelled and negotiated tirelessly. Yet the Elector's contemporaries did not accuse him of Calvinism, but rather of being corrupted by "the subtle Zwinglian poison". The thorough studies made by Walther Hollweg in Emden during recent years have revealed just how deeply Frederick was concerned with theological counsel from Zurich.

3. In 1566 Frederick was summoned to the Diet of Augsburg as the accused, in order to answer for his work of Reformation and for "his" Catechism. The situation was highly dangerous for the whole Reformation. The clever diplomacy of the Emperor Maximilian and the counter-reformation zeal of Albrecht of Bavaria succeeded in achieving a united front of the Catholics and Lutherans against Frederick. Their aim was that there should be an imperial ban, that an imperial war should be declared

against the palatinate, that Frederick should be deposed (there was talk of
the death penalty) and that the Reformation in the Palatinate should be
suppressed. Frederick saw clearly that the Reformation was endangered,
not only in his own state, but in the whole Empire. The suppression of the
Reformed church would be followed by that of the Lutherans, who were
already divided among themselves. Moreover, the moral authority of the
Diet in Europe as a whole was still so strong that if the reformed Palatinate
were condemned (because it stood outside the protection of the Confession
of Augsburg) then it could have provided the rulers in France, the
Netherlands and elsewhere with their long-sought legal pretext for the
persecution of the Protestants. But Frederick the Pious cleverly and pur-
posefully turned aside the weapons directed against him. Among the
Lutheran princes he awakened a sense of solidarity with foreign and Dutch
Protestants, as well as a concern for their "German liberty" if the strength
of the Habsburg-Spanish Imperial power should increase any further.
Among the Philippist party who were strong at the time, especially in the
Electorate of Saxony, he awakened a bad conscience about their becoming
ecclesiastically dependent upon the Gnesio-Lutherans, with their doctrine
of the ubiquity of the body of Christ, a doctrine which Melanchthon had
expressly rejected in later years. But it was the personal impression made
by Frederick, his earnestness concerning the faith and the clear Christian
confession which he made before his fellow electors and all his judges,
which were to be decisive. For his purposes Frederick required, and in
the shortest time possible, the formulation of a confession which would
be clear and concise yet sufficiently comprehensive, unambiguously
evangelical yet not polemical, so that either as many Protestant Churches
as possible, both in the Empire (including the Confederacy and the
Spanish Netherlands) and abroad could declare their agreement with it, or
else that the agreement between the confession and their own published
confessional standards would be clear to all. To this end, the document
should be supported only by ecclesiastical and not by state or civil
authorities. This was something quite unusual in the sixteenth century,
but was probably necessary because of the circumstances in Holland and
France, and in order not to burden with the semblance of any political
interference the already difficult political situation that confronted the
Emperor. It was such a statement, that would fulfil all these requirements,
that Frederick was seeking when he appealed to Henry Bullinger in
Zurich.

4.   The correspondence which now began found on all sides a great
readiness to help, yet also a sense of helplessness. Everyone knew that the

task required a great deal of time and care, and that it would be necessary, therefore, to fall back on existing materials. Among other possibilities, mention was made of the First Helvetic Confession of 1536 which, as the second Confession of Basle enjoyed an official status in the Rhine city. But this last attempt to achieve a concord had been concentrated wholly on the doctrine of the Lord's Supper. In Geneva, Beza suggested an immediate conference, to which Bern objected, quite rightly, that the congregations would become unsettled, "if they heard that the scholars were meeting yet again to come up with something new and to do a bit of polishing on the faith". Naturally, those in Bern also warned against "being in too much of a hurry in matters which required thought".

In this predicament, Bullinger turned to a manuscript which he had composed years earlier for his own quiet meditation. In essence it must have originated about 1562, when the exhausted chief minister had thought that his life was coming to an end. He had discussed it at the time with his Calvinist friend Peter Martyr (who died in November, 1562) and had obtained his agreement. No one else knew about the document. When the plague was raging in Zurich in 1564, Zwingli's successor decided that, after his death, the document should be handed over to the Zurich council as a testimony to his faithful doctrine and as his spiritual testament. But Bullinger now sent it to Heidelberg, together with a modest letter which suggested that they might like to have a look at it. In Heidelberg it was received with enthusiasm. According to the answer from Chancellor Ehem, it was exactly what was needed in the situation. The author was charged with seeing to the immediate preparation of prefaces and of accurate Latin and German texts for printing, and also with gathering declarations of agreement from home and abroad.

5. Henry Bullinger, of Bremgarten in Aargau, was by birth the son of a (Catholic) deacon, a man who was highly respected both for his efficient work and for his exemplary family life. He was brought up and educated at Emmerich am Niederrhein, in the pious atmosphere of the Brothers of the Common Life and then, while a young student at the University of Cologne (which was still humanistically orientated), he became a Protestant through reading Luther's writings. After his return he was entrusted by Zwingli with delivering lectures at the monastery of Kappel and, because of his knowledge of the Church Fathers, he was an indispensable assistant to the reformer in the controversy concerning the Lord's Supper. After the catastrophe of Kappel in 1531 the Zurich council named him as Zwingli's successor, whereupon he courageously insisted that the freedom

of the pulpit should remain undiminished. This man was not a mere "successor"; because of his achievements and his significance he stands in the front rank of the great reformers. By his theological and ecclesiastical wisdom and sense of purpose he led the German-Swiss reformation out of the state of isolation into which it had been thrown by military defeat. Among other things, we may mention his agreement with Calvin on the doctrine of the Lord's Supper (the Consensus Tigurinus of 1549), his magnificiently organised news-service (the so-called "Bullinger News"), and his astonishingly comprehensive correspondence, which made him the comforter, adviser and negotiator for great and small throughout all Europe (over twelve thousand of his letters are extant). His *Decades*, the "family book" consisting of ten didactic sermons on each of the five main topics, was translated into all the major languages and had more influence on popular theology than Calvin's more academic *Institutio*. It was discarded only after the Synod of Dordrecht (1618) because the Arminians appealed to it, much to the annoyance of the orthodox. But in the eyes of his contemporaroes in the sixteenth century, the man from Zurich stood on the same level as the Genevan.

6.   From this private document, which was to become an official confession, we get to know the author himself so well, because here was a theologian of high quality who was at the same time an excellent pastor who really understood his people. His theology was intended simply to serve the life of the congregation; any merely theoretical and speculative discussion was (ruthlessly) eliminated. Though one cannot resist a slight smile at a different (non-ecclesiastical) motive, when one observes how the printing of a text which had been stored away for years suddenly became so urgent a matter in Zürich. One assumes that the printer at Froschauer had got to beat his colleague in Heidelberg; otherwise there would be a (Palatinate) Confession instead of a Helvetic! At any rate, the work, printed in Latin and German, at the expense of the state, was ready for sending to the Elector on 12th March, 1566. Even that former colleague in the defence pact, Philipp of Hesse, was remembered, with a request to support Frederick at the Reichstag. The document was given the widest possible circulation. Beza translated it immediately into French. And it fulfilled its purpose at the dreaded Reichstag. The Roman and Lutheran opponents, as well as those who were wavering, were so strongly impressed by the vigorous courage of Frederick's confession that they could not bring themselves to condemn him to deposition and the ban. It is said that Frederick had his eldest son carry a Bible behind him as he was inter-

rogated, and that he defended his catechism with such a ready knowledge of Scripture that August of Saxony shouted: "What do you want? Fritz is more pious than all of us put together!" Even so, the decision had only been postponed: it was not until the Treaty of Westphalia in 1648 that the Reformed Church received legal recognition.

7.   There is no better way of showing the triumphant progress of the little book than by referring to the title-page and preface of the third edition: *Confessio et expositio simplex orthodoxae fidei.... A confession and simple exposition of the orthodox faith; and the catholic doctrines of the pure Christian religion unanimously published by the servants of the Church of Christ in the Confederacy...* with the intention of convincing all believers that they stand within the unity of the true and ancient Church of Christ, that they are propagating no new or false doctrines and that they have nothing in common, therefore, with any sects of heresies; made known at this time, so that all believers can form their judgment. Romans X: with the heart, one believes unto righteousness, but with the mouth confession is made unto salvation... All the servants of all the Churches of Christ in Switzerland have appended their signatures: Zurich, Bern, Schaffhausen, St. Gallen, Chur, and in the Three Federations on both sides of the Alps, Mülhausen and Biel; they have also been joined by the servants of the Church in Geneva and Neuchatel, etc. Following the publication of the confession, however, the servants of the Church of Poland in the Duchies of Zator and Auschwitz have declared their agreement; and also the servants of the Scottish Churches who, in a communication to the renowned Dr. Theodore Beza on 5th September, 1566, say, among other things: "All of us who were present at the assembly have signed and have ratified this by the academic seal". The Confession, together with certain other articles, was also published on 1st September, 1567, at Debrezen in Hungary, printed with a dedication to Johann II, by God's grace King of Hungary. This dedication contained, inter alia, the following words: "All of us, servants of the Church on both sides of the Theiss, at the Church assembly convened at Debrezen on 24th February, 1567, have signed, among other confessions, the Helvetic Confession, which was also signed by the servants of the Church of Geneva, etc." From 1644 onwards there appear, together with the cities of the Confederacy, the names of the ministers of Glarus, Basle and Appenzell also.

It is well known that in the sixteenth century there were endless disputations over dogmatic definitions, concerning statements which might serve to unite, or provide a compromise, or differentiate, or even condemn. Nor were matters in the Roman province, such as Trent, essentially different from the Protestant. Not infrequently unity was achieved (through only with difficulty), but sometimes there was total disagreement, and sometimes the formula of unity which had been arrived at actually had the effect of increasing the disunity. Therefore the course of events which we have described here is all the more remarkable. To *one* man, who himself stood in the shadow of death, a word was given which was then received by thousands, in both East and West, as their word of life in persecution and danger. Some minor changes were sought, and the man of Zurich cheerfully crossed out a few lines which might trouble the brethren in Geneva; but nobody quarrelled and everyone spoke straight from the heart.

8.   The *Expositio Simplex* is all of a piece. Its character can best be described by selecting some typical sections.

The Preface, which in its final version was edited by Bullinger's son-in-law Josias Simler, has some surprising statements on the development of Reformed confessions.

a) It is definitely accepted that it is an age characterised by the diligent editing of statements of faith. (So confession is clearly not unaffected by the changing peculiarities of time and place).

b) "Our" confessions have revealed certain deficiencies and are already almost forgotten; it is high time for a new one. (We are astonished by this—the well known Zurich, Berne and Basle confessions are just about 30 years old! So the obligation to fashion a confession is clearly never-ending).

c) The purpose is to demonstrate agreement in orthodoxy of faith and in brotherly love with the Churches of Christ, even when there are differences "in the expression and formulation of doctrine, in customs and ceremonies". (Most important—the real purpose of a confession is not to draw distinctions but to bind together!)

d) The indispensable proviso is that of better instruction "from the Word of God", which characterises and adorns all the Reformed confessions since Zwingli's *Introduction* (1523) and which makes all our confessions and our teaching subordinate to the freedom of the Holy Spirit.

9.   The Preface is followed by the religious edict of Theodosius (380 AD) and the Confession of Damasus who is mentioned in that edict.

The addition of these documents constitutes both a definite theological decision and a master-stroke of diplomacy. The ancient doctrines of the Trinity and of the two natures are thereby assumed, and it is emphasised that they have their roots in the Apostolic era; and at the same time an appeal is made to the protection of the imperial law. All who confess faith in the Trinity are orthodox in the sight of the imperial law. Therefore the Reformed Church does not merely protest against calumny and persecution, but demands from the emperor that civil protection to which it is entitled.

10.   The first chapter contains, as a marginal note, the most famous sentence of the whole second Helvetic Confession: *"Praedicatio verbi Dei est verbum Dei"* ("The preaching of the Word of God is the Word of God"). One can really say that the whole Reformation is summed up in this sentence, when one reflects that it points to the real presence of the Lord in the Word. However, this statement must not be misunderstood. For when seen aright, it is not a statement about the ministerial office, but rather about the Holy Spirit and Holy Scripture. When taken in its context, it means that the exposition and application of *Holy Scripture* is the Word of God, because through it God says to us today what He said formerly to the prophets and apostles: *loquitur adhuc nobis.* Praedicatio *verbi Dei* est verbum Dei. And conversely, in order to show itself to be the Word of God, the Bible has to be *preached.* The Bible is not a spiritual automaton. *Praedicatio* verbi Dei est verbum Dei! Thus preaching and faith are dependent upon the same *Spirit of God.* The old controversy about the priority of the external word (as Luther maintained) or the internal word (as Zwingli maintained) is resolved by reference to the fact that it is the one and the same Spirit who sends both.

11.   This same principle of the sovereignty of the Spirit of God governs the second chapter on the interpretation of *Holy Scripture.* Scripture may only be expounded according to Scripture, by considering the original language, by the context, and by comparison with unambiguous passages. As a guideline there is "the rule of faith and of love" and, above all "whatever emphasises the glory of God and the salvation of men". This method is simply a serious application of the fundamental principle that "God alone must be the judge in matters of faith". In this connexion, the old Zwinglian war cry against the "traditiones humanae", the traditions of men, is echoed.

12.   This pneumatological feature runs right through all the chapters. We find it even in Chapter XI on *"Jesus Christ,* true God and man, and only Saviour of the world" which *precedes,* moreover, the chapters on the Law of God (XII), the Gospel (XIII), Repentance (XIV) and Justification (XV). Accordingly, the classical doctrine of the two natures is stated with a

slight accentuation of the divinity as against the humanity of the person of
Jesus Christ and, as might be expected, there is the reformed emphasis
upon the identity of the glorified body of the Lord with His crucified body,
thus rejecting the doctrine of ubiquity. But the originality of this chapter
lies elsewhere. It has always been remarked that when one comes to the
end of the thirty chapters of the Helvetica posterior, the chapter on the
Last Things is missing. There have even been suggestions that a page was
lost. But is the eschatology missing? Not at all. There are flashes of it
everywhere. But it is expressly stated in this chapter; it is incorporated in
the witness to Christ. It is not a question of this or that apocalyptic
phenomenon, but of the coming Lord Himself—that is the hope of the
Church and of the world.

13.   One jewel in the Confession is the too often neglected definition of
Faith in Chapter XVI: "Christian faith is not merely an opinion or human
conviction, but rather an unwavering trust and an open and constant assent of the heart, as well as a sure laying hold of the truth of God, as it is set
forth in Holy Scripture and in the Apostles' Creed, indeed a laying hold of
God Himself as the highest Good, and especially of the divine promise,
and of Christ who is substance of all the promises. However, this faith is
wholly the gift of God, which God graciously grants to His elect according
to His pleasure, when, and to whom, and in what measure He will,
through the Holy Spirit by means of the preaching of the gospel and of
believing prayer".
   The impression that this rich description is just a bare recitation
vanishes immediately. After rejecting an intellectual or religious subjectivity, it moves in concentric circles towards an ever more essential grasp
of the heart of the matter. The Lutheran "fiducial faith", which is a
genuine subjectivity ("trust") as opposed to a false one, is supplemented
by the active "assent of the soul" (rather than the scholastic *assensus*)—
Bullinger is never afraid to talk about the psychological aspect of the life of
faith. But the objective basis of this life is stated at once: it is not a matter
of a pious disposition of the soul, but of a fundamentally clear and sober
grasp of "God's Truth". And we do not have to produce this by some
mystical, hermeneutic or existential act of creation, because it is given to
us historically; we have "Scripture and Confession", and they speak the
truth to us. Though a possible "objectivistic" misunderstanding is also
corrected immediately. The truth of God is not just this or that thing, but
rather "God Himself" in His personal presence. What a wonder this
is—that faith really "grasps" and "lays hold of" "God Himself"—but

only in that he thereby becomes everything to us. (Zwingli also had thus expounded the "highest good" of the scholastics). But nowhere is God more divine than in his "promises"—in that Word, therefore, in which He gives Himself to us. Yet even here we do not slip into objective relationships, for faith is an encounter, it lays hold of God in *Christ*, who is the incarnate promise, the self-revelation of God, in person, the "substance".

In the concluding sentence we observe once more the fundamental role of the Holy Spirit, who embraces both the objective and the subjective; preaching and prayer alike are his instruments. The deliberate lack of any logical consistency in the last words is splendid—an oratorio fidelis:—in order to believe, one must pray; and in order to pray, one must believe; faith is granted only to believing prayer: "Lord, I *believe*, help my *unbelief*!"

14.   It is in the realistic confidence which joyfully reckons on the Holy Spirit that there lies the reason why the short section about Divine Predestination and the *Election* of the Saints (Chapter X) is among the most reverent, clear and comforting of the Reformation writings on this theme. Whoever speaks of "Spirit" in the Biblical sense is talking about God's freedom and free gift for man-election, therefore. But at this point we are not confronted by an abstract principle; rather do we look into the face of Jesus Christ. He is the first of the elect, and the basis of all election. "We believe and teach that the Son of God, our Lord Jesus Christ, was predestined or foreordained by the Father from all eternity to be the Saviour of the world". All election is, therefore, election for Him, in Him and through Him. The chapter begins with Ephesians I: "God has chosen us in Him before the foundation of the world". Unfortunately, this relation of the doctrine of election to Ephesians I has not always been maintained in the old Reformed theology.

With that "in Him" and "through Him" the Holy Spirit comes into the picture again. But this comment requires further explanation. The attempt to see election reflected in the Holy Spirit is very old; or, to be more exact, to see it mirrored in the evidence of His gifts in my life, in my "sanctification". Is not the Holy Spirit promised to the elect? Indeed, is not the gift of the Holy Spirit the very consummation of election? When troubled by the question "Am I one of the elect?", to which we can be driven be an honest look at ourselves, one generation after another has looked for the inward working of the Spirit as the mark of election.

Now the Helvetica posterior belongs to those Reformation writings in which personal self-examination is treated with great seriousness as an indispensable part of the Christian life. But the attempt to discern my salvation in my sanctification would lead either to a greater legalism or to a mania for more mystical experiences. As the Holy Spirit sharpens our vision, to look at ourselves can only lead us into despair. Therefore the work of the Holy Spirit consists rather in setting us free from ourselves and from preoccupation with ourselves to contemplate, in joyous self-forgetfulness, the wonder of election itself, granted to us in Christ. As He is, and as He remains the *fundamentum electionis*, the ground of election, so is He for each of us that *speculum electionis*, the mirror of election. "This Christ is the mirror, in which we gaze upon our predestination. When we are united with Christ we have a clear and certain witness that our names are written in the book of life, and when He is ours *in true faith*, then we are His".

For this reason, the old wicked claim that one can possess something more in the Holy Spirit than can be had "just" by faith is to be resisted as a dangerous temptation. In pursuit of this one could miss Christ and the Holy Spirit and election. "Therefore we disapprove of the behaviour of those poeple who seek outside of Christ the answers to the question of whether they are elect and what God has determined before all eternity concerning them. For we have to listen to the preaching of the Gospel and to believe it and not doubt it. If you believe and are in Christ, then you are elect. For the Father has opened to us His eternal decree (His "sentence") concerning predestination in Christ". It must be said openly that this sounds different from the *horribile decretum* of Calvin.

I conclude with some observations on the question of confession in our church today.

15. Today, when we hear the word "Confession", we at once associate it with "compulsion". We have seen that this verdict would not be justified with regard to the origins of the Helvetica posterior. It was a manifestation of freedom, not of coercion; it was the declaration of free Protestants in Switzerland, in the Palatinate and in many lands. In the midst of mortal danger, it caused the enthusiastic jubilation of the brotherhood of faith to spring forth: "We have all signed:..."

It was not to be long, before it became "Sign!" What had once been a common word, which could be received with gratitude, became overnight the final word, which was hardly open to serious discussion any more, and which could be spoken only with restraint; it had been exalted above all discussion. Political, ecclesiastical and moral pressure crept in. No changes! No new confession! Thirty, sixty, three hundred, four hundred years ...

No doubt the fact that the confession is such a fine work contributed to its stability. Because it really is so excellent a teacher, this confession has, throughout the centuries, introduced congregations to the true sense of Holy Scripture and has shown preachers the great themes to be proclaimed; it has served to instruct individual church members, made them clear about their faith, and enabled them to reach their own independent decisions in their problems of faith and life.

16.   Times change, and we come to new periods in cultural history. So the day came, when resistance to all discipline gained the upper hand. This little book, which had for so long been "untouchable", suddenly became a bone of contention. The "Liberals" were "against", in regard both to the principle and the content of it, and cried "away with it!" The "Positives" were "for", it and cried "hold fast to it!" Gradually, commitment to the old book declined. Was this wholly a loss? I would say (with the recklessness of a necessary brevity) that it was not only a loss. Because the confession was seen by both parties as something historical—something past, which one should either set aside or hold fast. It had become a "standpoint" by which one stands firm or which one abandons as outdated. Whereas a true confession is not a standpoint, but rather a goal that is set *before* us, or, more exactly, a way to that goal. If a church has reached the point where its confession can be misunderstood by friend and foe alike, then it is no misfortune if the confession is no longer treated as valid.

17.   It is no misfortune because such a church, whether it will or not, is thrown back upon Holy Scripture. And that is precisely what the Reformation confessions wanted to achieve. If the Confessio leads to the Gospel—good! If the withdrawal of the Confessio leads to the Gospel—that is good as well! Though we may not be left without some sense of shame by the questions of our fathers:—"What do you confess? Do you know what you believe? Do you believe what you know?"

However, one cannot force a confession; the hour and the word are both matters of grace. This is not just because of our laziness and our foolishness, but because of the freedom of the Holy Spirit. More than forty years ago, at Barmen, five "Declarations" were submitted. One of these prevailed because of its inherent authority, just as the Helvetica posterior had done.

18.   When we come to the freedom of the Spirit we are dealing with the really fundamental question concerning confessions. The old confession itself poses this question, when it states: ''God Himself has ... spoken and speaks to us even now...'' (Chapter I). That is precisely the point in question. Does God really speak to us? Where God does not speak, man does not confess. But when a man has no confession—no real purpose, that is, on which he is prepared to stake his life, and for which he is ready to die, then he is truly poor.

The old book teaches us: wait upon the Holy Spirit. By virtue of its very existence it says: the Holy Spirit will give us our confession, our new, our very own confession, drawn from our own time and in our language, dealing with our arguments and offering us grace in our despair. Our fathers believed such things, so why should we not believe them?

19.   Four hundred years of the Confessio Helvetica posterior. A beautiful, old, worthy and still instructive book. The book of old Henry Bullinger—not our book. We are silent in the presence of the fathers of the sixteenth century, because we achieve nothing comparable for our own times. They set their hands to the task, so that states were moved, peoples were renewed, and western culture was thoroughly renovated, rebuilt and thereby saved—we hardly dare to attempt the task.

For Confession means coming out of the pious circles, the beautiful churches, the sacred gatherings and the holy, liturgical spheres, and coming into the world with Christ! Confession does not mean repeating and holding fast what was said by the pious fathers of the sixteenth century, but means saying what they would say today. This task is considerably more difficult. The fathers had to study Holy Scripture, venture everything with Christ, and depend on the illumination of the Holy Spirit. They were not disappointed.

And if we dare to do the same, why should there not be given to us also a manifesto that is at once both truly evangelical and ecumenical, so that the enlightenment of the church could take a further step forward?

20.   But that is not the most important thing. When Jesus Christ comes, to take home His disciples—and He will come, suddenly, and He already comes every day, by His Spirit—then He will not ask about confessions, but about confessors; about disciples who confess Him with a doubting and yet unshakable faith, in despair perhaps, or in a desperate world situation, yet in joyous hope, living in a world full of malice, ex-

ploitation, murder and hypocrisy, yet displaying sacrificial, loyal love. "Whoever confesses *me*, him will I also confess", He says.

His confession of us is always more important than our endeavours at confessing.

But we want to confess *that*. For as the Second Helvetic Confession of AD 1566 states on its title-page, quoting Romans 10:

"With the heart man believeth unto righteousness; and with the mouth confession is made unto salvation".

14

DISCORD AMONG GUESTS*

Lessons to be learned from the Reformers' debate about the Lord's Supper for a contemporary understanding and celebration

I. REFLECTIONS ON THE SITUATION

1. *Dialogue—a bounden duty*

The difference concerning the Lord's Supper and the fact that Christians, of all people, exclude each other from the communion table is an absurdity and the most hurtful wounding of the ecumenical movement. Moreover, it is a sin before God that the disciples of Jesus have created the greatest strife around his supper of peace. They have spoken wicked words, they have hated, and, in this context, have also shed blood. No wonder many, to this day, have difficulty in understanding one another. Humanly speaking, this disunity was possibly the reason for the reformation of the church encompassing only one third instead of the whole of Christendom.

A student of that reformation relates such facts penitently, without either reproaching the fathers of the past or the brethern of the present. No one ought to pass judgement on the controversy without appreciating that the disputants have been guided to their respective points of view and could not decide otherwise. A generation of historians and relativists does not have the right to reproach those forefathers who for the sake of truth staked and sacrificed life and work, and only those who are no longer moralistic know-alls are able to ask for forgiveness from the sin of schism and for release from its constraint.

Yet, this is what we must do and act accordingly. Therefore, it would be no genuine confession of sin if we would be satisfied, until the end of time, with separate tables as if they were an inevitable tragic destiny. Furthermore, some four hundred and fifty years have past since Marburg, around four hundred years since Trent, and about two hundred years since the counter-reformation, enough time, even in church history, for a certain

---

* A lecture given during 1970 to the theological faculties of the Universities of Helsinki and Abo/Turku (Finland). "Streit unte· Gästen. Die Lehre aus der Abendmahlsdebatte der Reformatoren für das Verständnis und die Feier des Abendmahls heute". *Theologische Studien* Heft 110. Theologischer Verlag Zürich 1972. Translation by Duncan Shaw.

pacification and reflection. After all, much has happened since then. Hopefully, we have learned a few lessons, and also forgotten others, and we believe that the Lord of the world has given his church some stern warnings within recent history.

We are compelled to resume discussion regarding the Lord's Supper: this time without squabbling. This, after all, is already happening in many places. The most noteworthy contemporary phenomenon, in this connection, is the Roman Catholic theologians' drawing nearer to their fiercest opponent—Calvin.[1] Naturally, most of the momentum for this new discussion, as well as its difficulties, comes from the exegetes. Today we would like to offer our contribution which we commence with a glance at the reformation.

2. The principal types of reformation teaching on the Lord's Supper

Actually, at this point, a survey of the whole controversy surrounding the Lord's Supper should be presented. However, it would require, even in short formate, a thick volume which no one has written yet.[2] But, even a mere description and analysis of the historical-dogmatic consequences arising from the most significant doctrinal formulations of all parties, would exceed the time available.

---

1. Cf. e.g., Otto Karrer, "Die Eucharistie im Gespräch der Konfessionen. Vortrag an der Una-Sancta-Varanstaltung beim Eucharistischen Weltkongress, München 1960" in *Una Sancta, Zeitschrift für interkonfessionelle, Begegnung*, 1960, 4, 229-250. (Further bibliography given there).—Leopold Schummer, *Le ministère pastoral dans l'Institution Chrétienne de Calvin à la lumière du Troisième Sacrement*, Veröffentlichungen des Instituts für europäische Geschichte, Mainz, Bd. 39, Abteilung für abendländische Religionsgeschichte, ed. Joseph Lortz, Wiesbaden 1965.—Alexandre Ganoczy, *Calvin théologien de l'église et du ministère*, Unam Sanctam, no. 48, Paris 1964.—Alexandre Ganoczy, *Ecclesia ministrans. Dienende Kirche und Kirchlicher Dienst bei Calvin*, Freiburg/Breisgau, Basel, Vienna, 1968.—Alexander Ganoczy, *Le jeune Calvin*, Wiesbaden 1966.— Alexander Ganoczy, "Calvin im Urteil der Katholiken von heute" in *Concilium*, 1966, 2, 245-249. (Further bibliography for the period before 1960 given there).—W. L. Beolens, *Die Arnoldshainer Abendmahlsthesen*, Assen 1964.—M. de Kroon, *De Eer van God et het heil van de mens*, Roermond 1968.—K. McDonnell, *John Calvin, the Church, and the Eucharist*, Princeton 1967.—J. L. Witte, "Calvinismus" in *Sacramentum Mundi*, Freiburg/Breisgau, Basel, Vienna, 1967, I 687-699.—Liselotte Höfer, "Eucharistie und Interkommunion im evangelisch-katholischen Gespräch" in *Kirchenblatt für die reformierte Schweiz*, Basel 1971, 19, 290-296. (Further bibliography given here).

2. For the beginnings, cf. the magisterial opus of Walther Köhler, *Zwingli und Luther, ihr Streit über das Abendmahl nach seinen politischen und religiösen Beziehungen*, I. Die religiöse und politische Entwicklung bis zum Marburger Religionsgespräch 1529, Quellen und Forschungen zur Reformationsgeschichte. Verein für Reformationsgeschichte. VI, Leipzig 1924. II. Vom Beginn der Marburger Verhandlungen 1529 bis zum Abschluss der Wittenberger Konkordie 1536, edd. Ernst Kohlmeyer and Heinrich Bornkamm, QFRG VII, Gütersloh 1953.—Hans Grass, *Die Abendmahlslehre* bei Luther und Calvin, Gütersloh, 2nd ed. 1954. G. W. L.: *Zw. Ref. i. Rahmen.*, 1979, ch. XV (Liter.).

Therefore, the only possibility is for us to forego consideration of all theological, christological, philosophical, morphological, and world conceptual implications and developments and briefly characterise the decisive doctrinal forms and their motivation. This procedure is justified because, during the period of orthodoxy, indeed throughout the entire history of confessionalism until now, they are always fundamentally the same motives, types and arguments which are being expressed, pondered, varied, combined and formulated.[3]

a) *Rome's pre-tridentine doctrine* was not as uniform as it seemed. The anti-Protestant front was rather disunited, especially in the defence of the mass from the time of the Sorbonne and Louvain statements through those of Aleander, Eck and Faber until about the time of Erasmus. Even their loyalty to the Fourth Lateran Council of 1215, with its mystically attuned doctrine of transubstantiation, was not unambiguous:

"In the One universal Church of the faithful, outside of which no one will have eternal life, Jesus Christ the Priest Himself is the sacrifice, whose body and blood in the sacrament of the altar under the species of bread and wine are really contained, because, through God's power the substance of the bread has been transformed into body, and the substance of the wine into blood; in order that the mystery of the union be completed and we receive ourselves from Him what the received from us"[4] (i.e. body and blood).

In the different interpretations and usages of this dogma of transubstantiation, the religious experience remained the same and has impregnated itself deeply into the feelings of late medieval men and indeed those of many "catholic" people even outside Rome, until the present time. Behind the much debated *transsubstantiatis pane et vino* remains the *potestas divina*. The mass is thus the main and central miracle, both in heaven and

---

3. One should compare, for example, Elert's comprehensive and systematic presentation which is typical of a wide circle or the brilliant historical and dogmatical account by Gollwitzer. There is hardly a theme or an argument in the contemporary debate which did not arise in the discussions between Zwingli and Luther.—Werner Elert, *Morphologie des Luthertums*, I. Theologie und Weltanschauung des Luthertums hauptsächlich im 16. und 17. Jahrhundert, Munich 1931. II. Soziallehren und Socialwirkungen des Luthertums, Munich 1932.—Helmut Gollwitzer, *Coena Domini. Die altlutherische Abendmahlslehre in ihrer Auseinandersetzung mit dem Calvinismus, dargestellt an der lutherischen Frühorthodoxie*, Munich 1937.

4. *Lateranense IV:* "Una vero est fidelium universalis ecclesia, extra quam nullus omnino salvatur, in qua idem ipse sacerdos est sacrificium Iesus Christus, cuius corpus et sanguis in sacramento altaris sub speciebus panis et vini veraciter continentur, transsubstantiatis pane in corpus, et vino in sanguinem potestate divina; ut ad perficiendum mysterium unitatis accipiamus ipsi de suo, quod accepit ipse de nostro". (Denzinger, new numeration 802, old numeration 430).

on earth: God's presence with us and among us. In this, the *mysterium unitatis* is perfected which had its beginning in the incarnation: Christ became man in order to die, and he has died so that the mass could be celebrated: Real Presence!

b) Alongside these lofty arguments, the details of the *Council of Trent* (1551) appear meagre. Indeed, they do not display such a notable achievement of the council fathers as, for example the *decretum de justificatione* does. They are merely orientated towards a contradicting of the reformers: Christ is perfectly capable of being simultaneously "in heaven", according to his existing naturally, and in other places with us, according to his existing sacramentally with his substance; there exists no contradiction to an illuminated intelligence and this must be steadfastly believed.[5] The total transubstantiation through consecration emanates from the words of institution.[6]

c) Meanwhile, the reformers had spoken. Although, until now, the *Confessio Augustana* represents the most official and most popular Lutheran Confession, we mention it only in passing. Article X, (*De coena domini*: the body and blood of Christ are really present and will be distributed among those who partake)[7] makes one most clearly aware of the diplomatic purpose of the whole Augsburg Confession. It says nothing about reformation motives and remains completely open to an interpretation in a transubstantiatory sense. Eck understood it in this way too.[8] The Reformed, who latterly often and partly with assent, considered or tried to account

---

5. Denzinger, 1636/874.

6. Denzinger, 1642/877. In contradistinction to all Reformation thinking, it is noteworthy that Trent relates the early church's christological definition of *unio hypostatica* to the *totus Christus* in the sacrament. Thus the divinity of Christ is also present under the species of bread and wine, and will be assimilated by the communicant; Denzinger, 1640-41/876); the bread and wine are therefore not simply body and blood: thus the intention of the definition of the fourth Lateran Council is thwarted.

7. *Confessio Augustana*, Art X. "Vom heiligen Abendmahl. Von dem Abendmahl des Herrn wird also gelehrt, daß wahrer Leib und Blut Christi wahrhaftiglich *unter der Gestalt* des Brots und Weins im Abendmahl gegenwärtig sei und da ausgeteilt und genommen werde. Derhalben wird auch die Gegenlehr verworfen". De coena Domini. De coena Domini docent, quod corpus et sanguis Christi vere adsint et distribuantur vescentibus in coena Domini; et improbant secus docentes". "The Holy Supper of our Lord, It is taught among us that the true body and blood of Christ are really present in the Supper of our Lord under the form of bread and wine and are there distributed and received. The contrary doctrine is therefore rejected". (*B.E.L.K.*, I, 62f.) The Latin and German versions of the Articles are compared in W. H. Neuser, *Die Abendmahlslehre Melanchthons .... 1519-1530*, Neukirchen 1968, 431-447.

8. *Ib.*, 63 n2. (H. Bornkamm).

themselves as being "religious relatives of Augsburg", have always sensed a serious gap in missing definitions against the mass.[9]

d) Before we bring under scrutiny the actual protestant doctrines of the Lord's Supper, we have to risk an attempt which has seldom been undertaken since Marburg, i.e., to delineate *two common basic concepts*.

Firstly, it is acknowledged that, for protestant justifying faith, particularly clearly in its Lutheran form, the *word* became fundamental and indeed as a word from without—an grant. That overturned the public worship of God.[10] The miracle and the power lay henceforth in the fact

9. Concerning the early period of the reformed church, cf. the account in, August Kluckhohn, *Friedrich der Fromme, Kurfürst von der Pfalz*, Nördlingen 1879, (among others), 258ff., in: A. A. van Schelven, *De nederduitsche vluchtelingskerken der XVIe eeuw in England en Duitschland in hunne beteekenis voor de Reformatie in de Nederlanden*, 's Gravenhage 1909; and in: Willem Nijenhuis, *Calvinus Oecumènicus, Calvijn en de eenheid der kerk in het licht van zijn briefwisseling*, 's Gravenhage 1958. (Consult the index under, Augsburg, Confessie van).

For Calvin, the problem played a prominent role for decades, not only in his correspondence with the refugee congregations in Frankfurt and Wesel, but also with those in France and Poland, and even with Bullinger in Zurich. Calvin's point of view was always that which he indicated in a letter to the Polish protestants, dated 24th October 1557. He does not reject the *Confessio Augustana*, but it is so vague that there arise constant differences of opinion as to its interpretation. In particular, suplementary explanations are essential in relation to its teaching on the Lord's supper. "Neque tamen haec erit ab Augustana confessione discessio, si clarior fidei vestrae expositio accedat ..." "It would not be to dissent from the Augsburg confession, if a clearer exposition of your faith were added to it ......" "Quid ..... obstat quominus in consensionem piam sanctam et dilucidam coalescatis simul omnes? Neque enim hoc modo violabitur confessio Augustana ..." "What is to keep you (namely, the adherents to the Augsburg and Bohemian (here referred to as the Waldensian) Confessions) from gathering together in order to come to a pious, pure and clear conviction held by all in common? Neither would the Augsburg confession be violated by this procedure ..." (*C. R., Calvini Opera*, XVI, coll. 676-77). The reference is to the *Confessio Bohemica* of 1535, which, in Article XIII, (*De Coena Domini*), expresses itself similarly to the *Confessio Augustana*, but in Article XI, (*De Sacramentis*), lays a "Reformed" foundation. H. A. Niemeyer, *Collectio Confessionum in ecclesiis reformatis publicatarum*, 1840, 804ff., 801ff.

John a Lasco even attempted to represent the Reformed understanding of the Lord's Supper as "true" interpretation of the *Confessio Augustana*, which naturally met with the severest displeasure of the fathers of the Formula of Concord. (*B.E.L.K.* II, 973 n2. Further bibliography is given there).

As late as 1647, in the negotiations for the legislation of the Reformed Church in the Empire at Münster and Osnabrück, the Great Elector sought for the recognition of the Reformed position as being akin to that of the Augsburg Confession. The result was a Latin sentence with a double meaning. Hans Leube, *Kalvinismus und Luthertum*, Leipzig 1928, I, 6 and 163-191.

10. Vilmos Vajta, *Die Theologie des Gottesdienstes bei Luther*, Göttingen, Vandenhoeck & Ruprecht 1952.—Julius Schweizer "Zur Ordnung des Gottesdienstes in den nach Gottes Wort reformierten Gemeinden der deutschsprachigen Schweiz", *Kirchliche Zeitfragen*, Heft 12, Zwingli Verlag, Zürich 1944.—Otto Weber, Artikel: "Der reformierte Gottesdienst", in *Evangelisches Kirchen-Lexikon*, Band I, Göttingen 1956, 1685-1687. Gottfried W. Locher, *In Spirit and in Truth*, above pp. 1-30.—Hermann Waldenmaier, "Die Entstehung der evangelischen Gottesdienstordnungen Süddeutschlands im Zeitalter der

that, in the word of man, the divine word of grace comes through, just as in man, Jesus, the eternal Son of God, has appeared. The same function, which belongs to the sacrament in the Romish divine service, is performed henceforward by preaching: real presence of the Lord. This as from old is named the Holy Ghost. Although Lutherans and Reformed describe the internal relationship between Word and Spirit differently,[11] this need not detain us here; at this point, we are confronted by their insoluble connection. From here on, the sacrament will be "relativised".

Then, "relativising" means here *relation*, connection not devaluation. The Word can exist without the sacrament, the sacrament never without the Word. It lives from the personal Word of promise which, according to Luther, appears in encapsulated power in the words of institution.[12] In spite of all respect for the 'sacrament of the altar' Luther would never agree with the argumentation of some High-churchmen that the Lord's Supper offers a grace over and above forgiveness.[13]

Reformation", *SVRG* 125/126, Leipzig 1916.—Simon van der Linde, *De leer van den Heiligen Geest by Calvyn*, Wageningen 1943, 166-198: "De Heilige Geest en het leven van der kerk".—Ronald S. Wallace, *Calvin's Doctrine of the christian Life*, Edinburgh & London 1959. 206-214: "The Church sanctified by the Word and Sacraments".—Bernhard Buschbeck, *Die Lehre vom Gottesdienst im Werk Johannes Calvins*, Marburg 1968.

11. Further material in: Gottfried W. Locher: *Die Lehre vom Heiligen Geist in der Confessio Helvetica Posterior* in Joachim Staedtke (Hsg): *Glauben und Bekennen, Vierhundert Jahre Confessio Helvetica Posterior, Beiträge zu ihrer Theologie und Geschichte*, Zwingli Verlag, Zürich 1966, 300-336, especially 320-322 (Comparison with Confessio Augustana).—*Id.*, *Praedicatio Verbi Dei est Verbum Dei*, above p. 277-287f.

12. Cf. V. Vajta, *op.cit.*, 182-195 (Die Konsekration als Verheißung der Gegenwart Christi durch das Wort).—Paul Althaus: *Die Theologie Martin Luthers*, Gütersloh, Mohn, 1962, 323-330 (Die Autorität der Einsetzungsworte).—Luther im Großen Katechismus: "... Denn obgleich das Werk am Kreuz geschehen und die Vergebung der Sund erworben ist, so kann sie doch nicht anders denn durchs Wort zu uns kommen. Denn was wußten wir sonst davon, daß solchs geschehen wäre oder uns geschenkt sein sollte, wenn man's nicht durch die Predigt oder mündlich Wort furtrüge? Woher wissen sie es oder wie können sie die Vergebung ergreifen und zu sich bringen, wo sie sich nicht halten und gläuben an die Schrift und das Evangelion? Nu ist je das ganze Evangelion und der Artikel des Glaubens: < Ich gläube eine heilige christliche Kirche, Vergebung der Sunde > etc. durch das Wort in dies Sakrament gesteckt und uns furgelegt". (*B.E.L.K.*, II. 713f.). Luther in the *Large Catechism*, V, 31-32, "Although the work was accomplished and forgiveness of sins was acquired on the cross, yet it cannot come to us in any other way than through the Word. How should we know that this has been accomplished and offered to us if it were not proclaimed by preaching, by the oral Word? Whence do they know of forgiveness, and how can they grasp and appropriate it, except by steadfastly believing the Scriptures and the Gospel? Now, the whole Gospel and the article of the Creed, "I believe in the holy Christian church, the forgiveness of sins", are embodied in this sacrament and offered to us through the Word".

13. Luther im Großen Katechismus: "Das Wort (sage ich) ist das, das dies Sakrament machet und unterscheidet, daß es nicht lauter Brot und 'Wein, sondern Christus' Leib und Blut ist und heißet ... Das Wort muß das Element zum Sakrament machen, wo nicht, so

e) Among the official Lutheran Confessions, the Smalkald Articles reproduce the voice of *Martin Luther* most accurately, "...that the bread and the wine in the Supper are the true body and blood of Christ".[14] The oft mentioned prepositions "in, with, and under"[15] state nothing but late

---

bleibt's ein lauter Element ... Das ist wohl wahr, wenn Du das Wort davon tuest oder ohn Wort ansiehest, so hast Du nichts denn lauter Brot und Wein, wenn sie aber dabei bleiben, wie sie sollen und müssen, so ist's laut derselben wahrhaftig Christus' Leib und Blut. Denn wie Christus' Mund redet und spricht, also ist es, als der nicht liegen noch triegen kann". (*B.E.L.K.* II, 709f.). Luther in the *Large Catechism*, V, 10-11, "It is the Word, I maintain, which distinguishes it from mere bread and wine and constitutes it a sacrament which is rightly called Christ's body and blood ... The Word must make the element a sacrament: otherwise it remains a mere element .... It is true, indeed, that if you take the Word away from the elements or view them apart from the Word, you have nothing but ordinary bread and wine. But if the words remain, as it is right and necessary, then in virtue of them they are truly the body and blood of Christ. For as we have it from the lips of Christ, so it is; he cannot lie or deceive.

Cf., further to this, Albrecht Peters, *Realpräsenz, Luthers Zeugnis von Christi Gegenwart im Abendmahl*, Berlin 1960, 153-156.

14. Luther in the Schmalkaldic Articles, "Vom Sakrament des Altars halten wir, dass Brot und Wein im Abendmahl sei der wahrhaftige Leib und Blut Christi und werde nicht allein gereicht und empfangen von frommen, sondern auch von bösen Christen". "The Sacrament of the Altar: We hold that the bread and wine in the Supper are the true body and blood of Christ and that these are given and received not only by godly but also by wicked Christians". It appears that Luther first dictated, "...dass unter Brot und Wein sei der wahrhaftige Leib und Blut im Abendmahl...", "...that under the bread and wine, the true body and blood of Christ are in the Supper...". This would be an expression of the doctrine of consubstantiation. The official Latin translation reads, "De sacramento altaris statuimus panem et vinum in coena esse verum corpus et sanguinem Christi et non tantum sumi et dari a piis, sed etiam a malis christianis et impiis". (*B.E.L.K.*, I, 450f.).

15. Luther im Kleinen Katechismus: "Was ist das Sakrament des Altars? Antwort. Est ist der wahre Leib und Blut unsers Herrn Jesu Christi, *unter* dem Brot und Wein uns Christen zu essen und zu trinken von Christo selbs eingesetzt". (*B.E.L.K.*, II, 519f.). "What is the Sacrament of the Altar? Answer: It is the true body and blood of our Lord Jesus Christ, under the bread and wine, given unto us Christians to eat and to drink, as it was instituted by Christ himself".

Im Grossen Katechismus: "Was ist nu das Sakrament des Altars? Antwort: Es ist der wahre Leib und Blut des HERRN. Christi, in und unter dem Brot und Wein durch Christus' Wort uns Christen befohlen zu essen und zu trinken". (*Ib.*, 709). Luther in the Large Catechism, V, 8, "Now, what is the Sacrament of the Altar? Answer: It is the true body and blood of the Lord Christ in and under the bread and wine, which we Christians are commanded by Christ's word to eat and drink".

In the Schmalkaldic Articles, cf., above n. 14.

Melanchthon in the *Confessio Augustana*, cf., above n. 7. The phrase "*Unter* der Gestalt" (under the form) of the German text is missing in the Latin. In the *Apologie*, Art. X, "...wir bekennen, daß unsers Herrn Christus Leib und Blut wahrhaftiglich im Nachtmahl zugegen und *mit* den sichtbaren Dingen, Brot und Wein, dargereicht und genommen wird..." "...confitemur nos sentire, quod in coena Domini vere et substantialiter adsint corpus et sanguis Christi et vere exhibeantur *cum* illis rebus, quae videntur, pane et vino, his qui sacramentum accipiunt". (*B.E.L.K.*, I, 247f.). In the Apology of the Augsburg Confession Art. X, "we confess our belief that in the Lord's Supper the body and blood of Christ are

Scholastic variations of the doctrine of consubstantiation[16] which, as already mentioned, was distinctly rejected at Trent. In fact, the reformer

truly and substantially present and are truly offered with those things that are seen, the bread and the wine, to those who receive the statement".

Confessio Augustana Variata 1540, Art. X: "De Coena Domini docent, quod *cum* pane et vino vere exhibeantur corpus et sanguis Christi vescentibus in Coena Domini".

Melanchthons Werke in Auswahl, Studienausgabe, herausgegeben von R. Stupperich, Gütersloh 1955, VI, 19.

Wittenberger Konkordie 1536 (Bucer, genauer: Formula Concordiae Lutheri et Buceri): "Sie (scil. Bucer und seine Gesinnungsfreunde) ... halten und lehren, das *mit* dem brot und wein, warhafftig und wesentlich zu gegen sey, und dargereicht und empfangen werde, der Leib und das blut Christi ... Sie halten nicht, das der leib und blut Christi Localiter, reumlich, ins brot eingeschlossen oder sonst leiblich damit vereinigt werde, außer der nießung des Sacraments, Doch so lassen sie zu, das durch Sacramentliche einigkeit, das brot sey der leib Christi, das ist, sie halten, so das brot dar gereicht wird, das *als denn zu gleich* gegenwertig sey, und warhafftig dar gereicht werde der leib Christi, etc. Denn außer der nießung ... halten sie nicht, das Christus leib zu gegen sey". In Ernst Bizer: *Studien zur Geschichte des Abendmahlsstreits im 16. Jahrhundert*, Gütersloh 1940, Nachdruck der Wissenschaftlichen Buchgesellschaft Darmstadt 1962, 118. "... Proinde sentiunt et docent *cum* pane et vino vere et substantialiter adesse, exhiberi et sumi corpus et sanguinem Christi. Et quanquam negant fieri transsubstantiationem, nec sentiunt fieri localem inclusionem in pane aut durabilem aliquam coniunctionen extra usum sacramenti: tamen concedunt sacramentali unione panem esse corpus Christi, hoc est, porrecto pane seniunt *simul* adesse et vere exhiberi corpus Christi. Nam extra usum ... sentiunt non adesse corpus Christi". Kürzende Zitierung der sog. Wittenberger Konkordie in der Konkordienformel 1580/84, Solida Declaratio, VII. Vom heiligen Abendmahl: (*B.E.L.K.*, II, 977). "The Wittenberg Concord of 1536 (Bucer, more accurately *Formula* Concordiae Lutheri et Buceri), They (that is, Bucer and his supporters) ... maintain and teach that, with the bread and wine, the body and the blood of Christ is truly and substantially present and is offered and received .... They do not hold that the body and blood of *Christi Localiter*, spacial, is contained in the bread or will be otherwise bodily united with it except in the usage of the sacraments. Yet, in this way, they allow that through sacramental unity the bread is the body of Christ, that is, they maintain that as the bread is administered at the same time the body of Christ is present and is truly administered etc. Thus, apart from the usage, ... they do not hold that the body of Christ is present".

Formula Concordie 1580/84: "... daß im heiligen Abendmahl der Leib und Blut Christi wahrhaftig und wesentlich gegenwärtig sei, *mit* Brot und Wein wahrhaftig ausgeteilt und empfangen werde". "... quod in coena Domini corpus et sanguis Christi vere et substantialiter sint praesentia et quod *una cum* pane et vino vere distribuantur atque sumantur". Epitome. (*B.E.L.K.*, II, 797.

Formula of Concord 1580/84, "We believe, teach, and confess that in the Holy Supper the body and blood of Christ are truly and essentially present and are truly distributed and received with the bread and wine".

"... daß der Leib und Blut Christi nicht allein geistlich durch den Glauben, sondern auch mündlich, doch nicht auf kapernaitische, sunder übernatürliche, himmlische Weise umb der *sakramentlichen Vereinigung* willen *mit* dem Brot und Wein empfangen werde ..."

"... corpus et sanguinem Christi non tantum spiritualiter per fidem, sed etiam ore, non tamen Capernaitice, sed supernaturali et coelesti modo, *ratione sacramentalis unionis, cum* pane et vino sumi". (*Ib.*, 799).

"We believe, teach, and confess that with the bread and the wine the body and blood of Christ are received not only spiritually, by faith but also orally—however, not in a Caper-

does not enter into an explanation of "how" the body of Christ is identical

---

naitic manner, but because of the sacramental union in a supernatural and heavenly manner".

"Daß neben den Reden (Ausdrucksweise) Christi und S. Pauli ... auch die Formen, < unter dem Brot, mit dem Brot, im Brot > gebrauchet (werden), ist die Ursach, daß hierdurch die papistische Transsubstantiation verworfen und des unvorwandelten Wesens des Brots und des Leibs Christi *sakramentliche Vereinigung* angezeigt würde..."

"Quod autem praeter illas phrases, quibus Christus et Paulus utuntur (cum dicunt panem in coena esse corpus Christi aut communicationem corporis Christi), etiam alias loquendi formas usurpamus, verbi gratia, cum dicimus *sub* pane, *cum* pane, *in* pane adesse et exhiberi corpus Christi, id non sine gravibus causis facimus. Primum enim his phrasibus ad reiiciendam papisticam transsubstantiationem utimur. Deinde etiam *sacramentalem unionem substantiae panis non mutatae et corporis Christi* hac ratione docere volumus". (*Ib.,* 983f.).

"In addition to the words of Christ and of St. Paul (the bread in the Lord's Supper "is true body of Christ" or "a participation in the body of Christ"), we at times also use the formulas "*under* the bread, *with* the bread, in the bread". We do this to reject the papistic transubstantiation and to indicate the sacramental union between the untransformed substance of the bread and the body of Christ".

In what follows, this *unio sacramentalis* of the elements with the body of Christ is expressly explained with the *unio* of both unaltered natures in Christ, except that here not *unio personalis* exists. The individual propositions have their exact meaning in their respective context of the discussion and of the texts. To go into them in detail, would lead too far and, for the present task would not produce very much. As a summary, we state,

a) "*Under* bread and wine" formulates most explicitly the real presence of the substance of the (transfigured) body and blood of Christ. Bread and wine are present only as *species*, they form only the outward garb. The substance of bread and wine is not considered. Questioning about it is actually dismissed. But "*sub speciebus panis et vini*" also expresses the doctrine of transsubstantiation. (cf., above n. 4). In the official texts, *Luther* prefers "under" except when he stands by "are".

b) "*In* bread and wine" raises the (unavoidable) question and constitutes the precise formulation of the doctrine of consubstantiation. The actual view of the *Formula of Concord* may be expressed here.

c) "*With* bread and wine", "*cum pane et vino*", distinctly separates the two substances and basically leaves open whether it is concerned with an instrumental or temporal togetherness (*unio sacramentalis: simul*). The first was held by *Melanchthon*. The latter depicts the compromise formula which *Bucer* and the Oberländer propose and which allowed them to approximate to Luther in expression and thereby theoretically to retain their fundamental Zwinglian difference, that actually "eating and drinking of the body and blood of Christ" is a spiritual process, namely faith.

d) The term *unio sacramentalis* in the Wittenberg concord of 1536 is used in the latter sense; thus the "union" reposes throughout in the carrying through of the celebration. The formula of concord of 1580, then annexes this expression for consubstantiation in which it makes the *unio sacramentalis* an act of divine power parallel to the christological *unio hypostatica.*

e) Note: Luther, moreover, did not acknowledge the so-called Wittenberg Concord as a concord but only as a concord proposal of Bucer and as a basis for discussion in a concord colloquy. Thus he felt justified in dismissing the "concord" in e.g. the Schmalcaldic articles of 1537. The Formula of Concord (1580) also treats the so-called Wittenberg Concord as an interim step.

16. From 1520 (*De captivitate Babilonica* ...), Luther rejects transsubstantiation: instead, he now takes up the old conception that the substance of the bread remains preserved, but the body of Christ is hidden and distributed in it. This goes back to the theory of impanation of

with the elements.[17] Thus, in spite of his strong rejection of the "abomination" of the mass,[18] one becomes aware in the mature Luther of the comparative indifference towards the doctrine of transubstantiation.[19] In order to understand Luther's teaching on the Lord's Supper, we must put it

the Berengar school, to Rupert von Deutz and Johannes Quidort of Paris. Duns Scotus then puts alongside the (seemingly) maintained *transsubstantiatio productiva* the *transsubstantiatio adductiva* as being much more plausible. The transsubstantiation occurs in that the body of Christ creates simultaneously in the substance of the bread a vacuity for itself. According to Ockham, the body of Christ exists in the Supper quantity-less although the body itself has quantity. Gabriel Biel also acknowledges the preservation of the substances of the elements and Pierre d'Ailly, to whom Luther explicitly refers, declares it to be definitely possible, and compatible with the Bible and with reason, that the substance of the bread "coexists" with that of the body of Christ. (Luther, W.A. VI, 508; also Cl. I. 438).—K. Algermissen, "Consubstantiation" in *L. Th. K.*, 1934, 1st ed., VI, col. 179.—J. Betz, "Consubstantiation" in *L. Th. K.*, 1961, 2nd ed., VI, col. 505 (a short but clear summary).—Reinhold Seeberg, *Lehrbuch der Dogmengeschichte*, 1930, 4th ed., III, 214f., 522f., 789f., 1933, IV, 399f.—Neuser, *Die Abendmahlslehre Melanchthons*, 371-385.

17. Luther im Grossen Katechismus, "Nu ist's nicht eins Fürsten oder Kaisers, sondern der hohen Majestät Wort und Ordnung, dafür alle Kreaturen sollen zu Füßen fallen und ja sprechen, daß es sei, wie er sagt, und mit allen Ehren, Furcht und Demut annehmen. Aus dem Wort kannst Du Dein Gewissen stärken und sprechen: wenn hunderttausend Teufel sampt allen Schwärmern herfahren: 'Wie kann Brot und Wein Christus' Leib und Blut sein?' etc., so weiß ich, daß alle Geister und Gelehrten auf einen Haufen nicht so klug sind als die göttliche Majestät im kleinsten Fingerlein. Nu stehet hie Christus' Wort: 'Nehmet, esset, das ist mein Leib', 'Trinket alle daraus, das ist das neue Testament in meinem Blut' etc., da bleiben wir bei und wöllen sie ansehen, die ihn meistern werden und anders machen, denn er's geredt hat". (*B.E.L.K.*, II, 709f.).

Luther in the Large Catechism, V, 11-13, "Now this is not the word and ordinance of a prince or emperor, but of the divine Majesty at whose feet every knee should bow and confess that it is as he says and should accept it with all reverence, fear, and humility. With this Word you can strengthen your conscience and declare: Let a hundred thousand devils, with all the fanatics, rush forward and say, 'How can bread and wine be Christ's body and blood?' Still I know that all the spirits and scholars put together have less wisdom than the divine Majesty has in his little finger. Here we have Christ's word, 'Take, eat; this is my body'. 'Drink of it, all of you, this is the new covenant in my blood', etc. Here we shall take our stand and see who dares to instruct Christ and alter what he has spoken".

18. "The mass in the papacy" is "the greatest and most horrible abomination" because of its character as a "sacrifice" and "work" by which it denies the "fundamental article" of justification by faith. (Schmalcaldic Articles in *B.E.L.K.*, I, 416; English translation in Book of Concord, ed. T. J. Tappert, Philadelphia 1959, 293).

19. Luther: "Von der Transsubstantiatio achten wir der spitzen Sophisterer gar nichts, da sie lehren, daß Brot und Wein verlassen oder verlieren ihr naturlich Wesen (naturalem suam substantiam) und bleibe allein Gestalt und Farbe des Brots und nicht recht Brot; denn es reimet sich mit der Schrift aufs best, daß Brot da sei und bleibe, wie es S. Paulus selbs nennet: 'Das Brot, das wir brechen' usw". (Schmal. Art., in *B.E.L.K.*, I, 452).

Luther Schmalcaldic Articles, part III, Article VI, 5, "As for transubstantiation, we have no regard for the subtle sophistry of those who teach that bread and wine surrender or lose their natural substance and retain only the appearance and shape of bread without any longer being real bread, for that bread is and remains there agrees better with the Scriptures, as St. Paul himself states, 'The bread which we break' (1 Cor. 10:16), and again, 'Let a man so eat of the bread' (1 Cor. 11:28)".

much more within the context of his entire theology and connect it to the central reformation questions of his, those concerning the certainty of faith and the comforting of the troubled conscience. "Therefore, we go to the sacrament so that we receive there such a great treasure, through and in which we receive forgiveness of sin".[20] Here it must be noticed how Luther, in consistent opposition to the current humanistic voices, puts the accent on the historicity, the concreteness and the worldly immediacy of the revelation of God's grace: in short, on the *humanity* of Jesus Christ. "We have to learn that there is no God apart from the one who is in this

---

20. Luther im Grossen Katechismus, "Nu siehe weiter auch die Kraft und Nutz, darümb endlich das Sakrament eingesetzet ist, welchs auch das Nötigste darin ist, daß man wisse, was wir da suchen und holen sollen. Das ist nu klar und leicht eben aus den gedachten Worten: 'Das ist mein Leib und Blut, FUR EUCH gegeben und vergossen zur Vergebunge der Sunde'. Das ist kürzlich soviel gesagt: darümb gehen wir zum Sakrament, daß wir da empfahen solchen Schatz, durch und in dem wir Vergebunge der Sunde überkommen. Warümb das? Darümb daß die Wort dastehen und uns solchs geben. Denn darümb heißet er mich essen und trinken, daß es mein sei und mir nütze als ein gewiß Pfand und Zeichen, ja eben dasselbige Gut, so fur mich gesetzt ist wider meine Sunde, Tod und alle Unglück ... Darümb ist es gegeben zur täglichen Weide und Futterung, daß sich der Glaube erhole und stärke, daß er in solchem Kampf nicht zurückfalle, sondern immer je stärker und stärker werde. Denn das neue Leben soll also getan sein, daß es stets zunehme und fortfahre. Es muß aber dagegen viel leiden. Denn so ein zorniger Feind ist der Teufel, wo er siehet, daß man sich wider ihn legt und den alten Menschen angreift und uns nicht mit Macht über- poltern kann, da schleicht und streicht er auf allen Seiten ümbher, versuchet alle Künste und lässet nicht abe, bis er uns zuletzt müde mache, daß man entweder den Glauben lässet fallen oder Hände und Füße gehen lässet und wird unlüstig oder ungedültig. Dazu ist nu der Trost gegeben, wenn das Herz solchs fühlet, daß ihm will zu schwer werden, daß er hie neue Kraft und Labsal hole". (*B.E.L.K.*, II, 711f.).

Luther in the Large Catechism, V, 20-27, "We have briefly considered the first part, namely, the essence of this sacrament. Now we come to its power and benefit, the purpose for which the sacrament was really instituted, for it is most necessary that we know what we should seek and obtain there. This is plainly evident from the words just quoted. 'This is my body and blood, given and poured out *for you* for the forgiveness of sins'. In other words, we go to the sacrament because we receive there a great treasure, through and in which we ob- tain the forgiveness of sins. Why? Because the words are there through which this is im- parted! Christ bids me eat and drink in order that the sacrament may be mine and may be a source of blessing to me as a sure pledge and sign—indeed, as the very gift he has provided for me against my sins, death, and all evils ... The Lord's Supper is given as a daily food and sustenance so that our faith may refresh and strengthen itself and not weaken in the struggle but grow continually stronger. For the new life should be one that continually develops and progress. Meanwhile it must suffer much opposition. The devil is a furious enemy: when he sees that we resist him and attack the old man, and when he cannot rout us by force, he sneaks and skulks about everywhere, trying all kinds of tricks, and does not stop until he has finally worn us out so that we either renounce our faith or yield hand and foot and become indifferent or impatient. For such times, when our heart feels too sorely pressed, this comfort of the Lord's Supper is given to bring us new strength and refreshment".

man (Jesus) who came down'',[21] here is meant, the one who humbled himself in our suffering, until the cross, who in the same embodiment follows us until today and offers himself to us in bread and wine. "In this, you have both, that it is Christ's body and blood and that it is yours as your treasure and gift".[22] Real Presence of the body of Christ with enfolds his divinity. The Lord's Supper is imparting grace.

f) You have learned concerning *Huldrych Zwingli*[23] that he "only" celebrates a meal of remembrance in which bread and wine "only" symbolise body and blood.[24] It should be noted in addition that, for the humanistic and Platonised student of Augustine, *"memoria"* *"remem-*

---

21. Luther: "Totus Christus est in carne. Nos apprehendimus nullum esse deum nisi illum, qui est in illo homine, qui descendit". WA·XX, 727, 5.—"Der Gott, der alles geschaffen hat und noch erhält, ... will sich nicht finden lassen, will auch nicht ... angetroffen werden, denn in diesem Fleisch und Blut des Sohns". (W.A. XXXIII, 185, 15f.). "God, who has created all things and still upholds them, ... will not let himself be found, nor likewise ... met, except in this flesh and blood of this Son".—"Wer das Fleisch trifft, der trifft Gott". (*Ib.*, 194, 23). "The one who meets the flesh, he meets God".—Paul-Wilhelm Gennrich, *Die Christologie Luthers im Abendmahlsstreit*, Königsberg 1929.—Albrecht Peters *Realpräsenz, Luthers Zeugnis von Christi Gegenwart im Abendmahl*, Lutherisches Verlagshaus, Berlin 1960.

22. Grosser Katechismus, (*B.E.L.K.*, II, 713), Luther, The Large Catechism, V, 29.

23. Alexander Barclay, *The Protestant Doctrine of the Lord's Supper*. A Study in the Eucharistic Teaching of Luther, Zwingli and Calvin. Glasgow 1927.—Cyril C. Richardson, *Zwingli and Cranmer on the Eucharist*. Evanston, III, 1949.—Walther Köhler, *Zwingli und Luther, ihr Streit über das Abendmahl* ... Bd. I, 1924, Bd. II, 1953; (cf. n. 2 above).

The leading thoughts of Köhler clearly emerge in his presentation in his posthumously published History of Christian Doctrine. (Walter Köhler, *Dogmengeschichte als Geschichte des christlichen Selbstbewustseins, Das Zeitalter der Reformation*, preface by Hans Barth, Zurich 1951, 70f., 262f., 360f.). Regarding Luther: "It is beyond all doubt, that obstinacy is not being expressed here but piety, which experienced its deepest and its most holy". (310). "With reference to Zwingli: "Zwingli obtained, from a critical exegesis, the original meaning of Jesus' celebration of the Lord's Supper as a meal of remembrance and set here the logic of thoughtful reason against Luther's doctrine of consubstantion ... It would be completely mistaken, because of that rational criticism, to see Zwingli's doctrine as mere rationalism. He had, at this point, no less then Luther, a most deeply religious interest: the preservation of the pure spirituality of the faith ..." (317). Concerning both, "The fundamental question for the history of Christian self-awareness was this, whether theology had the right to present the absurd as truth when it could be disguised as revelation: in other words, if the rent between reason and revelation is supportable. Zwingli expressed a definite No to this". (316).

24. Otto Ritschl, *Dogmengeschichte des Protestantismus*, Göttingen 1926, III, 85, describes Zwingli's view on the basis of Zwingli's interpretation of his 18th Article, "A memorial, however, in the ecclesiastical celebration of the Lord's Supper, should be a remembrance of what has once happened ... Thus Zwingli, in distinction to Luther, already from the beginning separated the sacrificial death of Christ as the sole ground for forgiveness of sins from the continually repeated recollection in the Lord's Supper. Zwingli found the testament of Christ in that event of the past; not, like Luther, in the ever recurrent, present, living, and faith-giving words of the institution". Further scholarly studies on Zwingli soon discovered that this description did not comprehend Zwingli's thought. Reinhold Seeberg, *Lehrbuch der Dogmengeschichte*, Leipzig 1933, 4th ed., IV, 460, thus already formulated Zwingli's view,

brance" does not mean retrospection but realisation, the authentic presence of the suffering of the Lord.[25] The miracle of the revelation lies in the fact that God himself was present in the man Jesus Christ and reconciled us with himself once and for all and thus brought us from our dependence upon the earthly to him.[26] The emphasis therefore is placed

---

"What concerns the Lord's Supper is, therefore, not a particular act of God's revelation and its apperception but a subjective act of faith and trust in Christ... While he executes this act of faith, he enjoys ideally the body of Christ. In this act, however, self realisation of Christ which grasps man, does not occur but a realisation of a past actuality which grasps Christ".

25. G. W. Locher, "The Characteristic Features...", cf. above pp. 222-224.

The difference between the common understanding of Zwingli and what Zwingli actually meant, is typified by the way in which a citation from the "Usslegen" of 1523, i.e. from the time before the controversy regarding the Lord's Supper, is handled. Reinhold Seeberg, *Grundriss der Dogmengeschichte*, Leipzig 1934, 6th imp., 144, cites without a reference, The Lord's Supper is "a remembrance of that which once happened". However, the place which was intended states (Zwingli), "This therefore will remain according to the great evidences of scripture: if the Holy Meal (*cibus*) of the soul is not an offering it is the recollection and remembrance of that which happened once, powerful to all eternity, and effects enough for our sin, satisfying the righteousness of God ... He says, Do this in remembrance of me, that is, put this into practice among you that you eat and drink my body and blood in remembrance of me, that is, that you renew with remembrance God's benefaction which I have bestowed upon you". (Z II, 136, 11-26); shortly before this paragraph, for the third time, "remembrance" is explained by "renewal". (R. Gwalther's translation of 1545 renders the process, "commemoratio", "recordatio et renovatio", "revocare in memoriam", "rememoratio".—"Attamen ista cum recoluntur, sacramentis non tantum ante oculos ponuntur, sed in mentem usque penetrant. Verum, quo duce? Spiritu". *De conv. Eccii*, S IV 32).

26. We wish to bring together two central texts from that early summary of Zwingli's preaching, the "Christlichen Ynleitung" ("Christian Introduction") ("Einleitung"—"Institutio"). In the explanation of the human, fallen, *sinful state*, one should note how the reformer closely relates the dogma to life in the psychological and sociological situation of his environment (renaissance man's desire for prestige and the first forms of exploitation emerging from early bourgeois capitalism).

"Nun ist der Präst und Val kummen uß unordenlicher Begird (ungezügelter Begehrlichkeit), namlich do Adam ouch wolt wüssend und groß, ja Gott glych werden. Also ouch hütbytag (heutzutage) ist ein ieder Mensch eygennützig, zühet im selbs fürer (drängt sich selbst vor) zuo Eer, Namen, Gwalt, Rychtag (Reichtum), Ruow (Ruhe, Bequemlichkeit); gevalt im selbs bas (gefällt sich selbst besser), denn er wardt ist; hat sich dafür, andrer Menschen Arbeit sölle im dienen, und ficht (strebt) darnach. Da hilfft kein Leugnen. Verhör ein ieder Mensch sin eygen Begird, so sind sy so groß, daß sy nieman ersettigen mag (befriedigen kann). Wo aber der Mensch in den (diesen) Stucken nit verhergt (kein Unheil anrichtet), ist nit siner, sunder Gottes Krafft ... Wir redend hie von dem Menschen und siner Vernunfft, Anschlag und Krafft; die sehend nach ihrer Natur allweg (stets) uff sich selbs zum ersten, zühend inen selbst zum ersten zuo. Kurtz, sy thuond nüt Rechts, sunder ytel (lauter) Eygennützigs". Z II 633, 7-19 (= I Zürich 1940, 253).

"Now, morbidity and the fall proceed from unrestrained covetousness, namely, that Adam also desired to become wise and great, indeed to be equal with God. In the same way, today, there is in each man selfishness thrusting himself forward to honour, name, power, riches, ease. He is better pleased with himself than he ought to be. He expects that other man should serve him and he strives thereafter. This cannot be denied. Everyman should

on the *divinity* of Christ[27] and the alternative is, either we have been redeemed at the cross or we have to receive redemption continually anew through the sacrament of the church.[28] But, where the congregation

---

cross-examine his own desires; they are so great that no one is able to satisfy them. But where man does not cause disaster through these things, it is not by his power but by God's ... We speak here of man and his reason, design and power, which in accordance with their nature, are primarily self-seeking. In short, they do nothing right, only manifold selfishness''.

In the exposition of the *gospel*, Zwingli always starts from the (satisfactorily effected) reconciliation through Christ.

"Sich (siehe) aber dagegen, wie wyßlich Got alle unsere Prästen in Christo Jhesu ersetzt (wiedergutgemacht) hat: I. Christus ist gedemuetiget biß in den schmächlichen Tod des Crützes, Philipper 2, 8, und hat der das getragen, durch den wir geschaffen sind, umb unsertwillen. Also sind wir durch die Wyßheit Gottes, durch die wir geschaffen sind und wider die Adam gesündet hat, widerumb erlößt. 2.... 3. Ewige Säligkeit hat er (Christus) allen Menschen erworben; denn sy sind alle, durch in geschaffen, durch in erlößt. Und wie er ein (= der) ewiger Gott ist, also ist er thür und wärd gnueg, aller Menschen Sünde in die Ewigkeit hinzunemmen und in ewig Säligkeit inzufueren, Hebr. 9 und 10''. Z II 637, 32-638, 10 (H I 259f.).

"See, however, in the face of this, how wisely God in Christ Jesus has restored all our morbidity: 1. Christ has been humiliated unto the shameful death of the cross (Philippians II, 8) and he has borne it through which we are created for our sake. In this way, by the wisdom of God through which we have been created and against which Adam has sinned, we are redeemed again. 2. ... 3. He (Christ) has attained eternal blessedness for all men, because, they have all been created through him and redeemed through him. And as he is (the) eternal God, so he is precious and worthy enough to take away into eternity all men's sin and to lead them into eternal blessedness, Hebrews 9 and 10''.

Concerning the term "Prästen" "morbidity" as "unheilbarer Bruch" "irreparable breach". Cf. G. W. Locher, *Die Theologie Huldrych Zwinglis im Lichte seiner Christologie*, Bd. I: *Die Gotteslehre*, Zürich 1952, 137ff.—G.W. Locher, *Zwingli's Message*, pp. 34-37.

27. Zwingli'; "Christus nobis ea parte salutaris est, qua de coelo descendit, non qua ex illibatissima quidem virgine natus est, tametsi secundum eam parti ac mori oportuerit; sed nisi deus simul fuisset, qui moriebatur, non potuisset toti mundo salutaris esse...Hactenus tantum est nobis salutaris, quatenus pro nobis mactatus est; at secundum carnem mactari tantum potuit, et secundum divinitatem tantum salutaris esse''. Z III 779, 18-22, 34-36. "Christus ist unser Heil, insofern er vom Himmel herabgekommen, nicht insofern er aus der allerdings unbefleckten Jungfrau geboren ist—obgleich er dementsprechend leiden und sterben mußte. Aber wenn der, der da starb, nicht zugleich Gott gewesen wäre, hätte er nicht für die ganze Welt das Heil sein können ... Christus ist nur insoweit für uns das Heil, als er für uns geopfert ist. Aber nur nach seinem Fleisch konnte er geopfert werden und nur nach seiner Gottheit unser Heil sein''. "Christ is our salvation by virtue of that part of His natures by which He came down from heaven, not of that by which He was born of an immaculate virgin, though He had to suffer and die by this part; but unless He who died had also been God He could not have been salvation for the whole world ... for He is only in so far salvation unto us as He was slain for us; but He could be slain only according to the flesh and could be salvation bringing only according to His divinity''. (*The Latin Works of Huldreich Zwingli*, ed. C. N. Heller. Philadelphia 1929, III, 204-205).—Cf. G. W. Locher, *Theologie Zwinglis*, I, (cf. n. 26 above), 33-43. "Christus noster''.

28. Zwingli: "Falsa ergo religio est, quae docuit huius symbolici panis usum peccata delere; nam Christus solus delet peccata, qum moritur''. Z III 803, 28f. "It is, therefore,

"remembers" its salvation, there the Lord is present to their faith by virtue of his divinity, also according to his humanity or more particularly according to his human-historic actions.[29] Real Presence of the divinity of Christ which his humanity brings about.

As a rule, one has not paid attention to Zwingli's differently apprehended but thorough doctrine of the real presence because one has adhered to a contrary exegesis of the words of institution. Instead, one omitted one, other, deeper difference. According to Luther, Christ remains the agent from beginning to end: the Christian the receiver. Zwingli, on the other hand, as a result of his understanding of the sacrament, recognises the Christian community as the actor of the celebration.[30] "Do this in

---

false religion which taught that the use of this symbolical bread destroys sins; for Christ alone destroys sins by His death". (Heller, *op. cit.*, 233).

To Ambrosius Blarer in Constance, in the letter of the 4th May 1528: "Ecclesiae Christi ipse caput est, ecclesiae Christi caput pontifex Romanus est: an iste duo diversa sunt? Morte Christi solo delentur peccata, esu corporis Christi corporeo delentur peccata: an non et ista aeque distant?" Z IX 461, 12-15. "He is head himself over the church of Christ. The pope in Rome is head over the church of Christ. Are not these two sentences indeed different? Sins are cancelled through the death of Christ alone. Sins are cancelled through the bodily eating of the body of Christ. Do these two sentences not fall apart too in the same way?"

To Wolfgang Capito and Martin Bucer in Strasbourg, in the letter of 12th February 1531, "Dati ergo, dati, dati, inquam, corporis in cibum animae sacramentum dedit ... Dati ergo Christi sacramentum est praebitum". Z XI 341, 10f., 20f. "For the given, the given, I say, that given body for the nourishment of the soul, he has given a sacrament ... indeed a sacrament (a holy sign) for the given Christ has been presented (to the disciples)".

29. "Divini homines ... eucharistiam ... adpellant corpus Domini, quod in ea commemoratur Christum pro nobis carnem et adsumsisse et morti obtulisse ... Quod panis signum sit, res autem ipsa Christus vere pro nobis traditus et oblatio factus, quae quidem res nunciatur, praedicatur et creditur ab his scilicet qui dominicam coenam agunt. Attamen huius rei panis symbolum est quod sensui offertur, res autem ipsa menti praesens est". S IV 117f. "The Holy Fathers call ... the eucharist ... the body of the Lord, because in it is commemorated the fact that Christ took upon Himself flesh and died for us ... Because the bread is a sign, and the thing itself is Christ who was really delivered up and made an offering for us. This thing is proclaimed, preached and believed by those who celebrate the Lord's Supper. Yet the bread is a symbol of this thing which is presented to the senses, the thing itself is present to the mind". (*The Latin Works of Huldreich Zwingli*, ed. W. J. Hinke, Philadelphia 1922, II, 191).

30. With individual Christian's in view, Zwingli can say, "Sunt ergo sacramenta signa vel ceremoniae ... quibus se homo ecclesiae probat aut candidatum aut militem esse Christi, redduntque ecclesiam totam potius certiorem de tua fide quam te". Z III 761, 22-25. "The sacraments are, then, signs or ceremonials by which a man proves to the Church that he either aims to be, or is, a soldier of Christ, and which inform the whole Church rather than yourself of your faith". (Heller, *op. cit.*, 184).

Luther detected this "subjectivism" sometimes, "Was meinest du, daß Gott nach unserm Tuen oder Gläuben fragt ...? ... Solchs muß man immerdar treiben (einprägen). Denn damit kann man fast (durchaus) aller Rottengeister Geschwätze zurückstoßen, denn sie die Sakrament außer Gottes Wort ansehen als ein Ding, das wir tuen." Großer Kat., *B.E.L.K.*, 1930, II, 709. "Do you think God cares so much about our conduct and believing? This

remembrance of me". Thus, the supper is a meal of thanksgiving, of remembrance, of obligation and of fellowship.[31] The debate in all directions finally leads Zwingli to distinguish between "spiritual eating" from John 6, namely, the faith, and sacramental eating.[32] "When you comfort

must always be emphasized, for thus we can thoroughly refute all the babbling of the seditious spirits who regard the sacraments, contrary to the Word of God, as human performances". (*The Large Catechism*, V, 6-7).

31. In August 1524, sometime prior to the outbreak of the controversy, the official "Christian answer of the Burgermeister and council of Zurich to bishop Hugo of Constance" already made it clear how they conceived of the Lord's Supper: instituted by Christ in memory of his death on the cross, fellowship meal, a sign of our obligation, an act of confession before God and man, and the way one is founded upon the other. (Z III 226-228).

"Εὐχαριστίας nomen dederunt Graeci coenae dominicae, pientiores semper ac doctiores, verbo absit invidia, Latinis homines, ut ipsorum monimenta sole clarius testantur. Dederunt autem indubie hac causa id nominis, quod tam ex fide quam verborum Christi apostolique vi intellegerunt, Christum hac coena voluisse iucundam sui commemorationem fieri, gratiasque publice haberi pro beneficio, quod in nos liberaliter expendit. Est enim eucharistia gratiarum actio. Qui ergo in hac publica gratiarum actione interesset, toti se ecclesiae probaret ex eorum esse numero, qui Christo pro nobis exposito fiderent, e quo se numero eximere, subducere aut alienare, sive desertione, sive impuritate vitae, summa esset perfidia. Unde et <communio> vel <communicatio> apud Paulum I. Corin. 10 (16) vocatur. Hinc etiam <excommunicatio>, qum scilicet alicui negabatur ad hanc fidelium communicationem accessus, propter vitae spuriciam. Tenemus ergo nunc ipso nomine, quid eucharistia, id est: coena dominica, sit, nempe: gratiarum actio et communis gratulatio eorum, qui mortem Christi annunciant, hoc est: ebuccinant, laudant, confitentur ac unice exaltant". Z III 775, 20-37.

"The Greeks gave the name Εὐχαριστία to the Lord's Supper, having always, if I may be permitted to say so, been more pious and more learned men than the Latins, as their written works bear witness clearer than day. And they undoubtedly gave it this name for the reason that they understood, both from faith and from the meaning of the words of Christ and the Apostle, that Christ wished to have a joyful commemoration of Himself made by this supper and thanks given publicly for the blessing which He has bountifully bestowed upon us. For the Eucharist is a thanksgiving. He, therefore, that would take part in this public thanksgiving should prove to the whole Church that he is of the number of those who trust in the Christ who died for us: to remove, to withdraw, or to estrange one's self from that number, whether by desertion or by uncleanness of life, would be the height of faithlessness. Hence, also, the Eucharist is called Communion or Communication by Paul. I Cor. 10:16. From this comes excommunication, too, or denying someone access to this communication of the faithful on account of impurity of life. We therefore now understand from the very name what the Eucharist, that is, the Lord's Supper, is: namely, the thanksgiving and common rejoicing of those who declare the death of Christ, that is, trumpet, praise, confess, and exalt His name above all others". (Heller, *op. cit.*, 199-200).

32. In the so-called *Fidei Expositio* of 1531. Because this was loaded with manifold problems and was posthumously published only in 1536 (G. W. Locher, "Zu Zwinglis 'Professio fidei'. Beobachtungen und Erwägungen zur Pariser Reinschrift der sogenannten Fidei Expositio", in *Zwingliana*, 1968/2, XII/10, 689-700) this distinction, in the Lord's Supper controversy, in the Zwinglian sense was not mentioned again. A summary is to be found in S IV S. 74, "Adserimus igitur non sic carnaliter et crasse manducari corpus Christi in coena ut isti perhibent, sed verum Christi corpus credimus in coena sacramentaliter et spiritualiter edi a religiosa, fideli et sancta mente". The difference was already developed there, pages 53f.: see the following note.

yourself in Christ, then you eat his body *spiritually*, that is to say, trusting in Him who assumed humanity for you sake, you remain unafraid taking a stand in God against all the arrows of despair. When you, however, come with this spiritual food, to the Lord's supper, and thank the Lord for this favour, for the redemption of the soul, whereby you are delivered from despair's destruction, and for the pledge, by which you are assured of eternal bliss; when you share, with the brethren, bread and wine which are the symbolic body of Christ, then, in a true sense you eat *sacramentally*, you indeed doing inwardly what you undertake outwardly. Then, the soul will be strengthened through the faith to which you bear witness with these symbols''.[33]

---

33. These sentences come towards the end of an explicit contrasting (S IV 53f) of "spiritualiter edere", "sacramentaliter edere ... quum proprie volumus loqui" and "sacramentaliter improprie dicuntur edere qui ...''. These distinctions do not only illuminate the core of Zwingli's teaching on the Lord's Supper but above all his piety; cf. the manifold founding on the experience of *Christus noster* (cf. Locher, *Die Theologie Huldrych Zwinglis*, 33f., 98f., 140f.). In order to clarify the above mentioned sentences we quote out of the section some definitions:

Zwingli: "Non editur itaque a nobis naturaliter, aut per essentiam corpus Christi; quanto magis non mensuraliter, sed solum *sacramentaliter* et *spiritualiter* ...

Spiritualiter edere corpus Christi nihil est aliud quam spiritu ac mente niti misericordia et bonitate dei per Christum; hoc est: inconcussa fide certum esse deum nobis peccatorum veniam et aeternae beatitudinis gaudium donaturum esse propter filium suum, qui noster totus factus, et pro nobis oblatus, divinam iustitiam nobis reconciliavit. Quid enim negare poterit qui unigenitum filium suum dedit? (Rom. 8).

Sacramentaliter autem *edere* corpus Christi, quum *proprie* volumus loqui, est adiuncto sacramento mente ac spiritu corpus Christi edere ...

Spiritualiter edis corpus Christi, non tamen sacramentaliter, quoties mentem tuam sic anxiam: Quomodo salvus fies?... Quum inquam sic anxiam mentem tuam sic solaberis: Deus bonus est: qui bonus est iustum et misericordem aut aequum esse oportet ... Istorum utriusque pignus habeo infallibile, unigenitum eius filium dominum nostrum Iesum Christum, quem ex misericordia nobis donavit ut noster esset ... Sic inquam cum Christo te solaris, iam spiritualiter corpus eius edis, hoc est, hominis propter te adsumpti fiducia imperterritus in deo stas contra omnia desperationis tela.

Verum quum ad coenam domini cum hac spirituali manducatione venis et domino gratias agis pro tanto beneficio, pro animi tui liberatione, qua liberatus es a desperationis pernicie, et pro pignore quo certus es de aeterna beatitudine; ac simul cum fratribus panem et vinum, quae iam symbolicum Christi corpus sunt, participias, iam *proprie sacramentaliter edis,* cum scilicet intus idem agis quod fore operaris, quum mens reficitur hac fide quam symbolis testaris.

At *sacramentaliter improprie* dicuntur *edere*, qui visible sacramentum sive symbolum publice quidem comedunt, sed domi fidem non habent. Hi ergo iudicium, hoc est, vindictam dei comedendo in se provocant, eo quod corpus Christi, hoc est, totum incarnationis passionisque mysterium, atque adeo ecclesiam ipsam Christi non habent pretio tanto quo a piis iure habetur ... Isti ergo sacramentaliter tantum edere dicuntur, qui symbolis gratiarum actionis utuntur quidem in coena, sed fidem non habent...''.

"Hence the body of Christ is not eaten by us naturally or literally, much less quantitatively, but *sacramentally and spiritually*. To eat the body of Christ *spiritually* is equivalent to trusting

That is indeed not insignificant. Yet, the Lutherans were of opinion that, as far as this view is concerned, the essential *gift* of the sacrament gets lost.

g) *John Calvin* also raises this objection.[34] [35] [36] Like Luther, he humbly admits that the sacrament is needed as "a support to the frailty of our

---

with heart and soul upon the mercy and goodness of God through Christ, that is, to have the assurance of an unbroken faith that God will give us the forgiveness of sins and the joy of eternal salvation for the sake of his Son, who gave himself for us and reconciled the divine righteousness to us. For what can he withhold from us when he delivered up his only begotten Son?

Properly said, To eat the body of Christ *sacramentally* is to eat the body of Christ with the heart and the mind in conjunction with the sacrament ...

You eat the body of Christ *spiritually*, but not sacramentally, every time your soul puts the anxious question: 'How are you to be saved?' But then you assure your anxious spirit: 'God is good: and he who is good must necessarily be righteous and merciful and kind'. Of both these things I have an infallible pledge, his only begotten Son our Lord Jesus Christ, whom of his own mercy God has given to us that he might be ours. On our behalf he has sacrificed himself to the Father to reconcile his eternal justice, that we might have assurance both of the mercy of God and of the atonement made to his justice for our sins by none other than his only begotten Son, whom of his love he gave to us". When your soul is troubled by anxiety and despair, confirm it with this confidence: 'Why are you cast down, O my soul? The God who alone gives salvation is yours, and you are his. You were his handiwork and creation, and you fell and perished. But he sent his Son and made him like yourself, except only for sin, that resting on all the rights and privileges of so great a brother and companion you might have boldness to lay claim to eternal salvation. What devil can frighten or terrify me when this helper stands by me to assist? Who can rob me of that which God himself has given, sending his own Son as pledge and surety? When you comfort yourself in Christ in this way, then you *spiritually* eat his body, that is, trusting in the humanity which he assumed for your sake, you stand unafraid in God against all the onslaughts of despair.

So then, when you come to the Lord's Supper to feed spiritually upon Christ, and when you thank the Lord for his great favour, for the redemption whereby you are delivered from despair, and for the pledge whereby you are assured of eternal salvation; when you join with your brethren in partaking of the bread and wine which are the tokens of the body of Christ, then, *properly said, you eat sacramentally*. You do inwardly that which you represent outwardly, your soul being strengthened by the faith which you attest in the tokens.

But of those who publicly partake of the visible sacraments or signs, yet without faith, *then improperly said they eat sacramentally*. By partaking they call down judgment upon themselves, that is, divine punishment, for they do not honour the body of Christ, that is, the whole mystery of the incarnation and passion and indeed the Church of Christ, as the faithful are always doing, and rightly so. Mere sacramental eating—that is to say, are those who make use of the signs of thanksgiving without having faith".

34. *Catechismus Genevensis* 1545: "Le ministre: Avons-nous en la Cène simplement le tesmoinage des choses dessusdictes, ou si elles y sont vrauyment données? L'enfant: Entant que Jesus Christ est la verité, il ne fault doubter que les promesses qu'il fait à la Cène, n'y soyent accomplies; et que ce qu'il y figure, n'y soit verifié. Ainsi, selon qu'il le promet et represente, je ne doubte pas qu'il ne nous face participans de sa propre substance, pour nous unir avec soy en une vie. Minister: Solamne corum, quae dixisti, beneficiorum significationem habemus in coena, an illic re ipsa nobis exhibentur? Puer: Quum Dominus noster Christus ipsa sit veritas, minime dubium est, quin promissiones, quas dat illic nobis, simul etiam impleat, et figuris suam addat veritatem. Quamobrem non dubito, quin sicuti

faith".[37] He acknowledged almost all of Zwingli's objections. He, too, stressed God's superiority and took over the figurative interpretation of

verbis ac signis testatur, ita etiam suae nos substantiae participes faciat, quo in unam cum eo vitam coalescamus". CR Calv. Opp. VI col. 127f.

"M: Have we in the Supper only a figure of the benefits which you have mentioned, or are they there exhibited to us in reality? S: Seeing that our Lord Jesus Christ is truth itself, there cannot be a doubt that he at the same time fulfils the promises which he there gives us, and adds the reality to the figures. Wherefore I doubt not that as he testifies by words and signs, so he also makes us partakers of his substance, that thus we may have one life with him". (John Calvin's Tracts and Treatises, edd., T. F. and D. W. Torrance, Edinburgh 19, II. 91).

On closer inspection, the whole discussion regarding the sacraments in the Catechism of Geneva presents one single debate with Zwinglianism and its arguments—which is proof of how strongly this attitude was represented in Geneva. Only a short delimitation from Luther follows temporarily. Viz à viz Zwingli, cf. especially n. 46 below.

35. Calvin: *Institutio*, IV, capp. XIV und XVII.—Herman Bavinck; "Calvyns leer over het Avondmaal (1887)" in H. Bavinck, *Kennis en leven*, Kampen 1922, 165-183.—Joachim Beckmann, *Vom Sakrament bei Calvin. Die Sakramentslehre Calvins in ihren Beziehungen zu Augustin*, Mohr/Siebeck, Tübingen 1926.—Wilhelm Niesel, *Die Theologie Calvins*, Chr. Kaiser, München 1938.—J. A. Cramer, "De avondmaalsleer by Calvyin" in *Nieuwe Theologische Studien*, 22. jaargang (1939), 266-282.—Ronald S. Wallace, *Calvin's Doctrine of the Word and Sacrament*, Oliver and Boyd, Edinburgh and London 1953.—G. P. Hartvelt, *Verum corpus. Een studie over een centraal hoofdstuk uit de avondmaalsleer von Calvijn*, Delft 1960. —Heinrich Janssen, "Die Abendmahlslehre Johannes Calvins", in Thomas Sarborg OSB (Hsg.), *Die Eucharistie im Verständnis der Konfessionen*, Paulus-Verlag, Recklinghausen 1961, 204-220.—Paul Jacobs, "Pneumatische Realpräsenz bei Calvin", in *Regards contemporains sur Jean Calvin*. Actes du Colloque Calvin Strasbourg 1964 (Cahiers de la Revue d'Histoire et de Philosophie Religieuses, publiés sous les Auspices de Faculté de Théologie Protestante de l'Université de Strasbourg, No. 39, Presses Universitaires de France, Paris 1965, 389-407).—Joachim Rogge, *Virtus und Res. Um die Abendmahlswirklichkeit bei Calvin*, Arbeiten zur Theologie I/18, Calwer Stuttgart 1965.—G. S. M. Walker, "The Lord's Supper in the Theology and Practice of Calvin", in *John Calvin. Courtenay Studies in Reformation Theology* I, The Sutton Courtenay Press Appleford, Abingdon, Berkshire 1966, 131-148.—Kilian McDonnell OSB, *John Calvin, the Church and the Eucharist*, Princeton University Press Princeton N.Y. 1967. Hughes O. Old, *The Patristic roots of reformed worship Dissertation*, Neuchâtel 1972.

36. *The Institutes* IV, xvii. It has a different meaning from Luther's "under" (cf., n. 15 above), when Calvin consistently says, "sub symbolis panis et vini". "Symbolum" always points from the *carnalia* to the *spiritualia*. cf., Institutio, IV, xvii, 32, "Pronunciat ille carnem suam esse animae meae cibum, sanguinem esse potam. Talibus alimentis animam illi meam pascendam offero. In sacra sua Coena iubet me sub symbolis panis ac vini corpus ac sanguinem suum sumere, manducare et bibere; nihil dubito quin et ipse vere porrigat, et ego recipiam". Calvini OS V 390. "He declares his flesh the food of my soul, his blood its drink (John VI, 53f.); I offer my soul to him to be fed with such food. In his Sacred Supper he bids me take, eat, and drink his body and blood under the symbols of bread and wine. I do not doubt that he himself truly presents them and that I receive them". (Calvin: *Institutes of the Christian Religion*, ed. J. T. McNeill and Trans. F. L. Battles, London 1961, 1403-4).

CR XX, c. 73. (In the letter no. 3986, to the Elector Frederick III of the Palatinate, of 23rd July 1563). "Christi carne et sanguine vere nos in sacra coena pasci, non secus ac panis et vinum corporum sunt alimenta, ingenue fatemur. Si quaeritur explicatio magis dilucida, carnis et sanguinis Christi substantia nobis vita est, eaque sub panis et vini symbolis nobis

the words of institution;[38] the elements are images[39] and the Supper is also
an act of confession of faith.[40] However, he determinedly applies to the

communicatur: quia Christus mysterium coenae instituens neque fallaciter quidquam pro-
misit, neque lusit inanibus spectris, sed quod se ipsa dabat externis signis repraesentavit".
"We sincerely confess that we will be truly nourished through the flesh and blood of Christ
in the Holy Supper, this is in no way different from bread and wine nourishing the body.
Should one require a clearer explanation; the substance of the flesh and blood of Christ is
our spiritual life and particularly it is being distributed to us under the symbol of bread and
wine. Because Christ instituted the sacrament of the Lord's Supper, he has neither given a
false promise nor played a game with empty concepts, but he has represented with visible
signs what he actually gave".

Inst. IV, XVII, 3: "... a rebus corporeis quae in sacramento proferuntur, quadam
analogia nos ad sprituales adduci". OS V 344. "And so as we have previously stated, from
the physical things set forth in the Sacrament we are lead by a sort of analogy to spiritual
things". (*Institutes*, 1363).

37. "Le ministre: L'imperfection donc ne nous empesche point d'en approcher. L'enfant: Mais au contraire, elle ne nous serviroit de rien, si nous n'estions imparfaictz. Car c'est
une aide et soulagement de nostre infimité". Minister: Non ergo ab accessu nos arcet im-
perfectio qua adhuc laboramus. Puer: Quin potius, si perfecti essemes, nullum amplius
usum inter nos haberet coena: quae sublevandae nostrae imbecillitati adminiculum esse
debet ac imperfectionis subsidium". Catechismus Genevensis 1545, CR Calv. Opp. VI col.
129ff.

"M.: Then the imperfection under which we still labour does not forbid our approach? S.:
On the contrary, were we perfect, the Supper would no longer be of any use to us. It should
be a help to aid our weakness, and a support to our imperfection". (*Tracts*, 92).

38. In his exegesis in the words of institution, *Calvin* explains that "consecration" no way
effects a substantiae mutatio of the bread involved, but it marks a *alius,* namely *spiritualis usus*
of the same. Then he continues, among other things, with reference to Augustine, "Fateri
necesse est, Sacramentum visibili signo constare, cui res signata coniuncta est, quae est eius
veritas. Iam et hoc satis tritum esse debet, rei signatae nomen ad signum transferri. Quare
nemo in Scriptura mediocriter versatus negabit, quin sacramentalis locutio metonymice
sumenda sit ..." *Johannis Calvini in Harmoniam ex Matthaeo, Marco et Luca compositam commentarii
... Ed. A. Tholuck*, Berlin 1833, Bd. II, p. 312. "We must state that a sacrament consists in a
visible sign to which the thing signified is conjoined and this is its reality (*veritas*). This
ground should be familiar enough by the name of the thing signified being transferred to the
sign. No one with a moderate aquaintance of scripture will deny that sacramental expression
must be taken metonymy. (*A Harmony of the Gospels of Matthew, Mark and Luke*, trans. A. W.
Morrison, Edinburgh 1972, III, 134).

39. E.g., "Figurant". Cf., n. 38 above.

40. The continuation of n. 37 of the aforementioned section states, "Le Ministre: Ces
deux Sacraments ne servent ilz point à autre fin? L'Enfant: Si font, d'autant que ce sont
signes et marques de nostre profession. C'est à dire, que par iceux nous protestons que nous
sommes du peuple de Dieu, et faisons confession de nostre Chrestienté". "Minister:
Nullumne praeterea alium finem propositum habent duo haec sacramenta? Puer: Sunt
etiam professionis nostrae notae et quasi tesserae quaedam. Illorum enim usu fidem apud
homines nostram profitemur, et testamur nos unum habere in Christo religionis
consensum". Catech. Genev. 1545, CR Calv. Opp. VI, col. 131f.

"M. Is no other end besides proposed by these two Sacraments? S. They are also marks
and as it were badges of our profession. For by the use of them we profess our faith before
men, and testify our consent in the religion of Christ". (*Tracts*, 92).

sacraments the terms, "seal" and "pledge of grace",[41] which Zwingli reserves for Christ himself.[42] Furthermore, Calvin explains, as Luther would be able to say, "the body of Christ, which had once been offered as a sin offering, will also now be given to us so that we know for certain that reconciliation applies to us as well".[43] Nevertheless, that is not to be found

---

41. Cf. Features, above p. 228.

42. "Minister: Quid est sacramentum? Puer: Externa divinae erga nos benevolentiae testificatio, quae visibili signo spirituales gratias figurant, ad obsignandas cordibus nostris Dei promissiones, quo earum veritas melius confirmetur". Cat. Genev., see note 40, col. 112.

"M.: What is a Sacrament? S.: An outward attestation of the divine benevolence towards us, which, by a visible sign, figures spiritual grace, to seal the promises of God on our hearts, and thereby better confirm their truth to us". (*Tracts*, 83-84).

Calvin often describes the sacraments as *tesserae*, marks; cf. n. 39 above, and *Institutes*, IV, xiv, 1, and *pignora*, pledges; *ibid.*, IV, xiv, 12 and xvii, 1. "Le Ministre: Tu entens donc qu'il y a deux choses en ce Sacrament: le pain materiel, et le vin que nous voyons à l'œil, touchons à la main, et savourons au goust; et Jesus Christ, dont noz ames sont interieurement nourries. L'Enfant: Voire. En telle sorte neantmoins que nous y avons mesme tesmoinage, et comme une arre de la resurrection de noz corps: entant qu'ilz sont faictz participans du signe de vie". "Minister: Ut in summam colligamus quae dixisti: duas in coena res esse asseris: nempe panem et vinum, quae oculis cernuntur, attrectantur manibus, percipiuntur gustu: deinde Christum, quo interius animae nostrae, tamquam proprio suo alimento, pascuntur. Puer: Verum, et eo quidem usque, et corporum etiam resurrectio illic nobis, quasi dato pignore, confirmetur: quum et ipsa vitae symbolo communicent". CR Calv. Opp. VI Col. 129f.

"M.: To collect the substance of what you have said—You maintain that there are two things in the Supper, viz, bread and wine, which are seen by the eyes, handled by the hands, and perceived by the taste, and Christ by whom our souls are inwardly fed as with their own proper aliment? S.: True; and so much so that the resurrection of the body also is there confirmed to us by a kind of pledge, since the body also shares in the symbol of life". (*Tracts*, 91-92).

43. The question wherein the proprium of the Lord's Supper exists beyond baptism and preaching of the Gospel is being answered in the Genevan Catechism in the following way:

"Minister: Quid amplius ex sacramento consequimur, aut quid praeterea utilitatis nobis confert? Puer: Hoc scilicet, quod illa, de qua dixi, communicatio nobis confirmatur et augetur. Tametsi enim tum in baptismo, tum in evangelio nobis exhibetur Christus: eum tamen non recipimus totum, sed ex parte tantum. Minister: Quid ergo in symbolo panis habemus? Puer: Corpus Christi, ut semel pro nobis ad nos Deo reconciliandos immolatum fuit, ita nunc quoque nobis dari: ut certo sciamus, reconciliationem ad nos pertinere. Minister: Quid in sanguinis symbolo? Puer: Christum, ut suum sanguinem semel in peccatorum satisfactionem, pretiumque redemptionis nostrae ipsum effudit, ita nunc eum nobis bibendum porrigere, ut fructum, qui inde pervenire ad nos debet, sentiamus". CR Calv. Opp. VI col. 125f.

"M.: What more do we obtain from the sacrament, or what other benefit does it confer upon us? S.: The communion of which I spoke is thereby confirmed and increased; for although Christ is exhibited to us both in baptism and in the gospel, we do not however receive him entire; but in part only. M.: What then have we in the symbol of bread? S.: As the body of Christ was once sacrificed for us to reconcile us to God, so now also is it given to us, that we may certainly know that reconciliation belongs to us. M.: What in the symbol of wine? S.: That as Christ once shed his blood for the satisfaction of our sins, and as the price of our redemption, so he now also gives it to us to drink, that we may feel the benefit which should thence accrue to us". (*Tracts*, 90).

as bread nor in the bread but "in the symbol of the bread; and it is our souls which,[44] "through the communion of his body and blood, are being nourished in the hope of eternal life".[45] The "awareness, that Christ dwells in us, and that we have communion with him of such a close kind that he is the head and we are the members",[46] will be "confirmed and in-

---

44. Cf. nn. 36 and 43 above.

45. "Minister: ... Quae est coenae significatio? Puer: Ideo a Christo instituta est, ut corporis et sanguinis sui communicatione educari in spem vitae aeternae animas nostras nos doceret, idque nobis certum redderet". "Le Ministre: ... Quelle est la signification de la Cène? L'Enfant: Nostre Seigneur l'a instituée pour nous asseurer que par la communication de son corps et de son sang, noz ames sont nourries en esperance de la vie eternelle". Cat. Gen. 1545, CR Calv. Opp. Vol. VI, col. 123f.

"M.: Let us now pass to the Supper. And, first, I should like to know from you what its meaning is. S.: It was instituted by Christ in order that by the communication of his body and blood, he might teach and assure us that our souls are being trained in the hope of eternal life". (*Tracts*, 89).

46. The decisive argumentation against Zwingli in the Genevan catechism which shows at the same time that in 1545 Calvin understood Zwingli very well and took him seriously and even used central Zwinglian concepts such as *christus noster*, states:

"Le ministre: Entens-tu qu'il nous faille communiquer vrayement au corps et au sang zu Seigneur? L'Enfant: Ie l'entens ainsi. Car puis que toute la fiance de nostre salut gist en l'obeissance qu'il a rendue à Dieu son pere: entant qu'elle nous est imputée, comme si elle estoit nostre, il faut que nous le possedions. Vue que ses biens ne sont pas nostres, sinon que premierement il se donne à nous. Le ministre: Mais ne s'est-il pas donné à nous, quand il s'est exposé à la mort pour nous reconciler à Dieu son Pere, et nous delivrer de damnation? L'enfant: Si est bien. Mais il ne suffit pas de cela, sinon que nous recevions, pour sentir en nous le fruict et l'efficace de sa mort et passion. Le ministre: La maniere de la recevoir, est-ce point par Foy? L'enfant: Ouy. Non seulement en croyant qu'il est mort et resuscité pour nous delivrer de la mort eternelle, et nous acquerir la vie: mais aussi qu'il habite en nous, et est conioinct avec nous en telle union que le chef avec ses membres, afin de nous faire participans de toutes ses graces, en vertu de ceste conionction". "Minister: Ergone corpore Domini et sanguine vescimur? Puer: Ita sentio. Nam quum in eo sita sit tota salutis nostrae fiducia, ut accepta nobis feratur obedientia ipsius, quam patri praestitit, perinde ac si nostra foret: ipsum a nobis possideri necesse est. Neque enim bona nobis sua aliter communicat, nisi dum se nostrum facit. Minister: Atqui, nonne tunc se dedit, quum se exposuit in mortem, ut nos a mortis iudicio redemptos patri reconciliaret? Puer: Id quidem verum est: sed non satis est nobis nisi eum nunc recipiamus: quo mortis eius efficacia fructusque ad nos perveniat. Minister: Recipiendi porro modus an non fide constat? Puer: Fateor. Sed hoc simul addo, fieri id, dum non solum mortuum credimus, quo nos a morte liberaret et suscitatum, quo nobis vitam acquireret: sed in nobis quoque habitare agnoscimus, nosque illi coniunctos esse eo unitatis genere, quo membra cum capite suo cohaerent: ut huius unitatis beneficio omnium eius bonorum participes fiamus". Cat. Genev. 1545 Calv. Opp. Vol. VI, col. 123ff.

M.: Do we therefore eat the body and blood of the Lord? S.: I understand so. For as our whole reliance for salvation depends on him, in order that the obedience which he yielded to the Father may be imputed to us just as if it were ours, it is necessary that he be possessed by us; for the only way in which he communicates his blessings to us is by making himself ours. M.: But did he not give himself when he exposed himself to death, that he might redeem us from the sentence of death, and reconcile us to God? S.: That is indeed true; but it is not enough for us unless we now receive him, that thus the efficacy and fruit of his death may

creased"[47] through the sacrament in a special way. The image instituted by Christ is a truthful promise. Therefore, "is with the image the object there"[48] that he makes us share in "his substance so that, through it, we are permitted to grow together into one life".[49] This takes place through the Holy Spirit who raises our souls to the transfigured Christ.[50] Christ's spiritual presence with us, and ours with him.[51]

We discern some of the important themes of Calvin's theology: God's divine freedom, the *unio cum Christo*, the upbuilding of the visible church. The Lord's Supper is completion, pledge, pardon's sign.

h) Now we venture to comprehensively summarise some main lines of thought: we do this with a carefulness appropriate to every schematisation and with the reservation of numerous additions and comments, several of which we have already indicated:

Luther expects, in the Lord's Supper, the *bodily* union of the receivers with
    the *body* of Christ (in the elements),

Zwingli expects, in the Lord's Supper, the union of the *soul* of the celebra-
    tors with the *divine nature* of Christ (present in human nature through
    remembrance of his suffering),

Calvin expects, in the Lord's Supper, the union of the *soul* of the receivers
    with the *body* of Christ (in heaven).

i) The pledge and sign are those which come to the forefront in the *Heidelberg Catechism*, which enjoyed the widest circulation within the

---

reach us. M.: Does not the manner of receiving consist in faith? S.: I admit it does. But I at the same time add, that this is done when we not only believe that he died in order to free us from death, and was raised up that he might purchase life for us, but recognise that he dwells in us, and that we are united to him by a union same in kind as that which unites the members to the head, that by virtue of this union we may become partakers of all his blessings". (*Tracts*, 89-90).

47. Cf. n. 43 above.

48. Cf. n. 34 above.

49. Cf. n. 34 above.

50. "Minister: Verum, qui hoc fieri potest, quum in coelo sit Christi corpus: nos autem in terra adhuc peregrinemur? Puer: Hoc mirificia arcanaque spiritus sui virtute efficit: cui difficile non est sociare, quae locorum intervallo alioqui sont disiuncta". Cat. Gen. CR Calv. Opp. VI, col. 127s.

"M.: But how can this be, when the body of Christ is in heaven, and we are still pilgrims on the earth? S.: This he accomplishes by the secret and miraculous agency of his Spirit, to whom it is not difficult to unite things otherwise disjoined by a distant space". (*Tracts*, 91).

51. Calvin counts on a real spiritual nearness of the soul to the transfigured Christ, simultaneously with a real spiritual radiating power of the transfigured body of the Lord. (cp., particularly, J. Rogge, *Virtus and Res*. (cf. n. 35 above).

52. *Heidelberger Katechismus* 1563, ed., H. Klugkist Hesse, in *Bekenntnisschriften und Kirchenordnungen der nach Gottes Wort reformierten Kirche*, ed. Wilhelm Niesel, EVZ, Zürich 1938, S. 149-181. *Von den heiligen Sakramenten* Fragen und Antworten 65-68. *Vom heiligen Abendmahl*

reformed churches, and which shaped the longest lasting piety while the Calvinist teaching, concerning the lifting up of the hearts to heaven, did not generally prevail everywhere.[53] Against the background of Luther's and Calvin's statements of the problem, the Heidelberg Catechism took over from Zwingli the term "sign" and that of "seal" from Calvin.[54] Thus it actually built a bridge as intended between the three reformers.

Jesu Christi FA 75-85.—*Catechesis Palatina* sive Heidelbergenesis. In: Collectio Confessionum in Ecclesiis Reformatis publicatarum, ed., H. A. Niemeyer, Lipsiae 1840, 430-461.—"The Heidelberg Catechism, 1563" in *Reformed Confessions of the 16th Century*, ed., with historical introductions, by A. C. Cochrane. Philadelphia 1966, 305-331.—Karl Sudhoff, *Theologisches Handbuch zur Auslegung des Heidelberger Katechismus*. Frankfurt a. M. und Erlangen 1862.—M. A. Gooszen, *De Heidelbergsche Catechismus*. Textus receptus met toelichtende texsten, Leipzig 1890.—Gerardus Oorthuys, *De Sacramenten*. Toelichting op de Zondagen XXIII tot XXXIII van den Heidelbergsen Catechismus. Nijkerk 1948.—Walter Hollweg, *Neue Untersuchungen zur Geschichte und Lehre des Heidelberger Katechismus*. Neukirchen 1961. Second part, Neukirchen 1968.—Pierre Ch. Marcel, "Die Lehre von der Kirche und den Sakramenten", in *Lothar Coenen* (ed.), *Handbuch zum Heidelberger Katechismus*, Neukirchen 1963, 135-158.—Ulrich Beyer, *Abendmahl und Messe. Sinn und Recht der 80. Frage des Heidelberger Katechismus*, Neukirchen 1965.

53. This doctrine is taken up in question and answer 76, although in a modified form, but it is, in my opinion, not clear, whether "it is to be so united more and more to his (Christ's) blessed body" happens by itself in the reception of the Lord's Supper (as in Calvin), or whether the Lord's Supper is also an image, a sign, a pledge of it. In the understanding of the reformed congregations, the "immediately as—that is" (sign, remembrance) and the "so indeed—so indeed" (assurance, seal, pledge) of the questions and answers 75, 77 (question), 78, 79, has impregnated itself.

54. *Von den heiligen Sacramenten*
65. Frag.—Dieweil denn allein der glaub vns Christi / vnd aller seiner wolthaten theilhafftig macht / woher kompt solcher glaube?
Antwort.—Der heilig Geist würckt denselben in vnsren hertzen / durch die predig des heiligen Euangelions / vnd bestätigt den durch den brauch der heiligen Sacramenten.
66. Frag.—Was seind die Sacrament?
Antwort.—Es seind sichtbare heilige warzeichen vnnd Sigill / von Gott darzu eingesetzt / daß er vns durch den brauch derselben / die verheißung des Euangelions desto besser zuuerstehen gebe / vnnd versigele: Nemlich daß er vns von wegen des einigen opffers Christi / am Creutz volbracht / vergebung der sünden / vnd ewiges leben auss gnaden schencke.
    Catechesis Palatina

    De Sacramentis
LXV. Quoniam igitur sola fides nos Christi atque omnium eius beneficiorum participes facit: unde haec fides proficiscitur? A Spiritu Sancto, qui eam per praedicationem Evangelii in cordibus nostris accedit, et per usum Sacramentorum confirmat.
LXVI. Quid sunt Sacramenta?
Sunt Sacra et in oculos incurrentia signa, ac sigilla, ob eam causam a Deo instituta, ut per ea nobis permissionem Evangelii magis declaret et obsignet: quod scilicet non universis tantum, verum etiam singulis credentibus, propter unicum illud Christi sacrificium in cruce peractum, gratis donet remissionem peccatorum, et vitam aeternam.

    Vom heiligen Abendmal Jesu Christi
75. Frag.—Wie wirstu im heiligen Abendmahl erinnert vnd versichert / daß du an dem einigen opffer Christi am Creutz / vnd allen seinen gütern gemeinschaft habest?
Antwort.—Also / daß Christus mir vnnd allen gläubigen von diesem gebrochnen brod zu

k) These doctrines have endured through times of controversy right down to the present day. They have deposited themselves in *liturgies,*

essen / vnnd von diesem Kelch zu trinken befohlen hat zu sienem gedechtniß / vnnd darbey verheißen Erstlich daß sein leib so gewiß für mich am Creutz geopffert vnd gebrochen / vnnd sein blut für mich vergossen sey / so gewiß ich mit augen sehe / daß das brod des HERRN mir gebrochen / vnd der Kelch mir mitgetheilet wird: Vnd zum andern / daß er selbst meine seel mit seinem gecreutzigten Leib vnnd vergoßnen Blut / so gewiß zu ewigen leben speise vnd trencke / als ich auß der hand des Dieners empfange / vnnd leiblich nieße das brod vnnd den Kelch des HERRN, welche mir als gewisse warzeichen des leibs vnd bluts Christi gegeben werden.

The Holy Sacraments

Q. 65. *Since, then, faith alone makes us share in Christ and all his benefits, where does such faith originate?*

A. The Holy Spirit creates it in our hearts by the preaching of the holy gospel, and confirms it by the use of the holy Sacraments.

Q. 66. *What are the Sacraments?*

A. They are visible, holy signs and seals instituted by God in order that by their use he may the more fully disclose and seal to us the promise of the gospel, namely, that because of the one sacrifice of Christ accomplished on the cross he graciously grants us the forgiveness of sins and eternal life.

Catechesis Palatina

De Sacramentis

LXV. Quoniam igitur sola fides nos Christi atque omnium eius beneficiorum participes facit: unde haec fides proficiscitur? A Spiritu Sancto, qui eam per praedicationem Evangelii in cordibus nostris accedit, et per usum Sacramentorum confirmat.

LXVI. Quid sunt Sacramenta?

Sunt Sacra et in oculos incurrentia signa, ac sigilla, ob eam causam a Deo instituta, ut per ea nobis promissionem Evangelii magis declaret et obsignet: quod scilicet non universis tantum, verum etiam singulis credentibus, propter unicum illud Christi sacrificium in cruce peractum, gratis donet remissionem peccatorum, et vitam aeternam.

The Holy Supper

Q. 75. *How are you reminded and assured in the holy Supper that you participate in the one sacrifice of Christ on the cross and in all his benefits?*

A. In this way: Christ has commanded me and all believers to eat of this broken bread, and to drink of this cup in remembrance of him. He has thereby promised that his body was offered and broken on the cross for me, and his blood was shed for me, as surely as I see with my eyes that the bread of the Lord is broken for me, and that the cup is shared with me. Also, he has promised that he himself as certainly feeds and nourishes my soul to everlasting life with his crucified body and shed blood as I receive from the hand of the minister and actually taste the bread and the cup of the Lord which are given to me as sure signs of the body and blood of Christ.

According to the Heidelberg catechism, the Holy Spirit is the active agent of the sacraments, who through their use (usus) confirms (confirmat) faith. The Kerygma is "sealed" "to give better understanding".

Cf. P. C. Marcel, *op. cit.*, in n. 52 (141f.): "The sacraments are not dealt with in a general abstract presentation but are directly connected to our faith ... Nevertheless, the Catechism expresses itself very precisely: the sacraments themselves do not confirm faith but their use accomplishes it, still better, the Holy Spirit utilises the usage of the sacraments in order to confirm faith. Thus, the condition is, that faith has already been at work in our hearts and is thus alive. Because the sacraments do not create it themselves ..." "The sacraments do not help God but us, us alone". This clarification and confirmation of the gospel, through the

whereby the liturgies often still introduce new motifs. We leave aside here the extraordinary similarity between the Calvinist and Greek-Orthodox interpretations of the eucharist;[55] similarly, the Anglican's powerful Book of Common Prayer, which, in its origin and doctrine belongs to the reformed family,[56] yet represents a particular type.[57]

3. The Congregation

However, today, more than ever before the question has to be put, "How does the *congregation* celebrate the Lord's Supper?" If it does not contradict its office bearers and theologians, that does not mean, that it thinks the same as they. Today, all churches experience the following. The local parishes remain loyal to their traditional mode of doctrine and they have been particularly conservative regarding their forms of worship. Yet, at the same time, the congregations are tolerant, indeed ecumenically open. They take delight in guests from afar and their rites: they are confessionally less anxious than their officials. Within protestantism, congregations have generally been ready for a union for the last hundred and fifty years and today the younger generation presses for bold experiments in face of changing home missionary responsibilities.

These brief and, in part, contradictory observations lead me to conclude that, in our parishes, across all confessions, we have throughout something

---

Holy Spirit by means of the sacraments is (questions and answers 75-85) specified for the Lord's Supper. Zwinglian concepts are here (alongside the term, sign), the strong concentration on the "sole offering of Christ is completed on the cross", as the embodiment of grace, i.e., at the invitation of the preaching of the gospel by which the sacraments "remembers". Thus, in comparison with Luther and Calvin, the definite departure from a greater content of the sacraments over against preaching. The recognition of the sacraments as assurance and confirmation, as seal and pledge, and as mystical union of the congregation as Christ's body is Calvinistio.

55. Paul Huber, "Die Auferstehungsfreude in der Liturgie der Ostkirche", in *Reformatio*, Jg. XVII, 1968, Heft 6/7, 388-408; 401f.

56. Cyrill C. Richardson, *Zwingli and Cranmer on the Eucharist.* Seaburg-Western Theological Seminary Evanston, Illinois 1949.—*Ib.*, "Cranmer and the Analysis of Eucharistic Doctrine", in *The Journal of Theological Studies*, New Series, Vol. VXI, Part 2, 1965, 421-437. Oxford, At the Clarendon Press.—Peter Brooks, *Thomas Cranmer's Doctrine of the Eucharist*, London, Macmillan & Co., 1965.—Richardson establishes, in my view, indisputably the Zwinglian foundation of the mature Cranmer. However, Brooks shows, partly by means of documents recently become available, how on these foundations new constructions have been erected in the course of the years. Yet, he overlooks the fact that Cranmer has taken over these thoughts in substantial parts, even to the extent of the actual wording, of Calvin.

57. Cf., e.g., Michael Bruce, "Die Eucharistie im Verständnis der Anglikaner", in Thomas Sartory OSB, *Die Eucharistie im Verständnis der Konfessionen*, Paulus-Verlag Recklinghausen 1961, 189-203.

like a particular lay confession which one could possibly even formulate dogmatically. In any case, it could well be described in a religious-psychological way. The example of the apostle forbids us to think lightly of this. Congregations experience today three things at the celebration of the Lord's supper: 1) The distinct nearness of the Lord, 2) The responsibility and preparedness for forgiveness, 3) The witnessing gathering of resolute Christians (in which bread and wine are signs of fellowship). These aspects are biblical and worthy of all consideration. In the resumption of discussion concerning the Lord's Supper, one must not have conversation exclusively with sixteenth century confessions but, in the first instance, with this confession.

4. *Exegesis*

The other authority with which we must reckon is to be found, as it were, at the opposite pole. It is almost unknown to the local congregation: modern *exegetical research*.[58] We are not now going to introduce wild mutually contradictory hypotheses, but we mention the most radical questions, characteristic of the situation, which we cannot ignore: 1) Is there, in fact, "the" New Testament doctrine of the Lord's Supper in which the reformers firmly believed and whose existence created the precondition for

---

58. A good insight into the main problems of research since the questionings of the literary critical, historical, critical, religious-historical and the form critical schools, are offered in the articles, "Abendmahl im Neuen Testament" in the different editions of *Religion in Geschichte und Gegenwart*, Tübingen.—Wilhelm Heitmüller, *RGG*[1], I, 1909, 20-52.—Karl Ludwig Schmidt, *RGG*[2], I, 1927, 6-16.—Eduard Schweizer, *RGG*[3], I, 1957, 9-21.—Ib., cf., thereto in *Theologischen Wörterbuch zum Neuen Testament*, Kohlhammer, Stuttgart, von Johannes Behm die Artikel δεῖπνον, *Th WBzNT* II, 1935, 33-35; und κλάω κτλ *Th WBzNT* III, 1938, 726-743; und von Leonhard Goppelt Artikel ποτήριον *Th WBzNT* VI, 1959. 141-144, 148-158.—Hans Lietzmann, *Messe und Herrenmahl*, Berlin 1926.—Joachim Jeremias, *Die Abendmahlsworte Jesu*, Göttingen 1935, 1967[4].—Ernst Gaugler, *Das Abendmahl in Neuen Testament*, Basel 1943.—Oscar Cullmann, *Urchristentum und Gottesdienst*, Basel 1944.—Franz J. Leenhardt, *Le sacrement de la sainte cène*, Neuchâtel-Paris 1948.—Werner Georg Kümmel, in H. Lietzmann: *An die Korinther I, II* (IINT IX), Tübingen 1949[4].—Wilhelm Michaelis, "Karfreitags- oder Ostercharakter des Abendmahls?" in *Das Wort sie sollen lassen stahn, Festschrift für Albert Schädelin*, Bern 1950, 57-66.—Rudolf Bultmann, *Theologie des Neuen Testaments*, Tübingen 1953, § 13, 2.—Ch. F. D. Moule, "The Judgement Theme in the Sacraments", in *The Background of the New Testament and its Eschatology. In honour of C. H. Dodd*, 1956, 464-481.—Ernst Fuchs, *Das urchristliche Sakramentsverständnis*. Schriftenreihe der Kirchlin-Theologischen Sozietät in Württemberg, Heft 8, Verlag Müllerschön, Bad Canstatt, 1958.—Max Thurian, *Eucharistie. Einheit am Tisch des Herrn?* Matthias-Gründewald-Verlag, Mainz 1963.—Willi Marxsen, *Das Abendmahl als christologisches Problem*. Gütersloh 1963/65.—Eduard Schweizer, "Abendmahl", in *Theologie für Nichttheologen*, Kreuz-Verlag, Stuttgart 1968, 17-23.—Walter Schmithals, "Abendmahl im Neuen Testament", *Ref. Kirchenzeitung*, 110. Jg. 1969, 118ff.—Björn Sandvik, "Das Kommen des Herrn beim Abendmahl im Neuen Testament", *AThANT* Bd. 58, Zürich 1970.

their controversy? 2) Did Christ celebrate the Lord's Supper with his disciples? 3) If so, did he celebrate the Jewish Passover? 4) Or, a meal of eschatological anticipation? 5) If so, did he solemnise an institution? 6) Or, does our Lord's Supper originate in an ecstatic, visionary celebration with the risen one? 7) Can the pre-Pauline meaning of I Corinthians 11, the oldest existing tradition, be clearly defined? 8) On the basis of existing texts can the original meaning of the synoptic tradition be determined? 9) Are or were the synoptic writers more or less agreed? 10) What was the information within the streams of tradition before the Evangelists? 11) What were the Aramaic words of institution and what did they mean? 12) How are they related to the early Christian "breaking of bread" in houses? 13) What was the relationship of Lord's Supper to Agape after the Acts of the Apostles? 14) How were these retained in the celebrations within the heathen-Christian congregations, particularly the Pauline ones? 15) Does Paul really wish to replace the celebration of Easter by a celebration of Christ's passion? 16) What did early Christendom consciously take over from heathen religious meals? 17) What concepts of the sacrament are reflected in the gospel of St John and the Johannine letters? (The interpretations of John 6 differ greatly). 18) Are therefore the texts in the New Testament already witnesses to conflicts concerning the Lord's Supper in early Christendom? 19) Or, in spite of all differences in tradition, interpretation and form, did they get on well together? 20) Because they were of the opinion that there was only one Lord's Supper, irrespective of interpretation and form?

As dogmatist and as historian, I incline to the final answer because faith in the living one, the εἰς Κύριος,[59] which makes people Christian, actually-holds all different traditions together.

5. *Arnoldshain and the Leuenberg Concord*

In America[60] and in the German speaking areas, some Lutherans, Calvinistic as well as Barthien Reformed,[61] and some members of the

---

59. Eph. 4, 5.

60. Paul C. Empie and James J. McCord (Editors), *Marburg Revisited, A Reexamination of Lutheran and Reformed Traditions*, Augsburg Publishing House, Minneapolis, Minnesota 1966.

61. As far as I see, with explicit excluding of the Zwinglian traditions, this in spite of all the above shown theological as well as historical Zurich contributions to the reformation debate, which should not be ignored; and in spite of the closeness of Zwingli's exegesis to many modern exegetical discussions. Wilhelm Niesel, in his fine book, *Das Evangelium und die Kirchen, Ein Lehrbuch der Symbolik*, Neukirchen 1953, 218, "ignores Zwingli's views as, today, they no longer play a role within the Reformed Churches". The opposite is true, e.g., the understanding of the elements as signs, the communical character of the Lord's Supper, and its power for witnessing and commitment, play, nowadays, an increasing role even among Lutherans and Roman Catholics.

United churches of Germany, have resumed theological negotiations.[62] Perhaps too early? Should one have waited first of all for a preponderant consensus among New Testament scholars? Nevertheless, the *"Arnoldshain Theses"* of 1957 have provided the basis for further discussion[63] and, in 1973, under the auspices of the World Council of Churches led to the Leuenberg Concord.[64] Yet, "Arnoldshain" has only just relaxed confessional boundaries. There are two reasons for this. In the first place, the doctrine of the Lord's Supper is not the most important difference between Protestant churches: certain diversities in tradition, which have never been considered as dogmatically divisive, have here and there characterised more strongly attuning and usage.[65] Secondly, "Arnoldshain" is predominantly orientated by the controversies outlined of the sixteenth century and, attempts to renovate them, indeed, through certain eschatalogical and ethical orientations reaches out beyond them. This is part of a necessary overcoming of the past, but the present poses new problems. The fourth article of the "Arnoldshain Theses" formulates: "the crucified and risen Lord imparts himself in his body, given up in death for all, and in his blood, shed for all, through his word of promise with bread and wine for us to take and takes us through the power of the Holy Ghost into the victory of his Lordship ..."[66]

---

62. Julius Schniewind und Ernst Sommerlath, *Abendmahlsgespräch*, Herausgegeben von Edmund Schlink; Töpelmann, Berlin 1952.—Reinhold Koch, *Erbe und Auftrag. Das Abendmahlsgespräch in der Theologie des 20. Jahrhunderts*, München 1957.

63. *Abendmahlsgespräch der Evangelischen Kirche in Deutschland 1947-57*, von G. Niemeier, Hannover 1958.—The Arnoldshain Theses are also found in *Auf dem Weg* (s. n. 64 below), 60-65; in Wolfgang Kung, *Liturgisches Wörterbuch*, Verlag Merseburger, Berlin 1964, 19-21; and elsewhere.—An insight into the debate resulting from these Theses is presented, among others, in G. Niemeier (ed.), *Lehrgespräch über das Heilige Abendmahl*. Stimmen und Studien zu den Arnoldshainer Thesen, München 1961.—Jürgen Wilhelm Winterhager, *"Luthererisch" und "Reformiert" im ökumenischen Dialog. Reformatio*, Bern, Jg. 1968, Nr. 6/7, 416-429.

64. André Appel (Lutherischer Weltbund), Marcel Pradervand (Reformierter Weltbund), Lukas Vischer (Faith and Order) (ed.), *Auf dem Weg. Lutherisch-reformierte Kirchengemeinschaft*. Polis Nr. 33, Zürich 1967. Bd. II: Nr. 41, Zürich 1971.—Wilhelm Dantine, *Der ökumenische Ertrag der lutherisch-reformierten Gespräche in Europa. Ökumenische Rundschau*, Stuttgart, 16. Jahrgang, Heft 4, Oktober 1967, 358-374.—Reinhard Groscurth, Ivar Asheim, Wilhelm Dantine, F. M. Dobias: *Zu den Thesen der lutherisch-reformierten Gespräche in Europa. Ökumenische Rundschau*, Stuttgart, 17. Jahrgang, Heft 4, Oktober 1968, 364-375.

65. E.g., the different doctrines of law and the related judgements of political and social problems.

66. *Auf dem Weg* (cf. n. 64 above) 62. The thesis nicely combines, the *scopus* which was common to the reformers. It further seeks, at the same time, to return to the New Testament and to enter into contemporary questioning. This is clearly expressed in the "Erläuterung" (explanation): "Thesis 4 speaks of the body and blood of Christ that becomes clear: body and blood of Jesus Christ are nothing other than Jesus Christ himself. They cannot be

6. *Doubts about the old formulas*

The content of such propositions may be correct—our *qualms* about the old doctrinal formulations and their further contemporary development are not lessening but increasing. If so far we have worked out the effective reformation motifs then we must now list the criticisms against a conserving and repristenising continuation of traditional formulations which emerge in the analysis of the situation: 1) Exegetical carelessness, 2) aristotelian-scholastic terminology on the part of Lutherans, 3) platonic anthropology on the part of the Reformed, 4) wrong topics on both sides, i.e., a late medieval fascinated fixation upon the elements of bread and wine instead of actively entering into the whole living operation of the communal supper, 5) alienness of congregations, all along the line.

II. REFLECTIONS ON A CONTEMPORARY UNDERSTANDING

We would be contradicting ourselves if we composed a modern formula in place of the old. For the present, we can only describe, in terms of the New Testament, what the church is beginning to apprehend. Nevertheless a church does not forget her actual origin. We only wish to pursue new ways which all confessions can justify. We are even entering into the main subject of the old controversy.

1. *The real presence*

For our generation, the question regarding the authentic presence of Christ is not, "How does the substance of bread and wine relate to the substance of a transfigured body?" But, "is He here in person?" Real presence means personal presence.

According to that, questioning infers the taking up of the most profound intentions of the reformers. Lutheran researchers have often stressed that

---

separated from the person and the destiny of Jesus Christ, just as the crucified and risen Lord cannot be separated from his body, given for all unto death, and his blood shed for all. If in Thesis 4 bread and wine are mentioned, so then this states that bread and wine in the Lord's Supper are the chosen means of Jesus Christ for the gift of his body and blood. The signatories have not attempted a closer definition of the connection of body and blood to bread and wine out of regard for the variety of New Testament witnesses". (*Ib.,* 65). In this final decision and with retained parallelism, "with bread and wine", Arnoldshain and the Leuenberg concord have omitted to free themselves resolutely from the old questioning (relationship of the elements to the substance) and have dispensed with stressing important exegetical understanding: "body" (not "flesh"), "cup on account of my blood", originally did not stand parallel. Whatever the original Aramaic form may have been, "my body" constitutes as much as "I myself" and embraces the entire meal. The rotating cup consummates the covenant of the disciples of the basis of the sacrifice on the cross, etc. Instead, Arnoldshain and Leuenberg have actually returned in their formula to Bucer and the Wittenberg Concord of the year 1536: "with bread and wine".

Luther's emphasis on the corporeality of Christ being right within the sacrament implies Christ's concrete historicity with us and for us.[67] Zwingli sought, in the categories of old idealism, to describe this same personative communion with us, when he stresses the divinity of the God-Man. He is always concerned about the *"Christus noster"*.[68] Calvin expresses himself with reverent discretion. In that he is not in a position to grasp conceptually the communion with Christ,[69] and assigns it decisively

---

67. E.g. Edmund Schlink, *Theologie der lutherischen Bekenntnisschriften*, Chr. Kaiser München 1948, 222-240.—Friedrich Brunstäd, *Theologie der lutherischen Bekenntnisschriften*, Bertelsmann Gütersloh 1951, 168-179.—Ernst Sommerlath, in *Abendmahlsgespräch* (cf., n. 62 above). 29f., 39-44.—Albrecht Peters in *Realpräsenz*, (cf., n. 21 above) 63ff., 125ff.—Paul Althaus, in *Die Theologie Martin Luthers*, 331-336. "The bodilyness ... is the same as the true historicity..." (332). "In the same way as the incomprehensible, all present God draws near to man in the humanity of Christ, so the incomprehensible all present humanity of Christ again draws near and is apprehendable for man in the Lord's Supper". (335f.).

68. Zwingli in "Brevis Commemoratio Mortis Christi ...": "Pii non solum symbola dentibus premunt, nec nuda habent symbola, sed ultra symbolorum manducationem quae ore corporis fit, intus in mentibus suis corpore et sanguine Christi per fidei manducationem pascuntur. Quam fidem spiritus Christi intus accendit, quando, quantum, et quibus ipse voluerit. Neque enim operatio eius symbolis alligata est, neque gratia indita, ut quasi vehiculo quodam et illis adferatur, sed Christus ipse summus et aeternus Pontifex corpore suo et sanguine pascit fideles ... Corpus ergo et sanguinem mens fidelis percipit, et percepta, spiritus dei calore concoquit, et in interiora animae viscera traiicit, ex quo intima et mirifica piae menti refectio exoritur. Coenam ergo seu eucharistiam quum celebramus, sacrificii illius unici in cruce oblati cum gratiarum actione recordamur ... Mors ergo Christi nunquam pectoribus nostris excidat, semper cogitemus *Christum totum nostrum factum*, ut nos simus ipsius per fidem et caritatem, proximi per caritatem, inque eo maneamus per fidem, et ipse in nobis per caritatem, omnia faciamus et feramus propter eum qui nostri causa mortuus est". S VI/II 10.

"The faithful have not the signs merely between their teeth, in fact, they possess not merely the signs but, over and above the eating of the signs with the physical mouth, they are being inwardly fed with Christ's body and blood in their soul through the eating of the faith. Christ's spirit kindles this faith when, how far, and in whom he will. In no way is his action bound to the signs, nor is grace embodied in it as in a vehicle with which it is delivered to the receiver. However, Christ himself, as the highest and eternal priest, feeds the faithful with his body and blood ... in this way the faithful soul receives the body and blood of Christ and, when he receives it, then he absorbs (digests) it completely in the glow of the Holy Spirit and leads it to the innermost organ of the soul, out of which grows an inner, glorious strengthening for the pious mind. Thus, when we celebrate the evening Meal, the Eucharist, then we remember thereby that single sacrifice accomplished on the cross and give thanks for it ... Thus, the death of Christ must never depart from our hearts. Let us always remember how Christ has become completely our own, so that we are his own through faith and love, and through love of our neighbour; and that we remain in him by faith and he in us by love; so that we do and bear everything for the sake of the one who has died for us".

69. Calvin: "Itaque nihil demum restat nisi ut in eius mysterii admirationem prorumpam, cui nec mens plane cogitando, nec lingua explicando par esse potest". Inst. IV, 17, 7.

"Therefore, nothing remains but to break forth into wonder at this mystery, which plainly neither the mind is able to conceive, nor the tongue to express". (*Institutes*, 1367).

to the Holy Spirit,[70] and gives weight most clearly to the mystery of the Lord's personal being-with-us.[71] *Spiritus Sanctus* always means personative presence.[72]

The contemporary discussion concerning the Christian concept of God with its existentialistic, anti-theistic tendencies creates directly and actually for us the sacrament as being a place of personal encounter. If that sounds too anthropomorphic, then it should be countered that revelation means an entering of God into the realm of human experience and comprehension. Of course, the spirituousness and the holiness of the divine presence always extends infinitely beyond the sphere of our encounters. However, everything depends on the fact that we perceive the elective, "you are mine".

---

70. Calvin: "Atqui Spiritui sancto non levis fit iniuria, nisi credimus fieri incomprehensibili eius virtute et cum carne et sanguine Christi communicemus". Inst. IV, 17, 33.

"Yet a serious wrong is done to the Holy Spirit, unless we believe that it is through his incomprehensible power that we come to partake of Christ's flesh and blood". (*Institutes*, 1405).

71. This, on the one hand, is established in Calvin's decidedly trinitarian description of the Holy Spirit and creates, on the other hand the *scopus* of his emphasis on the union of the faithful with the man Christ in the Lord's Supper. Dutch Calvin research has always laid particular importance on this point. cp., to this the articles by H. Bavinck (differences of opinion with A. Ritschl and W. Herrmann) and J. A. Cramer, mentioned in n. 35 above; further, Simon van der Linde: *De leer van den Heiligen Geest bij Calvijn*, Wageningen 1943, 25-31.

72. That Luther also in his insistence on the substantial and real presence of the body of Christ was fundamentally concerned about his personal presence, has come to light from time to time, e.g., in the so-called final union proposal at Marburg in 1529, "dass der leyb Christi im Abendmahl were". "That the body of Christ should be in the Lord's Supper". (Cf. Hans Joachim Iwand, "Coena Domini" in *Um den rechten Glauben, Gesammelte Aufsätze*, Munich 1959, 128f.).

The Swiss had to reject the formula because of its ambiguous nature (even the doctrine of transsubstantiation could have been read into it), but Zwingli mentioned it again in 1531 in a letter to Bucer. "Es handelt sich nicht darum, daß jemand uns nötigen müßte zu gestehen, daß wir glauben, daß Christus im Nachtmahl sei. Denn wäre er nicht dort, so würden wir vor dem Nachtmahl schaudern. Der Zwiespalt dreht sich nicht um Christus!" (Z XI 340, 7ff.). "It is not a question of our having to be pressed to admit that we believe that Christ is in the Supper. Because if he were not there, then we would tremble before the Supper. Divisions are not about Christ".

Further to this, G. W. Locher, "Die theologische und politische Bedeutung des Abendmahlsstreits im Licht von Zwinglis Briefen" in *Zwingliana*, 1971/1, xiii/5, 295f., n. 56).

The aspect of the personal presence of Christ becomes even clearer when Calvin describes the union with Christ as the real fruit of the Lord's Supper, "Magnum vero fiduciae ac suavitatis fructum ex hoc sacramento colligere possunt piae animae, quod illic testimonium habent in unum corpus nos cum Christo coaluisse, ut quicquid ipsius est, nostrum vocare liceat ..." Inst. IV, 17, 2. "Godly souls can gather great assurance and delight from this sacrament in that they have a witness of our growth into one body with Christ such that whatever is his may be called ours. (*Institutes*, 1361-62).

2. The congregation

No relationship with God without relationship to our neighbour—that is a law of life for Christian existence. Since the Lord's invitation, "drink ye all of it", the Lord's Supper has always been a manifestation of the *Communio sanctorum*—at least it is intended to be. At the Lutheran celebration for the individual too, and even in the Roman catholic private communion, the way in which the sacrament brings people together has always been underlined.

In the age of religious individualism, however, the onesided construction of the Lord's Supper concentrating on reception would be dangerous. In many churches, the moving about at communion is like being served at the post office: according rows, one after the other; no togetherness. Should the fellowship-building power of the celebration develop again, then the congregation must proceed from the assumption that it exists in essence according to its calling and rediscovers, recognises, and represents itself in the Lord's Supper. The more representation, the more benefaction.

Thus, our understanding must not only be related to "take" but equally to "remember!" and to "do this!" Then the real presence of the neighbour, the personal encounter of Christians, will effect again its healing action to a mutual strengthening and commitment. The majority of dogmatics and liturgies, of course, must be re-written with this in mind.

3. The individual

In this connection the individual cannot be forgotten. 1) It is implicit in the Lord's Supper that the congregation knows him, his name, his family, his lot, his character, and also his weaknesses. Where Christians are not concerned about one another, there is no fellowship; such a condition is the sin against the body of Christ which Paul brings to the fore.[73] 2) Present day Lutheran theology correctly interprets the Lord's Supper with the

---

73. Paul sees the destruction of the Lord's Supper in the fact that the Corinthians consider the "satisfying meal" with the poor brethren to be less important than the distribution of bread and wine which was pushed to the end of it. Thus he criticised not too little but rather too much "sacramentalism". "Indeed the well known sentence, that whosoever eats and drinks unworthily will be guilty of the body and blood of Christ (I Corinthians, XI, 27) has to be explained according to another part of the same letter (VIII, 11f.) in such a way that we are aware that we become guilty before Christ who gave his body and blood for the brother, as soon as we do not take very seriously the brother and the pure human relationship to him and only desire a sacramental assurance of our own salvation". (Eduard Schweizer in *Theologie für Nichttheologen*, 68 (cf. n. 58 above).

help of modern total psychology of body and spirit.[74] Yet, it nevertheless still exclusively conceives of the receiver as a sinner in need of forgiveness. Certainly, it must be made inexorably clear to him that he is such a one, however, he should feel himself accepted in the complicated, manifold, and often simultaneously, poor entirity of his existence, e.g., as a lost individual in the city or as a villager mistrusted on all sides, a badgered and overworked man or one whom no one needs and loves. All these types of existence are manifestations of sin. All their perpetrators and victims are called to the Table, not only with their sins, but also with their need.

4. *The gift of the Lord's Supper*

God gives us humans a great deal; in Christ he gives himself. Such high assertions are always in danger of remaining a theory. The action of the Lord's Supper, however, will immediately penetrate into life's experiences. Christ will daily become like meat and drink to us. Therefore, the celebration cannot remain in *mysterium*, but must allow what it represents to be experienced forthwith. Luther replied to this, "Forgiveness of sins", Calvin, "Knowledge and power from the resurrection". For our epoch, we add, on the basis of the New Testament: "Where the *church* bestirs itself to become an active fellowship, new beginnings of human society appear". Therefore, at that Table, one will be filled with eschatological joy; jubilation must not be lacking.[75] Subsequently, discipleship, with the remembrance of the Supper's earthly Lord, leads again to the thorny road of those who have taken up the cross. Nevertheless, it means, getting rid of the funereal atmosphere of our sacrament; and liturgy and praise should shine out as in the Easter splendour of early Christendom.

5. *The elements*

All protestants are agreed, bread is bread and wine is wine. What objectively changes this into the sacrament according to Luther involves the Word. As far as I can see, it was Melanchthon, who, after careful consideration introduced a more subjective terminology and transfered the effect of the sacraments to their "*usus*". This has been official Lutheran church doctrine from the time of the Augsburg Confession.[76] I know, that

---

74. Convincing because reserved: E. Schlink (cf. n. 67 above), 229.

75. Acts, II, 46.

76. C. A. Art. XIII. The terminology has been firmly taken over by the Heidelberg Catechism (possibly via Ursinus, a student of Melanchthon); cf. questions and answers 65, 66, 67, 73, 75, 78, 79. At the same time one is reminded of Zwingli's "aktion und Bruch des Nachtmahls" (1525). (Z IV).

all the problems regarding the relationship between Luther and Melanchthon are associated with this matter. We will not at this point turn back to the old debate. Yet, here for the first time, we are being admonished to avoid all staring at the host. We are concerned with the *Holy Supper* and not with eating and drinking holy substances. Today, many exegetes see in the so-called words of consecration the last parable of Jesus told, perhaps, within the framework of the obligatory custom of the celebration of the Jewish Passover.[77] In any case, the meaning of the action does not lie in the *mysterium*, but in the fact that Christ in it, has broken and is breaking through the sphere of the numinous.

6. *Coena Domini*

The difference therefore is important because is calls for a psychical decision which strikes deeper than a theological formula. The question is: who or what is here—*de facto!*—the centre? Bread and wine? Or a transubstantiation? Or a union of substances? Or our grasp of these things? Or, He, the Lord of the Table? Admittedly, we must investigate further: Who or what is the main thing? The congregation? The individual? Forgiveness? Redemption? Or He, who brings everything else with him?

This alternative has far-reaching ecumenical consequences. As long as we turn this or that into the main issue, we, in fact, elevate our interpretations to the criterion for admission. The opposite should apply. Where the churches do not invite and admit each other, they demonstrate that they are still not gathering unconditionally round the centre; that they are setting their own table or celebrating their own offering.

When we truly celebrate the *Lord's Supper*, then we are guests and have no right to allow another of His disciples to remain outside. The reformers have taught us that we, as a general principle, always find ourselves to be outside. Jesus has gone outside to eat with the outsiders and to demonstrate thereby the living fellowship with him.[78]

7. *Spiritus vivificans*

The phrase, we celebrate the Supper of the *Lord*, implies that there are effects of the celebration which we are unable to describe rationally and

---

77. J. Jeremias (cf. n. 58 above), 4th edition, 1967, 210.

78. Modern exegesis connects the traditions of Jesus' last Supper with his disciples closely with other passages in which he eats and drinks with various other people. Once again, we point here, and in any case with regard to these articles of Eduard Schweizer, yet also to the completely differently argued essay of Willi Marxsen (cf. n. 58 above).

which reach deeply into the subconscious. Lutherans have always attached
great importance to this dimension; whether this is a legitimate reference
to Luther, remains to be seen. What matters to us, is to mention once
again the congregation and its indissoluble, organic growing together as a
precondition, instrument and goal of the celebration. If one may speak of
the miracle of grace of a "transubstantiation" then it is here. Thus, the
mysterium, which is beyond our *ratio*, does not lie in the elements, nor even
in the *usus*, but here with the Lord of the Supper and His action. The congregation is the nascent and visible actualisation of the Spirit: the authorised bearer of word and sacrament, the embodied promise of human
humanity.

III. REFLECTIONS ON CELEBRATION TODAY

1. *Ceremonial freedom*

Freedom regarding ceremonies is strongly emphasised by all the
reformers. However, they drew contrary implications from it which have
more strongly determined the distinctiveness of the confessions than differences in doctrine. Generally, the Lutherans maintained that where the
church clings to familiar rites we have the freedom to let it keep them.
Thus, the structure of the *ordo missae* remained, the expression alone
became evangelical. According to the Reformed if the rites obscure our
understanding of the gospel, we have the freedom to reshape them. In the
first instance, the predominant objective is the unity of the Church, (*una
sancta*), in the latter its purity (*ecclesia semper reformanda*). Both points of view
are justified and the tension between them presents each generation with a
fruitful continuing responsibility.

For our generation the message of the church and its responsibility for a
clear public witness appear as a new guideline which does not leave any
room for confessional hobbies. Situation and mission are the same for all
churches. So, this guidance is an ecumenical. The mission concerns the
understanding of the church itself. Thus it is reformatory.

Today, has "freedom concerning ceremonies" to mean ecumenically,
circumstances permitting, "freedom from ceremonies"? Throughout the
world, the experience is remarkably opposite. We must enter in and we
must break out. The ancient proposition that the Lord's Supper must be
reserved for earnest and the sermon for mission is theologically false and
wastes the many opportunities of both. We also require both for the Lord's
Supper. We should offer it in changing variations, e.g.:

2. The exclusive celebration

Out of the loneliness, tension, and temptation of being a Christian, many Christians experience a great longing for sanctified quietness, meditation and order for their confused spiritual lives and, as a result, for a rich and relevant liturgy. The Table is prepared for such people and we should draw from the fulness of the traditional riches of prayers, hymns, music, and symbols.

3. The open festival and the agape

One appreciates that many serious laymen, including office bearers especially the younger, but also the older, working and thinking throughout the week in the rationalism of a technological era, require worship in the style of a dispassionate realism and a decisive commitment with which they can identify themselves and assume an inner responsibility without conceiving of it as an escapism. One recognises further that by far the greater proportion of our contemporaries live "outside" and that for such outsiders, as well as for good church people, the language and form of worship are so alien that they erect an unsuperable barrier. The Table is prepared for such people and we should have the courage to worship God in the most austere liturgical ways. The Lord's Supper, celebrated in an early Christian profane form as an actual meal, would be understood and immediately apprehended and a mighty power radiate in the world of the lovelessly feeded and of the hungering.[79]

Can we dare not only to teach and declare the presence of the Lord, but to count on it? If so, our forefathers did not struggle in vain. Our sons, however, will demonstrate again, in such experiments, the rebellious hope of the early Christian's eucharistic cry: "Grace is coming and this world is departing!"[80]

---

79. The department of Worldmission and Evangelism of the World Council of Churches in Geneva with Walter J. Hollenweger as executive secretary, devoted much time to the study of theological, ecclesiological, and social implications of new forms of worship and sacramental celebration. Several reports and interpretations have been presented by: W. J. Hollenweger, *Konflikt in Korinth*, Kaiser, Munic, 1978; amer. transl.: Paulist Press, New York.—W. J. Hollenweger: *Erfahrungen der Leibhaftigkeit*, ib. 1979.—W. Simpfendörfer, *Offene Kirche—Kritische Kirche*, Stuttgart, Kreuz-Verlag 1969.—Hartmut Löwe (ed.), *Abendmahl in der Tischgemeinschaft. Neue Möglichkeiten zur Feier der Eucharistie*, Stauda-Verlag, 1971.—Uwe Dittmer, *Im Blickpunkt: Abendmahl*, Evangelische Verlaganstalt. Berlin. 1973.

80. Ἐλθέτω χάρις καὶ παρελθέτω ὁ κόσμος οὗτος. Didache 10, 6.

15

ZWINGLI'S INFLUENCE IN
ENGLAND AND SCOTLAND*

Dates and Problems

I. A STATEMENT OF THE PROBLEM

The name of Huldrych Zwingli was soon almost forgotten in English Reformation history, and it seldom appears even in the flourishing literature of the present day. There are various reasons for this. In the 1530's and 1540's those who were of "reformed" views already had active connections with Martin Bucer and Peter Martyr Vermigli, with Henry Bullinger and Rudolf Gualther, and were soon to have contacts with John Calvin and Theodore Beza. These were the men who offered advice and assistance with their actual and (in part) novel difficulties and questions. The result was that in Britain, as happened almost everywhere outside Switzerland, the memory of the Zurich Reformer who died in 1531 was actually concealed by a Calvinism that was alive and advancing. What was of decisive moment was that nobody, when under the pressure of a deadly persecution, either felt the duty, or had the power and the time to burden himself with the dangerous name of the Zurich Reformer, a heretic who was a controversial figure among Protestants, and even among Calvinists and members of the Church of England.

In view of this silence concerning Zwingli, the question arises as to whether he had any influence upon the beginnings of the Reformation movement in England. Are there any traces to indicate his direct or indirect influence? Is it possible that such traces, having passed unrecognis-

* The task of gathering together the data and observations which form the basis of this essay has extended over many years. First of all, I am indebted to my friend Dr. Duncan Shaw of Edinburgh for advice, suggestions and discussions, who rightly requested the addition of this chapter for the English edition of this book, and who also contributed a great deal of the literature. Some years ago I received valuable help from Professor T. F. Torrance of Edinburgh and Professor J. K. Cameron of St. Andrews. More recently I have enjoyed three weeks' hospitality in Westminster and Chestnut College in the old Puritan centre of Cambridge. I am grateful to the Cambridge University Library for their help, and to Professors E. Gordon Rupp and Peter Brooks (both of Cambridge) for advice and information. The friendly evening conversations which I shared with Professor George Yule from Victoria, Australia, now in Aberdeen, proved especially instructive. Translation by Duncan Shaw. A supplement to this chapter: G. W. Locher, "'The most godly man Zuinglius.' Neuentdeckte Einflüsse Zwinglis in England" in *Kirchenblatt für die reformierte Schweiz, 1980/81*.

ed from the very beginning, have become deeply embedded in the character of the English Reformation tradition and so have influenced both the Established and the Nonconformist Churches right down to the present day?

We would emphasise that this is an enquiry into the effects of the work and the ideas of Zwingli himself, and of his friends such as Oecolampadius. The great significance of his successor Henry Bullinger, both for the Church of England and for the Puritan congregations, is well known to scholars, especially since the publication of the Parker Society edition of the Zurich Letters (1846ff.). In England (in distinction from Scotland) the authority of Bullinger surpassed even that of Calvin. And by virtue of their formative role in the development of evangelical piety in England, his *Decades* were of even more enduring influence than his correspondence. Not only were these by far the most widely-read book of sermons,[1] but they also served for a hundred and fifty years as a basic textbook in dogmatic and practical theology.[2]

However, as far as later Zwinglianism is concerned, we can only make occasional reference. The delimitation of the influence of Zwingli from that of Bullinger, or from that of Bucer or even Luther often appears difficult, if not impossible. But we shall hardly err, if we concentrate on the period from ca 1530 to 1555. Many of the confessors who appear in the reign of Mary Tudor (1553-1558) received their decisive evangelical

---

1. W. Hollweg, *Heinrich Bullingers Hausbuch. Eine Untersuchung über die Anfänge der reformierten Predigtliteratur*, Neukirchen, 1956, pp. 142-178, "Die Verbreitung der Decades in England"; cf. *ib.*, pp. 157-162 for the English and Latin editions printed in England.

2. I am indebted to Prof. G. Yule for this suggestion. Cf. Basil Hall, "Calvin against the Calvinists", in *John Calvin*, ed. G. E. Duffield, Courtenay Studies in Reformation Theology No. 1, Appleford, 1966. Hall writes (p. 33): "It is certainly arguable that Calvin had less real influence on English religion than Bucer of Strasbourg and Cambridge and Bullinger of Zürich. In the more settled conditions of Elizabeth's reign in the Universities and the dioceses Bullinger's *Decades* are referred to as required reading in the training of the clergy, whereas in Kennedy's account of Elizabethan episcopal administration Calvin's *Institutio* is referred to only once under this head. Moreover, Bullinger had been known to many of the English refugees from the Marian persecution, among whom were men of prominence in the Elizabethan Church, Bishops Jewel, Parkhurst, Grindal and Sandys. (W. F. M. Kennedy, *Elizabethan Episcopal Administration* (Alcuin Club Tracts), London, 1924, Vol. II, pp. 45, 46, 150, 249, 250)".

The use of the *Decades* in theological education would serve to confirm Hollweg's plausible conjecture that they actually arose out of work in connexion with the "Prophezey". Cf. Hollweg, *op. cit.*, pp. 57-60. According to David J. Keep (Zur Verbreitung von Bullingers Dekaden in England zur Zeit Elisabeths I., *Zwingliana 1976/2*, pp. 332-335) the sources do not prove such a long and wide official function of the Decades. However, Bullinger was estimated as "one of the Fathers of the Gospel". (p. 335).

impressions at a time when there could still have been genuine Zwinglian influences.

Finally, we would emphasise that the task of describing Zwingli's possible influences upon the British Isles, and of analysing their paths, connexions, changes and effects can only be carried out in Britain itself by those who are experts in English and Scottish Reformation history. What we offer here is only a preliminary list of facts and questions, a catalogue of problems which itself needs to be supplemented and corrected.

First, we provide an account of what we are actually seeking.

II. THE CHIEF CHARACTERISTICS OF ORIGINAL ZWINGLIANISM

The reader of this book[3] will concur if we summarise the characteristic features of the Zwinglian reformation movement as follows:[4]

1) The discovery of the Word of God, publicly preached on the basis of the Holy Scriptures of the Old and New Testaments, as providing both the power and the obligation for the renewal of life, and as constituting both the beginning and the very heart of the reformation itself.

2) The consequent opposition to human authority, teaching and tradition in divine things, to idolatry and superstition.

3) The essential recognition of Jesus Christ as the one who made atonement for us on the Cross, and who is the living and present Governor of His people by His Spirit.

4) The conscious will to reform both the church and society.

5) The attempt to realise the daily Christian life of the congregation in the form of democratic associations.

6) The evolutionary and possibly even revolutionary power which derives from these bases.

7) Corresponding to the radical nature of all these features, the characteristic concept of the celebration of the Lord's Supper as a confirmation of spiritual communion with Christ and with one another, and the consequent symbolic and spiritual understanding of the words of institution.

Explanation

When we consider the outworking in later generations, it is a question of tendencies, in part unconscious. We should not expect an exact copy of

---

3. See G. W. Locher, "Theokratie und Pluralismus—Zwingli heute", in *Wissenschaft und Praxis*, 62/1 (January 1973), pp. 11-24.

4. See "In Spirit and in Truth" (above, pp. 1-30).

the Zurich reformation. But when one or more of the aforementioned characteristics is seen to strive to take effect in programmatic form, then we may think in terms of relationship, repetition, or influence. And when a certain heresy, such as the denial of the corporal presence of Christ in the sacrament, is linked publicly and for all time with the name of Zwingli, then even an Edinburgh journeyman, questioned by the Bishop on account of making such a denial, knows that he stands in spiritual union with Zürich (or at least the street-preacher himself, from whom the journeyman learnt the doctrine of "by faith alone", understood this).[5]

It would not be difficult to show that these characteristics of the Zwinglian tradition appear individually with other Reformers as well, and partly even with the Anabaptists.[6] It is for this reason that we speak of programmatic tendencies. The fact that they are to be found with others "as well" is not sufficient to prove identity. In clarification, we would make several comments.

With regard to 1) and 2): The discovery of the viva vox belongs to the basic experience of the whole Reformation, and especially for Luther. But here we would underline the public, even judicial character of the sermon, which, with Luther, is secondary to the pastoral value of God's Word for the individual soul. We would also emphasise the conscious striving for a renewed communal life, which the Reformed Protestants did not simply leave to the spontaneity of gratitude for justification by faith, but regarded as the subject of settled principles for Christian living in state and church.[7]

With regard to 2): Luther's attack was directed against justification by works. Concerning 3): Because the people of God surround the justified sinner, social ethics predominate over individual ethics in Zwingli's thought. Concerning 4): Because of the Church's prophetic role vis-à-vis the state, Zwingli knows no separation between them. This distinguishes him from Calvinism, which renders the church independent and is prepared, when necessary, to go underground with her. Concerning 5): and 6): Bullinger was a faithful steward of Zwingli's heritage, and, indeed, one of the most significant promoters of the Reformation. But after the military defeat of 1531 the Zürich reformation had to give up its (revolutionary) aim of attaining autonomy for the Protestants in the common

---

5. Many similar examples are offered in John Foxe's *Acts and Monuments*.

6. Unfortunately we cannot include here the important connexions between the English Anabaptist movement and that on the Continent.

7. For the sake of clarification, it may be added that there developed from this a new legalism among reformed Christians, just as, on the other side, Lutheran individualism encouraged social conservatism.

dominions of the Confederacy and of achieving freedom for evangelical preaching in the Roman Catholic cantons. His concentration on protection and preservation and on the intellectual dissemination of the Gospel (through books!) furthered the development of a conservative form of church life which characterises Bullinger's work. This change also facilitated the acceptance of his sermons in the National Church of England. But we must still take Zwingli's own example into account whenever we find preaching that is energetically directed towards the criticism or reforming of society (and not merely social preaching); the same is true when we meet with concrete political suggestions for the defence of the Gospel.

III. THE CHIEF STAGES IN THE HISTORY OF THE ENGLISH REFORMATION[8]

It is not our task to relate the history of the struggle over the aim and the implementation of the reformation in England. It has to be divided among those who held civil and ecclesiastical authority, because the reformation is so entangled with political developments. Although abuses, corruption, formalism and social injustice were hardly less evident than on the continent, there was less discontent, bitterness, or inward rebellion. This could well be linked with the powerful position of the free city of London,[9] against which nobody could prevail in practice, and also with the protection of a free man as embodied in the conservative Anglo-Saxon legal tradition. Humanistic criticism was correspondingly less sharp in its effect, and the English humanism of Thomas More, John Colet, Desiderius Erasmus (in Cambridge from 1511 to 1514) and others sought to integrate the newly-awakened Biblical studies and actually strengthened the ancient Church.

Although Henry VIII (1509-1547), was a Renaissance figure, he was always scrupulous to appear orthodox. The Pope bestowed upon him the title of "Defensor fidei" for his reply to Luther's *De captivitate Babylonica ecclesiae* (1521). His endeavour to secure a rightful male heir to the throne was, from the purely political standpoint, a necessity; the wounds caused

---

8. W. A. Clebsch, *England's Earliest Protestants*, 1964; H. Maynard Smith, *Henry VIII and the Reformation*, 1948; W. K. Jordan, *Edward VI: the Young King*, 1968; Christina Garrett, *The Marian Exiles*, 1938; Patrick Collinson, *The Elizabethan Puritan Movement*, 1967. M. A. Simpson: *Defender of the Faith, Etcetera.* Elizabeth of England: her Church and Parliament, 1558-59, 1978.

9. G. M. Trevelyan, *A Shortened History of England*, 1942, (Pelican edition, 1972), see Index.

by the feud between the houses of York and Lancaster were scarcely healed, and there had never been a reigning Queen in England. The people
understood this, and their national pride was hurt by the way in which the
Pope, by delaying, exploited politically the divorce which the King was
seeking.[10] The Acts of Parliament of 1532-34, by which the Church of
England was separated from Rome, did not constitute a reformation, of
course. It may, indeed, be doubted whether it even marked the beginning
of the reformation. For the union of the Church with the increased power
of the monarch impeded the spread of the Protestant reformation as much
as it promoted it.[11] To prove that he was able to defend the true faith just
as effectively as the Pope, the King executed not only the martyrs of the
Catholic opposition, such as John Fisher and Thomas More, but also
Protestant martyrs like John Lambert. To a greater extent than in either
Germany or Switzerland, the reformation in England encountered bloody
persecution from the very beginning.

Henry VIII was aware of the need for a theological basis for his breach
with Rome, and he therefore allowed Archbishop Cranmer to make contacts with the Reformation movement on the Continent, but without
entering into any commitments. Under the boy King *Edward VI* (1547-53)
and his Protector Edward Seymour, the pent-up longing for Reformation

---

10. A new era in judicial and ethical thought was ushered in when Cranmer made the
ingenious suggestion that Henry should leave aside Rome's decision, and seek the opinions
of universities and scholars at home and abroad. These arrived within six months.

Apart from Luther and Melanchthon, the inquiry was addressed to Zwingli, Oecolampadius and Strasbourg. Zwingli's reply is not extant. But from the letters of Oecolampadius
it appears that while he and Zwingli recognised that the matter presented an opportunity for
the Reformation, for them the sanctity of marriage and the rights of Catherine had priority.
On the other hand, they recognised that Henry had genuine scruples ("conscientiae cryn
nide vexatur rex", Oecolampadius, Z XI 568, 9). From the very beginning the King had
had misgivings about marrying his brother's widow, because of Lev. 18:16. Of the seven
children, six had died, including three sons.

Wittenberg and Strasbourg advised bigamy, a suggestion which Oecolampadius angrily
denounced to Zwingli: "Far be it from us to listen to Mohamed rather than to Christ!"
Zwingli's detailed opinion has been missing in England since the middle of the nineteenth
century. But there is a summary, from which we can learn his conclusions, which were
endorsed by Oecolampadius: Lev. 18:16 must be respected; therefore the King's marriage
should be annulled; but the Queen should not simply be repudiated; instead, the marriage
should be formally dissolved, Catherine should retain the status of Queen, and Mary that of
a legitimate daughter. Z XI 1259, 1262, 1263, 1285; Z XI 582. D. W. Walther, *Heinrich VIII
von England und Luther*, 1908; E. Staehelin, *Das theologische Lebenswerk Oekolampads*, 1939,
pp. 631-633.

11. In France, Gallicanism hindered the success of the reformation even more clearly. In
Germany, on the other hand, the fact that the medieval Popes had weakened the central
power of the Empire actually prepared the way for evangelical preaching to have free opportunities at the courts of the princes and in the imperial cities.

was able to burst forth in full strength, and Cranmer, Bullinger and Calvin entertained high hopes. Martin Bucer, driven out of Strasbourg as a result of the Interim, spent his final years in Cambridge, from 1549-51; his book *De regno Christi*[12] was an attempt to recast in a theological form approriate to the Church of England the fruits of the thinking that lay behind the reformation in the Upper German-Swiss Imperial cities.[13] [14] In 1549 there appeared the first, conservative edition of the Book of Common Prayer; the second, which is generally regarded as more "Calvinistic", appeared in 1552. The Vestments Controversy involving Bishop Hooper, who had returned to England from Zurich, marks the beginning of "Puritanism" (i.e., the endeavour to achieve a Biblically "pure" Christianity) and this immediately began an attack upon all compromise with tradition, both inside and outside the Church of England. At the same time, however, under the regime of the Duke of Somerset, the nobility seized the opportunity to satisfy their greed for land, ruthlessly enriching themselves by means of the property of the monasteries which had been dissolved, thereby causing a great deal of suffering to the common people and also bringing the Reformation into disrepute.

The bloody Counter-Reformation under *Mary Tudor* (1553-1558) led to resistance, flight or trials in many places, and revealed the extent of protestant commitment.

Elizabeth I (1558-1603) wished to provide a home in the Church of England for those of both "Catholic" and "Puritan" tendency, in the spirit of the traditions of an all-embracing Christian state. Therefore, on the one hand she restored the "Calvinistic" Book of Common Prayer of 1552 and the Calvinistic "39 Articles",[15] while, on the other hand, she retained the hierarchical structure and the colourful liturgy—probably because she well knew that in England practice counts for more than theory. The Act of Uniformity of 1559 was intended to signify both the implementation and the conclusion of the Reformation—and, as a result of the total rejection of this standpoint by the revolutionary-inclined Puritans, this was to have far-reaching consequences, in both the ecclesiastical and political realms.

12. *Martini Buceri Opera Latina*. Vol. XV: *De Regno Christi Libri Duo*, 1550, ed. François Wendel, Paris/Gütersloh, 1955.

13. Bernd Moeller, Imperial Cities and the Reformation, Philadelphia, 1972.

14. C. Hopf, *Martin Bucer and the English Reformation*, Oxford, 1946; A. E. Harvey, *Martin Bucer in England*, Marburg, 1906; A. Lang, "Martin Bucer in England" in *Archiv fur Reformationsgeschichte*, 1941, xxxviii, 230-9.

15. For the Latin text see E. F. K. Müller, *Die Bekenntnisschriften der reformierten Kirche*, 1903, pp. XLIff., pp. 505-522.

IV. THE SPIRITUAL HISTORY OF THE ENGLISH REFORMATION[16]

As far as I am aware we do not possess, as yet, any clear and coherent picture of the spiritual path of the leaders of the English Reformation; apart, that is, from Thomas Cranmer, whose development has often been analysed yet variously interpreted—but which could well be representative of the majority of the most earnest and cultured leaders of the Church of England. There was the older tradition of Wyclif (1320-84) and the Lollards; they were to be found in semi-secret centres, without influencing the life of the people to any great extent, and soon went over to the Puritans. There were still pupils of the radical Augustinian Thomas Bradwardine (1290?-1349). There were Augustinian monks who, as elsewhere, proudly propagated the teaching of their brother from Wittenberg. As already stated, there was a mild, educated, critical humanism that nevertheless remained loyal to the church. As in many places, Luther's writings were at first spread abroad on the wave of humanism and were read with humanistic preconceptions. The fact that the University of Cambridge in particular became a centre for discussions and aspirations of reform is linked with Erasmus' having taught there. And Cambridge soon became the home of circles which were suspected of "Lutheran" heresy. In Oxford, in London and in other places also there were groups in which the reformation was discussed and debated; but the Whyte Horse Tavern was already, in a sense, unique—though at the same time typical.[17] Between about 1517 and 1527 a crowd of young people met there regularly for discussion—and this was the nest from which the future Reformers began their flight. Two members of the group (Heath and Parker) became Archbishops; seven became Bishops (Gardiner, Fox, Shaxton, Latimer, Coxe, Bale and Ridley); eight became martyrs (Bilney, Tyndale, Clark, Frith, Lambert, Barnes, Ridley and Latimer).[18] The diversity of the paths they followed in later life serves to confirm that for these men separation from Rome was not sufficient. The Reformation stimulus from the continent was turned into a demand for a more radical reformation. From the

---

16. John Chandos, ed., *In God's Name, Examples of preaching in England, 1534-1662*, 1971; W. M. S. West, *John Hooper and the Origins of Puritanism*, 1955; J. H. Primus, *The Vestments Controversy*, 1960; S. E. Lehmberg, *The Reformation Parliament, 1529-1536*, 1970; J. A. Devereux, "Reformed Doctrine in the First Prayer Book", in *The Harvard Theological Review*, 1965, pp. 49ff.; G. W. Bromiley, *Thomas Cranmer, Theologian*, London, 1952.

17. H. M. Smith, *op. cit.*, p. 254.

18. Smith continues: "They were very different men, who were to have very different careers, but in those early days they were kept together by the loving admiration which they had for Little Bilney, and they were all much more concerned with the knowledge of the Gospel than with the Babylonish Captivity of Martin Luther".

beginning this was the demand of the Reformed Protestants, as against the Lutherans. Now it was directed towards the Church of England, dating from (at the latest) the return of John Hooper from Zurich in 1549. So the debate about the aims of the Reformation must have begun early. The declaration of the autonomy of the Church of England could only serve to intensify it. Everyone knew that reformation is possible only through the temporal power. The Puritans received counsel and support from both Geneva and Zurich—from Geneva it was chiefly for the more revolutionary dissidents, while from Zurich it was for men both inside and outside the national church.

The measures taken during the reign of Henry VIII were quite comprehensible to the ordinary church people,[19] whereas the very different ideas of the Reformers, together with the reforms made during the short reign of Edward VI, which were inspired from abroad and ordered from above, remained alien to them. The majority of the clergy did not resist, but was unwilling, lazy or incapable of renewal. Cranmer had good reasons for proceeding in such a slow and patient way. He had to seek out the way carefully, not only for his church, but also for himself.[20]

It is, therefore, truly astonishing that all the evidence shows that, when the crisis came in the reign of bloody Mary, a definite and widespread Protestantism, could already stand the test. The Anabaptists were rejected, but otherwise the underground groups held closely together, as all the testimonies presuppose. As yet, no authoritative theology had been developed,[21] and no confession had gained universal acceptance; but there was a definite and generally unanimous spiritual brotherhood. Had the teaching of Huldrych Zwingli made any contribution towards this?

V. EARLY ZWINGLIANISM IN ENGLAND

1.   In the year 1543 there was published in Zurich an English edition of the *Fideo Ratio*, Zwingli's confession at the Diet of Augsburg in 1530.[22]

---

19. "The ordinary man, full of patriotic fervour, welcomed the punishment of traitors who adhered to a foreign power, but he was quite unwilling to accept a new religion made in Germany, and so rejoiced in the burning of heretics. He thought with the support of the King he would be able to walk in his old ways, observe his old customs, and worship God as his fathers had done". (H. M. Smith, *op. cit.*, p. 451).

20. At the time when he acted as a member of the court which condemned Latimer, Cranmer probably felt sympathy with him, but at that time he had not come so far theologically, personally or politically that it would have been possible for him to assist Latimer openly.

21. Or is it that we are not yet aware of it?

22. *The Rekening and declaratiō of the faith and beleif of Huldrik Zwingly ... sent to Charles V ...* Translated & Imprynted Zyryk ... 1543. Described in Z VI, II 787 as Edition G.

Further impressions followed in 1543[23] and 1548.[24] Although the name of Zurich was retained, these were probably printed in England. A fourth printing, in 1555,[25] provided a new translation of the text and named Thomas Cotsforde as its author; it states "Imprinted at Geneva". It would be interesting if this typical and important example of Zwinglian theology had been republished there, under the very eyes of Calvin, who belonged to the Commission of Censorship. But it is thought that this was a deliberate attempt to mislead, in order to protect the printer G. van der Erve of Emden in East Friesland and the authorities there from any difficulties.[26] In this case, John a Lasco would be the man behind this publication.[27]

In addition, there is: Ulrich Zwingli: *A short pathwaye to the ryghte and true understanding of the holye sacred Scriptures* ... translated ... by John Veron ... Worcester, J. Oswen, 1550.[28]

As regards the editions printed on the continent, it might be said that it was merely a question of propaganda material. But no printer would

---

23. *The rekenynge and declaracion of the fayth and belefe of Huldrike zwyngly* ... sent to Charles V ... Translated & Imprynted at Züryk ... 1543. At the end it states: "Imprynted by me Rycharde wyer". Described in Z VI, II 787 as Edition F.

24. *The rekenynge* ... etc. In wording and spelling the same title as the edition of Richard Wyer (note 23). "Translated and Imprynted at ziiryk ... 1548". Described in Z VI, II 788 as Edition H.

25. *The accompt, rekenynge and confession of the faith of Huldrik Zwinglius* ... Translated out of latyn by Thomas Cotsforde. And imprinted at Geneva ... 1555. Described in Z VI, II 788 as Edition I.

26. As in the catalogue entry in the University Library of South California, San Francisco. For the work of the printer Gillis van der Erven (Ctematius) in connexion with the reformation in England, see W. Hollweg, *Heinrich Bullingers Hausbuch*, Neukirchen, 1956, Index (Literature), and Duncan Shaw, "John Willock", in D. Shaw, ed., *Reformation and Revolution,* Edinburgh, 1967, pp. 52f. Cf. also F. Isaac, "Egidius van der Erve and his English Printed Books", in *The Library*, Fourth Series, London, 1932, XII, pp. 336-352.

27. From 1543 onwards the Polish nobleman John a Lasco, acting as the Superintendent in Emden, ordered the East Friesian Church on the pattern of Zürich. In 1549 he responded to Cranmer's call to come to London, where he built up the refugee congregation. In 1553, he fled from Mary Tudor together with his congregation, and found asylum in Emden. From 1556 onwards he worked as a reformer in Poland. Cf. U. Falkenroth in *Die Religion in Geschichte und Gegenwart*, 3rd ed., 1960, Vol. IV, column 236; H. Dalton, *John a Lasco.* London, 1886.

28. Ulrich Zwingli, *A short pathwaye to the ryghte and true understanding of the holye and sacred Scriptures* ... translated out of Laten, into Englysshe by John Veron...(Worcester, J. Oswen 1550).
The copy is in the University Library of South California, San Francisco. The text is Zwingli's *Von Klarheit und Gewissheit des Wortes Gottes*, 1522, (Z I 328-384) in Rudolf Gwalther's Latin translation, Opp. Zwinglii, Tom. I, 1545, pp. 160b-175a *De certitudine et claritate verbi Dei liber.*

plunge into pointless expense. The printings confirm that there was a demand for Zwingli's writings in England.

2.   This is further confirmed by Roman *polemic*. No bishop will unnecessarily draw public attention to an unknown heresy. When books are banned or a heresy is refuted, it is evidence that these are being disseminated. In lists of prohibited books issued in 1526 and 1531, the Archbishop of Canterbury forbade the importing and reading of numerous books by Oecolampadius and Zwingli, whose titles had been carefully compiled.[28a]

John Fisher (1459-1535), the Bishop of London, who had brought Erasmus to Cambridge, probably had a considerable share in Henry VIII's reply to Luther's *De captivitate Babylonica ecclesiae*, and in 1523 he produced a refutation of Luther's *Assertio* (1520). Of importance to us are his *Sacri Sacerdotii defensio* (1525) and *De eucharistia contra Joan. Oecolampadium libri quinque* (1527).[29] *Richard Smith* (1500-1563) a professor at Oxford, was regarded as "the greatest pillar for the Roman catholic cause in his time", and was most energetic of all in seeking the condemnation of Ridley and Latimer. His early writings, *The Assertion and Defence of the Sacrament of the aulter* (London, 1546) *and A defence of the sacrifice of the masse* (London, 1547) were both dedicated to Henry VIII and were specifically directed against Zwingli and Oecolampadius.[30] Later, he wrote against Cranmer, Melanchthon, Peter Martyr, Calvin, Beza and others.

28a. In 1526 the Archbishop of Canterbury proscribed Zwingli's work *Von der Taufe* (*On Baptism*) and his *Lehrbüchlein*. A list of imported "Books of the Lutheran sect", dating from about 1531, in London, contains an informative selection: 'Wycliffe comes first, then Luther comes next, followed by Oecolampadius and Zwingli and finally, various others. In the city where Colet was active, special attention is directed to exegetical works. We have here the fullest list of Zwinglian works to be found in indexes of prohibited books". These works, whose titles are recorded with a remarkable care, include the pedagogic work which the Reformer dedicated to his stepson in 1523 (*Of the Education of Youth*); his later writing against the Anabaptists, the *Elenchus in Catabaptistarum strophas* of 1527 (*Refutation of the Tricks of the Catabaptists*); his compendious dogmatic writings, the *Commentarius* and *De providentia* (1530), and, dating from the Diet of Augsburg, the *Fidei Ratio* against Eck; the statement of his eucharistic doctrine addressed to Billican and Rhegius in 1526, and that to Luther in the *Amica exegesis* of 1527; and above all his exegetical works, five of which are included: the *Annotations on Genesis*, the *Complanatio Isaiae*, the *Complanatio Jeremiae*, and the *Annotatiunculae* on the two Corinthian epistles and on Philippians. Cf. Johannes Ficker, "Verzeichnisse von Schriften Zwinglis auf gegnerischer Seite", *Zwa*. V/4 (1930/2), pp. 152-175; pp. 158f. follow Reusch, *Die Indices librorum prohibitorum des 16. Jahrhunderts*. Bibl. des Stuttgarter literarischen Vereins, No. 176, 1886.

29. *Dictionary of National Biography* (*DNB*), Vol. XIX, 1889, p. 62.

30. I am indebted to Dr. Duncan Shaw for pointing this out.

3.   But the most impressive evidence for the answer to our question is provided by a careful study of the *trial proceedings* reported in Foxe's *Book of Martyrs*.[31] The inquisition adapted the interrogation to each individual case with a deadly skill, but even with the most simple people there appears regularly and almost continuously the test question as to whether the sacrament is the true body of Christ.[32] We may choose some examples at random: "Over and besides, I find that in ... 1547, there was one John Hume, servant to Master Lewnax, of Wressel, apprehended, accused and sent up to the archbishop of Canterbury by the said Master Lewnax, his master, and Margaret Lewnax, his mistress, for these articles: I. First, for denying the sacrament (as it was then called) of the altar, to be the real flesh and blood of Christ. II. For saying that he would never veil his bonnet unto it, to be burned there-for. III. For saying that if he should hear mass, he should be damned".[33] An example from 1558: "Master Higbed (a worshipful gentleman in the country of Essex ... being zealous and religious in the true service of God) ... then Bishop Fecknam asked him his opinion in the sacrament of the altar. To whom he answered, 'I do not believe that Christ is in the sacrament as ye will have him, which is of man's making'. Later, in the same examination: "The Scriptures are full of figurative speeches ... the flesh profiteth nothing: for my words are spirit and life ... thus we see that Christ's words must be understood spiritually, and not literally ... in that Christ is God, he is everywhere; but that he is in man, he is in heaven, and can occupy but one place ..."[34] In both the argument and its formulation this belongs wholly to Zwingli's school.[35] It would be hard to accept that Higbed and his friend Causton had never read Zwingli. Again, in 1558: "Prest's Wife, a godly poor woman, suffered at Exter". For the sake of the faith she had left her family, but had then returned. " 'Thou foolish woman', quoth the bishop, 'I hear say, that thou hast spoken certain words against the most blessed sacrament of the altar, the body of Christ. Fie for shame! Thou art an

---

31. John Foxe (1516-1587), *Acts and Monuments of these latter and perilous dayes ("Book of Martyrs")*, 1563. The work enjoyed great popularity and appeared in many editions. There were several editions in the nineteenth century, including that of S. R. Cattley, in eight double volumes, 1858, (cf. J. F. Mozley, *John Foxe and his Book*, London, 1940).

32. It should be noted that this question could not be successful as far as genuine, consistent Lutherans were concerned, and the interrogators were well aware of this. Nevertheless, those found guilty on the basis of this question were all condemned as "Lutherans". Moreover, the same thing happened on the continent.

33. Foxe, *op. cit.*, V/II, p. 705.

34. Foxe, *op. cit.*, VI/II, pp. 729, 733, 735.

35. Not to Calvin's, nor to Bucer's.

unlearned person, and a woman ...' 'Yea, you caller, will you say that the sacrament of the Altar is a foul idol?' 'Yea truly', quoth she, 'there was never such an idol as your sacrament is made of your priests ...' " In the examination which follows, it comes to light that the woman, who was actually unable to read, had acquired, through small circles "of godly preachers and of godly books which I have heard read", some genuinely Zwinglian arguments and expressions, such as "that sacramental or significative bread instituted for a remembrance".[36] The books which were read in these groups must have been Zwinglian. And it would be easy to cite a dozen similar examples.

The inescapable impression is that a great deal of what has usually been termed "Lutheran" or "Calvinistic" in the history of the English Reformation was, in fact, genuine Zwinglianism, and that this was very widespread.

4.   There is an interesting illustration which serves to confirm this in the fact that in London on 4th March, 1550, Christopher Hales, an Englishman, placed an order for the portraits of Zwingli, Pellikan, Bibliander, Bullinger, Gualther and Oecolampadius with the famous Zurich painter Hans Asper.[37] In the end, only those of Oecolampadius and Zwingli were supplied—the latter might be the one which is now in Edinburgh.[38] The correspondence relating to this reflects the friendships, which had sprung up since the 1530s as a result of lively student exchanges between Cambridge, Oxford and Zurich.[39]

---

36. Foxe, *op. cit.*, VIII/II, pp. 497-499. "If his flesh is not profitable to be among us, why do you say, you make his body and flesh ..." (p. 499).

37. The brothers John (*DNB*, Vol. XXIV, 1890) and Christopher Hales were landed gentry from Kent who espoused the cause of the reformation. They had to flee in the reign of Mary. Cf. Georg Finsler, "Zwinglis Schrift 'Eine Antwort, Valentin Compar gegeben' von England aus zitiert", *Zwa.* III/4 (1914/2), pp. 115-117; Paul Boesch, "Der Zürcher Apelles. (scil. Hans Asper)", *Zwa.* IX/1 (1949/1), pp. 16-50; E. Staehelin, *Das Buch der Basler Reformation*, 1929, p. 263.

38. "Huldrych Zwingli", an oil painting by Hans Asper, in the National Gallery of Scotland, Edinburgh. Against Paul Boesch (see note 37), I believe that the Edinburgh painting is not a copy, but rather the original painting, which has been reduced in size, thereby losing the quatrain which Hales had requested. There is a good reproduction in *Zwa.* IX/1 (1949/1).

39. "In August 1536, Bullinger took into his home the young Englishman Nicolas Partridge, who had been taken ill as he was journeying to Italy. He then remained for some time for the purposes of study, as one of the seven students who came to Zürich in the thirties, as the centre of the Swiss reformation". Paul Boesch, "Rudolf Gwalthers Reise nach England im Jahr 1537", *Zwa.* VIII/8 (1947/2), pp. 433-471. Cf. Paul Boesch, "Von privaten Zürcher Beziehungen zu England im 16. Jahrhundert", in the "Neue Zürcher Zeitung", 19 July 1947, No. 1402/1405: Theodor Vetter, *Englische Flüchtlinge in Zürich*

Let us now consider some of the leading figures in the English Reformation.

5. *Thomas Bilney* (ca. 1495-1531).[40] "Little Bilney" was the widely respected and popular man who stood at the very centre of the youthful discussion group that met at the Whyte Horse in Cambridge. He was a humanistic Biblical scholar in the mould of Erasmus—or, perhaps more accurately, of Colet. He clearly seems to have aimed at the principle of Scriptural authority. At the same time, he took over Luther's own question and answer, and began to teach justification by faith. Although his utterances bear witness to the profound experience of freedom which this brought to him, he was like many others, in that he did not perceive that it involved a tension towards the programme of humanism. He proclaimed the worthlessness of all human effort apart from Christ, and added to it the humanist criticism of ritualism and ceremonialism. A merely outward service of God is vain and worthless, as are veneration of the saints and pilgrimages. Yet to the end he held firmly to the mediatorship of the church and the authority of the Pope, and he defended the sacrifice of the mass and transubstantiation. He was not a heretic; but Thomas More, who regarded him as a thoroughgoing Lutheran, brought him to the scaffold. The cause is instructive: under severe pressure, Bilney had promised to stop his preaching; but he had felt bound in conscience to resume it.

Bilney had understood Luther's doctrine of justification, but not its consequences. There do not seem to be any connexions with Zwingli, but there is a strong similarity in his path from humanism to a concentration on the Bible and opposition to ritualism. But despite Bilney's basic loyalty to the old church, the Reformation in England may rightly be said to begin with him. He embodied the duty and the promise of preaching.

6. *William Tyndale* (ca. 1491-1536).[41] The great Bible translator had heard John Colet at Oxford and Erasmus and Cambridge. According to

---

während der ersten Hälfte des 16. Jahrhunderts, Neujahrsblatt 1893 der Stadtbibliothek Zürich; Tagebuch des Pfarrers Josua/Maler, *Studienreise nach England im Jahre 1551*, Zürcher Taschenbuch, 1885; Salomon Rordorf-Gwalther, "Die Geschwister Rosilla und Rudolf Rordorf und ihre Beziehungen zu Zürcher Reformatoren", *Zwa.* III/6 (1915/2) pp. 180-193, especially pp. 183ff. No doubt a considerable amount of information about the reformation links between Zürich and England lies buried in the manuscript accounts and diaries of journeys which are deposited in British libraries.

40. *DNB*, Vol. V, 1886, pp. 40-42; E. G. Rupp, "Thomas Bilney", in *Studies in the Making of the English Protestant Tradition*, Cambridge, 1947, pp. 22-31.

41. *DNB*, Vol. LVII, 1899, pp. 424-431; J. F. Mozley, *William Tyndale*, London, 1937; C. H. Williams, *William Tyndale*, 1969; G. E. Duffield, ed., *William Tyndale*. Courtenay Library of Reformation Classics, Vol. I, 1964.

Foxe, he was already immersed in the study of Holy Scripture and the Biblical languages in the year 1515. He translated Erasmus' *Enchiridion* about 1522. From about the end of 1523 he struck up a friendship with John Frith in London, and came under the influence of the writings of Luther, whom he visited at Wittenberg in 1524. Then he stayed in Marburg, where he would become acquainted with Patrick Hamilton, the first Scottish martyr. Here Frith also joined up with him again. Tyndale had already taken to heart Luther's doctrine of justification and his distinction between Law and gospel, and was never to let go of them; at the same time, he adhered firmly to the doctrine of transubstantiation. But between 1528 and 1530 he accepted Zwingli's doctrine of the Lord's Supper, and that in its earliest form. It is reasonable to trace here the effect of the Marburg Colloquy between Luther and Zwingli in 1529,[42] in which Zwingli succeeded in winning many to his view. Tyndale rejected not only Luther's consubstantiation, but also Bucer's theory of a spiritual real presence. For him, the Lord's supper was a commemorative feast.

Tyndale's work, *The Obedience of a Christian Man, and how Christian rulers ought to governe,*[43] which appeared in Marburg in 1528, still bore a wholly Lutheran character, with its strict prohibition of all resistance to authority, and yet at many points there were already echoes of Zwingli's writings.[44] The "*Obedience*" established for the first time the two controversial principles of the English Reformation: the authority of Scripture in the Church, and the authority of the monarch in the state.

The *Brief declaration of the Sacraments,*[45] which was published in 1536, about the time of the Concord of Wittenberg, is in effect a private proposal for union, an attempt to achieve union with Luther, but on a Zwinglian rather than a Bucerian basis. It is conceded to Luther that those who

---

42. E. J. Carlyle (in *DNB*) maintained that it was "through the persuasions of Robert Barnes". That is improbable, for Barnes was a (somewhat uncertain) Lutheran (Cf. *The Reformation Essays of Dr. Robert Barnes*, ed. N. S. Tjernagel, London, 1963 and E. G. Rupp, "The Tragical History of Dr. Robert Barnes", *op. cit.*, pp. 31-46) (see Section 8).

43. W. Tyndale, *Doctrinal Treatises and Introductions to the different Portions of the Holy Scriptures*, ed. Henry Walter, Parker Society, Cambridge, 1848, pp. 131-344.

44. The basic aim of reforming the entire (political) society is Zwinglian. Among the individual Zwinglian elements are: the idea that God's Word is never free from persecution (p. 131); that the alternatives are either the Word of God or the authority of the "world" (pp. 132f.); the comparison of languages (p. 148); and that human wisdom produces idolatry. The Lord's Supper is still treated in the manner of Luther's early writings: the signs carry their promissio with them (p. 252). Although Luther's distinction between Law and Gospel underlies the treatise, it nowhere reflects Luther's horror of the Law, but rather comes down quickly on the side of Zwingli's delight in the Law.

45. *Op. cit.*, pp. 345-385.

receive the Lord's Supper in faith receive the gift of forgiveness of sins.[46] But we "believe" in what happened on the Cross, not in the sacrament itself.[47]

The *Prologue to the Pentateuch* (1534) introduced the concept of the covenant into English theological debate, and this was to have far-reaching consequences.

From 1529 onwards Tyndale was a Zwinglian, though he never repudiated what he had learnt from Luther. Luther's Preface to the Epistle to the Romans was retained in his translation of the New Testament; but from about 1528 onwards the Zürich Bible was of decisive influence for him. And the concepts which he derived from it[48] helped to form English Protestant religion; for Tyndale's work provided both the basis and the pattern for all the English translations of Holy Scripture right down to the New English Bible. "The Geneva Bible was eighty per cent based on Tyndale's version, and the Authorised (King James') Version ninety per cent".[49]

Before he could complete his work, Tyndale confided in a certain Henry Philipp, and became his benefactor. As a result of information provided by this traitor, he was executed near Antwerp in 1536.[50]

7. *John Frith (1503-1533).*[51] Frith was the first educated English reformer to raise the question of the real presence in the sacrament. He challenged publicly the biblical basis for transubstantiation. But what is

---

46. *Op. cit.,* p. 357.

47. "We be bound by these words only to believe that Christ's body was broken, and his blood was shed for the remission of our sins; and that there is no other satisfaction for sin than the death and passion of Christ". (*Op. cit.,* p. 367). That was Zwingli's basic position in the eucharistic controversy. Further Zwinglian elements are: the relation between baptism and circumcision (pp. 348ff.); the pattern of the Passover Meal as a Remembrance Meal (p. 354); and the statement that "Neither is idolatry any other thing than to believe that a visible ceremony is a service to the invisible God, whose service is spiritual, as he is spirit..." (p. 362). (Even Calvin took exception to this Zwinglian assertion. Cf. above p. 325). "The sign of the body of Christ is called by the name of Christ's body, which is there signified". (pp. 365, 368, 371). It is faith in Christ, not faith in the sacrament, which justifies us (p. 381).

The friendly arguments with Rome and with the Lutherans (pp. 366ff., 381ff.) show that Tyndale had a good knowledge of their writings.

48. There is a pressing need for a philological and theological study of this point. (cf. S. R. Mavecty, "Doctrine in Tyndale's New Testament. Translation as a tendentious Act" in *Studies in English Literature 1500-1900*, 1966, vi, pp. 151-8.

49. Professor George Yule.

50. C. H. Williams, *op. cit.,* pp. 50-54.

51. *DNB,* Vol. XX, 1899, pp. 278-280. H. M. Smith, *op. cit.,* *The Works of John Frith,* ed. N. J. Wright, Appleford, Abingdon, 1976.

most remarkable is the energy with which he contested the view that a particular interpretation of the words of consecration must be obligatory (and, therefore, divisive). It is well known that this is the viewpoint which Zwingli maintained in his dialogue with the Lutherans, in order that there might be ecclesiastical and political unity even if there were theological differences.

Frith lay imprisoned for three years in Oxford. He had come to know Tyndale and Hamilton in Marburg in 1528. After his return he was executed at the instigation of Thomas More. Among the plaintiffs was Thomas Cranmer, who felt some sympathy for him. In the course of his long imprisonment, in 1532, Frith set down in writing his own view of the sacrament.[52] Apart from the question of freedom of interpretation, to which we have already referred, he insists on the true humanity of Christ, which can only be present in one place, and he also insists that Christ's words must be understood "according to the analogy of scripture". These are Zwinglian ideas, even to their manner of formulation.

8. *Robert Barnes (1495-1540).*[53] He came to an evangelical faith about 1523, through the writings of Luther and under the influence of Bilney. At Christmas 1525 he delivered a biting sermon against superfluous festivals. In the consequent examination by Bishop Wolsey he appealed to the principle of Scriptural authority, but when threatened with burning he made the recantation required of him. He fled to Wittenberg and stayed with Luther. Henry VIII, needing both arguments and action against the Holy See, summoned him home in 1531. Barnes also undertook diplomatic missions to German princes and to Melanchthon on Henry's behalf. In 1539 he helped to negotiate Henry's marriage to Anne of Cleves, and therefore he fell out of favour when this marriage failed to turn out well. A sermon on justification, in which he defended Luther, provided the pretext for bringing him to trial. Bishop Gardiner convinced him that he was in error, and Barnes recanted. But when he finally began to preach the doctrine of sola fide once more, and as he also opposed Henry's separation from Anne of Cleves, he was sent to the stake.

Basically he was probably a true Lutheran (which means that he shared the Lutheran experience of inward trials and conflicts) and as such he was also a loyal servant of his King. He had decisively endorsed John

---

52. Reprinted in Foxe, *op. cit.*, V/I, p. 6.

53. *DNB*, Vol. III, 1885, pp. 253-256; A. G. Chester, "Robert Barnes and the burning of the books", in *Huntingdon Library Quarterly*, XIV, pp. 211-221.

Lambert's execution as a "Sacramentalist"; now he himself died as a sacrifice to that supremacy which he had furthered with all his powers.

9. *John Lambert (alias Nicholson) ?-1538.*[54] Lambert must have been very young when he first came into prominence, since he is looked upon as a pupil of Frith.[55] At times he worked as a schoolmaster, which was a common occurrence in Zwinglian circles. He preached most violently against the veneration of the saints, and his almost provocative insistence on disputations reminds one even more of Zwingli. Against Dr. Taylor, a Lutheran preacher, he drafted ten Zwinglian articles on the sacrament. Taylor passed these on to Barnes, who had Lambert brought to court. Lambert appealed to the King, seemingly with the naive hope that Henry would appreciate this acknowledgement of his supremacy. But instead Henry seized the opportunity once more to display his skill in theological disputation and to deliver a heretic to the scaffold.[56]

The defence which Lambert wrote begins with the Ascension of Christ, whose human nature can be in only one place. "Things corporal and spiritual are not to be compared".[57] The bread is a signum or figura for the Lord's body, and the words of consecration are to be understood spiritually and figuratively.[58] This follows from the analogy of Scripture.[59] When the sacrament is celebrated as a memorial feast, the sacrifice of Christ offered once-for-all upon the Cross is made mystically present.[60]

It indicates that Lambert had made a close reading of one of Zwingli's later writings (probably the *Fidei Ratio*) and made a careful note of its teaching.

10. *John Rogers, alias Thomas Matthew. 1500?-1555.*[61] Rogers also came from Cambridge, but was converted in Antwerp in 1534, through Tynedale, and then visited Wittenberg. Then he produced his

---

54. *DNB*, Vol. XXII, 1908, pp. 10f.; Foxe, *op. cit.*, V/I, pp. 237-250.

55. In both the older and the more recent literature, one finds the conjecture that Lambert was an Anabaptist (see, e.g. H. M. Smith, *op. cit.*, p. 360). But there is no foundation for this, either in the charges brought against him, or in his own statements.

56. There is a vivid account in H. M. Smith, *op. cit.*, pp. 446-450. It is interesting to note that Henry appeared in white robes—which only the Pope was entitled to do. But his arguments were soon at an end, and his prelates had to come to his assistance.

57. Foxe, *op. cit.*, V/I, p. 244.

58. *Ib.*, pp. 245-247.

59. *Ib.*, p. 248.

60. *Ib.*, pp. 248-250.

61. *DNB*, Vol. XLIX, 1897, pp. 126-129; J. L. Chester, *John Rogers*, London, 1861.

"Matthew's Bible" in Antwerp. This was basically Tyndale's work, supplemented by the Coverdale Bible, and slightly revised. It is hard to say what he had in mind after 1548 with his English translation of Melanchthon's "Interim Book". Before the court of Edward VI he recklessly delivered sharp attacks on the greed of the courtiers. Upon the arrival of Mary Tudor, before she was crowned, he was the one who sounded the trumpet warning: beware of the plague of Popery, of idolatry and superstition. As a result, he became the first of the "Marian martyrs".

While in prison he drew up, in collaboration with Hooper, Bradford, Coverdale and others, a confession of faith, dated 8th May, 1554.[62] This has been labelled extremely Calvinistic,[63] though it is, in fact, neither extreme nor Calvinistic. It starts with the principle of Scriptural authority and the doctrine of the "Catholic" Church, which listens only to the voice of Christ, her "husband" (Zwingli also likes to call Christ the "husband" of the Church, which is His "wife"). Then follow the Christian creeds. In speaking about "justification only through faith in Christ", a distinction is made between the justifying righteousness of God and that inner righteousness which is produced by the working of the Holy Spirit. Here one may trace points of contact with Zwingli as well as with Calvin. The article on the sacrament clearly rejects both transubstantiation and the sacrifice of the mass, but is otherwise careful in its expression: it is only in being used that the elements possess sacramental value.[64]

All things considered, it seems to me that John Rogers stands near to Melanchthon.

11. *John Bradford. 1510?-1555.*[65] Bradford also became a martyr under Mary Tudor. He was a close friend of Bucer and, among other things, translated one of Melanchthon's treatises. His very personal manner of preaching, in a pietistic, meditative style, pointed to Bucer and to the emergent Puritanism.[66]

Bradford declared that he had not read Luther, Zwingli or Oecolampadius on the Lord's Supper.[67] This lends even greater weight to the

62. Foxe, *op. cit.*, VI/II, pp. 550-553.
63. Sidney Lee in *DNB*, Vol. XLIX, 1897, p. 128.
64. Melanchthon had already emphasised this in the *Apology* for the Augsburg Confession in 1530, and John a Lasco said the same in debate with Calvin.
65. *DNB*, Vol. VI, 1886, pp. 157-159; John Chandos, ed., *In God's Name, Examples of preaching in England, 1534-1662*, 1971, pp. 36-38; Aubry Townsend, ed., *The Writings of John Bradford*, 2 Vol., Parker Society, Cambridge, 1848/53.
66. "Preface to the Places of Artopoeus", Townsend, Vol. I, pp. 5-12.
67. Vol. I, p. 525.

Zwinglian (rather than Bucerian or Calvinistic) content of his doctrine of the Lord's Supper. He acknowledges that the whole Christ, God and man, is truly present to the faith of the receiver.[68] The accusation of rationalism is thrown back to the Papists.[69] The *Sermon of the Lord's Supper*[70] describes Baptism as a sacrament of "initiation... wherewith we be enrolled, as it were, into the household and family of God".[71] This stems from Zwingli's *Commentarius de vera et falsa religione* (1525).[72] The Lord's Supper is compared to "when a loving friend giveth to thee a thing, or sendeth to thee a token (as for example, a napkin or such like)".[73] This may be compared to Zwingli's illustration of a ring in his *Apology*.[74] Without having read Zwingli, Bradford describes the presence of Christ's body as being spiritual rather than corporeal, real natural and carnal. This is pure Zwingli; Bucer's mode of expression was much nearer to Luther. Bradford's argument from "the nature of faith"[75] and his reference to the psychological force of the sacramental action, which speaks to all the senses at once, are also Zwinglian.[76] On the other hand, there is the Bucerian statement that in the sacrament the faithful really receive forgiveness.[77]

12. *Hugh Latimer. ca 1485-1555.*[78] With the Bishop of Worcester one finds a biographical link with Zurich, for Augustine Bernher,[79] who was for many years his servant, his friend, the publisher of his sermons, and the untiring attendant of Latimer and his fellow prisoners, was a Swiss.[80]

Latimer, son of a yeoman farmer and the "Apostle to the English", is one of the most significient of the English Reformers. In Cambridge he

---

68. Vol. I, p. 511.
69. Vol. II, pp. 271-277.
70. Vol. I, pp. 82-110.
71. Vol. I, p. 82.
72. Z III 759, 3, 19.
73. Vol. I, p. 93.
74. In *Ad Germaniae Principes de convitiis Eccii*.
75. Vol. I, p. 97.
76. Vol. I, p. 101. Cf. Zwingli, *Fidei Expositio* (1531), ed. 1536; S IV 56-58.
77. Vol. I, p. 99.
78. *DNB*, Vol. XXXII, 1892, pp. 171-179; H. S. Darby, *Hugh Latimer*, London, 1953; A. G. Chester, *Hugh Latimer, Apostle to the English*, Philadelphia, 1954; J. Chandos, *op. cit.*, pp. 10ff.; G. E. Corrie, ed., *Sermons and Remains of Hugh Latimer*, 2 Vol., Parker Society, Cambridge, 1844/45.
79. Arnold Lätt, "Austin Bernher, ein Freund der englischen Reformatoren", *Zwa.*, VI/6 (1936/2), pp. 327-336; *DNB*, Vol. IV, 1885, pp. 392f.
80. The literature is uncertain about his nationality, because Foxe states that he came from Belgium, but Bernher describes himself as "Helvetius" or "an Helvetian" (e.g. in Corrie, *Sermons of Hugh Latimer*, p. 455).

had delivered an oration against Melanchthon, but Bilney won him to the Gospel in 1524. He preached powerfully—throughout the land, and pleaded for Church services and a Bible in the language of the people. His support for Henry's divorce helped to protect him from repeated accusations. He became Bishop of Worcester in 1535, but resigned in 1539 when Henry took a pronouncedly catholic turn in his church policy. From 1547 to 1553, through his activity as a Biblical and social preacher, and as an advocate of the often unpopular measures taken by Cranmer, Latimer was the most important propagandist for the Gospel in England. He was burnt during Mary Tudor's reign.

There is a remarkable social-reforming ring about his sermons which is directed against the supporters of the Reformation as well as others. They clearly reveal a kindred spirit to Zwingli, not only in his doctrine of the Lord's Supper, but in his entire goal of a renewed Christian society; in his faith in the power of public preaching to bring this about; and not least in his fear of God's wrath if the call to renewal should not be heeded. This lends a prophetic note to his sermons, directed against idolatry on the one side, and social injustice on the other, as well as an urgent awareness that time is pressing for his country.[81] "London was never so ill, as it is now..."[82] "I say, repent, London, repent, repent!"[83] Everything must spring from the new, true faith—but this is itself dependent on the sermon. God's Word is the instrument, by which we are saved[84]—and, taken in the whole context of the sermon, this salvation does not primarily denote eternal bliss, but a life of righteousness, fellowship and faith here and now. Therefore society is dependent on the renewal of the church, and the basis of the Reformation is that the church begins to preach once more. Prelates should preach, and not rule.[85] If we do not bring ourselves to renew our church, and our life, the reason lies in our lack of gratitude for Christ's dying for our sins.[86] We may note how it is all interlarded with quotations from Augustin and the Latin classical authors and with many

---

81. "Now that the knowledge of God's word is brought to light". (Corrie, *Sermons*, p. 65). Cf. above ch. 6.

82. Corrie, *Sermons*, p. 64.

83. *Ib.*

84. "We cannot be saved without faith, and faith cometh by hearing of the word. *Fides ex auditu*". (Corrie, *Sermons*, p. 200).

85. Chandos, *op. cit.*, pp. 13, 22. Cf. Zwingli's *Christliche Einleitung* (1523), *Der Hirt* (1524) and *Vom Predigtamt* (1525). Zwingli's German writings were generally accessible after the appearance of Rudolph Gwalther's Latin edition of Zwingli's works in 1544.

86. Chandos, *op. cit.*, pp. 25-26. For the Cross of Christ is the "remedium" for all evil. Cf. Zwingli's Preface to the *Commentarius* (1525).

Biblical passages,[87] so that it is impossible to avoid the impression of Zwingli redivivus. Surely Latimer must know him, and be following his example, since there is such agreement, even in details. But even more important is their spiritual affinity, deriving from the similarity in their origins, their situation, their education and their encounter with the prophetic call of Scripture.[88] One difference is that the earlier sermons of Latimer are less Christocentric than those of Zwingli. But when he comes to speak of the Mass, everything becomes clear: either we trust in the cross of Christ—and that means in Christ himself—or else we trust in the sacrifice of the Mass-priest.[89]

His sermons before Edward VI, in 1549,[90] seek to set before the government the duty of freeing us from Pharaoh, the Pope.[91] Then they stress the

---

87. E.g. Chandos, *op. cit.*, pp. 16, 17, 19, 21.

88. The "Sermons on the Card" (about 1529) already demand true worship of God based on Holy Scripture. They call for an English Bible, and set the "triumph card", the heart, over against all external ceremonies and outward deeds of the letter only. The divine law of love, as set forth in the Sermon on the Mount, is set against the works commanded or appointed by men. (*Sermons and Remains*, Introduction, p. xi).

The sermons of 1536ff. attack superstition, mindless ceremonies and all kinds of abuses. The argumentation is not always christological and reformed, but it is always biblical.

The sermons of 1548 (*Sermons*, pp. 59ff.) distinguish between the Law and the Gospel, but they are no less concrete. The sermon which calls the rich citizens of London ("Nebo", *Sermons*, pp. 63ff) to repentance attacks the whole civil and ecclesiastical system. As a decisive measure towards reformation, Latimer demands that ministers should reside in their parishes, and they should preach (p. 62). The Apostles "preached and lorded not, and now they lord and preach not" (p. 66). As a consequence, souls starve, just as bodies starve when the ploughmen do not plough. The duty of the magistrates is to see to it that both ploughs are kept going "that the tranquillity of the commonweal may be confirmed". (p. 67). As part of the social reform for which he calls, the preacher asks for the establishment of schools in which men might be trained for their official duties. (p. 69).

Preaching means reformation, and reformation means preaching. It is necessary, because our rival is the most diligent preacher of all: the devil. We are compelled to choose between the true service of God, the Cross of Christ and "clothing the naked, the poor and impotent" or "new service of men's inventing", "purgatory pickpurse" and "decking of images" (p. 71). (Cf. Z II 47ff , and "In Spirit and in Truth", above, pp. 1f.).

Latimer deals with the problem of the Mass and the Lord's Supper from a strictly christological standpoint. Our Lord's own sacrifice of himself upon the Cross excludes the sacrifice offered by a mass priest (p. 72). "Then let us trust upon his only death, and look for none other sacrifice propitiatory, than the same bloody sacrifice, the lively sacrifice". (pp. 73-74).

The First Sermon preached before Edward VI (*Sermons*, pp. 84ff.) includes the comparison with the exodus from Egypt, of which Zwingli himself made frequent use. "King Edward ... now appointed in these our days to deliver us from danger, and captivity of Egypt and wicked Pharaoh; that is, from errors, and ignorance, and devilish antichrist, the Pope of Rome". (p. 84).

89. *Sermons*, pp. 72f.

90. *Ib.*, pp. 81-238.

91. *Ib.*, pp. 84, 92.

unity of the Christian society: the ruler bears the temporal sword, the preacher bears the spiritual sword of the Word;[92] all men are subject to both. Finally, he grasps the opportunity of raising at the highest level all kinds of abuses which have come to his knowledge. He demands tax relief for the poor—under pain of God's wrath![93] He scourges the avarice and corruption of the nobility—under pain of God's wrath![94] He gives examples of legal malpractices,[95] with the marginal comment that "Lawyers are like Switzers that serve where they have most money".[96]

It is remarkable that Latimer's sermons seldom discuss the Lord's Supper. But his "Protestation"[97] before the Queens Commissioners is a piece of pure Zwinglianism. The alternatives are the Cross of Christ or the sacrifice of the Mass. He casts back at his opponents, "the transubstantiators", the accusation of dividing the two natures of Christ (Nestorianism), which shows that he was well aware of this charge.[98] The Lord's Supper provokes us to thanksgiving for and remembrance of the death of Christ.[99] Latimer denies that he was ever a Lutheran.[100] Arguing from John 6, he distinguishes corporal, sacramental and spiritual eating as Zwingli does in his later writings.[101] He knows that the concept of the church is fundamental to the sacramental controversy: "It is one thing to say Romish church, and another thing to say catholic church".[102]

13.   *Nicholas Ridley,*[103] *ca. 1500-1555.* If Latimer stands alongside Zwingli, then Ridley stands alongside Bucer. This former student of Cambridge, Paris and Louvain became Chaplain to Archbishop Cranmer in

---

92. *Ib.*, p. 86.

93. *Ib.*, pp. 101ff.

94. *Ib.*, p. 107.

95. *Ib.*, p. 127.

96. An instructive remark, from the point of view of social history. We leave open the question as to whether it shows that Latimer or Bernher was aware of Zwingli's criticism of the mercenary system.

97. *Sermons and Remains*, pp. 251ff.; for the original Latin version, see pp. 479ff.

98. *Ib.*, p. 253.

99. *Ib.*, p. 255.

100. "No. I was a papist: for I never could perceive how Luther could defend his opinion without transubstantiation". (*Ib.*, p. 265).

101. *Ib.*, pp. 266-270; cf. Zwingli's *Fidei Expositio* (1531), ed. 1536, p. 74, pp. 53f.; also above p. 318-320.

102. *Sermons and Remains*, p. 290.

103. *DNB*, Vol. XLVIII, pp. 286-289; Henry Christmas, ed., *The Works of Nicholas Ridley*, Parker Society, Cambridge, 1841; Nicholas Ridley, *A brief Declaration of the Lord's Supper*, ed. H. C. G. Moule, London, 1895; J. G. Ridley, *Nicholas Ridley. A Biography*, London, 1957; G. W. Bromiley, *Nicholas Ridley, 1500-1555, scholar, bishop, theologian, martyr*, London, 1953.

1537. It is difficult to determine which of these two exercised the greater influence upon the other, whether to encourage or to inhibit reformation views. Ridley finally repudiated transubstantiation. He became Bishop of Rochester in 1547, and in 1550 was translated to London, where he did much for the alleviation of poverty. Earlier political remarks which he had made were taken as a personal slight by Queen Mary, and she had him imprisoned immediately. In 1555 he was burnt beside Latimer.

Ridley took his part in the slow process by which the gospel was accepted within the Church of England, and he shared in Bucer's efforts to make it possible, by means of ingenious formulae, for heterogeneous spirits to co-exist in peace. I do not find a clear evangelical confession on Ridley's part until after his imprisonment.

A brief declaration of the Lord's Supper, [104] which was written in prison, seems at first sight to be a Zwinglian exposition: the body of Christ is only in heaven; his sacrifice was made only on the Cross. That excludes both transubstantiation and the sacrifice of the Mass. [105] But then the argument becomes Bucerian: the body of Christ is also present on earth, "by grace", as the sun is present through its rays. [106] And in his extensive use of the concept of substance it remains uncertain whether he employs it polemically or ironically. [107]

His "Piteous Lamentation of the Miserable Estate of the Church of Christ in England" [108] makes a sharp attack on idolatry and disobedience to God's holy Word, [109] as does his "Treatise on the Worship of Images". [110]

In the disputation at Oxford, when the same questions were put to him as had been put to Latimer, Ridley's initial response was different. Shrewdly and skilfully following the scholastic method, he took apart the propositions of his accusers. Then, more positively, he acknowledged the "true presence of Christ's body in the sacrament... in the remembrance of him and his death". [111] That lies somewhere in between Bucer and Zwingli. It is interesting that Ridley expressly declares that he gained his

104. *Works of Nicholas Ridley*, pp. 5-45.

105. *Ib.*,,pp. 12f.

106. *Ib.*, p. 13.

107. "The natural substance of bread and wine is the true material substance of the holy sacrament of the blessed body and blood of our Saviour Christ". (*Ib.*, p. 15).

108. *Ib.*, pp. 47-80.

109. *Ib.*, pp. 52, 58.

110. *Ib.*, pp. 81-96 (The authorship is disputed. Cf. J. G. Ridley, *op. cit.*, p. 119 n.).

111. *Ib.*, p. 201.

understanding of the Lord's Supper solely from reading "Bertram". The latter (i.e. Rhabanus Maurus) is also quoted by Zwingli.[112] Like Bucer, Ridley also emphasises the (spiritual) objectivity of the gift of grace in the sacrament.[113]

14. *John Hooper, ca. 1495-1555.*[114] John Hooper was in Zürich from 1547-49, though this has more immediate reference to Bullinger, with whom Hooper entered into an intensive correspondence, than to Zwingli himself. This erstwhile Cistercian had learnt to know Zwingli and Bullinger through their writings. He fled to Zürich because he was suspected of heresy, and this resulted in his becoming the advocate of the Zurich church in England. Upon his return in 1549 he became the leader of the avant-garde of the radical reformation, from which Puritanism arose. This stern, unpopular man preached twice a day to enormous audiences. The young King liked him, Cranmer was irritated by him. He was hardened by the Vestments Controversy, when he refused for a long time to wear the prescribed vestments for his consecration as Bishop of Gloucester in 1551. Mary had him burnt at the stake.

In his work *Christ and his Office*, published in Zurich in 1547,[115] it is obvious that he owes a great deal to Zwingli: that the merits of Christ prevail over all the sins of the whole of mankind;[116] that Christ suffered only in his human nature;[117] the preaching office of the priest;[118] total reformation based on the Word of God;[119] and so on. Hooper's (Zwinglian) doctrine of the Lord's Supper is nicely derived from the doctrine of justification.[120] Therefore one should not expect from the sacrament what the Lord

---

112. *Ib.*, pp. 175, 206; cf. Z IV 805, 1.

113. *Ib.*, pp. 222, 274.

114. *DNB*, Vol. XXVII, pp. 304-306; M. Schmidt in *Die Religion in Geschichte und Gegenwart*, 3rd ed., Vol. III, 449; August Lang, *Puritanismus und Pietismus*, 1941, pp. 38ff.; Helmut Kressner, *Schweizer Ursprünge des anglikanischen Staatskirchentums*, Gütersloh, 1953; W. M. S. West, *John Hooper and the Origins of Puritanism*, Zürich Dissertation, 1955; J. H. Primus, *The Vestments Controversy*, Kampen, 1960; Samuel Carr, ed., *Early Writings of John Hooper*, Parker Society, Cambridge, 1843 (Cited as Vol. I); Charles Nevinson, ed., *Later Writings of John Hooper*, Parker Society, Cambridge (Cited as Vol. II). John Opie: The Anglicising of John Hooper. *Archiv für Reformations-Geschichte* 59/1 (1968) pp. 150-177.

115. Vol. I, pp. 1-96.

116. *Ib.*, p. 16; cf. S IV 7.

117. *Ib.*, p. 17.

118. *Ib.*, p. 19.

119. *Ib.*, p. 29.

120. *Ib.*, p. 60.

himself will do through his Spirit.[121] But already the social activism is lacking.

In Article 4 of his Visitation Book of 1551,[122] he defines the church in terms of the famous formula of Article VII in the Confession of Augsburg, but employs this against the concept of ecclesiastical office. Article 10 contests the Lutheran "in, with and under", maintaining instead a spiritual presence, known by faith; Article 11 rejects the concept of the communicatio idiomatum.

The *Lesson of the Incarnation*,[123] published in 1549 to controvert the Anabaptists, is prefaced by a fine English translation of Zwingli's "Prophecy prayer".

The *Brief Confession*, first published in 1550, includes Zwinglian teaching on the Lord's Supper (Article 28), a Calvinistic interpretation of the Descent into Hell (Article 24), and a late-Calvinistic doctrine of the Church, in which discipline is set alongside Word and Sacrament as an indispensable mark of the Church.[124] Articles 63-68 introduce Calvinistic elements into sacramental doctrine. In its general effect, the Brief Confession anticipates the Calvinistic Gallic and Belgic Confessions.

Overall, Hooper appears less Zwinglian than he has been represented in recent literature. This emerged in the path he followed in England. Bullinger was peaceable and basically politically loyal, but his pupil and friend, in adhering to Bullinger's puritan principles, ended in political opposition in England. Calvinism was built up on this basis.

15. *Miles Coverdale, 1488-1568.*[125] "One of the agents most responsible for bringing Lutheran ideas into England",[126] he was not a Lutheran in the confessional sense, however, but a man of Biblical-Protestant views.

He was a student and an Augustinian monk in Cambridge, who was brought under the influence of Luther by Robert Barnes. In 1535 he

---

121. *Ib.*, p. 76.

122. Vol. II, pp. 117-156.

123. *Ib.*, pp. 1-18; cf. "In Spirit and in Truth" (above, ch. 1) and Z IV 365, 702.

124. This was rejected by Calvin, cf. *Institutes* IV. i and IV. xii; but was included in the *Westminster Confession* (1647), Chapter XXX; and was stated even more clearly in the *Confessio Belgica* (1561), Article 29, and the *Confessio Scotica* (1560), Chap. 18. W. M. S. West (cf. n. 114) disputes Hooper's authorship of the Brief Confession. Don S. Ross (*ChH* March 1970) presumes John Garnier. In this case Hooper is indeed a follower of Zwingli's and Bullinger's.

125. *DNB*, Vol. XII, pp. 364-372; J. F. Mozley, *Coverdale and his Bibles*, London, 1953.

126. Martin Schmidt, in *Die Religion in Geschichte und Gegenwart*, 3rd. ed., Vol. I, column 1877.

brought to completion Tyndale's translation of the Bible. In 1539 there appeared the "Goostly Psalmes", which included many German hymns, among them 17 by Luther. His English version of Bullinger's "Christian Marriage" introduced the tradition of conduct books. He was a schoolmaster in Bergzabern from 1545 to 1547, and again pastor there from 1555 to 1557, after having received a passport to leave England from Mary Tudor, through the representations of the King of Denmark.

Coverdale kept to the line that had been followed by Tyndale. The Old Testament is largely based on the Zurich Bible of 1531, with headings and notes.[127] The New Testament follows Tyndale. In 1537 he translated a plague-sermon by Osiander. While in Bergzabern he took a keen interest in the work of the English congregations in Frankfurt-on-Main, in association with Calvin.

In 1550 he published an English version of *Spiritual Pearls* by the Zurich pastor Otto Werdmuller.

He was made Bishop of Exeter in 1551, and soon became a confident of Cranmer, and shared in the work of the Reformation Commission. While in prison in 1554 he subscribed Rogers' Confession.[128] During his stay with the refugee congregation in Wesel he was involved in the production of the Genevan Bible.

After the accession of Elizabeth he also returned to England with a more puritan outlook. The Queen appointed him Bishop of Llandaff, and closed her eyes to the nonconformist behaviour of the old man. As a preacher he enjoyed the complete confidence of all the puritans, and was among the leaders of those who strove for a purer church. The Act of Uniformity in 1559 broke his heart.

In addition to a translation of a work on the Lord's Supper by Calvin, mention may also be made of the *Fruitfull Lessons upon the Passion, Burial, Resurrection, Ascension and the sending of the Holy Ghost, gathered out of the four Evangelists*, an adaptation of Zwingli's *Brevis Commemoratio*.[129] In various excurses it provides a clear insight into important points of Zwingli's theology, and of his doctrine of the Lord's Supper in particular.

---

127. Ernst Nagel, "Die Abhängigkeit der Coverdale-Bibel von der Zürcher Bibel", *Zwa.* VI/8 (1937/2), pp. 437-457.

128. See above, Section 10.

129. *Brevis commemoratio mortis Christ ex quatuor Euangelistis per Huld. Zuinglium in unam seriem concinnata. Sequitur Historia Resurrectionis et Ascensionis Christi*, published posthumously by Leo Jud in *Opp. Zuinglii*, Tom. IV, 1544, pp. 347a-406b; cf. S VI, II, 1-75.

16.   *Thomas Cranmer, 1489-1556.*[130] It is not our task here to describe the character and the development of the central figure in the English reformation. Neither shall we analyse his wonderful gift to the Anglican tradition and to the church at large, the *Book of Common Prayer.* Richardson has argued strongly for a Zwinglian interpretation; Brooks' weighty attempt to refute this leads me to ask whether Calvinist texts could not be drawn upon for the purpose of comparison. It is probable that Cranmer consciously sought out (and found) a mode of expression which clearly says what is essential in worship, and yet leaves room for a variety of theological attitudes within the church. Therefore the question of the interpretation of the text of the Lord's Supper in the Prayer Book is not identical with the question of Cranmer's own doctrine. In my opinion, Willem Nijenhuis has proved conclusively that Cranmer's own views were originally Roman, then secretly Lutheran for a time, and finally Zwinglian; and his inquisitors realised this.[131]

This conclusion should not mislead us into regarding Cranmer as a "Zwinglian" without any qualification. The Archbishop of a powerful kingdom and a seafaring island race thinks and acts in a different dimension from the bourgeois, republican pastor of a minster. Though their criteria were remarkably similar.

VI. STAGES IN THE SCOTTISH REFORMATION[132]

From about 1525 onwards, reformation ideas and writings flooded into Scotland. The task of suppressing these was assigned by King James V to

---

130. G. E. Duffield, ed., *Work of Thomas Cranmer,* Courtenay Library of Reformation Theology, Vol. 2, 1964; G. Dix, *The Shape of the Liturgy,* 1944; G. B. Timms, "Dixit Cranmer", *Church Quarterly Review,* CXLIII, pp. 217-234 and CXLIV, pp. 33-51; G. Dix, "Dixit Cranmer et non timuit. A supplement to Mr. Timms", *Church Quarterly Review,* CXLV, pp. 146-176 and CXLVI, pp. 44-60; Cyril C. Richardson, *Zwingli and Cranmer on the Eucharist (Cranmer dixit et contradixit),* Evanston, Illinois, 1949; G. W. Bromiley, *Thomas Cranmer, Theologian,* London, 1956; Cyril C. Richardson, "Cranmer and the Analysis of Eucharistic Doctrine", *Journal of Theological Studies,* New Series, Vol. XVI/2, 1965, pp. 421-437; Peter Brooks, *Thomas Cranmer's Doctrine of the Eucharist,* London, 1965; W. Nyenhuis, "Traces of a Lutheran eucharistic doctrine in Thomas Cranmer", in W. Nyenhuis, *Ecclesia Reformata. Studies on the Reformation,* Leiden, 1972, pp. 1-22; C. H. Smyth, *Cranmer and the Reformation under Edward VI,* 1926 (reprinted with a Foreword by E. G. Rupp, London, 1973). (cf. for correction C. Hopf, *Martin Bucer and the English Reformation,* Oxford, 1946).

131. With reference to Cranmer's denial that he had ever held a Lutheran doctrine, Nyenhuis writes: "There can be only one answer: from his new eucharistic standpoint Cranmer no longer saw any difference in principle between the Roman and the Lutheran teaching regarding the sacrament". That would be a truly Zwinglian argument. Cf. Nyenhuis, *op. cit.,* p. 22.

132. John Knox, *The History of the Reformation in Scotland,* ed., W. C. Dickinson, London,

the Archbishop of St. Andrews, James Beaton, who was already under the influence of his clever but ambitious and cruel nephew David Beaton, who was later to become cardinal. In 1528 Beaton executed Patrick Hamilton, a 24 year-old "Lutheran" of royal blood,[133] who had returned home from Marburg. This marked the beginning of a constant and bloody persecution. Nevertheless, the evangelical influence went on spreading throughout all classes of society, from the nobility to the common people, and especially under the regency that was established after the death of James in 1542, as his daughter was still a minor. The first man who ventured to proclaim the gospel publicly in Scotland was the preacher George Wishart. When the Primate, David Beaton, had him burnt in 1546, this provoked a revolt that was as much political as religious in its motivation. Beaton himself fell victim to this. As a result, some of the leaders of the reformation, including John Knox, were taken as prisoners aboard the galleys which had been sent to the assistance of the regency by their French allies. The persecutions continued. A Provincial Council held in 1549, which decided on all kinds of reform, as well as the suppression of heresy, remained ineffective. Mary of Guise, the Regent, had to exercise restraint for some years, under the combined pressure of enmity towards the English-Spanish alliance that had been sealed by the marriage of Philip II and Mary Tudor, and the French plans for uniting the crown of Scotland with that of France. Yet there is something puzzling and elusive about the expansion and deepening of the Protestant movement during this period. It appears to have been a secret lay movement led almost exclusively by the noble or the middle-class[134] which nevertheless, when the hour came, could step forth as a powerful force able to represent democratically the whole people. Only a few of the spiritual leaders are known to us, including the popular William Harlow,[135] a former tailor, and John Willock, the most important Scottish reformer after Knox. Willock returned home from Emden early in 1555, and Knox returned (briefly) from Geneva in

---

1949 2 vols.; Friedrich Brandes, *John Knox, der Reformator Schottlands,* Elberfeld, 1862; P. Hume Brown, *John Knox. A Biography,* 2 Vol., London, 1895; Eustace Percy, *John Knox,* London, n.d. (ca. 1935) J. Ridley, *John Knox,* Oxford, 1968; *John Knox. A Quatercentenary Reappraisal,* ed. Duncan Shaw, Edinburgh, 1975; Duncan Shaw, "John Willock", in Duncan Shaw, ed., *Reformation and Revolution. Essays presented to … Hugh Watt,* Edinburgh, 1967, pp. 42-69; Gordon Donaldson, *The Scottish Reformation, 1560,* Cambridge, 1960.

133. "The Articles for the which he suffered, were but of Pilgrimage, Purgatory, Prayer to Saints, and for the Dead, and such Trifles", Knox, *History,* p. 13.

134. "The new Scottish congregations … had as yet no ministers". E. Percy, *op. cit.,* p. 235; cf. p. 278.

135. P. Hume Brown, *op. cit.,* Vol. I, p. 290.

the autumn of the same year. In 1557 the most influential of the nobles concluded the (first) Reformation "Covenant". In 1559 there was an uprising by the nobility and the cities; many churches began to reform their worship and to govern themselves by elders and deacons. On the advice of Willock, the Lords of the Congregation declared the Regent to be deposed, and besieged her French troops in Leith. In 1560, with the publication of the *Confessio Scotica* and the *First Book of Discipline*, the Scottish Parliament established a reformed national church. *The Book of Common Order* appeared in 1564.

Mary Stuart, who returned from France in 1561, had only private Catholic services. As a consequence of her breach of political and religious agreements, and her marriage to Bothwell, the murderer of her consort Darnley, she was compelled to renounce her crown in 1567 in favour of her son James. Her half-brother Moray, acting as Regent, helped to consolidate the reformed church. After Knox's death, Andrew Melville became the theological authority.

2.   In the sixteenth and seventeenth centuries, Scottish politics were determined according to archaic customs (loyalty to the clan; feuds etc.), through the struggles of the great feudal families, to which the Royal house itself belonged.

As regards *internal politics*, these families had an interest in the secularisation of the property of the churches and monasteries, while desiring that the bishoprics and the system of patronage should continue; whereas the self-government of the churches by elders and deacons (in synods) was the concern, both sociologically and psychologically, of the aspiring middle-classes. Neither in state nor in church could anything be carried through without the Lairds, but through the General Assembly of the "Kirk", the voice of the people gained a hearing. For centuries the tension between feudalism and democracy, episcopalianism and presbyterianism has remained the sad theme of Scottish church history. It may be remarked that neither Calvin nor Bullinger nor Knox were thoroughgoing democrats and presbyterians,[136] unlike Zwingli, à Lasco, Willock and Melville.[137]

---

136. The abolition of the episcopate was first postulated in Melville's *Second Book of Discipline* in 1581.

137. Janet G. MacGregor, *The Scottish Presbyterian Polity*, Edinburgh, 1926; Duncan Shaw, *The General Assemblies of the Church of Scotland, 1560-1600*, Edinburgh, 1964, pp. 75ff.

As regards *external politics*, the reformation meant turning away from the traditional alliance with France, which was threatening to turn into dependence, and, out of necessity, turning to England instead. But traditional Scottish nationalism naturally remained Francophile—which has for centuries proved a difficulty for the reformed church.

3.   Nobody can say for certain what was the real spirit of the secret yet powerful Scottish reformation movement in the years before 1560.[138] Humanism seems to have played only a minor role; the culture of the court and city, which it presupposes, was still not sufficiently developed. Genuine Lutheranism, with its individualism and its political abstention would not have been adequate for these conditions. Melanchthon and Bullinger were far too peace-loving and conservative. Calvin? The very fact that Knox could succeed with a generally Calvinistic theology in the Confessio Scotica suggests that there must have been a considerable preparation for this, though there are indications of Zwinglian influence also.

In any case, it did not result in Scotland's becoming a mere province of Geneva. With its puritan and politically revolutionary type of piety it became instead an independent centre within the framework of the manifold reformed churches, alongside Zürich, Geneva and Heidelberg. Together with English congregationalism, this Scottish type has exercised a decisive influence upon the ethic of the New World.

VII. EARLY ZWINGLIANISM IN SCOTLAND

The considerable part taken by the nobles and the people in the events of the Reformation, as well as certain similarities in the way in which Huldrych Zwingli and John Knox proceeded might deceive us into describing precipitate points of contract. But Scotland was remote, and was preoccupied with its own political and religious troubles. It is truly remarkable if we find traces of Zwingli's influence.

1.   *Libraries*. 1) The Library of *Clement Little,*[139] (admitted as an advocate in Edinburgh in 1560, died 1580), which he bequeathed to the

---

138. So far as I am aware, this question has never been seriously considered or systematically investigated. It would probably require researching numerous local archives. Duncan Shaw has rightly warned against the danger of seeing the history of the Scottish Reformation only through the eyes of John Knox's *History*, "for an excess of humility was no part of the Reformer's character" (W. C. Dickinson, quoted in D. Shaw, *op. cit.*, p. 42).

139. Charles P. Finlayson, *Clement Litill and his Library, the origins of Edinburgh University Library*, Edinburgh, 1980.

University, contained Zwingli's works in the 1545 Latin edition of Rudolf Gualther. In addition, it included many works by Musculus, Oecolampadius, Bibliander, Bullinger, Pellikan, Megander, Ochino, Sebastian Meyer and Capito.

2) The extant index to the library of *Adam Bothwell,*[140] the reformation-minded Bishop of Orkney from about 1560 to 1580, shows that his library contained books by Zwingli, Bullinger, Bucer and Oecolampadius.[141]

2. *Indirect Evidence* 1) In 1525 the Scottish Parliament prohibited the import of the writings "of the heretic Luther and his disciples".[142]

2) Among polemical works (which serve to indicate the significance of the opponent), there are those of *Ninian Winzett*, a priest and schoolmaster in Linlithgow, who in 1562 entered the lists against "Oecolampadius, Zwinglius and Calvin".[143]

3) Then, we possess an unforeseen and significent item: the remarkably detailed and sharp rejection and refutation of the Zwinglian doctrine of the Lord's Supper in Article XXI of the basically Calvinistic Confessio Scotica of 1560.[144] After the ebb of the first, so-called "Lutheran" wave of the reformation movement, which was not so confessional, Zwinglianism must have become very widespread in Scotland.[145]

This observation corresponds to activity of the first Scottish reformers.

3. *Patrick Hamilton.*[146] *1498-1528.* In 1527 Hamilton stayed in Wittenberg, and then in Marburg, at whose newly-opened University he

---

140. Gordon Donaldson, "Bishop Adam Bothwell and the Reformation in Orkney", in *Records of the Scottish Church History Society*, Glasgow, 1959, Vol. XIII, pp. 85-100.

141. A. J. Cameron, ed., *The Warrender Papers*, Vol. II, The Scottish History Society, Edinburgh, 1932; cf. also John Durkan and Anthony Ross, *Early Scottish Libraries*, Glasgow, 1961.

142. *The Acts of the Parliaments of Scotland*, ed. T. Thomson and C. Innes, Edinburgh, 1814, II., p. 295.

143. J. K. Hewison, ed., *Certain Tractates ... by Ninian Winzett*, Scottish Text Society, London and Edinburgh, 1888, p. 98; cf. also John Durkan, "Some Local Heretics", in *Transactions of the ... National History and Antiquarian Society*, Dumfries, 1959, pp. 67-77.

144. *Scots Confession, 1560 (Confessio Scoticana) and Negative Confession, 1581*, with Introduction by G. D. Henderson, Edinburgh, 1937; "The Confessioun of Faith ... Confessio Fidei et Doctrinae per Ecclesiam Reformatam Regni Scotiae receptae ...", ed. Theodor Hesse, in W. Niesel, ed., *Bekenntnisschriften und Kirchenordnungen der nach Gottes Wort reformierten Kirche*, Zollikon, 1938, pp. 79-117; cf. Friedrich Brandes, *John Knox*, 1862, pp. 476ff.; Karl Barth, *The Knowledge of God and the Service of God according to the Teaching of the Reformation, recalling the Scottish Confession* of 1560, London, 1938.

145. According to Prof. J. K. Cameron.

146. *DNB*, Vol. XXIV, pp. 201-203; P. Lorimer, *Precursor of Knox: or, Memoirs of Patrick Hamilton, the first Preacher and Martyr of the Scottish Reformation*, Edinburgh, 1857; *Patrick Hamilton*, ed. A. Cameron, Edinburgh, 1929.

became acquainted with Frith, Tyndale and the Dean of the Theological Faculty, Francis Lambert of Avignon. He had the honour of holding the first public disputation in the faculty. For this he compiled a series of Loci Communes, which he later enlarged, and which Frith published in an English edition after his death. Hamilton's "Places" are the first milestone on the road of the Scottish reformation.

After six months, he returned home in 1527 and gave evangelical lectures at the University of St. Andrews. Archbishop Beaton had him imprisoned, tried and burnt.

In content, Hamilton's theses present the Lutheran distinction between Law and gospel, and the doctrine of justification by faith. In structure, form and the didactic manner in which the doctrine of imputation is emphasised, they are clearly Melanchthonian. This accords with the fact that Hamilton's pupil at St. Andrews, Alexius Alesius, was later to appear in Leipzig as the leading Philippist in the dispute with the Gnesiolutherans.[147]

4.   *George Wishart.*[148] *1513?-1546.* Wishart travelled in Germany and Switzerland during 1539 and 1540. After his return he translated from Latin into English the First Helvetic Confession of 1536, which was intended as a unifying document, but was still characteristically Zwinglian.[149] It was not published until after his death, probably in 1548,

---

147. P. Hamilton's *Loci Communes* are printed in full in J. Foxe, *Acts and Monuments* (see Index).—For Alexander Alesius cf. J. H. Baxter, "Alesius and other reformed Refugees in Germany", in *Records of the Scottish Church History Society*, Glasgow, 1935, Vol. V, pp. 93-102, and A. F. S. Pearson, "Alesius and the English Reformation", in *ibid.*, Glasgow, 1950, Vol. X, pp. 57-87; also R. Buddensieg in *Realenzyklopädie für protestantische Theologie und Kirche*. 3rd ed., 1896, Vol. I, pp. 336-338; O. Clemen, "Melanchthon und Alexander Alesius", in *Archiv für Reformationsgeschichte*, Ergänzungsband 5, 1929, pp. 17ff. John T. McNeill, Alexander Alesius, Scottish Lutheran (1500-1565). *ARG* 55 (1964) 161-191.

148. *DNB*, Vol. LXII, pp. 248-251; Foxe, *op. cit.*, V/II, pp. 625-636, C. Rogers, *The Life of George Wishart,* London, 1876.

149. E. F. K. Müller, ed., *Die Bekenntnisschriften der reformierten Kirche*, 1903, pp. 101-109: Confessio Helvetica Prior, 1536. Müller states in the Introduction, "It is to be ascribed to the influence of Bucer and Capito if there sometimes occur, in this thoroughly Swiss confession, formulae which approximate to Luther's mode of expression. But apart from this, the very fact that the confession, while preserving its Zwinglian basis, should extol the gift of grace in the Lord's Supper in a deeply devotional manner, indicates how the tone of Swiss teaching was free of any one-sidedness" (p. xxvi). Cf. "The Confession of Faith of the Churches of Switzerland". Translated by George Wishart, 1536, in *The Miscellany of the Wodrow Society*, selected and edited by David Lang, Edinburgh, 1894, pp. 1-23. Professor J. Cameron thinks it likely that Wishart introduced a Zwinglian order of the Lord's Supper into Scotland, which would be in use until 1560.

but it could have been Wishart's own confession. In 1543 he stayed in Cambridge, and then returned to Scotland 1544. When he was banned from the churches, he preached in the fields: "Christ is as potent in the field as in the kirk"—which was by no means self-evident at that time. When there was an outbreak of the plague in Dundee, he hastened there in order to help the dying. After his arrest, he appealed at once to the authority of Scripture. When things became dangerous, he sent John Knox, his pupil and helper, back home; 'One sacrifice was enough'.

During the trial, whose proceedings are recorded by Foxe, he immediately launched a counter-attack upon ceremonialism. He was accused, among other things, of rejecting mass, auricular confession, the authority of the priest, the veneration of saints, and purgatory—a selection which was cleverly designed to arouse the antipathy of Lutherans also. In his answers, attention may be drawn to his remark that God seeks "the inward moving of the heart". In relation to the sacrament, he answered, *inter alia*, by recalling a conversation which he had once had with a Jew aboard a boat on the Rhine.[150] The Jew had linked the social injustice of Christendom with the idolatry of the mass. "We Jews are poor, but there are no beggars among us". This association of central questions of faith with social problems seems to have been characteristic of Wishart.[151]

His death at the stake unleashed a violent bitterness, and Archbishop Beaton suffered the fearful penalty of revenge.

5. *John Knox,*[152] *1502-72*. The mighty central figure of the Scottish reformation and his connexions with Zürich require a separate, detailed study. Yet one should not conceal the impression that this man, who was the pupil of Wishart, stood within the Zwinglian tradition throughout the period of his early activity, up to the time of his stay in Geneva. It was only after his arrival in Geneva in 1554 that he developed into a Calvinist; though he retained to the last his all-consuming sense of responsibility for

---

150. For centuries passengers sailing on the Rhine between Strasbourg and Basle found that conversation with the quick-witted Jews from Alsace provided a pleasant diversion. Cf. Johann Peter Hebel, "Schatzkästlein des Rheinischen Hausfreundes" in *Werke*, ed. Wilhelm Altweg, Vol. II, Zürich, n.d. (1958?), pp. 168ff.; also *ib.*, pp. 266f.

151. Zwingli also maintained that there was a connexion between sacramental and economic materialism.

152. *DNB*, Vol. XI, pp. 308ff.; Gordon Donaldson, *The Scottish Reformation, 1560*, Cambridge, 1960; James S. McEwen, *The Faith of John Knox*, London, 1961; Pierre Janton, *Concept et Sentiment de l'Église chez John Knox*, Paris, 1972.

political events, his sense of the unity of ecclesiastical and social reformation, the idea of the covenant, and his opposition to idolatry.[153]

6. *John Willock ?-1585.*[154] Willock, the most important reformer before
the return of John Knox, and his most prominent colleague, was a Zwinglian.

He was a monk until about 1540, and then acted for a time as chaplain
to the Duke of Suffolk, the father of Lady Jane Grey. He fled from Mary
Tudor, and settled in Emden, from where he paid two visits to Scotland,
and had a part in the abolition of the Mass. He returned home in 1555,
and although he was very ill, he urged on the "public reformation"
among the nobility, and secured the requisite petition to the Queen
Regent. She had him outlawed, but he was protected by the Lords.

In 1559 he became Knox' colleague in Edinburgh, and there he in-
troduced the Lord's Supper at St. Giles' in August, 1559. When Mary of
Guise, the Regent, broke the agreement he was the first to advocate her
deposition—that required a Zwinglian spirit.[155] He was a member of the
Reformation Commission, and participated in the drafting of the First
Book of Discipline in 1560.[156]

In 1562 he accepted a pastoral charge in Leicestershire. He had to leave
Edinburgh, in part, perhaps, on account of his Zwinglian sympathies.[157]
That the question was not yet resolved within the Scottish church is shown
by the fact that he was prevailed upon to retain his superintendency in
Glasgow, and that he was three times elected as Moderator of the General
Assembly. He died in office in Loughborough in 1585.

---

153. It remains to be explored whether Knox's dissatisfaction with Zürich might not have
been due to Bullinger's political conservatism; in which case Knox might be, in this respect,
the better Zwinglian. Dr. D. Shaw points out that Knox also describes Christ as the "Captain", e.g. in a sermon of August, 1565 (*The Works of John Knox*, ed. D. Laing, Edinburgh, 1864, VI, p. 271). Basil Hall goes so far as to say: "John Knox himself, contrary to
the received opinion about him, leaned more to Zurich than to Geneva in his theology and
something of his practice and he had been the disciple of George Wishart whose theological
interests were entirely German Swiss". ("Calvin against the Calvinists", in *John Calvin*, ed.
G. E. Duffield, Appleford, 1966, pp. 33-34).
154. *DNB*, Vol. LXII, pp. 30-31; Duncan Shaw, "John Willock", in D. Shaw, ed.,
Reformation and Revolution. Essays presented to ... Hugh Watt ... Edinburgh, 1967, pp. 42-69.
155. Calvin (*Institutes* IV. xx. 22-32) lays upon the legitimate representatives of the people
the duty of resisting despotic autocrats, whereas Zwingli says, "If they are unfaithful and
transgress the law of Christ, then they may be deposed in God's name". (Forty-second
Article, 1523; Z I 463; Z II 342-346).
156. James K. Cameron, ed., *The First Book of Discipline. With Introduction and Commentary*,
Edinburgh, 1972.
157. Cf. D. Shaw, *op. cit.*, pp. 59-61.

7. *The Confessio Scotica of 1560.*[158] The Scots Confession was a joint production, though it was the energy and leadership of John Knox that moulded its character, which is, on the whole, Calvinistic. Yet there is a striking divergence at a point which is usually typical of Calvinism. Article VIII, De electione does not present Calvin's doctrine of double predestination, nor that of Knox.[159] Instead, the doctrine of election appears within the context of Christology (Chapters 6-11), and not before it. Election is determined by faith in Christ, and not the other way round. Jesus Christ is the first of the elect, and whoever is bound to him by faith is elect in him. This is an important element in the Zwinglian tradition,[160] to which Bullinger, à Lasco and John Willock also adhered.[161]

In the preface, provision is made for the possibility of correction on the basis of Holy Scripture, and this casts a typically Zwinglian light upon the whole confession.[162] The accompanying challenge serves both to establish and to circumscribe the authority of a confession in a specifically reformed sense.

8. *The First Book of Discipline (1560).*[163] This form of church order signals the setting-up of the "prophecy" in Scotland,[164] similar to what existed already in Emden, Frankfurt on Main, Wesel and London, after the pattern of Zurich.[165] Following the rule that such ordinances mostly embody what has already been proved, I should like to think that the

---

158. See note 144.

159. John Knox's teaching on predestination is contained in his *An Answer to a great number of blasphemous Cavillations written by an Anabaptist, and adversarie to God's eternal Predestination. And Confuted*, printed by John Crespin, Geneva, 1560; cf. D. Shaw, "John Willock", pp. 59f. (See note 154).

160. See "Huldrych Zwingli's Doctrine of Predestination" (above, ch. 7). Cf. Bullinger's *Confessio Helvetica Posterior*, 1566, Article X; also Peter Walser, *Die Praedestination bei Heinrich Bullinger*, Zürich, 1957; Paul Jacobs, "Die Lehre von der Erwählung in ihrem Zusammenhang mit der Providenzlehre und der Anthropologie", in Joachim Staedtke, ed., *Glauben und Bekennen. Vierhundert Jahre Confessio Helvetica Posterior*, Zürich, 1966, pp. 258-277; G. W. Locher, "Bullinger und Calvin—Probleme des Vergleichs ihrer Theologien", in *Bullinger-Gedenkwerk*, Zürich, 1975.

161. Karl Barth (see note 144) speaks of Article VIII of the Scottish Confession as an important contribution, but does not recognise its Zwinglian origin.

162. Niesel, *op. cit.*, (note 144) p. 84, 2ff., p. 85, 2ff.; Henderson, *op. cit.* (note 144) pp. 40, 41. For Zwingli, cf. his *Schlussreden* (1523), ed. E. F. K. Müller, 2, 18f., Z I 457; the *Christliche Einleitung* (1523), Z I 629, 21ff.; and the *Fidei Ratio* (1530), ed., E. F. K. Müller, 79, 27ff. Cf. also D. Shaw, *op. cit.*, p. 60.

163. James K. Cameron, ed., *The First Book of Discipline. With Introduction and Commentary*, Edinburgh, 1972.

164. *Ib.*, pp. 187-191: "For Prophecying or Interpreting of the Scriptures".

165. See "In Spirit and in Truth" (above, ch. 1, pp. 27-30).

"prophecy" had long existed in Scotland also, having been introduced by Wishart, Willock and likeminded men.[166] This is also indicated by the fact that the Book of Discipline reveals a detailed practical knowledge of the difficulties that may arise with this institution, and provides for them.[167] The authors realised the valuable possibilities for the training and development of theologians and laity, for Bible exposition, discussion and forming of community.

9. *Covenant Theology*. Zwingli's covenant ideas were developed by Bullinger, Olevian and the Herborn School into a covenant theology, and issued finally in the great systems of Federal theology (Coccejus, Friedrich Adolf Lampe and others). In Scotland it followed its own peculiar path and had weighty consequences, for religion and for politics. This was because it became associated with the ancient and medieval institution of "covenants" which, like the covenants of the Swiss Confederates, had always had both a religious and a political character.[168]

---

166. Cf. Cameron, *op. cit.*, p. 187, note 30.

167. Beginning with the postulate that "learned men" take the lead (p. 188). Furthermore, the regular participants must know one another, and have respect for one another as individuals (*ib.*); even the more simple should be allowed to express their views (*ibid.*); unprofitable discussions should be avoided (p. 189); and all, including the leader, must keep to the text and beware of digressions (*ibid*).

168. The history of religious bands from 1557 onwards has been sketched by D. Hay Fleming in *The Story of the Scottish Covenants in Outline*, Edinburgh, 1904. Such bands have, however, a much older origin and very early bands of manrent were signed, to bind together families and individuals in mutual help by "council, help, supply, maintenance and defence" in common struggles. These bands were probably originally more common among the clans in the north. Many examples of bands, signed and witnessed, are still extant (cf. e.g. "The Manuscript History of Craignish by Alexander Campbell, Advocate", edited by H. Campbell in *Miscellany of the Scottish History Society*, Edinburgh, 1926, IV, pp. 277-283). Bands were appearing in the burghs as early as the fifteenth century. An Act of Parliament of 1457 forbade the formation of such leagues or bands within the burghs (*The Acts of the Parliament of Scotland*, Edinburgh, 1814, II, p. 50). It should be noted particularly that all leagues and bands were declared of no avail and prohibited by Parliament in 1555 (*ib.*, II, p. 495). (Note by Dr. Duncan Shaw).—J. W. Baker, *Covenant and Society: the Res Publica in the Thought of Heinrich Bullinger*, University of Iowa Dissertation, 1970. The federal theology of Piscator was brought to St. Andrews by Robert Howie, who became Principal of St. Mary's College. Here the leading representative became Andrew Melville (1545-1622). In 1564 he had been a pupil in Paris of the philosopher Petrus Ramus, who represented Zwingli's doctrine of the Lord's Supper against Beza. Melville became the Rector of the University of St. Andrews in 1570. He reformed the University of Glasgow in 1574, and the Universities of Aberdeen and St. Andrews in 1575. In 1581 he succeeded in carrying through the *Second Book of Discipline*, which broke with episcopacy, to which he was opposed. As moderator of the General Assembly he was uncompromising in maintaining the superiority of the divine-biblical-ecclesiastical law to the secular law, and the independence of the Church from the

VIII. LATER EFFECTS, RESULTS AND PROBLEMS

During the reign of Queen Elizabeth I the antagonism between Anglicans and Nonconformists, the tension between Puritans within the national church and those outside it, and the impatient demand for a true reformation all reached their first peak. At this point Archbishop Edmund Grindal, who was a perceptive theologian and also a sympathetic pastor, took a step which aroused universal enthusiasm and quickly achieved an unexpected measure of peace, trust and cooperation: he introduced "Prophesyings" into the Church of England.[169] The Queen, who was so shrewd politically, feared (not without reason) that the institution would promote the spread of Puritanism, and therefore forbade it. So England drove on towards revolution. Zwingli's last great proposal was declined.

2.   Names, facts, problems, and questions for research. Our questions even have something to do with the *Communio sanctorum*. The most enduring contributions made by the Zurich reformation go beyond late Zwinglianism, influencing the national church through Rudolf Gualther and Thomas Erastus,[170] and influencing Puritanism through Peter Martyr Vermigli and John Hooper; influencing both sides through *Henry Bullinger*, who should virtually be counted among the English reformers.[171] And beyond that, Bullinger (like Luther) had a decisive influence upon John Wesley.[172]

3.   And in that conscious, humanistic frankness, in that natural awareness that faith is not mere theory, but a practical religious and com-

---

state. He was imprisoned repeatedly, and had to flee to England, where he was imprisoned in the Tower for four years. He was released in 1611 and became a Professor in Sedan.— M. Schmidt in *Die Religion in Geschichte und Gegenwart*, 3rd ed., Vol. IV, 847f.; *DNB*, (1937/1938), XIII, pp. 230ff. *Realenzyklopädie für protestantische Theologie und Kirche*, 3rd ed., Vol. XII, pp. 570ff.; D. Shaw, *The General Assemblies of the Church of Scotland*, 1560-1600, Edinburgh, 1964, *passim*.

169. Patrick Collinson, *The Elizabethan Puritan Movement*, London, 1967, pp. 159ff., 168ff., 191ff.; also Patrick Collinson, "The Reformer and the Archbishop: Martin Bucer and an English Bucerian", in *The Journal of Religious History*, December 1971, pp. 305ff.

170. George Yule, "English Presbyterianism and the Westminster Assembly", in *The Reformed Theological Review*, May-August 1974, pp. 34-44; George Yule, *Puritanism and Politics* (in preparation).

171. In the nineteenth century, the Parker Society reprinted the English translation of the *Decades* in four volumes.

172. I am indebted to Professor T. F. Torrance for this point.

mon life, and in that strong sense of social responsibility that has characterised modern Anglo-saxon Christianity down to the present day, there lives (among many other factors) something of the spirit of the letters which were carried to and fro between London and Zurich in the sixteenth century.[173]

173. There is need for a further essay dealing with the question of what Swiss Church history owes to England and Scotland. It is by no means inconsiderable, and has the advantage of being more readily grasped and reviewed.

BIBLIOGRAPHY

To the best of my knowledge, there are no works which deal with our subject in the strictest sense. The following bibliography relates chiefly to the connexions between late Zwinglianism and England. But the works contain numerous details which refer to Zwingli and Oecolampadius themselves, including some which it has not been possible to examine or discuss in this chapter

SOURCES

Cameron, J. K., ed., *The First Book of Discipline. With Introduction and Commentary*, Edinburgh, 1972.

Townsend, A., ed., *The Writings of John Bradford*, 2 vol., Parker Society, Cambridge, 1848/53.

Bucer, M., *Opera Latina*, ed. F. Wendel, Paris/Gütersloh, 1955. XV: *De Regno Christi Libri Duo*, 1550.

Wright, D. F., ed., *Common Places of Martin Bucer*, Appleford, Abingdon, 1972.

Calvin, J., *Calvini Opera*, in *Corpus Reformatorum*, Vol. XXIX-LXXXVII, Berlin, 1863-1900.

Duffield, G. E., ed., *The Work of Thomas Cranmer*. With Introduction by J. I. Packer, Courtenay Library of Reformation Theology, Vol. 2, Appleford, Abingdon, 1964.

Bullinger, H., *Sermonum Decades quinque de potissimis Christianae religionis capitibus*, Zürich, 1552.

——, *Hausbuch ... fünfzig predigen Heinrychen Bullingers ... verdolmetschet durch Johansen Hallern...* Bern, 1558.

Lloyd, C., ed., *Formularies of Faith put forth by Authority during the Reign of Henry VIII*, Oxford, 1856.

Foxe, J., *Acts and Monuments of these latter and perilous dayes*, 8 double vol., ed. S. R. Cattley, London, 1858.

Hebel, J. P., *Werke*, ed. W. Altweg. Vol. II: *Schatzkästlein des Rheinischen Hausfreundes*, Zürich, n.d. (1958).

Carr, S., ed., *Early Writings of John Hooper*, Parker Society, Cambridge, 1843 (Cited as Vol. I).

Nevinson, C., ed., *Later Writings of John Hooper*, Parker Society, Cambridge, 1852 (Cited as Vol. II).

Knox, J., *The History of the Reformation in Scotland*, ed. W. C. Dickinson, London, 1949.

Kohlbrügge, H. F., *Bekenntnisschriften und Formulare der Niederländisch-reformierten Gemeinde in Elberfeld*,

Corrie, G. E., ed., *Sermons and Remains of Hugh Latimer*, 2 vol., Parker Society, Cambridge, 1844/45.

Müller, E. F. K., ed., *Bekenntnisschriften der reformierten Kirche*, Leipzig, 1903.

Niesel, W., ed., *Bekenntnisschriften und Kirchenordnungen der nach Gottes Wort reformierten Kirche*, Zollikon/Zürich, 1938.

Club, A., ed., *The English Prayer Book 1549-1662*, London, 1963.

Chandos, J., ed., *In God's Name. Examples of Preaching in England. 1534-1662*, London, 1971.

Ridley, N., *A brief Declaration of the Lord's Supper*, ed. H. C. G. Moule, London, 1895.

Christmas, H., ed., *The Works of Nicholas Ridley*, Parker Society, Cambridge, 1841.

Tyndale, W., *Doctrinal Treatises and Introductions to the different Portions of the Holy Scriptures*, ed. H. Walter, Parker Society, Cambridge, 1848.

Duffield, G. E., ed., *The Work of William Tyndale*. Courtenay Library of Reformation Classics, Vol. I, Appleford, Abingdon, 1964.

Cameron, A. J., ed., *The Warrender Papers*, Vol. II, Edinburgh, 1932. Publications of the History Society, Third Series, Vol. XIX.

Hewison, J. K., ed., *Certain Tractates ... by Ninian Winzett,* The Scottish Text Society, London and Edinburgh, 1888.
"The Confession of Faith of the Churches of Switzerland", translated from the Latin by George Wishart, 1536, in *The Miscellany of the Wodrow Society,* selected and edited by David Lang, Edinburgh, 1894, pp. 1-23.
Zwingli, H., Z, S and H (See list of Abbreviations).

LITERATURE

1. The Problem

Hall, B., "Calvin against the Calvinist", in *John Calvin,* ed. G. E. Duffield. Courtenay Studies in Reformation Theology, No. I, Appleford, Abingdon, 1966.
Hollweg, W., *Heinrich Bullingers Hausbuch. Eine Untersuchung über die Anfänge der reformierten Predigtliteratur,* Neukirchen, 1956. Beiträge zur Geschichte und Lehre der Reformierten Kirche, Vol. VIII.

2. The Chief Characteristics of Original Zwinglianism

Locher, G. W., "In Spirit and in Truth" (above, ch. 2).
——, "Theokratie und Pluralismus—Zwingli heute", in *Wissenschaft und Praxis,* 62/1 (January 1973), Göttingen, 1973, pp. 11-24.
McNeil, J. T., *The History and Character of Calvinism,* New York, 1954.
Thompson, B., "Zwingli's Eucharistic Doctrine", in *Theology and Life,* 4 (1961), 2.
Walton, R. C., *Zwingli's Theocracy,* Toronto, 1967.
Weerda, J. R., *Nach Gottes Wort reformierte Kirche,* Munich, 1964.

3. The Chief Stages in the History of the English Reformation

Bailey, D. S., *Thomas Becon and the Reformation of the Church in England,* Edinburgh, 1952.
Chapman, H. W., *Lady Jane Grey. October 1537-February 1554,* London, 1962.
Clebsch, W. A., *England's Earliest Protestants,* Yale, 1964.
Collinson, P., *The Elizabethan Puritan Movement,* London, 1967.
Dugmore, C. W., *The Mass and the English Reformers,* London, 1958.
Elliott-Binns, L. E., *The Reformation in England,* London, 1937.
Garrett, C., *The Marian Exiles,* Cambridge, 1938.
Hopf, C., *Martin Bucer and the English Reformation,* Oxford, 1946.
Hughes, P., *The Reformation in England,* 3 vol., London, 1950ff.
Jordan, W. K., *Edward VI: The Young King,* London, 1968.
Kennedy, W. F. M., *Elizabethan Episcopal Administration,* 2 vol., Alcuin Club Tracts, London, 1924.
Knappen, M. M., *Tudor Puritanism,* Chicago, 1939.
Knox, D. B., *The Doctrine of Faith in the Reign of Henry VIII,* London, 1961.
Krumm, J. J., "Continental Protestantism and Elizabethan Anglicanism (1570-1595)", in *Reformation Studies. Essays in Honor of R. H. Bainton,* Richmond, U.S.A., 1962, pp. 129-198.
Loades, D. M., *The Oxford Martyrs,* London, 1970.
Meissner, P., *England im Zeitalter von Humanismus, Renaissance und Reformation,* Heidelberg, 1952.
Moeller, B., *Reichsstadt und Reformation,* Schriften des Vereins für Reformationsgeschichte 180, Gütersloh, 1962.
Morgan, I., *The Godly Preachers of the Elizabethan Church,* London, 1965.
Porter, H., *Reformation and Reaction in Tudor Cambridge,* Cambridge, 1958.
Rupp, E. G., *Studies in the Making of the English Protestant Tradition,* Cambridge, 1947.
Smith, H. M., *Henry VIII and the Reformation,* London, 1948.

Smithen, F. J., *Continental Protestantism and the English Reformation*, London, 1927.
Staehelin, E., *Das theologische Lebenswerk Oekolampads*, Leipzig, 1939.
Trevelyan, G. M., *A Shortened History of England*, London, 1942.
Walther, D. W., *Heinrich VIII von England und Luther*, Leipzig, 1908.

4. The Spiritual History of the English Reformation

Anson, P. F., *Bishops at Large*, London, 1964.
Boesch, P., "Die englischen Flüchtlinge in Zürich unter Königin Elisabeth I", in *Zwa.* XI, pp. 531-535.
Bromiley, G. W., *Thomas Cranmer, Archbishop and Martyr*, London, 1955.
——, *Thomas Cranmer, Theologian*, London, 1956.
——, *Nicholas Ridley, 1500-1555, Scholar, Bishop, Theologian, Martyr*, London, 1953.
Cowell, H. J., "The sixteenth century English speaking refugee churches at Strasbourg, Basle, Zurich, Aarau, Wesel and Emden", in *Huguenot Society Proceedings*, London, XV, 1937, pp. 612-665.
Denis, P., "John Veron: The first known French Protestant in England", in *Huguenot Society Proceedings*, London, XXII, 1973, pp. 257-263.
Devereux, J. A., "Reformed Doctrine in the First Prayer Book", in *The Harvard Theological Review*, 1965, pp. 49ff.
Haas, R., "Engländer und Schotten an der Universität Marburg in den ersten Jahren ihres Bestehens", in *Jahrbuch der Hessischen Kirchengeschichtlichen Vereinigung*, XXIII, pp. 23-31.
Hill, C., *The World Turned Upside Down. Radical Ideas during the English Revolution*, London, 1972.
——, *Intellectual Origins of the English Revolution*, Oxford, 1965.
——, *Society and Puritanism in Pre-Revolutionary England*, London, 1964.
——, *Puritanism and Revolution*, London, 1958.
Hopf, C., ed., "Bishop Hooper's notes to the King's Council", in *The Journal of Theological Studies*, London, XLIV, 1943, pp. 194-199.
Kittleshon, J. M., "W. Capito, the Council and Reformed Strasbourg", in *Archiv für Reformationsgeschichte*, 1972, pp. 127-133.
Lehmberg, S. E., *The Reformation Parliament 1529-1536*, Cambridge, 1970.
Lindeboom, J., *Austin Friars. History of the Dutch Reformed Church in London 1550-1950*, The Hague, 1950.
Mozley, J. F., *Coverdale and his Bibles*, London, 1953.
——, *John Foxe and his Book*, London, 1940.
——, *William Tyndale*, London, 1937.
Primus, J. H., *The Vestments Controversy*, Kampen, 1960.
Read, E., *Catherine, Duchess of Suffolk, A Portrait*, London, 1962.
Schelven, A. A. van, *Nederduitsche Vluchtelingen-kerken der 16. eeuw in Engeland en Duitschland*, The Hague, 1909.
Staedtke, J., ed., *Glauben und Bekennen. Vierhundert Jahre Confessio Helvetica Posterior*, Zürich, 1966.
West, W. M. S., *John Hooper and the Origins of Puritanism*, Dissertation, Zürich, 1955. (Cf. also *The Baptist Quarterly*, XV, 1954 and XVI, 1955).
Wyatt, T., "Aliens in England before the Huguenots" in *Huguenot Society Proceedings*, London, XIX, 1953, pp. 74-94.

5. Early Zwinglianism in England

Boesch, P., "Von privaten Zürcher Beziehungen zu England im 16. Jahrhundert", in *Neue Zürcher Zeitung*, 19th July, 1947, No. 1402/1405.
——, "Rudolph Gwalthers Reise nach England im Jahr 1537", in *Zwa.* VIII/8 (1947/2), pp. 433-471.

——, "Der Zürcher Appelles (scil. Hans Asper)", in *Zwa.* IX (1949), pp. 16-50.

Brooks, P., *Thomas Cranmer's Doctrine of the Eucharist*, London, 1965.

Darby, H. S., *Hugh Latimer*, London, 1953.

Dix, G., *The Shape of the Liturgy*, London, 1944.

——, "Dixit Cranmer et non timuit. A supplement to Mr. Timms", in *Church Quarterly Review*, London, CXLV, 1948, pp. 146-176; CXLVI, pp. 44-60.

Finsler, G., "Zwinglis Schrift 'Eine Antwort, Valentin Compar gegeben' von England aus zitiert", in *Zwa.* III/4 (1914/2), pp. 115-117.

Foxe, J., *Acts and Monuments of these latter and perilous dayes*, 8 double vol., ed. S. R. Cattley, London, 1858.

Hollweg, H., *Heinrich Bullingers Hausbuch. Eine Untersuchung über die Anfänge der reformierten Predigtliteratur*, Neukirchen, 1956.

Isaac, F., "Egidius van der Erve and his English Printed Books", in *The Library*, Fourth Series, London, 1932, XII, pp. 336-352.

Kressner, H., *Schweizer Ursprünge des anglikanischen Staatskirchentums*, Schriften des Vereins für Reformationsgeschichte 170, Gütersloh, 1953.

Lamont, W. M., *Godly Rule, Politics and Religion 1603-1660*, London, 1969.

Lang, A., *Puritanismus und Pietismus*, Neukirchen, 1941.

Lätt, A., "Austin (Augustin) Bernher, ein Freund der englischen Reformatoren", in *Zwa.* VI/6 (1936/2), pp. 327-336.

Locher, G. W., *Streit unter Gästen. Die Lehre aus der Abendmahlsdebatte der Reformatoren für das Verständnis und die Feier des Abendmahls heute*, Theologische Studien 110, Zürich, 1972.

Macklem, M., *God have mercy. The Life of John Fisher of Rochester*, Ottawa, 1968.

Maler, J., *Tagebuch. Studienreise nach England im Jahre 1551*, Zürcher Taschenbuch, 1885.

Moller, J. G., "The Beginnings of Puritan Covenant Theology", in *The Journal of Ecclesiastical History*, London, April 1963, pp. 46ff.

Nagel, E., "Die Abhängigkeit der Coverdale-bibel von der Zürcher Bibel", in *Zwa.* VI/8 1937/2, pp. 437-457.

Nyenhuis, W., "Traces of a Lutheran eucharistic doctrine in Thomas Cranmer" in W. Nyenhuis, *Ecclesia Reformata. Studies on the Reformation*, Leiden, 1972.

Pollard, A. W., ed., *The Beginning of the New Testament Translated by William Tyndale, 1525*. Oxford, 1926.

——, *Thomas Cranmer and the English Reformation*, London and New York, 1926.

Richardson, C. C., *Zwingli and Cranmer on the Eucharist (Cranmer dixit et contradixit)*, Evanston, III., 1949.

——, "Cranmer and the Analysis of Eucharistic Doctrine", in *The Journal of Theological Studies*, London, XVI/2, 1965, pp. 431-437.

Ridley, J. G., *Nicholas Ridley. A Biography*, London, 1957.

——, *Thomas Cranmer*, London, 1962.

Rordorf-Gwalther, S., "Die Geschwister Rosilla und Rudolf Rordorf und ihre Beziehungen zu Zürcher Reformatoren", in *Zwa.* III/6 (1915/2), pp. 180-193.

Schmidt, M., Article "John Hooper" in *Die Religion in Geschichte und Gegenwart*, 3rd ed., 1960, Vol. III, column 449.

Shaw, D., "John Willock", in D. Shaw, ed., *Reformation and Revolution. Essays presented to ... Hugh Watt*, Edinburgh, 1967, pp. 42-69.

Smyth, C. H., *Cranmer and the Reformation under Edward VI*, 1926. Reprinted with Foreword by E. G. Rupp, London, 1973.

Staehelin, E., *Das Buch der Basler Reformation*, Basle, 1929.

Timms, G. B., "Dixit Granmer", in *Church Quarterly Review*, London, CXLIII, pp. 217-234; CXLIV, pp. 35-51.

Vetter, T., *Englische Flüchtlinge in Zürich während der ersten Hälfte des 16. Jahrhunderts*. Neujahrsblatt 1893 der Stadtbibliothek Zürich.

——, *Literarische Beziehungen zwischen England under der Schweiz im Reformationszeitalter*, Zürich, 1901.

Walton, R. C., "Zwingli and the Anglo-Saxon World", in *The Reformed and Presbyterian World*, XXX, 1969, pp. 214-218.

Williams, C. H., *William Tyndale*, London, 1969.

6. Stages in the History of the Scottish Reformation

Brandes, F., *John Knox, der Reformator Schottlands*, Elberfeld, 1862.

Brown, P. H., *John Knox. A Biography*, 2 vol., London, 1895.

Donaldson, G., *The Scottish Reformation 1560*, Cambridge, 1960.

Kuipers, C. H., *Quintin Kennedy (1520-1564): Two Eucharistic Tracts*, Nymegen, 1964.

Lorimer, P., *John Knox and the Church of England*, London, 1875.

MacGregor, J. G., *The Scottish Presbyterian Polity*, Edinburgh, 1926.

Percy, E., *John Knox*, London, (1935).

Ridley, J. G., *John Knox*, Oxford, 1968.

Shaw, D., *The General Assemblies of the Church of Scotland 1560-1600*, Edinburgh, 1964.

——, "John Willock", in D. Shaw, ed., *Reformation and Revolution. Essays presented to ... Hugh Watt*, Edinburgh, 1967, pp. 42-69.

——, ed., *John Knox, A Quatercentenary Reappraisal*, Edinburgh, 1975.

Taylor, M., *A Doctrinal Defence of the Mass and the Sacraments during the Scottish Reformation (1549-1564)*, Unpublished Dissertation, Gregorian University, Rome, 1954.

7. Early Zwinglianism in Scotland

Baker, J. W., *Covenant and Society. The Res Publica in the Thought of Heinrich Bullinger*, University of Iowa Dissertation, 1970.

Barth, K., *The Knowledge of God and the Service of God according to the teaching of the Reformation, recalling the Scottish Confession of 1560*, London, 1938.

Cameron, A., ed., *Patrick Hamilton*, Edinburgh, 1929.

Donaldson, G., "Bishop Adam Bothwell and the Reformation in Orkney", in *Records of the Scottish Church History Society*, Glasgow, 1959, Vol. XIII, pp. 85-100.

Durkan, J., "Some Local Heretics", in *Transactions of the National History and Antiquarian Society*, Dumfries, 1959, pp. 67-77.

Durkan, J. and Ross, A., *Early Scottish Libraries*, Glasgow, 1961.

Finlayson, C. P., *Clement Little and his Library*, MS in the University Library, Edinburgh.

Jakobs, P., "Die Lehre von der Erwählung in ihrem Zusammenhang mit der Providenzlehre und der Anthropologie", in J. Staedtke, ed., *Glauben und Bekennen. Vierhundert Jahre Confessio Helvetica Posterior*, Zürich, 1966, pp. 258-277.

Janton, P., *Concept et Sentiment de l'Église chez John Knox*, Paris, 1972.

Locher, G. W., "Bullinger und Calvin—Probleme des Vergleichs ihrer Theologien", in *Bullinger-Gedenkwerk*, Zürich, 1975

Lorimer, P., *Patrick Hamilton*, Edinburgh, 1857.

McEwen, J. S., *The Faith of John Knox*, London, 1961.

Wasler, P., *Die Praedestination bei Heinrich Bullinger*, Zürich, 1957.

Warfield, B. B., "Predestination in the Reformed Confessions", in *Presbyterian and Reformed Review*, New York, January 1901, pp. 49-128.

8. Effects, Results and Problems

Collinson, P., "The Reformer and the Archbishop. Martin Bucer and the English Bucerian", in *Journal of Religious History*, December 1971, pp. 305ff.

Yule, G., "English Presbyterianism and the Westminster Assembly", in *The Reformed Theological Review*, May-August 1974, XXXIII, pp. 33-44.

——, *Puritanism and Politics* (In preparation).

SELECTED BIBLIOGRAPHY

GERMAN

Finsler, G., *Zwingli-Bibliographie*, Zürich 1897.
Gäbler, U., *Huldrych Zwingli im 20. Jahrhundert*. Annotierte Bibliographie 1897-1972. Zürich 1975.
Locher, G. W., *Ergänzungen*. *Zwingliana* XV/1, 1979, 54-56.
Zwingliana: *Beiträge zur Geschichte Zwinglis...* Zürich 1897ss (Zwa).

Huldreich Zwinglis Werke. Ausgabe M. Schuler & J. Schulthess. 8 Volumes. Zürich 1828-1842. Supplementum 1861. (S)
Huldreich Zwinglis Sämtliche Werke. Edited by E. Egli e.a. Corpus Reformatorum Vol. 88ss. Berlin 1905, Leipzig 1908ss. Zürich 1961ss. (Z)
Zwingli — Hauptschriften. 8 Volumes. Edited by O. Farner e.a. Zürich 1940-1963. (H)
Künzli, E., (ed.), *Huldrych Zwingli — Auswahl seiner Schriften.* Zürich 1962.

Escher, H., (ed.), *Ulrich Zwingli. Zum Gedächtnis der Zürcher Reformation 1519-1919.* Zürich 1919.
Köhler, W., *Das Buch der Reformation Huldrych Zwinglis.* München 1926.

Köhler, W., *Huldrych Zwingli.* Leipzig 1943.
Farner, O., *Huldrych Zwingli.* 4 volumes (Vol. 4 ed. by R. *Pfister*). Zürich 1943-1960.
Büsser, F., *Huldrych Zwingli.* Göttingen 1973.
Haas, M., *Huldrych Zwingli und seine Zeit.* 2 d. ed. Zürich 1976.
Locher, G. W., *Die Zwinglische Reformation im Rahmen der europäischen Kirchengeschichte.* Göttingen & Zürich 1979.

Baur, A., *Zwinglis Theologie.* 2 volumes. Halle 1885-1889.
Wernle, P., *Der evangelische Glaube nach den Hauptschriften der Reformatoren.* Vol. 2: Zwingli. Tübingen 1919.
Köhler, W., *Zwingli und Luther, ihr Streit über das Abendmahl...* Vol. 1. Leipzig 1924, Vol. 2 (ed. by E. Kohlmeyer). Gütersloh 1953.
Locher, G. W., *Die Theologie Huldrych Zwinglis...* Vol. 1. Die Gotteslehre. Zürich 1952.
Grötzinger, E., *Luther und Zwingli.* Gütersloh 1980.
Staedtke, J., (ed.), *Glauben und Bekennen. 400 Jahre Confessio Helvetica Posterior.* Zürich 1966.
Gäbler, U., & Herkenrath, E., *Heinrich Bullinger 1504-1575.* Gesammelte Aufsätze zum 400. Todestag. Zürich 1975.

Schmidt-Clausing, F., *Zwingli als Liturgiker.* Göttingen 1952.
Schweizer, J., *Reformierte Abendmahlsgestaltung in der Schau Zwinglis.* Basel s.a. (1954).
Jenny, M., *Die Einheit des Abendmahlsgottesdienstes bei den elsässischen und schweizerischen Reformatoren.* Zürich 1968.

Escher, H., *Die Glaubensparteien in der Eidgenossenschaft...* Frauenfeld 1882.
Moeller, B., *Reichsstadt und Reformation.* Gütersloh 1962.
Locher, G. W., *Zwinglis Politik — Gründe und Ziele.* Theol. Zeitschrift Basel 36/2, März 1980, 84-102.

ENGLISH

Wayne Pipkin, H., *A Zwingli Bibliography*. Pittsburgh Theol. Seminary, 1972.
Jackson, S. M., *The Latin Works of Huldreich Zwingli*. (Philadelphia 1901). Introduction by Edward Peters. Philadelphia 1972.
Bromiley, G. W., *Zwingli and Bullinger, Selected Translations with Introductions and Notes...* London 1953.
Meyer, C. S., *Luther's and Zwingli's Propositions for Debate (...The 67 Articles of 1523)*. Leiden 1963.
Potter, G. R., *Huldrych Zwingli. Documents*. Edward Arnold, London 1978.
McNeill, J. T., *The History and Character of Calvinism*. New York 1954, Part I Zwingli, 1-89.
Potter, G. R., *Zwingli*. Cambridge 1976.
Davies, R. E., *The Problem of Authority in the Continental Reformers*. London 1946, Ch. II, p. 62-92.
Courvoisier, J., *Zwingli, a reformed Theologian*. Richmond Vi., 1963.
Richardson, C. C., *Zwingli and Cranmer on the Eucharist*. Evanston, Illinois 1949.
Garside, Ch., *Zwingli and the Arts*. New Haven 1966.
Walton, R. C., *Zwingli's Theocracy*. Toronto 1967.
Baker, J. W., *Heinrich Bullinger and the Covenant*. Athens, Ohio 1980.

FRENCH

Huldrych Zwingli: De la justice divine et de la justice humaine. Traduction... (avec introduction) par J. Courvoisier. Paris 1980.
Brüschweiler, P., *Les rapports de Zwingli avec la France*, Paris 1894.
Courvoisier, J., *Zwingli*. Neuchâtel 1947.
Rilliet, J., *Zwingli*. Paris 1959.
Pollet O.P., J. V. M., Article "Zwinglianisme". *Dict. Théol. Cath.* XV/2, 1951, 3745-3928.
Pollet O.P., J. V. M., *Huldrych Zwingli et la Réforme en Suisse*. Paris 1963.
Courvoisier, J., *Zwingli Théologien Réformé*. Neuchâtel 1965.
Stauffer, R., *La Réforme (1517-1564)*. Paris 1970.
Meylan, H., *Zwingli et Erasme. Colloquia Erasmiana Tyronensia*. Paris 1972, vol. II, 849-858.
Stauffer, R., *Interprètes de la Bible, Etudes sur les Réformateurs du XVIe Siècle*. Paris 1980.

DUTCH

Huldrich Zwingli's Zeven en zestig Artikelen en zyn Korte Christelyke Inleiding. Vertaald en toegelicht door G. Oorthuys, Nykerk 1913.
Tichler, J., *Huldrich Zwingli de kerkhervormer*. 2 dlen Utrecht 1857/1858.
Cramer, S., *Zwingli's leer van het godsdienstig geloof*. Middelburg 1866.
Bruins, J. A., *Het leerstuk over de kerk volgens Luther, Zwingli en Calvyn*. Leiden 1869.
Bavinck, H., *De ethiek van Ulrich Zwingli*. Kampen 1880.
Oorthuys, G., *Zwingli*. In: G. O.: *Kruispunten op den weg der kerk*. Wageningen 1935, 1-104.
Witteveen, K. M., *Het evangelie tussen pacifisme en geweld, Huldrych Zwingli*. Kampen 1974.
Tukker, C. A., *Vast vertrouwen en Onberispelyk leven. Over de 67 stellingen van Huldrych Zwingli...* Utrecht 1979.
Balke, W., *De avondmaalsleer van Zwingli*. In: W. van 't Spyker e.a.: *Bij brood en beker*, Goudriaan 1980, 149-177.
Lindeboom, J., *De confessioneele ontwikkeling der reformatie in de Nederlanden*. Den Haag 1946.

INDEX OF SUBJECTS

Absolution (see confession), 25, 61
Acts of Uniformity, 346, 366
Acts of Parliament, 345
Ad fontes, 235 s
Allegory, 190, 245 s, 251
Alloiosis, 173 n, 176
Anabaptists, 19, 70 s, 73 n, 91, 114 n, 153, 210, 218, 284, 343, 348, 357 n, 365
Analogy, 121, 216 s, 356, 357
Anthropology, 53 ss, 76 n, 178, 203, 205, 223, 234, 241, 244, 263
Antichrist, 18, 109, 112, 144, 210, 361 n
Antiquity, 114, 241
Apocalypse, 189, 245
Apocrypha, 189
Apostles, 185, 188, 218
"Apostle's Creed", 18, 212, 248, 257
Arnoldshain Theses, 330 s, 332 n
Ascension, 22, 37, 225, 357
Aseity, 170
Assumptio carnis, 173
Astrology, 11
"Athanasianum", 172
Atonement, 56, 134, 230
Authority, 103, 111, 174, 188, 189, 239, 267, 271, 354, 356, 375
Ave Maria, 60, 91

Baden Disputation, (151) 268
Baptism, 60, 76, 135, 218-219, 359
Beginnings of Reformation, 53, 66, 104, 146 n, 152, 238
Bern Disputation, 151, 256-258, 268
Bible, 6, 10, 28 s, 113, 155, 239, 245, 360
  Translations, 29, 245, 353, 355, 358, 366
Biblicism, 29, 71, 188
Biographies, 48-53, 150-153, 154-155, 156-160
Bishop, 212, 248, 253, 369 n, 376 n
Book of Common Prayer, 328, 345 (bis)

Calvinism, 1, 56, 64, 68, 71, 149, 210, 263, 280, 289, 326, 340, 365, 373 s, 375
Celibacy, 109 n, 112, 113, 145
Ceremonialism, 4, 21, 59, 361, 364
Canon Law, 113
Character indelibilis, 287
"Christ our Captain", 10, 72-86, 104, 142, 166, 374 n

Christendom, 33, 34, 102, 103, 212, 242, 253
Christian Civic Union (Christliche Burgrecht), 109, 269, 270
Christian Life, 31 s, 85 s, 104, 123, 137, 139-141, 167, 184 s, 195, 262-266, 335, 339, 360
Christianismus (Christus) renascens, 15, 52, 101 s, 108 n, 235, 241 s, 253
Christology, 3, 10, 15, 37, 57, 59, 66, 67, 90, 94, 102, 106, 132 ss, 142, 143, 155, 157, 173-178, 180, 209, 224, 226 s, 244, 252, 308, 336
Church, 8, 25 n, 38, 143, 149, 180, 210-213, 232, 247, 252, 257, 267, 287, 336, 338, 358, 360, 362
  Church History, 111 ss
Church Fathers, 157, 235, 241, 246, 251, 292
Church of England, 29, 71, 187, 290, 328, 340, 341, 344, 344-367, 346, 348, 377
Church of Scotland, 290, 341, 367-376, 370
Cities, 65, 109, 269, 270, 271, 274, 275, 289, 344, 346
Common Weal, 155 n, 271
Communicatio idiomatum, 176, 365
Communion of Saints, 20, 140 n, 212, 335, 377
Conduct Books, 366
Confessio Augustana, 283 n, 289, 291, 306 s, 309 n, 336, 365
Confessio Belgica, 56, 133 n
Confessio Bohoemica, 307 n
Confessio Helvetica posterior, 187 s, 278-287, 288-302, 375 n
Confessio Helvetica Prior, 279 n, 292, 372
Confessio Scotica, 369, 371, 375 (n)
Confession of Faith, 83, 215, 221, 279, 299 s, 322, 329
Confession of Sin, 18, 23-27, 26, 61, 212
Congregation, 185, 210 ss, 212, 222, 248, 293, 328 s, 332, 335, 338, 368, 376
Conscience, 19 n, 111, 112, 143, 144, 155, 216, 254, 259, 260 s, 266, 313, 345 n, 353
Consensus Tigurinus, 293
Consubstantiation, 221, 310 ss, 354, 365
Corpus Christianum, 63, 100, 163, 231, 265, 346

Council, 108
Covenant, 55, 67, 114, 210, 218, 221, 355, 374
Covenant Theology, 29, 114, 135, 219, 376 s
"Covenants" in Scotland, 369, 376
Creation, 113 s, 169 s, 178
Creature, 14, 15, 67, 101, 110 n, 147, 163, 180, 204, 241

Damnation, 135, 136, 145
Death, 36
Decades, 293, 341
Deification, 14, 15, 67
Deity, Divinity, 37, 66, 90, 122, 125, 174, 175, 178, 185, 274, 316 s, 321, 333
Development, 244, 245 s
Devotio moderna, 235, 280, 292
Discipline (and "power of the keys"), 212, 268
Divorce of King Henry VIII, 344 s, 345 n, 356, 360
Dordrecht (Dort) Synod, 135 n, 235, 277, 293
Dualism, 53, 206
Dyophysitism, see Nestorianism

Economics, 39-40
Editions, 44-48
Education, 62 s, 77 (n), 107 n, 229 s, 236, 237, 245 s, 253, 254
Election see Predestination, 54, 55 s, 123, 125, 129, 130, 145, 183 s, 210, 230, 231, 298 s, 375
Emperor, 58, 100, 116, 119, 256, 269, 275, 288, 290 s
Enthusiasts, 284
Eschatology, 11, 95, 101 ss, 104, 105, 107, 109, 119, 155, 253, 297, 336, 360
Essentia, 170
Eternity, 125
Eucharist see Lord's Supper, 20-23, 57-59, 220-228, 221, 317 n, 318 s, 328, 361 s
Europe, 115-117, 256, 269, 276, 290
Exaltation, 57, 177
"Existo", 168 n
Exploitation, 40, 101 n, 112, 315 n, 373 n
"Extra Calvinisticum", 176

Faith, 19, 21, 25, 26, 33, 37, 40 s, 55, 59, 65, 84, 136-139, 143, 148, 165-167, 180, 182-185, 190, 216, 223, 227, 252, 253, 254, 276, 297 s, 323 s, 359, 360
Fasting, 112

Fear, 33, 104 s, 143, 144, 145 s, 360
Fides historica, 113 s, 185
First Book of Discipline, 369, 374, 375 s
Fons bonitatis, 169
Forgiveness, 23 s, 111, 180, 183, 212, 252, 253, 308, 329, 336, 355, 359
Freedom, 11, 13-15, 17, 117 s, 154, 179, 180, 183 s, 186, 198, 210, 219, 231, 234, 237, 241, 254, 260, 265 s, 268, 270, 271 s, 276, 286, 291, 292, 301, 325, 338 s, 344, 353, 356, 376

Germans, 116
Glory (Honour) of God, 20 n, 114, 149, 155, 180, 189
God, 14, 24 s, 41, 101, 125, 137, 168-172, 185, 206 s, 208, 286
    Summum bonum, 14, 122, 126 n, 162, 168 s, 298
Gospel, 9 s, 11, 15, 16, 34, 35-37, 122, 137, 142, 145, 147, 164 s, 182 ss, 199, 252, 256, 272
Grace, 8, 9, 36, 76 sn, 122 s, 126-235, 132, 142, 143, 145, 152, 163, 171, 183, 208, 215 s, 227 s, 242, 246, 252, 264, 300, 338
"Gratia infusa", 143, 214

Harmony, 7, 8 s
Heathen, 54 s, 108, 114 s, 135, 166, 179, 242, 258
Heidelberg Catechism, 25 n, 201, 212, 279, 288, 290, 325 s, 336 n
Heresy, 113, 190, 269, 340, 348 n, 350, 357, 368
Hermeneutics, 69 s, 113, 158
History, 95-120, 111 s, 114 ss, 248, 252
Holy Spirit see also Sp. of God, 19, 21, 22, 24, 56, 69, 136, 142, 179, 181, 186, 210, 223, 285, 287, 299, 308, 334, 337 s
Human Doctrines, 112, 148, 157, 160
Human justice, 229
Humanism, 14, 16, 28, 43, 53, 57, 58, 65, 67, 107, 113, 152, 153, 157, 205, 233-255, 344, 347, 353
Humanity, 76 n, 182, 242 ss, 245, 252, 253, 266, 338
Humanity of Christ, 173, 176, 177, 313, 317, 333, 356, 357, 364
Hymn's, 61

Iconoclastic movements, 18
Idolatry, 14, 15, 19, 25, 34, 41, 59, 94 n, 148, 160, 161 n, 181, 259, 358, 360, 363, 373, 374

Images, 5 n, 260, 361 n
Imitatio, 75, 245
Incarnation, 10, 36, 60, 244
Infant Baptism, 218
Influence, 29, 70 s, 135, 293, 340 n, 340-383, 375 s
Infralapsarianism, 134, 135
Interim, 288 s, 346, 358
Interpretation of Scripture, 11, 28-30, 113, 143 ss, 189, 219, 245, 246, 251, 264

Judaism, 14, 111
Judgment of God, 3, 11, 14, 15, 33-35, 102 n, 104 s, 118, 147, 253, 271 s, 273 s, 360
Justice, 36, 56, 123, 126-135, 140, 171, 209, 229
Justification, 25, 131, 142, 143 ss, 161, 183, 242, 250, 287, 307, 353, 354, 356, 358, 364, 372
Justification by works, 161, 184, 250, 288

Kappel, Battle of, 31, 34, 65, 82, 86, 151, 276, 289, 292, 343

Last Day, 95, 103, 297
Law, 122, 186, 188 n, 195, 196-201, 264, 376 n
Legalism, 19
Leuenberg Concord, 330 ss, 332 n
Liturgy, 5, 6-8, 17-18, 23, 60, 60-62, 71, 212, 327 s, 336, 339, 346
Lord's Supper see Eucharist, 57-59, 61, 76, 149, 220-228, 268, 303-339, 354, 359, 362, 364, 365, 366, 371
Lordship of Christ, 3, 37, 77, 108, 254, 261, 331
Love, 148, 184, 230
Lutheranisme, 23, 65, 144, 145, 188, 205, 263, 284, 286, 289, 290 s, 330 s, 335, 336 s, 338

Magistrates, 106, 109, 182 n, 210, 229, 260, 267, 361 n
Manducatio infidelium, 224 n
Marburg Colloquy, 57 s, 64, 151, 205 n, 271, 284, 307, 354
Marignano, Battle of, 34, 74
Mariology, 36, 87-94, 175, 316
Memoria see Remembrance, 59, 314 s
Mercenary Service, 16, 33 s, 79-83, 115, 117 s, 146, 267, 268, 272, 362
Militia Christi, 73, 76

Monasticism, 112, 146
Monophysitism, 176, 177
Morbus, 54, 135 n, 202, 315 n, 316 n

Natural Law, 196
Nature, 140, 174 s, 234, 241, 252, 286
"Nestorianism", 67, 174, 176, 362
Nicaeno-Constantinopolitanum, 172, 248 n
Nonconformists, 29, 341, 347, 348, 377

Office, 25, 210, 285
Omnipotence, 140, 167, 178, 287
Orthodoxy, 71, 188, 293

Paganism, 14, 67, 111
Pantheism, 67, 123
Pastors, 106, 146, 154, 201, 210 s, 262
Pavia Campaign, 16 n
Peace of Augsburg, 289
Perfection, 125, 269
Permission, 127
Perseverance, 258 ss, 262-266
Petition, 17
Philosophia Christiana, 52, 53, 76 n, 107, 242, 242-250, 253
Philosophy, 108, 225
Pictures, 5, 352
Platonism, 58, 203, 222 s, 226, 235, 241, 244, 332
Pledge of Grace, 21, 228, 323
Pneumatology, 178-180, 188, 230, 231, 263, 274
Politics, 34, 38, 64, 108 s, 117, 148, 229, 265, 266, 267-276, 274, 275 s, 374
Pope, 16, 34, 100, 101 n, 112, 116, 117, 144, 210, 248, 253, 269, 272, 275, 288, 344, 345, 353, 357 n, 358, 361
Portraits, 50 s
Preaching, Sermon, 1, 8-20, 11, 12 s, 13, 15, 59, 102 s, 143, 186 s, 210, 265, 269, 271, 274, 283, 286, 353, 360
Prestination, see Election, 29, 54-56, 68, 121-141, 170 s, 179, 208 s, 298 s, 375
Princes, 109, 267, 270, 289, 291
"Pronous", 66
Property, 39 s
Prophesy, 27-30, 62 s, 71, 151, 254, 270, 375, 377
Prophet, 15, 18, 67, 98, 106 s, 146, 210, 260, 264, 265, 271, 273, 360
Protestation of Speyer, 270
Providence, 10, 11, 123 s, 139 ss, 166, 167, 170 s, 206 s, 208 s, 261

"De Providentia", 64, 108 n, 126-132, 137 n, 169

Puritanism, 30, 341, 346, 347, 348, 359, 364, 366, 377

Real Presence, 20 s, 21, 33, 58, 61, 220, 284, 308, 314, 317, 325, 332-334, 335, 339, 355, 357, 358, 359, 363, 365

Reason, 121, 122, 148, 162 n, 189, 251, 252, 316 n

Reconciliation, 9, 10, 21, 33, 36, 37, 59, 252, 315, 323

Redemption, 9, 56, 134, 136, 164, 175, 208, 266

Reformation, 3, 4, 11, 13, 14, 21, 32 s, 44, 53, 63 s, 66, 102, 105, 109, 110, 142-149, 157, 158, 159, 160-164, 228, 233-255, 250, 252, 260, 267, 284, 332, 338, 347, 353, 360, 374, 377

  Accomplishing the Reformation, 18-20, 108 s, 289, 344, 361 n, 363, 366, 377

Reformed Faith, Church, Theology, 37 s, 70, 107, 123, 235, 253, 276, 277, 286, 287, 288, 290, 294, 307, 330 s, 338, 348, 370, 375

Rejection see Repropation

Religion, 5, 14, 180, 180-182, 270, 274

Remembrance, 220 s, 222 s, 314 s, 354, 362

Renaissance, 64, 108, 205, 315 n

Repentance, 25, 26, 190-195, 250, 360

Reprobation, 56, 123, 125, 127, 129, 131, 209

Responsibility, 205, 234 s, 328, 329, 338, 378

Resurrection, 15, 297, 325, 336

Revelation, 55, 108, 111, 114, 119, 122, 128, 129, 173, 180, 287, 298, 334

Right Hand of God, 58, 177, 210

Righteousness, 65, 360

Sacrament, 8, 21, 59, 76 n, 143, 145, 180, 187 s, 214-217, 225, 227, 327 n, 357, 364

Sacramental Eating, 318-320 (n), (352)

Sacramentalism, 4 s, 219, 241, 283, 373

Sacrifice of Christ, 56, 135-139, 220, 223, 357, 361 n

Salvation, 13, 37, 55, 90, 102, 123, 124, 130, 133, 134, 135, 148, 187, 201, 208, 230, 316

Satisfaction, 9, 10, 36 s, 56, 126-135, 129, 165, 252, 316 n

Scholasticism, 58, 67, 92 n, 124, 157, 169, 225, 235, 245, 332

Scripture, Holy, 27, 53, 66, 92, 108, 113, 143, 157, 180, 188-190, 242, 251, 267, 271, 283, 356, 373

"Secret Advice", 272-274

Sermon see Preaching, 5, 9, 18, 338

Servum arbitrium, 76 n, 166 n, 208, 234 s, 240

"Significat", 221, 317

Simplicitas Dei, 121, 131, 171, 209

Sin, 8, 10, 25, 33, 36, 54, 109 s, 127, 146, 165, 178, 202-208, 315 n, 336

  Original Sin, 54, 135, 193, 202 ss, 315 s n

Sin against the Holy Spirit, 15, 208

Smalcald Articles, 142, 144, 285 n, 309, 312 n

Smalkaldic War, 65, 275, 288

Society, 155, 211, 252, 267, 270, 276, 354 n, 360, 374

Soteriology, 157, 180

Spirit of God/Holy Spirit, 4, 5, 12-14, 19, 25, 34, 37, 38, 61, 148, 156, 162, 179, 189, 252, 286 s, 338, 365

Spiritualism, 21, 67, 178, 284

State, 37 s, 63-65, 155, 211 n, 228 s, 252, 346, 376

Stoicism, 243, 244, 262, 263

Summum bonum see God

Supralapsarianism, 134

Svabian War, 79, 116

Swiss Confederation, 3, 4, 33, 73, 117-119, 146, 253, 256, 258, 268 s, 271, 272, 273 s

Swiss Humanism, 237, 241, 247

Syllogismus practicus, 139, 185

Synergism, 235

Theocraty, 37 s, 66, 97, 163, 211 n, 228, 229, 230, 231

Thirtynine Articles, 346

Tradition(s), 14, 26, 110 s, 147 s, 160, 241, 290

Transformatio, 244, 245, 255

Transsubstantiation, 33, 61, 220, 284, 305 s, 312, 337, 338, 355, 358, 362, 363

Trent, Council of, 306

Trinity, 67, 172, 174, 178, 185

Turks, 100, 116, 249, 275, 289

Typology, 190

Ubiquity, 58, 176, 226 n, 291, 297

Unity of the Church, 58, 290, 337, 338, 356

Universalism, 136, 179

Unio cum Christo, 305, 324, 325, 333 s

"Usus", 336, 338, 358

Verbum internum/externum, 12 s, 186, 188, 264, 282, 285, 286
Vestments Controversy, 346, 364
Via antiqua, 59, 112, 153
Via moderna, 59

"Watchman's Duty", 38, 63, 211 ss, 265
Whyte Horse Tavern, 347, 353
Wittenberg Concord, 311 n, 332, 354

Word of God, 4, 11, 12, 13, 15, 35-37, 71, 145, 148, 149, 162, 178, 185-188, 250-253, 257, 282 s, 286 s, 307 s, 336, 360
Work, 39 s, 118 s
Worship, 1-30, 3 s, 23, 328

Zurich Disputation, 103 n, 150, 259, 267, 357
Zwinglianism, 65, 66 s, 210, 230-232, 280, 290, 293, 341, 342-344, 371, 374, 377

Index of Writings by Zwingli

Apology... Ad Germaniae Principes, 225, 359
"Appeal", 271
"Archeteles", 27, 111 n, 155 n, 156-160, 239
Articles, 67, and "Exposition", 4, 9, 10, 19, 25, 38, 48, 103 n, 142, 150, 189 s, 216 n, 220, 252, 374 n, 375 n
Brevis Commemoratio, 333 n, 366 n
Christian Introduction, 46, 190, 194 n, 197 n, 201 n, 267, 315 n, 360, 375 n
Of the Clarity and Certainty of the Word of God, 158 n, 164 n, 189 n, 349
Commentarius see Exegetica
Commentarius de vera et falsa religione, 147 n, 151, 182, 208, 239, 240, 259 n, 359, 360, 154 n, 155 n, 174 n, 190 n

Epistola ad Matthaeum Alberum, 221
Exegetica, 262, 270
"Exhortation", 4, 155 n, 271
Fidei expositio, 55, 165 n, 318 n, 362 n
Fidei Ratio, 132 ss, 172, 348 s, 357, 375 n
"Lehrbüchlein", 47, 62
Letter to Lambert, 201
Letter to the Toggenburgers, 160 n
"plague song", 51, 152
Second Sermon at the Bern Disputation, 256-266
"Sermon on the maid Mary", 84, 87 n, 87-94
"The Shepherd", 146 n, 147, 201, 360
Supplicatio ad Hugonem episcopum, 145 n

INDEX OF NAMES

Apart from significant exceptions this index is based on the text proper.

Abraham, 54
Adam, 164, 165, 181, 203, 205, 207
Aeneas, 236
Albrecht of Bavaria, 290
Alexander the Great, 97
Alesius, Alexius, 372
Anne of Cleves, 356
Aristotle, 112
Asper, Hans, 352
Athene, Pallas, 237
Aubigné, Agrippa de, 263
Augustinus, Aurelius, 99, 100, 101, 107, 124, 127, 132, 154, 202, 203, 222, 241, 250, 251, 314, 360
August of Saxony, 294

Bale, 347
Barnes, Robert, 347, 356, 365
Barth, Karl, 69, 121, 123, 201
Baur, August, 156
Beaton, David, 368
Beaton, James, Archbiship, 368, 372, 373
Bernher, Augustine, 359
Bertram, see Rhabanus Maurus
Beza, Theodore, 29, 290, 293, 294, 340, 350
Bibliander, Theodorus, 28, 29, 47, 352
Bilney, Thomas, 353, 356, 360
Blanke, Fritz, 19, 45, 53, 70
Blaser, Ambrosius, 257
Bothwell, Adam, 369, 371
Bradford, John, 358
Bradwardine, Thomas, 347
Breitinger, Antistes, 17, 120
Bromily, G. W., 48
Bucer, Martin, 20, 58, 257, 340, 341, 346, 354, 358, 362, 364, 371
Buchmann, Heinrich, 47
Buchli, Johannes, 72
Budaeus, 219
Bullinger, Henry, 17, 29, 48, 53, 114, 135, 151, 187, 239, 277, 280, 283, 285, 286, 291, 295, 340, 341, 344, 346, 352, 364-366, 369-371, 375-377
Bultmann, Rudolf, 252

Caesar, Julius ("Emperor"), 76, 97, 115, 119, 236
Calvin, John, 12, 20, 29, 44, 45, 54, 64, 65, 70, 87, 107, 111, 127, 131, 132, 142, 144, 149, 183, 187, 188, 191, 200, 210, 219, 222, 225, 231, 233, 234, 236, 277, 280, 282, 283, 286, 287, 290, 293, 299, 304, 320, 323, 325, 326, 333, 336, 340, 341, 346, 349, 350, 358, 366, 369, 370, 375
Capito, Wolfgang Fabricius, 371
Causton, 351
Coccejus, 376
Colet, John, 344, 353
Cato, 54
Celtes, Konrad, 233
Ceporin, 29
Cicero, 114, 236
Charles V, 83, 256, 263, 275
Claus, Brother, 119
Coligny, Gaspard de, 263
Constantin, 99, 112
Cornelius, 282
Cotsforde, Thomas, 349
Courvoisier, Jaques, 50, 68, 69
Coverdale, Miles, 358, 365, 366
Coxe, 347
Cranmer, Thomas, Archbishop of Canterbury, 345-348, 350, 356, 360, 362, 364, 366, 367
Cromwell, Oliver, 64

Dante, 140, 141
Darnley, 369
David, 76, 91, 98, 207, 259
Dencalion, 115
Domitian, 115
Dürer, Albrecht, 50, 77

Eck, Johannes Dr, 72, 177
Eekhof, 71
Edward VI, 345, 348, 358, 361
Egli, Emil, 45, 47
Eli, 240
Elijah, 239
Elisabeth I, 346, 366, 377

Erasmus, Desiderius, 52, 53, 66, 76, 77, 107, 208, 233-236, 238, 241, 243, 245-250, 251, 253, 254, 282, 344, 350, 353, 354
Erastus, Thomas, 377
Erve, G. van der, 349

Faber, Johann, 68, 72
Farner, Alfred, 63
Farner, Oskar, 2, 47-49, 51, 53, 61, 156
Fecknam, Bishop, 351
Federer, Karl, 88, 89, 91
Fendt, Leonard, 17, 60
Fischer, John, 345, 350
Foxe, 347, 354, 373
Frederick III ("the Pious"), 278, 289, 290, 291, 293, 294
Frith, John, 347, 355, 357, 372
Froben, Johann, 237

Galen, 236
Gardiner, Bishop, 347, 356
Gasser, Thomas, 257
George, Duke of Brunswick, 200
Gestrich, Christof, 69
Glareanus, Heinrich, 237, 241
Göldli, Jörg, 82
Goethe, Johann Wolfgang, 74
Grebel, Conrad, 237
Grey, Lady Jane, 374
Greyerz, Hans von, 236, 237
Grindal, Edmund, Archbishop, 377
Groot, Gerard, 245
Grossmann, Kaspar, 257
Gualther, Rudolph, 29, 340, 352, 371, 377
Guggisberg, Kurt, 257
Gustavus Adolphus, 275
Gut, Walter, 62

Hales, Christopher, 352
Haller, Berchtold, 256, 257
Hamilton, Patrick, 354, 356, 368, 371, 372
Hannibal, 115
Harlow, William, 368
Hector, 115
Higbed, Master, 351
Heliogabalus, 115
Henry VIII, 345, 348, 350, 356, 357, 360
Hercules, 54
Herodotus, 96, 97, 98
Hoen, Cornelius, 58, 221
Hoffmann, Hans, 51
Hohenlandenberg, Hugo von, Bishop of Constance, 27, 150, 156

Holl, Karl, 63
Hollweg, Walther, 290
Homer, 114
Hooper, John, Bishop, 346, 348, 358, 364, 365, 377
Horace, 237
Hospinian, 29
Hume, John, 351
Hutten, Ulrich von, 240

Isaiah, 91, 92, 116
Israel, 218

James V, 367
Jenny, Markus, 61
Jeremiah, 116, 271
Jerome, 241, 246, 251
Joachim II of Brandenburg, 288
Joachim of Fiore, 112
Johann II of Hungary, 294
John the Baptist, 248
Joseph, 88
Josua, 76
Jud, Leo, 17, 28, 47, 151
Jugurtha, 115
Julius II, 248
Junius Franciscus, 29
Jupiter Sol Invictus, 99

Kant, Emanuel, 234, 265
Karlstadt, 284
Karrer, Otto, 89
Kittel, Gerhard, 28
Knox, John, 368-370, 373-375
Kohlbrügge, Hermann Friedrich, 2
Köhler, Walter, 42, 43, 49, 51, 53, 55, 57, 58, 63, 65, 156, 233, 238
Kolb, Franz, 256
Kressner, Helmut, 65
Künzli, Edwin, 46

Lambert, Francis, 201, 372
Lambert, John (alias Nicholson), 345, 347, 357
Lampe, Friedrich Adolf, 376
Lasco, John à, 29, 349, 369, 375
Latimer, Hugh, 347, 350, 359, 360-363
Lavater, Johann Caspar, 120
Lavater, Ludwig, 29
Lessing, Gotthold Ephraim, 99
Lewnax, Margaret, 351
Lewnax, Master, 351
Lortz, Joseph, 68

Luther, Martin, 3, 12, 13, 17, 20-25, 32, 33, 37, 43, 44, 52, 54, 55, 57, 58, 59, 60, 63, 65, 68, 69, 72, 96, 101, 103, 109, 112, 115, 122, 142, 144, 145, 148, 149, 151-153, 171-173, 176, 177, 183, 186, 187, 189, 191, 194, 198, 199, 200, 203, 205, 208, 212, 221, 222, 225, 227, 231-234, 239, 240, 249-251, 280, 282-286, 308, 309, 312, 313, 317, 320, 323, 325, 326, 333, 336-338, 341, 343, 344, 347, 350, 353-356, 358, 365, 371, 377

Manasseh, 39, 229
Manuel, Niclaus, 275
Mars, 237
Mary, 60, 87-94
Mary Stuart, 369
Mary of Guise, 368, 374
Mary Tudor ("bloody Mary"), 341, 346, 348, 358, 360, 363, 366, 368, 374
Masaryk, 263
Maximilian, 290
Megander (Grossmann), Kaspar, 371
Meister, Willi, 62
Melanchthon, Philipp, 234, 291, 337, 350, 358, 360, 370
Melville, Andrew, 369
Menelaus, 115
Meyer, Paul, 63
Meyer, Sebastian, 371
Moeller, Bernd, 65, 71
Moray, 369
More, Thomas, 344, 345, 353, 356
Moritz of Saxony, 289
Mose, 54, 259
Müntzer, Thomas, 284
Muralt, Leonhard von, 45
Muras, Gerhard G., 46
Musculus (Müslin), Wolfgang, 371
Myconius, Oswald, 51, 237, 240

Näf, Werner, 237
Nero, 115
Numicidus, Mettellus, 115

Occam (see William)
Ochino, Bernardino, 371
Oecolampadius, Johannes, 221, 240, 256, 257, 341, 350, 353, 358, 371
Olevianus, Caspar, 29, 376
Orange, Williame de, 263
Oorthuys, Gerardus, 48
Origen, 241, 246, 251

Osiander, 366
Ottheinrich of the Palatinate, 288, 289

Paris, 115
Paul, 167, 179, 201, 248, 250, 265, 282, 330, 335
Pellikan, Conrad, 352, 371
Pestalozzi, 120
Peter, 248, 282
Philipp, Henry, 355
Philip II, 368
Philipp von Hessen, 58, 269, 293
Pfister, Rudolf, 49, 54-56
Pindar, 28
Plato, 43
Piscator, 29
Plimy, 114
Pollet, J. V. M., 66, 67, 68

Ragaz, Leonhard, 120
Rhabanus Maurus, 364
Rich, Arthur, 51-53, 156, 233, 251
Richardson, Cyril C., 367
Ridley, Nicholas, 347, 350, 362, 363
Rilliet, Jean, 50
Rogers, John (alias Thomas Matthew), 357, 358, 366
Rogge, Joachim, 52, 233
Rother, Siegfried, 64
Rückert, Oskar, 62
Rüsch, Gerhard, 47, 62

Sardanapalus, 115
Saul, 76
Scotus, Duns, 67
Seneca, 114, 262, 263
Seymour, Edward, Duke of Somerset, 345, 346
Shaxton, 347
Simmler, Josiah, 29, 295
Smith, Richard, 350
Socrates, 54, 136
Spillmann, Kurt, 62
Suffolk, Duke of, 374
Surgant, Johann Ulrich, 66
Schiner, Cardinal, 16
Schmid, Heinrich, 64
Schmid, Konrad, 257, 259
Schmidt-Clausing, Fritz, 17, 60, 178
Schultess, Johannes, 44
Schuler, Melchior, 44
Schweizer, Julius, 17, 23, 60, 61

Taylor, Dr., 357
Tertullian, 76
Theodosius, 295
Theseus, 54
Thomas Aquinas, 54, 59, 67, 127, 131, 241
Thomas à Kempis, 245
Tilly, 17
Tossanus, 29
Troeltsch, Ernst, 63
Tyndale, William, 354, 355, 356, 358, 366, 372

Uriah, 207
Usteri, John Martin, 233

Vadianus, Joachim, 233, 237
Vermigli, Peter Martys, 29, 278, 292, 350, 377

Veron, John, 349
Virgil, 236

Weisz, Leo, 47
Wenger, John C., 70
Werdmüller, Otto, 366
Wernle, Paul, 42, 51, 55, 65
Wesley, John, 377
William of Occam, 59
William of Orange, 275, 290
Williams, George W., 70
Willock, John, 368, 369, 374, 375, 376
Winzett, Ninian, 371
Wishart, George, 368, 372, 373, 376
Wolsey, Bishop, 356

Xylotectus, 237

Zébédée, 20